Y0-BQS-970

DICTIONARY OF BANKING TERMS

by

Thomas P. Fitch

Consulting Editors

Irwin Kellner
Senior Vice-President & Chief Economist
Manufacturers Hanover Trust Company

Donald G. Simonson
Anderson School of Management
University of New Mexico

Ben Weberman
Senior Editor
Forbes Magazine

BARRON'S

ACKNOWLEDGMENTS

This book would never have reached completion without the assistance of many individuals who graciously gave their time and expertise. The author would like to acknowledge the contributions by the reviewers of the Banking Dictionary, Irwin Kellner, Donald Simonson and Andrew Zamora, who made numerous comments and suggestions. Ben Weberman, who acted as consultant to the project, drew from his years as a financial writer in making many important contributions. Don Reis, Sally Strauss, and John Berseth at Barron's have been invaluable in bringing the book into final form and shaping up the author's prose. Finally, the author wishes to offer a personal note of thanks to several individuals who suggested meaningful changes in the manuscript: Joseph Feher, Larry Frieder, Richard Leech, Patricia Murphy, and Theodore W. Volckhausen. Special thanks are offered to Antonio Marfia, who made numerous contributions to the international terms in the Dictionary, and to my wife, Kathy, for her guidance and support over the last few years.

— THOMAS P. FITCH

© Copyright 1990 by Barron's Educational Series, Inc.

All rights reserved.
No part of this book may be reproduced
in any form, by photostat, microfilm, xerography,
or any other means, or incorporated into any
information retrieval system, electronic or
mechanical, without the written permission
of the copyright owner.

All inquiries should be addressed to:
Barron's Educational Series, Inc.
250 Wireless Boulevard
Hauppauge, New York 11788

Library of Congress Catalog Card No. 89-18315

International Standard Book No. 0-8120-3946-7

Library of Congress Cataloging-in-Publication Data

Fitch, Thomas.
    Dictionary of banking terms / by Thomas Fitch; consultants,
Irwin Kellner, Donald Simonson, Ben Weberman.
        p.   cm.
    ISBN 0-8120-3946-7
    1. Banks and banking—Dictionaries.   I. Title.
HG151.F57 1990
332.1'03—dc20   89-18315
                                                           CIP

PRINTED IN THE UNITED STATES OF AMERICA
    123   9770   98765

INTRODUCTION

by Ben Weberman

Banking industry changes have been roaring along in the decade of the 1980s without slowing in the '90s. Integration of business, along with diversification and technological advance, has been the hallmark of progress. Soon it will be difficult to differentiate a commercial bank from a savings institution or a securities firm. Concurrently, financial institutions have entered an era of product innovation unprecedented in history.

Banks can no longer be characterized as institutions that take deposits and make loans. In today's market, credits are arranged in a variety of ways to provide the basic seasonal capital or capital asset needs. As an example, banks are arranging senior debt, intermediate (or intermezzo) financing, and even subordinated credits. Mergers, leveraged buyouts, and takeovers can all be arranged through the banking system.

Meanwhile, computer-generated information is being used to set terms for interest rate swaps and currency swaps. Borrowers and lenders can more easily move between floating rate and fixed rate, between dollars or pounds or any other combination of exchanges. Balance sheet assets, once fixed and illiquid, are now securitized so participations can be sold to other institutions or to the public.

Lest it be forgotten, the sprawling, trillion-dollar mortgage market is the ancestor of securitization, and is well represented in the list of definitions. First there was pooling of residential mortgages for resale to investors. Then pools of mortgage loans were separated into tranches, with each tranche possessing different payment characteristics, through the medium of Collateralized Mortgage Obligations (CMOs).

CMOs and other derivative mortgage-backed securities (such as Interest Only and Principal Only securities) can trace their history to the creation of U.S. Treasury stripped bond issues. The first such securities were arranged by securities firms that bought large blocks of bonds and had a bank trustee separate all semiannual interest payments from the principal, or corpus.

Even as banks are leaping into new fields, they are also merging into larger institutions. Regional banking companies are crossing state lines to join with other institutions of similar size, creating super-regional banks. The competition between these super-regionals and money center banks is on an equal footing.

An entirely new range of banking organizations has arisen from efforts to support and retain the thrift industry. Many savings and loan associations are being merged out of existence, acquired by healthy savings institutions or by commercial banks. The Federal Savings and Loan Insurance Corporation (FSLIC) has had its existence terminated by Congress, but new supervisory organizations have arisen to regulate and indemnify the thrift industry.

The securities industry is experiencing the thrust of banks into its deepest confines through the securities subsidiaries of bank holding companies. Underwriting of corporate debt securities, formerly barred by the Banking Act of 1933—widely known as the Glass-Steagall Act—is no longer forbidden to commercial banks.

Deposit insurance is mostly responsible for these changes in banking. Prior to the Banking Act of 1933, which initiated federal insurance of bank deposits, banks were using their own assets to bail out failing corporate financings through purchase of securities for their own account. They thus established conditions for loss of confidence in the banking system. The backing of deposit insurance has prevented public loss of large sums even though institutions have failed, thus maintaining public confidence in banks and savings institutions.

While commercial bankers and investment bankers may debate the merits of whether loans or investments hold the greater risk, banking regulators, including the Federal Reserve Board, the Comptroller of the Currency, and the Federal Deposit Insurance Corporation, are aligning with thrift regulators to create a wholly new set of capital rules. Banking institutions are being asked to post reserves whose size is determined by the risk of various categories of bank assets. Higher levels of capital are required for higher risk assets.

In sum, the banking system has been made over and the transition is not yet complete. A new industry has emerged. While most participants and observers are familiar with the terminology of what they have been doing, they have encountered new and strange worlds in other parts of their daily business lives.

This book is designed to provide a key source of information about all activities in banking, traditional as well as ones newly created. It will be of considerable value and benefit to the long time professional as well as the novice. Those interested in investment banking as well as commercial banking will find the book a necessity.

HOW TO USE THIS BOOK EFFECTIVELY

Alphabetization: All entries are alphabetized by letter rather than word, so that multiple-word terms are treated as single words. For example, **asset management account** follows **asset-liability committee (ALCO), Dun & Bradstreet** follows **due-on-sale clause, goodwill** follows **good money,** and **selling group** follows **seller-servicer** and precedes **sell short.**

Many terms commonly used in banking have distinctly different meanings depending on the context in which they are used. Readers must determine the context relevant to their purpose. When a term has several entries, subentries are presented in alphabetical sequence. In some entries the various meanings are presented as simple numerical headings. Numbers in entry titles are alphabetized as if they were spelled out—for example **x.9** follows **x-mark.**

Abbreviations and Acronyms: A separate list of abbreviations and acronyms follows the Dictionary. It contains a shortened version of terms defined in the book, plus related business terms.

Cross-References: To add to your understanding of a term, related, or contrasting terms are sometimes cross-referenced. The cross-referenced terms will appear in SMALL CAPITALS either in the body of the entry (or subentry) or at the end of the definition. These terms will be printed in SMALL CAPITALS only the first time they appear in the entry. When a term is fully defined by another term, a reference rather than an entry is provided; for example, **community bank** see INDEPENDENT BANK.

Italics: Italic type is used to indicate that another term has a meaning identical or very closely related to that of the entry. Italic type is also used to highlight words or phrases that have a special meaning to the trade. Italics are also used for the titles of publications.

Parentheses: Parentheses are used in entry titles for two reasons. The first is to indicate that a word or phrase has a meaning so closely related to the term defined that only one entry is necessary; for example **capital gain (or loss).** The second is to indicate that an abbreviation is used with about the same frequency as the term itself. For example: **certificate of deposit (CD),** or **Federal Deposit Insurance Corporation (FDIC).**

Examples, Illustrations, and Tables: The examples in the Dictionary are designed to help readers gain understanding and to help them relate abstract concepts to the real world of banking. Line drawings are presented in some entries in addition to text to clarify concepts best understood visually. Tables supplement definitions where essential detail is more effectively condensed and expressed in tabular form; for example, an AMORTIZATION SCHEDULE shows how a loan is paid down through regular payments of principal and interest.

Special Definitions: Some entries are given expanded treatment to enhance their reference value. Examples are **Depository Institutions Deregulation & Monetary Control Act of 1980** and **Financial Institutions Reform, Recovery & Enforcement Act of 1989.** Organizations and associations that play a role in the industry are included in the Dictionary along with a brief statement of their mission.

A

AAA highest rated corporate or municipal bond, with full payment of principal and interest expected at maturity. Bonds rated AAA, AA, A, and BBB by Standard & Poor's, and Bbb or better by Moody's Investors Service, are considered investment grade bonds, eligible for purchase by banks and savings institutions as INVESTMENT SECURITIES. See also BOND RATING.

abandonment voluntary surrender of property, or a right to property, without attempting to reclaim it or name a successor. In most states, ownership of abandoned property reverts to the party holding a prior interest, or to the state if no owner is found. In bankruptcy law, abandonment is a means for returning collateral to secured creditors, provided the bankruptcy trustee agrees. See also DORMANT ACCOUNT; ESCHEAT.

ABA transit number Numerical Transit System of two-part coding assigned to banks and savings institutions by the AMERICAN BANKERS ASSOCIATION. The first part shows the city, state, or territory where a bank is located; the second part (separated by a hyphen) identifies the bank itself. The ABA number is the numerator of a fraction appearing in the upper right corner of a check; the denominator is the bank's CHECK ROUTING SYMBOL, identifying the FEDERAL RESERVE BANK clearing checks drawn on that bank and funds availability. Every depository financial institution in the United States has a unique transit number, assigned from a list of ABA numbers maintained by Rand McNally & Co. of Chicago. See also BANK IDENTIFICATION NUMBER; MAGNETIC INK CHARACTER RECOGNITION.

ability to pay capacity to meet future obligations from earnings or income.
1. **Banking.** A borrower's capacity to make principal and interest payments from disposable income. When making loans, lenders look closely at a credit applicant's current salary and expected future earnings, and at an organization's CASH FLOW

from conversion of assets into cash. See also BALANCE SHEET RATIOS; FIVE C's OF CREDIT; QUALIFYING RATIO.

2. Securities, municipal bonds. The issuer's capacity to generate sufficient income from taxes or other sources, based on property taxes, bond rating, and so on.

3. Finance. The ability to meet DEBT SERVICE payments on bonds and other long-term obligations.

above par price of a stock or bond above its face value. Most bonds have a par value of $1,000 or $5,000. Bond prices are expressed in terms of a 100 scale (100 = par or face value). A $1,000 bond priced at 105 is 105% of $1,000 or $1,050. The value above par is the PREMIUM value. The par value for stocks is vastly different than for bonds. Most stocks have no par value at all, or have a nominal value (for example, 10 cents per share) that has no relation to market or book value, unless the issuer is near failure. See also AT PAR; PAR VALUE.

absolute priority rule see BANKRUPTCY.

absolute title clean title, free of liens or attachments, replacing all previous titles. Accepted as the sole document of title, it is defensible against claims by third parties.

abstraction of bank funds wrongful taking of bank funds from a teller's cash drawer, escrow account, or trust account for unauthorized use, in violation of a bank's responsibility as a FIDUCIARY. Also called DEFALCATION or EMBEZZLEMENT.

accelerated cost recovery schedule (ACRS) see ACCELERATED DEPRECIATION.

accelerated depreciation accounting method of reducing the book value of an asset at a higher rate than comparable methods in the early years of ownership. It is based on the theory that an asset's value is highest during its early years, when it is new and has greater earnings potential than in subsequent years. Since 1981, the most common form of accelerated depreciation is the accelerated cost recovery system (ACRS), which later was modified by the TAX REFORM ACT OF 1986. The Internal Revenue Service must approve accelerated methods of depreciation, which are arithmetically more complicated than straight line asset depreciation allocating an equal portion of the asset value to each year. Accelerated depreciation also has the undesirable effect of reducing income in the early years, although offsetting advantages include the deferral of taxes until later years. Under ACRS, depreciation is more a method of allocating costs over multiple accounting periods than an attempt to match costs with income. Previous methods of accelerated depreciation included the declining balance method and the sum-of-the-years digits method.

acceleration clause clause in a bond mortgage, bond, or promissory note stating that the unpaid balance is due and payable if specified conditions of default, defined in a loan COVENANT or bond INDENTURE, should occur. Acceleration, at the option of the lender, calls for immediate payment of the remaining balance, plus interest due, if the borrower fails to make timely payments, maintain insurance on mortgaged property, pay property taxes, and so on.

acceptance promise to pay created when the drawee of a TIME DRAFT stamps or writes the word "accepted" above his signature and a designated payment date. Once accepted, the draft is the equivalent of a promissory note; the drawee becomes the ACCEPTOR, and is obligated to pay the amount shown at maturity. Acceptances are NEGOTIABLE INSTRUMENTs, which means they can be sold to another holder before maturity.
1. **Banking.** A time draft accepted by a bank, known as a BANKER'S ACCEPTANCE. It is used primarily in financing international trade, for example, an overseas manufacturer selling goods to an importer, although a domestic acceptance is not uncommon. See also DOCUMENTARY CREDIT; THIRD COUNTRY ACCEPTANCE.
2. **Finance.** Trade acceptance issued by a finance company affiliated with a manufacturer, for example, General Motors Acceptance Corp. or by an importer acting as agent for a manufacturer. It is often backed by a bank LETTER OF CREDIT.

acceptor person or party, normally the DRAWEE, who accepts a bill of exchange or TIME DRAFT, and becomes responsible for payment at maturity to the party named in the draft.

access

1. right to use banking services. Specifically, the right to make deposits to, or withdrawals from, a checking or savings account, verify an account balance, use a safe deposit box, or make electronic transfers using a bank card or other ACCESS DEVICE.
2. bank card organization in Great Britain formed in 1972, a member of MASTERCARD INTERNATIONAL and Eurocard.

access device

bank card or personal security code giving consumers the means to make deposits, withdraw funds, transfer funds, or pay bills electronically. As defined by Federal Reserve Board Regulation E, an access device is any DEBIT CARD, PERSONAL IDENTIFICATION NUMBER, telephone transfer code, or telephone bill payment code used by a consumer to initiate an electronic transfer of funds. Financial institutions may issue an access device only at the consumer's request.

accommodation endorser

person who endorses a PROMISSORY NOTE as a favor to the borrower, without compensation or benefit. An endorser or cosigner's signature enables the borrower to qualify for credit, or to obtain credit at more favorable terms. The endorser is a GUARANTOR or surety, and remains secondarily liable in event of default. Accommodation endorsements are widely used in banking. A parent company may endorse the bank loan of a subsidiary; banks sometimes endorse the ACCEPTANCE of other banks to make these instruments more readily marketable in the SECONDARY MARKET. See also CO-MAKER.

accommodation paper

PROMISSORY NOTE or NEGOTIABLE INSTRUMENT signed by a third party, who acts as accommodation maker, endorser, or party. Banks, before advancing funds to corporations of uncertain credit strength or to closely held corporations, often require corporate officers to personally guarantee repayment of bank loans by endorsing the note evidencing the loan. See also ACCOMMODATION ENDORSER.

account

contractual relationship between two parties involving an exchange of funds at a later date, as between buyer and seller, or an agreement by one party to hold funds in trust for the other. It also is the continuously updated record of transactions, yielding the current balance, or AVAILABLE BALANCE. For example, a charge account, checking account, or trust account.

1. **Accounting.** A bookkeeping entry in a ledger. Examples are accounts receivable, accrued interest, allowance for bad debt.

2. **Banking.** (1) A record evidencing funds on deposit under a particular name or ACCOUNT NUMBER, including a checking account, also called a DEMAND DEPOSIT account, which pays no interest but allows the account holder to withdraw funds by writing checks; a NEGOTIABLE ORDER OF WITHDRAWAL (NOW) account, a check-like account that pays interest; a PASSBOOK account, a savings account with no specified maturity; and a TIME DEPOSIT account, which pays interest on funds deposited for specified periods (7 days up to seven years or more), and is subject to an EARLY WITHDRAWAL PENALTY if funds are taken out before the maturity date. The MONETARY CONTROL ACT of 1980 phased out deposit interest ceilings by March 1986, allowing banks and thrifts to pay competitive rates on savings accounts, sharply reduced penalties for early withdrawal, but maintained the prohibition on paying interest on checking accounts. See also ALL SAVERS CERTIFICATE; AUTOMATIC TRANSFER OF SAVINGS (ATS); DRAFT; MONEY MARKET DEPOSIT ACCOUNT; ORDER; PAYABLE THROUGH DRAFT; SAVINGS ACCOUNT; SMALL SAVER CERTIFICATE; STATEMENT SAVINGS ACCOUNT; SUPER NOW ACCOUNT; TRUST ACCOUNT; (2) A transaction record of an OPEN-END CREDIT plan, such as a CREDIT CARD or home equity credit line, or a commercial open account relationship, as in ACCOUNTS RECEIVABLE FINANCING or ASSET-BASED LENDING. In commercial finance the term account generally refers to the indebtedness, not the borrower or account holder.

3. **Securities.** A contractual arrangement under which securities, mutual fund shares, futures and options, and so on are bought and sold; a brokerage account.

accountabilities deposits, stock certificates and other items held in trust by one party for another. A bank's TRUST DEPARTMENT or other fiduciary is required by law in many states to give a periodic accounting of the assets, or liabilities, comprising a TRUST.

account activity deposits, withdrawals, earnings credits for deposit balances, and service charges on a bank account during a particular time period. These are summarized in an ACCOUNT STATEMENT, which banks are required by banking regulation to issue every month, to give customers an opportunity to correct posting errors. A recent trend in banking is the COMBINED STATEMENT, listing activity on several related accounts, for example, checking, statement savings, money market savings account, and so on. See also ACCOUNT ANALYSIS.

account analysis monthly statement evaluating the adequacy of COMPENSATING BALANCES or fees paid by a corporate account for banking services, taking into account a company's AVERAGE DAILY BALANCE, AVERAGE DAILY FLOAT, EARNINGS CREDIT note on collected balances, and other factors. When servicing costs exceed the bank's compensation from fees or balances, the extra cost is passed on to the customer as service charges or higher balance requirements. An analytical tool mostly used in pricing corporate CASH MANAGEMENT services, account analysis is also used by banks to evaluate profitability of CORRESPONDENT banking services, such as check clearing, performed for other financial institutions.

accountant's opinion statement describing results of an examination of a firm's books and records, following accepted auditing standards. Most banks, except for the smallest commercial banks, have their records and accounts audited annually by a certified public accountant. The opinion may be qualified or unqualified, depending on the scope of the examination and the accountant's confidence in the information reviewed. A qualified opinion, although not necessarily negative, indicates information that the accountant was not able to directly confirm, normally because of limitations in the scope of the audit. See also GENERALLY ACCEPTED ACCOUNTING PRINCIPLES; REGULATORY ACCOUNTING PRINCIPLES.

account balance see BALANCE.

account history
1. bank's summary of a deposit account's activity, including interest earned, during a particular period.

2. internal summary of transaction activity by a credit card or other OPEN-END CREDIT account, including late payments, overlimit activity, average daily balance, and so on. See also ACCOUNT STATEMENT; CREDIT FILE.

account hold

1. CHECK HOLD, or the number of days that a bank legally can hold uncollected balances before giving customers use of those funds. The EXPEDITED FUNDS AVAILABILITY ACT of 1987 accelerates the AVAILABILITY SCHEDULE requiring banks to make the first $100 available for withdrawal at the opening of business the day after the funds are deposited, remaining funds on the third day after a deposit if drawn on a local bank and within six days if drawn on nonlocal banks, starting in 1990. See also LOCAL CHECK; REGULATION CC.

2. notation limiting an account owner's access to funds in the account, as when a time savings account is used as collateral for a loan.

account inquiry request for a copy of an individual's AC-COUNT HISTORY, usually in connection with a credit approval or renewal of an existing line of credit. See also CREDIT REPORT.

account in trust account managed by one party for use by another, who is named the BENEFICIARY. A parent or guardian opening a child's savings account under the UNIFORM GIFTS TO MINORS ACT approves any withdrawals until the child reaches legal age.

account number numeric code identifying the holder of an account. Account numbers are generally issued sequentially by the date an account is opened, have a standardized number of characters, and may contain coded information for internal security purposes. Bank credit cards, for example, have 16 digit account numbers, as required by MasterCard and Visa. See also CHECK DIGIT.

account reconcilement bookkeeping service offered by banks, usually for a fee, to assist customers in balancing their checkbooks. Some banks provide, as a cash management service to corporate customers, an electronic reconcilement service that automatically balances a checking account, lists checks paid and deposits posted, and summarizes all account activity for an accounting period. This service reduces the company's clerical costs, and also functions as an outside AUDIT control over funds collection and disbursement.

accounts receivable financing

form of ASSET-BASED LENDING in which businesses obtain short-term financing by selling their trade receivables or pledging receivables as collateral for a loan. Direct sale of accounts receivable is a nonrecourse type of financing called FACTORING. An accounts receivable loan from a bank is a DISCOUNT: the borrower draws against a line of credit that is less than the full dollar value of his trade credits. Accounts receivable financing is a rather flexible way of obtaining credit, since the borrower's financing costs are directly related to his business cycle, but is often priced at spreads above the bank PRIME RATE and is relatively expensive compared to other forms of credit. See also BORROWING BASE; INVENTORY FINANCING; SECURITY INTEREST.

accounts receivable turnover

ratio of total credit sales to average accounts receivable during an accounting period, a measure of an organization's ability to convert inventory into cash, and thus, financial efficiency. Close attention should be paid to credit terms, billing procedures, and company and industry trends. See also BALANCE SHEET RATIOS; RATIO ANALYSIS.

account statement

any summary of transaction activity occurring during an accounting period, usually monthly, but sometimes quarterly, or at other intervals.

1. **Banking.** A listing of deposits, withdrawals, checks paid, interest earned, and service charges against an account—called a bank statement. It is issued monthly, as required by Federal Reserve regulations, to give customers an opportunity to review their financial records and correct any errors. Many financial institutions issue consolidated bank statements to save postage expense, and also to give customers a single statement showing all of their account relationships with a bank. See also CONSOLIDATED FINANCIAL STATEMENT; PERIODIC STATEMENT.

2. **Securities.** A record of transactions showing status of an account maintained at a broker-dealer firm, net market value of securities owned, cash and securities positions, and so on

Brokerage statements are issued monthly or quarterly, depending on the level of activity in the account.

accounts uncollectible loans in DEFAULT that have been charged off, or are likely to be charged off, as losses. Lenders are required to report the condition of loans with principal and interest in arrears in quarterly CALL REPORTS to bank regulatory agencies. See also ADVERSELY CLASSIFIED ASSETS; LOAN LOSS RESERVES.

accretion of discount accounting process for adjusting the book value of a bond purchased at a discount (the ORIGINAL ISSUE DISCOUNT) to the PAR VALUE at maturity. Accretion is, in effect, a noncash payment of interest, reflecting interest earned while a bond is owned. Accretion is calculated through the "straight line" method, which increases the bond price at a fixed rate per year (a bond purchased at 90, repayable at par in five years, accretes at 2 points per year); and the scientific or constant interest method, which accelerates the accretion as the bond redemption date approaches. Contrast with AMORTIZATION.

accrual basis basis of accounting in which revenues and expenses are recognized in the period in which they arise, regardless of when the cash for the revenue or the expenditure actually occurs. Matching revenues and expenses in the appropriate periods, it is considered superior to any other basis of accounting. The CASH BASIS form of accounting, on the other hand, is more susceptible to manipulation. Accrual accounting is the only basis of accounting approved under GENERALLY ACCEPTED ACCOUNTING PRINCIPLES, and is used by public companies and most privately owned companies.

accrual bond long-term, deferred interest COLLATERIZED MORTGAGE OBLIGATION (CMO) bond that pays no interest until all prior bonds in a CMO bond offering have been retired. Also called a Z-Bond. An accrual bond is similar to a ZERO-COUPON BOND, except that it has an explicit coupon rate and pays both principal and coupon interest. These bonds, backed by residential mortgages, have maturities of 20-25 years, and are most often purchased by investors desiring protection from call risk caused by early prepayments of underlying mortgages, or who seek the price leverage afforded by these deep-discount bonds. See also STRIP; STRIPPED MORTGAGE BACKED SECURITIES.

accrued interest interest earned but not paid on a bond, certificate of deposit, or time deposit. Fixed income security after the most recent interest payment. When securities are sold, the buyer pays, in addition to the purchase price, any interest earned by the seller up to, though not including, the settlement date. Accrued interest is calculated, ordinarily using the 360-day year, by multiplying the coupon rate times the bond par value and the number of days elapsed since the last interest payment. (Interest = rate x par value x number of days/360). Accrued interest on bank owned securities is carried as an asset account on the balance sheet. See also UNEARNED DISCOUNT; UNEARNED INTEREST.

acid test ratio SEE BALANCE SHEET RATIOS.

acknowledgment admission of the truth of a statement or validity of a document. See also ATTEST.
1. **Banking.** A notification by a paying bank that an item presented for payment has been paid, or that it cannot be honored. See also WIRE FATE ITEM.
2. **Securities.** A verification, by an authorized official, that a customer's signature is genuine, required when transferring accounts to another broker or fiduciary.

acquirer
1. in bank cards, a bank that purchases merchant sales drafts. Also called the MERCHANT BANK. Merchants receive credit for the dollar value of credit card receipts, less a processing fee (the MERCHANT DISCOUNT RATE).
2. in AUTOMATED TELLER MACHINE networks, the financial institution that dispenses the cash, collecting a transaction fee from the card issuing bank.
3. bank gaining control over another financial institution, either through an exchange of stock, payment in cash, or a combination.

acquisition purchase of an asset, such as real estate, chattels, securities, and so on, with title and rights of ownership passing to the new owner.

Banking:

1. addition of new accounts through marketing, resulting in deposit growth or new money. Deposit growth is accomplished by direct mail promotion, advertising, in-branch promotions, and so on. The term also applies to credit accounts, such as the addition of new credit card customers through direct mail marketing or purchasing the credit portfolios of other banks.

2. takeover of one company by another through a PURCHASE ACQUISITION, a mostly cash transaction, or a POOLING OF INTERESTS in which two banks agree to swap common stock. Bank regulators sometimes provide generous assistance to banks that take over failing institutions, paying the acquirer the difference between the book value of the acquired bank's assets and the purchase price. See also BAILOUT.

acquittance document or receipt evidencing full payment of an obligation, releasing the lender's SECURITY INTEREST. When a borrower has made the last payment in a mortgage, the lender issues a SATISFACTION OF MORTGAGE document, indicating that the debt has been fully repaid. See also TERMINATION STATEMENT.

active account account with frequent deposits or withdrawals posted during an accounting period. Also, a credit card account or bank line of credit showing principal and interest payments due on the customer's ACCOUNT STATEMENT. Contrast with INACTIVE ACCOUNT

active trust trust account in which the trustee has a specific duty to perform, for example a TESTAMENTARY TRUST created by a WILL. The trustee has authority to sell assets to meet claims of creditors and distribute the estate to beneficiaries. Contrast with GRANTOR TRUST or passive trust, which has no discretionary duties to perform.

activity charge fee charged to a bank account to cover servicing costs. Some activity fees are triggered when the account balance falls below a certain level, for example, a monthly service charge on a checking account. Others are transaction fees based on account usage, for example, an item charge for checks written or a service charge for automated teller machine withdrawals. See also ACCOUNT ANALYSIS; BREAK-EVEN YIELD; MINIMUM BALANCE; TARGET BALANCE.

act of bankruptcy behavior deemed an admission of bankruptcy—generally the failure to pay obligations when due. Creditors who believe a borrower has committed an act of bankruptcy can file an INVOLUNTARY BANKRUPTCY petition, asking a bankruptcy court to dispose of the debtor's assets to meet their claims. The Bankruptcy Reform Act of 1978 simplified the filing of involuntary petitions by eliminating specific tests of bankruptcy, such as transferring assets to defraud creditors. Under the new code, inability to pay bills on time is sufficient grounds for filing a creditor's petition. See also CREDITORS' COMMITTEE.

actuals any physical commodity or financial instrument (Treasury bills, bonds, currencies) that is sold at the SPOT rate at the expiration of a contract. In FINANCIAL FUTURE, it is the commodity underlying the futures contract, as distinguished from the futures contract itself. In the futures market, delivery of the physical commodity or financial instrument rarely occurs, as most traders close out their forward positions before a contract expires.

additional collateral see SIDE COLLATERAL.

add-on interest finance charges computed by adding the interest payable to the full amount of loan principal. The add-on interest is applied to the original principal amount, and a portion of the interest due is charged to each loan payment. This results in an annual interest rate (the ANNUAL PERCENTAGE RATE) that is higher than the rate stated in the loan agreement because the add-on method does not take into consideration the reduction of principal as installment payments are made. As a general rule, the more frequent the loan payments, the higher the EFFECTIVE RATE of interest the borrower pays.

Computing interest due under the add-on interest method is fairly simple. The loan PRINCIPAL is divided into a number of fixed payments, and each payment is multiplied by the finance charge, to calculate the interest cost to the borrower: Add-On Interest = Principal x Rate x Number of Months in the loan/12. This method of interest computation differs from the SIMPLE INTEREST method in that the add-on method allocates a higher portion of the total interest cost to the early months of a loan, whereas simple interest allocates an equal portion of interest to each installment. See also AMORTIZATION; DISCOUNT; RULE OF THE 78'S.

adequate notice printed notice clearly stating terms and conditions of a consumer loan or extension of credit. Lenders are required by the TRUTH IN LENDING ACT to disclose key credit terms, such as the ANNUAL PERCENTAGE RATE, annual fee, GRACE PERIOD, and other pertinent information when a new account is opened, and notify customers of any subsequent changes in credit terms.

adjudication settlement of opposing arguments by notice and trial in a court of law; also a court's ruling, such as adjudication of bankruptcy. Contrast with ARBITRATION.

adjustable rate mortgage (ARM) mortgage with periodic adjustments in interest rate, usually every six months. ARM rates are calculated against a money index, such as the six-month Treasury bill rate or the Federal Home Loan Bank of San Francisco cost of funds, or a lender's internal cost of funds. These mortgages often have consumer protections against rapid escalation in borrowing costs, such as an annual CAP on interest rate increases in any single year, or over the life of the loan (LIFE OF LOAN CAP). An adjustable mortgage with an initial rate of $8\frac{1}{2}\%$, an annual increase cap of 2%, and a lifetime cap of 5%, cannot rise higher than $13\frac{1}{2}\%$.

Lenders generally set the introductory rate on ARMs below those on comparable fixed rate mortgages, as an incentive to get borrowers to take variable rate loans, and also because they know they can adjust the rate later on, should interest rates rise. This initial rate is also known as a TEASER RATE.

Adjustable mortgages first appeared in the 1960s, but did not gain legislative or regulatory approval nationally until the early 1980s when volatile interest rates made it unwise for lenders to make 30-year mortgages at fixed rates of interest. ARMs are a useful asset-liability management tool, as they pass on to the borrower some of the interest rate risk associated with long-term lending. Adjustable rates also offer mortgagors potentially lower rates if rates happen to decline. See also ALTERNATIVE MORT-

GAGE INSTRUMENT; BIWEEKLY MORTGAGE; CONVERTIBLE; PAYMENT CAP.

adjustable rate preferred stock cumulative preferred stock with dividends paid and adjusted quarterly. The investor appeal of adjustable rate preferred stock, issued by commercial bank holding companies since 1982, is largely dependent on the reset price above or below yields on Treasury securities, for example, the three-month T-Bill, used in calculating dividends. Adjustable rate issues have no maturity date, but may be called at the option of the issuer. Shareholder dividends are nonaccruing, and are paid on scheduled dividend dates.

adjusted capital ratio ratio of adjusted capital to total assets, used in computing CAPITAL ADEQUACY. A bank's adjusted capital includes LOAN LOSS RESERVES for bad debt, securities gains or losses, less loans classified as DOUBTFUL LOANS or LOSS. The risk-adjusted capital guidelines, adopted by banking regulators in 1988, are aimed at developing uniform bank capital guidelines. See also CAPITAL ADEQUACY; RISK-BASED CAPITAL.

adjusted gross estate value of an estate after payment of administrative expenses, debts of the decedent and losses, but before estate taxes are paid. Fifty percent of the adjusted gross estate is the maximum value of a MARITAL DEDUCTION in computing death taxes.

adjusted gross income individual's income from all sources, as reported on the IRS 1040 tax return, after certain allowable deductions—IRA or KEOGH contributions, moving expenses, and alimony.

adjustment accounting entry for ledger entries not previously posted and transfers to subsidiary accounts, or to correct bookkeeping errors. In computation of equity CAPITAL, a bank writes down the book value, or original value, of loans when they were made by 100% for loans classified as LOSS, and 50% for DOUBTFUL LOANS, with the difference being charged to the LOAN LOSS RESERVE for bad debt. See also ADJUSTED CAPITAL RATIO; RISK-BASED CAPITAL.

adjustment credit short-term ADVANCE by a Federal Reserve Bank, secured by a bank's own promissory note—the most common form of borrowing from a Federal Reserve Bank to meet RESERVE REQUIREMENTS and support short-term lending. Adjustment credit advances have a maximum maturity of 15 days. Usage is heaviest during periods of TIGHT MONEY and high interest rates.

administrator

1. bank or party appointed by a probate court to distribute an estate of a person who dies INTESTATE, that is, without leaving a WILL or who fails to name an EXECUTOR. The administrator has legal authority to pay claims against the estate, and to distribute assets to the heirs.
2. person who manages any business.

ad valorem valuation based on monetary worth of an asset, from the Latin phrase *ad valorem*, meaning to "the value," and is a widely accepted basis for tax assessments (ad valorem taxes)—sales taxes, property taxes, and import tariffs.

advance

1. PRINCIPAL amount available when a borrower draws from a line of credit, takes a CASH ADVANCE against a bank credit card, or disburses a loan at specific periodic stages. Advances may be secured or unsecured. See also OVERDRAFT.
2. to draw against a preapproved line of credit.
3. in international banking, disbursement of funds to finance payment of collections or refinance a maturing loan, as in a bridge loan.
4. DISCOUNT WINDOW loan from a FEDERAL RESERVE BANK to a commercial bank maintaining a RESERVE ACCOUNT at one of the 12 district Fed banks. These loans are made on a bank's own promissory note, backed by U.S. Treasury securities or acceptable collateral.

Most Federal Reserve credit is by advances, as this form of credit is easier to execute than rediscounting loans, and also because banks are reluctant to let their customers know they occasionally have to borrow. Contrast with REDISCOUNT. See also ADJUSTMENT CREDIT; EMERGENCY CREDIT; EXTENDED CREDIT; SEASONAL CREDIT

advance commitment written promise or agreement to take some future action. The most common example is a contractual commitment a financial institution makes to lend funds to a borrower at a future date on terms agreed upon in advance, for example, a REVOLVING CREDIT agreement. The lender ordinarily charges a COMMITMENT FEE and may require the borrower to keep part of the loan as a COMPENSATING BALANCE in a checking account at the lending institution. A FIRM COMMITMENT is absolutely binding on the lender, whereas a conditional commitment is binding only if certain terms are met in the future, such as meeting certain tests of creditworthiness. In mortgage banking, an advance commitment is called a STANDBY COMMITMENT.

advance option short-term credit facility allowing a bond underwriter to make an unsecured advance to an issuer in the event that the issuer's bond offering is not subscribed fully. The bank acting as underwriter makes a short-term loan based on the conditional sale of the bond. The corporation wants to issue bonds, but is not sure how much it can sell, so it obtains a STANDBY LETTER OF CREDIT from a bank covering, say, 50% of the proposed bond offering. Compare to SWINGLINE.

advance refunding in MUNICIPAL BONDS, sale of new bonds prior to the first call date of previously issued bonds. This is done by selling a new issue at market rates of return and turning over to a bank trustee enough proceeds to buy Treasury issues or other high-quality debt that comes due on the first call date of the original bond, a process known as DEFEASANCE. At that time, the collateral held by the trustee is converted to cash to retire the original bond issue, which has become callable.

adverse action in consumer credit, denial of an applicant's request for credit. Under the Fair Credit Billing Act, creditors who decline a request for credit must advise the applicant of the reason. If turned down because of DEROGATORY INFORMATION in a CREDIT REPORT, the applicant is entitled to examine, without cost, his or her credit report and request that any negative information reported by a lender, if incorrect, be changed. See also EFFECTS TEST; REGULATION B.

adversely classified assets loans and other assets that are at risk to some degree. Such assets fail to meet acceptable credit standards, and are reported separately in bank CALL REPORTS. State and national banking examiners have adopted uniform guidelines (the National Bank Examiners risk classification system), listing rating poorly performing loans as follows, from worst to least serious: LOSS, or complete write-off; DOUBTFUL LOAN, where repayment in full is questionable; SUBSTANDARD, where some loss is probable unless the corrective actions are taken; and SPECIAL MENTION, indicating potential problems, such as missing documentation or insufficient collateral.

Supervisory agencies require that lenders write down loans classified as doubtful to 50% of the original book value, and loans classified as loss by 100% in calculating their net capital (adjusted capital plus reserves for possible loan losses) available for making new loans. See also NONACCRUAL ASSET; NONPERFORMING LOAN.

advice written confirmation of payment received, funds transferred, service performed, or payment made. Examples in banking include a credit advice, indicating a deposit made; a debit advice, a withdrawal or transfer; a payment advice, and so on.

affidavit Latin for "has pledged his faith," a sworn statement in writing, witnessed by a notary public or other public official. Federal agencies, such as the Federal Housing Administration, or the Veterans Administration sometimes require affidavits from borrowers to show eligibility for a mortgage loan. Depository institutions may require affidavits before distributing assets of trust. See also ATTEST.

affiliate any firm closely related to another through ownership by a parent company. If only two companies are involved and one owns more than 50% of the stock in the second, the preferred term is SUBSIDIARY.

Banking:
1. bank that is owned or controlled by a MULTIBANK HOLDING COMPANY; also, under the the Banking Act of 1933, any organization owned by a bank through stock holdings, or whose officers are also directors of the bank. See also CHAIN BANKING; INTERLOCKING DIRECTORATE.
2. company performing any service, except deposit taking, owned or controlled by an insured bank or bank holding company. Bank service affiliates engage in a wide range of activi-

ties, from check clearing to securities underwriting, and are regulated by the Bank Service Corporation Act and the 1970 amendments to the Bank Holding Company Act. The Garn-St. Germain Act of 1982 expanded these powers by allowing service corporations to engage in any nonbank activities approved by the Federal Reserve Board for bank holding companies. See also REGULATION Y; SERVICE CORPORATION.

3. bank participating in either or both of two national bank card systems (MASTERCARD INTERNATIONAL or VISA) that issues cards and accepts merchant sales drafts, but does not own any credit card receivables. Also called an AGENT BANK.

Finance:

1. any company directly or indirectly owning 5% or more of the voting stock in another company, as defined by the Investment Company Act.

2. company whose actions are controlled by another company through a joint agreement, or a company that, with others, controls the accounting company, as determined by Interstate Commerce Commission (ICC) Account 706.

affinity card credit card promoted under a sponsoring agreement between an organization and a card issuing bank. In exchange for making available its membership list, the sponsor receives some compensation from the issuing bank, usually part of issuer's net interest income. The issuer may waive annual fees for affinity cardholders, or even offer the card at a lower rate than ordinary bank cards. See also CO-BRANDED CREDIT CARD.

afghani national currency of Afghanistan.

African Development Bank regional financial institution created by agreement among independent African countries in 1964. The United States' membership is authorized by the African Development Bank Act. Membership, originally restricted to African countries, became open to nonregional countries in 1981. The bank provides long-term development loans, primarily for agriculture and capital improvement projects.

after acquired clause

1. clause in a mortgage bond stating that any property acquired by the mortgagor after the mortgage is signed will be in cluded as collateral in the mortgage lien. Such clauses provide additional protection for lenders and may also help borrowers obtain financing at a better rate, although they limit a mortgagor's ability to raise capital through new borrowings. This situation often leads to debt swaps of new loans for old ones and rewriting of indenture agreements securing mortgage backed bonds.

2. in ASSET-BASED LENDING, lien extending the lender's security interest to any additional inventory or receivables acquired by the borrower. Sometimes called a FLOATING LIEN, this gives the lender adequate protection against loss when the loan collateral is constantly changing.

agency relationship between a principal and another party, named as agent, who is authorized to carry out the principal's instructions in transactions with a third party. For example, giving another person POWER OF ATTORNEY to negotiate a contract.

1. Securities. Federal agency securities other than those issued by the U.S. Treasury Department, such as obligations of the Government National Mortgage Association, the Federal Intermediate Credit Banks, the Export-Import Bank. These are exempt from Securities and Exchange Commission registration requirements. Some agency securities, such as Government National Mortgage Association participation certificates, are backed by the full faith and credit of the federal government.

2. Finance. Account managed by one party for another, as by a bank trust department for an institutional client, such as a pension fund. A bank, acting as agent, can also purchase or sell securities for individuals.

agency bank organization commonly used by foreign banks entering the U.S. market. Agency banking offices are exempt from interstate banking laws, but they cannot accept deposits or make loans under their own names. They are permitted to offer banking services of a parent, such as foreign exchange trading, letters of credit, and so on. Agency banks arrange loans to other banks and corporations, rather than to consumers.

Agency for International Development (AID)

federal agency created in 1961 to administer assistance programs to less developed countries (LDCs) by making loans or more favorable terms than private banks, and arranging technical assistance, distribution of surplus agricultural commodities, and direct grants. AID financings, arranged through letters of credit drawn on commercial banks, are fully backed by the U.S. government.

agent bank

1. bank named by members of a multibank lending syndicate to protect the interests of the participating banks in administering a loan to a foreign or domestic borrower. Its role is similar to a bond trustee. The agent bank is responsible for notifying other banks of advances or drawdowns by the borrower and changes in interest rate. Often synonomous with LEAD BANK or lead manager.
2. bank that participates in the credit card program of another bank, by issuing cards and acting as a merchant depository, but does not finance the card receivables. Most financial institutions participating in bank card programs are agents rather than principal issuers.
3. bank acting as agent for a foreign bank in collecting money due on a bill of exchange or a bankers' acceptance authorized by an import letter of credit.

aggregate demand (aggregate supply) consumer
spending plus government spending and investment spending by producers, considered a measure of total demand for goods and services in the economy. Aggregate demand is a measure of month-to-month growth or contraction of consumer spending, often used as an indicator of economic prosperity. Both monetary policy and fiscal policy attempt to influence aggregate demand to meet desired objectives of economic growth and employment. Aggregate supply is the economy's overall production of goods and services to meet anticipated demand.

aging schedule classification of accounts receivable, inventory or loans by the time intervals in which they are held. In a loan portfolio, aging shows the distribution of accounts from the date they are acquired, and is an indication of overall ASSET QUALITY or probability of repayment. Aging of accounts also reveals delinquency patterns, for example, any loans past-due 30 days, 60 days, 90 days or more—a useful guide in planning collection efforts. Loans 90-days delinquent are listed as NONACCRUAL loans, which means the bank is no longer posting interest

due on the income statement. If this situation persists these loans may have to be charged off as BAD DEBT.

In ASSET-BASED LENDING, aging of accounts is a listing of accounts receivable by invoice date, and is used in determining the BORROWING BASE of eligible receivables against which funds are advanced. See also ADVERSELY CLASSIFIED ASSETS; LOAN GRADING.

agio difference in value payable for exchanging one kind of money for another, for example, coins or bullion for paper money of equivalent face value. Also, a fee charged by a bank for exchanging coins for paper money. The term is used almost exclusively in Europe.

agreement language defining the terms and conditions of a legally binding contract between two parties, such as an extension of credit, or a loan secured by collateral. Examples include a deposit agreement as specified by an account SIGNATURE CARD, lease agreement, loan agreement, and credit card agreement.

agreement among underwriters contract between members of an UNDERWRITING GROUP offering a new issue of securities by which rights and responsibilities are assigned. Also called a *syndicate agreement*. A syndicate is a group of bankers who underwrite and distribute an offering of securities. The agreement designates the MANAGING UNDERWRITER and additional participating underwriters; the ALLOTMENT or portion of the offering to be assigned each member; the life of the syndicate; and the method for offering the securities, that is, whether the underwriters agree to purchase the securities from the issuer or try to place them on a BEST EFFORT basis. Ordinarily, the offering syndicate dissolves after the securities have been placed, usually within 60 days, or sometimes earlier if by mutual consent.

agreement corporation state chartered corporation engaged in international banking. These banking offices agree to limit their activities, under Federal Reserve Board regulations, to those permitted EDGE ACT CORPORATIONS, but have more liberal capital guidelines. Agreement corporations are chartered to conduct international operations through domestic offices, thereby allowing local firms access to international markets through local banks. In practice, the activities of these banks are similar to those of Edge Act banks.

agricultural credit credit extensions, notes, bills of exchange, and bankers' acceptances financing agricultural transactions. Banks lend to farmers for a variety of purposes, including (1) short-term credit to cover operating expenses; (2) intermediate credit for investment in farm equipment and real estate improvements; (3) long-term credit for acquisition of farm real estate and construction financing; and (4) debt repayment and refinancing. Commercial banks are the largest source of agricultural credit, followed by the Farm Credit Banks. FEDERAL LAND BANKS are the largest source of farm real estate lending, followed by insurance companies. See also FARM CREDIT SYSTEM; FARMER MAC; FARMERS HOME ADMINISTRATION.

algorithm set of rules for solving a problem in a finite number of steps using a mathematical formula, for example, a computer program. In banking, algorithms are used in loan pricing, financial modeling and asset-liability management, transfer pricing, and data security. See also DATA ENCRYPTION STANDARD; MODULUS 10 DIGIT.

alienation clause type of acceleration clause allowing the lender to demand full payment when mortgaged property is conveyed to another owner. An example is a DUE-ON-SALE clause in a mortgage deed. See also ASSUMABLE MORTGAGE.

alien corporation company incorporated in a foreign country. The term is sometimes used interchangeably with FOREIGN CORPORATION, although there is a technical distinction between the two. In state laws throughout the United States, the term foreign corporation is used to refer to a corporation chartered in another state. A Delaware corporation is a foreign corporation in every state except Delaware itself. In general business usage and in the federal tax laws, however, the term foreign corporation is used to refer to a company incorporated in a country other than the United States.

all-in cost total cost, whether explicit or implied. The all-in cost of a certificate of deposit is the rate of interest paid the depositor, the deposit insurance premium, and the opportunity cost of maintaining a noninterest bearing RESERVE REQUIREMENT balance at a Federal Reserve Bank. In bank lending, the term refers to borrower's total cost of credit, including net interest charged, origination fees, service fees, utilization fees, and so on. See also COST OF FUNDS; MARGIN; SPREAD; TOTAL RETURN.

allocated transfer risk reserve (ATRR) special portion of a bank's LOAN LOSS RESERVE against losses to foreign borrowers. The ATRR, required by the International Lending Supervision Act of 1983, is a reserve account covering so-called COUNTRY RISK, for example, a private borrower's inability to raise the necessary foreign exchange to pay external debt. The three federal banking regulators, the Comptroller of the Currency, the Federal Reserve Board, and the Federal Deposit Insurance Corporation, decide how much in transfer risk reserves is necessary. See also SOVEREIGN RISK.

allonge paper attached to a NEGOTIABLE INSTRUMENT for additional endorsements, as when a check is signed over to a third party. When a bank borrows at the Federal Reserve DISCOUNT WINDOW, it may put its own endorsement on a slip attached to promissory notes, bills or drafts offered as collateral.

all or none (AON) securities term used to indicate that no part of an order should be executed unless the full order can be filled. The issuer of new securities with an all or none agreement is entitled to cancel the entire offering unless the offering is fully subscribed. Similarly, a broker whose customers make an all or none order to buy securities must execute the entire order all at once or leave it unfilled. The order is not cancelled, however, unless it is marked FILL OR KILL (FOK).

allotment allocation, or share, usually of securities in an underwriting of new issues. Also, a method of filling bids in U.S. Treasury security auctions. In corporate securities, the most common usage occurs in "syndicated underwriting" where members of the syndicate subscribe to underwrite and distribute a certain number of shares. If the issue is over-subscribed, a portion of the entire issue is assigned to each participant. Formal notice is given in an allotment notice. In a "ratable allotment," for example, if 20 million subscriptions are received for a new issue of only 10 million shares, a participant in the underwriting syndicate who subscribed to 5 million shares would receive an allotment of 2.5 million shares to offer for sale.

allowance
1. **Accounting.** An account for adjusting the value of an asset through charges to current income; a reserve for depreciation.
2. **Banking.** LOAN LOSS RESERVE for anticipated charge-off of bad debt.
3. **Trusts.** A probate court's award to a fiduciary, for example, a WIDOW'S ALLOWANCE.

allowance for bad debt see LOAN LOSS RESERVES.

all savers certificate one-year certificate account, paying a rate tied to Treasury bill yields, authorized by the Economic Recovery Tax Act of 1981 to attract funds to mortgage lenders, primarily thrifts. Certificate holders received an exemption from federal income taxes for interest income up to $1,000 for individuals and $2,000 for a married couple filing jointly. None have been issued after December 1982.

altered check check or other NEGOTIABLE INSTRUMENT with the date, dollar amount, or payee's name changed or erased, usually for fraudulent purposes. Banks may refuse to honor checks if tampering is suspected.

alternative minimum tax flat rate federal tax to ensure that wealthy individuals, limited partnerships, trusts, and estates pay at least some tax. The tax is payable on capital gains from exercising stock options, for example, if taxes due using the alternative method are higher than the federal income taxes due on ordinary income. A corporate alternative minimum tax, enacted in the Tax Reform Act of 1986, is applied to a broad number of TAX PREFERENCE ITEMS such as depreciation charges on equipment, and also deductions from current income for LOAN LOSS RESERVES.

alternative mortgage instrument (AMI) any residential mortgage that differs from a conventional fixed-rate mortgage in interest rate charged, the periodic payment, or

terms for repayment. Included are ADJUSTABLE RATE MORTGAGES with interest rates tied to a money market index, GRADUATED PAYMENT MORTGAGES with payment increases at scheduled intervals, and mortgages with equity participation by the lender (SHARED APPRECIATION MORTGAGES). Designed to make housing more affordable to first-time home buyers, these loans were popularized by banks and savings and loans in the early 1980s, when high interest rates made conventional 30-year mortgage financing unattractive for borrowers. Many of the alternative forms of mortgage financing involved NEGATIVE AMORTIZATION of interest. Monthly payments in the early years of a loan are not sufficient to pay the interest due, thereby increasing the lender's credit exposure; in later years, payments are gradually raised or the repayment schedule extended to recover the unpaid interest. See also ANNUAL CAP; BALLOON MORTGAGE; CREATIVE FINANCING; GROWING EQUITY MORTGAGE; HOME EQUITY CREDIT; INTEREST ONLY LOAN; REVERSE MORTGAGE; ROLLOVER.

amendment addition, deletion, or change to a legal document. All parties to the agreement must formally consent to an amendment by signing it. Only then does the amendment become an integral part of the document and is binding on all parties to the original agreement.

American Bankers Association (ABA) national trade association of commercial banks in the United States, organized in 1875. The majority of the 14,000 U.S. banks are members of the association, which sponsors conferences and seminars, and promotes professional development in banking through ABA banking schools and the ABA educational arm, the AMERICAN INSTITUTE OF BANKING. ABA also represents the banking industry before Congress and federal regulatory agencies. See also TRADE ASSOCIATION.

American depositary receipt (ADR) negotiable certificate issued by a U.S. bank for shares of stock issued by a foreign corporation. The securities are held in a custodial account, either at the issuing bank or an agent. ADRs are registered with the Securities and Exchange Commission, and give the holder the same benefits of ownership as shareholders. Two types of American Depositary Receipts include sponsored ADRs, which are approved and promoted by the issuing corporation; and unsponsored ADRs, which are not backed by the issuer. ADRs are priced in dollars, and traded on stock exchanges and over-the-counter in the same fashion as U.S issued securities. See also INTERNATIONAL DEPOSITARY RECEIPT.

American Institute of Banking (AIB) educational division of the AMERICAN BANKERS ASSOCIATION. AIB promotes professional advancement in banking through classroom instruction, seminars, study groups, and correspondence courses, and is supported by participating financial institutions through 600 local chapters.

American National Standards Institute (ANSI) nonprofit organization, based in New York City, which sponsors industry standards for information management and financial communication between firms. The AMERICAN BANKERS ASSOCIATION has responsibility for the ANSI financial industry standards committee (ANSI X9).

American rule see PRUDENT MAN RULE.

American Stock Exchange (AMEX) second largest stock exchange in the United States in trading volume; it lists securities of more small- to medium-sized companies than the New York Stock Exchange, and handles options trading for a large number of New York Stock Exchange listed companies. It also handles the largest volume of foreign securities traded in the United States, which are purchased and sold as AMERICAN DEPOSITARY RECEIPTS.

amortization reduction in the value of an asset over the period owned; also the liquidation of debt through payments to a creditor or to a sinking fund.
1. **Banking.** The payment of a loan by periodic payments of principal and interest, resulting in a declining principal balance and eventual repayment in full. This form of debt repayment is LEVEL PAYMENT AMORTIZATION. Other amortization methods have repayment schedules in which the early loan payments don't fully cover the interest due, a situation called NEGATIVE AMORTIZATION.

  Even though level payment amortization calls for the same payment in every installment, the loan payments are divided unequally between principal balance and interest owed. In the early years of a 30-year mortgage, a higher portion of early loan payments goes toward payment of interest than reducing the principal; as the loan is gradually paid down, an increasing portion of each loan payment is allocated to the loan PRINCIPAL until a zero-balance is eventually reached. See also ADD-ON INTEREST; AMORTIZATION SCHEDULE; BALLOON MORTGAGE; REBATE; RULE OF THE 78's; SIMPLE INTEREST.

2. **Securities.** An accounting process for adjusting the book value of bonds purchased above PAR VALUE to the face value during the period owned. Compare to ACCRETION OF DISCOUNT.

3. **Accounting.** A gradual reduction in book value of GOOD WILL and other intangible assets. The preferred term for writing off fixed assets such as plant or equipment is DEPRECIATION.

amortization schedule table commonly used in mortgages and installment loans, showing the number of payments due, the amount due in each installment, the declining principal balance, and the number of years needed to fully extinguish the debt.

AMORTIZATION OF ONE-YEAR LOAN AT 10%, SIMPLE INTEREST

Monthly Payment (P&I): 87.92

To Principal	To Interest	Balance
79.59	8.33	920.41
80.25	7.67	840.16
80.92	7.00	759.24
81.59	6.33	677.65
82.27	5.65	595.38
82.96	4.96	512.42
83.65	4.27	428.77
84.35	3.57	344.42
85.05	2.87	259.37
85.76	2.16	173.61
86.47	1.45	87.14
87.19	.73	−.05

amount financed credit or advance actually made available to a borrower, repayable according to terms of the loan. It is equal to the loan PRINCIPAL less any prepaid finance charges, and does not include payments such as prepaid DISCOUNT POINTs that are not included in the finance charge. See also ADD-ON RATE; AMORTIZATION.

analyst see CREDIT ANALYST.

announcement effect market reaction to reports from regulatory agencies, such as growth in the money supply, borrowing by the Treasury Department, or changes in key interest rates, as when the Federal Reserve Board raises the DISCOUNT RATE, potentially a warning of tight credit and higher interest rates. Also known as *signal effect*. Policymakers in Washington often publicly announce changes in key borrowing rates, regulatory policy, and so on, in anticipation of their easing or tightening credit, which sends a signal to the credit markets. Other forms of signal effect are market reactions to the news.

annual cap clause in an ADJUSTABLE RATE MORTGAGE limiting any increase in the interest rate during a calendar year adjustment period to a preset amount or ceiling, giving the borrower a cushion against a sudden increase in mortgage payments and PAYMENT SHOCK when the loan rate is adjusted, particularly in periods of rising interest rates. A 10% mortgage with a 2% annual cap will increase only to 12% even if the mortgage INDEX rate goes up by 3%. See also LIFE OF LOAN CAP; PAYMENT CAP.

annual clean up see CLEAN-UP REQUIREMENT.

annual percentage rate (APR) cost of credit in consumer loans, expressed as a percentage rate per year. The APR is a more accurate measure of the cost of credit than the INTEREST RATE charged by the lender, because the APR takes into consideration the amortizing of loan balances through periodic payments. Under the federal TRUTH IN LENDING ACT, the APR must be stated in loan agreements, and disclosed with great accuracy—within $^{1}/_{8}$th of one percentage point (.125%). In OPEN-END CREDIT plans, however, the annualized rate (computed by multiplying the periodic rate by 12; for example, a monthly rate of 1.5% x 12 months = an 18% APR) is less accurate, as it assumes the current balance will be kept for a full year without any additional charges, and is for information purposes only. Consumer finance charges disclosed under Truth in Lending are usually never the same as interest charges under state USURY laws, because APR finance charges include not only interest, but application fees and other charges that are excluded from the definition of interest under state law. The APR does, however, allow consumers to do more comparison shopping when applying for a loan. See also EFFECTIVE RATE; NOMINAL INTEREST RATE.

annual report audited annual disclosure of performance to shareholders of a public corporation, as required by the Securities and Exchange Commission. It contains management's review, the corporate income statement, balance sheet, as well as other schedules, such as flow of funds and changes in capital accounts. Also in the annual report is the auditor's letter, a statement containing the ACCOUNTANT'S OPINION. See also FORM 10K.

annuity investment contract, usually purchased from an insurance company, making a series of payments over a period of time, for a fixed number of years or the life of the annuitant. Payments at scheduled intervals (monthly, quarterly, annually, or semi-annually) begin when the annuitant reaches a certain age. For individual investors, the most common annuities are fixed dollar annuities, guaranteeing repayment of invested principal, plus interest; variable annuities, devised as an inflation hedge, that pay an amount based on capital appreciation of a portfolio. See also BANK INVESTMENT CONTRACT.

antedate see BACK DATING.

anticipated balance estimated balance of a SAVINGS ACCOUNT or TIME DEPOSIT account at maturity or other future date, including compounded interest, assuming no additional deposits or withdrawals occur.

anticipated interest estimated interest a savings account will earn as of a future date, assuming that there is normal compounding of interest and no additional deposits or withdrawals occurring during the interest period.

anticipation any advance payment of an obligation prior to the date payment is due, usually to save interest costs.
1. **Banking.** Borrower's legal right, if allowed by a mortgage instrument, to repay the outstanding principal and interest on a loan, as when refinancing the loan at a lower rate. Also, deposit of funds for payment of an ACCEPTANCE prior to the maturity date, reducing the customer's liability.
2. **Accounting.** Charges to income or future earnings before these earnings are realized.

antitrust laws legislation designed to prevent monopolies or business practices limiting free market competition. Although some 40 states have adopted such legislation, the more important acts are these federal laws: (1) the Sherman Antitrust Act of 1890, which outlawed monopolies, restraints of trade, and business combinations (called trusts) created for the sole purpose of restricting competition, though it did not define these terms; (2) the Federal Trade Commission Act of 1914, creating the Federal Trade Commission, a federal agency with power to regulate interstate commerce, investigate business activities (except those by banks) and issue enforcement orders; (3) the Clayton Antitrust Act of 1914 and amendments, which banned tie-in contracts, interlocking directorates, and certain types of HOLDING COMPANY acquisitions.

   In banking, antitrust legislation is enforced by the U.S. Department of Justice, which has authority to review pending mergers, holding company acquisitions, and stock purchases, and by state attorneys general or judicial departments. The Bank Merger Act of 1960 gives banking regulatory agencies the authority to approve or reject mergers of banks or bank holding companies, and the Justice Department may intervene if it disagrees. An evolving area in antitrust regulation is the concept of *market power*, which relates specifically to JOINT VENTURE activities by groups of financial institutions such as an automated teller machine (ATM) network. The prevailing view, supported by arbitration cases, holds that network operators cannot bar nonmember banks if the service provided (for instance, access to ATMs owned by other banks) is so widely accepted by the public that limiting bank participation will harm other banks wishing to join. See also HERFINDAHL INDEX.

apportionment proportional division of rights, ownership, or expenses, as between buyer and seller in a real estate conveyance. In trusts and estates, it applies to the division of income and administration expenses between two or more accounts, for example, principal and interest income, or the division of estate taxes among heirs of an estate. Contrast with allocation, which assigns income earned or expenses paid to a single account for accounting purposes.

appraisal written estimate of market value by a qualified appraisor, based on an analysis of relevant data. A market value estimate, often used as the basis of determining collateral value in bank lending, may be based on replacement cost, sales of comparable property, or expected future income from income producing property. See also LOAN TO VALUE RATIO.

appreciation
1. increase in the value of an asset through a rise in market price, appraised value, or income earned, as compared to an earlier period. The opposite is DEPRECIATION.
2. increase in the value of one currency vis-a-vis another, without any change in official value occurring. It results from growth in market demand for either currency rather than official action such as a currency revaluation.

approved list
1. **Banking.** Bonds or other securities that a bank may hold as investments, usually based on ratings from bond rating firms such as Standard & Poor's, Moody's, Fitch's, and others. Federal Reserve regulations limit investments by national banks to investment grade securities as determined by a ratings service. For example, Standard & Poor's Triple B (BBB) or higher. State chartered banks are subject to the same investment requirements as national banks by the Federal Reserve Act. Also, bond investments of mutual savings banks are closely regulated by statute in several states.

2. Investments. A list of investments authorized for a fiduciary, by state statute, or by directors of a mutual fund

arbitrage profit making by buying a security, currency, or commodity at a low price in one market and simultaneously selling in another market at a higher price. Alternately, an arbitrageur borrows in one market and lends in another. The effect is to diminish price differences between markets.

There are several forms of arbitrage transactions. In the cash market, an arbitrage deal usually involves money market instruments issued in one money center and invested in another at a higher rate. For example, a bank issues a three-month $100,000 certificate of deposit in the United States at 10% and buys a three-month Eurodollar CD bearing the same face value at 10.50%. It also refers to switching similar assets, e.g., CERTIFICATES OF DEPOSIT or TREASURY BILLS denominated in different currencies; if the exchange risk is covered by a forward agreement the transaction is known as COVERED INTEREST ARBITRAGE.

In the futures market, arbitrage is sometimes called maturity arbitrage, for example, buying three-month delivery contracts and selling six-month contracts in a particular currency (also known as a FORWARD FORWARD).

Arbitrage also relates to SWAP transactions where similar issues of fixed-income securities are exchanged and later resold. See also COVERED INTEREST ARBITRAGE; CURRENCY SWAP; HEDGE/HEDGING; INTEREST RATE SWAP.

arbitration
1. settlement of a dispute after a hearing of opposing arguments by an arbitrator, rather than a court of law. If binding arbitration is accepted, the parties involved agree to follow the arbitrator's decision, which is binding only on the parties to the dispute, and is not a legal precedent, unlike a judicial ruling. In deciding complex issues, arbitration can be a more expedient way of resolving disputes than formal litigation and adjudication before a court of law.
2. in the securities industry, a method for settling disputes between member firms, or between member firms and nonmembers. Securities arbitration generally follows rules set by the National Association of Securities Dealers, the Municipal Securities Rulemaking Board, and the securities exchanges. The opinion of a three- to five-member board of arbitration is

considered final and binding. Arbitration of disputes involving broker-dealers and their customers is often part of a brokerage agreement, but can often limit a brokerage client's right to sue a broker-dealer.

arm's length transaction transaction carried out by unrelated or unaffiliated parties, as by a willing buyer and a willing seller, each acting in his own self-interest. Pricing based on such transactions is the basis of fair market valuations. Transactions involving parent companies and subsidiaries are not made at arms length.

arrears
1. debt, installment loan payment, or bond interest due but unpaid. Loans unpaid after an allowed GRACE PERIOD are considered delinquent. The term also applies to unpaid preferred stock dividends.
2. mortgage or installment loan interest payable at specific dates for the use of borrowed money in the previous period.

articles of incorporation document stating the purpose of a private corporation, filed by founders of a CORPORATION at a designated state office, e.g., with the Secretary of State. When approved, it becomes the firm's certificate of incorporation, giving the corporation its legal existence, subject to the laws of the state where incorporated. The filing lists the names of incorporators and amount of authorized shares of stock. After the charter is granted, corporate directors adopt by-laws stating, among other things, the operating rules of the corporation.

articles of partnership written agreement by persons establishing a partnership, stating, among other things, the nature of the business being formed, the capital contribution of each partner as well as their duties and responsibilities, and the share in net profits of the organization. Also called PARTNERSHIP AGREEMENT.

In a business partnership, a common form of organization in law and accounting firms, profits and losses flow through to the partners of the firm, who pay taxes as individuals. Unless otherwise stated in the articles of partnership, partners share equally in the profits and surplus of the partnership. See also GENERAL PARTNER; LIMITED PARTNERSHIP.

Article XII company investment company chartered under New York state law to finance international banking transactions. An Article XII company cannot accept deposits, but can hold credit balances and offer other banking services. These companies, which can be owned by foreign banks, do not maintain reserve requirements or have access to the Federal Reserve's Fed Wire, but can be members of privately operated funds transfer systems, such as the Clearing House Interbank Payments System in New York.

Asian currency unit (ACU) unit of account for dollar denominated deposits held in separate accounts in banks in Singapore, Hong Kong, and other Asian financial centers. The term refers to nonresident dollar deposits in Asian financial centers. Contrast with EUROPEAN CURRENCY UNIT.

Asian Development Bank international development finance institution, organized in 1966, to lend economic assistance and technical support to developing countries in Asia. Membership is open to members and associate members of the United Nations Commission for Asia and the Far East, renamed the Economic and Social Commission for Asia and the Pacific in 1974. The United States' membership is authorized by the Asian Development Bank Act. The bank lends capital assistance through the Asian Development Fund, a SOFT LOAN window established in 1973, and supported by member contributions, and transfers from its own capital. See also MULTILATERAL DEVELOPMENT BANKS.

asked price lowest price at which a seller is willing to offer securities or financial futures, also called a QUOTATION. It is then compared against the BID price, the highest price offered by a potential buyer.

assessed valuation appraisal of real and personal property by taxing authorities for computation of AD VALOREM taxes. This is used to determine debt limits for municipal governments, as set by charter or by statutory limit, depending on the municipality or the state where it is located. Local property taxes are computed from an assessment ratio that sets taxes payable against a percentage of fair market value.

assessment
1. tax on real property, whether an annual property tax based on current fair market value, or special assessments for sewers or public improvements.
2. amount sometimes levied by banks, corporations, and insurance companies on stockholders to cover an impaired capital position or unanticipated losses.
3. in bankruptcy, special charge to the holders of stock not fully subscribed, payable to the bankruptcy trustee for benefit of creditors.

asset anything owned by a person or organization having monetary value, usually its cost or fair market value. An asset may be a specific property, such as title to real estate or other tangible property, or enforceable claims against others.
1. **Banking.** Loans, discounts, investment securities (government bonds, municipal bonds), and claims against other banks. Loans account for the largest portion of interest earning assets held by banks and thrift institutions. Also included in this category are FEDERAL FUNDS sold to other banks; checks in the process of collection. See also REAL ESTATE OWNED; TRADING ACCOUNT ASSETS.
2. **Finance.** There are several major asset categories: (1) current assets—cash and short-term items convertible into cash within one year; (2) FIXED ASSETS—furniture, plant, and equipment owned by a firm, which are depreciated over their useful life; INTANGIBLE ASSETS—patents, trademarks, or goodwill, which have a value and carry a cost; and (3) pledged assets—collateral for a bank loan or purchase of securities on margin.

asset-backed securities bonds or debt securities collateralized by the cash flow from a pool of auto loans, credit card receivables, vehicle and equipment leases, consumer loans, and other obligations. The bonds give the holder an UNDIVIDED INTEREST in the securitized assets, and are funded by the cash flows received by the issuer from regular payments of principal and interest from borrowers.

The process of converting loans into marketable securities is known as SECURITIZATION. When mortgage loans, consumer loans, commercial loans, and leases are securitized, the pools of assets backing a particular issue are transferred to a GRANTOR

TRUST, a passive entity that issues the securities that are purchased by investors. Virtually any debt obligation with regularly scheduled principal and interest payments can be securitized: auto loans, credit card receivables, home improvement loans, leases, residential mortgages, and second mortgages. Examples are COLLATERALIZED AUTO RECEIVABLE SECURITIES (CARS), CERTIFICATES FOR AMORTIZING REVOLVING DEBT (CARDS), and MORTGAGE-BACKED SECURITIES, such as COLLATERALIZED MORTGAGE OBLIGATIONS (CMOs), and REAL ESTATE MORTGAGE INVESTMENT CONDUITS (REMICs). Securitizing bank debt also gives lenders another source of funds for making new loans, and is a technique actively used in ASSET-LIABILITY MANAGEMENT. See also ASSET SALES; SECONDARY MORTGAGE MARKET.

asset-based lending financing that advances credit secured by a firm's balance sheet assets, such as inventory, receivables, or collateral other than real estate. Also called asset-based financing. The most common forms are ACCOUNTS RECEIVABLE FINANCING, in which the lender advances funds against trade receivables, inventory lending, and equipment leasing. The lender takes a lien against the pledged collateral under Article 9 of the UNIFORM COMMERCIAL CODE, and may seize the collateral if the borrower defaults. Asset-based lending covers a broad range of secured lending activities, and is used to support the credit needs of firms that cannot obtain bank financing on a fully unsecured basis. See also FACTORING; WAREHOUSE RECEIPT.

asset card transaction card giving the holder access to an underlying asset, such as a brokerage margin account or financial institution deposit account. Often used to draw down funds from a centralized ASSET MANAGEMENT ACCOUNT. Also, a bank DEBIT CARD.

asset coverage measure of an organization's SOLVENCY or its ability to pay back bank debt and other credit obligations from earnings, usually expressed as a ratio of balance sheet assets to long-term debt. The ratio of assets to long-term debt is computed by dividing total assets (less intangible assets, current liabilities, and existing senior debt) by the debt or equity being considered. The result can be expressed as a ratio, a percentage, or in dollar terms. Direct asset coverage per share of common stock is called net book value per share of common stock. See also DEBT SERV-ICE RATIO.

asset ledger subsidiary ledger of asset accounts in which journal entries of transactions affecting the assets are summarized and classified into debits and credits. Depending on the size of an organization and the complexity of its accounting system, it may have one sub-ledger for all assets or many different ledgers for different types of assets, for example, fixed assets.

asset-liability committee (ALCO) senior management committee in a bank or thrift institution, responsibile for coordinating the institution's borrowing and lending strategy, and funds acquisition to meet profitability objectives as interest rates change. This committee also monitors actions by the Federal Reserve that may affect interest rates, such as a change in the Federal Reserve DISCOUNT RATE. When interest rates are rising, lenders shorten loan maturities; when rates are falling, they are more likely to fund new lending through longer-term Certificates of Deposit (CDs), or fixed-income debt such as U.S. Treasury securities.

asset-liability management active management of a financial institution's BALANCE SHEET with the objective of maintaining balanced growth in net interest income and earnings and control of interest rates risk as rates change. Interest rate risk results from the time difference in the maturities of assets (primarily bank loans) and liabilities (interest earning deposit accounts), or when the rates paid depositors and yields earned on loans change at different speeds. For example, financing 30-year fixed rate mortgages with shorter maturity time deposits. When more loans reprice during a given period of time, the balance sheet is said to be asset-sensitive. If more deposit liabilities reprice the balance sheet is liability-sensitive.

When general interest rates are rising, the result is favorable growth in the bank's net interest income. If rates are falling, banks are more likely to lengthen the maturities on new loans, or invest in longer-term certificates of deposit or fixed income debt to take advantage of prevailing higher yields and low securities prices. Asset-liability management is designed to manage the impact of these interest rate fluctuations on the balance sheet.

Because bank loans are valued for accounting purposes at the original cost when loans are booked, rather than current market value, the balance sheet can hide paper losses. These losses would have to be realized if loans earning less than current market rates are sold to a third party, or if the borrower pays off a loan early and the lender cannot relend those funds at the same rate because interest rates have gone up. For example, a 30-year fixed rate mortgage earning 12%; if the borrower prepays the loan when mortgage rates are at 10%, the lender may not be able to redeploy those funds in 12% assets. Differences in book values of assets and liabilities are measured in several ways. One method is GAP measurement, which shows the concentrations of assets and liabilities, and the net difference—the gap—between them. Gap is a measure of funding MISMATCH, that is, whether there is a funding surplus or deficit for a particular time period. For example, a four-month funding surplus occurs if a bank has more available deposits than loans and investments in the coming four months. This bank is liability sensitive; to close the gap, then, more loans are needed. Gap is an imprecise measuring tool, however, because it does not take into account the effect of interest rate changes on either deposits or loans, as borrowers pay off loans when rates fall, and reinvest in higher earning deposits when interest rates are rising. A more precise measure of interest rate risk is DURATION, which measures the impact of changes in interest rates on the expected maturities of both assets and liabilities. In essence, duration takes the gap report data and converts that information into present-value worth of deposits and loans, which is more meaningful in estimating maturities and the probability that either assets or liabilities will reprice during the period under review. See also DYNAMIC GAP; GAPPING; LIQUIDITY; MATCHED MATURITIES; MISMATCH; NEGATIVE GAP; POSITIVE GAP; REFINANCE RISK; REINVESTMENT RISK; REPRICING OPPORTUNITIES; STATIC GAP; ZERO GAP.

asset management account money-management account combining an array of investment services with convenient access by check writing, credit or debit card, and a combined statement of financial position. Brokerage accounts, such as the Merrill Lynch Cash Management Account™, combine a margin account for securities purchases with a money market fund for investing idle balances. Bank sponsored accounts require lower initial balances, are usually built around a checking or NOW account, and allow securities buying, usually from discount brokers.

asset quality estimation of the quality of bank assets (principally loans and leases) as measured by a lender's credit standards, and the liquidity of securities held in the investment portfolio. Originally, asset quality was defined as the lender's estimate of full repayment of principal and interest, as measured by generally acceptable credit standards. If assets are packaged for resale to investors in the secondary market, the criterion for determining quality of assets is, "What can I expect to get in the market if I sell my loans?" In this context, asset quality has less to do with charge-off analysis than the marketability of the credit portfolio.

asset sales nonrecourse sale of bank receivables to a third party, either through the sale of WHOLE LOANS or WHOLE POOLS of loans, or SECURITIZATION, that is, issuing securities collateralized by the receivables of bank credits (residential mortgages, auto loans, leases, credit card receivables). Accounting treatment of asset sales is complicated, and determines whether a transaction is a sale of assets. In general terms, the test of an asset sale is whether the seller gives the buyer control over the assets transferred, and also any residual interest, without recourse to the seller. Transfers with recourse, allowing the buyer to resell a portion of the assets back to the seller, are treated by Financial Accounting Standards Board Rule 77 as a financing rather than a sale of assets.

If the agreement requires the seller to take back any bad loans, it is not considered for accounting purposes a true sale of assets and the seller cannot deduct the value of loans sold from its loan portfolio. See also ASSET-BACKED SECURITIES; PRIVATE PLACEMENT.

asset swap exchange of one asset for another, often done to improve the quality of a bank's loan portfolio by, for example, converting a fixed rate asset into an asset with a floating rate. There are numerous examples: converting a EUROBOND into a synthetic floating rate note through an exchange of interest payments; an exchange of one commodity for another, as in a commodity swap; or a DEBT FOR EQUITY SWAP.

assignment
1. signing over title, rights, or other interests to another person.
2. in Letters of Credit, transfer by a BENEFICIARY of all or part of the credit to another party, which must be confirmed by the advising bank.
3. writing on the back of a stock certificate transferring ownership to another holder.
4. transfer of debtor's property to creditors, called an assignment for the benefit of creditors. Transfers in the 90 days prior to a bankruptcy petition may, however, be set aside by a bankruptcy trustee. See also VOIDABLE PREFERENCE.
5. option writer's notice to the Options Clearing Corp. of his intention to fulfill an offsetting buy, resulting in an assignment in favor of the seller.

associate bank bank that is a member of a corporation or joint venture providing common benefits. Examples include banks that are members in a clearing house association and those affiliated with a bank card system such as Visa or MasterCard International. Typically, associations have different classes of membership, depending on equity ownership, and other factors. Also called an associate member.

association number see ABA TRANSIT NUMBER.

Association of Bank Holding Companies see TRADE ASSOCIATION.

Association of Reserve City Bankers see TRADE ASSOCIATION.

Association of Thrift Holding Companies see TRADE ASSOCIATION.

assumable mortgage MORTGAGE giving the borrower the right to assign the unpaid balance of his obligation, without prepayment penalty, to another person upon sale of the mortgaged property. The buyer assumes payment of the loan at the same rate and terms for the remainder of the mortgage, and the seller remains secondarily liable for the obligation. Department of Veterans Affairs mortgages and mortgages insured by the

Federal Housing Administration are generally assumable by the buyer. Contrast with PORTABLE MORTGAGE. See also ASSUMPTION; DUE-ON-SALE CLAUSE.

assumption mortgage clause stating the terms under which an existing mortgage or deed of trust may be conveyed to another party. Generally, a mortgage cannot be transferred at the same rate and terms without written consent of the lender. See also ASSUMABLE MORTGAGE.

at par security issued or sold at nominal face value. The term generally applies to newly issued bonds, preferred stock, or debt securities. A $1,000 bond that is actually issued, or later re-sold, for $1,000 is sold at par. Although common stock usually carries a par value, it is usually set at an arbitrarily low amount ($1, for example) that bears little relation to the actual market price. This practice is followed because common stock that is originally issued at prices below par creates a contingent liability on the books of the original purchasers for the amount of the discount. See also PAR VALUE.

at sight denotes a negotiable instrument, such as a bill of exchange or draft payable when presented to the drawee.

attachment
1. writ authorizing seizure of property after a court approved judgment in favor of a creditor. After the court adjudicates its claim, the creditor must obtain a property execution authorizing garnishment of wages or seizure of personal assets, such as bank accounts, in a jurisdiction where the borrower resides, usually a municipality or county.
2. creditor's lien, which is said to attach to the borrower's assets in exchange for a loan or advance against a line of credit. See also SECURITY INTEREST.

attest sworn statement of fact or condition, duties or responsibilities, signed by person making the statement, often in the presence of a notary public or another indifferent person. In the case of a will, the testator signs in the presence of two or more witnesses, or before a notary public.

at the market see MARKET ORDER.

at the money refers to the STRIKE PRICE of an option contract when the option is about equal in price to the current market price of the underlying security or futures contract. See also IN THE MONEY; OUT OF THE MONEY.

attorney at law person licensed by a state to practice law, give legal advice, and represent clients in legal proceedings before a court or administrative agency. Generally, a lawyer.

attorney in fact person named by another to act as an agent in his behalf. Assignment is in writing, and is commonly referred to as a POWER OF ATTORNEY assignment, and may be general or limited to specific acts.

auction market system by which securities are bought and sold at the best possible price through competitive bidding. Prices are established by brokers acting as agents of buyers and sellers, as well as principal dealers acting for their own accounts. In the securities market, the best example is the New York Stock Exchange, where buyers and sellers make competitive bids for exchange listed securities by submitting order tickets to the exchange. The commodity futures market where interest rate futures are traded, is in contrast, an open outcry market, where market prices are set by direct interaction of exchange members standing in a pit on the trading floor.

The U.S. Treasury Department sells new issues of Treasury bills on a DISCOUNT YIELD basis through competitive auction bidding in which the price of bills offered for sale is gradually lowered, starting with the lowest yield (and highest price) until the entire amount being offered is sold. See also COMPETITIVE BID; DUTCH AUCTION.

audio response interactive voice communication system allowing bank customers to make financial transactions, as in telephone banking or telephone bill payment. A series of voice prompts programmed into the system gives the customer verbal instructions for making balance inquiries, transferring funds between accounts, and making bill payments to third parties. Also called *audiotex*. Contrast with VIDEOTEX.

audit examination and verification of a company's books and records by a qualified accountant. An auditor's letter of opinion, which may be qualified or unqualified, is included in the annual report. Community banks have generally been exempted from the requirement by bank regulators for an annual audit. Audits are also required by the Securities and Exchange Commission for companies with registered securities. Banks are exempt from this requirement, though bank holding companies are not.

audit department internal management control group responsible for maintaining accuracy of financial data through periodic inspections of branch offices and bank departments. The internal audit department also insures adherance to law, regulation, and policy.

auditor's opinion see ACCOUNTANT'S OPINION.

audit trail chronological record of a transaction, loan, or investment, including credit memos and related documents. Such a record reveals the step-by-step history of a transaction as it flows through the organization, enabling an after-the-fact review to determine the time and place where errors occurred. See also CREDIT REVIEW.

austral national currency of Argentina, replacing the peso in 1984.

authentication legal verification of the genuineness of a bond, document, or signature. In electronic funds transfers, authentication is a method of verifying that a payment instruction has in fact originated at the sending bank, and has not been tampered with by an unauthorized party. See also ATTEST; MESSAGE AUTHENTICATION CODE.

authority to purchase advice used in Far East trade, authorizing a correspondent bank to purchase drafts drawn on an importer rather than the importer's bank. Many banks add their own guarantee, giving the advice the same authority as a LETTER OF CREDIT.

authorization issuance of approval to complete a transaction or pay funds, for example a bank card authorization or payment authorization. In bank cards, the card issuing bank notifies the merchant processing bank, the merchant bank, that a cardholder has available credit and issues an AUTHORIZATION CODE for the transaction.

authorization code in bank cards, a message from a merchant processing bank, the acquirer bank, to a card accepting merchant approving transactions against the card presented by the cardholder. See also NEGATIVE AUTHORIZATION; POSITIVE AUTHORIZATION; ZERO-FLOOR LIMIT.

authorized investment investment by a fiduciary or trustee, following written instructions in a trust instrument. Contrast with legal investment conforming with regulations by state banking authorities or state law concerning permissible investments by fiduciaries and mutual savings banks.

authorized settlement agent bank that is authorized to submit checks or CASH ITEMS to a Federal Reserve Bank for collection. In bank cards, a bank authorized to honor clearing drafts for the settlement of interchange.

authorized stock (shares) maximum number of shares in each class of capital stock that a corporation can legally issue. (It may not actually issue all of the shares authorized.) The total shares per class of stock, for example, common stock, or preferred stock, is specified in the corporate charter or ARTICLES OF INCORPORATION. The number of authorized shares can be increased by amending the articles of incorporation or charter, which is usually accomplished by shareholder vote.

automated clearing house (ACH) computer-based clearing and settlement facility for interchange of electronic debits and credits among financial institutions. ACH entries can be substituted for checks in recurring payments such as mortgages, or in DIRECT DEPOSIT distribution of Federal and corporate benefits payments, including Social Security payments. Since the mid-1970s the ACH has functioned as a unified payment clearing system consisting of regional clearing house associations owned by financial institutions. The ACH, while used extensively in the early years as a payment system for fixed amount, recurring payments, is being used increasingly as a payments processor for business-to-business trade payments. The Federal Reserve Banks furnish the data processing services for most ACHs, although a few, notably the New York Automated Clearing House and the Cal-Western Automated Clearing House, are privately operated. Final settlement, or NET SETTLEMENT, of ACH transfers is made against Reserve Accounts at Federal Reserve banks. See also CASH CONCENTRATION & DISBURSEMENT; CORPORATE TRADE EXCHANGE; CORPORATE TRADE PAYMENT; ELECTRONIC DATA INTERCHANGE.

automated teller machine (ATM) computer terminal activated by a magnetically encoded BANK CARD, allowing consumers to make deposits, obtain cash from checking or savings accounts, pay bills, transfer money between accounts, and do other routine transactions as they would at a bank teller window. Nationwide automated teller machine networks make it possible for consumers to obtain cash from ATMs across the country by using ATM codes issued by their financial institutions and their PERSONAL IDENTIFICATION NUMBERS. ATMs in shared networks involving out-of-state banks are not considered branch offices, so long as the banking services offered do not include accepting deposits.

automatic bill payment see TELEPHONE BILL PAYMENT.

automatic deposit see DIRECT DEPOSIT.

automatic transfer of funds arrangement that moves funds between checking or savings accounts under prearranged conditions, usually to take advantage of higher rates offered on investment accounts. See also AUTOMATIC TRANSFER SERVICE; SWEEP ACCOUNT.

automatic transfer (of savings) (ATS) prearranged transfer of funds from a savings account to checking, allowing the depositor to earn interest until funds are needed to cover checks written or to maintain a minimum balance.

availability time period, expressed in days, from the day of deposit until funds are credited to an account's COLLECTED BAL-

ANCE, are available for spending or investment. Funds availability is determined by average clearing time, allowing for MAIL FLOAT and FEDERAL RESERVE FLOAT. See also AVAILABILITY SCHEDULE; CHECK HOLD; DEFERRED AVAILABILITY.

availability schedule table showing the number of days needed to clear a deposited check. Under the Expedited Funds Availability Act, financial institutions must give their customers access to deposited funds within a fixed number of days, depending on whether a check is drawn on a local or nonlocal bank. Local checks (checks deposited at a bank in the same Federal Reserve Regional Check Processing Center as the paying bank) must be available for use three business days after the day of deposit. See also CHECK HOLD.

available balance checking account balance a customer actually has use of: the current balance, less deposits not yet posted to the account. A bank may sometimes include checking account CASH RESERVE in computing the available balance.

available credit credit ready for use in new purchases, sometimes called open to buy. In bank cards, it is the difference between the AVERAGE OUTSTANDING BALANCE and the cardholder's preapproved credit limit. Also, the unused portion of a bank LINE OF CREDIT.

available funds
1. funds that a bank can put to use in meeting loan demand or hold in its investment portfolio, depending on market competition, demand for credit, interest rates, and other factors. The total is equal to cash on hand (VAULT CASH) and checks payable by other banks (cash and due from banks on the balance sheet) plus aggregate loans and investments.
2. AVAILABLE BALANCE in a depositor's account, which is the amount that can be invested readily, disbursed to pay creditors, or transferred to another account.

available reserve net difference between EXCESS RESERVES balances maintained in a RESERVE ACCOUNT at a Federal Reserve Bank or branch office, and funds borrowed at the DISCOUNT WINDOW.

AVAILABILITY OF FUNDS

Type of Deposit	When Funds Are Available for Use
—Cash —First $100 of any deposit of checks —Government checks, cashier's checks, certified checks, teller's checks —Checks written on another account at the same institution —Direct deposit and other electronic credits	Next business day after the day of deposit
—Checks written on local institutions*	Third business day after the day of deposit (second business day after Sept. 1, 1990)
—Checks written on nonlocal institutions — Deposits made at an automated teller machine owned by another institution	Seventh business day after the day of deposit (fifth business day after Sept. 1, 1990)

*Under the Expedited Funds Availability Act, a check is a local check if deposited in an institution in the same Federal Reserve check processing region as the paying bank. There are 48 check processing regions in the United States.

aval European term for a third party guaranty of payment on a bill of exchange or promissory note, endorsed by the guarantor's signature. Compare to ACCOMMODATION ENDORSER.

average annual yield average return per year for the entire term of a multiyear CERTIFICATE OF DEPOSIT (CD), assuming that compound interest earned remains on deposit. The average annual yield of a CD will be higher than the EFFECTIVE ANNUAL YIELD because it includes interest earned over a longer period of time.

average balance see AVERAGE DAILY BALANCE.

average collected balance average dollar amount on deposit in a checking account during an accounting period, equal to daily ledger balances less uncollected checks, divided by the number of days. See also AVAILABLE BALANCE; UNCOLLECTED FUNDS.

average daily balance
1. average amount in a deposit account, equal to the sum of daily deposit balances during an accounting period, usually a month, divided by the number of days.
2. method of computing CREDIT CARD finance charges, computed by taking the daily beginning balance, adding new charges for that day, and subtracting any payments applied to purchases. The resulting total, divided by the number of days in the billing period, is multiplied by the finance charge.

average daily float average dollar amount of checks or drafts in the process of collection, and not credited to the account as collected funds or available funds. Also referred to as items in collection.

average life number of years until the date when one half of each dollar of principal in a security will be paid. Average life is a shorthand method of computing a bond's retirement date, which determines its YIELD TO MATURITY. This calculation is only an approximation, as it depends on borrower prepayments and other factors. For example, some 30-year conventional mortgages will prepay much faster than others. Average lives of corporate and municipal bonds frequently are determined by prepayments into a sinking fund. Also called WEIGHTED AVERAGE LIFE in mortgage backed securities or AVERAGE MATURITY in corporate and municipal bonds. See also CASH FLOW YIELD; DURATION; HALF LIFE.

average outstanding balance average unpaid balance in a credit card portfolio, including interest-paying balances carried over from previous billing periods. The average outstanding balance, a measure of profitability and account usage, is equal to the total number of accounts divided by the number of accounts with balances.

average ticket average merchant transaction in a bank card program. Also called average draft. Computed by dividing total dollars charged in a time period by the number of sales drafts, it is indicative of account activity and indirectly is a measure of bank card INTERCHANGE fees payable by other banks.

award

1. decision by a board of arbitration, after hearing arguments presented by the parties to a dispute, in favor of either of the parties.
2. acceptance of a competitive bid in AUCTION MARKET sale for U.S. Treasury securities or municipal bonds.

away broker's expression for a trade or quote originating with a broker other than the one quoting the price. For example, "The bid is 1.7890 for deutschmarks away (from me)." It may also refer to trades executed outside the quoted market price "away from the market."

B

back contracts futures contracts farthest from expiration. Contracts that will not soon mature. Also known as back months or distant contracts. Contrast with front contracts or nearby contracts.

back dating writing a check or draft with a date earlier than today's date. This does not affect its negotiability, as long as the check is cashed or deposited within six months of the date written. The opposite is a POST-DATED check.

back end load mutual fund that charges a sales commission, or LOAD, if the investor disposes or sells shares in the fund. Also called trail commissions. Compare with FRONT-END LOAD.

back office area in a bank where checks are paid, deposits and withdrawals are posted to accounts, and interest earned on deposits is credited to the account holders. Also known as a bank's operations center. The back office may, in fact, be in a separate building where loan payments are received, checks drawn on other banks are bundled and sent out to the issuing bank for payment, customer ACCOUNT STATEMENTs are prepared for mailing; and activity by a bank or its customers is reconciled periodically against the bank's central accounting system. See also AUTOMATED CLEARING HOUSE; CUSTOMER INFORMATION FILE; PROOF AND TRANSIT; PROOF OF DEPOSIT; WIRE TRANSFER.

back-to-back commitment two-part commitment by a lender. The first part is an advance on a construction loan; the second is a long-term commitment, also called the TAKE-OUT COMMITMENT, by the same bank lender for permanent mortgage financing on the property.

back-to-back letters of credit two letters of credit, one in favor of the buyer's agent and one financing the seller. A back-to-back credit is created when an exporter holding an irrevocable LETTER OF CREDIT persuades the buyer's bank (the advising bank) to open a second credit in favor of the merchandise supplier. The two credits are identical in all respects, except that the supplier becomes the BENEFICIARY of the back-to-back credit, and amount of the second credit is less than the original export credit. The difference is the import agent's commission.

back-to-back loan two-party loan between a parent company in one country and subsidiaries in another. Similar to a PARALLEL LOAN, with the important difference that a back-to-back loan gives the lender the right to OFFSET claims against pledged collateral if the borrower defaults, while the parallel loan does not. The two-party, or parallel, loan, is less risky for the lender because the parent company is obligated to step in if a foreign subsidiary fails to pay the note.

backup sudden reversal of a market trend. When interest rates are rising, prices of fixed-income MONEY MARKET instruments (for example, Treasury bonds) fall, and bond yields automatically rise. The market is said to back up because bond holders cannot liquidate their holdings as easily as they could before the reversal. When an investor, anticipating a market shift, switches from longer-term to shorter-term bonds, he is said to back up or shorten his portfolio.

backup line bank line of credit serving as an alternate source of liquidity for an issuer of commercial paper, and a source of credit for the buyer, or purchaser in the event the issuer is unable to rollover the paper at maturity. The amount of backup varies from as little as 50% for some AAA rated issuers to 100% for lower quality paper. Ordinarily, the line is a confirmed letter of credit or a contractual facility (revolving credit agreement or revolving underwriting facility) in place at issue time. Or, it may be cash set aside by the issuer. A bank line typically is a SWING LINE. Bank credit lines are paid for by compensating balances or by straight fee.

backup withholding IRS rule requiring banks to withhold a percentage of interest or dividends payable to taxpayers who did not pay taxes on interest or stock dividends in a prior tax year, or who did not disclose their Social Security number to their financial institutions—withholding at the 20% level in 1988.

bad bank specially chartered bank, acting as a self-liquidating trust, chartered by a bank holding company to hold nonperforming assets owned by a federally insured bank. Transfer of bad loans improves the ASSET QUALITY of the seller. Also known as a *collection bank*.

bad check any check dishonored, for wrong endorsement, lack of endorsement, insufficient funds, account closed, and so on. Also called a RETURN ITEM. State laws vary on penalties that banks can charge for bad checks. See also CHECK KITING.

bad debt loans classified as a probable LOSS and having no economic value. These loans, past-due as to payment of interest and principal, are removed from the loan portfolio and their book value loss is charged to a reserve account (the LOAN LOSS RESERVE). Usually, an offsetting charge to current income is made to adjust for the deduction from the reserve account. See also BAD DEBT RECOVERY; LOAN LOSS PROVISION.

bad debt recovery collection of loans written off as uncollectible and charged to the lender's LOAN LOSS RESERVES account. Recoveries may come from several sources: the borrower's voluntary payment of some or all of the principal or interest payments due; FORECLOSURE and sale of the borrower's assets pledged as loan COLLATERAL; or GARNISHMENT of the borrower's wages, salary, or bank assets. See also REAL ESTATE OWNED; WORKOUT AGREEMENT.

baht national currency of Thailand.

bailment delivery of personal property for safekeeping by another, with control and possession passing from the bailor (the owner) to the bailee. For example, personal items or stock certificates, held in trust in a bank SAFE DEPOSIT BOX. The bailee has no knowledge of the items delivered and no fiduciary relationship is created, as in a TRUST agreement.

bailout financial assistance given to an insured bank or savings institution suffering a loss of earnings resulting from loan losses, deteriorating market conditions, or a sudden outflow of deposits in a depositor RUN. When the infusion of funds is from a federal deposit insurance agency (the BANK INSURANCE FUND, insuring

commercial bank deposits, or the SAVINGS ASSOCIATION INSUR-
ANCE FUND, insuring deposits in savings and loan associations),
the depositors actually get bailed out. The insurance agency may
arrange open bank assistance to a troubled bank, or arrange an
acquisition by a healthy financial institution. In either case, the
deposit insurance fund gives enough assistance, usually in the
form of promissory notes, to cover the difference between the
estimated market value of the bank's assets and its liabilities (the
bank's negative net worth), thereby recapitalizing the institution
so it may continue in operation. See also BRIDGE BANK; INSURED
DEPOSIT; MODIFIED PAYOFF; PURCHASE AND ASSUMPTION; RESO-
LUTION TRUST CORPORATION.

balance

1. amount available in an account after payment of service
   charges, less withdrawals or debits and deposits not credited.
   In a checking account, the most important figure is the account's COLLECTED BALANCE representing the total of deposits cleared, less checks paid and bank service charges.
2. to reconcile a checking account by comparing bank statement
   with check book register.
3. amount payable in a mortgage or installment loan payment.
   Also called the BALANCE DUE.

balance due
amount payable at regular intervals in a mortgage, installment loan or open-end credit account. In credit
cards, a nominal payment called the MINIMUM PAYMENT is due,
although the cardholder may pay any amount, up to the full
amount advanced against the account.

balance of payments
accounting of a country's eco-
nomic transactions with foreign countries in a stated period of
time, normally one year. The balance of payments for any country is divided into two broad categories: the CURRENT ACCOUNT,
representing import and export trade, plus income from tourism,
profits earned overseas, and interest payments; and the capital
account, representing the sum of bank deposits, investments by
private investors, and debt securities sold by a central bank or
official government agencies.

In economic terms, a balance of payments surplus means a
nation has more funds from trade and investments coming in
than it pays out to other countries, resulting in an APPRECIATION

in the value of its national currency versus currencies of other nations. A deficit in the balance of payments has the opposite effect: an excess of imports over exports, a dependence on foreign investors, and an overvalued currency. Countries experiencing a payments deficit must make up the difference by exporting gold or HARD CURRENCY reserves, such as the U.S. dollar, that are accepted currencies for settlement of international debts. See also INTERNATIONAL RESERVES; SPECIAL DRAWING RIGHTS.

balance reporting reporting of an organization's collected balances, by telephone or personal computer connection with a reporting bank's back office, usually on a daily basis. Daily reporting of account balances in one or more banks, normally done early in the business day, is a major component of CONTROLLED DISBURSEMENT services sold by banks to corporate cash management customers.

balance sheet statement of financial position listing assets owned, liabilities owed, and owner's equity as of a specific date. Banks accept deposits (counted as bank liabilities) and make loans (counted as bank assets), giving the balance sheet a more accurate snapshot of a bank's financial condition than the INCOME STATEMENT. This explains the importance of ASSET-LIABILITY MANAGEMENT in managing bank profitability and stability in earnings. Banks are required by regulation to combine earnings of a bank and affiliated companies in a CONSOLIDATED FINANCIAL STATEMENT, and to submit a periodic REPORT OF CONDITION, listing balance sheet assets and liabilities, to bank supervisory agencies.

　　Bank accounting systems differ from corporate accounting in that bank ledger accounts are balanced daily, resulting in a daily statement of condition, providing verification that a bank's books are in balance that day. This balance sheet information is reported quarterly to stockholders and the public, and to banking regulatory agencies in a bank's CALL REPORT or report of condition.

balance sheet ratios
1. ratios used in examining the financial condition, and changes in financial position, of any company, based on data reported in the BALANCE SHEET. Certain ratios are particularly applica-

ble to banks. The most important are the CAPITAL RATIOS (measuring the ratio of equity capital to total assets) and LIQUIDITY RATIOS (measuring a bank's ability to cover deposit withdrawals and pay out funds to meet the credit needs of its borrowers). Other useful ratios are the loan-to-deposit ratio (total loans divided by total deposits) the charge-off ratio (net charge-offs as a percentage of total loans), the loan loss reserve ratio (LOAN LOSS RESERVES for potential bad loans as a percentage of total loans), and the ratio of NONPERFORMING LOANs to total loans. See also NET INTEREST MARGIN; RETURN ON ASSETS; RETURN ON EQUITY.

2. accounting ratios used by bank credit officers in evaluating creditworthiness of borrowers. The most widely used are: the *acid-test ratio* or *quick ratio* (short-term assets divided by current liabilities); the *current ratio* (current assets divided by current liabilities); and the *debt coverage ratio* (working capital divided by long-term debt). Financial ratios can be measured against ratios in prior years, or industry averages, for quick, easy comparison. Key performance ratios, such as the leverage ratio (long- term debt as a percentage of shareholder net worth), are frequently used in pricing commercial loans. A loan might have an interest spread over a BASE RATE, for example, the bank PRIME RATE plus 25 basis points if financial leverage is kept at, or below, a certain level. See also PRICE EARNINGS RATIO; RATIO ANALYSIS.

balboa national currency of Panama.

balloon maturity bank loan, usually a mortgage, requiring a large, lump-sum payment at maturity. The balloon extinguishes the debt. Also, a bond issue requiring larger payments at the later maturity dates. See also BALLOON MORTGAGE; BALLOON PAYMENT.

balloon mortgage mortgage that does not fully repay principal and interest by the maturity date. A balloon mortgage, also known as a nonamortizing mortgage has a lower debt repayment than a conventional fixed rate mortgage loan, and thus is attractive to new home buyers whose incomes may be expected to increase, or to people who expect to sell their property and pay off the loan in a much shorter period than if they had borrowed with a conventional, fully-amortizing mortgage. The two types of balloon mortgages are the INTEREST-ONLY LOAN—a mortgage with payments that cover only the interest owed and the partially amortizing mortgage, also known as a ROLLOVER mortgage—a short-term mortgage that must be refinanced at the end of a stated term, usually three to five years. See also ALTERNATIVE MORTGAGE INSTRUMENTS; NEGATIVE AMORTIZATION.

balloon payment final lump-sum payment of unpaid principal remaining at the end of a BALLOON MORTGAGE and in certain types of leases. The extra payment extinguishes the debt.

bank organization that accepts deposits, makes loans, pays checks, and performs related services for the public. A bank acts as a middleman between suppliers of funds and users of funds, substituting its own credit judgment for that of the ultimate suppliers of funds, collecting those funds from three sources: demand deposits (checking), savings and time deposits; short-term borrowings from other banks; and equity capital. A bank earns money by reinvesting these funds in longer-term assets. A COMMERCIAL BANK invests funds gathered from depositors and other sources principally in loans. An investment bank does much the same with its investment portfolio of securities managed on behalf of clients and for its own trading account. In making loans, a bank assumes both interest rate risk and credit risk; market rates may rise above the NET INTEREST MARGIN a bank earns on its loan portfolio, and borrowers may default.

In addition to their role as credit intermediaries, banks act as agents for customers in a number of bank-related functions: initiating payment orders to third parties, either by check or electronic funds transfer; purchasing or selling securities, as for a trust account customer; and operating cash management for corporate customers. These NONCREDIT SERVICES are an important, and growing, source of fee income. Banks also offer safe deposit boxes; manage trust accounts for individuals and endowment funds; clear checks and drafts for other financial institutions; underwrite securities through SECURITIES AFFILIATES; and, in general, perform other bank related services as permitted by federal and state banking regulations. Deregulation in the banking industry since the mid-1970s has removed many of the distinctions between COMMERCIAL BANKs and THRIFT INSTITUTIONS (a category that includes CREDIT UNIONS, FEDERAL SAVINGS BANKs, SAVINGS AND LOAN ASSOCIATIONs and SAVINGS BANKs). Thrift institutions make consumer and commercial loans and offer checking accounts, NEGOTIABLE ORDER OF WITHDRAWAL (NOW) ACCOUNT, and compete openly with full-service banks in most states.

See also: AFFILIATE; AGENT BANK; AGREEMENT CORPORATION; ASSOCIATE BANK; BANK EXAMINATION; BANK HOLDING COMPANY; BANKERS' BANK; BANKING POWER; BRIDGE BANK; CENTRAL BANK; COMPTROLLER OF THE CURRENCY; COOPERATIVE BANK; CORRESPONDENT; COUNTRY BANK; DE NOVO; DEPOSITORY INSTITUTION; DUAL BANKING; FEDERAL; RESERVE BANK; FEDERAL RESERVE SYSTEM; FEDERAL HOME LOAN BANK SYSTEM; FULL-SERVICE BANK; GARN-ST GERMAIN ACT; GLASS-STEAGALL ACT; INDEPENDENT BANK; INDUSTRIAL BANK; INSURED BANK; INTERSTATE BANKING; MCFADDEN ACT; MEMBER BANK; MONEY CENTER BANK; MUTUAL SAVINGS BANK; NATIONAL BANK; NONBANK BANK; NONMEMBER BANK; REGIONAL INTERSTATE BANKING; RETAIL BANKING; REGULATION A; REGULATION D; RELATIONSHIP BANKING; RESERVE CITY BANK; RESPONDENT; STATE BANK; SUPER-REGIONAL BANK; UNIT BANKING; UNIVERSAL BANKING; WHOLESALE BANKING.

Bank Administration Institute nonprofit organization, based in Rolling Meadows, Illinois, that promotes banking industry standards in bank operations and auditing through professional schools, technical conferences, and a research affiliate, the Foundation for Financial Institutions Research. The Bank Administration Institute, founded in 1924, is the oldest and largest technical organization serving the U.S. banking industry.

bank call see CALL REPORT.

bank capital see CAPITAL.

Bank Capital Markets Association see TRADE ASSOCIATION.

bank card transaction card giving a bank's customer the ability to pay for goods and services at retail merchants, and get cash at bank teller windows or at automated teller machines. A bank card may be a CREDIT CARD, tied to a pre-approved line of credit, or a DEBIT CARD, drawing funds from the holder's checking or savings account. A bank card is also a useful form of identification when cashing a check.

Bank Card Association organization, owned by financial institutions, that licenses a bank card program or performs transaction processing for its owners. The present-day national card associations, MASTERCARD INTERNATIONAL and VISA (USA), perform four key functions: licensing bank cards and service marks to card issuing banks; authorizing transactions by cardholders; settling interchange transactions when the transaction processing bank (called the MERCHANT BANK) is different from the card issuer; and setting the INTERCHANGE rate, or the transaction processing fee paid by association members. Mailing of new cards and billing to cardholders is done by the banks themselves.

bank check see CASHIER'S CHECK.

bank credit
1. sum of bank LOANS and DISCOUNTS (loans with the interest deducted when the loan is made) extended by commercial banks and savings institutions, and is a major source of EARNING ASSETS in banks. Bank lending is influenced mostly through OPEN MARKET OPERATIONS of the Federal Reserve System, and to a much lesser extent through DISCOUNT WINDOW lending by Federal Reserve Banks directly to banks and savings institutions. When the Fed purchases securities from dealers in the open market, bank credit is expanded; credit is drained from the banking system when the Fed sells securities.
2. FEDERAL RESERVE CREDIT, a credit the Federal Reserve Banks contribute to depository financial institutions, either directly, from Reserve Banks loans through the DISCOUNT WINDOW facility, or indirectly, from securities owned by Reserve Banks through open market operations, plus FEDERAL RESERVE FLOAT.

bank debits checks paid, drafts honored, and other instruments drawn against deposited funds of individuals, partnerships, corporations, and other legal entities, during a given period of time—usually reported daily. On a national basis, used by economists to forecast national trends.

bank discount rate

1. rate quoted by dealers for short-term noninterest bearing money market instruments, such as commercial paper and U.S. Treasury bills. When a bank accepts or agrees to pay a time draft, thus creating a BANKER'S ACCEPTANCE, the difference between what the bank pays and the face value of the instrument is the bank's charge (called a DISCOUNT) for honoring the draft. The rate is the bank discount rate.

2. rate that banks charge on discount loans (loans with the interest deducted when the loan is made). The borrower receives the face value of the note, less the discount. For example, a borrower taking out a $1,000 one-year loan that pays the lender $50 in interest receives $50 for use over the year. The rate of interest is 5.263%. ($50 ÷ $950).

bank draft

check drawn by a bank against its own funds deposited in another bank. Banks frequently use bank drafts when it is more convenient to write a bank check than to use a customer's check. For example, a bank's customer needing funds payable the next day in New York can instruct his bank to write a check drawn on its New York CORRESPONDENT. Banks charge a fee for the service. In international banking, a sight draft or demand draft drawn on a foreign bank allows payment in a local currency at the SPOT exchange rate, minimizing foreign exchange risk in import/export trade financing. Contrast with CASHIER'S CHECK.

bank endorsement

bank's endorsement of checks paid and presented to the check writer's bank for collection. Generally, all checks passing through a bank, except those written by its own customers (called ON-US items), checks bundled together in CASH LETTERS, or checks cleared with other banks through a local CLEARING HOUSE are stamped with the bank's ABA TRANSIT NUMBER. This identifies the bank to other financial institutions and indicates the words "pay any bank" and the date the check is paid.

banker's acceptance

time draft or bill of exchange drawn on a bank and accepted by that bank. The draft is stamped "accepted" and signed by a bank officer. By accepting the draft, the bank agrees to pay the face value of the obligation if the issuer (the DRAWER of the draft) fails to pay, hence the name two-name paper. By lending its name to the transaction, the accepting bank makes it easier for an importer or exporter to obtain trade financing. A bank, once it has accepted a draft, can either hold the paper until maturity or sell it in the money market. The accepting bank assumes some risk, although in most cases the credit risk is minimal as banks generally deal only with top-rated companies. Maturities on accepted drafts generally range from 30 to 180 days; payment is due at maturity, which usually coincides with delivery of goods to the buyer.

Bankers' acceptances are most widely used in international trade, although domestic acceptances are not uncommon. Acceptances used in trade finance are eligible for REDISCOUNT at a Federal Reserve Bank, and are not subject to RESERVE REQUIREMENTS. Bankers' acceptances are more marketable than trade drafts issued by finance companies, and there is an active secondary market for bank accepted paper. Some banks even purchase acceptances nearing maturity to increase their liquidity. See also DOLLAR EXCHANGE ACCEPTANCE; FINANCE BILL; RISK PARTICIPATION; THIRD-COUNTRY ACCEPTANCE.

Bankers Association for Foreign Trade (BAFT) see TRADE ASSOCIATION.

bankers' bank depository institution, usually a commercial bank, organized and chartered to do business with other banks and owned by the banks it services. These banks do not take deposits or make loans to the public. They may be chartered as NATIONAL BANKS, invest in an EXPORT TRADING COMPANY, and may be exempted from RESERVE REQUIREMENTS.

banker's blanket bond fidelity bond purchased from an insurance broker that protects a bank against losses from a variety of criminal acts: employee fraud, robbery, burglary, and forgery. Some states require blanket bond coverage as a condition of operating a bank.

bank examination periodic review of a bank's balance sheet assets and liabilities by chartering agency or bank supervisory agency. Bank examiners focus their attention on three main areas: the competence of bank management; the quality of bank assets, principally loans; and compliance with state or federal banking regulations. Today, examiners also look closely at OFF-BALANCE SHEET LIABILITIES such as loan commitments or guarantees, which are contingent claims on the bank's assets.

Supervisory examinations are carried out by both federal and state agencies. National banks are examined by the Comptroller of the Currency, state chartered banks by the Federal Deposit Insurance Corporation or the state banking department, and bank holding companies by the Federal Reserve Board. Thrift institutions, which offer many of the same services as commercial banks, also face periodic scrutiny by a supervisory agency. Savings and loan associations are examined by the Office of Thrift Supervision, savings banks and credit unions by state banking departments. See also COMPLIANCE EXAMINATION.

Bank Export Services Act of 1982 federal legislation authorizing bank holding companies, bankers' banks and Edge Act corporations to operate EXPORT TRADING COMPANY subsidiaries. The act also directed the EXPORT-IMPORT BANK of the United States to provide loan guarantees to export trade subsidiaries, and permitted Federal Reserve member banks, and agencies and branches of foreign banks, to accept drafts or bills of exchange financing imports or exports of trade merchandise.

bank failure closing of an insolvent bank by the chartering agency. Only a state banking commissioner, the primary regulator of a state chartered bank, or the COMPTROLLER OF THE CURRENCY, who regulates NATIONAL BANK, can make the decision to close a bank. If the bank is federally insured—by now nearly all bank deposits are covered by federal deposit insurance—the bank is placed in receivership with the FEDERAL DEPOSIT INSURANCE CORPORATION, which then settles any claims against the bank by its creditors, including the claims of insured depositors up to the $100,000 per account. The FDIC has the authority to liquidate, if necessary, the bank's assets to meet these claims, and by law is obligated to dispose any creditor claims by selecting the failure-resolution method bearing the lowest cost to the BANK INSURANCE FUND, managed by the FDIC.

The least disruptive way of disposing a failed bank is a PURCHASE AND ASSUMPTION, a transaction in which another bank steps forward and purchases some or all of the failed bank's assets and assumes its deposit liabilities. In drastic situations where a failed bank has almost no salvageable value, and thus no willing bidders are willing to acquire it, the insurance fund pays the insured depositors of the liquidated bank the value of their claim, up to the $100,000 limit per account. This form of depositor protection is known as a MODIFIED PAYOFF; the insurance payout to depositors is modified in the sense that an UNINSURED DEPOSITOR, someone who has deposits in the failed bank greater than the insurance limit, may suffer some loss of principal or interest. The major difference between the two methods is, in a purchase transaction, the acquiring bank assumes the claims of both insured and uninsured depositors are fully covered, since the acquirer assumes all the deposit liabilities.

Since federal deposit insurance began in the 1930s, no major bank in the United States has been allowed to fail by banking regulatory agencies, mainly out of fear that a failure by a large REGIONAL BANK or a MONEY CENTER BANK would be too disruptive to financial markets. In 1984, when the FDIC rescued the Continental Illinois National Bank of Chicago, the insurance fund acquired an equity position in Continental and became its largest creditor. Since 1982, federal legislation has permitted takeovers of failing banks and savings institutions by out-of-state acquirers if no in-state purchaser can be found.

FDIC assisted mergers of failed banks into healthy institutions and acquisitions of troubled savings institutions assisted by the Federal Savings and Loan Insurance Corp. have accelerated the INTERSTATE BANKING movement of the 1980s, allowing regional and money center banks to establish a presence in markets outside their home state by acquiring and restructuring troubled institutions. Generally, these merger transactions involve some form of insurance fund assistance, which usually takes the form of a payment (or loan) representing the difference between the book value of bad loans in the failed bank and the price paid by the acquiring institution. See also BAILOUT; BRIDGE BANK.

Bank for International Settlements (BIS) international organization, based in Basel, Switzerland, that acts as a bank for central banks of major industrial countries. Chartered in 1930 by a group of European central banks, the BIS has evolved since the 1960s into an influential monetary institution, assisting central bankers in investing monetary assets. It acts as a trustee for the International Monetary Fund in loans to developing countries. The RISK-BASED CAPITAL standard, adopted by banks in the GROUP OF 10 countries by 1988, in which loans and other bank assets are classified by risk, was formulated by cen-

tral bankers attending BIS meetings. Although the United States has declined any official role in the BIS, the Federal Reserve Board of Governors regularly takes part in its meetings, and the bank is a member of the Federal Reserve's SWAP NETWORK with other central banks.

The BIS also holds the central clearing account for the EUROPEAN CURRENCY UNIT, a monetary unit adopted by the European Community as a common currency. See also BASEL CONCORDAT.

bank giro see GIRO.

bank holding company company owning or controlling one or more banks, often identifiable by the word *Bancorp* or *Bancshares* in the corporate name. Companies owning 25% or more of the voting stock in a bank or controlling a majority of its directors are required by the BANK HOLDING COMPANY ACT to register with the Federal Reserve Board of Governors. This federal law defines a bank as any depository financial institution that either accepts demand deposits (checking accounts) or makes commercial loans, and whose depositors' funds are insured by a federal deposit insurance agency. Commercial paper issued by a bank holding company is exempt from reserve requirements and federal deposit insurance premiums. The Federal Reserve Board closely supervises the nonbank activities of registered bank holding companies to maintain the legal separation between banking and commerce. See also MULTIBANK HOLDING COMPANY; ONE BANK HOLDING COMPANY; PERMISSIBLE NONBANK ACTIVITIES; REGULATION Y.

Bank Holding Company Act federal legislation, enacted in 1956, requiring any company owning a bank to register as a BANK HOLDING COMPANY with the Federal Reserve Board of Governors. The act also made it unlawful for a registered holding company to acquire more than 5% of the shares of any bank without board approval and own or control nonbanking companies except in situations where the proposed activity is closely related to banking or has a public benefit, and prohibits nonbank companies from owning a bank. The DOUGLAS AMENDMENT, to the 1956 Act, adopted in the 1960s, prohibited banking companies from acquiring banks in more than one state, although Congress allowed the states to decide for themselves whether or not to allow interstate banking. Other amendments to the Bank Holding Company Act set standards (in 1966) for bank acquisitions, extended the act's coverage (in 1970) to holding companies owning a single bank, and brought U.S. branches or agency offices owned by foreign banks (in 1978) under Federal Reserve supervision as regulated holding companies. See also INTERSTATE BANKING; PERMISSIBLE NONBANK ACTIVITIES; REGIONAL INTERSTATE BANKING.

bank holiday

1. uniform schedule of national holidays honored by financial institutions. State holidays are not standardized, however. Under the Uniform Commercial Code, interbank payments delayed by a holiday are payable the next business day.
2. temporary closing of a bank by government officials. The most famous "bank holiday" is the one-week nationwide closing in 1933, ordered by President Franklin D. Roosevelt to control a wave of bank failures and restore confidence in the banking system.

bank identification number (BIN)

1. ABA TRANSIT NUMBER.
2. numeric code identifying bank card issuing financial institutions affiliated with Visa or MasterCard International. The BIN number is the first six digits of the ACCOUNT NUMBER. Banks use BIN tables in routing transactions to the appropriate bank for credit approval and final settlement.

Banking Act of 1933 major banking reform legislation enacted by Congress as a remedy to the financial instability in the banking system during the Great Depression, creating the FEDERAL OPEN MARKET COMMITTEE, and the FEDERAL DEPOSIT INSURANCE CORPORATION. The act gave effective control of MONETARY POLICY to the Federal Reserve Board of Governors. Sections 16, 20, 21, and 32 of the act, separating commercial banking from investment banking, are more commonly known as the GLASS-STEAGALL ACT.

banking enterprise zone economic zone established by state legislation, often accompanied by tax abatements. Several states in the early 1980s adopted legislation encouraging out-of-state banks to relocate their credit card businesses, offering lower corporation taxes in exchange for a promise by the banks to create a certain number of new jobs. With the exception of Delaware, which managed to attract several major credit card banks, and South Dakota, most such efforts have had only marginal success. See also INTERNATIONAL BANKING FACILITY.

banking power

1. ability of a bank to lend, specifically its power to "create money" by depositing a portion of a new loan in a bank account. The borrower doesn't take out the loan in cash; instead, the loan proceeds are deposited in a new or existing checking account. The lender agrees to honor checks drawn against the account, and, can use part of that balance to make new loans.

   Unlike most other corporations, which are free to engage in almost anything not prohibited by law, U.S. banks may undertake only those activities specifically approved by law or regulation. Banking powers generally fall into two categories: express powers, including the ability to lend money, granted by state legislatures or Congress; and implied powers given by the courts through judicial rulings. See also MONEY MULTIPLIER.

2. PERMISSIBLE NONBANK ACTIVITIES of bank holding companies are activities considered closely related to authorized powers of banks, and are approved by the Federal Reserve Board on a case-by-case basis. See also BANK HOLDING COMPANY ACT; REGULATION Y.

banking syndicate See SYNDICATION; TENDER PANEL.

Bank Insurance Fund (BIF) deposit insurance fund
operated by the FEDERAL DEPOSIT INSURANCE CORPORATION, insuring deposits in commercial banks and savings banks up to $100,000 in interest and principal per account. All assets, debts, and obligations of the FDIC were transferred by the Financial Institutions Reform, Recovery and Enforcement Act of 1989 to the Bank Insurance Fund. The act also authorized increases in deposit insurance premiums to build up reserves in the insurance fund.

bank investment contract (BIC) contract issued by
a bank to a corporate investor, usually a company-sponsored profit sharing plan or 401(k) plan, guaranteeing a fixed rate of

return on invested capital over the life of the contract. A bank investment contract is similar to a guaranteed investment contract (GIC) sold by insurance companies, has a maturity of one to ten years, and the added protection of federal deposit insurance up to the $100,000 limit per insured account. As with an insurance company GIC, the selling bank assumes all market and interest rate risk of the invested portfolio but can make money by investing the funds in higher yielding securities such as U.S. Treasury bills.

bank line bank's moral commitment to lend, as distinct from its contractual, legal, commitment; alternate name for a LINE OF CREDIT. A bank line is an indication of a bank's willingness to lend to a particular borrower up to a predetermined amount, usually for working capital purposes, and for a one-to-three-year period. The line is renewable at the option of the lender, so long as the borrower meets certain conditions, for example, agreeing to keep a portion of the line in a COMPENSATING BALANCE with the lender to maintain his business in sound financial condition. In some cases, the borrower may be asked to demonstrate his ability to operate without bank financing by periodically reducing the borrowed amount to zero (called a CLEAN-UP REQUIREMENT).

Ordinarily, no commitment fee is charged, although the lender may assess a usage fee on funds actually advanced. An advised line of credit is disclosed to the borrower, whereas a guidance line is used for internal credit monitoring by the lender and is not disclosed. See also EVERGREEN LOAN; REVOLVING CREDIT.

Bank Marketing Association see TRADE ASSOCIATION.

bank merger consolidation of two or more banks in a single entity. Banks and bank holding companies must obtain written approval from a federal supervisory agency, as required by the Bank Merger Act of 1960, before acquiring another bank.

For example, the FEDERAL DEPOSIT INSURANCE CORPORATION, which supervises state chartered NONMEMBER BANKs, has the authority to reject mergers that lessen competition unless the potential benefits of a merger outweigh any anticompetitive effects. Amendments to the Bank Merger Act in 1966 gave the

U.S. Department of Justice the right to review, during a 30-day period, pending mergers for possible violations of federal ANTI-TRUST LAWS.

Mergers of failed banks and savings institutions are frequently arranged by federal deposit insurance agencies to protect depositors' assets, and transfer assets to a healthy institution. See also BAILOUT; BANK FAILURE.

bank note

1. non-interest bearing promissory note, issued by an authorized bank for payment of debts. The FEDERAL RESERVE NOTE is the only officially authorized circulating note. Synonomous with currency and LEGAL TENDER.
2. unsecured interest-bearing notes issued by banks in denominations of $100,000 and up, and sold to institutional investors. These notes are similar to CERTIFICATES OF DEPOSIT, except that these obligations are not protected by deposit insurance. Bank notes resemble bonds more than deposits, paying semiannual interest, and are liabilities of issuing banks rather than bank holding companies. See also DEPOSIT NOTE.

bank of first deposit bank where a check in the process of collection is initially deposited to an account. If the check is drawn on another bank, the collecting bank presents the check directly to the paying bank, or to a Federal Reserve Bank, for settlement against the paying bank's RESERVE ACCOUNT. See also CASH ITEMS; COLLECTION ITEMS; DIRECT SEND.

bank quality bonds given one of the top four ratings by bond rating firms, for example, a Standard & Poor's rating of BBB or better. Commercial banks are permitted to purchase these securities, also known as INVESTMENT GRADE bonds, for their own account. These bonds also are considered acceptable investments for fiduciaries, such as trust departments and pension funds. Bonds with a lower rating are known collectively as JUNK BONDS, and are considered speculative investments.

Bank Rate Monitor Index index of money market rates on consumer deposit accounts paid at 100 banks around the country, compiled weekly and reported in daily newspapers. The Bank Rate Monitor Index is compiled weekly by Bank Rate

Monitor Inc., Pompano Beach, Florida, and lists the average rate paid on a variety of consumer savings deposits and time deposit accounts.

bank reserves bank deposits allocated for a specific purpose. LEGAL RESERVES are funds that banks maintain in a noninterest earning account at a Federal Reserve Bank or at a correspondent bank, plus vault cash, to meet their RESERVE REQUIREMENTS. Legal reserves protect depositors' assets, and also permit the Federal Reserve System to more easily regulate bank credit, the funds that banks have available for lending, by controlling the total supply of reserves in the banking system through Federal Reserve MONETARY POLICY.

LOAN LOSS RESERVES, a percentage of outstanding loans, are kept in a separate account to cover anticipated loan losses. When interest payments on a loan have not been made for a reasonable period, usually 90 days, the loan is no longer considered an earning asset, and a reserve is set aside to cover the expected loss. If the loan is later written off as a worthless asset, a charge is made against the reserve for loan losses.

PRIMARY RESERVES are checking account balances in a Federal Reserve Bank, vault cash, plus checks in the process of collection; SECONDARY RESERVES are mostly marketable short-term securities, such as U.S. Treasury bills, that are easily convertible to cash. See also EARMARKED RESERVES.

bank run series of unexpected cash withdrawals, caused by a sudden decline of depositor confidence or fear that a bank will be closed by the chartering agency. Today, the silent run is much more prevalent than bank runs in the past, when customers lined up in front of tellers' windows and demanded their savings in cash. Today, depositors simply transfer their interest-sensitive funds—called HOT MONEY deposits—to other institutions. Also called a run on a bank.

bankruptcy legal proceedings for adjusting the debts of an individual or business unable to meet obligations to creditors. The debtor is placed under control of a BANKRUPTCY TRUSTEE, who manages the debtor's affairs for the benefit of creditors. Whereas most debtors seeking protection from creditors have more liabilities than assets, a bankruptcy petition is not necessarily an admission of INSOLVENCY, i.e., inability to pay debts as they come due. Corporations, in recent years, have used bankruptcy as a strategy: filing a bankruptcy petition directs all pending legal claims to a single court—the bankruptcy court.

Bankruptcy courts deal with two broad types of cases: VOLUNTARY BANKRUPTCY by debtors seeking a fresh start, and INVOLUNTARY BANKRUPTCY filed by a sufficient number of creditors, who believe the debtor has committed an ACT OF BANKRUPTCY by concealing assets or favoring one creditor over another. In both cases, the objective is a fair and equitable settlement of claims and distribution of assets. Filing a petition initiates an automatic stay against further debt collection until a debt is discharged, the petition is dismissed, or a repayment plan is accepted by creditors. Once a petition is filed, the bankruptcy remains on a debtor's credit bureau report for a 10-year period.

The Bankruptcy Reform act of 1978, the first major revision in the bankruptcy code in four decades, brought about several important changes: the new code simplified the procedures for filing petitions, modified the *absolute priority rule* giving secured creditors seniority over other creditors, limited creditor rights to SET-OFF claims against a debtor's assets, and expanded the powers of federal bankruptcy judges to decide cases. Amendments to the code in 1984 curtailed some of the more liberal provisions in the '78 law dealing mostly with consumer bankruptcies; The Bankruptcy Reform Act of 1984 added an ABILITY TO PAY test to Chapter 13 debt repayment plans filed by individuals with income, gave bankruptcy courts the power to dismiss so-called abusive petitions by debtors concealing assets, and also modified the status of bankruptcy judges.

The important chapters in the revised code are the following:

Chapter 7: called a LIQUIDATION, allows a court-appointed trustee with broad discretionary powers to distribute assets among creditors and arrange interim financing. In general, the trustee represents the interests of the unsecured creditors, or general creditors. If, however, there are no assets, the debt is discharged, and the creditors receive nothing.

Chapter 9: a rarely used section of the code, designed for adjustment of debts of a municipality. Also called a municipal reorganization.

Chapter 11: a REORGANIZATION, normally by a business, allowing the debtor (called a DEBTOR-IN POSSESSION if no trustee is named) to maintain operating control of a business, while restructuring debts and working out a repaymant schedule acceptable to a committee of creditors. Creditor loans to Chapter 11 debtors are permitted under certain conditions.

Chapter 12: a new provision dealing with agricultural bankruptcies, allows small family-owned farms with debts under $1.5 million to repay obligations based on fair market value of the loan collateral rather than the loan book value when the credit was originally extended.

Chapter 13: a debt repayment plan, called a WAGE EARNER PLAN, filed by individuals earning regular income. The debtor files a budget with the court, and agrees to make partial payment (less than 100%) of obligations owed to creditors over a three-to-five year period, normally within three years. See also COMPOSITION; CRAMDOWN; DISCHARGE OF BANKRUPTCY; PREFERENCE; PRIORITY OF LIEN; REAFFIRMATION; REDEMPTION; VOIDABLE PREFERENCE.

bankruptcy trustee person named by a bankruptcy judge, with the consent of creditors, to manage the affairs of a debtor in bankruptcy. The trustee has legal authority to file claims on behalf of the debtor, set aside a PREFERENCE to one or more creditors, and also represent the interests of unsecured creditors or general creditors. Certain bankruptcy courts have a U.S. Trustee, a permanent trustee who handles all cases filed in that jurisdiction.

Bank Secrecy Act federal law enacted in 1970, intended to discourage the use of currency in illegal transactions, requiring banks to microfilm all checks written for amounts above $100, and report all cash deposits, withdrawals, or transfers of $10,000 to the Internal Revenue Service. International transactions are reportable to the U.S. Customs Department. Banks are required to fill out a CURRENCY TRANSACTION REPORT within 15 days of the transaction date to avoid having to pay stiff penalties. See also MONEY LAUNDERING.

banks for cooperatives See FARM CREDIT SYSTEM.

bank statement
1. REPORT OF CONDITION, financial statement discloses a bank's income and condition of its balance sheet, filed quarterly with its primary regulator. These statements are also availa-

ble on request for public inspection. See also FORM 8K; FORM 10K.

2. customer's ACCOUNT STATEMENT of deposits, withdrawals, transaction activity and bank service charges, usually mailed monthly.

3. bank's statement of deposit accounts subject to RESERVE REQUIREMENTS, filed every other week with a Federal Reserve Bank.

Bank Wire privately-owned bank communication service, organized in the 1970s as a private sector alternative to the Federal Reserve's FED WIRE payment network. Due to funding problems, however, Bank Wire and its Cashwire net settlement service ceased operations in 1986, and are now defunct.

banque d'affaires see MERCHANT BANKING.

Banxquote Money Markets Index index of rates paid by investors on negotiable certificates of deposit and high yield savings accounts, compiled weekly by Banxquote On-Line Inc., New York, New York. The index offers a side-by-side comparison of rates paid by selected banks and savings institutions on small-denomination (under $10,000) savings accounts. The High Yield Jumbo Index lists rates paid on a variety of negotiable CDs with maturities from one month to five years.

barbell portfolio portfolio of INVESTMENT SECURITIES concentrating the bulk of assets in bonds or other securities with very long or very short-term maturities. This is a more sophisticated form of investing than *laddering* (the practice of buying bonds in each maturity range, producing a higher return), but it may create liquidity risk if a bank wants to restructure its portfolio. More frequent adjustments are necessary to maintain the desired asset mix, especially when rates change.

Barbelling an investment portfolio through the heavy use of short-term and long-term issues, with few securities of intermediate maturity, is designed to maximize liquidity, with minimal market impact from the short-term issues, while the long-term debt brings the highest yield and the highest return. This strategy, of course, does not make much sense when the yield curve is flat, that is, when short-term rates are roughly the same as long-term rates, or when the yield curve is inverted, and short-term rates are higher than those at the long end. See also LADDERED PORTFOLIO.

barren money cash or money earning no interest, such as cash in a safe deposit box or reserve account balances in a Federal Reserve Bank.

barter exchange of goods or services without the use of MONEY. In the absence of an acceptable currency, the parties involved set a price through private agreement. Barter is frequently used in less developed countries as a substitute for payment in hard currency. For example, an exporter may agree to take partial payment in trade goods or commodities, instead of money, a form of barter known as *counter-trade*.

Basel Concordat agreement in 1975 by a committee of central bankers, representing the Group of 10 countries affiliated with the BANK FOR INTERNATIONAL SETTLEMENTS, that set guidelines for international bank supervision. The guidelines, initiated by the Committee on Banking and Regulation, also known as the Cooke Committee (named after its chairman, Peter Cooke), called on central banks to support branches, agencies, and bank subsidiaries in foreign countries, have never been fully tested, and are a moral obligation of the participants. The Concordat was revised and published in 1983 when the failure of the Banco Ambrosiano, a major Italian bank, shook up the international financial markets.

Base I data processing network operated by VISA (USA) for authorization of bank card transactions by banks affiliated with the Visa card system. See also BASE II.

Base II data processing network operated by VISA (USA) for clearing and settlement of bank card transactions between card honoring merchant banks and card issuers for net daily account settlement among Visa member institutions.

base rate interest rate used as an index for pricing a bank loan or line of credit, for example, the banker's acceptance rate, CERTIFICATE OF DEPOSIT rate. LONDON INTERBANK OFFERED RATE (LI-

BOR), or the PRIME RATE. A MARGIN is added to, or subtracted from, the base rate.

base year analysis
examination of an organization's financial statements by a bank credit department, by which financial data reported in a prior year are compared to data reported in the period under review. The prior year is called the base year. See also BALANCE SHEET RATIOS; TREND ANALYSIS.

basis
1. original cost of an asset plus capital improvements, from which any taxable gains (or losses) are determined, after deducting depreciation expenses. In investments, the purchase price, plus out-of-pocket costs such as brokers' commissions, is used in computing short-term or long-term capital gains reportable to the Internal Revenue Service.
2. in the futures market, the difference between the SPOT price, or cash market price, of a security (or commodity) and its price in the futures market. As the delivery date of a FUTURES CONTRACT approaches, this difference gradually disappears, and at maturity the cash market and futures market price should be the same. Most investors use financial futures only as a hedging tool to limit possible losses as interest rates change. More active investors buy and sell financial futures contracts with the expectation of making a profit from the price differential between cash and futures market prices, and are said to be trading the basis.
3. number of days used in calculating the interest earned in an investment or interest payable on a bank loan. Also called the *accrual base*.

There are different interest calculation methods.

365-day year base—savings and time deposit accounts paying interest from date of deposit to date of withdrawal, U.S. Treasury bills, and bank loans (interest computed using actual days in the loan). Also called *money market basis*.

360-day year base—federal agency securities, municipal bonds, corporate bonds, and LIBOR (London Interbank Offered Rate) based instruments. Also called *corporate bond equivalent basis*.

The difference in interest earned, comparing a 360-day year and 365-day year, can be substantial with a larger principal invested. For example, $100 invested at 8%, using a 360-

day year earns $8.00 at 360 days, whereas $100 invested at 8% using a 365-day year earns $7.89 at 360 days. Comparing interest yield on an investment with a 365-day yield basis to one with a 360-day year is easy; to convert from 365 to 360 day interest, simply multiply the 365-day interest by 1.0139; to convert from 360 to 365-day interest, multiply the 365-day interest by .98630.

4. in FOREIGN EXCHANGE, adjustment in the forward market price of different currencies for differences in interest rates. For example: if U.K. interest rates are 5% above U.S. rates, British pound sterling is priced at a 5% discount vis-a-vis the U.S. dollar, allowing different currencies to be traded on a comparable basis. See also PURCHASING POWER PARITY.

basis point smallest measure in quoting yields on bonds, mortgages, and notes, equal to one one-hundredth of one percentage point, or .01 per cent. A bond whose yield to maturity changes from 8.50% to 9.25% is said to move 75 basis points in yield.

basis price price of a bond expressed as an annual percentage rate; the YIELD TO MATURITY expected by the purchaser. Contrast with dollar price, the price actually paid by the investor. See also BOND TABLE.

basis risk in ASSET-LIABILITY MANAGEMENT, the risk that changes in interest rates will cause interest-bearing deposit liabilities to reprice at a different rate than interest-bearing assets, creating an asset-liability MISMATCH. For example, a 1% rise in 30-day money market rates may produce a 0.5% increase in the yield on bank loans and a full 1.0% rise in rates paid on corresponding deposit accounts. Also, the risk that prices on financial instruments in the cash market will react differently to changes in rates than prices on futures market contracts.

basis swap swap agreement involving exchange of two floating rate financial instruments denominated in the same currency, one pegged to one reference rate and the other tied to a second reference rate. Contrast with CURRENCY SWAP and INTEREST RATE SWAP.

BASIS SWAP

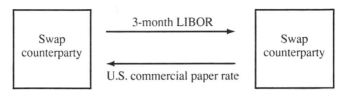

Notional amount: $5 million.
Maturity: 3 years.
Payment schedule: every three months.

Source: Recent Innovations in International Banking (Bank for International Settlements, 1986).

batch group of checks, drafts, or items handled as a unit for back office processing later during the day. Also called *block*. Contrast with ON-LINE processing.

batch header record
1. 94 character format, the bank address for sending Automated Clearing House (ACH) payments. This may not be the same as the ABA TRANSIT NUMBER if payments ordinarily are processed through a correspondent bank.
2. identifier for any group of accounts processed as a unit.

bear bond bond considered likely to increase in value in a bear market, that is, when interest rates are rising. The typical bond pays the investor a stream of cash fixed in terms of the dollar amount and the dates paid, and will decline in price when rates increase. Certain bonds, for example, an INTEREST-ONLY (IO) STRIP, or a mortgage-backed security paying interest only, are likely to rise in value in a bear market because prepayments on the underlying mortgages slow down. This slowing in loan prepayments increases the cash the investor can expect to receive. RESIDUALs in Collateralized Mortgage Obligations have similar characteristics.

bearer bond bond payable to holder rather than an owner registered on the books of the issuer's bank or agent. These bonds are negotiable instruments with no record of ownership. Title is held by anyone who possesses the security and holds it in good faith. Bond interest is paid semiannually when detachable coupons are clipped and mailed to a bank for collection, just like a check. Contrast with REGISTERED BOND.

bear spread trading strategy in which a trader sells contracts (goes short) in nearby months and buys contracts (goes long) in months further out, acting in the belief that short-term interest rates are rising faster than long-term rates and market prices of currencies, financial instruments, and so on, are falling. Called *selling the spread* in futures trading. In options trading, a combination of puts and calls intended to take advantage of falling prices. The opposite is a BULL SPREAD.

bear squeeze official INTERVENTION by central banks in the foreign exchange markets to force currency speculators short selling a currency to cover their positions, preventing the speculators from making quick profits. This generally is done by bidding to purchase more of a local currency than is available in the exchange markets, usually causing large losses to currency speculators.

belly up slang expression for a borrower, corporation, or development project that has failed, and is unable to pay obligations to creditors. Also, an insolvent bank or savings institution, in particular a financial institution closed down by its financial regulator.

below market rate rate below conventional rates in a given market, may be designed to assist low or moderate income buyers, as in mortgages financed by MORTGAGE REVENUE BONDS. Also, a low introductory rate in an ADJUSTABLE RATE MORTGAGE, known as a TEASER RATE.

belt and suspenders slang expression for an overly cautious lender, who takes an assignment of collateral plus personal guarantees from a borrower. The term also characterizes a lender who follows loan policies to the letter, saying, "When in doubt, file," meaning a new lien is filed at nearly every opportunity.

beneficiary

1. person named to receive income from a trust, insurance policy or endowment.
2. in trade finance, the person or company in whose favor a LETTER OF CREDIT is opened or a DRAFT is drawn.
3. the last-named party receiving payment in a transaction. Also called *ultimate beneficiary*.
4. person to whom an estate passes, as provided by a WILL.

bequest

gift of personal property according to a WILL, synonomous with legacy. A gift of real property is a *devise*.

best effort

securities term for underwriting on an AGENCY basis, usually involving a new offering of securities. The distributor of the securities offered for sale pledges to sell as much as can be sold, but makes no guarantee to purchase the entire offering from the issuer. It may, in fact, be agreeable to sell only part of the total offering, so long as the sale meets the issuer's minimum subscription requirements. If, for example, only three fifths of an offering is actually sold, the underwriter receives a pro rata share of the total commission and has no further obligation to the issuer. Best effort underwriting is seen most often in the over-the-counter market for initial public offerings by DE NOVO companies and financial institutions, as opposed to established companies. In FIRM COMMITMENT underwriting, the underwriter has given a commitment to purchase the entire offering as PRINCIPAL in the public offering, and the underwriting risk is borne entirely by the underwriter or investment banking group.

beta

1. analytical term describing price differences in financial instruments, generally comparing the price volatility of a particular issue to the movement of the market in general. If the difference is great, a security is said to have a high beta, relative to another; if low, it is said to have a low beta.
2. initial market installation of a new banking system, equipment or computer software, called the "beta site" test.

bid

1. price at which market participants are willing to buy securities, futures contracts or foreign currencies. The bid price, in other words, is the highest price a prospective buyer is will-

ing to pay at a particular time. The difference between the bid price and the OFFER price (the lowest price a seller will accept) is known as the SPREAD, which is a dealer's commission in buying and selling securities. See also COMPETITIVE BID; NONCOMPETITIVE BID; QUOTATION.

2. offer to acquire a failed bank at a liquidator's auction.

bid and asked range of price quotes in the OVER-THE-COUNTER market, the bid price being the highest price a buyer is willing to pay; the asked price being the owner's proposed selling price. When combined, the two prices are a broker's QUOTATION.

bid wanted indicates the owner of a security or financial instrument is seeking bids by interested buyers, generally when prices are rising. The settlement price will be negotiated later. Potential sellers of securities frequently ask a bond broker who deals only with other dealers, not the public, to seek a bid from other dealers. A bid wanted quote is signified by the notation BW in published market sheets.

big bang reorganization of the London Stock Exchange on October 27, 1986 that removed several barriers to competition in the London financial markets. It eliminated a system of fixed commissions on traders and introduced a graduated fee schedule; it eliminated the distinction between jobbers, or stock brokers who bought and sold stocks as order takers, and brokers who executed client orders with the jobbers as intermediaries; and it allowed non-British traders on the London Stock Exchange floor.

bilateral credit limit agreement by member banks in the CLEARING HOUSE INTERBANK PAYMENTS SYSTEM (CHIPS) in New York to limit the payments they are willing to accept from each other to an agreed-upon level. This limits their intraday credit risk when they authorize payments to other CHIPS members, but have not yet collected funds from other banks to back up those transfers. In CHIPS, interbank payments due to or due from each bank are settled on a net basis at 4:30 P.M. daily, and until net settlement takes place, banks are at risk if another bank, for any reason, is unable to meet its obligation to other banks in the network. See also DAYLIGHT OVERDRAFT; SENDER NET DEBIT CAP; SYSTEMIC RISK.

bill

1. **bill of exchange,** a payment order written by one person (the drawer) to another, directing the latter (the drawee) to pay a certain amount of money at a future date to a third party. An important document in international trade, a bill of exchange is a bank draft when drawn on a bank or, a trade draft when drawn on another party. Sometimes used interchangeably with DRAFT (although drafts are negotiable instruments transferable by endorsement) whereas bills of exchange are not always negotiable. See also BANKERS ACCEPTANCE.

2. **bill of lading,** a receipt issued by a common carrier for transporting trade goods from one point to another. When presented to a collecting bank along with an accepted bank draft, the bank releases the goods after it has been paid by the paying bank. A bill of lading is a title document and a receipt for goods transported. See also DOCUMENTARY DRAFT.

3. TREASURY BILL, a security with a maximum maturity of one year, issued by the U.S. Treasury Department. Three-month and six-month bills are auctioned weekly by the Treasury; one-year bills are auctioned monthly. In all cases, bills are sold at a discount from principal amount and redeemed at face value.

4. **due bill,** a statement of money owed, as when a bank sells a security and receives payment but has not delivered the security or equivalent asset. Outstanding due bills are considered borrowed funds by a bank issuing a bill, and a loan by the holder of the obligation. In the securities industry, a due bill indicates the amount owed by a buying broker to a selling broker. It can also be an IOU for interest or dividend payments to the owner of record, if such payments are owned by the buyer.

bill discounted See BANK DISCOUNT RATE; DISCOUNT.

billing cycle interval between periodic payment-due dates on a consumer installment loan or credit card account, usually every 25 or 30 days. Billing periods are considered roughly equal if they vary by no more than four days from the regular statement date.

billing error charge to a customer's ACCOUNT STATEMENT disputed by the account holder, resulting from unauthorized use, incorrect billing date, payments to a credit card account not credited, or errors in computation, such as transposition of numbers or late mailing of the periodic billing statement. These BONA FIDE ERRORS are corrected through ERROR RESOLUTION procedures in the Fair Credit Billing Act and the Electronic Funds Transfer Act.

bill payment See TELEPHONE BILL PAYMENT.

bills payable
1. trade obligations of a firm, such as a trade acceptance or BANKER'S ACCEPTANCE, payable at maturity.
2. a bank's indebtedness to other banks, principally an ADVANCE from a Federal Reserve Bank, backed by the bank's own promissory note and a pledge of government securities as collateral. See also BORROWED FUNDS.

birr national currency of Ethiopia.

biweekly mortgage mortgage with an amortization schedule calling for level payments every two weeks, rather than once a month as in most conventional and government guaranteed home mortgages. Biweekly mortgages have advantages for both financial institutions and consumers. Lenders are often willing to make a biweekly mortgage at a lower rate than a conventional 30-year mortgage, as the biweekly loan has an accelerated cash flow. A biweekly payment schedule will pay off a 30-year mortgage in about 17 years, substantially reducing the finance charges paid by the borrower. See also ALTERNATIVE MORTGAGE INSTRUMENTS.

Black Scholes model mathematical formula widely used in pricing option contracts. The model attempts to gauge whether option contracts are fairly priced, by comparing the price of the instrument and the STRIKE PRICE (or exercise price) of the option, the volatility of the instrument, the time remaining until the expiration of the option contract, and current interest rates. The Black Scholes model has also been adapted to bank asset-liability management and also the pricing of interest rate CAPS and COLLARS.

blank endorsement endorser's writing on a check, promissory note, or bill of exchange without indicating the party to whom it is payable. The endorser merely signs his name, making the instrument "payable to bearer" and negotiable by delivery alone. Also called endorsement in blank.

blanket lien expression loosely describing a floating lien, covering all personal property owned by a borrower, as opposed to real property. As used by some lenders, it is meant as a catch-all security interest covering every imaginable type of collateral owned by the borrower. Also called Mother Hubbard clause or dragnet clause. Compare to CROSS-COLLATERAL.

blanket mortgage mortgage secured by two or more parcels of property, frequently used by developers who acquire a single large tract of land for subdivision and resale to individual homeowners. Also called a "blanket trust deed."

blended rate
1. rate in an assumable mortgage (also a WRAPAROUND MORTGAGE) combining a first and second mortgage), combining the old, below market rate and the new higher rate.
2. in commercial loan refinancings, a formula rate used to adjust for the current rate; a fair and equitable composite rate. For example, if the borrower's old rate is 7%, and the current market rate is 12%, the lender may agree to make the loan at 9%, provided the borrower maintains a compensating balance and/or brings in additional collateral.
3. in cost of funds accounting, a POOLED COST OF FUNDS, for example, a blend of the Federal Funds rate and the bank certificate of deposit rate.

blind brokering form of securities trading that promises anonymity to either side to a transaction, common in the primary dealer market for U.S. government securities. The broker, who acts as agent for an unnamed third party, assumes the responsibilities of a PRINCIPAL to a trade.

blind trust trust created to avoid appearance of conflict of interest by an individual whose job involves a conflict with investing. Money in the trust is put in the hands of a trustee, who may not divulge the portfolio to the donor because knowledge of the holdings would compromise the independence and integrity of job performance. The party named as trustee can be a bank trust department or any third party, other than a relative, employee, or business partner, who is independent of the donor in name and in reality.

block

1. **Banking.** A group of checks, or checks and cash, collected during business hours and submitted, along with relevant deposit slips, for sorting into the check collection system, and also for proving (reconciling) deposits with deposit slips. For example, a teller's block. Checks are routinely processed as single units. See also BATCH.
2. **Securities.** The shares of a security bought or sold in a single transaction, the most common unit being 10,000 shares.

blocked account

1. bank account in a currency subject to EXCHANGE CONTROLS by monetary authorities. Some countries restrict or prohibit out-of-country transfers from domestic bank accounts in the local currency. The result is an overvalued currency, in relation to free-market currencies that are not inhibited by currency controls. For example, an exporter may be prohibited from drawing against an account in a blocked currency, except for internal transfers of funds.
2. any bank account frozen for political reasons, usually during wartime or national emergency. In the United States, funds in these blocked accounts owned by foreign governments or private individuals may not be touched, unless released by executive order of the president or the U.S. Treasury. See also FROZEN ACCOUNT; WARNING BULLETIN.

blocked currency trading
trading in currencies whose convertibility is limited by EXCHANGE CONTROLS. Currencies of nations that restrict exchange at free market prices normally are traded at a discount from the official exchange rate. Importers and exporters who have bank accounts in blocked currencies dispose of their blocked account holdings through brokers specializing in blocked currency trading.

blotter
original journal of accounting entries recorded in chronological order, which is later posted to a ledger. Banks that

do not have automated record keeping systems maintain pen and ink journals for loans, teller transactions, and so on, although the practice is becoming less common.

Blue List trade publication, "The Blue List of Current Municipal Offerings," listing par value, coupon rate, and yield to maturity of municipal bonds and notes, compiled daily by a Standard & Poor's affiliate since 1935. The Blue List covers about 40% of the municipal bonds offered in the dealer market. Dealers pay a fee for each daily listing.

Blue Sky laws popular name for state securities laws designed to safeguard investors from buying worthless securities. Blue sky laws vary from one state to another, although most have similar prohibitions against fraud and require registration of most securities offered for sale, with the exception of municipal bonds. Many states have patterned their securities laws after federal legislation.

board

1. official governing body of an organization; the BOARD OF DIRECTORS of a bank or corporation, the BOARD OF TRUSTEES of a mutual savings bank or savings and loan association.
2. shorthand reference for the BOARD OF GOVERNORS of the Federal Reserve System.
3. popular name for a stock exchange, in particular the New York Stock Exchange or the Big Board.

board of directors governing body of a corporation, elected by shareholders to represent their interests in managing the firm. Directors adopt the bylaws and operating rules of a corporation, appoint its operating officers, and set the stock dividend rate paid to shareholders. Directors of national banks are required to own shares of stock in the bank and are elected by shareholders at an organizational meeting before the bank opens for business, and at regular annual meetings afterwards.

Most large corporations have a certain number of INSIDE DIRECTORS who are also officers of the firm, and outside directors who are elected from the community at large.

Each FEDERAL RESERVE BANK is governed by a nine-member board elected by MEMBER BANKS that own stock in the Reserve Bank in that region of the country. These boards have three separate classes of directors, who are named to serve three-year terms: Class A Directors, representing the member banks, and are usually bankers; and Class B Directors and Class C Directors, representing the interests of business, labor and consumers. Class A and Class B directors are elected by member banks in a Federal Reserve district; Class C directors are named by the BOARD OF GOVERNORS of the Federal Reserve System. Directors appoint each Reserve Bank's president, and first vice president, who serve for five-year terms, and name the district's representatives to the FEDERAL ADVISORY COUNCIL, which advises the Board of Governors on policy issues relating to bank supervision and regulation.

Board of Governors seven-member board, appointed by the President of the United States and confirmed by the Senate, governing the Federal Reserve System. Full name: Board of Governors of the Federal Reserve System. Federal Reserve governors, who serve for 14-year terms, set RESERVE REQUIREMENTS for depository financial institutions; approve the DISCOUNT RATE for short-term Reserve Bank loans to financial institutions, as proposed by each of the 12 Federal Reserve Banks; regulate state chartered MEMBER BANKS and bank holding companies; and cast a majority of the votes on the influential FEDERAL OPEN MARKET COMMITTEE, through which the Federal Reserve directs MONETARY POLICY. The chairman of the Board of Governors is the senior policy maker in the Federal Reserve System, and represents the Federal Reserve before Congress and federal agencies.

board of trustees group of individuals named to manage a nonstock corporation, for example a mutual savings bank, mutual fund, foundation, or university. The trustees of a mutual savings bank are elected by depositors to establish operating rules, set lending policies, appoint its executive officers, and have a fiduciary duty to protect assets of depositors.

boiler plate slang term for standard clauses in loan agreements, insurance policies, wills, and other official documents. Some states have adopted so-called plain English laws, requiring lenders to write consumer credit agreements in everyday language so consumers have a clear understanding of their rights and responsibilities when borrowing from a bank.

boliviano national currency of Bolivia.

bona fide error bank's error in billing or record keeping that may result in over-billing to a customer's account. Banks are legally required to investigate alleged errors, and are exempt from civil money penalties under the Truth in Lending Law if the error was clearly unintentional. See also BILLING ERROR; TRANSPOSITION ERROR.

bond interest-bearing or discounted certificate of indebtedness, paying a fixed rate of interest over the life of the obligation, hence the name *fixed income security*. The issuer is obligated by a written agreement (the bond INDENTURE) to pay the holder a specific sum of money, usually semiannually but sometimes at maturity, as is the case with ZERO-COUPON BONDS, and the face value, or PAR value, of the certificate at maturity. Bonds are long-term obligations, meaning they have maturities of five years, and frequently, ten years or longer.

Bondholders have different rights than stockholders; the holder of a bond has a claim against the issuer, but has no ownership rights, as stockholders have. The only exception is a CONVERTIBLE bond, which may be swapped for common stock usually at the option of the issuer. Most convertibles are DEBENTURES, or unsecured promises to pay.

Bonds, even though they pay only a fixed rate of interest, and thus are vulnerable to a decline in price when interest rates are rising, are popular with financial institutions for a number of reasons. They allow the issuer to raise additional capital without selling stock, through the financial technique known as LEVERAGE; issuers, by selling bonds secured by loans, are able to liquify the balance sheet, by converting balance sheet assets (residential mortgages, leases, credit card receivables) into marketable securities; and, when loan demand is slack, banks frequently invest excess funds in U.S. government and municipal securities, including bonds.

Typically, bonds are classified by several different categories:

Collateral Backing—fully unsecured promise to pay a DEBENTURE or bonds secured by mortgages or claims to specific assets, for example, ASSET-BACKED SECURITIES.

Maturity—single maturity term bond or SERIAL BOND having several maturities.

Method of transfer—book entry registered on the books of a central depository; BEARER BOND payable to the holder; or REGISTERED BOND.

Price—Discount bond, sold at an ORIGINAL ISSUE DISCOUNT from face value or premium bond, sold ABOVE PAR.

See also ACCRUAL BOND; BOND EQUIVALENT YIELD; BOND RATING; BOOK-ENTRY SECURITY; CONTROLLED AMORTIZATION BOND; EUROBOND; INDUSTRIAL DEVELOPMENT BOND; JUNK BOND; MORTGAGE BACKED BOND; PRIVATE PURPOSE BOND; PUBLIC PURPOSE BOND; SAVINGS BOND; STATE AND LOCAL BONDS; SURETY BOND; TREASURY BOND; YANKEE BOND; YEN BOND.

bond anticipation note (BAN) short-term debt instrument with a maturity under a year, issued by a municipality or local government, usually for capital improvement projects, that is paid off when long-term bonds are issued.

Bond Buyer Index index published by The Bond Buyer, a daily newspaper covering the municipal bond market. Actually, there are several Bond Buyer indices:

—the Bond Buyer average of 40 long-term bonds, compiled daily from quotations by five municipal bond brokers, is used by the Chicago Board of Trade as the basis for long-term municipal bond contracts. The index is adjusted to an 8% average yield.

—the Bond Buyer 20 bond index, estimating the composite yield of 20 general obligation bonds rated A or better.

—the Bond Buyer 11 bond index of select AA rated bonds, several of which are included in the 20 bond index.

bond circular see PROSPECTUS; REGISTRATION STATEMENT.

bond equivalent yield investment yield of a bond purchased at discount from face value, such as a U.S. Treasury bill or municipal bond, expressed as a percent. These securities do not pay monthly, quarterly, or semi-annual interest, as interest-bearing securities do. For Treasury bills with maturities of three or six months, the formula for converting discount yield basis to the bond equivalent is as follows:

Yield equals face value minus the purchase price, divided by the purchase price; multiplied by the number of days in the year following the issue date/the number of days to maturity.

Also called *coupon equivalent yield* or *equivalent bond yield*.

bond power a type of assignment by the registered owner of securities, allowing transfer to another holder. Bond assignments often are executed in blank, when the bond owner cannot sign the certificates in person. When securities are pledged as loan collateral, a bond power assignment allows the lender to sell the securities if the borrower defaults.

bond rating evaluation by rating company of the probability that a particular bond issue will default. Bonds are rated by Standard & Poor's, Moody's Investors Service, Fitch Investor's Service, and Duff & Phelps and are given bond ratings from AAA (least likely to default) to D (default). Bonds rated BBB by Standard & Poor's and Baa by Moody's are rated BANK QUALITY bonds, or investment grade bonds suitable for purchase by commercial banks, fiduciaries, mutual savings banks, and trust companies. Bonds given lower ratings are considered speculative investments

BOND RATING—CORPORATE AND MUNICIPAL BONDS

	Bond Rating Service	
Explanation of Rating	Moody's Investors Service	Standard & Poor's
Highest quality	Aaa	AAA
High quality	Aa	AA
Upper medium grade	A	A
Medium grade	Baa	BBB
Predominantly speculative	Ba	BB
Speculative, low grade	B	B
Poor quality	Caa	CCC
Highest speculation	Ca	CC
Lowest quality, no interest paid	C	C
In default		DDD
In arrears		DD
Questionable value		D

bond swap selling a bond prior to its maturity and purchasing another. Bond swapping is a popular portfolio management technique. There are several types of swaps: A maturity swap exchanges bonds of different maturities, such as long-term bonds for bonds of shorter maturities; a quality swap upgrades safety by purchasing high-grade bonds; a yield swap aims to maximixe return on invested capital by, say, purchasing deep discount bonds when rates are falling; and a tax swap creates a tax loss offsetting capital gains earned by a substitute bond while preserving the original investment. See also ASSET SWAP; CURRENCY SWAP; INTEREST RATE SWAP; WASH SALE.

bond tables mathematical tables showing the purchase price of a bond, or what an investor would have to pay, at a given YIELD TO MATURITY. The tables show the net present value of any bond, and are particularly useful in pricing municipal bonds. For example: a 16-year bond paying 8% coupon interest has a price of 95.67 and a YIELD TO MATURITY of 8.5%. Bond tables have been outmoded by electronic calculators with built-in formulas for computing bond price and yield to maturity.

bond trustee financial institution with trust powers, such as a commercial bank trust department or trust company, given fiduciary powers by a bond issuer to enforce the terms of the bond INDENTURE. The trustee sees that bond interest payments are made as scheduled, and protects the interests of the bondholders if the issuer defaults.

book
1. trader's log of purchases and sales creating a market position. Also called a *position sheet*. A trader's book may be LONG (an excess of assets or forward market purchases over liabilities in the same asset), SHORT (an excess of liabilities or forward sales contracts over assets), or matched in which assets are roughly equivalent to liabilities of the same maturities. A trader who has more liabilities than assets, or vice versa, is said to be running an open book or UNMATCHED BOOK.

In the securities industry, specialists on the New York Stock Exchange maintain a book of stocks in which they are authorized to make markets.

2. to originate a loan.
3. shorthand expression for BOOK VALUE of a bank's common stock in relation to market value, as in "ABC Bank is selling at twice book."

book entry security

security represented by an account entry on the records of a private depository or, in the case of U.S. government securities, a Federal Reserve Bank, instead of a paper certificate. Nearly all Treasury securities are issued in book entry form, as are one third of municipal bonds. Book entry securities are less vulnerable to theft, can't be counterfeited and don't require accounting or recording by certificate number. Also, owners don't have to worry about clipping coupons to collect bond interest payments.

Book entry accounting records for privately issued securities are kept by the Depository Trust Company in New York City and the Midwest Exchange in Chicago.

book profit (or loss) See UNREALIZED PROFIT (OR LOSS).

book value

1. current value of an asset as it appears on the balance sheet. It can be the same as market value, or it can represent the difference between the purchase price and market price, less accumulated depreciation.
2. NET WORTH of a corporation, sometimes expressed in terms of value dollars per share of common stock, after deducting the outstanding preferred stock outstanding.
3. original purchase price of an asset.

borrowed funds

generic term for funds loaned to a bank, generally on a short-term basis, by another bank. It covers the following: BILLS PAYABLE; EURODOLLARS purchased and FEDERAL FUNDS purchased; REDISCOUNTS of promissory notes and business paper at a Federal Reserve Bank; and REPURCHASE AGREEMENTS with other financial institutions and securities dealers. Also called *borrowings*. See also BORROWED RESERVES; MANAGED LIABILITIES.

borrowed reserves

loans by a Federal Reserve Bank to a bank or thrift institution to maintain the required RESERVE RATIO. These loans are generally in the form of short-term advances collateralized by government securities. Because reserve balances earn no interest, banks try to minimize their borrowings from the Federal Reserve System, except when needed to support additional lending. An increase in net borrowed reserves, indicates heavy loan demand, potentially higher short-term interest rates and a period óf TIGHT MONEY for borrowers. See also DISCOUNT WINDOW; NONBORROWED RESERVES; REDISCOUNT.

borrower person or organization obtaining funds from another, called a LENDER, normally repayable with INTEREST at a future date. An extension of credit by a financial institution, for example a bank LOAN, is evidenced by a PROMISSORY NOTE, a legally enforceable agreement to repay. A credit applicant whose ability to meet the obligation is uncertain may be asked to have a second party sign the note as co-borrower or CO-MAKER. See also MORTGAGOR.

borrowing base amount a lender is willing to advance against the dollar value of pledged collateral. The borrowing base is determined by multiplying the value of the assigned collateral (receivables, inventory, equipment) by a discount factor, a process known as *margining*. In accounts receivable financing, the lender may agree to advance funds against 80% of current receivables. For example, the borrowing base of a customer pledging receivables of $200,000 is $160,000. As a rule, receivables qualify for a higher borrowing base (and a smaller margin) than inventory because receivables are one step closer to being converted into cash. See also FLOATING LIEN.

bourse French for stock exchange. A generic term for European exchanges trading listed securities, and in some countries, foreign exchange. It is used most often in France and Belgium. Called *borsa* in Italy and *borse* in Germany.

boutique popular name for a bank-owned company or holding company affiliate that acts as an INVESTMENT ADVISOR for pension funds and other institutional investors. In the securities industry, the term refers more generally to investment bankers specializing in serving a particular segment of the industry, e.g., mergers and acquisitions, money management for institutional clients, and so on.

bow-tie loan variable rate loan so-called because it defers all interest rate increases above a certain level to maturity. For example, a construction loan deferring interest payments when the loan rate exceeds a preset level to the date when the construction loan is refinanced by a permanent loan from a TAKE-OUT lender.

branch automation see PLATFORM AUTOMATION.

branch banking multioffice banking. A branch is any banking facility away from a bank's main office that accepts deposits or makes loans. State laws strictly control the opening of new banking offices by both state chartered banks and national banks, although savings and loans and other thrift institutions have generally been exempted from such restrictions. Savings and loans have, however, infrequently used this power to open branches statewide. Some states in the Midwest and Southwest limit commercial banks to offering banking services at a single office, called a *unit bank*. Many banks have gotten around this limitation by forming a multibank holding company owning several independently operated banks.

Commercial banks in several states have used a federal court ruling, the so-called Mississippi decision, to expand their franchise through branching. In that ruling, a 1987 decision by the U.S. Fifth Circuit Court of Appeals, the court invalidated Mississippi's restrictive branching law, ruling that commercial banks should have the same ability to open branches as savings and loans, since S&Ls offer the same banking services to the public.

Branch banking should not be confused with INTERSTATE BANKING. Interstate branching is still prohibited by the McFADDEN ACT, a 1927 federal law limiting branching to the boundaries of a bank's home state. Interstate banking addresses the ownership of banks and the power given state legislatures by the DOUGLAS AMENDMENT to the Bank Holding Act to approve acquisitions of in-state banks by bank holding companies in another state. In most states, the legal prohibitions on interstate deposit taking are still in force and are unaffected by the interstate expansion of banking.

Since the mid-1970s, as inflation drove up the cost of maintaining large branch networks, many banks supplemented their branch systems with AUTOMATED TELLER MACHINE (ATM) networks, began closing unprofitable branches, and modernized remaining branch offices to provide more cost-effective service to their customers.

See also CHAIN BANKING; GROUP BANKING; REGIONAL INTERSTATE BANKING; UNIT BANKING.

break-even yield yield required to cover the cost of bringing to market a new product or banking service. In COST ACCOUNTING, it is the point at which a sale covers the cost of a product or service. Each additional sale brings profit to the bottom line, considering the cost of offering the service, normally the fully loaded cost that includes fixed costs, such as building rent, and equipment costs, and variable costs such as the bank cost of funds. For example, credit card accounts are not expected to yield anything for the first year; afterward, the cost of opening the account, plus any fraud or credit losses, is offset by the card annual fee and interest payments.

breakpoint

1. deposit account balance below which zero reserves are required. In December 1988, the first $3.4 million in deposit balances were exempt from RESERVE REQUIREMENTS. This figure is adjusted annually.
2. account balance where the interest rate earned (or paid) is raised or lowered. Graduated interest loans allowed in some states charge a higher rate on the initial portion of an open-end loan or credit card outstanding balance, up to, say $500, and a lower rate on higher balances.

   Some banks also have made a practice of tiering interest rates on time deposit accounts, paying higher rates as the balance increases, to encourage depositors to put more of their income toward savings.
3. in mutual funds, the point at which the sales commission charged is lowered, because of the size of the transaction. Most funds have several breakpoints.

Bretton Woods System international monetary system created in 1944 at an international conference of 44 nations in Bretton Woods, New Hampshire. A direct result of this conference was the creation of the INTERNATIONAL MONETARY FUND (IMF), the INTERNATIONAL BANK FOR RECONSTRUCTION AND DEVELOPMENT (known informally as the World Bank), and the FIXED EXCHANGE RATES that existed until the 1970s. The original agreement, which became law in the United States in 1945, was modified in 1971 when the par value exchange system was abandoned and replaced by a system of FLOATING EXCHANGE RATES.

bricks and mortar popular name for the fixed assets owned by a bank, either owned or leased, including branch offices, ATMs, and the back office. Generally it refers to retail offices or branch offices in conventional multibranch banking. Branch banking has a high number of distribution points for retail customers, at a high fixed cost.

bridge bank national bank organized to assume the deposits and secured liabilities of an insolvent bank. The FDIC was given authority to charter these temporary banks by the Competitive Equality Banking Act of 1987. The FDIC has the authority, using a bridge bank, to operate a failed bank for up to three years until a buyer can be found.

bridge loan
1. short-term loan to cover a home buyer's financing costs when selling one house and purchasing another. The loan provides funds to buy a new house before proceeds are available from sale of the old house.
2. in corporate finance, interim financing covering the time lag between redemption of a bond or commercial paper issue, and replacment by a new one. Bridge loans, commonly replacing short-term debt with longer term financing, are an integral part of corporate restructurings, mergers and leveraged buy-outs. Banks and insurance companies supply funds to pay off old debts before proceeds are raised from new debt or issuance of stock. Also known as *gap financing* or SWING LOAN.
3. short-term multinational credit extended to a LESS DEVELOPED COUNTRY, arranged through the International Monetary Fund and the World Bank, in anticipation of longer-term financing by private banks.

broken date term used in FOREIGN EXCHANGE trading and the Euromarket for a forward exchange contract or money market contract with delivery of currency, CDs, and so on, to take place on a nonstandard date; for example 28 days instead of 30 days. Also called *cock date*.

broker person or firm that acts as intermediary between buyer and seller, charging a commission or fee. A broker is an agent, rather than a PRINCIPAL, in a transaction, and does not buy for its own account or make markets, as opposed to a DEALER. A broker can work directly with the public or act as a middleman between two dealers. A real estate broker brings together buyer and seller when real property is placed on the market. A MORTGAGE BROKER helps a mortgagor shop around for the best rate and terms in obtaining mortgage financing. A stockbroker, also called a registered representative, account executive, or, more recently, a financial planner, specializes in stocks and bonds, and is registered with the Securities and Exchange Commission. See also DISCOUNT BROKERAGE; FULL SERVICE BROKER.

brokered deposit deposit, usually a CERTIFICATE OF DEPOSIT (CD), purchased from a broker acting as an agent for depositors seeking the highest rates offered by insured financial institutions. The broker, often a securities broker-dealer, pools CDs from many small investors and markets them to financial institutions, usually in blocks nearing $100,000, and negotiates a higher rate for CDs placed with the purchaser. The broker issues a receipt, a SAFEKEEPING CERTIFICATE, to the investor and charges a commission to the purchasing financial institution.

broker's call loan short-term demand loan to a broker secured by pledged securities. Brokers use the loans to finance underwriting or to secure advances to customers who maintain margin accounts. The broker loan rate usually is a percentage point or so above such short-term rates as the federal funds rate or the Treasury bill rate. Broker loans are usually callable on 24-hour notice, hence the term call loan rate.

building and loan association see SAVINGS AND LOAN ASSOCIATION.

bulk filing check processing operation involving the high-speed sorting of checks and storage of cancelled checks by statement preparation cycle, rather than by ACCOUNT NUMBER. Bulk filing saves time and labor as checks paid are grouped by customer account number only once, when checking ACCOUNT STATEMENTs are printed and mailed to a bank's customers.

bull bond bond considered likely to increase in value in a bull market, that is, when interest rates are falling. Whereas most bonds will increase in value in a declining rate market, bonds that perform especially well in a bull market are PRINCIPAL-ONLY (PO) STRIP mortgage-backed securities. POs, which consist entirely of mortgage principal payments, do well in a falling rate market because mortgagors refinance their loans at lower interest rates. Investors are repaid their original investment more quickly, increasing the CASH FLOW YIELD of the security.

bullet loan loan that has a one-time payment at its termination. A bullet loan is similar to a BALLOON MATURITY loan, with the important difference that a bullet loan, unlike a balloon loan, has no obvious source of repayment. To pay off the bullet loan the borrower may have to refinance at the current rate, liquidate assets, or sell collateral. Despite this disadvantage, bullet loans have their merits.

Some commercial loans written as revolving lines of credit (revolvers) become de facto EVERGREEN LOANS. They are renewed without reducing the loan principal if the lender merely extends the maturity date, or rolls over the loan, instead of requiring the borrower to pay down the loan. Certainty of payment in a bullet loan, as compared against evergreen revolving credit facilities, gives rise to the expression, "Bullets are better than revolvers."

bullion gold or other precious metals in bar or coin form. The major gold trading centers are London and Zurich, with gold futures trading based in New York. Monetary reserves of central banks are kept mostly in gold bullion. See also EARMARKED RESERVES; GOLD FIX.

bull spread trading strategy in which a trader buys contracts in nearby months (goes long), and sells contracts in future months (goes short), expecting to realize a profit if prices rise. Also called *buy a spread*. The opposite is BEAR SPREAD.

bundling packaging several related banking services as a single account, for which the customer pays an annual fee or monthly fee, plus applicable monthly service charges. The concept is borrowed from the ASSET MANAGEMENT ACCOUNTS in the brokerage industry —a group of services including a checking account, debit card, and securities margin account in a single package. Contrast with UNBUNDLING. See also EXPLICIT PRICING; RELATIONSHIP BANKING.

business credit loans made to corporations and partnerships, as distinct from consumer loans or personal loans. A TERM LOAN provides financing for short-term working capital or long-term capital improvements, and is repaid in a lump sum. A LINE OF CREDIT allows businesses to borrow repeatedly up to a certain amount. Most lenders ask for business financial statements, and usually want personal guarantees, even when making loans to established small businesses. See also CORPORATE RESOLUTION; DEMAND LOAN; FINANCING STATEMENT; TIME LOAN.

business day
1. day on which a bank is open for business, ordinarily most calendar days other than Sundays and legal public holidays.
2. day that two related markets, for example, futures exchanges or stock exchanges in different cities, are open for business.

business plan document required of new businesses or corporations in REORGANIZATION, where the business is planning a major change in operations. This plan may be a chronological explanation of how the firm will use the bank loan, plus management goals and earnings objectives over the next three to five years. This statement usually is accompanied by a PRO FORMA STATEMENT of anticipated earnings and expenses over the same period. The two statements should complement each other.

butterfly spread options strategy designed to profit from stable or decreasing volatility. The spread involves trades in four call options, all with the same expiration date: an option with a low exercise price; the sale of two call options with an intermediate exercise price; and the purchase of a call option with a high exercise price.

buy a spread See BULL SPREAD.

buyback
1. in a foreign debt restructuring, an agreement by a debtor nation to buy outstanding loans from creditor banks at fair market value. Funds to purchase unpaid loans, normally at a deep

discount from face value or book value, come from a variety of sources: export earnings, tourism, and direct loans or grants from the International Monetary Fund and other international credit agencies.

2. offer by a corporation to repurchase its own stock from shareholders, done to raise the price of its stock or fend off a hostile takeover.

3. REPURCHASE AGREEMENT.

buy contract contract to purchase Treasury bills, money market instruments, or other assets in the future.

buydown money advanced, usually by a builder, to reduce the borrower's monthly payment in the early years of a mortgage, below the level required for normal amortization. Buydowns are most prevalent in periods of high interest rates, when prospective home buyers might otherwise not qualify for a mortgage loan.

buy in

1. **Futures.** Covering a futures market short position by purchasing an offsetting long position, or taking delivery of securities or commodities.

2. **Securities.** The process whereby a broker or dealer bank, after purchasing securities that a selling broker cannot deliver, completes the transaction with another source at current market prices and charges the original selling broker the difference in cost.

buying forward buying money market instruments or currencies in anticipation of a price rise or future demand. The opposite side is a sell contract by a counter-party.

buy on margin buying an asset by making an initial payment—called the MARGIN—and borrowing the balance needed to cover the purchase price from a bank or broker. When securities or commodities are purchased on margin, there is no need to borrow any funds from a bank or broker to cover the rest of the cost. The margin represents a down payment. There are numerous examples: buying a house by making a down payment and financing the rest through a mortgage, buying securities through a broker, and so on. In securities purchasing, the amount of margin needed is regulated by the Federal Reserve Board.

buy-sell agreement

1. agreement between a bank or MORTGAGE BANKER making a construction loan for a project and the permanent lender assigning to the latter the long-term mortgage on the completed project. Many lenders providing interim financing during the construction phase will not advance funds without a permanent TAKE-OUT lender, who in effect buys out the original lender's interest in the project.
2. agreement in a closely held corporation or partnership, whereby, in the event of death of one of the partners, the survivor offers to buy the interest of the deceased owner from his estate.

C

cable
1. international bank draft transmitted by cable transfer between correspondent banks, as opposed to payment through the mail.
2. trader's jargon for the British POUND STERLING, dating to the 1930s when international money transfers were done mostly in sterling.

calamity call
clause in a COLLATERALIZED MORTGAGE OBLIGATION (CMO) requiring the issuer to retire a portion of the CMO issue on a monthly basis if prepayments by mortgagors can reach a level high enough to cause an insufficient cash flow to meet scheduled payments of principal and interest. A calamity call reduces the issuer's REINVESTMENT RISK, although that risk can also be covered by a prepayment reserve fund.

calendar
schedule of upcoming securities that will be brought to market. For example, the weekly auctions of U.S. Treasury securities, municipal bonds offered by dealers, and also ASSET-BACKED SECURITIES offered for sale by banks and investment banks.

call
1. lender's demand for early payment of a loan, because the borrower has failed to meet contractual commitments such as maintaining adequate insurance or making timely payments; or, in a DEMAND LOAN, the lender's exercise of his right to ask for repayment in full at any time.
2. comptroller's call issued to NATIONAL BANK by the COMPTROLLER OF THE CURRENCY, to file a CALL REPORT or Report of Condition.
3. regulatory agency's order to a distressed bank to raise more capital, sometimes referred to as a capital call.

   4. broker's demand for additional MARGIN or collateral when
   the value of customer's pledged collateral falls below a stated
   value, known as a margin call.
   5. REDEMPTION privilege exercised by a bond issuer, as permitted in the INDENTURE agreement of a mortgage backed bond
   or issue of asset-backed securities. It permits the issuer to
   retire the bonds if only a small portion of the issue
   is outstanding, in order to keep servicing costs from becoming unreasonable. Also called *nuisance call*.

callable bond containing a clause in the indenture agreement
giving the issuer the right to redeem all or part of the issue before maturity, but no earlier than the FIRST CALL DATE. Early
redemptions are made at a premium above par value. In corporate debt, bonds may be nonrefundable or noncallable. The
former means they can be called, but not with proceeds of another issue carrying a lower rate of interest.

call date see FIRST CALL DATE.

call loan see BROKER'S CALL LOAN.

call option contract giving the buyer of an option contract the
right to purchase a specified amount of securities, currencies, or
financial futures at a predetermined price, called the EXERCISE
PRICE or STRIKE PRICE, on or before a specified future date.

call protection
   1. provisions in a bond INDENTURE limiting redemption of callable bonds for a specified period, usually ten years for municipal and corporate bonds.
   2. feature in MORTGAGE BACKED SECURITIES designed to minimize prepayment risk during a so-called LOCK-IN PERIOD. If
   loans are prepaid during this period, funds are not passed
   through immediately to the investor. Buyers of mortgage
   backed securities like this feature because it provides a more
   consistent cash flow. See also CALAMITY CALL.

call report
   1. quarterly report of income and condition required by a financial institution's primary supervisory agency: the Comptroller of the Currency for National Banks; Federal Reserve

Banks for state member banks; the Federal Deposit Insurance Corp. for insured nonmember banks; or state banking agencies for state chartered banks and trust companies. Abstracts from call reports are printed and published by the Comptroller of the Currency and the FDIC.

2. bank calling officer's written report of business development.

CAMEL rating measure of the relative soundness of a bank. CAMEL ratings—the term stands for CAPITAL, ASSET, *management, earnings,* and LIQUIDITY—are calculated on a 1-5 scale, and are used by bank supervisory agencies to evaluate bank condition. A rating of 1 is given to banks with the strongest performance ratings; banks given a CAMEL rating of 4 or 5 are placed on the watch list of banks in need of supervisory attention. Individual CAMEL ratings are disclosed to bank management, though not to the general public.

Canadian rollover mortgage see ROLLOVER MORTGAGE.

cancel to endorse or mark a check in such a way that it is no longer negotiable. A check paid by a bank, charged to the check writer's account, and endorsed so the check is no longer negotiable. Cancelled checks are the property of the drawer, but the paying bank is permitted to keep them until the account is settled and a statement of account is mailed to the customer.

cancelled check check voided by endorsement, indicating it has been paid by the drawee bank and cannot be renegotiated. Cancelled checks are normally returned to the check writer, who holds them as receipt for payment. Some banks, however, hold cancelled checks (or microfilmed copies of checks), a service known as CHECK SAFEKEEPING, and furnish a copy on demand when proof of payment is needed.

cap
1. INTEREST RATE CAP in a commercial loan negotiated at loan origination. The lender agrees to fix the maximum interest rate charged on a floating rate loan, for which the borrower pays a fee. By paying a cap fee the borrower obtains the

lender's guarantee that a loan made at 10% will not exceed an annual rate of 15% over the life of the loan.

2. clause in a residential mortgage loan agreement limiting any interest rate or payment increases to a specified amount until the loan is fully paid. An ANNUAL CAP limits yearly increases; a LIFE OF LOAN CAP remains in force throughout the term of the loan; a PAYMENT CAP limits month-to-month increases in loan payments.

3. upper end of a COLLAR, a two-way credit agreement protecting both borrower and lender against fluctuating interest rates; the lower end is a FLOOR.

4. in a wire transfer payment system, the originating bank's net debit cap, placing a limit on its aggregate DAYLIGHT OVERDRAFT exposure it is willing to accept during a single business day.

capacity one of the FIVE C'S OF CREDIT—the borrower's ability to pay an obligation when due, normally determined by verifying salary given on a credit application with an employer and considering probability of continued employment.

capital

1. **Banking.** Funds invested in a bank, including COMMON STOCK and qualifying PREFERRED STOCK, MANDATORY CONVERTIBLE securities, such as CAPITAL NOTES, plus retained earnings. Equity capital is the initial funding (called contributed capital or PAID IN CAPITAL) needed to charter a bank, a cushion against operating losses, such as BAD DEBT, and a source of protection for depositors' money.

In 1989 banking regulatory agencies revised the capital standards for banking institutions after the FINANCIAL INSTITUTIONS, REFORM, RECOVERY & ENFORCEMENT ACT required savings and loan associations to meet the same standards for CAPITAL ADEQUACY as national banks. Under the revised guidelines, there are two broad requirements: a minimum level of equity capital (called *core capital* equal to 3% of total assets; and a RISK-BASED CAPITAL ratio equal to 7.25% of total assets (rising to 8% after December 31, 1992). Banking institutions are required to meet the higher of the two ratios in determining their capital adequacy, as defined by banking regulations. Under the Risk-Based Capital guidelines, to be fully in force by 1992, bank assets are classified by risk (because they represent loans and investment of funds) and capital requirements are determined from the risks assigned to each asset category. Thus, an asset defined as needing 100% of capital would require 100% of the prevailing 8% risk-based capital requirement. In other words, for every $100 in loans and investments, a bank would need, on average, $8 in capital coverage. See also CAPITAL RATIO; PRIMARY CAPITAL; TOTAL CAPITAL.

2. **Finance.** The funds raised by a firm through sale of stock or debt securities plus retained earnings; also, any long-term asset producing income.

capital adequacy ability of a bank to absorb operating losses or shrinkage in asset values. Banking supervisory agencies have for years defined bank CAPITAL in terms of target levels of PRIMARY CAPITAL and SECONDARY CAPITAL that commercial banks should maintain at all times to meet claims of creditors, including depositors. Primary capital, consisting of stockholders' equity, is given greater weight. The uniform capital guidelines adopted in 1988 by bank regulatory agencies in the United States, Great Britain and Japan, and phased in over a four-year period ending in 1992, raised the minimum capital level from 6% of total bank assets to an 8% capital-to-assets ratio. See also CAPITAL RATIO; RISK BASED CAPITAL.

capital asset pricing model technique for measuring securities risk by measuring co-variance with a market portfolio, or *beta* (which measures systematic patterns of risk), and for comparing expected risk against expected return. The model determines yield based on variance of a specific security (stock, asset-backed security, mortgage backed bond, and so on) on the basis of variance from the market as a whole. According to the model, investors seek a risk premium over yields on investments that are generally regarded as risk-free, such as U.S. Treasury bills.

capital gain (or loss) difference between selling price of an asset and its cost when purchased. If the difference is positive, a gain is realized; if negative, a loss results. IRS rules require a holding period of at least one year before claiming long-term capital gains on investment securities purchased after January 1, 1988.

capital lease long-term lease of capital equipment that for accounting purposes is treated as a borrowing of funds and a balance sheet asset to be amortized. A capital lease, also called a FINANCE LEASE, is similar to owning the leased asset. It conveys the tax benefits of ownership if written for a period equal to 75% of the asset's economic life, transfers ownership to the lessee at the end of the lease term, or allows the lessee to purchase the asset at fair market value. Contrast with OPERATING LEASE.

capital market financial market where corporations and governments raise funds by selling stocks, bonds, and other kinds of investments, mostly to long-term savers and investors. A very decentralized market, it is divided into three major parts: the stock market, the bond market and the MONEY MARKET where short-term IOUs are traded. Securities, either debt or equity, are marketed through organized exchanges or sold directly to investors, as U.S. Treasury bills and notes are often sold.

capital note any NOTE or DEBENTURE issued by a bank or bank holding company that qualifies as bank capital. Capital notes are unsecured liabilities that are considered supplementary capital or Tier 2 capital in meeting a bank's required capital-to-asset ratio. Under regulatory capital guidelines, notes qualify as capital if they have original maturities of at least seven years, are noncallable before the maturity date, and have a mandatory conversion clause requiring the issuer to exchange the notes for common stock at a future date at a preset price. Included are the following: EQUITY CONTRACT NOTES, requiring the holder to purchase shares of common stock at a conversion price equal to the face value of the notes; and EQUITY COMMITMENT NOTES, requiring the issuer to redeem the notes with new shares of common stock sometime before the final maturity. Capital meeting these tests are hybrid securities having the qualities of both equity and debt; a bank can increase its capital-to-asset ratio, while leveraging equity capital to give shareholders a higher return on investment. Some banks have sold retail capital notes in denominations as low as $500. See also BANK NOTE; DEPOSIT NOTE.

capital ratio key financial ratio measuring a bank's CAPITAL ADEQUACY. As a general rule, the higher the ratio the more sound the bank. A bank with a high capital-to-asset ratio is protected against operating losses more than a bank with a lower ratio, although this depends on the relative risk of loss at each bank.

There are several standard measures of capital adequacy:

—PRIMARY CAPITAL to assets ratio: primary capital divided by average total assets plus the allowance for loan and lease losses.

—TOTAL CAPITAL ratio: PRIMARY CAPITAL plus secondary capital divided by average total assets plus allowance for loan and lease losses.

—capital to risk assets ratio: TOTAL CAPITAL divided by average total assets, less cash, bank balances, and U.S. government securities.

—loans to capital ratio: aggregate bank credit divided by total capital.

cardholder agreement written statement of terms and conditions relating to a bank card, as required by Federal Reserve regulations. In credit cards, the agreement states the ANNUAL PERCENTAGE RATE, the monthly minimum payment, annual card fee if any, and the cardholder's rights in billing disputes.

card recovery bulletin see WARNING BULLETIN.

carry forward/carry back
1. excess bank reserves (up to 2%) that may be carried over from one week to the next reserve maintenance period to help meet that period's reserve requirements. Deficiencies in reserves must also be carried forward to the next accounting period.
2. TAX LOSS CARRY FORWARD.

carrying charges
1. portion of the FINANCE CHARGE in bank loans covering the lender's costs in booking the loan and collecting payments plus a portion of bad debt expense.
2. broker's charge to customers for a MARGIN account financing securities purchased on credit.
3. dealer's out-of-pocket expenses, usually bank loans, for holding a cash security or commodity until sold or delivered. Carrying charges can also refer to storage, insurance, and other costs.

cash

1. currency (including bills and coin) in circulation, including checking account deposits. Cash held by a bank, for example VAULT CASH, requires no capital backing under Risk-Based Capital rules adopted by bank regulatory agencies.

2. to convert a check to cash by endorsing and presenting to a bank. Also called negotiating a check.

   See also CURRENCY IN CIRCULATION.

cash advance

cash loan against a personal line of credit, obtained by presentment of a BANK CARD at a bank teller window, at an automated teller machine, or by mail. Finance charges are paid from the transaction date.

cash basis

basis of accounting in which revenues are recognized only when the related cash is received, or realized and expenses only when they actually are paid. This form of accounting is more susceptible to manipulation than the ACCRUAL BASIS, in which income and expenses are recognized in the period in which they arise. Under cash basis accounting, income for the year can be increased or lowered simply by delaying or accelerating payment of expenses. The TAX REFORM ACT OF 1986 prohibits corporations, partnerships involving partners that are corporations, and trusts with unrelated business income from using the cash basis if their average gross annual receipts are more than $5 million.

cash basis loan

loan on which interest payments are recorded when collected from the borrower. These are loans in which the borrower has fallen behind in interest payments, and are classified as NONACCRUAL ASSETS. In extreme situations, where the lender reasonably expects that only a portion of the principal and interest owed ultimately will be collected, payments are credited directly to the outstanding principal. See also NONPERFORMING LOAN.

cash card

alternate name for bank automated teller machine DEBIT CARD.

cash collateral

cash, negotiable instruments, documents of title, securities, bank deposits, and other short-term assets that readily are convertible into cash.

cash concentration & disbursement (CCD)

corporate electronic payment used in business to business and intracompany transfers of funds. Vendors, including numerous federal agencies, have used the CCD payment format, an electronic payment record developed by the National Automated Clearing House Association, to make single invoice payments to suppliers. Funds are cleared on an overnight basis through the nationwide AUTOMATED CLEARING HOUSE network. See also CONCENTRATION ACCOUNT; CORPORATE TRADE EXCHANGE; CORPORATE TRADE PAYMENT.

cash discount

reduced price offered by a merchant as an inducement for cash payment. The Cash Discount Act of 1969 encouraged merchants to offer discounts to customers paying by cash rather than a credit card, though it prohibited merchant SURCHARGEs for accepting bank credit cards. The act expired in 1983. A small number of merchants, mostly oil retailers, still offer consumers a cash discount for paying by bank DEBIT CARD or in cash.

cash dispenser

card activated banking terminal similar to an AUTOMATED TELLER MACHINE, that dispenses currency in various denominations, but does not accept deposits. The earliest ATMs were cash dispensers only.

cash flow

Banking:
1. flow of funds representing the movement of cash through a bank. Bank cash flow is usually summarized by a cash flow report indicating the sources of bank funds (mostly deposits), and uses of funds (mostly bank loans), and is an important measure of overall LIQUIDITY. A bank's internal cash flow measures turnover in the loan portfolio, among other things. Cash flow applies only to the actual movement of funds into or out of the accounts on a bank's books. In other words, only actual revenues and disbursements are counted, as opposed to bookkeeping entries, such as depreciation and reserve accounts, which are recorded in the INCOME STATEMENT. See also CASH POSITION.
2. flow of funds from borrower repayment of principal and interest on bank loans underlying in MORTGAGE-BACKED BONDS and ASSET-BACKED SECURITIES. Timely payment of interest to

bondholders depends on the cash stream represented by borrower payments. If mortgagors pay their loans early, the cash flow is accelerated and bondholders receive less than the COUPON RATE of interest in mortgage backed bonds. The unpredictability of the cash flows from mortgage backed securities led issuers of securities to break out mortgage bonds into distinct classes of securities, some paying at a faster rate than others to appeal to different groups of investors. See also COLLATERALIZED MORTGAGE OBLIGATION; DISCOUNTED CASH FLOW.

Finance: cash available in an organization, summarized as net after-tax income plus expenses, usually asset depreciation. A *cash flow statement* shows *the sources of cash* and *uses of cash* for an accounting period.

cash flow loan short-term loan that normally is unsecured by pledge of assets or collateral, and is repayable from cash generated by sale of assets. A cash flow loan sometimes can be secured by personal property, as opposed to real estate. Distinguish from WORKING CAPITAL loan, because the note may not be repaid from cash receipts from sale of inventory, or conversion of receivables into cash. In a cash flow loan, the ultimate source of repayment may be the income generated from NONRECURRING GAINs such as a sale of assets through DIVESTITURE or sale of common stock. See also COLLATERAL LOAN.

cash flow yield monthly rate of return of a mortgage-backed security, based on principal and interest mortgage payments and an estimated rate of loan prepayment. Cash flow yield is the monthly INTERNAL RATE OF RETURN of a mortgage backed security, assuming a standard rate of mortgage prepayments. The cash flows from mortgages are discounted to their net present value, producing the rate of return that approximates the actual return to the holder. Prepayment assumptions are adjusted according to differing types of collateral, for example, Federal Housing Authority insured loans or conventional mortgages. Because some mortgage pools are paid off faster than others, cash flow yield offers a more realistic way to price mortgage backed securities than the 12-year prepayment assumptions prevalent in the 1970s.

cashier bank officer responsible for custody of the bank's earning assets, and whose signature is required on official bank checks, called CASHIER'S CHECKS and all official correspondence.

cashier's check check drawn by a bank on itself, signed by a bank officer, authorizing payment of the amount shown to the PAYEE. Cashier's checks serve a variety of purposes: disbursing loans to customers, paying bank suppliers, and so on. Also called *official check* or *treasurer's check*. A cashier's check, because it is drawn on a bank, rather than a private person, is generally regarded as good as cash. Contrast with CERTIFIED CHECK.

cash items any check given immediate credit to a customer's account, before a bank has received payment from the paying bank. A check processed as a cash item is, in effect, a short-term loan from the bank to creditworthy customers. A DEBIT TICKET, listing the check in the process of collection as a balance sheet liability, is prepared when the item is sent out for collection. When payment is received, a credit is posted on the bank's general ledger. Generally, a fee is charged for handling checks as cash items. See also COLLECTION ITEMS.

cash journal book of original accounting entries, where transactions are recorded in chronological order. Entries from the cash journal are later entered in the balance sheet ledger. A cash journal is a basic service to bank MASTER TRUST customers.

cash letter group of checks, accompanied by a paper listing sent to a clearing house or the Federal Reserve check collection system. A cash letter contains a number of negotiable items, mostly checks, accompanied by letter that lists the amounts and instructions for transmittal to other banks. Also called a *transit letter*.

cash management
1. financial management technique used by corporate treasurers to control the use of cash balances, accelerate the collection of checks and decelerate disbursements to trade creditors. Managing bank FLOAT on checks in the process of collection is an integral part of corporate cash management. Large cor-

porations collect funds from many different accounts into a single CONCENTRATION ACCOUNT, and invest excess funds in the MONEY MARKET. The local accounts are frequently drawn down to zero-funds every day. In disbursing payments to trade creditors, treasurers attempt to control the outflow of funds by timing payments with the receipt of invoices from trade creditors. A frequently used tool in cash management is CONTROLLED DISBURSEMENT of corporate payments to match the collection of accounts receivables against disbursements to trading partners. See also BALANCE REPORTING; DELAYED DISBURSEMENT; ELECTRONIC DATA INTERCHANGE; LOCK BOX; TREASURY WORKSTATION; ZERO-BALANCE ACCOUNT.

2. personal financial management account combining checking, a money market account, a brokerage margin account, and usually a bank debit card. The first account of this type—the Merrill Lynch "Cash Management Account" (CMA)—broke new ground in personal funds management; idle cash automatically was swept into a money market account and taken out when securities were bought. The CMA, patented by Merrill Lynch & Co., has since been emulated by other brokerages, and the name is commonly used as a generic term.

cash management bill short-term debt instrument normally issued with maturity up to 50 days by the U.S. Treasury as an alternative to Treasury notes or Treasury bills. Cash management bills are sold to money market investors in minimum denominations of $1 million. These bills are issued to cover temporary cash shortages, for example, just before a major tax collection date, such as April 15 or June 15.

cash market market where securities, financial instruments, or currencies are transferred from buyer to seller, and paid for at the current market price. Also called the *spot market*. Cash market transactions are for immediate, on the spot delivery, as opposed to financial futures, forward market contracts, options, and swaps, which call for delivery at some future date.

cash position

1. cash assets in a bank, synonomous with LIQUIDITY. Specifically, cash position is a measure of cash on hand, including vault cash and teller cash, and cash that can be raised from

the sale of short-term assets, such as certificates of deposit, government securities, repurchase agreements, and so on. Also included are excess RESERVE ACCOUNT balances with a Federal Reserve Bank or correspondent, deposits with other banks, and checks in the process of collection.
2. reserve position in a bank's reserve account at a Federal Reserve Bank or a correspondent.

cash ratio ratio of total cash plus short-term investment securities to total bank assets; a LIQUIDITY ratio.

cash reserve
1. bank's vault cash that may be used to satisfy RESERVE REQUIREMENTS of member banks. Cash on hand, including currency and coin, may be used to meet legal reserve requirements. The Monetary Control Act of 1980 phased in reserve requirements for nonmember banks and thrift institutions over an eight year period.
2. revolving LINE OF CREDIT attached to a checking account allowing a consumer to write checks for amounts greater than the account balance without paying overdraft charges. Also called *cash reserve checking* or *overdraft protection*.

cash settlement
1. settlement provision in some options and futures contracts that do not require delivery of the underlying instrument. For options, the difference between the settlement price on the underlying instrument or security and the option's exercise price is paid to the option holder at the exercise date. For futures contracts, the exchange establishes a settlement price on the final day of trading and all remaining open positions are marked to market at that price.
2. in securities trading the optional delivery of stocks purchased on the trade date, rather than the settlement date. See also DELIVERY VERSUS PAYMENT.

cash surrender value accumulated paid-in value of a life insurance policy that qualifies as collateral on a bank loan. Banks usually will advance amounts up to the cash surrender value of a life insurance policy, less the interest charged on the loan. Besides taking an ASSIGNMENT of the insurance policy, which transfers title to the policy to the lender, the lender usually will ask the borrower to sign a separate contract stating the lender's rights. Loans secured by life insurance are a commonly used way to obtain bank credit. The lender usually advances up to 90% of paid-up cash value, as of the most recent payment date. Cash value is determined from a schedule, which may be in the policy itself or from the insurance company issuing the policy. The paid-up value may be used as collateral for a bank loan, although bank rates are often higher than rates insurance companies charge for policy loans. See also KEY MAN INSURANCE.

cause related marketing consumer credit marketing whereby a portion of the net profits are set aside for a designated public charity or cause. Such marketing efforts have become more common in credit card marketing in recent years, as more credit card issuers pursue market segmentation strategies based on consumers' identification with specific public interest causes.

caveat venditor Latin for "let the seller beware." Financial institutions selling loans in the SECONDARY MARKET are bound by written agreement to see that loans delivered to a buyer are documented properly and meet contract specifications. The opposite of caveat emptor (let the buyer beware).

cease and desist order order issued by a bank regulatory agency, after notice and opportunity for hearing, requiring a depository institution or a bank officer to suspend any unlawful, unsafe, or unsound practices, such as excessive lending to an insider. These orders are issued by the appropriate regulatory agencies under the FINANCIAL INSTITUTIONS REGULATORY ACT of 1978 and are enforceable in the courts.

ceiling

1. maximum DEPOSIT INTEREST RATE permitted on interest-bearing deposit accounts by Federal Reserve REGULATION Q. The Regulation Q rate ceiling gradually was phased out in the 1980s, when deposit interest rates were decontrolled, allowing banks and savings institutions to compete openly for deposit dollars by paying depositors market rates for savings accounts and certificates of deposit. The legal interest rate ceiling, jointly administered by banking regulatory agencies, was originally intended to ensure that all financial institutions, no matter how large or small, had equitable access to

consumer deposits. See also DEPOSITORY INSTITUTIONS DE-REGULATION & MONETARY CONTROL ACT; MARKET RATE OF INTEREST.

2. USURY ceiling, the highest rate of interest permitted by state law on consumer installment loans and other extensions of credit.

3. in FOREIGN EXCHANGE, the price level of a particular currency that triggers INTERVENTION by central banks in the exchange markets.

central bank central monetary authority, usually an agency of a national government, that performs a number of key functions: 1) issues the nation's currency; 2) regulates the supply of credit in the economy; 3) manages the external value of its currency in the foreign exchange markets; 4) holds deposits representing reserves of other banks and other central banks; 5) acts as FISCAL AGENT for the central government, when the government sells new issues of securities to finance its operations; and 6) attempts to maintain an orderly market in these securities by actively participating in the government securities market.

The FEDERAL RESERVE SYSTEM, the central bank in the United States, regulates BANK CREDIT by raising or lowering the DISCOUNT RATE, and by buying and selling government securities in the open market. This process, known as OPEN MARKET OPERATIONS, aims to promote stable economic growth while controlling the rate of inflation. Other major central banks are the Bank of England, the Bundesbank in West Germany, and the Bank of Japan.

See also BANK FOR INTERNATIONAL SETTLEMENTS; BASEL CONCORDAT; INTERVENTION; LENDER OF LAST RESORT; MONETARY POLICY; SWAP NETWORK.

central information file see CUSTOMER INFORMATION FILE.

central liability list combining all of a borrower's liabilities with a lender, including direct and indirect loans, letters of credit, guarantees, and other accommodations. Grouping all related credit with a borrower gives the lender a history of the borrower, and is useful in controlling credit overextensions.

Central Liquidity Facility (CLF) government corporation within the NATIONAL CREDIT UNION ADMINISTRATION that lends funds to member credit unions. Membership is voluntary. The CLF, which began operating in 1979, is capitalized by credit union contributions of capital stock and is authorized to make short-term and long-term loans to credit unions needing temporary financial assistance.

certificate paper establishing an ownership claim; also, an assertion of facts.
1. bank CHARTER or certificate of authority issued by a chartering agency, authorizing a newly organized bank to open for business.
2. CERTIFICATE OF DEPOSIT, a receipt for a time deposit.
3. certificate of accounts, an auditor's opinion, filed by a certified public accountant after examination of an organization's books and records.
4. CERTIFICATE OF TITLE evidencing ownership of real estate or personal property.
5. CERTIFICATE OF CLAIM, a borrower's written promise to reimburse a lender for certain credit costs, for example, debt collection costs.
6. SAFEKEEPING CERTIFICATE issued by custodian for a certificate of deposit, stock certificate,or other security assigned to a new nominee.
7. PROTEST certificate issued by a bank refusing to honor a check.
8. CERTIFICATE OF INDEBTEDNESS.

certificate account see SAVINGS CERTIFICATE.

certificate for amortizing revolving debt (CARD) ASSET-BACKED SECURITIES consisting of bank credit card receivables, issued in 1986 by Salomon Brothers. The expected life of the securities is short, about two years, and securities pay only interest for a specified period.

certificate of claim borrower's agreement to reimburse a lender for out-of-pocket expenses associated with a foreclosure auction on a defaulted mortgage loan. This depends, of course, on the proceeds of a sale being sufficient to cover these expenses.

certificate of deposit (CD) receipt for a TIME DEPOSIT issued for a stated time period and normally paying a fixed rate of interest. Bank CDs, issued in negotiable and non-negotiable form, have maturities as short as seven days to seven years or longer, and pay a market rate of interest. The interest earned on consumer CDs, which are non-negotiable debt instruments protected by federal deposit insurance up to $100,000 in interest and principal, is stated as an annual rate and an EFFECTIVE RATE that shows the effect of interest compounding. Since 1983, when time deposit rates were deregulated and minimum deposit requirements were lowered, CDs have been enormously popular investment accounts with consumers. Banks and savings institutions also have issued zero-coupon CDs, which pay no interest until the maturity date, much like ZERO-COUPON BONDS.

A NEGOTIABLE CERTIFICATE OF DEPOSIT has a principal of $100,000 (frequently $1 million or more), and can be sold to a new owner before maturity. Negotiable CDs are generally purchased by institutional investors, rather than individuals, and are actively traded in the secondary market.

Cashing in a bank CD before the maturity date can trigger an EARLY WITHDRAWAL PENALTY, which can be as little as partial loss of interest or complete loss of interest earned from the date of deposit, depending on the original maturity of the CD. Penalties are set by the issuing bank or savings institution. See also AVERAGE ANNUAL YIELD; BROKERED DEPOSIT; EURODOLLAR CERTIFICATE OF DEPOSIT; JUMBO CERTIFICATE OF DEPOSIT; MONEY MARKET CERTIFICATE; VARIABLE RATE CERTIFICATE; YANKEE CERTIFICATE OF DEPOSIT.

certificate of indebtedness

1. short-term IOU issued by the U.S. Treasury Department until 1981 when the government borrowed from the Federal Reserve System to cover Treasury obligations. These special certificates, with maturities of 90 days to one year, have since been replaced by six-month and one-year Treasury bills; none are currently outstanding.
2. unsecured promissory note issued by a corporation, giving the holder a claim to the unpledged assets of the issuer.

certificate of title opinion by an attorney or title searcher, after an inspection of public tax and land records, of the condition of the title to a specific piece of property. It does not provide warranties as to the authenticity of a title; that is done by a title insurance company.

certified check business or personal check stamped with the paying bank's certification that: 1) the maker's signature is genuine; and 2) there are sufficient funds in the account to cover the check. Once certified, a check becomes an obligation of a bank, and is paid out of bank funds. Banks charge a fee for certifying customer checks. Contrast with CASHIER'S CHECK.

chain banking control of three or more independently chartered banks by a few individuals, usually through stock ownership or interlocking directorates. Chain banking is found mostly in Midwestern states with restrictive branching laws, and differs from BRANCH BANKING, or multioffice banking within a single institution and GROUP BANKING by affiliate banks within a bank holding company. Its importance in the banking system has been declining in recent years, the result of state laws enabling INTERSTATE BANKING acquisitions by holding companies and, in several states, more liberalized branching laws.

character one of the five elements (the FIVE C's OF CREDIT) in credit analysis. A loan backed by only a borrower's reputation in the community is called a *character loan* or GOOD FAITH loan.

chargeback paying bank's refusal to honor a check or draft, causing the check to be returned to the presenting bank. Bank card sales drafts are sometimes charged-back by the cardholder's bank to the merchant bank, or to the merchant in certain situations, for example, when a card transaction is not processed according to specifications. Visa and MasterCard have elaborate rules for handling chargebacks. See also RETURN ITEMS.

charge-off

1. loans written off as uncollectible bad debt. When full repayment is considered unlikely, loans are removed from the lender's balance sheet and charged against the LOAN LOSS RESERVES account for bad debt. Loans removed from the lender's books may be partially or fully recovered by the lender's collection department or an outside debt collection agency if the loan is secured by collateral or the borrower has additional assets that are not secured by the debt. Closed

bank accounts are also removed from bank records by charging them off. Also called *write-off*. See also BAD DEBT; WORKOUT AGREEMENT.

2. process of removing uncollected loans or closed accounts from a bank's balance sheet.

charitable trust trust created for educational, scientific, or other purposes, organized as a legal charity. Also called a public trust. There are two types: a *charitable lead trust* pays income to a charity for a period of time, say 20 years, after which the property is distributed to noncharitable beneficiaries; a *charitable remainder trust* pays its income to taxable beneficiaries and the principal to charity when the trust ends.

charter legal authorization from a state or federal agency giving a bank the authority to commence business. To obtain a charter, a bank must have sufficient capital to support normal business activity, have competent management, be able to obtain deposit insurance and demonstrate a commitment to the local community.

charter conversion see CONVERSION.

charting see TECHNICAL ANALYSIS.

chattel mortgage lien giving a lender a security interest in personal property, as opposed to real estate (land, buildings) pledged as collateral for repayment of a loan. Chattels can be any kind of movable property, such as automobiles, jewelry, and so on. A chattel mortgage is normally used in financing big-ticket consumer goods, such as household appliances; the lien terminates when the obligation is paid. See also CONDITIONAL SALES CONTRACT.

cheap money said of credit available when interest rates are low and banks are willing to lend their EXCESS RESERVES, presumably with minimal repayment risk, to a creditworthy borrower.

check demand draft drawn on a bank, payable to the maker or to a third party. Checks are NEGOTIABLE INSTRUMENTS, transferable to another person. A check signed by the DRAWER, or MAKER, can be voided only by a STOP PAYMENT order. The ability to offer checking accounts is one of the criteria determining whether a financial institution is, in fact, a bank, as defined by the Bank Holding Company Act: See also CASHIER'S CHECK; CERTIFIED CHECK; DRAFT; NEGOTIABLE ORDER OF WITHDRAWAL (NOW) ACCOUNT; PAYMENT ORDER; SUPER NOW ACCOUNT; THIRD PARTY CHECK.

checkable deposits deposit accounts that may be drawn against by writing CHECKs or DRAFTs. The term includes, in addition to DEMAND DEPOSIT ACCOUNTS, any negotiable payment order, such as a NOW account—Negotiable Order of Withdrawal—or a SUPER NOW ACCOUNT. The Monetary Control Act of 1980 places all check-like bank deposits under the same category for the purpose of calculating Reserve Requirements.

check credit unsecured revolving line of credit, often used as a substitute for bank credit cards. Check credit functions as a cash advance against a bank card line of credit, but the drafts are processed as checks. Check credit may be a CASH RESERVE line of credit, or a special set of drafts that access a credit line. See also OVERDRAFT.

check digit final character in the nine-digit bank transit/routing number (ABA TRANSIT NUMBER plus CHECK ROUTING SYMBOL) printed on checks. The check digit, derived by computer from the other digits in the number, is used to validate a bank's transit and routing numbers in check processing. Some banks also use check digits to verify the accuracy of ACCOUNT NUMBERS.

check guarantee merchant service that, for a fee, guarantees that a customer's check will be paid. Check guarantee services compare check account numbers against a file of known bad check writers.

check hold number of days a bank can legally hold uncollected funds before crediting deposited funds to a customer's account. The Expedited Funds Availability Act of 1987 limits check holds to two business days for LOCAL CHECKs and five days for nonlocal checks after September 1, 1990. The first $100 of any check must be available for use the next business day. See also AVAILABILITY SCHEDULE; REGULATION CC.

check kiting drawing against balances credited to uncollected checks. By writing checks drawn on two or more out-of-town banks, a person temporarily short of cash can write an interest-free unauthorized bank loan or temporarily inflate his account balance to improve his chances of getting a loan. For example: a person deposits a $1,000 check in bank ABC, drawn on funds in bank XYZ. Before the first check clears he deposits a $1,000 check in bank XYZ, drawn on the first bank, and a $2,000 check drawn on bank XYZ in bank ABC. By carefully timing the checks, he has accumulated $3,000 in fictitious balances. Check kiting schemes can be very elaborate, and have been known to cause bank failures. Kiting is best controlled by monitoring unpaid checks in the process of collection.

checkless society notion that ELECTRONIC FUNDS TRANSFER (EFT) would someday replace check writing as the accepted way of transferring economic value. First advanced in the 1960s when banks were beginning to automate their back offices, the terms checkless society and cashless society are used most often as a reminder that changes in the payment system seldom induce corresponding changes in traditional banking habits. The U.S. banking system handles more checks and check-like instruments than ever, the result of payment innovations such as the Negotiable Order of Withdrawal account and the SUPER NOW ACCOUNT.

check routing symbol denominator (lower number) of a fraction appearing in the upper right corner of checks paid through the Federal Reserve System. The ABA TRANSIT NUMBER is the upper number. The routing symbol is a three- to four-digit number identifying the Federal Reserve district of the drawee (paying) bank, the Federal Reserve facility through which the check is collected, and the funds availability assigned by the Fed. Checks given IMMEDIATE AVAILABILITY, indicated by a 0 as the final digit in the routing symbol, are payable the same day as presented to a Federal Reserve Bank for collection. A DEFERRED AVAILABILITY check (identifiable by the numbers 1 through 9 in the final digit) is paid by a Federal Reserve Bank in two business days.

check safekeeping service in which a bank holds, or safe-keeps, cancelled checks or a copy of the checks, instead of re-turning them to the check writer. The customer receives a de-scriptive statement listing checks paid, the amount, and to whom they were paid. The major incentive for offering safekeeping is savings in labor costs and postage associated with statement preparation and mailing. Also called *check retention*. See also MICROFILM; TRUNCATION.

check, stop payment see STOP PAYMENT.

Chicago Board of Trade see FUTURES EXCHANGES.

Chinese Wall
1. popular name for the legal separation between a commercial bank and its trust department, designed to prevent conflicts of interest that may influence the trust department's role as a FIDUCIARY and investment advisor for trust accounts.
2. legal separation between commercial banking and investment banking dating to the GLASS-STEAGALL ACT of 1933, which directed commercial banks to divest their investment banking subsidiaries. Commercial banks may not underwrite any se-curities, other than ASSET-BACKED SECURITIES, consisting of bonds collateralized by bank obligations and certain types of GENERAL OBLIGATION BONDs issued by state and local govern-ments.

chip card see SMART CARD.

Christmas club see CLUB ACCOUNT.

churning
Banking:
1. lending and refinancing, replacing old debt with new debt to collect commitment fees and other fees.
2. in collection of past-due loans, extracting token payments from delinquent borrowers, without curing the delinquency (restoring the debt to current paid status). The best example is in credit cards, where a borrower whose account is ex-tended to the CREDIT LIMIT agrees to send three $10 pay-ments, or takes a cash advance against the credit line to pay down the outstanding balance.

3. in a loan portfolio, replacing expired accounts with new accounts, without increasing the number of accounts. This happens most often in a highly competitive market, as in bank credit cards.

Securities: excessive trading in a customer's account designed solely to increase broker's commissions—an illegal practice under SEC rules.

city bank see RESERVE CITY BANK.

claim

1. rights to assets held by another, for example, a depositor's claim to assets of a bank or a creditor's claim represented by a LIEN.
2. rights to an estate, for example, a life interest in the property of a deceased spouse.
3. owner's right of possession, represented by a CERTIFICATE OF TITLE.

class

1. securities issued as part of a group, or having similar characteristics, such as bonds issued under the same INDENTURE. Synonomous with TRANCHE.
2. one of several types of stock issued by a corporation, for example, Class A or Class B. Usually only one class has voting rights.
3. group of creditors in a bankruptcy case, ranked by seniority of claim. For example, secured creditors holding liens or mortgages.

classified loan see ADVERSELY CLASSIFIED ASSETS; NONACCRUAL ASSET.

clean

1. **Accounting.** Auditor's certificate in which no irregularities are disclosed. Also called an *unqualified opinion*.
2. **Banking:** To be free of debt, as during a borrower's annual clean-up period when bank lines of credit are paid down to a zero balance owed. See also CLEAN-UP REQUIREMENT.
3. **International Trade.** A bill of exchange, draft, or LETTER OF CREDIT without shipping documents attached, usually issued to organizations with good credit.

clean float market condition in which the value of a nation's currency in relation to other currencies is determined purely by free market forces. There are almost no cleanly floating Western currencies, i.e., currencies that are not supported one way or another through INTERVENTION by central banks. Currencies that trade with a minimum of intervention by central banks or central monetary authorities are the Swiss franc, the West German deutschmark, and the Canadian dollar. See also DIRTY FLOAT.

clean-up requirement contractual requirement that a borrower pay off any outstanding balance on a one-year renewable LINE-OF-CREDIT and reduce usage of the line to zero for a specified period. Once required as a proof that the borrower is not dependent on the lender for permanent financing, these provisions are becoming less common in banking. Also called *annual clean-up*.

clear
1. COLLECTION of checks deposited in a bank, with payment to the depositor. See also CLEARINGS.
2. matching of trades between buyers and sellers of securities, financial futures contracts, and so on, by an exchange or clearing house.
3. clear TITLE, or marketable title, without liens or encumbrances.

clearing house
1. **Banking.** Central collection site where banks exchange checks with one another. The arrangement is less costly than presenting checks directly to paying banks, and allows participants to maintain one clearing account, against which its debits or credits are posted. See also CLEARING HOUSE FUNDS.
2. **Futures.** An agency affiliated with a commodities exchange through which transactions are settled, through delivery of the commodity or purchase of offsetting futures positions.

Clearing House Automated Payments System (CHAPS) private telecommunication and payment system for interbank clearing of British POUND STERLING payments, operated since 1984 by the Bankers Clearing House of London.

clearing house funds funds available to collecting banks by settlement of checks, drafts, and other payment orders through a bank-owned clearing house association. Funds are usually available for use after one business day, except for transfers through the Clearing House Interbank Payments System (CHIPS), which are available for investment the same day. Paper checks and drafts are available in one to three business days, if drawn on a local bank, whereas large-dollar transfers of corporate funds are available for use the same day or the next day, depending on the payment system used. Contrast with FEDERAL FUNDS.

Clearing House Interbank Payments System (CHIPS) computerized funds transfer system for international dollar payments linking 140 depository institutions with offices or subsidiaries in New York City. Funds transfers through CHIPS, operated by the New York Clearing House Association, account for 90% of all interbank payments relating to international trade. Final settlement occurs through adjustments in special account balances at the Federal Reserve Bank of New York. Since 1981, settlement has occurred at the close of each business day when CHIPS members who owe payments to other banks transfer funds to a special settlement account at the Federal Reserve Bank of New York and others receive payments due. CHIPS members send and receive payments from other U.S. banks through the Federal Reserve's FEDERAL WIRE (Fed Wire), the Fed's electronic funds transfer and securities transfer network. See also SOCIETY FOR WORLDWIDE INTERBANK FINANCIAL TELECOMMUNICATIONS (SWIFT).

clearing house proof daily settlement sheet listing checks exchanged by members of a clearing house association. The proof sheet lists the total amount of debits and credits due to or due from each bank, and serves as the basis for adjusting RESERVE ACCOUNT balances of clearing house members kept at a Federal Reserve Bank. The weekly report to members is a clearing house statement.

clearings movement of checks from banks where they are deposited back to those on which they were written, and funds movement in the opposite direction. This results in credit to the banks where funds are deposited and corresponding debits to the

accounts of the paying institutions. The Federal Reserve operates a nationwide check clearing system, including numerous
REGIONAL CHECK PROCESSING CENTERS. Many checks are cleared
by private sector arrangements either by DIRECT PRESENTMENT
to the payor bank or, if the check is drawn on a local bank,
through a CLEARING HOUSE association. Check-like Negotiable
Order of Withdrawal (NOW) accounts and share draft payment
orders may also be cleared through the Federal Reserve Banks,
under the Monetary Control Act of 1980. The act also requires
the Federal Reserve to charge fees for its check clearing services. International clearings between countries are settled
through the FOREIGN EXCHANGE market.

Clifford trust trust allowing a transfer of income generating
assets for a period at least ten years and a day, for example, from
a parent to a child. Afterward, the assets in trust are returned to
the donor. Before the Tax Reform Act of 1986 eliminated the tax
benefits of Clifford trusts, they were often used for specific purposes, such as financing a college education, because trust income was transferred to a beneficiary, who usually is in a lower
tax bracket. Trust income is tax free, but may be taxable if income from the trust for each child exceeds $1,000 a year. Also
called a *ten-year trust*. See also INTER VIVOS TRUST.

close to consummate an agreement, sale, or transfer of assets.
  1. **Accounting.** The transfer of final entries from subsidiary
     ledgers to a balance sheet ledger, a process known as closing
     the books.
  2. **Real Estate.** The rights of ownership are transferred in ex-
     change for monetary and other considerations. At a loan clos-
     ing, promissory notes are signed and checks exchanged.
  3. **Securities.** End-of-day trading, referring to trades occurring
     within half an hour of the closing bell. Also, the final price of
     a security traded on a public exchange.
  4. **Underwriting.** Exchange of checks and securities after an
     offering of securities has been placed with investors.

closed account account with a zero-balance, debits equaling credits.

closed-end credit consumer installment loan made for a
predetermined amount, calling for periodic payments of princi-

pal and interest over a specified time period or term. The finance charge may be a fixed or variable rate. The borrower does not have the option of obtaining extra funds under the original loan agreement, as in OPEN-END CREDIT.

closed-end fund investment trust that pools the assets of investors and issues a fixed number of shares. In contrast, an open-end fund or a MUTUAL FUND that continuously offers new shares to the public or offers to repurchase shares at NET ASSET VALUE. Shares of closed-end funds are traded over-the-counter or on stock exchanges. Non-bank affiliates of commercial banks are authorized by the Federal Reserve Board to offer closed-end investment trusts.

closed-end lease consumer lease that does not give the lessee the option of buying the leased property when the lease expires. The lessee makes a fixed monthly payment for a specified number of months, and has no further obligation afterward. This type of lease is most common in automobile leasing. Contrast with OPEN-END LEASE, which may have a BALLOON PAYMENT at the end of the lease.

closed-end mortgage bond secured by a mortgage on real estate prohibiting the borrower from using the mortgaged property as collateral for any other debts or repaying the debt early except with consent of the bondholders.

closing costs borrower's out-of-pocket expenses in closing a mortgage loan as listed in the CLOSING STATEMENT. These costs include origination fees and closing points, title insurance, attorney fees, land survey, and such prepaid items as taxes and insurance escrow payments. See also REAL ESTATE SETTLEMENT PROCEDURES ACT.

closing date date on which ASSET-BACKED SECURITIESS are first authenticated and delivered by the issuer. The bond indenture or indenture supplement is finalized, collateral is delivered to the trustee, legal documents are executed, and cash is received by the issuer on this date.

closing points sum paid by a home buyer to the mortgage lender at loan closing to increase the loan's effective yield. One point is equal to one-percent of the loan amount. Also called a *discount point*.

closing statement document listing all charges payable by either buyer or seller at a real estate closing, under the REAL ESTATE SETTLEMENT PROCEDURES ACT. The borrower has a right to request a copy of the statement one day before the property transfer takes place. This statement lists real estate commissions, lender's fees and discount points charged, title insurance costs, and the amount the lender is willing to hold in escrow for taxes and insurance.

cloud on title TITLE that is encumbered by prior liens, attachments, or court judgments, impairing the owner's ability to transfer title to someone else. Distinguish from *clean title*.

club account
1. deposit accounts of unincorporated voluntary associations.
2. special purpose savings account, often issued with a coupon book. These accounts normally pay interest and have a one-year maturity. Examples are Christmas club, Chanukkah club, holiday club and vacation club.

co-branded credit card Visa or MasterCard credit card jointly sponsored by a bank and retail merchant, such as a department store. Co-branded cards can be issued at less cost than conventional retail private label cards, and give issuing banks access to new customers. Cardholders may be given incentives, such as discounts on merchandise, rebates, or discounts off purchases. A co-branded card has a tie-in with a specific merchant rather than an association or professional group. It also can be used at other merchants. Contrast with AFFINITY CARD.

code of ethics rules and procedures of professional conduct, for example, the Robert Morris Associates Code of Ethics, which sets voluntary standards for exchange in credit information between banks. The code also includes prohibitions on lender take-backs, and so on.

collar two-sided interest rate guaranty protecting both the borrower and lender. It consists of a FLOOR and an INTEREST RATE CAP. The lower end, the floor, assures the lender the rate will not fall below a fixed amount; the upper end, the cap, assures the borrower that the cost of credit will not rise above a stated level. The cap protects the borrower from interest rate risk if rates rise quickly. Often, the lender is willing to reduce the cost of an interest rate cap if the borrower accepts an interest rate floor as well. For example, a bank may agree, in exchange for an up-front fee, not to charge a rate below 9% or above 14% over the life of the loan.

collateral asset pledged as security to ensure payment or performance of an obligation. In bank lending, it is generally something of value owned by the borrower. If the borrower defaults, the asset pledged may be taken and sold by the lender to fulfill completion of the original contract. Four types of collateral, as recognized by the Uniform Commercial Code, are commonly used in secured lending: trade goods, paper (negotiable instruments and title documents), intangibles, and business proceeds (cash). Collateral assigned to the lender can even be the asset being financed, as in ASSET-BASED LENDING, where a loan might be secured by business inventory or accounts receivable. In a home mortgage loan, the borrower gives the lender a MORTGAGE on the house being purchased.

When bank assets are securitized, or converted into marketable securities in the SECONDARY MARKET, the PRINCIPAL and INTEREST payments serve as collateral for the securities offered for sale to investors. Examples are Ginnie Mae pass through securities, which are backed by residential mortgages.

See also ASSET-BACKED SECURITIES; COLLATERAL LOAN; SECURITY AGREEMENT; SECURITY INTEREST; SIDE COLLATERAL.

collateralize to secure a debt in part or in full by pledge of COLLATERAL. See also ASSIGNMENT; HYPOTHECATION.

collateral auto receivable securities (CARS) ASSET-BACKED SECURITIES backed by automobile loan receivables, pioneered by Salomon Brothers in 1985. Securities are issued on a nonrecourse basis and sold by several commercial banks and captive finance companies owned by auto manufacturers.

collateralized mortgage obligation (CMO)
mortgage-backed bond secured by the cash flow of a pool of

mortgages. In a CMO, the regular principal and interest payments made by borrowers are separated into different payment streams, creating several bonds that repay invested capital at different rates.

A given pool generally secures several different classes of CMO bonds. A CMO pays the bondholder on a schedule that differs from the mortgage pool as a whole, and includes fast pay, medium pay, and slow pay bonds to suit the needs of different investors. The common arrangements include: a fast-pay bond with a maturity much shorter than the total pool; a bond paying interest only for a period that may be contingent on how prior CMOs perform, before payment of principal begins; and a bond paying variable interest based on an index, typically the London Interbank Offered Rate (LIBOR), even though the mortgages themselves may be fixed rate loans.

Fast paying bonds appeal mostly to savings and loans seeking short-term liquidity investments, whereas longer-term CMOs appeal to the investment needs of pension funds and institutional investors. The first CMOs were issued by the Federal Home Loan Mortgage Corp. (Freddie Mac) in 1983. CMOs manage the prepayment risk associated with mortgage-related securities by splitting the pools of mortgage loans into different categories. CMOs pay principal and interest semiannually.

A CMO can be a nonrecourse sale of assets by the issuer, or a liability of the issuer, depending on how a transaction is arranged. The accounting rules in issuing these securities are complex.

See also ACCRUAL BOND; PASS-THROUGH SECURITY; PAY-THROUGH SECURITY; REAL ESTATE MORTGAGE INVESTMENT CONDUIT.

collateral loan loan secured by a pledge of assets. Loans secured by collateral are primarily commercial loans where the ultimate source of repayment is the borrower's assets, rather than the borrower's character or reputation in the community. The lender's FINANCING STATEMENT lists the collateral securing the loan, and the location and condition of the collateral. When filed with a public records office, a LIEN is created, giving the lender priority over other creditors. See also ASSET-BASED LENDING; CASH FLOW LOAN; MORTGAGE; PERFECTED LIEN; SECURITY AGREEMENT; SECURITY INTEREST; UNIFORM COMMERCIAL CODE.

collateral trust note

1. short-term COMMERCIAL PAPER issued by a mortgage banker to finance its inventory of loans. These notes are issued under a trust indenture, and are collateralized by a pool of mortgages. Holders of the notes have equal claim with lenders originating the mortgages.

2. short-term notes secured by pledged bonds or other securities, most often issued by railroads, holding companies, and investment trusts.

collateral value

estimate of value of borrower's pledged collateral as determined by APPRAISAL. If marketable securities are pledged, the lender is restricted by Federal Reserve Board regulations on MARGIN lending. See also LOAN-TO-VALUE RATIO.

collateral value insurance

business insurance that guarantees the value of appraised collateral and establishes a minimum liquidation value. Generally, the machinery, inventory or equipment offered for collateral is appraised, and a certificate of guarantee is then issued. This form of lender protection is available from insurers and is used mostly in ASSET-BASED LENDING.

collected balance

checking account cash balance after deducting checks drawn on other banks. Generally defined as account ledger balances, less unpaid checks in the process of collection. A bank may count a deposited check as funds available for use by its customer in two business days, but usually will not include it in the depositor's collected balance for five or six days. This allows time for the drawee bank to return the check because of insufficient funds in the check maker's account or for other reasons. Contrast with AVAILABLE BALANCE.

collection

1. PRESENTMENT of checks, drafts, and other negotiable instruments to the point of origin, and receiving payment from the paying bank. The term covers CASH ITEMS such as checks and drafts, and also *noncash items*, including acceptances, bonds, and notes, which are referred to as COLLECTION ITEMS. Cash items receive immediate credit; collection items are credited to the owner's account only when paid.

2. handling of past-due accounts by specialists, who attempt to get a promise to pay from the delinquent borrower and ultimately recover all or part of the debt.

collection items any check or negotiable instrument that is not credited as collected funds to the customer's account until payment has been received from the paying bank. Also called *noncash items*. Collection items are not processed through the normal check clearing system, and generally a special handling fee is charged by the paying bank, the collecting bank, or both. Included are a broad range of financial instruments: negotiable certificates of deposit, commercial paper, drafts, notes, and acceptances. Processing of collection items may be done by a correspondent bank if the customer's bank does not have a collection department. See also WIRE FATE ITEM.

collection period period of time required to convert deposited checks into collected balances. This varies according to the type of instrument, the distance between the paying and collecting bank, and statute. The Expedited Funds Availability Act of 1987 requires banks to credit funds to a customer's account within two days from the date of deposit for local checks, and within five days for nonlocal checks, as of September 1, 1990.

collective investment fund pooled fund operated by a bank or trust company for investment of the assets of separate trust accounts. Also known as MASTER TRUST accounting. Pooling helps the investors obtain diversification of investments, improved earnings, and economies of scale. National banks and many state chartered banks are authorized to invest trust assets in a master trust account.

colon national currency of Costa Rica and El Salvador.

co-maker person who signs a borrower's PROMISSORY NOTE to give a loan additional security or to enhance the quality of a loan. A co-maker has a liability similar to an ENDORSER or GUARANTOR, although in a strict legal sense a guarantor or endorser cannot be compelled to honor the note until certain conditions are met.

combined statement ACCOUNT STATEMENT listing account activity in demand deposit, including statement savings; time deposit account and balances owed on revolving credit lines, telephone banking transactions, and so on. Combined statements save postage and the costs of printing and mailing separate statements. See also DESCRIPTIVE STATEMENT.

comfort letter

1. in UNDERWRITING, a letter from an independent auditor reporting the procedures followed in reviewing unaudited financial statements and other data in preparing the registration statement and prospectus. Sometimes called *cold comfort letter*.

2. letter indicating that a bank holding company will honor its end-of-day net settlement position in an electronic payment system. Comfort letters are commonly used in the Clearing House Interbank Payments System network in New York to reduce the possibility that a CHIPS member will fail to meet its payment obligations to other banks.

commercial and industrial (C&I) loan

LOAN to a corporation, commercial enterprise, or joint venture, as opposed to a loan to a consumer. C&L loans can be a source of working capital, or used to finance the purchase of manufacturing plants and equipment. These loans are generally short-term, are secured by COLLATERAL pledged by the borrower or can be fully unsecured, and usually are made at flexible rates. Generally, the rate is pegged to the bank PRIME RATE or money market rate, such as the LONDON INTERBANK OFFERED RATE (LIBOR). If the borrower defaults, the lender may try to seize the collateral and sell it to pay off the loan or may demand repayment if the borrower suffers a decline in financial condition. See also CONTINUATION STATEMENT; CORPORATE RESOLUTION; COVENANT; DEMAND LOAN; FINANCING STATEMENT; SECURITY AGREEMENT; SECURITY INTEREST; TERM LOAN; TIME LOAN.

commercial account

bank account maintained by a business, generally a demand deposit or checking account. Business checking accounts generally have higher monthly activity fees and service charges than accounts owned by individuals but receive an EARNINGS CREDIT based on average collected balances. Banks are prohibited by Federal Reserve REGULATION Q from paying interest on demand deposit accounts, although many corporations maintain interest-bearing savings accounts. In most states, sole proprietor owners of a business may open interest bearing NEGOTIABLE ORDER OF WITHDRAWAL (NOW) ACCOUNTS and SUPER NOW ACCOUNTS. See also ACCOUNT ANALYSIS; BUSINESS CREDIT; NONPERSONAL TIME DEPOSIT.

commercial bank state bank or NATIONAL BANK, owned by stockholders, that accepts demand deposits, makes commercial and industrial loans, and performs other banking services for the public. The term commercial bank is synonomous with FULL SERVICE BANK, because many commercial banks supply trust services, foreign exchange, trade financing, and international banking. Most state chartered trust companies are also commercial banks. Commercial bank deposits are issued by the BANK INSURANCE FUND, a federal insurance fund managed by the Federal Deposit Insurance Corporation. See also INDEPENDENT BANK; NONBANK BANK; SECURITIES AFFILIATE.

commercial letter of credit see LETTER OF CREDIT.

commercial loan see COMMERCIAL & INDUSTRIAL LOAN.

commercial mortgage loan secured by commercial real estate, usually with a 20- to 40-year term. Commercial mortgages differ in many ways from residential mortgage loans. These are highly customized financings and are usually pegged to a BASE RATE such as the bank PRIME RATE, and are sometimes made at fixed rates. Rates and payment terms are negotiated in each loan by the borrower and the lender. Commercial mortgages have commitment fees and can be quite profitable for mortgage lenders, although there is some default risk. Commercial mortgage financing is frequently arranged through multilender SYNDICATES or LOAN PARTICIPATIONS arranged by a lead bank. See also INTEREST ONLY LOAN; ZERO-COUPON MORTGAGE.

commercial paper short-term IOU, or unsecured money market obligation, issued by prime rated commercial firms and financial companies, with maturities from 2 days up to 270 days. The most active market is in issues under 30 days.

Commercial paper is, in effect, a promissory note of the issuer used to finance current obligations, and is a NEGOTIABLE

INSTRUMENT as defined by the Uniform Commercial Code. Interest rates on commercial paper are often lower than bank loan rates, which makes the commercial paper market an attractive alternative to issuers, particularly in periods of TIGHT MONEY and high interest rates.

Bank-related paper accounts for about 25% of the commercial paper market, and is an obligation of bank holding company or nonbank subsidiary, but not the bank itself. Commercial banks are permitted by the Federal Reserve Board to act as agent in placing commercial paper directly with investors and underwrite limited amounts of paper through SECURITIES AFFILIATES.

Most commercial paper rates are quoted on a discount basis, although some paper is interest-bearing. Issuers market their paper through dealers, or alternatively through direct placement with an investor. Commercial paper is rated by debt rating agencies and generally is backed by a bank LINE OF CREDIT. Secondary market sales are limited, as issuers are able to closely match the maturity needs of investors. See also SECURITIES AFFILIATE.

commingled funds
1. **Asset-Based Lending.** A borrower's cash collateral account mixed with other accounts kept by the lender.
2. **Trusts.** A fund managed by a bank trust department for employee benefit plans, retirement plans of self-employed workers. These funds give the participants greater investment diversification and safety of principal, at lower operating cost for the bank. The Federal Reserve Board has permitted bank trust departments to offer commingled accounts, much like MUTUAL FUNDS, to customers with INDIVIDUAL RETIREMENT ACCOUNTS. See also MASTER TRUST.

commission
1. broker's charge for executing a trade.
2. fee, a percentage of the selling price of property, paid to a real estate broker.
3. fee paid to a bank's TRUST DEPARTMENT, normally a percentage of the income from a trust account.

commission house see FUTURES COMMISSION MERCHANT.

commissioner of banking see STATE BANKING DEPARTMENT.

commitment

1. lender's agreement to make a loan at a quoted rate during a specific future period. Usually, a COMMITMENT FEE is charged for this service. See also LOCK-IN PERIOD.
2. mortgage originating bank's contractual agreement to deliver a specified number of mortgage loans to a secondary market CONDUIT. See also STANDBY COMMITMENT.

commitment fee lender's charge for holding credit available. The fee may be waived for some borrowers, and usually is replaced with interest when funds are advanced, as in a REVOLVING CREDIT. In business credit, commitment fees often are charged for an unused portion of a LINE OF CREDIT.

commitment letter form letter from a lender stating willingness to advance funds to a named borrower, repayable at a specified rate and time period. This is a common notice in loans that are real estate secured, such as home equity lines of credit and second mortgages, subject to an escape clause allowing the lender to rescind the agreement in event of materially adverse changes in the borrower's financial condition.

Committee on Uniform Securities Identification Procedures (CUSIP) see CUSIP NUMBER.

Commodities Futures Trading Commission (CFTC) independent federal agency created by Congress in 1974 to regulate the commodity futures market. Traders engaged in the commodities markets are required to register with the CFTC. The CFTC has authority to set margin requirements, regulate options contracts in commodities, and supervise registered FUTURES COMMISSION MERCHANTs.

Commodity Credit Corporation government corporation under the U.S. Department of Agriculture that finances public price supports for farm commodities. The agency gives its financial backing to bank letters of credit supporting commodity exports.

commodity paper note, bill of exchange, or trade acceptance secured by shipping documents or a warehouse terminal receipt, which is payable on demand. Bank endorsed commodity

paper is eligible for REDISCOUNT under Federal Reserve REGULA-
TION A.

common law body of law based on judicial decisions and
precedent that has become the basis of the legal system in Great
Britain and the United States (except in Louisiana, where *civil
law* is the legal foundation). Many of the legal concepts in use
today, including the law of contracts, are derived from common
law.

common stock security representing equity ownership in a
corporation. Holders of common stock have the right to elect
directors and collect dividends. Common stock claims are subordinate to bondholder claims, preferred stockholders, and general
creditors.

common trust fund See COMMINGLED FUNDS.

community bank see INDEPENDENT BANK.

community property property shared by husband and
wife, each having a half-interest in the earnings of the other; the
form of joint property ownership in several states. Most states
adhere to common law rules of property ownership where each
spouse owns what he or she earns.

Community Reinvestment Act (CRA) federal law
adopted in 1977 requiring mortgage lenders to demonstrate their
commitment to home mortgage financing in economically disad-
vantaged areas. Specifically, the CRA prohibits redlining or
credit allocation based on geographic region, and requires
lenders to file annual compliance statements.

co-mortgagor see CO-MAKER.

compensating balance demand deposit balance maintained by a corporate borrower. Its purpose is to compensate for
bank expenses in servicing a loan or line of credit. A loan
contract, for example, may call for 10 and 5 compensating balances—10% of the credit line at commitment time and an additional 5% when the borrower draws against the credit.

competitive bid public auction bid containing prices and terms offered by an underwriter for a new issue of securities. Issuers select the underwriter bidding the best (highest) price and lowest interest cost. The highest price must be combined with the interest coupon to arrive at NET INTEREST COST or NIC. Sometimes the issuer specifies the interest coupon, or sometimes allows bidders to specify the coupon rate, especially in municipal general obligation (G-O) bonds.

Underwriting proposals for most municipal general obligation bonds, railroad bonds, and public utility bonds are submitted in this bid form. U.S. Treasury securities also are marketed through competitive bidding by dealer banks bidding the highest price (and lowest yield) for new Treasury bills, notes, and bonds. Contrast with NEGOTIATED UNDERWRITING. See also NONCOMPETITIVE BID.

competitive bid option commercial loan SYNDICATION where banks submit auction bids for a loan, and have the option of selling loan participations to other banks or investors. The borrower has the option of selecting the banks from which it chooses to borrow, and can reject bids from lenders whose bid rates are too high. Typically, these credit facilities are priced at thin spreads over a base lending rate, for example, the lender's internal cost of funds or LIBOR. The lead bank in the syndicate generally retains only a small portion of the financing in its own portfolio. Competitive bidding by U.S. banks for commercial and industrial (C&I) loans is similar to TENDER PANEL bidding in the Eurocredit market where a group of banks make bids to purchase short-term corporate notes through a REVOLVING UNDERWRITING FACILITY.

Competitive Equality Banking Act federal legislation of 1987 that did the following: established the Financing Corporation, a federal agency to recapitalize the Federal Savings and Loan Insurance Corporation by issuing 30-year bonds; gave the Federal Deposit Insurance Corporation authority to charter a BRIDGE BANK to assume the deposits and secured liabilities of an insolvent bank; authorized banking regulatory agencies to charter mutual holding companies; imposed a one-year moratorium on new insurance and securities activities of commerical banks, expiring March 1, 1988; prohibited new charters of NONBANK BANKs and restricted existing nonbank banks to 7% annual growth; and required faster clearing of checks deposited in banks and savings institutions. This section of the law, the EXPEDITED FUNDS AVAILABILITY ACT, is implemented by Federal Reserve REGULATION CC.

compliance examination periodic bank examination by a federal regulatory agency to ensure compliance with consumer protection regulations, such as the Community Reinvestment Act, the Equal Credit Opportunity Act, or the Truth in Lending Act. Financial institutions are required by law to issue reports at regular intervals, for example, an annual statement of mortgage lending in the lender's market area. Compliance exams are intended to uncover any violations of consumer protection regulations so that remedial action can be taken.

composition agreement between an insolvent debtor and his creditors, whereby the creditors accept less than the full value of their claims. Considered an expedient alternative to bankruptcy, composition plans are most often agreed to in small, unincorporated businesses rather than larger firms. Creditors are inclined to accept the composition repayment in the belief that a going concern is better than one that liquidates to pay off its creditors.

compound interest interest added to interest previously earned on a principal balance. Compounding increases the depositor's rate of return on bank balances and the lender's effective yield on the unpaid principal of outstanding loans. For example: take a $1,000 savings account paying 5% interest, compounded monthly; the EFFECTIVE RATE earned is 5.116%, assuming the $1,000 remains on deposit for a full year and no additional deposits are made. The more frequently interest is compounded, the higher the effective rate earned. In bank lending, compounding occurs when interest is charged faster than it is paid, or, more commonly, when the borrower misses payments or makes late payments. Under certain circumstances, compounding of interest may lead to violations of state USURY laws, depending on how the accrued interest is computed, if the effect is to raise the lender's yield above the statutory ceiling, or if state laws prohibit any form of compounding. See also DAILY INTEREST; RULE OF 72.

COMPOUND INTEREST

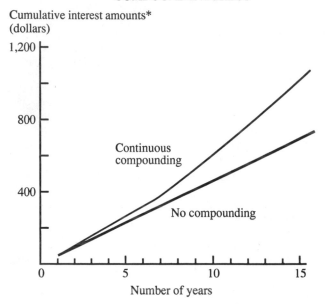

Cumulative interest amounts*
(dollars)

*Amount paid on $1000 at 5% annual interest rate.

Source: John R. Brick, ed., *Bank Management* (Richmond, Virginia: Robert F. Dame, Inc., 1980), p.475.

Comptroller of the Currency chief regulator of national banks, appointed by the President for a five-year term, with Senate confirmation. The Office of the Comptroller of the Currency is the supervisory agency for nationally chartered banks. Each NATIONAL BANK is required to file a statement of condition not less than four times a year. National bank examiners, under the direction of 14 regional administrators of national banks, conduct national bank examinations at least three times every two years. The Comptroller of the Currency also serves as one of the three directors of the Federal Deposit Insurance Corp. See also FEDERAL FINANCIAL INSTITUTIONS EXAMINATION COUNCIL.

Comptroller's call see CALL REPORT.

computerized loan origination (CLO) mortgage origination network linking mortgage lenders to realtors via computer terminals. The first was First Boston Corp.'s Shelternet (now defunct), which began operating in 1983. Mortgage originators use CLO networks to offer home buyers rapid approval of mortgage applications, and also to pool mortgages for resale in the SECONDARY MORTGAGE MARKET.

concentration

1. condition of a bank's loan portfolio measured by the number of loans extended to a particular industry. Excessive lending to a single industry (agriculture, oil and gas exploration, real estate) indicates a lack of DIVERSIFICATION in the loan portfolio, and potential credit risk. Many Texas and Oklahoma banks suffered enormous losses in the mid-1980s when the oil exploration industry bottomed out; many were later taken over by other banks. In general, most banks report loan concentrations above 50% of equity. The Securities and Exchange Commission requires banks to disclose in financial reports any concentration exceeding 10% of loans. See also ASSET QUALITY; LIQUIDITY.

2. share of deposits owned by a bank in a given market. The U.S. Department of Justice uses a statistical yardstick, the HERFFINDAHL INDEX, in gauging the anticompetitive effects of bank mergers. The index is calculated by adding the market shares of a product, such as deposits, owned by banks in a market and squaring the results. The index indicates both the number of firms in a market and their relative size. For example, a market with five firms, each having individual market shares of 30, 20, 20, 20, and 10 percent would have an index of 2200. Generally, the Justice Department will not challenge a merger unless the post-merger index is at least 1800 and the merger causes an increase of at least 200 on the scale.

concentration account deposit account into which funds are periodically transferred from various local banks, via wire transfer or automated clearing house debit, from other accounts in the same bank, or in different banks. See also LOCK-BOX; ZERO-BALANCE ACCOUNT.

concentration bank bank that maintains a CONCENTRA-TION ACCOUNT for a corporate customer. Usually this bank is also the corporation's LEAD BANK, having the firm's primary deposit account, and may offer investment advice, funds transfer, and other NONCREDIT SERVICES. See also TREASURY WORKSTATION.

conditional commitment

1. lender's agreement to provide financing to a qualified borrower, provided the borrower obtains insurance or satisfies other requirements.
2. notice from a federal loan guaranty agency, such as the Federal Home Administration, that it has agreed to insure a mortgage loan, subject to the limitations in the guarantee.

conditional prepayment rate (CPR) mortgage prepayment model in which the average monthly prepayment rate is annualized by multiplying by 12. CPR expresses prepayment as ratio of prepayments to outstandings, usually a percentage of the mortgage balance outstanding at the beginning of the year that will be prepaid that year. A variation is single monthly mortality, which expresses expected prepayments as a monthly rate. CPR is a predictor of CASH FLOW YIELDs from Collateralized Mortgage Obligation issues.

conditional sales contract agreement commonly used in real estate finance and commercial finance, whereby the seller retains title to the equipment through a purchase money security interest. Ownership passes to the purchaser when installments are fully paid. See also FINANCE LEASE.

condominium single housing unit in a multiple-unit building. The owner holds legal title to the unit and pays property taxes plus a share of the building's common charges for maintenance and upkeep. The owner may sell, rent, or mortgage the unit just as if it were a single-family house. Compare to COOPER-ATIVE.

conduit government or private organization that assembles mortgage and other loans into a large pool, and issues pass-through or pay-through securities in its own name to investors. The first mortgage conduits were established by the Government National Mortgage Association and the Federal Home Loan Mortgage Corp. Private sector conduits have since been orga-nized by mortgage insurance companies and financial institu-tions to issue securities backed by mortgages, credit card receiv-ables, boat loans and other loans, without federal agency guarantee. Mortgage conduits make it easier for a large number of banks and thrifts to sell their loans to secondary market inves-tors, as smaller lenders are not limited by pool size or eligibility restrictions. See also ASSET BACKED SECURITIES; COLLATERAL-IZED MORTGAGE OBLIGATION; PASS-THROUGH SECURITY; PAY-THROUGH SECURITY.

Conference of State Bank Supervisors (CSBS) see TRADE ASSOCIATION.

confession of judgment loan clause by which the bor-rower waives his claim to mortgaged property without hearing or notice if the lender obtains a DEFICIENCY JUDGMENT in event of default. This credit practice was prohibited by regulation in 1985. Also called *cognovit agreement*.

confirmation
1. written communication to the counterparty reciting all the relevant details of a transaction, as agreed by telephone or telex.
2. audit function whereby a bank requests customers to verify account balances; a means of detecting deposit fraud. *Posi-tive confirmation* requests that every balance be checked; *negative confirmation* requests a reply only if errors or ac-count differences are found.
3. in bankruptcy, acceptance of a debt repayment plan by credi-tors

confirmed letter of credit LETTER OF CREDIT in inter-national trade guaranteed by a second bank, in addition to the bank originally issuing the credit. The confirming bank agrees to pay or accept drafts against the credit even if the issuer refuses. A confirmed letter of credit also protects against unfavorable exchange regulations and shortages of foreign currency in the importing country.

conservator

1. court appointed person to manage and protect the interests of an estate or the affairs of a person judged incompetent.
2. official appointed by a banking regulator to protect the assets of a troubled bank or savings institution while a permanent solution to its financial problems is worked out. A bank declared to be insolvent is placed under control of a RECEIVER, and assets sold to pay its creditors.

consideration something of value voluntarily exchanged by parties to an agreement, making the agreement a legally binding CONTRACT on all of the parties involved. In banking, the lending of money in exchange for a borrower's promise to repay the loan, put up collateral, or both. A lender cannot take a lien without advancing funds to the borrower.

consolidated financial statement

1. accounting statement combining the assets and liabilities of a bank, its domestic branches, and major subsidiaries in a single statement. Major commercial banks report changes in their financial position weekly to the Federal Reserve Board of Governors. Banks and bank holding companies, but not finance companies, are required by regulation to file consolidated statements. See also REPORT OF CONDITION.
2. FINANCIAL STATEMENT combining assets, liabilities, and shareholder's equity of affiliated companies for reporting or disclosure purposes.

consolidation loan installment loan that enables a borrower to combine several outstanding loans under one loan, rather than several smaller ones, often with a lower monthly payment.

consortium bank European MERCHANT BANK owned by banks from different countries, and engaged primarily in international banking. Consortium banks, originating in the 1960s and 1970s, are less active in Euromarket lending than they once were, and also have domestic operations lending to business customers.

constant payment periodic payment of a fixed amount that includes interest and principal. Any loan with a declining principal balance. As the loan is paid off, a greater portion of each payment is allocated to reducing the principal. For example, fixed-rate home mortgage loan.

constant percent prepayment annualized estimate of mortgage loan prepayments, computed by multiplying the average monthly prepayment rate, also called the Single Monthly Mortality, by 12. See also CONDITIONAL PREPAYMENT RATE.

construction loan see CONSTRUCTION MORTGAGE.

construction mortgage interim loan covering construction and development costs, secured by a MORTGAGE on the property financed. Also called a *construction loan*. Funds are advanced at specific stages of construction, in so-called progress payments, with a portion held back until completion of the project, a certain percentage of the building has been leased, or other criteria have been met. Construction financing is paid off from the proceeds of a permanent mortgage by an INSTITUTIONAL LENDER, for example a life insurance company or pension fund or bank. However, some lenders have made construction loans on speculation, without a FIRM COMMITMENT by a take-out lender. Many of these construction loans financing speculative real estate developments have, as a result, become long-term permanent mortgages on the books of the original lender.

constructive notice notice in a newspaper or public record presumed to be legally sufficient notice of actions taken, for example, the recording of liens, escheats of abandoned property to the state, and so on. Constructive notice is enforceable under the law if given in a legally prescribed manner. Distinguish from actual notice, in which a person is notified of a pending action by letter or in person.

consular invoice certification by a consul or government official covering an international shipment of goods. A consular invoice, obtained from the consul of the importing country at the point of shipment, insures that the exporter's trade papers are in order and the goods being shipped do not violate any laws or trade restrictions. AD VALOREM or specific import duties are determined from a consular invoice.

Consumer Advisory Council group established by Congress in 1976 to advise the Federal Reserve Board on its responsibilities under the Consumer Credit Protection Act and other credit related issues. The council, drawn from a diverse group of consumers and lenders, meets three times a year, but has no real power.

Consumer Bankers Association see TRADE ASSOCIATION.

consumer credit credit extended to individuals for personal or household use, rather than businesses. Broadly defined, consumer credit includes all forms of INSTALLMENT CREDIT other than loans secured by real estate (home mortgages, for instance) plus OPEN-END CREDIT such as credit cards. New forms of credit, however, have blurred these distinctions; a HOME EQUITY CREDIT line is a revolving line of credit secured by real estate—a lien on the borrower's home.

Many traditional forms of consumer credit, such as auto loans, have standard monthly payments—fixed repayment schedules of one to five years or more—and are made at either fixed interest rates or variable rates that are based on an INDEX. Consumer loans fill a variety of needs: financing the purchase of an automobile or household appliance, home improvement, debt consolidation, and so on. These loans may be unsecured or secured by an assignment of title, as in an auto loan, or money in a bank account. Consumer debt is monitored by the Federal Reserve Board, and is one of the leading indicators of growth in the economy. See also AMORTIZATION SCHEDULE; CLOSED-END CREDIT; HOME EQUITY CREDIT; RULE OF THE 78's; REGULATION B; REGULATION Z; SIMPLE INTEREST.

Consumer Credit Protection Act see TRUTH IN LENDING ACT; REGULATION Z.

consumer lease contract for a lease of personal property, such as an automobile, boat, or household appliance with a total obligation under $25,000. Lease financing has a fixed schedule of monthly payments, usually over a three- to five-year period, and may include an option to purchase the leased property at maturity. Bank lessors are required by Federal Reserve REGULATION M to disclose the actual cost to the consumer. This includes security deposits, monthly payments, taxes, and registration costs, and in an OPEN-END LEASE, whether a BALLOON PAYMENT is due at maturity.

consumer related receivables securities bond or debt instrument backed by the CASH FLOW from consumer credit receivables, such as auto loans or credit cards. These securities are more commonly called ASSET-BACKED SECURITIES because a pool of credit receivables is the collateral backing the securities. Commercial banks are authorized by the Federal Reserve Board to underwrite limited amounts of securities through holding company affiliates. See also SECURITIES AFFILIATE; SECURITIZATION.

consummation actual time where a credit agreement becomes a legally binding contract between a financial institution and a borrower. Depending on state laws, this may occur when the loan documents are signed, as in a mortgage closing, when the lender accepts a credit application, or when the lender makes a firm commitment to extend credit.

contemporaneous reserves method of calculating bank RESERVE REQUIREMENTS for deposit accounts based on currently outstanding balances. Since 1984, banks and savings institutions have reported their transaction account balances (checking, Negotiable Order of Withdrawal (NOW), and Super-Now accounts) every Wednesday, based on average balances in the 14-day period ending Monday of that week. A bank experiencing deposit growth during that period will have to put more funds in its RESERVE ACCOUNT, a noninterest earning account at a Federal Reserve Bank or correspondent bank. The change in reporting, intended to give the Federal Reserve Board a more up-to-date view of growth in the MONEY SUPPLY, does not affect TIME DEPOSITs, which are still reported on a LAGGED RESERVES basis, i.e., with a two-week delay.

contingent interest see FUTURE INTEREST.

contingent liability

1. obligation of a person who signs a promissory note as an ACCOMMODATION ENDORSER, CO-MAKER, or GUARANTOR, becoming liable for payment in the event the original borrower defaults.
2. financial obligation of a bank that is dependent on future events or actions of another party, such as a standing agreement to lend money if a borrower cannot obtain alternate financing. Included are standby letters of credit, commitments to make or purchase loans, and participations in acceptances, financial futures, and forward contracts. These are ordinarily reported as OFF-BALANCE SHEET LIABILITIES in a bank's CALL REPORT.

contingent reserve funds set aside from net earnings to cover unexpected needs, such as unanticipated loan losses, future taxes, and interest expense. See also LOAN LOSS RESERVE'S.

continuation statement amendment to a financing statement that protects a lender's lien on personal property, as distinguished from real property—real estate. A lender's FINANCING STATEMENT granting a security interest in pledged collateral ordinarily expires after five years under the UNIFORM COMMERCIAL CODE. It may be extended beyond that period by filing a continuation statement with the secretary of state and other public officials, as specified in the laws in the jurisdiction where the property is located. See also PERFECTED LIEN.

contract

1. **General.** An agreement backed by lawful consideration to carry out actions, exchange assets, or refrain from doing things. A legally valid contract is reached through mutual agreement by persons with the capacity to negotiate, in which each gives up something of value. It must be for a lawful purpose.
2. **Futures.** (1) A trading unit in a financial future; (2) An agreement between buyer and seller of a futures contract, as defined by a commodities exchange or exchange clearing house.

3. Foreign Exchange. An agreement by two parties to exchange one currency for another at a specified future date.

contract month month in which contracts to deliver commodities or financial instruments in a futures exchange are satisfied by making or taking delivery. Also called *delivery month*. In reality, most commodity and interest rate futures contracts are closed out or liquidated before the contract delivery date by reversing the original transaction.

contract of sale agreement to transfer title to real property or tangible assets at a given price. Actual delivery is effected by delivery of a signed, sealed, and acknowledged deed. This may happen days or months later, normally when the buyer has fulfilled certain conditions, such as making a certain number of payments. See also CONDITIONAL SALES CONTRACT.

controlled amortization bond (CAB) mortgage backed bond with a SINKING FUND provision. The CAB bond has prior claim to cash flows from underlying mortgages and has predictable AVERAGE LIFE over a wide range of mortgage prepayments.

controlled disbursement in corporate CASH MANAGEMENT, a funds management technique designed to maximixe the funds available for investment in the money market or for payment to trade creditors. Typically, the corporate cash manager receives a listing early in the day, usually before 10 A.M., of all checks expected to clear that day, representing available funds to the corporate treasurer. Controlled disbursement is designed to control the flow of checks through the banking system to meet corporate investment and funds management requirements. Excess funds can be invested in the money market. Contrast with DELAYED DISBURSEMENT, which emphasizes clearing of checks through remote locations to extend check clearing time and FEDERAL RESERVE FLOAT on uncollected checks. See also TREASURY WORKSTATION.

conventional mortgage fixed rate or adjustable rate MORTGAGE not backed by federal insurance or guarantee. These mortgages are generally fixed term loans, for example a 30-year fixed rate loan, and are not insured by the FEDERAL HOUSING

ADMINISTRATION or guaranteed by the Department of Veterans Affairs. In the secondary mortgage market, the Federal National Mortgage Association and the Federal Home Loan Mortgage Corp. are the major purchasers of conventional loans.

conversion

1. exchange of banking charter by a bank or thrift institution, for example, a state chartered bank applying for a national charter from the Comptroller of the Currency, or vice versa. Charter conversions allow a bank to take advantage of differences in banking regulation, such as more liberal LEGAL LENDING LIMITS for state chartered banks in some states.
2. switching from mutual ownership to stock ownership through a common stock RIGHTS offering, done by a savings bank or savings and loan association to raise equity capital.
3. switching an ADJUSTABLE RATE MORTGAGE to a fixed rate loan, often at no additional charge to the borrower if done within a specified period.
4. exchange of a convertible security, such as a CAPITAL NOTE or a DEBENTURE for a specified number of common stock shares.
5. exchange of mutual fund shares for shares in another source of funds, often at no charge if the transfer is within a family of funds.
6. in tort law, the wrongful taking of property that belongs to someone else, as when a TRUSTEE uses assets in a trust fund for personal benefit.

conversion privilege

feature in some ADJUSTABLE RATE MORTGAGES allowing the borrower to switch to a fixed rate loan. Convertible mortgages usually have option of conversion after three to five years and have become increasingly popular with mortgage borrowers.

convertible

1. ADJUSTABLE RATE MORTGAGE that can be exchanged, at the borrower's option, for a fixed rate mortgage, usually in the first one to five years. The borrower pays a conversion premium, but the cost of switching to a fixed rate loan is generally less than the cost of refinancing.

2. DEBENTURE or PREFERRED STOCK that can be exchanged at a set price for a predetermined number of common stock shares of the same issuer.

3. currency easily exchanged for another currency or an equivalent amount of gold.

convexity in bonds and other fixed-income securities, a measure of the rate of change in DURATION. It is called convexity because the shape of the typical yield curve measuring price versus maturity of a security, for example, a ten-year Treasury bond, is somewhat rounded or convex in shape. The ten-year Treasury bond is said to have *positive convexity*.

In contrast, mortgage backed securities and pools of mortgage loans have *negative convexity* because when current interest rates drop to a certain point below the rate at which the loans were made, borrowers tend to refinance their loans, paying off their old mortgages and taking out new loans. Mortgage prepayments shorten the duration of mortgage backed securities, causing a drop in price. Thus, convexity tries to explain the difference between estimated prices of a security and market prices that are influenced by changes in interest rates.

conveyance transfer of TITLE to real property from buyer to seller by MORTGAGE or deed of trust. Also the document effecting a legal transfer.

cooperative form of multiple ownership real estate in which property units are owned by a nonprofit corporation or business trust, which grants occupancy rights to individual tenants. Also called a co-op. Property owners buy shares in the corporation representing their ownership of an apartment or office, and pay the corporation a share of real estate taxes, building maintenance, and other overhead expenses. Loan interest and property taxes paid by the corporation are tax deductible by individual tenants. Property transfers from the old owner to a new owner are subject to approval by a tenant board.

cooperative bank member-owned organization, similar to SAVINGS AND LOAN ASSOCIATION, that makes loans and pays interest on pooled deposits. Cooperatives in the United States are

CONVEXITY

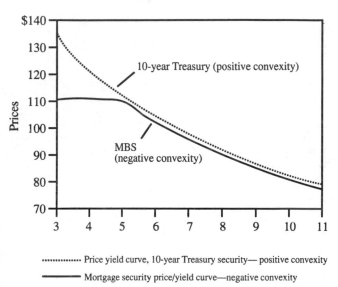

.... Price yield curve, 10-year Treasury security— positive convexity

———— Mortgage security price/yield curve—negative convexity

Source: William W. Bartlett, *Mortgage Backed Securities* (New York: Institute of Finance, 1989), p.203

CREDIT UNIONs, Federal Intermediate Credit Banks and Banks for Cooperatives in the FARM CREDIT SYSTEM, and state chartered savings associations in several New England states.

cordoba national currency of Nicaragua.

core deposits deposits acquired in a bank's natural market area, counted as a stable source of funds for lending. These deposits have a predictable cost, imply a degree of customer loyalty, and are less interest rate sensitive than short-term CERTIFICATES OF DEPOSIT and MONEY MARKET DEPOSIT ACCOUNTS.

Included are small denomination TIME DEPOSITs and all noninterest bearing DEMAND DEPOSIT accounts.

corporate agent banking services performed on an agency basis for corporations and government entities. Among these are check clearing, dividend and interest payment, stock registration and redemption, and tax collection for government agencies. These generate fee income for the providing bank. See also NON-CREDIT SERVICES.

corporate resolution legal document adopted by a corporation's board of directors and signed by the corporate secretary, specifying who may sign checks, borrow money, and otherwise do business with a bank. Many banks have adopted standard corporate resolution forms to facilitate the loan documentation in commercial credit. The corporate resolution, and often a copy of a corporation's charter and bylaws, are kept in the loan files at the various lending institutions where it does business. Also called corporate *borrowing resolution.*

corporate trade exchange (CTX) electronic funds transfer used by corporations and government agencies to pay trading partners through the AUTOMATED CLEARING HOUSE (ACH) system. The CTX payment format combines payment information and a variable length record (called an *addendum record*) with related information, such as invoice numbers, allowing multiple payments to trade creditors in a single transfer of funds. The CTX payment format follows the American National Standards Institute (ANSI) X.12 payment standard for intercorporate data communication. See also CASH CONCENTRATION & DISBURSEMENT; CORPORATE TRADE PAYMENT; ELECTRONIC DATA INTERCHANGE.

corporate trade payment (CTP) electronic funds transfer used by corporations and government agencies to pay trade creditors through the AUTOMATED CLEARING HOUSE (ACH). The CTP payment format, combining a standard ACH payment and additional records (up to 4,990 addenda records) for remittance information, is used mostly by large corporations in paying suppliers. As a corporate-to-corporate payment, the CTP is less flexible, and consequently less popular, than the newer payment options, such as the CORPORATE TRADE EXCHANGE. See also CASH CONCENTRATION & DISBURSEMENT; ELECTRONIC DATA INTERCHANGE.

corporation business organization treated as an entity—an artificial person distinct from its owners—in the eyes of the law. Ownership is represented by shares of stock. A corporation has three distinguishing characteristics: 1) separation of ownership from management and limited liability, i.e., its liability to creditors is limited to its resources, unlike partnerships or sole proprietor businesses that have unlimited personal liability; 2) the ability to negotiate contracts and own property; and 3) transferable ownership, assuring its existence beyond the lives of its stockholders. Stockholders elect corporate directors, who in turn decide its policies. See also ARTICLES OF INCORPORATION; SUBCHAPTER S.

corpus
1. PRINCIPAL of a trust, as distinct from interest income, which may consist of stocks, bonds, bank accounts, real estate, or other property contributed by the donor.
2. principal amount of an investment note. Compare to COUPON.
3. principal in a zero-coupon debt issue, which pays no interest to the holder until final maturity.

correspondent bank that holds deposits owned by other banks and performs banking services, such as check clearing for banks in other cities. The deposit balance is a form of payment for services. Many community banks clear checks drawn on out-of-town banks through RESERVE ACCOUNTS at a larger bank. Correspondent banks also buy participations in loans exceeding the LEGAL LENDING LIMIT of a smaller bank, called the RESPONDENT, and give these banks access to financial markets, such as the foreign exchange market or financial futures market, that are ordinarily beyond the reach of smaller financial institutions.

co-signer see ACCOMMODATION ENDORSER; CO-MAKER.

cost accounting accounting system allocating direct and indirect costs of bank services to various departmental units. Internal cost accounting considers various factors in pricing bank services, and typically includes the following: overhead, including building rent, utilities, administrative support, and executive salaries; selling costs, which include advertising, promotional expenses, and salaries of account executives and branch employees; and interest cost, or the cost of acquiring funds for lending or investing. Some bank expenses have fixed costs that remain more or less constant, such as employee salaries and rent; others have variable costs and are volume sensitive.

The MARGINAL COST OF FUNDS measures the cost of expanding deposits at the margin, that is the cost of one additional dollar unit of deposit or loan volume. Fully absorbed costing, takes into consideration both interest expense and noninterest expenses, such as rent, insurance, and taxes, and frequently it is the basis of pricing banking services. A bank carries out a cost analysis of the product or service being considered and determines the yield required to meet its required return. Fully absorbed costing, also called *cost plus pricing*, often disadvantageously ignores customer demands and competitive pricing by other financial institutions.

See also BREAK-EVEN YIELD; COST CENTER; COST OF FUNDS; QUADRATIC PRICING MODEL; PROFIT CENTER; RELATIONSHIP BANKING; TRANSFER PRICE.

cost center organizational unit within a company that doesn't generate income. Its primary function is providing services for other centers.

cost of funds dollar cost of interest paid or accrued on funds acquired from various sources within a bank, and BORROWED FUNDS acquired from other banks, including time deposits, advances at the Federal Reserve DISCOUNT WINDOW, Federal Funds purchased, and Eurodollar deposits. A bank may use its internal cost of funds in pricing the loans it makes. See also COST OF FUNDS INDEX.

cost of funds index (COFI) measure of interest paid on funds borrowed from depositors, or from other banks. The index is expressed as a percentage, such as the Federal Home Loan Bank index in mortgage lending, or the eleventh district Federal Home Loan Bank index. A cost of funds index published by the Office of Thrift Supervision is often used by mortgage lenders as the basis for adjusting rates on ADJUSTABLE RATE MORTGAGES.

counterfeit security, currency or bank card made to appear genuine, with the intention of defrauding an unsuspecting person. Counterfeiting U.S. currency and bank cards is a felony under federal law, punishable by fines and prison terms. The U.S. Secret Service, a bureau of the Treasury Department, has responsibility for detecting and arresting counterfeiters.

counter-party

1. person at the opposite side of a repurchase agreement or swap agreement. The person who agrees to sell back securities sold in a repurchase agreeement, or exchange at a later date currency values or interest rates in a swap agreement with another party.
2. bank that either purchases or sells back overnight Federal Reserve (Fed Funds).

countersign signature vouching the authenticity of another's handwriting; a form of dual control when corporate checks are signed by more than one MAKER. A company's authorized check writers are listed in its CORPORATE RESOLUTION.

counter-trade See BARTER.

country bank bank whose main office is outside a city with a Federal Reserve Bank or branch. Country banks do not receive overnight credit on checks cleared through the Federal Reserve System, and generally have lower RESERVE REQUIREMENTS than RESERVE CITY BANKS, which are located in major cities having a Federal Reserve Bank. The term *country collections* is often used in reference to all banks outside the region where the sending bank is located.

country club billing credit card billing system in which copies of the original sales drafts are included with the monthly statement. Bank card issuers abandoned country club billing in the 1970s in favor of less costly DESCRIPTIVE STATEMENT billing—an itemized listing of account charges.

country exposure lending survey quarterly report released by the INTERAGENCY COUNTRY EXPOSURE REVIEW COMMITTEE disclosing information on foreign lending of U.S. banks on a consolidated basis. Borrowers are ranked by loan type (public or private, maturity, cross-border, and nonlocal currency loans). The report, detailing loans to 190 countries, is issued quarterly.

country limit limit placed by a bank on the amount of money it is willing to lend to all borrowers, both public and private, in one country.

country risk risk that economic or political changes in a foreign country, for example, lack of currency reserves (FOR-EIGN EXCHANGE), will cause delays in loan payments to creditor banks, EXCHANGE CONTROLS by monetary authorities, or even repudiation of debt. Country risk is broader in scope than SOVER-EIGN RISK as it takes into account the probability of debt repayment by private borrowers as well as central governments. Banks set aside funds in a reserve account, called the ALLOCATED TRANSFER RISK RESERVE, as a cushion against possible bad debt losses from foreign loans. See also COUNTRY EXPOSURE LENDING SURVEY; COUNTRY LIMIT.

coupon detachable certificates attached to a note or bond showing the dollar amount of interest payable to the holder at regular intervals, ordinarily semiannually. Coupons on a BEARER BOND are negotiable instruments, paying a fixed amount to the holder when sent to the issuer's agent for payment or a bank for collection, just as checks are processed. The bank charges a fee for this service.

coupon rate nominal annual rate of interest the issuer of a note or bond promises to pay the holder during the period the securities are outstanding. In mortgage banking, it refers to the contract rate of interest on a MORTGAGE BACKED SECURITIES.

coupon stripping process of separating a security, usually a bond, or a loan into different cash flows. The intention is to produce securities tailored to specific investor needs: for example, interest only and principal only mortgage backed securities, or zero coupon bonds. See also STRIP; STRIPPED MORTGAGE BACKED SECURITIES.

coupon swap see INTEREST RATE SWAP.

covenant

1. language in a loan agreement by which the borrower pledges to do certain things and refrain from others. *An affirmative covenant* requires the borrower to maintain adequate property insurance, make timely loan payments, and keep his business in sound financial condition. A *negative covenant* (also called a *restrictive covenant*) prohibits the borrower from selling or transferring assets, defaulting, or taking specific actions that would diminish the value of the collateral or impair the value of the lender's ability to collect the loan. Failure to perform as agreed might cause the lender to accelerate the loan, or call (demand full payment of) the loan.

2. enforceable clause in a bond contract protecting the interests of bondholders. There are various kinds of bond covenants: an agreement to charge sufficient fees, common in municipal bonds, to produce the required revenue (*a rate covenant*); an agreement not to sell or encumber the project (*a negative covenant*); an agreement to maintain adequate insurance and debt service (*a protective covenant*).

cover

1. taking assignment of collateral as protection against borrower default. Synonomous with security. Also, allocating a part of net income against possible BAD DEBT losses.

2. to offset an account withdrawal by making a DEPOSIT.

3. purchase of currency or financial futures to offset or close a previously taken position. A short cover involves buying against contracts expiring in the same delivery month.

4. buying back securities previously sold in a SHORT SALE.

5. in corporate finance, ability of a corporation to service its debt obligations out of earnings.

6. in UNDERWRITING, the second highest bid in competitive bidding for a bond issue, called the *covering bid*.

coverage ratio
financial ratio measuring a bank's ability to absorb potential losses from nonperforming loans. The ratio is calculated by dividing the ending balance of the LOAN LOSS RESERVES balance by total nonperforming loans.

covered interest arbitrage
currency arbitrage carried out by purchasing financial instruments in different currencies and using a FORWARD EXCHANGE CONTRACT to lock in a yield.

An investor buying a two-year bond dominated in West German deutschmarks, yielding 5%, might exchange D-marks for dollars in the forward market to buy a U.S. dollar denominated security of comparable maturity yielding 9%.

covered option call option backed by the security underlying the option contract. The writer, or seller, of the option collects a premium for writing the option, and has the securities to deliver if the option is exercised. Contrast with NAKED OPTION

cramdown confirmation of a Chapter 11 REORGANIZATION by a bankruptcy court against the wishes of dissenting creditors. The confirmation is approved, provided that at least one class of adversely affected creditors agrees, and the debtor's repayment plan does not discriminate.

creative financing
1. **In general.** Any funds acquisition, bank lending, or capital raising technique that differs from standard industry practices. Borrowers often resort to innovative financing when financing from conventional sources is unavailable or can be arranged at more favorable terms using nonstandard financing techniques. Such techniques have become more common in the fixed income and equity markets in recent years.
2. **Mortgages.** Any mortgage that differs from a 30-year CONVENTIONAL MORTGAGE in rate, credit terms, or other factors. Creative financing allows a lender to tailor mortgage financing to suit a borrower's income and financial situation, making home ownership more affordable by a wider group of borrowers. Reduced interest rate loans, seller buydowns, or jumbo loans are examples. Creative financing also can involve taking out a SECOND MORTGAGE at loan origination to lower the required down payment. Most creative mortgages are ineligible for purchase by federal agencies in the SECONDARY MORTGAGE MARKET. See also ALTERNATIVE MORTGAGE INSTRUMENT; SALE AND LEASEBACK.
3. **Commercial lending.** A customized loan in which the rate paid and credit terms are negotiated by borrower and lender. The lender may agree to arrange financing at an attractive rate and terms if a borrower assumes part of the credit risk in funding a loan. So-called performance based loan pricing

also allows a lender to tailor a line of credit or revolving credit so that pricing is set according to the borrower's usage of the credit.

credit faith, from the Latin *credito*. An agreement by which something of value—goods, services, or money—is given in exchange for a promise to pay at a later date.

Banking:

1. lender's agreement to advance funds, based on an estimation that the debt will eventually be repaid, or to refrain from collecting a previously existing debt, as in a refinancing.

   Bank credit is classified by: type of borrower, for example, loans to consumers (mortgages, auto loans, credit cards) as opposed to loans to businesses (commercial lines of credit, working capital loans); type of collateral pledged, if any; and terms of repayment. Some bank loans are repaid according to a fixed schedule, for example, a 30-year mortgage; others, such as a DEMAND LOAN to a business that may be called at any time by the lender.

2. used by bank credit analysts and lenders instead of BORROWER or LOAN. A lender might say, "I'll approve the credit if it's a four-year loan," or "I think the credit is good."

3. bookkeeping entry representing a deposit of funds into an account. In accounting, a credit entry notes an increase in liabilities, owner's equity, and revenues, and a decrease in assets and expenses. See also ABILITY TO PAY; CLOSED-END CREDIT; CREDIT ENHANCEMENT; CREDIT LINE; CREDIT RATING; CREDIT REPORT; CREDIT RISK; EQUAL CREDIT OPPORTUNITY ACT; EXTENSION AGREEMENT; FAIR CREDIT BILLING ACT; FAIR CREDIT REPORTING ACT; FORBEARANCE; INSTALLMENT CREDIT; LINE OF CREDIT; OPEN-END CREDIT; REGULATION B; REGULATION G; REGULATION T; REGULATION Z; REVOLVING CREDIT; SECURED LOAN; USURY.

credit analyst

1. person who evaluates the financial history and financial statements of credit applicants, with an eye toward assessing creditworthiness. An analyst is trained to evaluate: 1) the applicant's financial strength; 2) the probability of full repayment; and 3) whether collateral or a co-signer is needed to adequately secure the loan.

2. person who evaluates the earnings and financial performance of corporations. The preferred term is financial analyst or securities analyst.

credit application oral or written request for an extension of credit, following the lender's procedures for the credit requested. Information regarding the cost of credit must be disclosed, such as the ANNUAL PERCENTAGE RATE, under Federal Reserve REGULATION Z, when a consumer formally applies for credit. A completed application means the lender has received all the information ordinarily received in evaluations for the amount and type of credit requested, including credit reports from a credit bureau, government guarantees, or approvals to insure or provide security for the credit. An application fee may be charged to cover loan processing and property appraisal costs, as in a mortgage. Advances under an existing credit arrangement, or rate shopping generally are not considered applications for credit, and do not require TRUTH IN LENDING disclosures by the lender.

credit balance account with payments exceeding the principal balance owed, as when a customer pays down a loan by making extra payments. In FACTORING, the amount owed to a customer when accounts receivable are purchased by a factor.

credit bureau See CREDIT REPORTING AGENCY.

credit card payment card issued to a person with a satisfactory CREDIT RATING for making retail purchases or obtaining a CASH ADVANCE from a preapproved CREDIT LINE. Credit cards are a convenient substitute for checks, which explains their wide popularity over the last 30 years. The SECURED CREDIT CARD, a recent innovation backed by a deposit account, is issued to marginally qualified borrowers. A credit cardholder has the option of paying off the entire outstanding balance due on a credit card account, or paying off the loan in several installments. See also TRAVEL & ENTERTAINMENT CARD.

credit clinic popular name for an organization that purports to help consumers clean up unfavorable credit ratings by advising consumers to dispute all negative credit reports. It assumes that creditors will be unable to respond in the 60-day period required by the FAIR CREDIT BILLING ACT for answering these challenges, and, as a result, will have to purge the questioned records.

credit control regulatory powers of the Federal Reserve Board in carrying out MONETARY POLICY. The Fed controls credit availability, which in turn stimulates or limits economic growth, by (1) raising or lowering the DISCOUNT RATE; (2) buying or selling government securities through OPEN MARKET OPERATIONS; adjusting RESERVE REQUIREMENTS on deposit account balances; and setting MARGIN requirements for securities lending. The Federal Reserve's power to impose SURCHARGES on bank reserves, and also impose reserve requirements on nonbank financial companies, authorized by the Credit Control Act of 1969, expired in 1982.

credit counseling credit advisory service offered to persons with excessive debts as an alternative to bankruptcy. Debt counselors affiliated with the National Foundation for Consumer Credit charge only a nominal monthly fee for helping consumers work their way out of debt. Consumers are budgeted a portion of take-home income to pay off current obligations and voluntarily curb their use of credit until debts are repaid.

credit criteria factors employed to determine CREDITWORTHINESS, or ability to repay debt, including the following: income, amount of personal debt carried, number of accounts from other credit sources, and credit history. A lender is free to use any credit-related factor in approving or denying a credit application so long as they do not violate the equal credit protections of Federal Reserve REGULATION B prohibiting credit discrimination on the basis of race, sex, or other factors.

credit denial turndown of an application for credit. Also called a credit decline or rejection. The EQUAL CREDIT OPPORTUNITY ACT requires lenders who deny consumer credit applications to state in writing the reasons why the applicant was rejected. Reasons for denial can vary from insufficient information in the credit application or lack of previous borrowing experience to a poor credit history. If turned down on the basis of information supplied by other creditors, the applicant has the opportunity, under REGULATION B, to obtain at no cost a copy of the credit report. In any event, the lender must respond to the applicant's credit request within 30 days of receiving it. See also ADVERSE ACTION; CREDIT SCORING; EFFECTS TEST.

credit department department in a bank that evaluates the financial condition of credit applicants and maintains a log of loan payments on currently outstanding loans. Credit information is gathered on a confidential basis and stored for future reference. The credit department also responds to requests by other lenders for credit information on a particular borrower. See also CREDIT REVIEW.

credit enhancement enhancement to the creditworthiness of loans underlying an asset-backed security or a municipal bond, generally to get an investment grade rating from a bond rating agency and to improve the marketability of the debt securities to investors. There are two general classifications of credit enhancements: third-party enhancement, in which a third party pledges its own creditworthiness and guarantees repayment in exchange for a fee; and self-enhancement, which is generally done by the issuer through OVER-COLLATERALIZATION, i.e., pledging loans with a book value greater than the face value of the bonds offered for sale.

Third party enhancements take the form of a STANDBY LETTER OF CREDIT or COMMERCIAL LETTER OF CREDIT issued by a bank, a surety bond from an insurance company, or a special reserve fund managed by a FINANCIAL GUARANTEE firm. The type of enhancement used and the amount of credit protection purchased varies according to the characteristics of the portfolio. Holders of the securities issued have recourse against the guarantor to the extent of the guarantee. Lines of credit are sometimes referred to as *soft capital* because they would not ordinarily be called upon. See also BACKUP LINE.

credit file record containing historical data on open or fully paid credit accounts. Credit files may contain personal financial statements, credit applications, and comments by credit analysts, as well as the current status of the account, payment history, current balance, credit limit, and so on.

credit history see CREDIT FILE.

credit insurance various types of insurance purchased by the borrower, and in some instances by the lender. If purchased by the bank, insurance is a hedge against abnormal credit losses. In consumer credit, credit life insurance or disability insurance purchased by the borrower pays the creditor in event the borrower suffers an accident or dies before the debt is repaid. See also MORTGAGE INSURANCE; SINGLE INTEREST INSURANCE.

credit investigation appraisal of a prospective borrower's ability and willingness to repay a loan, carried out by a CREDIT ANALYST. Before approving a loan, a lender may ask for credit references and personal or corporate financial statements, obtain a copy of the applicant's CREDIT REPORT, and also verify the applicant's salary with his or her employer.

credit line
1. maximum amount of credit available in an open-end credit arrangement such as a bank credit card, which the lender may change at any time. The line is disclosed in the credit card agreement.
2. funds available to a borrower for a specified period, subject to review before renewal, for example, a revolving LINE OF CREDIT.

credit money money not backed by hard currency or bullion. Money backed by the full faith and credit of the issuing country. Most currencies in circulation today are credit money. Also called *fiat money*.

creditor any lendor who, in the course of business, regularly extends credit, repayable by agreement, by a second party, the DEBTOR. The loan may be repayable in several equal installments over a specified period, or in certain business loans repayable in full at the option of either the borrower or the lender. A lender who takes an assignment of collateral has a claim on the borrower's assets, whereas a lender who lends on the strength of a borrower's character can look only to the borrower's future income.

creditors' committee group representing a class of creditors holding secured claims against a company in REORGANIZATION under Chapter 11 of the Bankruptcy Code. Large companies in bankruptcy, for example, a New York Stock Exchange listed company, may have several committees of creditors. The debtor company must offer an acceptable repayment plan to its creditors before a reorganization can be approved. See also CRAMDOWN; INVOLUNTARY BANKRUPTCY.

credit quality see ASSET QUALITY.

credit rating

1. lender's estimate of an individual's creditworthiness, based on past history of borrowing and repaying, employment, and information supplied by the prospective borrower in a credit application, as well as the applicant's CREDIT REPORT. Lenders often ask businesses to furnish tax returns and financial statements.
2. evaluation of creditworthiness of individuals and businesses by a CREDIT REPORTING AGENCY. Many organizations are active in assigning credit ratings, including consumer credit bureaus, such as TRW Inc. and Trans Union Credit Information, and mercantile agencies, such as DUN & BRADSTREET. See also BOND RATING.

credit reference previous borrowing history offered as demonstration of creditworthiness in a CREDIT APPLICATION. Credit references are a source of supporting documentation in applying for bank credit.

credit report

1. **Banking.** A report furnished by a CREDIT REPORTING AGENCY when requested by a lender or the individual named in a report. A credit report lists available credit and a borrower's payment history including on-time payments, late payments, and the number of times a loan payment was missed. It also may include judgment liens to collect a debt, bankruptcy petitions, and tax liens. Credit reports retain adverse credit information for seven years, and bankruptcy petitions for a ten-year period. Federal law requires credit reporting agencies to give consumers the right to inspect their credit report and write comments if they disagree with it.
2. **Asset-Based Lending.** A form the borrower is asked to deliver periodically that lists merchandise returns, credit allowances, and so on, allowing the lender to monitor collateral backing the loan.

credit reporting agency private organization that collects information on debt and repayment records of participating credit granting institutions. Also called *credit bureau*. Account activity information kept on file at credit bureaus is made available in a CREDIT REPORT to lenders or to individuals listed in bureau files. Credit grantors make extensive use of credit bureau reports when they mail preapproved credit applications for installment credit, such as bank credit cards.

credit review follow-up monitoring of a loan or extension of credit by a senior loan committee, bank auditor, or regulatory agency. Credit review is intended to determine whether the loan was made in accordance with the lender's written credit standards and in compliance with banking regulations. Missing documentation or signatures on loan documents, if detected by the credit review process, can then be corrected by the lending officer, thus preventing a deterioration in credit quality and possible loss. Also called *loan review*.

credit risk risk that a borrower will not pay a loan as called for in the original loan agreement, and may eventually DEFAULT on the obligation. Credit risk is one of the primary risks in bank lending, in addition to INTEREST RATE RISK.

credit scoring predicting the creditworthiness of credit applicants by use of a statistical model. A commonly used methodology is multiple discriminant analysis (MDA), which is widely used by research firms. Credit scoring estimates the repayment probability based on the information in the credit application and a credit bureau report. The two main types of credit scoring include application scoring for new accounts and behavior scoring for accounts that have activated and are carrying balances.

Application point scoring systems assign points to various credit criteria, such as income, number of existing credit accounts, time at residence, and so on. An applicant who scores enough points to pass the CUTOFF SCORE is considered creditworthy. Another application scoring technique, DECISION TREE SCORING, also calculates the repayment probability, though it does not assign points to credit criteria. Behavior scoring models, on the other hand, measure a borrower's ability to repay debt, giving an early warning about potentially delinquent accounts. Banks and other credit grantors use credit scoring to increase the profitability of a loan portfolio, reduce the number of unprofitable accounts, and systematically process a large number of applications at lower cost.

See also EFFECTS TEST; EQUAL CREDIT OPPORTUNITY ACT; JUDGMENTAL CREDIT ANALYSIS; PROHIBITED BASIS; REGULATION B.

credit slip document reversing a credit card charge to a cardholder's account, indicating the cardholder returned merchandise to the retailer where it was purchased. Also called *credit voucher*.

credit ticket bookkeeping memo for a credit transaction. For example, a deposit to a checking account or savings account. See also DEBIT TICKET.

credit tranche see TRANCHE.

credit union nonprofit savings institution that makes personal loans and offers other consumer banking services to persons sharing a common bond, typically employment at the same firm. Deregulation in the banking industry since the late 1970s has allowed credit unions to offer many of the same banking services as commercial banks, savings banks, and savings and loan associations. Federally chartered credit unions can write residential mortgages and issue credit cards. Many credit unions also offer interest-bearing transaction accounts (called a SHARE DRAFT ACCOUNT). Credit unions can charge below-market rates on loans while paying higher rates to savers, as they are exempt from federal and state taxes. In 1984, membership eligibility— the common bond rule—was greatly relaxed, allowing credit unions to solicit accounts from a member's immediate family, significantly expanding potential membership in credit unions. Individuals living in the same community can even start their own credit union. Credit unions get their operating funds from shares purchased by individual owners, who are called members, and pay dividends (representing the payment of interest) out of earnings.

The NATIONAL CREDIT UNION ADMINISTRATION, an independent federal agency chartered in 1970, is the primary regulator of national (federally chartered) credit unions. It also operates the National Credit Union Share Insurance Fund, which offers share insurance up to $100,000 per account for qualifying federal and state credit unions, and the CENTRAL LIQUIDITY FACILITY, a lender-of-last resort for credit unions. See also SHARE ACCOUNT; SHARE DRAFT.

Credit Union National Association see TRADE ASSOCIATION.

creditworthiness general qualification for borrowing, based largely on a borrower's credit history, in the opinion of a lender or as determined by a CREDIT SCORING system if credit scoring is used.

cross-border outstandings aggregate total of dollar-denominated loans and contingent obligations to foreign borrowers, including loans, bankers' acceptances, and standby letters of credit, plus deposits with foreign banks. Excluded are local currency transactions in foreign countries and deposits with branches of U.S. banks.

cross-collateral collateral covering several loans under a single security agreement, also called a *dragnet clause* and sometimes a Mother Hubbard clause. In essence, collateral for each loan backs the entire package of loans.

Also, language in a second mortgage loan stating the loan is in default if the borrower defaults on other loans secured by the same property.

cross-currency swap see CURRENCY SWAP.

cross-hedge hedge against interest rate risk by purchase of a financial future in a different, but related, asset. A cross-hedge is used when there is no futures market for the asset owned or when it is more profitable not to use the same market. It assumes that similar financial instruments show correlation in their price movements. For example, hedging corporate bonds with Treasury bond futures.

cross-rate currency EXCHANGE RATE computed by pricing two currencies against a third, usually the U.S. dollar. For example, if $1 (U.S.) = $1.1923 (Canadian) or .55540 British

CROSS RATE TABLE

	British pound sterling	Canadian dollar	Japanese yen	Swiss franc	Deutsch-mark
Pound sterling	—	.7132	.004445	.3874	.3207
Canadian dollar	1.402	—	.00914	.5433	.4496
Japanese yen	224.99	109.42	—	87.184	72.150
Swiss franc	2.5810	1.8407	.01147	—	.8278
Deutsch-mark	3.1184	2.2240	0.1386	1.208	—

pound sterling, a dealer would need .46582 British pounds to buy one Canadian dollar. Foreign exchange dealers use currency cross-rate tables to look for arbitrage opportunities. Each major currency, such as the U.S. dollar or the British pound, has its own cross-rate.

cross-sell selling more than one banking product at the customer service desk, for example, check OVERDRAFT protection to a customer opening a checking account. Banks often give employee bonuses, such as cash incentives to branch employees to meet sales objectives. Cross-marketing is perfectly legal as long as there are no tie-in arrangements, i.e., making the sale conditional on acceptance of the add-on product.

crowding out theory that heavy borrowing by the federal government displaces private sector borrowing in the capital markets. If, for example, the Treasury Department were to auction a long series of Treasury bills or Treasury bonds, government borrowing would soak up investor demands. Because the government can afford to pay any rate, nongovernment issuers of debt would be forced to pay higher rates than they can afford, and thus be crowded out. In practice, it has never worked that way because new sources of credit are found at each successive increase in interest rates.

Crummey trust trust allowing tax-free gifts to minors and limited withdrawals of interest or principal by the BENEFICIARY during a specified period, say 30 days a year, while the trust is in effect. A Crummey trust, unlike a *minor's trust*, does not require distribution of trust assets by age 21.

cruzado national currency of Brazil, replacing the cruzeiro in 1985.

curing of delinquency see REINSTATEMENT.

currency
1. circulating money accepted as a medium of exchange for payment of debts. Also called LEGAL TENDER. Generally, the term applies only to paper money—FEDERAL RESERVE NOTES in the United States—not coins. See also CURRENCY IN CIRCULATION.
2. NATIONAL CURRENCY, such as the U.S. dollar and the British pound sterling.

currency band range of upper and lower prices within which currencies are allowed to move against a reference currency or currencies of major trading partners. Although currency bands mostly are irrelevant in the current system of FLOATING EXCHANGE RATES, central banks attempt to keep key currencies, such as the U.S. dollar or the German deutschmark or the Japanese yen from getting out of line vis-a-vis other key currencies through MARKET INTERVENTION. In the European Monetary System SNAKE, currencies of Western European countries are allowed to float up or down in relation to the West German deutschmark, the strongest currency in the European community. See also PEG (PEGGING).

currency basket currency unit consisting of specific amounts of currencies from several nations. These artificial currencies, used as reference rates for international monetary transactions, cannot be owned privately. Nominal values of currency baskets vary as the prices of constituent currencies fluctuate. Examples are the ASIAN CURRENCY UNIT (ACU), the EUROPEAN

CURRENCY UNIT (ECU) and International Monetary Fund SPECIAL DRAWING RIGHTS (SDRS).

currency futures contract in the futures markets for exchange of currencies at a specific exchange rate. A futures contract is a standard contract, hedging against currency risk, for purchase of standard amounts of a specific currency (normally major currencies, such as the U.S. or Canadian dollar, British pound sterling, Japanese yen, West German mark or Swiss franc). Contrast with FORWARD EXCHANGE CONTRACT.

currency in circulation paper money and coins in the hands of consumers and businesses, as opposed to cash (VAULT CASH) held by financial institutions, or currency reserves of Federal Reserve Banks and the U.S. Treasury. Circulating currency is only a small fraction of the cash available for spending and it understates the MONEY SUPPLY, which is largely demand deposits or checking accounts in banks and savings institutions.

Currency held by the public is one of the key factors affecting BANK RESERVES. It is one of the statistical measures watched by the FEDERAL OPEN MARKET COMMITTEE trading desk at the Federal Reserve Bank of New York when the Fed decides to add or drain reserves from the banking system to stay within monetary policy targets.

currency options contract giving the right, not the obligation, to buy or sell a specific quantity of one foreign currency in exchange for another at a fixed price, called the EXERCISE PRICE or STRIKE PRICE. The buyer of a currency option pays a premium to the seller. American-style options are exercisable on any date up to the contract expiration date; in contrast, European style options only can be exercised at specific future dates.

Foreign currency options for U.S. dollar, deutschmark, Canadian dollar, pound sterling, Swiss franc, and Japanese yen are traded OVER-THE-COUNTER by banks in major financial centers around the world. Exchange-traded currency options (British pound sterling, Canadian dollar, deutschmark, French franc and Swiss franc, and Japanese yen) are traded in the United States on the Philadelphia Stock Exchange. OTC trading in some markets coincides with the quarterly expiration cycles—March, June, September, and December—of exchange traded currency options.

CROSS-CURRENCY INTEREST RATE SWAP

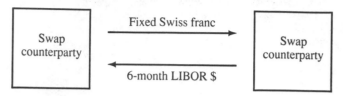

Source: Recent Innovations in International Banking (Bank for International Settlements, 1986).

currency swap agreement to exchange one currency for another at an agreed upon exchange rate. In a currency swap, the holder of an unwanted currency exchanges that currency for an equivalent amount of another currency to improve the market liquidity of a currency owned or to obtain bank financing at a lower rate. For example, company ABC obtains five-year below market financing from a German bank, and swaps deutschmarks for dollars with company ZYX, which has more U.S. dollars than it needs. At maturity, the swap is reversed. A *cross currency swap* involves the exchange of a fixed rate obligation in one currency for a floating rate obligation in another. Swaps are technically borrowings, but unlike bank loans they are not ordinarily disclosed on the balance sheet. See also INTEREST RATE SWAP.

currency translation process of restating balance sheet amounts denominated in one currency in terms of a second currency at current exchange rates. No actual exchange of funds takes place. Multinational corporations are required by Statement 52 (SFAS 52) of Financial Accounting Standards Board, to restate assets and liabilities, plus earnings of foreign subsidiaries in terms of a national reference currency. The resulting foreign currency translation exposure is recorded as an equity account on the balance sheet. At large banks, adjusted foreign currency translation is included as part of equity capital.

currency transaction report (CTR) Internal Revenue Service (IRS) form 4789 report that banks and thrift institutions are required by the Bank Secrecy Act to fill out detailing currency transactions of $10,000 or more.

currency warrants detachable options in securities issues giving the holder the right to purchase additional securities denominated in a currency different from that of the original issue. The coupon and the price of the securities covered by the warrant are fixed at the time of the sale of the original issue.

current account portion of the BALANCE OF PAYMENTS consisting of exports and imports of goods and services, as well as transfer payments such as foreign aid grants. A current account surplus (or deficit) is the amount by which exports of goods and services plus inward transfers exceeds, or falls short of, imports of goods and services. It is the most widely accepted definition of international payment flows between countries. The U.S. accounting practices include income paid or received from foreign investments as part of services.

current coupon bond interest rate comparable to that earned by newly issued bonds with a similar COUPON RATE and maturity, and is the rate closest to prevailing market rates of interest. In other words, the bond is selling at a price close to its PAR VALUE. Its YIELD TO MATURITY is the same or nearly the same as its interest rate, or, in the case of floating rate bonds, the interest payable in the current period.

current pool factor ratio of the outstanding principal of pass-through securities or COLLATERALIZED MORTGAGE OBLIGATIONS in relation to the original principal amount issued, expressed as a percent. The ratio indicates the prepayment experience of different classes (called TRANCHES) of asset-backed securities issued under the same indenture, or comparable issues.

current yield annual rate of interest paid by a bond, computed by dividing the coupon interest by original purchase price. The current yield of an 8% bond selling at $800 is 10%. Current yield is different from YIELD TO MATURITY, which includes the annual accretion of interest as the price rises from $800 to $1,000 at maturity. Current yield is useful in comparing year-to-year changes in bond yield.

curtesy legal interest, referred to as a LIFE ESTATE, of a husband in the property of his wife after her death. The legal interest held by a widow is a DOWER.

cushion

1. interval between the issue date of a security and the earliest CALL DATE. Also referred to as CALL PROTECTION; also, the degree of protection given investors holding discount pool Mortgage Backed Securities, which are essentially COLLATERALIZED MORTGAGE OBLIGATIONS backed by low-rate mortgages.
2. *cushion bond*—a bond with a high coupon selling at a price below what might be considered a market price. This occurs when a bond is trading at a high premium but is callable at a lower price. The call option holds down the market price, creating a cushion between the market price and what could justifiably be a higher price.
3. function served by a reserve account, such as a bank's LOAN LOSS RESERVES for possible bad debt.

CUSIP number nine-digit identifier—seven numbers and two letters—identifying all U.S. securities issued in book-entry or certificate form after 1970. Full name: Committee on Uniform Securities Identification Procedures (CUSIP). The CUSIP numbering system, developed by the American Bankers Association, was expanded in 1989 to include foreign securities, to be identified by a nine-digit CUSIP International Numbering System (CINS).

custodian CORPORATE AGENT, usually a commercial bank, that holds securities under a written agreement for a corporate client and buys or sells securities when instructed. Custody services include securities safekeeping, and collection of dividends and interest. Custodian banks, and their agents in various countries called subcustody banks, also buy, sell, and deliver securities when instructed by a bank's corporate clients. The bank acts only as transfer agent and makes no buy-sell recommendations.

custody account

1. account held in trust by a parent for a minor under the UNIFORM GIFT TO MINORS ACT. Minors cannot transfer assets without approval of the account trustee.

2. account held by a CUSTODIAN for an institution such as a mutual fund, pension fund, or a corporate customer. The bank holds the customer's property in safekeeping, as provided by a written agreement, collects dividends and interest payments, and sells or delivers securities when instructed by the principal. See also MASTER TRUST.

customer activated terminal (CAT) any card activated terminal that gives customers access to balance accounts information; also any video interactive terminal that gives rate and current balance information, and so on.

customer information file (CIF) computerized accounting system that maintains a record of a bank's customers, including such information as deposit accounts owned, credit relationships, trust accounts, joint ownership of accounts, and so on. The CIF is a bank's customer control file, allowing the bank to look at its customers by total relationship, rather than single accounts (checking, savings). It is updated periodically, frequently daily, to reflect changes as new accounts are opened, checks written, and loan payments made. When used in product marketing, a CIF can help identify CROSS-SELLING opportunities at the new accounts desk, produce customer lists for direct mail marketing, and analyze the profitability of customer relationships. See also GEODEMOGRAPHIC MARKETING; PLATFORM AUTOMATION; RELATIONSHIP BANKING.

customer initiated entry (CIE) banking transaction from a self-service banking terminal, for example, an automated teller machine, or from a telephone in the case of telephone bill payment. Customer initiated entries substitute customer labor for bank labor, and in theory are less costly to process at higher transaction levels. See also ELECTRONIC FUNDS TRANSFER.

customer service representative (CSR) bank employee who opens new accounts, accepts loan applications, and assists customers with service related questions. In recent years, some banks have upgraded the customer service representative to PERSONAL BANKER.

cut-off date predetermined date in a billing or processing cycle when account activity for the previous reporting period is summarized (when checks written against an account are collected and summarized in a monthly statement). Checks paid or deposits received after the cut-off date are included in the next month's statement.

cut-off score minimum number of points needed in a CREDIT SCORING system to qualify as creditworthy. Applicants scoring below the cut-off score are denied credit, unless the credit grantor decides to approve the credit request anyway and OVERRIDE the score. Those whose scores exceed the cut-off generally are approved.

cut-off time

1. point in the business day before which electronic payments, such as Federal Reserve Fed Wire transfers or automated clearing house (ACH) entries, must be submitted to a processing bank for entry into the interbank clearing system.
2. transaction processing time, measured in seconds, at which an electronic banking terminal automatically disconnects from a host computer or INTERCEPT PROCESSOR if unable to approve a transaction. Also called *time-out*. An automated teller machine or electronic point-of-sale terminal is said to time-out if no approval code is received within 15 to 30 seconds.
3. latest time of day a bank will credit deposits made to a customer's account. Also called *ledger credit cuttoff.*

cycle

1. grouping of accounts in batches, which are processed as a single unit, to distribute the work load and make identification of accounts easier. Checking account statements are processed in batch cycles, as are credit cards, and installment loans.
2. business cycle—the periodic expansion and contraction of the economy, as measured by growth in the U.S. Gross National Product. According to the U.S. Bureau of Economic Research, which tracks economic trends, business cycles, on average, last about 52 months or 2½ years. Among the factors affecting the rate of economic expansion (as the economy moves from recession to growth and stable employment)

are expansion and contraction in bank credit, which is influenced by Federal Reserve MONETARY POLICY. See also LAGGING INDICATORS; LEADING INDICATORS.

cy pres doctrine rule applied to trust agreements, for example a TESTAMENTARY TRUST created by a will, which says that in the event the agreement cannot be carried out as intended, it should be followed as closely as possible— literally *near to it*.

D

daily interest interest earned from date of deposit to date of withdrawal. Also, deposit account interest compounded daily and credited to the depositor's account monthly, quarterly, or at other intervals. For example, $100 deposited for a year (365 days) earns $.84 in daily compound interest at 30 days, $2.53 at 90 days, $5.13 at 180 days, and $10.67 after a full year. See also COMPOUND INTEREST.

data capture electronic collection of merchant bank card sales draft receipts directly from the merchant's point-of-sale terminal or electronic cash register. Bank card data capture, also called *draft capture*, accelerates collection of funds for card processing merchant banks and their merchant accounts by eliminating mail float in bank card ticket processing.

data encryption standard (DES) adopted by the financial industry for protection of sensitive transaction information, including account balances, bank identification codes (called issuer keys), and consumer account access codes. The DES is a public standard, published by the National Institute of Standards and Technology, and is also known as the Data Encryption Algorithm (DEA), as accepted by the financial industry. See also ALGORITHM; KEY MANAGEMENT; PERSONAL IDENTIFICATION NUMBER.

dated date date from which a newly issued bond begins to accrue interest, ordinarily one month after the closing date of a mortgage backed bond or municipal bond. The securities actually may be delivered after the closing date.

date of record see RECORD DATE.

dating

1. **Banking.** The period of time from issuance of a TIME LOAN or DISCOUNT and maturity of the note.

    2. **Factoring.** An extension of the payment period in which payment is expected.

3. VALUE DATING.

day cycle daytime processing cycle for transmitting AUTOMATED CLEARING HOUSE debits or credits between regional clearing house associations, ordinarily from 8 A.M. to 1 P.M. Eastern time. Also called daytime window. Compare with NIGHT CYCLE.

daylight overdraft intraday loan that occurs when a bank transfers funds in excess of its RESERVE ACCOUNT. Daylight overdrafts, which can add up to more than $100 billion a day in credit exposure, are caused by the provisional settlement feature in private sector payment systems, such as the CLEARING HOUSE INTERBANK PAYMENT SYSTEM (CHIPS), the New York City-based clearing house that handles the majority of worldwide banking transactions in international trade. CHIPS payments are not considered final payments until the end of the day, in contrast with funds transferred through the Federal Reserve's FEDERAL WIRE (Fed Wire), which are guaranteed by the Fed when posted. This creates daylight exposure until CHIPS participants settle accounts with each other at the end of the day.

Daylight overdrafts also occur on Fed Wire, and generally arise from the fact that the Federal Reserve Banks do not monitor reserve account activity on a real-time basis. Financial institutions are required by Federal Reserve regulation to limit daylight overdrafts to certain multiples of capital, which are set by each bank and monitored by the reserve banks. See also BILATERAL CREDIT LIMIT; EX POST MONITORING; NET SETTLEMENT; SENDER NET DEBIT CAP.

day loan bank loan to a broker for purchase of securities, usually arranged in the morning, hence the name morning loan. Securities delivered to the broker later that day become the collateral for a regular BROKER'S CALL LOAN.

day order order to purchase securities or financial futures good for one day only. If the order cannot be filled that day it is automatically cancelled.

days of grace see GRACE PERIOD.

dealer person or firm that acts as a PRINCIPAL, buying (or selling) from his own account for position and risk, as opposed to a BROKER, who acts as an agent for customers and is paid a commission. Dealers expect to make a profit by selling at a higher price or by correctly guessing future interest rate movements. In a new offering of securities, the dealer's profit is the difference (or SPREAD) between the price paid by the dealer to the issuer and the price at which investors buy the securities from the dealer, who underwrites the offering by buying part or all of the offering.

Commercial banks are permitted by the Glass-Steagall Act and the Securities Act of 1934 to act as principals in auctions of U.S. Treasury securities and sales of municipal general obligation bonds; bank holding companies can deal in limited amounts of commercial paper and corporate bonds through SECURITIES AFFILIATEs owned by a bank holding company.

In the securities industry, investment banking firms often act as both broker or dealer, depending on the transaction, and the term broker-dealer commonly is used. See also DEALER BANK; PRIMARY DEALER.

dealer bank commercial bank that underwrites and makes markets in securities of the U.S. government and federal agencies, municipal general obligation bonds, and other debt securities. Banks that deal in municipal securities are registered dealers with the Municipal Securities Rulemaking Board.

dealer financing financing arrangement where a bank purchases, at a discount, loans originated by a car dealer or other retailer. In dealer financing, also called INDIRECT LENDING, the dealer's customer becomes a customer of the bank because the bank. See also DEALER RESERVE; INDIRECT LOAN.

dealer reserve reserve account maintained by a bank arranging DEALER FINANCING. The reserve is the dealer's portion of the finance charge. The dealer reserve is collateral for the installment notes and is a deposit account in the dealer's name. As loans are paid, a portion of the reserve account is disbursed to the dealer.

death taxes generic name for state estate taxes assessed on property transferred at the death of an owner, including estate and inheritance taxes.

debenture unsecured promise to pay, backed only by the general credit of the issuer. Debentures, like corporate bonds, are issued under a deed of trust or INDENTURE. Some debentures can be exchanged for common stock at a specific price and are called CONVERTIBLE debentures. Contrast with BOND.

debit bookkeeping entry on the left-hand side of a balance sheet. A debit transaction increases an asset account or an expense, and decreases a liability, equity account, or valuation account.

debit balance
1. **Banking.** The amount owed by a bank customer who writes checks greater than the balance in his checking account, creating an OVERDRAFT.
2. **Securities.** The balance owed by a broker's customer with insufficient margin in a trading account. See also CREDIT BALANCE.

debit card bank card that draws funds from a deposit account as opposed to a line of credit. Purchases made with a debit card are charged directly to a consumer's checking or savings account. Sometimes called an ASSET CARD. There are two types of debit cards currently in use in the United States: national debit cards—for example, the *Visa* debit card and MasterCard "MasterDebit" card—and bank issued AUTOMATED TELLER MACHINE (ATM) debit cards. The main difference is that the national debit cards were designed specifically as retail payment cards; bank debit cards were used first as ATM access cards and later as general purpose transaction cards.

debit ticket bookkeeping memo for a debit transaction. When a bank processes a check as a cash item, it credits the customers's account and writes a debit ticket, charged to the general ledger account for "cash items in the process of collection." When it receives payment from the paying bank, a corresponding credit entry cancels the debit entry.

debt for bond swap exchange of old debt owed by a developing country for bonds issued by the central government in the debtor nation. Normally, the debt is converted at a discount from face value. For example, in 1988 Mexico swapped part of its external debt for bonds backed by 20-year, zero coupon U.S. Treasury securities. This swap guaranteed only repayment of loan principal. The repayment of principal, interest, or both on outstanding bank loans may be guaranteed by the International Monetary Fund. See also DEBT FOR EQUITY SWAP.

debt for equity swap agreement between a lender and borrower involving a swap of commodities, raw materials, or tangible assets in exchange for old debt owed by a less developed country (LDC). Federal Reserve Board REGULATION K revisions allows U.S. bank holding companies and subsidiary banks to take equity positions in assets of foreign borrowers. In a debt for equity swap, a lender holding a dollar-denominated loan would exchange that debt at a discount for equity positions in local companies in the debtor nation, acquired with local currencies.

debt instrument written promise to repay a debt, evidenced by an acceptance, promissory note, or bill of exchange. Also formal debt securities, such as bonds and debentures.

debt limit maximum borrowing power of a government entity, as set by the state constitution or legislative authority. The federal debt ceiling is adjusted by joint congressional resolution, whereas debt limits of most state governments are established by state constitution, and borrowing limits of municipal governments are imposed by state legislatures. In municipal securities, an issuer's debt limit is normally stated as a percentage of ASSESSED VALUATION.

debt loading adding up personal debts in anticipation of BANKRUPTCY. Personal debts, if acquired within 90 days of a bankruptcy filing, may be excluded from bankruptcy protection by a bankruptcy court. See also INSOLVENCY.

debtor in possession legal name for a firm or business concern filing for protection from creditors under Chapter 11 of the Bankruptcy code, acting as its own BANKRUPTCY TRUSTEE.

Financing arrangements given to an insolvent borrower under court supervision may have some attractions to lenders because these are supervised closely by the bankruptcy court.

debtor nation nation that is in arrears in interest or principal payments on debts to bank lenders and, in some situations, international development agencies such as the World Bank. Debtor nations have an unfavorable balance of trade, that is, an excess of imports over exports, or have a net inflow of capital from foreign investors.

debt repayment schedule
1. consumer loan AMORTIZATION SCHEDULE showing the number of payments needed to pay off a loan.
2. WAGE EARNER PLAN in a Chapter 13 bankruptcy calling for the debtor to pay a certain amount every month to the court for distribution to creditors over a three-year period in partial repayment of debts owed.

debt rescheduling see RESCHEDULING.

debt service
1. cash outlay needed to meet principal and interest payments on a mortgage or other note, usually expressed as a monthly or annual payment. Fixed rate consumer loans, including mortgages, are often referred to as CONSTANT PAYMENT obligations, as the regular payments needed to fully amortize the debt remain the same through the life of the loan.
2. amount needed in a calendar year or fiscal year to meet bond interest payments, retire the principal on maturing bonds, or make payments to a sinking fund.

debt service ratio
1. financial ratio measuring a borrower's ability to meet payments on a loan after paying expenses. The ratio, also called *debt coverage ratio*, measures the number of times loan principal and interest are covered by net (after tax) income. It is generally applied to income property such as apartment buildings and multitenant office buildings. For example, an income property generating $1,455,000 in annual income qualifies for an mortgage of $11,525,000 carrying a debt service cost of $1,265,000, or a debt coverage ratio of 1.15

($1,455,000 divided by $1,265,000). But if the loan interest rises anytime during the loan, the borrower may not have sufficient income to repay the loan. Contrast with LOAN-TO-VALUE RATIO, which looks at the ratio of debt to property value at loan origination.

2. foreign debt repayments, including interest and servicing costs made by a country as a percentage of the country's export earnings. The ratio measures the ability of a debtor country to repay debts from foreign exchange earnings.

debt-to-equity ratio

1. financial ratio showing the ability of shareholders' equity to meet creditors' claims in event its assets are liquidated.

   2. ratio measuring financial LEVERAGE, the long- term debt-to-equity ratio or an organization's use of long-term funds borrowed in the capital markets to enhance owner's equity.

deceased account deposit account whose owner is deceased. Once notified of the death, a bank places a hold on the account and withhholds payment until authorized by court to make payment to the legal heirs.

decedent person who has died. The term is used in connection with wills, estates, and inheritances. A person leaving a valid will is a TESTATOR; if there is no will, the decedent is said to have died INTESTATE.

decision tree

1. diagram in financial analysis showing the interaction of financial ratios, and how one ratio affects another ratio, allowing a financial analyst or bank examiner to see the cause and effect relationship in different ratios.

2. CREDIT SCORING model that examines the interaction between different factors of credit, for example, a borrower's age, income, type of residence, by means of a tree-like chart. Differs from the more widely accepted point scoring analysis, which assigns points to each credit factor considered in approving or rejecting a credit application.

declining yield curve See NEGATIVE YIELD CURVE.

dccd see QUITCLAIM DEED; WARRANTY DEED.

deed of trust legal document used in some states in lieu of a mortgage. Title to the property passes from seller to a trustee, who holds the mortgaged property until the mortgage has been fully paid and then releases the title to the borrower. The trustee is authorized to sell the property if the borrower defaults, paying the lender the amount of the mortgage loan and any remaining balance to the former owner.

deep discount bond trading at less than 80% of its stated PAR VALUE, that is, assuming it was issued at or near its nominal face value. As a general rule, the longer the maturity, the greater the discount. Also, a loan sold in the secondary market at a price well below its book value or acquisition cost. This ordinarily results when fixed-rate loans originated at rates below current market rates are removed from the lender's books and sold to investors at a loss.

defalcation wrongful diversion of funds held in trust by a FIDUCIARY. Usually said of public officials or officers of corporations. See also EMBEZZLEMENT.

default failure to meet a contractual obligation, such as repayment of a loan by a borrower or payment of interest to bond holders. Default gives the note holder, or the holder of a mortgage bond, rights and recourse under the mortgage indenture to institute foreclosure proceedings or to accelerate the maturity date.

defeasance
1. **Banking.** A clause in a loan agreement, such as a MORTGAGE, giving the borrower the right to redeem the title to property securing the debt when the loan is fully paid.
2. **Finance.** A refinancing technique in which a bond issuer, instead of redeeming the bonds at the call date, continues to make coupon interest payments from an IRREVOCABLE TRUST. The cash flow from trust assets, ordinarily U.S. Treasury securities or zero-coupon securities, must be sufficient to service the bonds until the expected maturity. Defeasance effectively removes the bonds from the issuer's balance sheets, even though the issuer continues to meet bond interest payments.

   In mortgage banking defeasance allows a bond trustee to

protect mortgage-backed bonds from early redemption, if the issuer fails to keep sufficient collateral or defaults. See also ADVANCE REFUNDING.

deferred availability temporary delay in crediting transit checks drawn on out-of-town banks to a bank's RESERVE ACCOUNT at a Federal Reserve Bank. Checks with 0-day availability are credited the same day as received. Checks with 1-day or 2-day availability—the average time it takes to clear checks drawn on distant banks—are posted to the sending bank's deferred account, and funds from this account are moved on a daily basis to the reserve account as these checks are paid. Even so, a bank may get credit for transit checks before funds are collected from the paying bank, which in turn creates FEDERAL RESERVE FLOAT.

deferred credit see DEFERRED AVAILABILITY; UNEARNED DISCOUNT.

deferred interest
1. bond paying interest at a later date, at maturity in the case of a ZERO-COUPON SECURITY. Interest payments accumulate during the holding period but no interest is actually paid until the redemption date. See also ACCRETION OF DISCOUNT.
2. posting delay in crediting DEFERRED AVAILABILITY checks to an interest-bearing account. In effect one to two days' interest is lost during the collection period.

deferred payments
1. deferral of principal and interest payments in a GRADUATED PAYMENT MORTGAGE.
2. skip payment privilege sometimes offered credit card or installment loan customers, a consumer convenience though less common today than in the years before credit cards became popular.

deficiency judgment court order authorizing a lender to collect part of an outstanding debt from foreclosure and sale of the borrower's mortgaged property or repossession of property securing a debt, after a finding that the property is worth less than the book value of the outstanding debt.

defined contribution plan any of a number of savings plans allowing employers, and also employees, to make periodic contributions on a tax-deferred basis, for retirement income. Included are profit sharing plans and 401K PLANs. Some plans allow matched funding by employers, sometimes on a dollar-for-dollar basis with employee contributions. See also DEFINED BENEFIT PENSION PLAN.

defined benefit pension plan retirement income plan set up by a corporation to pay a specified sum to qualified employees, based on the number of years in service. Corporate contributions are placed in a separate trust account. These plans pay no taxes on their investments, and are managed according to federally mandated standards under the EMPLOYEE RETIREMENT INCOME SECURITY ACT.

definitive securities securities issued in certificate form, as distinguished from BOOK-ENTRY SECURITY, where ownership is indicated by entries in a computer. Most Treasury securities are in book-entry form. Also, a permanent bond issued by a corporation, replacing a temporary bond. See also BEAREP BOND; REGISTERED BOND.

deflation decrease in the general level of prices, usually the result of an economic downturn brought on by TIGHT MONEY policies of the Federal Reserve System. Deflation may result from (1) tight money monetary policies causing a rise in interest rates and shrinkage in the money supply; or (2) changes in fiscal policy, such as increases in taxation. Deflation is not the same as DISINFLATION, which is characterized by a lower growth in prices.

delay See PAYMENT DELAY.

delayed disbursement practice in cash management whereby firms pay vendors and other corporations by disbursing the payments from a bank in a remote city. Delayed disbursement, also called *remote disbursement*, maximizes clearing FLOAT, and differs from CONTROLLED DISBURSEMENT.

delinquency failure to pay an obligation when due. Consumer installment loans are normally considered delinquent if two consecutive payments are missed; an OPEN-END CREDIT account, such as a bank credit card, is often treated as a delinquent account if a payment is not received within the allowed 15- to 25-day grace period. A delinquent loan payment is subject to a LATE CHARGE penalty and can be noted on the borrower's credit report as a past due payment. Loans with more than two missing payments (60 to 90 days past due) are regarded as seriously delinquent and debt collection efforts are initiated to recover the amount due.

delivery
Banking.
1. PRESENTMENT of a check or negotiable instrument, endorsed by the payee, to the paying bank.
2. in the secondary market, forwarding of loan documents by a selling bank to the purchaser, under the terms of a FORWARD COMMITMENT or STANDBY COMMITMENT.

Futures. taking possession of the financial instrument, security, or commodity underlying a futures market contract at specified times, normally at the beginning of a contract delivery month.

delivery date
1. day in the month when financial instruments or commodities are deliverable under a financial futures contract. This may occur any day during the contract month at the seller's option, so long as proper notice is given. Actual delivery normally takes place two days after the seller's DELIVERY NOTICE. See also FIRST DAY NOTICE.
2. day that a purchaser of securities takes possession. Delivery may take place under five-day regular way delivery, cash basis delivery, or seller's option delivery at a later date. See also SETTLEMENT.
3. maturity date of a FORWARD EXCHANGE CONTRACT in foreign exchange, at which time the exchange of currencies takes place.

delivery notice in financial futures, a written notice given by a seller to a clearing house stating the date when a commodity or financial instrument will be delivered. The futures clearing house assigns the contract to the longest-standing buyer on record. Also called notice of intention to deliver.

delivery versus payment securities industry term indicating payment is due when the buyer has securities in hand or a book entry receipt. Also called *delivery against cash*, *cash on delivery*, or from the sell side, *receive versus payment*. Commonly used by institutional accounts, payment can be made to the seller, or a bank acting as the seller's agent, by check, wire transfer, or cash.

delta TECHNICAL ANALYSIS term used in measuring the interaction between the price of an option premium and the price of the underlying security or futures contract. An option that changes in premium by $1 for every $2 in the price of the underlying security has a delta of 0.05. An AT THE MONEY option has a delta value near 0.05. The delta rises toward 1.0 for IN THE MONEY options and approaches zero for options that are OUT OF THE MONEY. Compare with gamma, which is the sensitivity of an option's delta to small changes in the price of the underlying instrument.

demand deposit account paying funds on demand without notice of intended withdrawal. Also called a *checking account*. Federal and state banking laws define a demand deposit as any bank deposit payable within 30 days. Bank demand deposit drafts, or checks, are NEGOTIABLE INSTRUMENTS, as defined by Article 3 of the UNIFORM COMMERCIAL CODE. See also CHECK; NEGOTIABLE ORDER OF WITHDRAWAL (NOW) ACCOUNT; SUPER NOW ACCOUNT.

demand draft written order directing that payment be made, on sight, to a third party. The person writing the draft is called the drawee; the bank making the payment is the drawer, or the payor bank. The beneficiary of a demand draft, the person receiving the payment, is the payee. Drafts may be payable at some future date (time drafts) or on sight (demand drafts.) Demand drafts drawn on banks are known as CHECKS.

demand loan loan with no specific maturity date, but payable at any time. Only interest is paid until the principal is paid off, or until the lender demands repayment of principal. The borrower may, however, pay off the loan early, without incurring a prepayment penalty. If the funds are advanced to a broker, it is referred to as a call loan. See also TERM LOAN; TIME LOAN.

denomination face value of coins, currency, or securities. FEDERAL RESERVE NOTES, the legal currency in the United States, are issued with values of $1 to $100. Bonds typically are $1,000 or $5,000.

de novo newly chartered bank, as opposed to a bank acquired through an ACQUISITION. Also, a newly opened branch banking office, in contrast to a branch purchased from another bank. Banking expansion can take place through chartering of new banks and approval of new branch offices by state banking departments, or through the acquisition of existing banks (and banking offices). In states where de novo branching is tightly regulated, for example, the UNIT BANKING states in the Midwest where branching is prohibited by state law, banking companies have frequently been able to expand geographically by forming a MULTIBANK HOLDING COMPANY, which then acquired other banks. State INTERSTATE BANKING laws have permitted banking expansion only through holding company acquisitions, rather than de novo charters of new banks.

deposit

1. funds placed with a bank in a savings account, or in a demand account subject to withdrawal by check. A deposit balance in a deposit accepting bank—a depository financial institution—is merely a credit, representing the depositor's right to an equivalent amount of money from the bank. The opposite is a WITHDRAWAL, removing funds from an account.
2. crediting of cash, checks, or drafts to a customer's account at a depository financial institution.
3. EARNEST MONEY given as intention of fulfilling a contract, for example, a DOWN PAYMENT towards purchase of a house.

depositary an agent authorized to place funds, securities, and so on in safekeeping in a DEPOSITORY institution.

depositary receipt see AMERICAN DEPOSITARY RECEIPT; INTERNATIONAL DEPOSITARY RECEIPT.

deposit insurance see BANK INSURANCE FUND; FEDERAL DEPOSIT INSURANCE CORPORPORATION; GUARANTY FUND; SAVINGS ASSOCIATION INSURANCE FUND.

deposit interest rate interest rate paid on deposit accounts by commercial banks and other depository financial institutions. Depository institutions are prohibited by Federal Reserve REGULATION Q from paying interest on checking accounts. Interest-bearing deposit accounts have been completely deregulated since March 31, 1986, when the old interest rate ceilings under Regulation Q were abolished. Rate ceilings were phased out over a six-year period by the DEPOSITORY INSTITUTIONS DEREGULATION COMMITTEE.

deposit note debt security issued by a bank, backed by federal deposit insurance up to $100,000 in principal and interest, and carrying an original maturity of two to five years. Deposit notes, which pay a fixed rate of interest, can be issued in book entry or certificate form, and typically are issued for sale to institutional investors in denominations of $250,000 or more. Some banks have, however, issued retail deposit notes in denominations as low as $1,000.

   As bank issued debt, rather than bank holding company debt, deposit notes are subordinate to claims of depositors, and are exempt from Securities and Exchange Commission registration. These notes are similar to certificates of deposit, with the exception that certificate of deposit interest is computed on a 365-day money market year and deposit notes pay interest on a 360-day year. Deposit notes easily are marketed through brokers, have an active secondary market, and hold some appeal with investors unwilling to buy bank holding company debt. Compare to BANK NOTE.

depository
   1. bank holding funds or marketable securities, usually under a specific agreement. Distinguish from DEPOSITARY.
      2. bank authorized to accept public deposits for state and local governments, or federal tax payments in a TREASURY TAX AND LOAN ACCOUNT.
   2. CORRESPONDENT bank holding deposits for other banks, used for check clearing or meeting RESERVE REQUIREMENTS.

Depository Institutions Act of 1982 see GARN-ST
GERMAIN DEPOSITORY INSTITUTIONS ACT.

**Depository Institutions Deregulation and
Monetary Control Act** federal law, enacted in 1980,
deregulating deposit interest rates and expanding access to the
Federal Reserve DISCOUNT WINDOW in the first major reform of
the U.S. banking system since the 1930s. The act has two main
sections: Title 1, the Monetary Control Act, which extends RE-
SERVE REQUIREMENTS to all U.S. banking institutions and also
deals with the banking services furnished by the Federal Reserve
System; and Title 2, the Depository Institutions Deregulation
Act of 1980, phasing out Federal Reserve REGULATION Q deposit
interest rate ceilings.

The following are highlights of the act:

(1) mandatory reserve requirements that banks keep in noninterest earning accounts at Federal Reserve Banks were lowered. State chartered banks that are not members of the Federal
Reserve System, as well as thrift institutions, were required to
maintain reserve account balances. Mandatory reserves for all
depository institutions were phased in over an eight-year period
ending in 1988.

(2) Federal Reserve Banks were required to begin charging
banks for clearing checks through the Federal Reserve System,
and pricing reserve bank services at levels competitive with private sector pricing.

(3) a five-member committee, the DEPOSITORY INSTITUTIONS
REREGULATION COMMITTEE, was created to phase out federal interest rate ceilings on deposit accounts over a six-year period
ending in 1986.

(4) nationwide NEGOTIABLE ORDER OF WITHDRAWAL (NOW) accounts were authorized.

(5) federal deposit insurance coverage was raised from
$40,000 to $100,000 per insured account.

(6) all depository institutions, including savings and loans
and other thrift institutions, were given access to the Federal
Reserve DISCOUNT WINDOW for credit advances.

(7) savings and loan associations were authorized to make
consumer loans, including auto loans and credit card loans, up to
20% of total assets.

(8) savings and loans were authorized to offer TRUST accounts.

(9) state USURY laws limiting rates lenders could charge on residential mortgage loans were pre-empted.

(10) state chartered, federally insured banks were allowed to charge the same interest rates on bank loans as national banks.

(11) Federal Reserve REGULATION Z, implementing the consumer credit protections in the Truth in Lending Act, was simplified.

(12) authorized federal credit unions to originate residential mortgages. See also GARN-ST GERMAIN DEPOSITORY INSTITUTIONS ACT; MONEY MARKET DEPOSIT ACCOUNT; PRIVATE SECTOR ADJUSTMENT FACTOR; SUPER NOW ACCOUNT.

Depository Institutions Deregulation Committee (DIDC)

five-member committee established by the Banking Act of 1980 (the DEPOSITORY INSTITUTIONS DEREGULATION AND MONETARY CONTROL ACT) to gradually phase out interest rate ceilings on deposit acccounts over a six-year period. The DIDC's authority ended when Federal Reserve REGULATION Q interest rate ceilings on passbook savings accounts, the last to be deregulated, expired on March 31, 1986.

Depository transfer check (DTC)

preprinted DEMAND DRAFT used by corporations to make transfers of cash from a checking account at one bank to a CONCENTRATION ACCOUNT at another bank. This nonnegotiable instrument requires no signature. Also called a *depository transfer draft*.

Depository Trust Company (DTC)

corporation owned by Wall Street brokerage firms that acts as a go-between in securities settlement. Ownership of stock and bond certificates is kept on the DTC's computerized record keeping system, allowing most securities transfers to take place in a virtually paperless environment. DTC charges and credits are netted against each member firm's account on a daily basis.

deposit slip

two-part form listing checks deposited into a customer's account. One copy is the customer's transaction receipt, the other serves as an audit trail and is a record of original entry legally admissable in a court of law.

depreciation

1. **Accounting.** The amortization of fixed assets, such as furniture and fixtures, allocating the purchase cost of the asset over its useful economic life. ACCELERATED DEPRECIATION allows faster write-off than would ordinarily occur under "straight-line" depreciation.

2. **Foreign Exchange.** A decline in price of one currency relative to another without market INTERVENTION by central banks.

depth of the market
amount of a currency (commodity, security) that can be traded in the market at any given time without causing a price distortion. Thin markets usually are characterized by wide spreads and substantial price fluctuations during a short period of time. Strong markets tend to be characterized by relatively narrow spreads and stable prices.

deregulation
business environment in which market competitors are controlled more by market forces rather than by government regulation, with the aim of creating a more efficient marketplace by substituting MARKET DISCIPLINE for the hand of government. The regulatory framework in the financial services industry, created by the BANKING ACT OF 1933, was modified substantially in the 1980s. Deposit interest rate ceilings were abolished and financial institutions were permitted to offer a wider range of new services, allowing commercial banks and thrift institutions to pay market rates for deposits and compete more effectively with nonbank financial companies. See also DEPOSITORY INSTITUTIONS DEREGULATION AND MONETARY CONTROL ACT; GARN-ST GERMAIN DEPOSITORY INSTITUTIONS ACT.

derivative mortgage-backed securities
mortgage-backed securities formed by dividing the cash flows from a pool of mortgages into obligations with payment characteristics substantially different from the underlying mortgages. Innovation in the mortgage market has led to numerous derivative mortgage instruments: the COLLATERALIZED MORTGAGE OBLIGATION, consisting of a series of bonds with different maturity classes; the INTEREST-ONLY (IO) STRIP, receiving only interest payments; the PRINCIPAL-ONLY (PO) STRIP, a security receiving only loan principal payments; and mortgage RESIDUALS, which are the excess cash flow after debt service payments. Derivative se-

curities often are used as hedging devices to immunize a loan portfolio against interest rate risk. See also ACCRUAL BOND; CONTROLLED AMORTIZATION BOND; INVERSE FLOATER; STRIPPED MORTGAGE-BACKED SECURITIES.

derogatory information adverse information on accounts that have not paid accounts with other creditors according to payment terms, as reported to a credit bureau. In addition, derogatory information may be any of the following: loans charged off; bankruptcy filings; or court judgments, such as garnishment or attachment of wages.

descriptive billing credit card billing system in which monthly statements list the merchant name and location, transaction amount, and date of purchase. Bank credit card systems also include a merchant reference number to identify and investigate charges disputed by a cardholder. Contrast with COUNTRY CLUB BILLING. See also COMBINED STATEMENT.

descriptive statement ACCOUNT STATEMENT listing deposits, withdrawals, and account service charges in chronological order, or as they are posted to the customer's account. If the transaction was initiated by an ELECTRONIC FUNDS TRANSFER, Federal Reserve regulations require financial institutions to disclose the transaction date, location of the terminal, and amount of the transaction. This rule also covers preauthorized payments, direct payroll deposits, and automated teller machine transactions.

desk
1. money desk at the Federal Reserve Bank of New York, where Federal Open Market Committee buy-sell orders are executed, increasing or reducing the supply of available bank reserves
2. any trading desk where orders are executed for bank customers, correspondent banks, or a bank's own account. For example, a foreign exchange desk, Federal Funds (Fed Funds) desk, loan sales desk, and so on.

deutschmark national currency of West Germany. Abbreviated DM.

devaluation downward adjustment by monetary authorities
in the official exchange rate of a nation's currency in relation to a
KEY CURRENCY, such as the U.S. Dollar or an established monetary standard such as gold. Devaluation occurs when a government increases the amount of its currency it is willing to exchange with other currencies at current exchange rates. Contrast
with DEPRECIATION. See also REVALUATION.

differential
1. **Banking.** Refers to the 1/4 of 1 % difference between deposit
   interest rates paid by commercial banks and rates paid by
   savings and loans. The rate differential on time deposit accounts, created in the 1960s to give thrift institutions a stable
   funding source for mortgage lending, was phased out in January 1984.
2. **Finance.** A broker's commission for handling small, odd-lot
   orders, which normally is higher than with regular orders.

dinar national currency of Algeria, Bahrain, Iraq, Jordan,
Libya, Tunisia, Yugoslavia, and Kuwait.

direct debit PRE-AUTHORIZED PAYMENT used in collecting recurring bills by electronic means. Generally, the borrower signs
a pre-authorization agreement giving his bank the right to debit
an account for the amount due on a designated day. Direct debit
payments, also called *reverse wire transfers*, are most often used
by banks to collect loan or mortgage payments.

direct deposit automatic deposit of wages or benefits (such
as Social Security payments) into a consumer's bank account.
Direct deposit payments are processed through the AUTOMATED
CLEARING HOUSE.

direct investment equity investments by state chartered
banks and thrift institutions. State chartered banks are permitted
by state regulations in about 20 states to take equity positions in
real estate development. Direct investments by savings and loan
associations in speculative real estate projects contributed to
heavy losses in savings and loan associations in the late 1980s
and a federal bailout of the S&L deposit insurance fund in 1989.
National banks are prohibited by law from making such invest-

ments. The Financial Institutions Reform, Recovery and Enforcement Act of 1989 restricts direct real estate investments by savings institutions to separately capitalized subsidiaries.

direct loan loan by a bank to its own customer without the use of third parties, such as dealers. Direct lending gives the lender more opportunities to screen credit applicants than indirect lending, and to monitor the loan through the CREDIT DEPARTMENT once a loan is approved and funds are disbursed.

director persons elected by shareholders of a corporation at the annual meeting to represent their interests, select the firm's officers, and carry out company policy. Directors name operating officers, such as president, and decide when dividends are paid. See also INSIDE DIRECTOR.

directors & officers' (D&O) insurance liability insurance protecting a bank director or officer against lawsuits by third parties, for example, shareholders, loan customers, or banking regulatory agencies seeking damages for losses caused by errors in loan administration or negligent acts. For example, directors can be held personally responsible for imprudent lending practices, such as excessive loans to a single industry, causing a loss to the bank's shareholders. Inside directors and officers of failed banks and savings institutions have also been sued by the federal insurance funds to recover costs absorbed by the insurance fund in liquidating the failing institution or arranging a friendly takeover by another bank. Due to the high cost of coverage, some banks have funded their own coverage through SELF-INSURANCE via a pooling arrangement sponsored by the American Bankers Association.

direct placement sale of new securities to a long-term institutional investor such as a life insurance company or pension fund, without the use of underwriters. Also, the sale of loans, such as mortgages directly to an investor, bypassing a CONDUIT that packages loans for sale in the secondary market. The preferred term is PRIVATE PLACEMENT.

direct send private agreement among banks to exchange checks drawn on accounts at each other's bank, bypassing local clearing houses or the Federal Reserve check collection system.

Direct presentment between large correspondent banks accelerates check presentment to issuing banks, and thus increases the funds availability. Contrast with TRANSIT LETTER.

direct verification see CONFIRMATION.

dirham national currency of Morocco and the United Arab Emirates.

dirty float foreign exchange rate that is influenced to one degree or another by market INTERVENTION by the issuing country's monetary authority. Most western currencies, including the French franc, Italian lira and, to a lesser extent, U.S. dollar and Japanese yen, fall into this category. The opposite is CLEAN FLOAT.

disbursement
1. payment of funds that partially or fully settles a debt. Also, an outflow of cash that reduces a liability.
2. periodic release of construction loan in installments, called progress payments, at specific phases of construction. A portion of the loan is normally held back until completion of the project. See also CONTROLLED DISBURSEMENT; DELAYED DISBURSEMENT.

discharge of bankruptcy bankruptcy court's order releasing a debtor from his obligations, except for obligations the debtor voluntarily agreed to assume. Although the debtor is no longer liable for discharged obligations, the bankruptcy will remain on his CREDIT REPORT for 10 years. A discharge of obligations is available only to individual debtors, but not to corporations.

discharge of lien notification to a borrower of a lender's release of a lien on property securing performance of a loan after payment of the debt, for example, a SATISFACTION OF MORTGAGE document. The discharge is also noted in public land records.

disclosure

1. **Banking.** Information on credit terms required by federal or state laws to give their customers. Disclosure is normally required in all consumer loans and residential mortgages. Items subject to disclosure are the ANNUAL PERCENTAGE RATE, method of interest rate computation, minimum monthly payment, and also procedures for error resolution in billing disputes. In an ADJUSTABLE RATE MORTGAGE, for instance, the lender is required to disclose additional information, such as the INDEX, and how often the rate is adjusted.

2. **Securities.** The release of relevant information to a buyer of securities. The Securities Act of 1933 and other regulations require issuers to give buyers sufficient information to make an informed decision. It is up to the customer to evaluate the information and make a purchase decision. The SEC and securities exchanges do not care what is sold, only that all the relevant information is presented to the buyer.

3. **Accounting.** A fact or condition stated on the balance sheet or in footnotes.

discount

1. bank loan with interest deducted from the face amount of the note when the credit is extended. Generally used only for short-maturity business loans. The borrower repays the full amount indicated on the note.

2. price difference between a bond's current market price and its stated PAR VALUE, when the market price is lower.

3. BANK DISCOUNT RATE, or a bank's quoted price when it accepts payment liability for a bill of exchange, which then becomes a BANKER'S ACCEPTANCE.

4. Treasury Department's method of issuing U.S. Treasury bills at less than face value, with redemption at par at maturity. The discount on the bill represents interest.

5. price difference between two currencies, when one is trading at less than par value in relation to another currency.

6. fee charged by a bank for processing and crediting credit card receivables to a merchant's bank account.

7. CASH DISCOUNT offered by merchants for payment in cash. See also DEEP DISCOUNT; MERCHANT DISCOUNT RATE.

discount brokerage
cut-rate brokerage service, involving execution of securities buy or sell orders, without giving

investment advice. Discount brokerage through affiliated companies has been an approved banking activity for bank holding companies since 1983, by an amendment to Federal Reserve REGULATION Y. Trades executed by a discount broker are cleared through a securities exchange, normally by a clearing broker.

discounted cash flow accounting technique for estimating the present value (market value) of anticipated future income and expenditures, such as earnings from loan principal and interest payments, and income from investment securities. It is calculated as either net present value, which expresses future cash flows in terms of current money by applying a discount rate to future receipts, or INTERNAL RATE OF RETURN, which figures the average annual yield or return on capital of an investment or a bank loan over its expected lifetime.

discount house organization that purchases and discounts bankers' acceptances and trade acceptances, bills of exchange, and commercial paper. Acceptances are money market instruments. They are counted as loans when held by the reporting bank, through discounting its own acceptances of purchases in the market. Discount houses are financial intermediaries in Great Britain and several European countries, but not in the United States.

discount point amount paid by a home buyer to the lender at the outset of a mortgage, typically at loan closing, to increase the loan's effective yield. One point equals 1% of the principal; on a $100,000 mortgage loan, one discount point is $1,000.

discount pool pool of loans originated under current market rate; these pools tend to have slower prepayment characteristics, because the borrower is unlikely to be able to refinance at a comparable rate unless rates drop dramatically. As such, these are a CUSHION for long-term investors, such as pension funds. Lower rate is a kind of built-in CALL PROTECTION.

discount rate
1. rate charged by Federal Reserve Banks for loans at the Federal Reserve DISCOUNT WINDOW. The discount rate is set by each Federal Reserve Bank and approved by the Federal Reserve Board of Governors in Washington. Each Reserve Bank

submits its own rate to the board, which then either approves the rate or denies it. The discount rate is not necessarily the same across all 12 Federal Reserve Banks. Occasionally, one or more of the district Fed banks has insisted on a different rate than other Fed banks. This situation could persist for several weeks, although in recent years the Reserve Banks have tended to fall into line with a uniform discount rate, reflecting the emergence of a national market for bank credit. The discount rate is one of the policy tools the Federal Reserve Board employs to carry out monitory objectives; the others are OPEN MARKET OPERATIONS and RESERVE REQUIRE-MENTS. As of March 31, 1980, when the MONETARY CONTROL ACT OF 1980 became law, all depository financial institutions holding transaction accounts were able to borrow at the discount window.

2. BANK DISCOUNT RATE, quoted by banks when they accept acceptances and bills of exchange. The best names, those holding prime paper, qualify for the lowest rates.

discount window Federal Reserve facility for direct loans to a financial institution with a deficiency in its RESERVE ACCOUNT. The term originated with the practice of sending a bank representative to a reserve bank teller window when a bank needed to borrow money. The discount window provides credit through discounts (actually, rediscounts) of notes and acceptances already accepted, and discounted by a bank, and advances that are collaterized by a bank's holdings of Treasury securities. Today, most Federal Reserve credit is in the form of advances, which are a more convenient way of borrowing. On occasion, banks have used the discount window facility to build up their reserves position, anticipating future demand, rather than cover a deficiency in a reserve account. See also ADJUSTMENT CREDIT; EXTENDED CREDIT; SEASONAL CREDIT.

discount yield yield computation based on face amount of a security rather than the purchase price. Treasury bill yields are calculated this way, and also yields on most commercial paper and some municipal notes. Discount yield is calculated by:
discount / face amount x 360 / days to maturity.

discretionary account account managed by a bank acting as an ATTORNEY IN FACT, usually through its TRUST DEPART-

MENT. The bank has the right to buy or sell assets, usually securities, without prior consent.

discretionary trust trust that gives the trustee a degree of latitude in paying income from the trust to a beneficiary, usually to keep the beneficiary from wasting the trust's assets.

discrimination denial of credit to an applicant, based on factors prohibited by federal credit laws. The EQUAL CREDIT OPPORTUNITY ACT allows credit denials if the applicant cannot demonstrate creditworthiness, but forbids discrimination on the basis of race, color, age, religion, national origin, or other factors specified by law. Discriminating means treating that applicant less favorably than similarly qualified applicants. See also COMMUNITY REINVESTMENT ACT.

dishonor
1. refusal by a drawee bank to accept a promissory note, or to pay a check or draft, as might happen if the check writer's account has insufficient funds. To collect payment, the holder of the instrument must look to the endorsers or guarantors through a legal process known as PROTEST. But, unless the drawee bank gives prompt notice, by returning the check the same day, the endorser's liability is voided.
2. refusal by a check writer or maker to pay a check or other negotiable instrument. See also NOTICE OF DISHONOR; WRONGFUL DISHONOR.

disinflation slowing of the rate of increase in consumer and wholesale prices. Federal Reserve monetary policy is designed to contain the rate of inflation by controlling the supply of credit available for borrowing and keeping the inflation rate at a manageable level.

disintermediation withdrawal of funds from interest-bearing deposit accounts when rates on competing financial instruments, such as money market mutual funds, stocks, bonds, and so on, offers the investor a better return. Disintermediation was at its peak in 1966 when REGULATION Q interest rate ceilings prevented banks and savings institutions from competing effectively with nondepository institutions, such as brokers, disrupting the banks' ability to lend. The double-digit inflation of the late 1970s, which caused many consumers to put their liquid assets in short-term money funds, led to federal legislation in 1980 deregulating deposit interest rates, allowing banks and thrifts to compete more effectively with nonbank financial intermediaries.

disposable income net income remaining after state, federal, and local taxes are paid, and available for consumption or saving. Distinguish from discretionary income, which is income remaining after meeting essential household expenses, such as food and housing costs.

diversification

1. **Banking.** The allocation of a bank's assets over a wide group of borrowers to keep ASSET QUALITY of the loan portfolio at an acceptable level and maintain consistent earnings, while minimizing CREDIT RISK, or potential losses from borrower defaults. The LEGAL LENDING LIMIT prevents a bank from making excessive loans to a single borrower, but a lender can still "put too many eggs in one basket" by lending to many borrowers in a particular industry. Losses could result from an excessive CONCENTRATION of loans if borrowers as a group, for example, real estate developers or oil drilling companies, suffer an economic downturn. Lenders also guard against loss of earnings by operating branch offices to service a geographically diverse group of customers, and by offering NONCREDIT SERVICES, such as trust accounts, to commercial and retail customers.

2. **Investments.** The distribution of assets in a portfolio among different types of securities, such as bonds, stocks, commercial paper, and so on, and also by buying securities of the same type with different maturities. See also BARBELL PORTFOLIO; IMMUNIZATION; LADDERED PORTFOLIO.

divestiture sale of an asset to achieve a desired objective. A bank may sell branch offices, or even an entire operating division, to cut operating expenses or carry out its business plan for long-term growth. In a merger with another bank, it may be required to sell branches to gain the approval of state or federal banking supervisors. Assets sold without recourse are taken off the selling bank's balance sheet and transferred to the purchaser. In accounting terms, the sale is treated as a nonrecurring gain (or loss). See also ANTITRUST LAWS; ASSET SALES.

dividend

1. quarterly payment to stockholders of record, as a return on investment. Dividends may be in cash, stock, or property, and are declared from profits (surplus). If there is no surplus, the payment is considered a return on capital. Dividend payments are, in effect, taxed twice—once when corporate profits are taxed and again when the dividend is received by a taxpaying stockholder.
2. money paid to the holder of a SHARE ACCOUNT in a credit union; the payment is the equivalent of INTEREST.

dividend paying agent
corporate agent, often a commercial bank, assigned the responsibility for paying quarterly dividends to stockholders of record. This agent may or may not be the same as the TRANSFER AGENT, the firm that keeps track of securities redemptions and new issues.

documentary commercial bill
draft accepted by a bank with bills of lading and other documents attached, as opposed to a clean draft. The attached documents are delivered to the drawee when it accepts or pays the draft, and ordinarily controls title to the merchandise.

documentary credit
commercial letter of credit provided for payment by a bank to the named beneficiary, usually the seller of merchandise, against delivery of documents specified in the credit.

documentary draft
DRAFT in international trade with shipping documents such as a bill of lading, attached, as opposed to a CLEAN draft. The draft is deliverable to the DRAWEE of the instrument when that party accepts or pays the draft.

documents against acceptance
instructions given by an exporter to a bank that the documents attached to the draft for collection are deliverable to the drawee only against his or her acceptance of the draft.

documents against payment instructions by an exporter to a bank that the documents attached to the draft for collection are deliverable only after his or her payment of the draft.

dollar national currency of the United States and 14 other countries. Since 1971, when the U.S. officially abandoned the gold exchange standard and convertibility of the dollar into gold, the value of the U.S. dollar has been allowed to float freely against other currencies in foreign exchange markets.

dollar bond

1. popular name for a municipal revenue bond quoted and traded in dollar price, rather than YIELD TO MATURITY. Dollar bonds are usually municipal bonds with a single large amount due at one time, usually the TERM BOND portion of a financing, as opposed to SERIAL BONDS, which consist of numerous maturities of smaller amounts. Dollar bonds come in the same $5,000 principal amounts as other bonds.
2. EUROBOND denominated in U.S. dollars and issued in a financial center outside the United States. See also DUAL CURRENCY BOND.

dollar-day collected balance of one dollar, held for one day. The term is often used as a measure for quantifying the comparative benefits of alternative CASH MANAGEMENT systems.

dollar exchange acceptance time draft drawn by central banks in different countries and accepted by banks for the purpose of furnishing foreign exchange.

dollar roll sale of a mortgage backed security to a dealer, with an agreement to repurchase a substantially identical security at a future date and at a specified price. This normally is done as a short-term financing technique or to generate income from arbitrage by borrowing at below market rate in the mortgage backed securities market and reinvesting in another market, say the U.S. Treasury bond market, at a higher rate. A dollar roll term of investment can be anywhere from one to three months. Contrast with REVERSE REPURCHASE AGREEMENT.

domestic exchange checks, drafts, and acceptances drawn in one city and payable in another in the United States. Checks cleared through the Federal Reserve System are exchanged at par, or face value, i.e., without discount. Before the Federal Reserve check collection system was established in 1916, many banks imposed an exchange charge, or a fee deducted from the face amount of checks drawn on other banks. This practice, known as nonpar banking, has virtually disappeared, with the exception of some small state chartered banks in rural areas. Contrast with FOREIGN EXCHANGE.

Donoghue's Money Fund Average weekly index of rates paid by money market mutual funds. Donoghue's Money Fund Average is the simple average of the 7-day, 30-day, and compounded 7-day annualized rate paid by more than 400 taxable money market mutual funds, reported weekly by the Donoghue Money Fund Report of Holliston, MA 01746, a money market newsletter.

donor person making a gift; a voluntary transfer of property to another, who accepts the gift without CONSIDERATION. A GIFT INTER VIVOS is an irrevocable transfer occurring during the donor's lifetime.

don't know securities term for a questioned trade, indicating refusal to complete a transaction due to a disagreement on the trade details or because errors are discovered in the comparison sheets exchanged by broker-dealers.

dormant account savings account showing no activity, other than posting of interest for a specified period. These are generally low balance accounts. If unclaimed for a certain number of years, ownership reverts to the state under ESCHEAT laws.

double leverage use of holding company debt to finance bank equity. Double leveraging occurs when a bank holding company borrows in the debt market, and transfers the proceeds to a subsidiary bank. The practice is discouraged by bank regulators if an excessive proportion of bank net income is used to retire holding company debt.

doubtful loan loan in which full repayment is considered uncertain. Some losses are expected. A loan classified as doubtful has all the characteristics of a SUBSTANDARD loan (well-defined credit weaknesses), with the added characteristic that credit weaknesses make full collection or liquidation in full highly questionable and improbable. Fifty percent of loans classified as doubtful are deducted from adjusted bank capital in computing regulatory CAPITAL ADEQUACY. See also ADVERSELY CLASSIFIED ASSETS.

Douglas Amendment amendment to the BANK HOLDING COMPANY ACT enacted in 1966, prohibiting a bank holding company from acquiring a bank in another state unless the acquisition is expressly authorized by that state's laws. Without enabling legislation from the states—authorization that did not appear until the mid-1980s—the Federal Reserve Board did not have the authority to approve interstate bank mergers. Reciprocal state legislation, beginning in New England and the southeastern United States, initially opened the door to regional interstate banking and nationwide banking.

dower right of a widow to some or all of the property of her deceased husband. Years ago some states have recognized a common law dower, giving a widow a fixed portion of the estate; today this right has generally been abolished.

Dow Jones Industrial Average price-weighted average of 30 leading industrial stocks traded on the New York Stock Exchange, compiled by Dow Jones & Co. and published daily in the *Wall Street Journal*. The industrial average is one of four securities averages computed by Dow Jones; the others are a 20-stock transportation average, an average of 15 utility stocks, and a composite averaging all of these securities. The industrial average is the most popular, and is widely quoted as an indicator of stock prices and investor confidence in the securities market.

down payment initial good faith deposit made by a home buyer, indicating intention to purchase real estate offered for sale and obtain financing from a bank or mortgage company. Also called *earnest money* or a GOOD FAITH deposit.

downstream

1. RESPONDENT bank, generally a community bank, in a CORRESPONDENT banking relationship.

2. funds borrowed by a bank holding company for use as a subsidiary, generally to obtain a more favorable rate; a downstream loan. Contrast with UPSTREAM.

drachma national currency of Greece.

draft payment order in writing that directs a second party, the DRAWEE, to pay a specified sum to a third party (the payee). A draft is actually a bill of exchange, although the term draft is ordinarily used if it is drawn on a bank. A CHECK is a bank draft payable when presented (a SIGHT DRAFT). Drafts may also be payable at a future date (a TIME DRAFT). See also DOCUMENTARY DRAFT; PAYABLE THROUGH DRAFT.

dragnet clause see CROSS-COLLATERAL.

draining reserves see TIGHT MONEY.

draw down

1. to activate a LINE OF CREDIT.

2. bank customer's instructions to transfer funds to another bank, as when a corporation transfers temporarily idle funds into a CONCENTRATION ACCOUNT for reinvestment at market interest rates.

drawee person or organization who is expected to pay a check or draft when the instrument is presented for payment.

drawer party instructing the drawee to pay someone else, by writing, or drawing a check or draft. The drawer is also known as the maker or writer.

dual banking banking system in the United States, consisting of STATE BANKs, chartered and supervised by state banking departments, and NATIONAL BANKs, chartered and regulated by the Office of the Comptroller of the Currency. The side-by-side existence of state banks and national banks accounts for wide variations in credit regulation, LEGAL LENDING LIMITS, and investment policies from one state to another, and even within a state.

dual control actions requiring approval by two persons, each being held accountable. When a teller cashes a check for a noncustomer, a bank officer's signature is often required. If authorization by two individuals working together is required, the preferred term is joint custody. For example, access to a safe deposit box requires approval by banker and customer, each possessing a key to the box. Dual control differs from dual posting, a bookkeeping system where ledger entries are recorded independently by two bank employees.

dual currency bond bond paying interest in one currency, but convertible into another at redemption. A dual currency bond might be issued by a German bank, paying interest in deutschemarks, but is repaid in dollars at redemption.

duality membership in both of the two national bank card organizations. Prior to 1976, credit card issuing banks belonged to either Visa (then National BankAmericard Inc.) or MasterCard (Interbank Card Association).

due bill see BILL.

due diligence
1. **Banking.** The responsibility of bank directors and officers to act in a prudent manner in evaluating credit applications; in essence, using the same degree of care that an ordinary person would use in making the same analysis.
2. **Securities.** The responsibility of securities underwriters to explain relevant details of a new issue of securities to interested purchasers. Called a due diligence meeting.

due from account general ledger asset account representing funds on deposit at another bank. In international banking, the term Nostro (*due from* in Latin) is often used.

due-on-sale clause language in a mortgage contract stating that the outstanding balance is due and payable if the home owner sells the property to another, or if certain other conditions are met. The mortgage cannot be assumed by another buyer, as in an ASSUMABLE MORTGAGE, without approval of the lender, and normally only at current market rates. The GARN-ST GERMAIN DEPOSITORY INSTITUTIONS ACT of 1982 was enacted during a period of high interest rates when rates on conventional mortgage loans were as high as 15 to 16%. It allowed federal preemption, for a three- year period ending October 15, 1985, of state laws enforcing due-on-sale provisions in mortgage contracts. As a practical matter, due-on-sale clauses are common in most conventional mortgages, aside from mortgages insured by the Federal Housing Administration or guaranteed by the Department of Veterans Affairs, and are required in mortgage loans sold in the secondary market to the Federal National Mortgage Association (Fannie Mae) and the Federal Home Loan Mortgage Corp. (Freddie Mac). The due-on-sale provision insures secondary market conduits have a continuous supply of loans originated at market interest rates.

due to account general ledger liability account representing funds payable to other banks. In international banking, the term Vostro, (*due to* in Latin), is often used.

Dun & Bradstreet (D&B) company that supplies corporate credit reports and ratings, based on industry reported information and its own analytical data. D&B furnishes ratings on estimated financial strength, promptness of trade payments, and capital adequacy, plus statistical data, such as financial performance ratios of rated companies. Dun & Bradstreet clients receive extracts of balance sheet and income statement data, as reported by D&B listed companies. Credit information on some three million U.S. and Canadian companies is listed in a ratings directory, *The Reference Book*. The absence of a D&B rating for a particular company means that Dun & Bradstreet did not have sufficient information available to classify a company.

Dun & Bradstreet's bond rating subsidiary, MOODY'S INVESTORS SERVICE, rates corporate and municipal bonds, bank certificates of deposit, and commercial paper.

Credit analysts, when evaluating publicly traded companies, supplement D&B reports with audited financial statements.

duration calculation measuring the price sensitivity (INTEREST RATE RISK) of a financial instrument to changes in interest rates. Duration attempts to determine the true maturity, as opposed to final maturity, of a security, by measuring the average time required to collect all payments of principal and interest. The duration of a callable bond, also called its *effective duration*, may be considerably shorter than its stated maturity in a period of rising interest rates. Thus, as market interest rates rise, the duration of a financial instrument decreases. For example, a 30-year conventional mortgage may have an effective duration of only 11 to 12 years, which means the loan will probably be paid off in about one third of the time it is supposedly carried by the originating lender as an earning asset. Duration differs from other measurements such as AVERAGE LIFE and HALF LIFE. Duration measures the time required to recover a dollar of price in present value terms (including principal and interest), whereas average life computes the average time needed to collect one dollar of principal.

Although duration is also used in bank ASSET- LIABILITY MANAGEMENT, it is difficult for many banks to analyze the volatility of everything on the balance sheet. They don't have access to all of the information necessary to do the calculations. In contrast, *gap analysis* is a more simplistic measurement that looks only at the maturity difference between balance sheet assets and liabilities. See also DYNAMIC GAP; GAPPING; IMMUNIZATION; STATIC GAP.

Dutch auction auction system in securities underwriting where the issuer gradually lowers the price until a responsive bid is met. Winning bids are filled at the lowest price moving the entire lot or purchase of a specified amount. Bidders can bid any price they want, and securities are sold to all bidders whose price is at, or lower, than the set price. The Dutch auction technique is not used in auctions of U.S. Treasury securities. See also MONEY MARKET PREFERRED STOCK.

dynamic gap asset-liability gap model that takes into account projected future balances or the difference between INTEREST SENSITIVE ASSETS and INTEREST SENSITIVE LIABILITIES at specific future time periods, as opposed to STATIC GAP.

E

early withdrawal penalty forfeiture of interest or service fee charged depositors for withdrawing money from a savings or time deposit prior to maturity. Under current Federal Reserve regulations, banks may still require 30 days' notice before withdrawing funds, but penalties for early withdrawals have been sharply reduced from levels prior to interest rate deregulation.

earmarked reserves funds set aside for a specific purpose. For example, a bank's LOAN LOSS RESERVES for possible bad debt. The Federal Reserve Bank of New York holds gold bullion in trust for foreign central banks and various international organizations. Earmarked gold is used to back up monetary agreements, such as currency swaps to stabilize exchange rates. See also EXCHANGE STABILIZATION FUND; GOLD STOCK.

earnest money good faith sum of money given to bind a contract, for example an agreement to purchase real property, or a commitment fee to assure an advance of funds by a lender. In a real estate transaction, the money is applied to the purchase price and is forfeited if the purchaser fails to carry out the terms of the agreement.

earning assets any asset generating INTEREST or yielding FEE income—the major source of a bank's net income. Included are loans and leases, but not UNEARNED INTEREST income; U.S. government, corporate, and municipal securities held as INVESTMENT SECURITIES; securities purchased under agreements to resell (REPURCHASE AGREEMENTS); TIME DEPOSIT accounts in other banks; FEDERAL FUNDS sold to other banks; and TRADING ACCOUNT ASSETS.

earnings allowance see EARNINGS CREDIT.

earnings credit adjustment factor that reduces bank service charges on deposit accounts, for example, a checking account calculated by multiplying the AVERAGE DAILY BALANCE by the factor for an accounting period. Large banks often peg their earnings credit rate to the U.S. Treasury bill rate.

earnings per share net income allocated to a share of common stock after payment of taxes and preferred stock dividends. Corporations usually express earnings per share on a fully diluted basis, taking into account what might happen if holders of stock options exercised their purchase rights, and all outstanding convertible bonds and convertible preferred stock were exchanged for shares of common stock.

earning the points in foreign exchange, market condition that exists when the buying price of a currency in the forward market is cheaper than the SPOT MARKET price. For example, when the spot market rates are U.S. $1 = 1.6510 deutschmarks, and the one-month forward rate is $1 = 1.6450, the difference is .0050. A trader selling at the spot rate and buying at a cheaper one-month forward rate is earning the points. The opposite is LOSING THE POINTS.

easy money said of credit available to the public through the banking system when the Federal Reserve allows bank credit to expand. When the Federal Reserve allows reserves to accumulate, interest rates are stable, if not declining. Easy money policies could encourage economic growth and, eventually, inflation, if carried out for a sustained period. Contrast with TIGHT MONEY.

E bond see SAVINGS BOND.

econometrics economic modeling technique that seeks to explain in mathematical terms the relationships between key economic variables such as capital spending, wages, bank interest rates, population trends, and also government fiscal and monetary policies. An econometric model helps business planners test different hypotheses explaining why the economy acts as it does, for example, the relationship between bank RESERVE REQUIRE-

MENTS and interest rate volatility. This helps organizations explore various options available in forecasting business growth. See also TECHNICAL ANALYSIS.

Economic Recovery Tax Act federal law enacted in 1981 that cut taxes across-the-board, modified the depreciation tables used by businesses in writing off capital equipment, and indexed tax brackets to the inflation rate. The act reduced the individual tax rate by 23%, cut the corporate capital gains tax to a maximum of 20%, and introduced the accelerated cost recovery system used by businesses in calculating ACCELERATED DEPRECIATION.

To encourage individual savings, the act made INDIVIDUAL RETIREMENT ACCOUNTS (IRAS) available to anyone earning regular income, and introduced the ALL SAVERS CERTIFICATE, a one-year savings certificate free of federal taxes. (IRA eligibility rules have since been modified substantially by the TAX REFORM ACT OF 1986, eliminating the tax deferral on IRA accounts of individuals covered by a corporate pension.)

The act also reduced the federal tax on estate and gift taxes, making the first $600,000 tax free after 1987, and allowed an unlimited MARITAL DEDUCTION on property transfers as provided by a will.

Edge Act corporation banking corporation financing international commerce, chartered by the Federal Reserve Board under a 1919 amendment to the Federal Reserve Act. These corporations, owned by state chartered or national banks, may operate interstate branches, accept deposits outside the United States, and invest in non-U.S. firms. A nonbanking Edge Act corporation makes equity investments under Federal Reserve REGULATION K in foreign corporations, such as merchant banks or finance companies. A banking Edge buys and sells notes, drafts, and bills of exchange, and basically complements the international banking activities of its parent bank. The International Banking Act of 1978 approved ownership of Edge corporations by foreign banks. See also AGREEMENT CORPORATION; EXPORT TRADING COMPANY.

education loan loan made for college or vocational training expenses, often at a BELOW MARKET RATE. Loans backed by the Student Loan Marketing Association (Sallie Mae) are 90% guaranteed for repayment of principal and interest. A guaranteed student loan (renamed a Stafford Student Loan, after Sen. Robert T. Stafford of Vermont) is insured by a state guarantee agency and reinsured by Sallie Mae. Repayment of principal and interest in a Stafford Student Loan is deferred until after college graduation.

EE bond SEE SAVINGS BOND.

effective annual yield depositor's yield earned on a savings account or time deposit, including compounded interest, assuming the funds remain in the account for a full calendar year. Rates on bank certificates of deposit are stated in advertisements as ANNUAL PERCENTAGE RATE (APR), and as an effective rate, indicating the rate earned if a CD with a maturity of less than a year remains on deposit for a full year. Effective yield may overstate the actual yield on CDs with original maturities under a year, because the calculation assumes the funds will be automatically reinvested (rolled over) at the original rate. Contrast with AVERAGE ANNUAL YIELD.

effective date date on which a transaction is posted, or an agreement becomes effective.
1. **Banking.** The time when an expiring CERTIFICATE OF DEPOSIT is renewed at the current rate, and interest paid is adjusted accordingly. Also, the date on which a bank card becomes valid.
2. **Securities.** The date on which a registered offering of securities may be sold, ordinarily 20 days after filing of the issuer's registration statement with the Securities and Exchange Commission. See also SHELF REGISTRATION.

effective net worth stockholder's equity in a corporation, plus subordinated debt, such as debentures or loans to the firm by an owner. Credit analysts sometimes count loans by a principal toward a company's worth, provided the principal owners sign a SUBORDINATION AGREEMENT assuring that bank loans are paid first. This is especially true of closely held corporations where officers and owners are often the same.

effective rate

1. rate of interest paid on a loan, or earned on an interest-bearing deposit, including COMPOUND INTEREST, as distinguished from the NOMINAL INTEREST RATE. In a bank loan, the ANNUAL PERCENTAGE RATE. See also ADD-ON INTEREST; SIMPLE INTEREST.

2. investor's yield realized on a bond or security, which is different from the COUPON RATE. The effective rate takes into account the price paid, the time to maturity and the amortization of premium or accretion of a discount. Also called *effective yield*.

3. weighted average cost of Federal Funds purchased in the inter-bank market, calculated by the Federal Reserve Bank of New York. Banks that are short in their RESERVE ACCOUNTS are charged at a rate equal to the effective Fed Funds rate.

effects test method of assessing the discriminatory impact of supposedly neutral credit policies. In general, the effects test works this way: a person who alleges illegal discrimination need only establish a prima facie case by showing that the action in question has a disproportionately discriminant effect on a member of a protected class, and therefore is discriminatory in effect. The statutory basis of the effects test is the EQUAL CREDIT OPPORTUNITY ACT, which prohibits credit denials on the basis of marital status, national origin, age, or whether applicants are receiving public assistance, and also the Fair Housing Act. The effects test is most frequently applied in evaluating the fairness of statistically based credit scoring systems and alternative mortgages, such as graduated payment mortgages, where future income is considered.

efficient market theory that financial markets fully reflect all publicly available information. This theory, which has its detractors, holds that the prices paid today will correlate with what investors expect market prices will be in the future. In foreign exchange, it means the forward exchange rate on currencies deliverable next month will be roughly equal to the expected SPOT rate, assuming the currencies are freely exchangeable.

electronic banking form of banking where funds are transferred through an exchange of electronic signals between financial institutions, rather than an exchange of cash, checks, or other negotiable instruments. The ownership of funds and transfers of funds between financial institutions are recorded on computer systems connected by telephone lines. Customer identification is by access code, such as a password or PERSONAL IDENTIFICATION NUMBER, instead of a signature on a check or other physical document. Electronic banking systems can be low-dollar retail payment systems, such as AUTOMATED TELLER MACHINE networks and POINT-OF-SALE systems; and large-dollar interbank payment systems, such as the Federal Reserve Fed Wire or the CLEARING HOUSE INTERBANK PAYMENT SYSTEM operated by the New York Clearing House Association. See also AUTOMATED CLEARING HOUSE; BOOK ENTRY SECURITY; ELECTRONIC FUNDS TRANSFER; WIRE TRANSFER.

electronic data interchange (EDI) electronic communication of business transactions, specifically, the exchange of trade related documents, such as purchase orders and invoices in a standard format and corporate electronic funds transfer. With EDI, electronically transmitted data replaces paper documents in the business accounts receivable cycle. Electronic messages are sent through public data transmission networks or the banking system. When payments also are made through EDI, the payment instructions flow through the banking system. See also CORPORATE TRADE EXCHANGE; CORPORATE TRADE PAYMENT; ELECTRONIC FUNDS TRANSFER; X. 12.

electronic funds transfer (EFT) transfer of funds between accounts by electronic means rather than conventional paper-based payment methods, such as CHECK writing. As defined by the ELECTRONIC FUNDS TRANSFER ACT of 1978, an electronic funds transfer is any financial transaction originating from a telephone, electronic terminal, computer, or magnetic tape.

There are two categories of EFT systems:

1. large dollar WIRE TRANSFER systems such as Fed Wire, the Federal Reserve communication system linking Federal Reserve Banks, member banks, and the Treasury; and the Clearing House Interbank Payment System (CHIPS), a private wire network that handles most of the U.S. dollar volume in foreign trade.
2. consumer electronic payment systems, including AUTOMATED TELLER MACHINE networks, retail merchant POINT-OF-SALE (POS) debit card systems, and telephone bill payment systems. See also ELECTRONIC DATA INTERCHANGE.

Electronic Funds Transfer Act federal law enacted in 1978 providing the legal framework for ELECTRONIC FUNDS TRANSFER into, or out of, a consumer's bank account. These payments are not regulated by the UNIFORM COMMERCIAL CODE, which limits its coverage of consumer payments to negotiable instruments, such as checks or drafts. The act specifies protections available to consumers sending or receiving funds electronically, and limits consumer liability for UNAUTHORIZED TRANSFER to $50, provided the bank is notified promptly.

The act requires financial institutions to inform consumers of their financial rights under the act, provide written receipts of all electronic transfers, list transfers on an ACCOUNT STATEMENT, and develop procedures for error resolution. These guidelines are implemented in Federal Reserve REGULATION B. See also PERSONAL IDENTIFICATION NUMBER; PROVISIONAL CREDIT.

eligible paper notes, drafts, bankers' acceptances, and so on that are acceptable collateral for DISCOUNT WINDOW loans at a Federal Reserve Bank. To be acceptable for rediscount, paper must arise from a commercial transaction, have a maturity not exceeding 90 days, and bear the member bank's endorsement. The Monetary Control Act of 1980 extended discount window access to all financial institutions holding transaction accounts or nonpersonal time deposits.

embezzlement unlawful conversion of assets held in trust, as when a bank teller diverts money in a cash drawer to personal use. Misappropriation of bank funds can take many forms, which makes detection more difficult.

emergency credit extended term loan, usually more than 30 days, from a Federal Reserve Bank to nonbank financial institutions when assistance is not available from other sources. Savings and loan associations, for example, must look first to one of the Federal Home Loan Banks for credit advances. Reserve Banks are also authorized by the Federal Reserve Act to extend credit to corporations other than banks, although this power has not been used in many years. See also EXTENDED CREDIT.

Employee Retirement Income Security Act (ERISA) federal law enacted in 1974 that set investment guidelines for management of private pension plans and profit sharing plans, including employee vesting and conduct of plan administrators. The act also established an insurance fund, the Pension Benefit Guaranty Corp.

employee savings plan group savings plan, involving tax-deferred employee contributions to a pooled investment account. Contributions are often matched, up to a certain dollar amount, by employers. Other examples of defined contribution plans are 401(k) plans and profit sharing plans.

employee stock ownership plan (ESOP) stock ownership plan whereby employees purchase shares in their company's stock. Shares can be sold directly through a STOCK PURCHASE OPTION, or through a company sponsored 401(k) PLAN. A leveraged ESOP allows a company to raise its capital-to-asset ratio by issuing new shares of stock to an employee trust, which finances the transaction with a loan from a bank. The ESOP loan is repaid in pretax corporate dollars, and dividend payments to employees and the dividends reducing the bank loan are tax deductible expenses. An ESOP is often used as a retirement benefit to current employees. Employees receive shares of stock and future dividends that can be reinvested in new stock. These plans often are started by companies seeking to avoid hostile takeover by keeping company stock in friendly hands.

employee trust pension or profit-sharing plan set up by an employer, usually a corporation, to provide retirement income for its employees. Known as an employee benefit trust, or DEFINED BENEFIT PENSION PLAN, the plan is managed by a trustee, often a bank, which pays out funds at retirement or as instructed by the plan's corporate sponsor.

encoding imprinting of the dollar amount, in machine readable characters—MAGNETIC INK CHARACTER RECOGNITION (MICR), on checks sent through the banking system for collection, as well as checks deposited at the same bank from which the items are drawn. All preprinted checks have standard MICR line coding on the bottom edge, and for a good reason; the Federal Reserve refuses to handle unencoded checks as CASH ITEMS, which means delayed funds availability for the depositor.

encryption scrambling of sensitive information, such as account numbers or access codes, to prevent unauthorized use. The DATA ENCRYPTION STANDARD (DES), the encryption format adopted by the financial industry, requires that information scrambling take place in a computer or terminal before transmission. See also MESSAGE AUTHENTICATION.

encumbrance right or claim to real property that passes with title, for example, easements, judgment liens, and mortgages. An encumbrance does not hinder transfer of ownership, though it may reduce the market value of the property.

endorsement signature on the back of a negotiable instrument, such as a CHECK. Endorsement legally transfers ownership to another party. The UNIFORM COMMERCIAL CODE recognizes five kinds of endorsement: (1) BLANK ENDORSEMENT or unqualified endorsement; (2) special endorsement; for example, "Pay to the order of ABC Company"; (3) restrictive endorsement, writing limiting further negotiation, such as "for deposit only"; (4) qualified endorsement, "Pay to ABC Bank, without recourse"; and (5) conditional endorsement, "Pay XYZ Company upon completion of contract." (Rarely used.)

The Expedited Funds Availability Act of 1987 imposes certain restrictions on check endorsements, requiring endorsers to write their names in the top 1-1/2 inches on the back of a check, leaving space for bank endorsements.

endorser person who, by signing a check or negotiable instrument, transfers his ownership interest to another party. The endorser promises to make good on the check if it is dishonored for any reason.

end-to-end foreign exchange term for the end-of-month working date against another end-of-month working date, regardless of the actual number of days in between. The forward maturity dates (the SPOT dates for delivery) in future months are fixed at the last business day in a given calendar month. Also known as *fixed dates*. The only exception is when the maturity date falls on a nonbusiness day; then the spot date is moved ahead to the next business day. The term also can apply to the

ENDORSEMENT

ENDORSE HERE

X

DO NOT WRITE, STAMP OR SIGN BELOW THIS LINE
RESERVED FOR FINANCIAL INSTITUTION USE*

Space for
Bank
Endorsements

* FEDERAL RESERVE BOARD OF GOVERNORS REG. CC

forward maturities in a CURRENCY SWAP. For example, an end-to-end January-February forward contract would go from January 31 to February 28, not 30 days from January 31.

Equal Credit Opportunity Act (ECOA) federal law enacted in 1974 requiring lenders to give businesses and consumers equal access to credit. The act specifically prohibits credit discrimination on the basis of race, marital status, national origin, age, or dependence on public assistance. Borrowers who exercise their consumer rights under the Consumer Credit Protection Act are also protected from credit discrimination. Lenders are required to respond to credit applications within 30 days, and if the application is rejected, to offer reasons for denying credit. The act is implemented by Federal Reserve REGULATION B. See also EFFECTS TEST; PROHIBITED BASIS.

equity
1. value of stockholders' ownership interest in a corporation after all claims have been paid, and thus a claim on its assets in proportion to the number, and class, of shares owned. Equity, also called net value or net worth, is total assets less total liabilities. Common stock equity of a bank is counted as part of its PRIMARY CAPITAL.
2. fairness in settling legal disputes, as opposed to a strict interpretation of common law rules.
3. residual value of a brokerage or futures margin account, assuming its liquidation at the current market prices.
4. credit union member's ownership interest, represented by a SHARE ACCOUNT.
5. market value of real property, less any outstanding mortgages.

equity commitment notes CAPITAL NOTES issued by a bank or bank holding company requiring redemption by the issuer sometime before the maturity date from the proceeds of a new offering of common stock. First issued by J. P. Morgan & Co., Inc. in 1982, equity commitment notes are similar in structure to equity contract notes. Federal Reserve rules stipulate the notes must be redeemable at specific intervals, generally one third of the total offering every four years. These securities are treated as debt from an accounting standpoint, paying tax de-

ductible interest, and count towards the issuer's required capital-to-assets ratio. See also EQUITY CONTRACT NOTES; MANDATORY CONVERTIBLE.

equity contract notes note or debenture issued by a bank or bank holding company, convertible into common stock at a stated conversion price at a future date. Also called a CAPITAL NOTE. Equity notes with a MANDATORY CONVERTIBLE clause requiring the issuer to exchange the notes for common stock shares, qualify as supplementary capital or Tier 2 capital under the RISK-BASED CAPITAL guidelines approved by banking regulatory agencies. See also EQUITY COMMITMENT NOTES.

equity kicker in real estate finance, a participation in future earnings from income property. Kickers supplement the normal cash flow yield, and generally are more common in periods of tight credit, when developers are more willing to give up a share of future earnings in return for development financing. See also WARRANT.

equity of redemption mortgagor's right to redeem property after DEFAULT, and avoid a FORECLOSURE sale, by paying the outstanding principal, plus interest and other costs, to the mortgagee. Some states permit redemptions even after a foreclosure auction.

equity participation see KICKER.

equivalent bond yield see BOND EQUIVALENT YIELD.

equivalent taxable yield see TAXABLE EQUIVALENT YIELD.

error resolution process for correcting disputed transactions to a consumer's bank account, under Federal Reserve REGULATION E. A consumer claiming that funds were taken from an account by another person's UNAUTHORIZED TRANSFER without prior consent, or a transaction was posted improperly due to a bank bookkeeping error, can have the error corrected by notifying the financial institution holding the account. Once notice is given, the financial institution has from 10 to 45 days to investigate the complaint and recredit funds debited in error. The consumer's account liability is limited by regulation to $50 if the bank is notified of the error, but otherwise can be as high as $500. See also PROVISIONAL CREDIT.

errors and omission insurance liability insurance protecting a lender against losses due to negligence, improper documentation, and other errors, but not gross negligence or fraud. An example is TITLE INSURANCE. Errors and Omission coverage is required of financial institutions originating mortgage loans for resale in the secondary mortgage market.

escheat reversion of property to the state under certain prescribed conditions, for example, if the owner dies without heirs or if a depositor's account remains inactive for many years and the owner cannot be located. Property may be redeemed if the owner reappears.

escrow written agreement authorizing the holding of funds by a custodian, usually a bank or trust company. These accounts usually pay the same rate of interest as passbook accounts. Banks typically hold escrow accounts for real estate taxes and property insurance due on mortgaged property.

escudo national currency of Portugal.

estate ownership rights or claims to property, both real estate and personal property, at the time of death. The total of a person's assets passes to his heirs, according to the terms of a will, or is disposed of at the discretion of a probate court if no will is left. Individuals plan for the orderly distribution of an estate through *estate planning*, which involves the drawing of wills and setting up trusts, to achieve maximum benefit for heirs or trust beneficiaries in event of death.

estoppel certificate contract clause in which one party asserts that mortgage debt, collateral pledged, and so on, is correct on the date the agreement was made. This prevents the borrower from claiming differently at a later date. Also called an *estoppel clause*.

Eurobond corporate or government bond denominated in a currency other than the national currency of the issuer. These bonds are ordinarily issued in bearer form by international syndicates of commercial banks and investment banks that bid on securities offered for sale through a TENDER PANEL. Eurobonds may be issued in a single currency, in multicurrency form, or a unit of account, such as the EUROPEAN CURRENCY UNIT. An important capital source for multinational companies, Eurobonds are cleared and settled through Euroclear and Cedel, two bank-owned clearing houses. Borrowing in the Eurobond often makes it possible to obtain financing at lower interest rates. See also SAMURAI BOND; YANKEE BOND; YEN BOND.

Eurocheque multicurrency European payment system giving bank customers check cashing privileges in 39 countries. A debit card system managed by Eurocheque International in Brussels, it allows cardholders to buy merchandise or cash checks with presentment of the Eurocheque card.

Eurocommercial paper short-term unsecured promissory note issued in London and other European financial centers for same-day settlement in U.S. dollars in New York. Paper is issued in either discount or interest-bearing form, and distributed through dealers on a best-effort basis, in contrast to EURONOTE facilities, which are issued through a TENDER PANEL. Eurocommercial paper gives issuers quicker access to funds than Euronotes, sometimes even same day funds.

Eurocredit see FLOATING RATE NOTE; REVOLVING UNDERWRITING FACILITY.

Eurocurrency deposit in a bank outside the country of origin. Most Eurocurrency deposits are U.S. dollar deposits, although nearly all major Western currencies are also represented. Eurodeposits are time deposits that can be loaned from one owner to another, ordinarily on a short-term basis. Eurocurrency deposits are not subject to RESERVE REQUIREMENTS or domestic interest rate ceilings. See also LONDON INTERBANK OFFERED RATE.

Eurodollar dollar denominated deposit in a bank or bank branch outside the United States. Deposits in an INTERNATIONAL BANKING FACILITY in the United States, permitted since 1981 for both domestic and foreign banks, and in Asian financial centers are also Eurodollars. However, the majority of Eurodollar deposits are still found outside the United States, primarily in London based banks, where there is an active secondary market for large Eurodollar deposits. Banks holding Eurodollar deposits also use them to make loans, denominated in dollars, to corporations, foreign governments and government agencies, domestic U.S. banks, and others.

Eurodollar certificate of deposit certificate of deposit issued by a U.S. bank branch located outside the United States. Virtually all Euro CDs are issued in London at rates pegged to the LONDON INTERBANK OFFERED RATE.

Euro feds overnight advances of Eurodollars between U.S. based banks, transmitted by FEDERAL WIRE. For a U.S. bank with insufficient reserves, borrowing in the Eurodollar market is an alternative to buying FEDERAL FUNDS. U.S. banks with excess reserves may find a Euro placement (a deposit of dollars in the Euromarket) more attractive than selling Fed funds. Consequently, the rate on overnight Euros closely tracks the Fed funds rate.

Euronote short-term unsecured promissory notes issued by high quality corporate, financial, or sovereign borrowers. An alternative to syndicated credit facilities, Euronotes have maturities of 7 to 365 days. The most active sector is notes of 30-to 180-day maturities. Typically, Euronotes are issued in bearer form and sold at discount. Euronotes are denominated in dollars or the EUROPEAN CURRENCY UNIT.

European currency unit (ECU) monetary unit created in 1979 by nine European nations to promote currency stability in the European Economic Community. The ECU consists of weighted amounts of the national currencies of members of the EUROPEAN MONETARY SYSTEM, an organization created in 1979 to fix the parity exchange value of European currencies. This has certain advantages to lenders, as ECU-based loans are protected from currency devaluations. The monetary value of ECUs in relation to other currencies is published in daily newspapers.

European Economic Community (EEC) economic union known informally as the Common Market, organized in 1957 by France, Italy, Luxembourg, the Netherlands, and West Germany, to foster economic cooperation among European nations. Trade barriers were gradually abolished and import duties standardized with non-EEC countries. In 1973, Great Britain, Ireland, and Denmark became members, followed by Greece, Spain, and Portugal in the 1980s. Also called the European Community. The agreement by EEC member countries to abolish trade barriers and EXCHANGE CONTROLS in currency movement between member countries by 1992 is a further extension of this process.

European Monetary System monetary arrangement of the European Economic Community (the Common Market) formed in 1979 to provide greater exchange rate stability, economic cooperation, and encouragement of internal trade and development in the European community. A key point involved the creation of a common unit of account, the EUROPEAN CURRENCY UNIT (ECU), made up from fixed amounts of each member's currency, plus the pound sterling, and a reserve fund containing 20% of each member's gold and dollar reserves—initially, Ireland, Belgium, Denmark, Italy, France, and West Germany— from which a central bank would borrow when it wanted to stabilize its currency by making purchases in the open market.

evergreen loan revolving line of credit with no CLEAN-UP REQUIREMENT requiring the borrower to pay off the outstanding balance periodically. Evergreen loans are generally made for specific terms, for example three years, and may be renewed or cancelled at the end of that period. Also, a de facto condition of short-term loans that are constantly renewed without a reduction in loan principal. See also BULLET LOAN; REVOLVING CREDIT.

exact interest deposit account interest calculated on a 365-day year, as opposed to a 360-day year, which is known as ORDINARY INTEREST. Banks use the 365-day basis in paying DAILY

INTEREST—interest from date of deposit to date of withdrawal on certificates of deposit and other time deposits. U.S. Treasury notes and bonds, and municipal bonds, earn exact interest.

exception item check that cannot be paid for one reason or another, such as a customer's STOP PAYMENT order, closed account, missing endorsement, and so on. Also, any item requiring special handling by the paying bank.

excess cash flow payments from loans or mortgages underlying mortgage backed bonds or other asset-backed bonds in excess of the amount needed to retire the bonds. This additional cash flow, from overcollateralization, mismatched coupons, prepayments, or reinvestment income, may be used toward bond redemption or passed to investors who purchased a residual interest in the securities.

excessive purchases credit card charges deviating from normal usage. Frequent use of a bank card in a 24-hour period is an alert to the possibility that a card has been stolen or is being used fraudulently.

excess loans loans exceeding the LEGAL LENDING LIMIT for loans to a single borrower. State banks are limited to making loans to a single borrower equal to 10% of their available capital, and national banks are limited to a 15% maximum. Bank directors may be held personally accountable for losses resulting from excessive loans. See also INSIDER LENDING.

excess reserves surplus balances above what banks are legally required to hold to meet RESERVE REQUIREMENTS. Excess reserves can be held as vault cash, reserve account balances in a Federal Reserve Bank, or in a pass-through account at a correspondent. Excess reserves in the banking system can result from weak loan demand or high interest rates and TIGHT MONEY by the Federal Reserve. Banks sell excess reserves to one another in the Federal Funds market.

exchange controls restrictions on currency flows between countries, imposed by central banks or monetary authorities. A country may: (1) prohibit residents from owning a bank account denominated in another currency or an account in a foreign bank; (2) prohibit exporters from drawing against a bank account except for internal transfers; and (3) limit bank trading in a domestic currency to discourage currency speculation. Exchange controls are common in some European countries and in most developing countries; a bank account in one of these currencies is known as a BLOCKED ACCOUNT. These currencies frequently are overvalued in relation to unimpeded currencies, and may not be CONVERTIBLE easily into other currencies or a monetary standard, such as gold. See also DIRTY FLOAT; RESTRICTED MARKET.

exchange rate conversion price for exchanging one currency for another. Exchange rates are influenced by a number of factors, including domestic interest rates and inflation rates, and whether central banks are attempting to influence the market price through INTERVENTION in the exchange markets.

Exchange Stabilization Fund currency reserve fund managed by the Federal Reserve Bank of New York, for the U.S. Treasury Department, to arrange interim financing for foreign governments and central banks. The Fed uses the Exchange Stabilization Fund to arrange currency swaps through the Federal Reserve SWAP NETWORK with other central banks.

ex-coupon see COUPON STRIPPING.

executor person or institution, often a trust company, named in a WILL to distribute the assets of a decedent. The executor assumes control of the assets of an estate, pays estate taxes, debts, and expenses.

exempt securities securities exempt from registration and reporting rules of the Securities and Exchange Commission, and also Federal Reserve margin requirements. U.S. Treasury securities, as well as federal agency issues, municipal bonds, commercial paper and private placements are exempt from these rules. Direct obligations of a bank or savings institution, for example, Ginnie Mae pass-through certificates, are exempt from SEC registration; but SEC registration is required if mortgage securities are issued through a subsidiary company.

exercise price dollar price at which a call option or put option is exercised. Also called STRIKE PRICE.

ex-legal denotes the absence of a legal opinion. Municipal bonds issued without the customary legal opinion of a bond counsel printed on the certificates, which may hinder the marketability of the bonds when they are traded.

exotic currency currency that is not traded easily; there is no depth to the market. Large institutions might assign trading in these currencies to one trader. See also WEAK CURRENCY.

expectations theory interest rate theory that says the anticipated YIELD on successive maturities of the same security is determined by investor expectations of future interest rates. An investor is said to be motivated by rational expectations when an investment decision is based on all available information. The expectations theory tries to explain the term structure of interest rates by saying that any combination of maturities produces roughly the same average yield. Investors willing to accept 6% on one-year certificates of deposit, anticipating next year's one-year rate will be 8%, expect the current rate on two-year CDs will be 7%, the average of the two rates (6% + 8% / 2 = 7%). Contrast with the MARKET SEGMENTATION THEORY. See also LIQUIDITY PREFERENCE THEORY.

Expedited Funds Availability Act federal law enacted by Congress in 1987 limiting CHECK HOLDs on checks deposited into a bank account, and requiring banks and other depository financial institutions to follow a uniform funds availability schedule in processing checks or drafts deposited into an account. Financial institutions must also inform their customers of the estimated clearing time for a check to become AVAILABLE FUNDS for spending or investment. Banks must disclose in writing the time needed for LOCAL CHECKs, or checks drawn on financial institutions serviced by the same Federal Reserve Regional Check Processing Center as the depositor's bank, and nonlocal checks drawn on more distant banks. Under the Expedited Funds Availability Act, the first $100 of a check is to be available for use at the opening of business the day after a deposit is made, remaining funds on the third day after the deposit if payable by a local bank, and within six days if drawn on more distant banks, as of September 1, 1990. Cash deposits, U.S. Treasury checks, official bank checks (cashier's checks, certified checks, and teller's checks), and checks paid by government agencies are also included in checks subject to next day availability. The act also imposed new rules for check ENDORSEMENTS, requiring depositors to endorse their names in a 1 1/2 inch space on the back side of checks. The Expedited Funds Availability Act is implemented by Federal Reserve Regulation CC.

expiration date

1. last date a bank CREDIT CARD can be used. The date is embossed on the card.
2. in options trading, the last date an options contract can be exercised. In American style options, options can be exercised any time during the option cycle; in European style options, they can be exercised only on the maturity date.

explicit pricing pricing system in which the customer is charged the exact cost of providing a bank service (cost-plus pricing) plus a markup for profit. Federal Reserve Banks are directed by the 1980 Monetary Control Act to price check collection and other reserve bank services at actual cost, plus a markup called the PRIVATE SECTOR ADJUSTMENT FACTOR to bring Fed pricing into line with what banks would charge for the same or similar services. In bank service pricing, explicit pricing is a bank charge for value added services, for example, a $1 transaction fee at an Automated Teller Machine (ATM) for access to a national ATM system. Contrast with RELATIONSHIP BANKING.

Export-Import Bank independent federal agency set up by Congress in 1934 to finance exports of U.S. products by making intermediate and long-term nonrecourse loans when financing is unavailable from private lenders. The Eximbank borrows from the Treasury Department to make direct credits and discount loans to foreign borrowers, and also provides credit guarantees and insurance against political risk. The bank competes with similar financing agencies in other industrialized nations. See also FOREIGN CREDIT INSURANCE ASSOCIATION.

export trading company (ETC) trading organization supplying support services required for export trade. An ETC may warehouse, ship, and insure goods, as well as supply clients with market information. U.S. commercial banks are permitted to own and operate export trading companies under the BANK EXPORT SERVICES ACT of 1982.

ex post monitoring after the fact measurement of credit advances for purposes of compliance with banking regulations. To qualify for an OVERDRAFT CAP; a bank must have a computerized monitoring system to control transfers of funds into and out of customer accounts.

exposure
1. total amount of credit committed to a single borrower, or to a single country if EXTERNAL DEBT is considered.
  2. in foreign exchange and futures market trading, the potential for suffering a gain or loss from fluctuations in market prices.
3. bank's risk of suffering a loss when it credits a customer's account before funds are collected from the payer. Called a DAYLIGHT OVERDRAFT in wire transfer systems.

express trust trust created by explicit instructions, given either orally or in writing, as opposed to a constructive trust created by a court of equity.

extended credit advance from a Federal Reserve Bank for a longer period than the customary ADJUSTMENT CREDIT arranged at a discount window. Extended credit is often for periods longer than 30 days, priced at a surcharge above the Fed's discount rate, it fills the needs of seasonal credit by small banks lacking direct access to money markets and credit to meet the liquidity needs of banks holding long-term fixed rate assets. See also EMERGENCY CREDIT; SEASONAL CREDIT.

extension agreement agreement by a lender to roll back the due date on a loan. Lenders are sometimes willing to do this when they believe a borrower's financial condition will eventually improve, and that extending the maturity is preferable to calling the loan. See also STANDSTILL AGREEMENT.

external debt

1. funds obtained from outside an organization, including bank loans and subordinated debt—a measure of financial leverage. In general, external debt is anything that is not equity capital such as common stock or preferred stock

2. total amount of bank debt owed by debtor nations to foreign lenders and creditor banks.

F

face value principal of a security, insurance policy, or unit of currency. In securities, the face value (or the PAR VALUE) and market value are usually different until maturity. That price difference is the premium or discount.

facilities management operation of a bank's data processing department by a third party, usually under multiyear contractual agreement. This relieves the bank of the burden of maintaining complex computer systems and competing with other firms for data processing professionals, and makes it easier for the bank to meet the regulator's requirements for EDP security.

facility fee lender's charge for making a line of credit or other credit facility available to a borrower, for example, a COMMITMENT FEE.

facsimile draft computer generated copy of an original sales draft. In a disputed credit card transaction, for example, a facsimile draft shows enough information—account number, signature, transaction amount—to validate a transaction

factoring short-term financing from the nonrecourse sale of accounts receivable to a third party, known as a factor. The factor assumes the full risk of collection, including credit losses. Factoring is most common in the garment industry, but has been used in other industries as well. There are two basic types of factoring: (1) discount factoring, in which the factor pays a discounted price for the receivables prior to the maturity date; and (2) maturity factoring, where the factor pays the client the purchase price of the factored accounts at maturity.

   Factoring can be on a notification, or a non-notification basis. The typical method in accounts receivable factoring is nonnotification financing, in which the client's debtors are not notified and the client remits payments to the factor as they are received. Factoring is normally done WITHOUT RECOURSE, meaning that the factor does the credit evaluation before credit is extended and assumes the risk of nonpayment. Financing carried out on a RECOURSE basis is called ACCOUNTS RECEIVABLE FINANCING. See also ASSET-BASED LENDING.

fail

1. **Banking:** The inability of a bank to meet its credit obligations to other banks in private wire transfer systems, possibly causing settlement failures at other banks. This is known as SYSTEMIC RISK.
2. **Securities:** A trade in which delivery does not take place on the settlement date. If it is the fault of the seller, that is, the seller fails to present the securities, the trade is noted as a fail to deliver. If the buyer fails to pay because securities have not been delivered by the seller's broker, it is a fail to receive. Fails normally occur when the buyer and seller disagree on whether the securities delivered meet the specifications of the purchase order.

Fair Credit Billing Act

federal act specifying procedures for resolution of billing disputes in consumer installment credit and credit cards. Enacted by Congress in 1974, the Fair Credit Billing Act amends the Truth-in-Lending Act by: (1) requiring lenders to correct billing errors within 90 days of receiving a consumer complaint; (2) prohibiting credit card issuers from offsetting an unpaid bill against a deposit account without obtaining a court order; and (3) limiting the cardholder's liability to a maximum of $50. Consumers must be given a statement of their credit rights. See also PROVISIONAL CREDIT; REGULATION Z.

Fair Credit Reporting Act

federal law enacted in 1970 to ensure confidentiality of consumer credit information held by lenders and credit reporting agencies. The act prohibits disclosure of credit files, other than for specific purposes, such as employment, insurance, and bona fide credit applications; requires credit bureaus to give consumers a copy of their credit report when requested; and specifies procedures whereby consumers can dispute any DEROGATORY INFORMATION in a credit report.

fair market value

price at which an asset passes from a willing seller to a willing buyer, each having access to all the relevant facts and acting freely—frequently the basis for tax assessments and judicial awards.

Fannie Mae see FEDERAL NATIONAL MORTGAGE ASSOCIATION.

Farm Credit System (FCS) nationwide cooperative system of banks and associations providing credit to farmers, agricultural concerns, and related businesses. The system is comprised of the Banks for Cooperatives, which makes loans to farmer-owned marketing, supply, and service cooperatives, and rural utilities; the Farm Credit Banks, which make short and intermediate term farm loans secured by real estate; and the Federal Farm Credit Banks Funding Corp., which acts as a conduit through which the FCS issues debt in the credit markets. The Farm Credit Banks were created by merger of the old Federal Intermediate Credit Banks, making intermediate term farm loans, and the Federal Land Banks. A new agency, the Federal Agricultural Mortgage Corporation (FARMER MAC) was established by the Agricultural Credit Act of 1987 to create a secondary market for farm credit. Bonds, notes, and other obligations issued by Farm System institutions, other than the FAC, are insured by the Farm Credit System Insurance Corporation. Another federal agency, the Farm Credit Financial Assistance Corporation, provides capital assistance by issuing government guaranteed bonds. The Farm Credit System, originally capitalized by the federal government, is now self-funding and owned by its member- borrowers.

Farmer Mac nickname for the Federal Agricultural Mortgage Corp., a quasi-government agency created by the Agricultural Credit Act of 1987 to guarantee farm loans up to $2.5 million sold to investors in the secondary market. Farmer Mac, a stock corporation owned by agricultural lenders, operates in much the same fashion as the Government National Mortgage Association (Ginnie Mae), by certifying private loan packagers who assemble pools of loans for resale and guaranteeing timely payment of principal and interest. Unlike Ginnie Mae passthrough securities, Farmer Mac securities are not exempt from SEC registration requirements.

Farmers Home Administration (FmHA) agency of the U.S. Department of Agriculture supplying loans, including operating loans, water conservation loans, and residential mortgages to farmers in rural areas. Farmers Home Administration loans are funded by annual appropriations by Congress, and by private lenders, whose loans are guaranteed up to 90% of principal and interest by the Farmers Home Administration.

Federal Advisory Council advisory group consisting of one member from each Federal Reserve District, usually a banker, selected annually by the board of directors in each of the 12 Fed districts. Members meet with the Federal Reserve Board at least four times a year to make recommendations on business and financial issues relating to banking, but have no real power.

Federal agencies interest-bearing debt securities of U.S. departments and agencies. Among these are the 12 Federal Home Loan Banks the Export-Import Bank, the Government National Mortgage Association, and the Federal Housing Authority. The Federal National Mortgage Association (Fannie Mae), which buys residential mortgages in the secondary market, is technically a quasi-federal agency as it is a publicly owned stock corporation.

Federal agencies lend directly to qualified borrowers or guarantee loans made by private lenders. Some agency securities are backed by the FULL FAITH AND CREDIT of the U.S. government, for example, Government National Mortgage Association pass-through securities and participation certificates, whereas Fannie Mae debentures are backed only by the issuer.

Federal Credit Union (FCU) consumer cooperative chartered by the National Credit Union Administration. Federal credit unions which hold the majority of credit union assets in the United States, originate a wide variety of consumer credit, from auto loans to residential mortgages at competitive rates. In 1984, the definition of membership in federal CUs was liberalized to include a member's immediate family, making federal CUs more competitive with other financial institutions.

Federal Deposit Insurance Corporation (FDIC) federal agency that manages the BANK INSURANCE FUND, insuring deposits in commercial banks, and the SAVINGS ASSOCIATION INSURANCE FUND, insuring deposits in savings and loan associations (S&Ls), up to $100,000 per account in interest and principal. Federal deposit insurance is mandatory for federally chartered banks and savings institutions. The FDIC has a five-member board of directors, including the chairman of the FDIC, the Comptroller of the Currency, the director of the Office of Thrift Supervision, and two members appointed by the President and confirmed by the Senate. The FDIC, acting as conservator or receiver for troubled banks, can repudiate contracts and borrow from the Federal Home Loan district banks. The FDIC is also manager of a separate fund, the FSLIC Resolution Fund, to manage the assets and liabilities of insolvent savings and loans taken over by the Federal Savings and Loan Insurance Corporation (FSLIC) prior to 1989. See also RESOLUTION TRUST CORPORATION.

Federal Financial Institutions Examination Council
interagency group of federal banking regulators formed in 1979 to maintain uniform standards for the federal examination and supervision of federally insured depository institutions, bank holding companies and savings and loan holding companies. Its members are: the Comptroller of the Currency, the chairman of the Federal Deposit Insurance Corporation, a member of the Board of Governors of the Federal Reserve System, the chairman of the Office of Thrift Supervision, and the chairman of the National Credit Union Administration. The council also produces the UNIFORM BANK PERFORMANCE REPORT.

Federal Financing Bank (FFB)
agency in the U.S. Treasury established by Congress in 1973 to centralize borrowing by federal agencies. Instead of selling securities directly to the financial markets, all but the largest federal agencies raise capital by borrowing from the U.S. Treasury, through the Federal Financing Bank. The FFB makes loans at favorable rates to agencies that do not have ready access to the credit markets; its debt is a direct obligation of the U.S. Treasury.

federal funds
unsecured advances of immediately available funds from excess balances in RESERVE ACCOUNTS held at Federal Reserve Banks. Technically, Fed Funds are not borrowings, but purchases of immediately available funds. A bank advancing Fed Funds sells excess reserves; a bank receiving Fed Funds buys excess reserves from the selling bank. Federal Funds sold are credit transactions on the account of the selling banks. Al-

though most Fed Funds sales are made on an overnight basis, some are negotiated for much longer periods as Term Fed Funds. Contrast with CLEARING HOUSE FUNDS. See also FEDERAL FUNDS RATE.

federal funds rate rate charged in the interbank market for purchases of EXCESS RESERVE balances. The rate of interest paid on overnight Fed Funds, the Fed Funds rate, is a key money market interest rate, and correlates with rates on other short-term credit arrangements. Because the Fed Funds rate reprices with each transaction, unlike the Federal Reserve DISCOUNT RATE, it is the most sensitive of the money market rates and is watched carefully by the Federal Reserve Board.

Federal Home Loan Bank Board (FHLBB) federal agency established by the Federal Home Loan Bank Act of 1932 to supervise a reserve credit system, the FEDERAL HOME LOAN BANK SYSTEM, for savings institutions. The Bank Board also acted as chartering agency and primary regulator of federal savings and loan associations, under the Home Owners Loan Act of 1933. The FINANCIAL INSTITUTIONS REFORM, RECOVERY AND ENFORCEMENT ACT of 1989 abolished the Federal Home Loan Bank Board, transferring its powers in examination and supervision of federally chartered savings institutions to a new agency, the OFFICE OF THRIFT SUPERVISION, a bureau of the U.S. Treasury Department. Regulatory oversight of the district Home Loan Banks was transferred to a five-member board, the FEDERAL HOUSING FINANCE BOARD. See also SAVINGS ASSOCIATION INSURANCE FUND.

Federal Home Loan Bank System system of 11 regional banks established by the Federal Home Loan Bank Act of 1932, acting as a central credit system for savings and loan institutions (S&Ls). The district Home Loan Banks make short-term credit advances to savings institutions, much like the Federal Reserve System acts as lender of last resort to commercial banks. Each Home Loan Bank operates independently, and has its own board of directors.

The FINANCIAL INSTITUTIONS REFORM, RECOVERY AND ENFORCEMENT ACT of 1989 restructured the Federal Home Loan Bank System, placing the district banks under supervision of a five-member board, the FEDERAL HOUSING FINANCE BOARD. The act also required district banks to establish an Affordable Housing Program to finance below-market mortgages to low income borrowers, designate a community investment office, and contribute a portion of their reserves to the retirement of long-term bonds issued by the RESOLUTION FUNDING CORPORATION, the federal agency financing the closing of insolvent S&Ls. Commercial banks and credit unions holding at least 10% of their assets in residential mortgages are also eligible for membership in the Federal Home Loan Bank System. Commercial banks are eligible for credit advances, but only for use in residential mortgage lending.

Federal Home Loan Mortgage Corporation (FHLMC) corporation, also known as Freddie Mac, authorized by Congress in 1970 as a SECONDARY MARKET conduit for residential mortgages. The Federal Home Loan Mortgage Corp. purchases loans from mortgage originators. It sells its own obligations and mortgage backed bonds issued by the GOVERNMENT NATIONAL MORTGAGE ASSOCIATION to private investors, namely bank trust funds, insurance companies, pension funds, and thrift institutions. The corporation's PARTICIPATION CERTIFICATES collateralized by mortgage loans are considered agency debt, even though they are not guaranteed by the U.S. government. Payment of principal and interest are guaranteed by the U.S. government. The Financial Institutions Reform, Recovery, and Enforcement Act (FIRREA) of 1989 restructured Freddie Mac as a quasi-public corporation with an 18-member board, 13 of whom are elected by shareholders and 5 appointed by the president. Stockholders are given voting rights by FIRREA and have the option of exchanging preferred stock for common stock. The act also exempted Freddie Mac from compliance with state Blue Sky Laws regulating the issuance of securities.

Federal Housing Administration (FHA) federal agency that insures residential mortgages. Created by the National Housing Act of 1934, the FHA is now a part of the Department of Housing and Urban Development. Both the FHA and the Department of Veterans Affairs have single family mortgage programs to assist home buyers that are unable to obtain financing from conventional mortgage lenders (banks, savings and loans and other financial institutions). Private lenders are the

sources of funds for FHA loans, but the FHA loans often have a rate ceiling below prevailing market rates. There are also limits on the loan amount the FHA will insure for a single borrower.

Federal Housing Finance Board (FHFB) independent federal agency regulating the credit advance activities of the 11 Federal Home Loan Banks. The board, established by the FIRREA of 1989, has five members, including the secretary of Housing and Urban Development, and four directors appointed by the president with Senate confirmation to serve seven-year terms. At least one director must represent the interests of community groups.

Federal Intermediate Credit Bank see FARM CREDIT SYSTEM.

Federal Land Bank see FARM CREDIT SYSTEM.

Federal National Mortgage Association (FNMA) federally chartered, stockholder owned corporation that purchases residential mortgages insured or guaranteed by federal agencies, as well as conventional mortgages, in the SECONDARY MORTGAGE MARKET. Also called Fannie Mae, the corporation raises capital to support its operations through collection of insurance and commitment fees, issuance of stock, and sale of debentures and notes. First established as a government agency in 1938, Fannie Mae became a private corporation in 1968. Fannie Mae guarantees timely payment of principal and interest on mortgage backed securities issued by the corporation.

Federal Open Market Committee (FOMC) policy committee in the Federal Reserve System that sets short-term MONETARY POLICY objectives for the Fed. The committee is made up from the seven governors of the Federal Reserve Board, plus the presidents of six Federal Reserve Banks. The president of the Federal Reserve Bank of New York is a permanent FOMC member. The other five slots are filled on a rotating basis by the presidents of the other 11 Federal Reserve Banks. The committee carries out monetary objectives by instructing the Open Market Desk at the Federal Reserve Bank of New York to buy or sell government securities from a special account, called the OPEN MARKET ACCOUNT, at the New York Fed. When the

FOMC purchases securities, it adds reserves to the banking system, expanding the supply of credit and allowing banks to make more loans; when it sells securities, it drains reserves and tightens credit.

The Federal Open Market Committee generally buys and sells securities, normally U.S. Treasury bills, for longer-term impact. For short-term adjustment of bank reserves, it will sell securities to a securities dealer with an agreement to repurchase (a MATCHED SALE REPURCHASE AGREEMENT), or buy securities from a dealer, followed by a subsequent resale back to the dealer (a REPURCHASE AGREEMENT). Open market operations are one of three monetary policy tools of the Federal Reserve; the others are the discount rate and reserve requirements on transaction and time deposit accounts. See also DISCOUNT WINDOW; OPEN MARKET OPERATIONS; REPURCHASE AGREEMENT; RESERVE REQUIREMENTS.

Federal Reserve Bank one of 12 regional banks in the FEDERAL RESERVE SYSTEM. These banks are located in Boston, New York, Philadelphia, Cleveland, Richmond, Atlanta, Chicago, St. Louis, Minneapolis, Kansas City, Dallas, and San Francisco. The role of each bank, and its branches, is to provide central bank services, such as check collection, access to the the Federal Reserve Wire Network (FEDERAL WIRE or Fed Wire) and credit advances at the Fed DISCOUNT WINDOW. In addition, Federal Reserve Banks establish monetary policy along with the Federal Reserve Board of Governors, and monitor commercial and savings banks to ensure that financial institutions follow Federal Reserve regulations. Reserve banks act as depositories for member banks in their regions. Each Federal Reserve Bank is owned by commercial banks in its Federal Reserve district that hold stock in the Fed district bank. These commercial banks are MEMBER BANKs in the Federal Reserve System. See also FEDERAL RESERVE BOARD; REGIONAL CHECK PROCESSING CENTER.

Federal Reserve Board (FRB) seven-member board governing the FEDERAL RESERVE SYSTEM. Its members are appointed by the president, subject to Senate confirmation, and serve 14-year terms. The board supervises the banking system by issuing regulations controlling the activities of bank holding STARTcompanies, and also issues regulations implementing federal laws regulating banking; holds a voting majority at meetings of the influential FEDERAL OPEN MARKET COMMITTEE, which exercises control over the supply of credit in the banking system; and sets RESERVE REQUIREMENTS for NATIONAL BANKS and state chartered banks that own stock in Federal Reserve Banks. See also FEDERAL RESERVE BANK.

Federal Reserve credit credit contributed to the banking system by Federal Reserve Banks. This is derived from a variety of sources (1) Reserve Bank discounts and advances at the DISCOUNT WINDOW, secured by bank endorsed business paper (discounts) or credit advances secured by government securities put up as collateral (advances); (2) Treasury and federal agency securities owned by reserve banks through OPEN MARKET OPERATIONS of the Federal Reserve System; and (3) additional sources of credit, including longer-term EXTENDED CREDIT to financial institutions having liquidity problems, and FEDERAL RESERVE FLOAT on checks presented to Reserve Banks for collection.

Reserve Banks exert more influence over lending by financial institutions through the actions of the FEDERAL OPEN MARKET COMMITTEE than the Fed DISCOUNT WINDOW loans. See also MONETARY BASE.

Federal Reserve float temporary credit to a bank's reserve account caused by the time lag in the collection of checks. Float is checkbook money on the books of both the paying bank and the depositing bank, in effect fictitious reserves created when a Federal Reserve Bank credits a DEFERRED AVAILABILITY check to a bank's Reserve Account at the Fed but before it has collected payment on the check from the paying bank.

Checks drawn on banks in cities with a Federal Reserve Bank or branch office are treated as IMMEDIATE CREDIT AVAILABILITY checks and no Fed float is created. Processing and transportation delays are the major causes of Fed float, the largest source of collection float in the U.S. banking system.

Federal Reserve note circulating currency issued by Federal Reserve Banks to meet the public's seasonal needs for money. Federal Reserve notes are non-interest bearing promissory notes issued in denominations of $1 to $100, and are official LEGAL TENDER for payment of debts. The notes are liabilities on the books of issuing reserve banks, identifiable by the letter code on the face of the notes: A for the Federal Reserve Bank of Boston, B for the Federal Reserve Bank of New York, and so on.

Federal Reserve regulations see REGULATION A through REGULATION CC.

Federal Reserve System central banking system in the United States, the "Fed," established by the Federal Reserve Act of 1913 and comprising the 12 district Federal Reserve Banks and their 24 branch offices, the Federal Reserve Board of Governors in Washington, D.C., the Federal Open Market Committee, the Federal Advisory Council, and member banks owning stock in one of the 12 Federal Reserve Banks. National banks are required by law to own stock in the Federal Reserve Bank in their region. State chartered banks have the option of becoming member banks, although only about 1,100 state chartered banks have done so.

As its name implies, the Federal Reserve System differs from European central banks in an important way: it is a federal central bank, with operational responsibilities shared by the Board of Governors and the 12 regional banks. The Federal Reserve System regulates the cost and availability of bank credit through MONETARY POLICY decisions of the Federal Open Market Committee; sets the DISCOUNT RATE banks pay when borrowing from a Federal Reserve Bank; approves interstate banking mergers; supervises bank holding companies, and oversees international banking operations through agreements with other central banks. See also FEDERAL RESERVE BANK; FEDERAL RESERVE BOARD; FEDERAL WIRE.

Federal Savings and Loan (S & L) Association
savings and loan association chartered and supervised by the OFFICE OF THRIFT SUPERVISION. Federal savings and loans (S & L) derive their funds mostly from consumer deposits and invest primarily in long-term residential mortgages. Congress authorized federally chartered savings institutions to serve the needs of home buyers under the Home Owners' Loan Act of 1933. Since the early 1980s, deregulation in the banking industry gave federal savings institutions the right to offer checking accounts and Negotiable Order of Withdrawal (NOW) accounts. The Garn-St Germain Act of 1982 allowed federal savings institutions to

make consumer loans, offer discount brokerage accounts, and invest up to 5% of assets in commercial loans. Even with these expanded powers, federal S&Ls are required to keep at least 70% of assets in residential mortgages or mortgage securities.

See also FEDERAL SAVINGS BANK; THRIFT INSTITUTION.

Federal Savings and Loan Insurance Corporation (FSLIC) federal agency established by Congress in 1934 to insure deposits in savings and loan associations and savings banks. During the 1980s, heavy losses by savings institutions depleted the reserves of the FSLIC, causing it to become insolvent. The FINANCIAL INSTITUTIONS REFORM, RECOVERY AND ENFORCEMENT ACT of 1989 transferred the assets and liabilities of the FSLIC to a new deposit insurance fund, the SAVINGS ASSOCIATION INSURANCE FUND, a deposit insurance fund operated by the Federal Deposit Insurance Corporation. See also RESOLUTION TRUST CORPORATION.

Federal Savings Bank (FSB) savings bank, chartered and supervised by the Office of Thrift Supervision. Federal savings banks, designated by the letters FSB in an institution's name, were authorized by a 1978 amendment to the Home Owners' Loan Act of 1933. Federal savings banks can put up to 10% of assets in commercial, business, or agricultural loans, and can be chartered as mutual or stockholder-owned institutions.

Federal Wire (FED WIRE) high-speed electronic communications network linking the Federal Reserve Board of Governors, the 12 Federal Reserve Banks and 24 branches, the U.S. Treasury Department, and other federal agencies. The Federal Reserve Wire Network, more commonly known as Fed Wire, is used by the Reserve Banks and the Treasury for large dollar time-sensitive payments, such as funds transfers between Reserve Banks, purchases or sales of FED FUNDS, transfers between correspondent banks, and sales of book entry form U.S. government securities.

Federal Reserve MEMBER BANKS and other depository financial institutions also have access to the Fed Wire network to their own account and in transferring funds on behalf of a customer, when timeliness and certainty of payment are important. The

Treasury Department and federal agencies make extensive use of the Fed Wire in collection of funds from Treasury TAX AND LOAN ACCOUNTS in commercial banks, and in disbursement of funds.

Fed Wire transfers are immediate transfers of funds, and are effective usually within minutes of the time a payment is initiated. They are guaranteed as final payments when the receiving financial institution is notified of the credit to its reserve account. See also AUTOMATED CLEARING HOUSE; CLEARING HOUSE INTERBANK PAYMENTS SYSTEM; SOCIETY FOR WORLDWIDE INTERBANK FINANCIAL TELECOMMUNICATIONS.

Fed funds see FEDERAL FUNDS.

Fed Wire see FEDERAL WIRE.

fee a charge for services performed.
1. **Banking.** A lender's charge for making credit available, for example, a COMMITMENT FEE or credit card annual fee. Also, charges for noncredit services, such as a trust department's allowance or commission.
2. **Estates.** An inheritable estate in land, usually referred to as a fee simple estate or freehold estate. A fee simple absolute is an estate to which the holder has unquestioned ownership, whereas a fee tail is inheritable only by a limited group of heirs.

fiat money paper money that is backed only by the issuing government's decree that it is acceptable as LEGAL TENDER currency. Its value stems from public confidence, rather than convertible into gold or other hard currency.

fidelity bond see BANKER'S BLANKET BOND.

fiduciary person or legal entity that administers investments for the benefit of others. A fiduciary is legally obligated to safeguard assets in trust in the best interests of those for whom it acts. State law, the Uniform Fiduciaries Act, controls what fiduciaries can or cannot do with entrusted assets.

field warehouse see WAREHOUSE.

fill or kill limit order indicating whether a specified security should be filled immediately or cancelled.

finality of payment guaranty of payment to the party receiving an electronic funds transfer. Also called *receiver guarantee*. Interbank payments over the Federal Reserve Wire Network (Fed Wire) are final and irrevocable when transmitted, and are credited to the receiving bank's reserve account at the time of the transaction. Fund transfers in private wire transfer networks, such as the Clearing House Interbank Payments System (CHIPS), and also AUTOMATED CLEARING HOUSE transfers, are final when the sending bank's reserve account is debited by the Fed. See also NET SETTLEMENT; SAME DAY FUNDS.

finance bill bill of exchange that, when accepted by a bank, becomes a source of short-term credit for working capital rather than import or export finance. Also called a *bankers' bill* or *working capital acceptance*. Finance bills, which usually have maturities longer than 60 days, are sometimes issued in tight money periods. They are subject to reserve requirements, unlike ordinary bankers' acceptances, and cannot be rediscounted at the Federal Reserve window.

finance charge borrower's total cost of credit, including loan interest, commitment fees, and prepaid interest, in a consumer loan. Under the Truth in Lending Act, the finance charge must be disclosed as the total dollar cost of credit. Contrast with ANNUAL PERCENTAGE RATE.

The finance charge does not include late payment fees, annual charges, such as a credit card annual fee, and credit insurance, except in situations where the lender requires insurance before a loan is made.

finance company financial intermediary, often affiliated with a holding company or a manufacturer, that makes loans to individuals or businesses. As a group, finance companies service several distinct segments of the financial services market. Captive finance companies owned by manufacturers finance their dealers' inventory and provide direct financing, sometimes at below-market rates, to consumers buying the manufacturer's goods. Sales finance companies purchase, at a discount, the installment sales contracts of retail merchants. Commercial finance companies, also known as commercial credit companies, make loans to wholesalers and manufacturers, secured by the assets of the business (ASSET-BASED LENDING), and engage in lease financing. Credit receivables of finance companies are the basis of many ASSET-BACKED SECURITIES that are traded in the capital markets as ordinary bonds and notes. Some diversified finance companies, such as General Electric Capital Corp., are among the largest financial intermediaries and are involved in all phases of credit, from private label credit for retailers to aircraft leasing.

Consumer finance companies, formerly known as small loan companies because they extended credit in loans as low as $500 to people who had trouble getting a bank loan, today offer many banking services, including Visa and MasterCard credit cards, home mortgages, and home equity credit. Some even accept federally insured consumer deposits through a NONBANK BANK, and operate full-fledged consumer banking networks that are virtually indistinguishable from commercial banks and savings institutions. Unlike banks, though, finance companies raise most of the funds needed for lending from sale of commercial paper and short-term debt in the capital markets, rather than directly from depositors. See also FACTORING; FINANCIAL INSTITUTION; INDUSTRIAL BANK.

finance lease fixed-term lease, usually noncancellable, used by businesses in financing capital equipment. The lessor's service is limited to financing the asset, whereas the lessee pays all other costs, including maintenance and taxes, and has the option of purchasing the asset at the end of the lease for a nominal price. Also called a *full-payout lease* because the lease is fully paid out (amortized) over its lifetime. Contrast with OPERATING LEASE.

Financial Accounting Standards Board (FASB) seven member independent board, based in Norwalk, Connecticut, that sets accounting rules for certified public accountants. Organized in 1973, its Statements of Financial Accounting Standards are the basis for GENERALLY ACCEPTED ACCOUNTING PRINCIPLES.

financial counseling see CREDIT COUNSELING; FINANCIAL PLANNING.

financial future FUTURES CONTRACT on a financial instrument, allowing the holder to take advantage of price movements in currencies and interest rates. Financial futures contracts are traded in U.S. Treasury bills, notes and bonds, and Government National Mortgage Association pass-through securities. Futures are used as a hedging device against changes in interest rates or for speculation.

There are several basic types of financial futures instruments: CURRENCY FUTURES, INTEREST RATE FUTURES, and stock index futures (for example, futures contracts based on the Standard & Poor's 500 index). Both parties make a good faith deposit to cover any changes in market premiums, instead of having the full premium paid by the option buyer to the seller.

financial guarantee noncancellable indemnity bond guaranteeing the timely payment of principal and interest due on securities by the maturity date. If the issuer defaults, the insurer will pay a fixed sum of money to holders of the securities. Financial guarantees are similar to a STANDBY LETTER OF CREDIT, but are issued by an insurance company. Financial guarantees are also written by banks allowed to stay in the insurance business by the Garn-St Germain Act of 1982, which prohibited banks from entering the business. While banks may or may not be allowed to write insurance guarantees directly, they can own shares of bond insurance companies. For example, Citicorp in New York owns American Municipal Bond Insurance Corp. Insurance companies selling bond insurance must be monoline underwriters, which eliminates direct ownership by property and casualty insurance companies. See also CREDIT ENHANCEMENT; MUNICIPAL BOND INSURANCE.

financial innovation payment system advances altering or modifying the role of banks, and financial institutions in general, as intermediaries between suppliers and users of funds. Technological innovations, such as ELECTRONIC FUNDS TRANSFER payments, replace checks with electronic debits and credits. Risk transferring innovations, such as ADJUSTABLE RATE MORTGAGES, transfer credit risk from one party to another. Credit generating innovations, for example, HOME EQUITY CREDIT lines, give borrowers new ways to use financial assets, increasing the supply of available credit. Equity generating innovations, such as MANDATORY CONVERTIBLE notes, give banks a less costly way to raise equity capital than issuing new shares of common stock.

financial institution government agency or privately owned entity that collects funds from the public, and from other institutions, and invests those funds in financial assets, such as loans, securities, bank deposits, and income generating property. Broadly defined, financial institutions act as intermediaries between saver and borrowers and are differentiated by the way they obtain and invest their funds. Depository financial institutions—a group that includes commercial banks, savings and loan associations, mutual savings banks, and credit unions— conduct business by accepting public deposits, which are insured by the federal government against loss, and channeling their depositors' money into lending activities. Nondepository financial institutions, such as brokerage firms, life insurance companies, pension funds, and investment companies, fund their investment activities directly from the financial markets by selling securities to the public or by selling insurance policies, in the case of insurance companies. Increasingly, the boundaries between depository and nondepository institutions have become less distinct. Brokerage firms can invest their customers' money in bank CDs, whereas banks and savings institutions offer securities brokerage and mutual funds.

Financial Institutions Reform, Recovery and Enforcement Act (FIRREA) federal legislation of 1989 providing government funds to insolvent savings and loan associations, and mandating sweeping changes in the examination and supervision of savings and loans. The act required savings and loans to adopt new capital standards; transferred the regulatory powers of the Federal Home Loan Bank Board to a new agency, the OFFICE OF THRIFT SUPERVISION, a bureau within the U.S. Treasury Department; and placed the 12 district Federal Home Loan Banks under control of an oversight board, the FEDERAL HOUSING FINANCE BOARD. The act also abolished the defunct Federal Savings and Loan Insurance Corporation (FSLIC).

Among its major provisions:

(1) established two new federal deposit insurance funds, the BANK INSURANCE FUND, insuring deposits in commercial banks, and the SAVINGS ASSOCIATION INSURANCE FUND, insuring deposits

in savings institutions, up to $100,000 per account. Both funds are to be managed by the Federal Deposit Insurance Corporation.

(2) authorized a new federal agency, the RESOLUTION FUNDING CORPORATION (REFCORP), to finance the liquidation of insolvent savings associations. Refcorp is to issue $30 billion in zero-coupon bonds with funds from the retained earnings of the Federal Home Loan Banks. An additional $20 billion to be used in closing insolvent thrifts will be raised directly by the U.S. Treasury Department through the sale of Treasury obligations.

(3) established a new federal agency, the RESOLUTION TRUST CORPORATION (RTC), to dispose of assets of failed savings associations. The RTC's activities as liquidator of defunct S&Ls will be financed by securities issued by the Resolution Funding Corporation, direct Treasury borrowings, and assessments on the district Federal Home Loan Banks.

(4) expanded the board of directors of the Federal Deposit Insurance Corporation from three to five members, including the director of the Office of Thrift Supervision, and two others appointed by the President and confirmed by the Senate.

(5) required savings and loans to meet minimum capital standards: tangible capital of 1.5% of total assets; "core capital," which is tangible capital plus supervisory goodwill acquired in a merger of a troubled savings institution; and RISK-BASED CAPITAL equal to 6.4% of risk-weighted assets (rising to 8% by January 1, 1993). Goodwill is excluded from inclusion in core capital after 1994.

(6) authorized a new insurance logo for savings and loans including the words "backed by the full faith and credit of the United States Government."

(7) required savings and loans to meet a new "qualified thrift lender" test of 70% of portfolio assets in residential mortgages or mortgage related securities by July 1, 1991.

(8) raised deposit insurance premiums paid by commercial banks to $1.50 per $1,000 in insured deposits and premiums paid by savings and loans to $2.30 per $1,000 by 1990 to recapitalize the federal deposit insurance funds.

(9) permitted commercial banks and savings and loans to acquire financially sound savings associations in other states.

(10) prohibited, with certain exceptions, state chartered savings associations from activities not permissible for savings institutions.

(11) banned, with certain exceptions, savings and loans from

converting from the Savings Association Insurance Fund to the Bank Insurance Fund for a five-year period ending in 1994.

(12) required savings associations to adhere to the same risk-based capital standards as national banks.

(13) required savings associations to adhere to the same lending limit in loans to a single borrower as national banks: a legal loan limit equal to 15% of capital in unsecured loans and 25% of capital in secured loans.

(14) required savings associations to divest their holdings in junk bonds by July 1, 1994, and generally follow the same investment guidelines as commercial banks. Junk bonds and direct investments of savings and loans must be held in separately capitalized subsidiaries.

(15) permitted the district Federal Home Loan Banks to accept commercial banks as member institutions and make credit advances to commercial banks with at least 10% of assets in residential mortgages.

(16) banned the use of brokered deposits by savings associations failing to meet minimum capital requirements.

(17) required the district Home Loan Banks to establish an Affordable Housing Program, and pledge a percentage of their retained earnings to mortgages to low income borrowers.

(18) banned tax breaks to acquirers of insolvent savings associations.

(19) directed the Treasury Department and the General Accounting Office to conduct studies of risk-based deposit insurance, market valuation accounting, and other matters.

(20) allowed commercial banks to market bank services directly to nonbank affiliates and bank-owned affiliates.

(21) restructured the Federal Home Loan Mortgage Corporation as a stockholder owned corporation with an 18-member board of directors. Holders of Freddie Mac preferred stock were authorized to exchange shares of preferred stock for voting common stock.

(22) amended the Home Mortgage Disclosure Act to require mortgage lenders to collect and report to their primary regulator data on mortgage activities by census tract.

(23) amended the Community Reinvestment Act to require federal banking regulators to disclose lender compliance annually on an A-B-C-D scale.

(24) directed that real estate appraisals comply with state certification and licensing standards.

(25) expanded the enforcement powers of banking regula-

tors, authorizing banking agencies to assess civil money penalties up to $1 million a day and criminal penalties up to $5 million a day, and added bank fraud to crimes covered under the Racketeer Influenced and Corrupt Organizations Act (RICO).

Financial Institutions Regulatory Act federal law enacted in 1978 that made several important changes in regulation and supervision of depository financial institutions. The act: (1) created the FEDERAL FINANCIAL INSTITUTIONS EXAMINATION COUNCIL to coordinate the supervisory activities of federal supervisory agencies; (2) authorized banking regulators to issue CEASE AND DESIST orders against officers and directors of financial institutions; (3) required banks to make loans to directors, officers, and major stockholders on the same terms as other borrowers; created a credit union CENTRAL LIQUIDITY FACILITY to meet short-term liquidity needs of insured credit unions; and (4) placed ELECTRONIC FUNDS TRANSFERS between financial institutions and consumers under federal regulation. See also ELECTRONIC FUNDS TRANSFER ACT.

financial intermediary financial institution, such as a commercial bank or savings and loan association, that accepts deposits from the public and makes loans to those needing credit. By acting as a middleman between cash surplus units in the economy (savers) and deficit spending units (borrowers), a financial intermediary makes it possible for borrowers to tap into the vast pool of wealth in federally insured deposits—accounting for more than half the financial assets held by all financial service companies—in banks and other depository financial institutions. The movement of capital from surplus units through financial institutions to deficit units seeking bank credit is an indirect form of financing known as intermediation—consumers are net suppliers of funds, whereas business and government are net borrowers. A bank gives its depositors a claim against itself, meaning that the depositor has recourse against the bank (and, if the bank fails, the deposit insurance fund protecting insured deposits), but has no claim against the borrower who takes out a bank loan. See also DISINTERMEDIATION.

financial leverage see LEVERAGE.

financial planning

1. **Banking.** Capital budgeting and profit planning carried out by a bank's senior management committee, with the aim of managing asset growth, net income, and expenses to meet specific objectives in future time periods. Financial planning is broader in scope than ASSET-LIABILITY MANAGEMENT, which is largely concerned with pricing interest sensitive deposits and bank loans and managing interest rate risk and liquidity risk. In a larger sense, bank financial planning is synonymous with strategic planning and market planning, both of which are concerned with setting specific targets for deposit growth, net income, and expected payback or return from new branch offices, automated teller machines, and other facilities. Through financial planning, a bank's senior management committee formulates plans for meeting competition from other financial services companies and sets objectives for profitability, growth in market share, types of customers to be served, and so on, all of which determine the future direction of the bank.

2. **Investments.** Financial counseling designed to help individuals make the best use of their financial assets and achieve specific economic objectives, such as adequate funding of a child's college education expenses, or post-retirement needs. Financial planning entails writing down objectives, setting up budgets, and periodically reviewing a plan. Many banks offer financial planning services to help private banking or retail customers select customized financial services suiting their individual needs, charging an hourly rate or a flat fee for writing a financial plan. Professional financial planners are certified by the College of Financial Planning, Denver, Colorado.

financial privacy consumer protections expressed in the Right to Financial Privacy Act of 1978. Depository institutions may give federal agencies access to financial account information in connection with a law enforcement action if the request is: (1) authorized by a consumer, or (2) obtained by formal written request, subpoena or search warrant. Banks are permitted to give financial information to government authorities in filing a lien, perfecting a security interest, proving claims in bankruptcy court, and handling consumer applications for federally guaranteed loans.

financial statement report summarizing the financial condition of an individual, partnership, or business organization. Statements that bank lenders use most often in making loans are the BALANCE SHEET (assets, liabilities, and net worth as of a certain date); the INCOME STATEMENT summarizing income and expenses; and a corporation statement of retained earnings or partnership's statement of capital accounts.

financial supermarket popular name for a company offering a market basket of financial services under one roof. Financial supermarkets, both depository financial institutions, such as banks and savings associations and nonbank brokerage firms, aim to provide their customers with one-stop-shopping. They offer a wide array of financial products, ranging from brokerage services and mutual funds to financial planning and banking services, plus asset-management accounts that combine related accounts in a single account having transaction capabilities much like a bank credit card. The financial supermarket became part of the banking industry's vocabulary in the early 1980s, when nonbanking financial companies, unrestricted by banking regulations, began offering financial services in competition with banks and thrifts.

Despite its marketing appeal, one stop financial shopping can be a costly venture for financial institutions that plan to offer one-stop-shopping to the general public. Financial supermarkets have to balance their desire for more of the public's business against consumers' reluctance to put all of their eggs, financially speaking, in one basket.

financing statement document filed with a lender detailing personal property taken as collateral from a borrower. Also called the UCC-1 statement. The financing statement, a standard document under the UNIFORM COMMERCIAL CODE, is filed with the secretary of state or other designated public official. The document is time stamped, the filing date is noted, and a file number is assigned, securing the lender's claim to the assigned collateral. See also CONTINUATION STATEMENT; PRIORITY OF LIEN.

finder's fee

1. fee paid by a lender to a broker, or sometimes by a borrower to a broker, for obtaining a loan, usually a mortgage, or for referring business to a lender.
2. fee paid by a lender to a third party, and sometimes to a bank's own customers, for referring new business.
3. in real estate, a commission paid to a broker for locating a property.

firm commitment

Banking:

1. lender's agreement to fund a commercial loan, installment loan, or mortgage loan at a quoted rate for a specific period of time. Called a LOCK-IN PERIOD in mortgage lending. A COMMITMENT FEE is often required; is usually forfeited if the borrower does not take the loan.
2. in the secondary mortgage market, a lender's agreement to sell loans to a buyer in a specific future time period. Secondary market conduits, such as the Federal National Mortgage Association or the Federal Home Loan Mortgage Corporation, buy loans with a 60- to 120-day forward delivery. See also GOING LONG; GOING SHORT.

Securities: securities offering in which the underwriters assume all the risk, as opposed to a BEST EFFORT deal in which the underwriter acts as agent for the issuer.

first call date earliest date the issuer of a municipal or corporate bond may redeem all or part of the issue at a price specified in the indenture. The first exercisable call date is noted in the bond offering sheets. Mortgage backed bonds may become callable if original principal falls to a certain level, even if no call date is given. The issue may also be called early if a percentage of the amount raised, say 80%, is not reinvested in mortgages within a two-year period. The purpose is to keep tax-exempt mortgage financings from being classified as arbitrage deals, and losing the tax exemption on interest. See also YIELD TO CALL; YIELD TO MATURITY.

first day notice first date on which a seller in the futures market notifies a clearing house of his intention to deliver a financial instrument, in fulfilment of a futures contract. Also, the date on which a clearing house notifies a buyer.

first mortgage mortgage creating a primary lien against real property, and having priority over subsequent mortgages, which are known as junior mortgages. It is the first to be paid when the property is sold. See also HOME EQUITY LOAN; SECOND MORTGAGE.

fiscal agent

1. bank or trust company named to handle collection and disbursement of trade related payments, and pay stock dividends and bond interest payments to holders of securities. Every federal agency, for example, the Federal National Mortgage Association or the Government National Mortgage Association, has a fiscal agent to handle its financial arrangements when it issues debt securities.

2. financial institution named to collect tax revenues and remit payments to vendors for a national, state, or municipal government. For example, the Federal Reserve Banks act as fiscal agents for the U.S. Treasury Department.

fiscal policy taxation and spending policies of the federal government. Fiscal policy is carried out by adjusting budgetary deficits (or surpluses) to achieve desired economic goals. When federal expenditures grow at a faster rate than tax revenues, the U.S. Treasury raises additional funds by borrowing in the capital markets. When tax revenues exceed federal spending, surplus funds can be used to reduce the national debt. In practice, Congress has found it difficult to adjust the federal budget to balance revenues and expenditures. The Gramm-Rudman-Hollings Deficit Reduction Act of 1985 sets annual targets for reducing the size of the federal deficit and has automatic spending cuts if deficit reductions are not achieved. The federal budget itself is more of a legislative process than a single budget, and is not signed into law by the President. What the Congress approves each year is a concurrent budget resolution, providing funding for various federal programs, and is actually made up from separate budgets passed by many Congressional committees.

Fiscal policy is administered independently of the Federal Reserve System's MONETARY POLICY, although the two have similar goals—balanced economic growth and stable employment at low rates of inflation—and together exert considerable influence over the demand for bank credit and pricing of bank loans. Deficit spending by the federal government must be financed through periodic borrowings in the public debt market by the Treasury Department. These auctions of new Treasury debt are closely watched by the Federal Reserve, and by the financial markets in general. See also CROWDING OUT; KEYNESIAN ECONOMICS; MONETARY ACCORD OF 1951; SUPPLY SIDE ECONOMICS.

fiscal year any 12-month period or period of 52 weeks, designated by a corporation, government agency, or any other organization as the time period for filing financial reports, balance sheets, and income statements. This period may differ from the calender year.

five c's of credit judgmental method of evaluating a potential borrower's creditworthiness, based on five criteria: character, capacity, capital, collateral and conditions. The first four deal with a borrower's ABILITY TO PAY, whereas the last point refers to general business conditions in the borrower's industry.

fixed asset tangible property used in the operation of a business. Fixed assets are stated on the balance sheet by their net depreciated value. Plant, machinery and equipment, furniture and fixtures, and leasehold improvements are the fixed assets of most companies.

fixed exchange rates FOREIGN EXCHANGE rate system that existed under the BRETTON WOODS SYSTEM, in which the value of national currencies is set vis-a-vis the value of other currencies. Also called *pegged exchange rates*. Each country is required to maintain its currency at or near this fixed rate. Fixed exchange rates, established at the Bretton Woods International Monetary Conference of 1944, were used until the early 1970s, when the United States abandoned the gold standard and a system of FLOATING EXCHANGE RATE was adopted. A modified form of fixed exchange currency rates continues today in the European Monetary System SNAKE, a monetary system adopted in the 1970s to hold currency fluctuations to a band of exchange rates with upper and lower limits. See also EUROPEAN CURRENCY UNIT; SMITHSONIAN AGREEMENT.

fixed rate loan loan with an interest rate that does not vary over the term of the loan, as opposed to a variable rate loan or ADJUSTABLE RATE MORTGAGE. Fixed rate loans generally are constant payment, fully-amortizing loans, for example, a 30-year fixed rate mortgage repayable through equal monthly payments of principal and interest. Many consumer installment loans, such as auto loans, boat loans, and home improvement loans, are made at fixed rates. Fixed rate loans often have a higher initial cost than adjustable rate loans because the lender isn't protected against increases in money costs—the lender's cost of funds—but the borrower has the comfort of knowing the rate and payment will not vary over the life of the loan.

flat

1. bond traded without accrued interest. This happens if the transaction settlement date is the same as the semiannual interest payment date. Income bonds issued by companies in reorganization—interest is paid only if earned—and bonds in default usually are traded flat.
2. market maker's position that is neither short nor long at the end of a trading session. The net exposure is zero.
3. underwriter's position if all securities are sold from inventory.
4. in the foreign exchange market, broker's position in which commitments to buy a particular currency are identical to commitments to sell that currency. Also called a SQUARE POSITION.

flat bed imprinter manual device that copies the embossed characters of a bank card or charge card on all copies of a sales draft. These are used most often by smaller merchants with low sales volume. See also POINT-OF-SALE TERMINAL.

flexible rate mortgage see ADJUSTABLE RATE MORTGAGE.

float dollar value of cash balances created by the time lag in processing unpaid checks. Collection float is interest that may be lost to the depositor; payment float is interest that may be gained by the payer. The largest component of float is FEDERAL RESERVE FLOAT, created when a Federal Reserve Bank credits the reserve account of a collecting bank before it has collected from the paying bank. Other kinds of float are MAIL FLOAT, caused by delays in mail handling betweeen cities; holiday float created when a bank is not open for business due to a state or national holiday; and return item float, created when checks are returned for insufficient funds or other reasons. At greater distances between paying and receiving banks, bank clearing float tends to increase, although federal legislation enacted in 1987 requires banks to adhere to uniform funds availability on out-of-town checks, which will give banks an incentive to hold clearing float at a minimum. A bank customer's AVERAGE DAILY FLOAT is often calculated for purposes of ACCOUNT ANALYSIS. See also AVAILABLE BALANCE; REGULATION CC.

floater debt instrument with a variable coupon, paying a rate indexed to a money market rate. For example, a floating rate tranche in a Collateralized Mortgage Obligation pays a coupon rate usually tied to the three-month or six-month London Interbank Offered Rate (LIBOR). Floating rate obligations have also been indexed to U.S. Treasury bill rates. Many floating rate consumer loans, for example, Adjustable Rate Mortgages, have been tied to a cost of funds index, such as the 11th District Federal Home Loan Bank Index, reflecting the cost of money for savings associations. See also FLOATING RATE NOTE.

floating debt one-year to five-year municipal notes issued to meet short-term financing needs, for example, Revenue Anticipation Notes and Tax Anticipation Notes. Municipal obligations that have been rolled into longer-term bonds are known as *funded debt*.

floating exchange rate EXCHANGE RATE system in which rates of each national currency are determined by interaction of market supply and demand. Factors affecting demand and supply of each currency include a country's CURRENT ACCOUNT balance, the general strength of its economy, its rate of INFLATION, and interest rates as compared against other nations.

In the years since 1971 when the United States finally abandoned the fixed exchange rate system and convertibility of the dollar into gold, most world currencies have traded at floating, or flexible, exchange rates. A downside to the floating exchange rate system is that central banks have to intervene in the markets from time to time, by buying or selling currencies to keep exchange rates from getting too high or too low. CLEAN FLOAT currency has a minimum of official intervention, except to maintain market stability, and its exchange rate is mostly determined by market demand. DIRTY FLOAT, on the other hand, denotes a varying amount of official INTERVENTION to keep a nation's currency within a desired range of currency prices in relation to other currencies. See also CONVERTIBILITY; EXCHANGE CONTROLS; FIXED EXCHANGE RATES.

floating interest rate loan interest rate that changes whenever an index rate, or BASE RATE, such as the bank PRIME RATE, the LONDON INTERBANK OFFERED RATE (LIBOR) or Federal Home Loan Bank index rate changes. There are numerous examples: (1) consumer loan rate, for example, the rate charged on adjustable rate mortgages or variable rate auto loans, that is indexed to another rate, such as the commercial bank prime rate, a COST OF FUNDS INDEX, or a lender's internal cost of funds; (2) key lending rate, such as the PRIME RATE that moves upward or downward, depending on market demand for funds, available reserves in the banking system, and other factors. Contrast with FIXED RATE LOAN.

floating lien loan or credit facility secured by inventory or receivables. This type of security agreement gives the lender an interest in assets acquired by the borrower after the agreement, as well as those owned when the agreement was made. When the agreement covers proceeds from sales, the lender also has recourse against receivables. See also BORROWING BASE; INVENTORY FINANCING.

floating rate certificate of deposit large dollar certificate of deposit (CD) paying a rate tied to a money market rate. Commonly used in the Euromarket to finance interbank lending, floating rate CDs or floaters are usually denominated in units of $250,000 with a coupon rate tied to the six-month London Interbank Offered Rate (LIBOR).

floating rate loan see VARIABLE RATE LOAN.

floating rate note (FRN) variable rate bonds with an interest rate that is periodically reset, usually every three to six months, and that carry a fixed spread, usually over the six-month London Interbank Offered Rate (LIBOR). Floating rate notes, also called FLOATERS, have been an important source of medium-term international credit for commercial banks active in

Euromarket lending. Competition in the Euromarket has led to a wide variety of notes: a perpetual floating rate note is a variable rate note with no stated maturity; a capped floating rate note sets an upper limit on the borrower's interest rate; and a mini-max FRN carries a rate that can fluctuate only within a preset range. Floating rate notes are usually subordinated to the claims of the depositors, and usually count toward a bank's capital base.

flood insurance federally subsidized hazard insurance protecting home owners against property damage from flooding. Coverage is mandatory when lenders make federally insured or guaranteed mortgages to home buyers purchasing property in designated flood hazard areas. Flood insurance coverage, obtained from private insurers, is available only to residents of communities participating in the National Flood Insurance Program, administered by the Federal Emergency Management Agency.

floor minimum rate that a bank can impose on a floating rate or variable rate loan. A floor rate is often negotiated together with a rate ceiling, called an INTEREST RATE CAP; the two financial guarantees are collectively referred to as an interest rate COLLAR. The floor protects the lender from a sharp drop-off in rates; the cap assures the borrower that financing costs will not rise excessively.

floor limit largest credit card a retail merchant may accept without obtaining authorization by the card issuer. Contrast with ZERO-FLOOR LIMIT.

floor loan initial funding of a CONSTRUCTION MORTGAGE that a lender agrees to advance without regard for tenant leasing, or requiring the builder to substantially complete the project and have a certificate of occupancy. For example, the lender may fund 80% of the total cost of a project, with the remainder, called a HOLDBACK, held aside until the builder has leased the majority of units or has the building ready for occupancy. A floor to ceiling loan, in contrast, has two separate fundings: one at satisfactory completion of the project, and a second funding when the building is fully occupied or meets cash flow requirements set by the lender.

floor planning bank loan made to finance a dealer's inventory. The dealer issues a TRUST RECEIPT to the bank, and the bank is repaid when the inventory is sold. Floor planning has a lower profit margin and is less desirable than other forms of commercial lending. In addition to bearing the financing risk, the bank stands to lose money if the dealer makes a sale without notifying the lender, known as *selling out of trust*. Dealer financing is usually done only on goods for which broad consumer demand exists.

flow of funds

1. economic report showing movement of funds between funds surplus and funds deficit sectors of the economy—households, businesses, governments, and financial institutions—reported monthly by the Federal Reserve Board in the Federal Reserve Bulletin. A periodic summary, the "Flow of Funds Accounts" report, is issued quarterly.
2. statement in the bond resolution of a municipal bond issuer stating how municipal revenues are to be applied, generally giving priority to maintenance and operations, and bond debt service.

footings expression for the bottom line figure on a bank's balance sheet: total assets or liabilities, plus equity capital.

forbearance

1. lender's decision not to exercise a legally enforceable right against a borrower in default, in exchange for a promise to make regular payments in the future. For example, a mortgage lender will agree not to initiate foreclosure proceedings against a mortgagor whose loan is in arrears.
2. temporary relief granted a bank by a regulatory agency from compliance with minimum capital requirements or other banking regulations, extended to financial institutions in economically depressed areas. Banks given capital forbearance must file a plan to restore their capital base within a specified period.

forecasting

1. in ASSET-LIABILITY MANAGEMENT, an estimate of future expectations based on historical information, current and projected market conditions, and management assumptions

about interest rates and market demand for credit. As used in an asset-liability model, forecasting is a planning tool that estimates the amount of interest earning assets and interest sensitive liabilities to try to determine whether the balance sheet will be asset sensitive or liability sensitive during specific time periods in the future. The forecast is normally revised periodically as market conditions or management assumptions change. See also DYNAMIC GAP.

2. in corporate CASH MANAGEMENT, an estimate of future cash receipts from conversion of assets into cash. Forecasting tries to anticipate changes in cash flow for purposes of funds management and debt management.

3. projecting corporate earnings, financial institutions, sales, and so on in future time periods. See also ECONOMETRICS.

foreclosure legal proceeding initiated by a creditor to take possession of collateral securing a defaulted loan. Some states allow lenders to reclaim property by simply declaring the borrower has defaulted, a process known as *strict foreclosure*. Most states, though, require lenders to file a foreclosure suit and obtain a judgment before seizing and auctioning off a borrower's property. Proceeds from a foreclosure sale are applied first to pay off the mortgage debt and foreclosure expenses, with the remainder, if any, going to the borrower. A borrower in default has the legal right, in most states, to redeem his property, called the RIGHT OF REDEMPTION, by paying the lender the balance of the outstanding debt, plus out-of-pocket expenses.

foreign branches branches of U.S. banks in foreign countries or branches of foreign banks in the United States. By reciprocal agreement among central banks, foreign branches are subject to the banking laws and regulations in their host country. The International Banking Act of 1978, for example, requires U.S. offices of foreign banks to maintain reserve accounts with a Federal Reserve Bank, choose a home state as their U.S. base of operations, and comply with the provisions of the BANK HOLDING COMPANY ACT of 1956 and the DOUGLAS AMENDMENT to the 1956 act dealing with interstate banking. This means that U.S. offices of foreign banks are subject to the same limitations on interstate expansion as U.S. banks. The International Banking Act did, however, contain a generous grandfather clause allowing non-U.S. banks to keep their existing multistate branches networks.

foreign corporation legal term for a corporation chartered in a state other than the one where it does business. A bank chartered in New York, but owning a loan production office in California, is a foreign corporation in California. The less confusing designation, *out-of-state corporation*, is preferred in general usage. Contrast with ALIEN CORPORATION.

Foreign Credit Insurance Association (FCIA) voluntary association of some 50 U.S. insurance companies formed in 1961 under the sponsorship of the EXPORT-IMPORT BANK. Acting as agent for the EximBank and its member companies, it provides insurance coverage for credits extended by U.S. exporters to foreign purchasers. FCIA provides some degree of insurance for commercial risk, whereas EximBank assumes coverage for political risk.

foreign currency futures see CURRENCY FUTURES

foreign currency options see CURRENCY OPTIONS.

foreign currency translation see CURRENCY TRANSLATION.

foreign deposits deposits at branch offices of domestic banks outside the United States or its overseas territories. Such deposits are not subject to deposit insurance premiums or reserve requirements, and are not included in computing the net demand deposits of domestic banks. This freedom from bank regulation was one reason the INTERNATIONAL BANKING FACILITY was authorized by state governments—mostly in New York and California—to create a domestic environment competitive with the relatively unrestricted Bahamas and Cayman islands Offshore Banking Centers.

foreign exchange currency—literally foreign money—used in settlement of international trade between countries. Trading in foreign exchange is the means by which values are established for commodities and manufactured goods imported or exported between countries. Creditors and borrowers settle the resulting international trade obligations, such as bank drafts, bills of exchange, bankers' acceptances, and letters of credit, by exchanging different currencies at agreed upon rates.

FOREIGN EXCHANGE VALUE DATES

TODAY (Transaction Date)	TOMORROW	NEXT DAY	BEYOND TWO DAYS
Cash delivery date (U.S. dollar, Canadian dollar, Mexican peso)	Spot date for Canadian dollar tomorrow / next	Spot delivery date Tomorrow / next delivery date	Forward delivery date

The result of all this international trade is that financial institutions accumulate surpluses of different currencies from loan repayments by foreign borrowers, and also from import-export trade financing on behalf of bank customers.

The interbank foreign exchange market is an over-the-counter market, a network of commercial banks, central banks, brokers, and customers who communicate with each other by telex and telephone throughout the world's major financial centers. Foreign exchange traders also make markets or speculate in different currencies, usually anticipating future appreciation of stronger currencies against weaker ones, through the foreign exchange FORWARD MARKET and the CURRENCY FUTURES market.

See also FORWARD EXCHANGE CONTRACT; FORWARD FORWARD.

foreign items check drawn on any bank other than the bank where it is presented for payment. Also called TRANSIT ITEMS.

forgery alteration of a document or negotiable instrument with intent to defraud; signing another's signature to a document with intent to defraud. See also ALTERED CHECK; RAISED CHECK.

forint national currency of Hungary.

Form 8K report disclosing significant events potentially affecting a corporation's financial condition or the market value of its shares, required by the Securities and Exchange Commission. The report is filed within 30 days after the event (a pending merger, an amendment to the corporate charter, a charge to earnings for loan losses) took place, and summarizes information that any reasonable investor would want to know before buying or selling securities.

Form 10K annual financial report filed with the Securities and Exchange Commission. Issuers of registered securities are required to file a 10K, as well as corporations with 500 or more shareholders, assets of $2 million, and exchange listed corporations. The report, which becomes public information once filed with the SEC, summarizes key financial infomation, including sources and uses of funds by type of business, net pre-tax operating income, provision for income taxes and loan losses, plus comparative financial statements for the last two fiscal years. A summary of the 10K report is included in the annual report to stockholders.

Form 1099 Internal Revenue Service form disclosing interest dividends earned by time deposit savings accounts, escrow accounts, and other interest-bearing deposits during a calendar year. Banks and other organizations paying interest or dividends are required by law to mail a 1099 form to all customers with interest-earning deposits early in a new year for income tax reporting.

Form 10Q quarterly financial report filed by companies with listed securities and corporations required to file an annual 10K report with the Securities and Exchange Commission. The 10Q report, which does not have to be audited, summarizes key financial data on earnings and expenses, and compares current financial information to data reported in the same quarter in the previous year.

forward book total of a foreign exchange dealer's forward contracts in various maturities for a given currency or for all currencies.

forward commitment agreement by a lender to make a loan at a quoted rate, purchase a loan from another lender, or sell a loan to a secondary market CONDUIT in the future. The commitment, spelled out in a binding contract, may expire if unexercised by a certain date. See also LOCK-IN PERIOD.

forward delivery

1. agreement between two parties whereby currency or other financial instruments are exchanged at a specified future date beyond the SPOT settlement date.
2. agreement by a mortgage originating bank to deliver mortgages at a specific future date, for example, 30, 60, or 120 days, to a secondary market purchaser. Also called *deferred delivery*.

forward discount price for future delivery of a currency that is lower than the SPOT price for immediate delivery. For example, if a dealer is quoting $1.7510 and $1.7520 (BID AND ASKED) for current delivery of British pound sterling, and the discounts for six months' forward delivery are .0040 and .0030, the forward quotes would be adjusted to $1.7470 and 1.7490. The forward discount normally adjusts for the difference in interest rates between two countries, but also can indicate market expectation of a lower price.

forward exchange contract agreement between two parties to exchange one currency for another at a forward or future date. Forward contracts call for delivery on a date beyond the SPOT contract settlement, which ordinarily takes place within ten days of the transaction date. Unlike a futures contract, forward contracts do not take place on regulated exchanges and do not involve delivery of standard currency amounts. They are cancellable only with consent of the other party to a trade. A forward contract allows a bank, or a bank's customer, to arrange for delivery (or sale) of a specific amount of currency on a specified future date, at the current market price. This protects the buyer against the risk of fluctuating rates when acquiring foreign exchange needed to meet future obligations.

forward exchange rate price quoted for delivery of a currency beyond the SPOT delivery date, or delivery in two business days. The forward rate may be quoted with a discount (FOR-

WARD DISCOUNT) or with a premium (FORWARD PREMIUM), depending on interest rates, market demand, and so on, or as an OUTRIGHT FORWARD transaction without an offsetting purchase or sale in the SPOT MARKET.

forward forward forward market contract where the dealer takes two different forward positions at opposite sides of the market. For example, a purchase of three-month dollars and simultaneous sale of six-month dollars in the foreign exchange market.

forward margin see FORWARD DISCOUNT; FORWARD PREMIUM.

forward market market where dealers agree to deliver currency, commodities, or financial instruments at a fixed price at a specified future date. Most forward contracts are made for delivery at specific future dates, for example, one week from the transaction date, one month, and so on. Longer term contracts are more speculative in nature, and are substantially more risky. See also ROLLOVER; SPOT NEXT; TOMORROW NEXT.

forward premium price for future delivery of a currency or a financial instrument that is higher than the immediate delivery price, or SPOT market price. A dealer quoting $1.7110 and $1.7120 (bid and asked) for British pound sterling and the premiums for six months forward delivery are .0025 and .0030, respectively, the bid and asked prices would be adjusted to $1.7135 and $1.7150. See also FORWARD DISCOUNT.

forward rate agreement (FRA) contract by which two parties agree on the interest rate to be paid at a future settlement date. The contract period is quoted as, for example, six against nine months, the interest rate for a three-month period commencing in six-months time. The principal amounts are agreed, but never exchanged, and the contracts are settled in cash; exposure is limited to the difference in interest rates between the agreed and actual rates at settlement.

forward spread price difference between SPOT price and one-month FORWARD RATE. Say the spot rate is $1 = 1.6510 DM, and the one-month forward rate is $1 = 1.6460. The difference, or .0050, is the forward spread.

401(k) plan employee savings plan that allows an employee to contribute pretax dollars to an investment pool managed by his employer. Also known as a *salary reduction plan*. An employee can contribute up to 10% of gross salary, up to $7,000 a year, adjusted annually for inflation. Employers often match individual contributions up to a certain dollar amount. Federal income taxes are deferred until an employee retires, or leaves a sponsoring company and loses eligibility. Under IRS rules, an individual must begin withdrawals from a qualified 401(k) between ages 59½ and 70½, and when leaving a qualified plan, and reinvest the account within 60 days in a rollover Individual Retirement Account or other tax qualified plan to avoid paying a tax penalty. Investors can put 401(k) assets in bank certificates of deposit, mutual funds, stocks, bonds, etc.

fractional reserves proportion of bank deposits that must be kept as LEGAL RESERVES. Bank reserves are a tool of central bank monetary policy; an increase in the ratio of required reserves to deposits indicates a tightening in credit policy by the Federal Reserve. Large banks are required to keep up to 12% of checking account deposits in a noninterest earning account at the Fed. Smaller banks have lower reserve requirements. The *multiplier effect* of money allows a bank to re-lend most (88¢ of $1 in deposits, at a 12% reserve requirement) of the funds in new deposits, in effect, creating new deposits. Because only a portion of deposits are backed by reserves, banks can suffer losses, or even fail, due to a sudden runoff of deposits, as in a BANK RUN. This risk is known as LIQUIDITY RISK. See also BANK RESERVES; MONEY MULTIPLIER.

franc national currency of Belgium, France, and Switzerland.

fraud intentional deception resulting in injury to another, as when a person makes false statements, conceals or omits material facts. A false statement is fraudulent if it is made knowingly, without believing it to be true, or carelessly stated, without regard for the truth. Persons suffering a loss from a fraudulent transaction have legal recourse under the UNIFORM COMMERCIAL CODE only if the contract is a written agreement, is valued at $500 or more, and is signed by the person owing the money or his agent. Legal protections against consumer credit fraud, for example, credit card fraud, are enforceable under federal and state laws. See also STATUTE OF FRAUDS.

Freddie Mac see FEDERAL HOME LOAN MORTGAGE CORPORATION.

free balance see MINIMUM BALANCE.

freehold legal estate in land, giving the owner the right to hold the property for life, passing it down to his or her legal heirs. There are three types of freehold estates: LIFE ESTATE, an estate limited to the life of the holder; fee simple, an estate without any restrictions; and fee tail, an estate inherited by the donor's direct descendents. Contrast with LEASEHOLD.

free period in credit cards, the time interval in which interest is charged for current purchases. This period usually runs anywhere from 10 to 25 days after the billing date. Also called GRACE PERIOD or *days of grace*.

free reserves funds available to banks for lending or investment, widely regarded as an indicator of available BANK CREDIT. Excess reserves are the amount remaining after required reserves are subtracted from reserve balances deposited with a Federal Reserve Bank. The total of free reserves is computed by subtracting from a bank's EXCESS RESERVES (or reserve account balances above its reserve requirements) any borrowings from the Federal Reserve.

front-end load

1. mutual fund that charges the investor an above normal management fee, called a LOAD in the mutual fund industry, at the time an investment is made to cover servicing costs over the life of the investment. Front-end fees also apply to certain annuities and other investments. Contrast with BACK-END LOAD.

2. loan disbursement schedule that is higher in early years of a loan and lower in subsequent years. This is a fairly common arrangement in construction lending.

3. loan structured with above normal usage fees in the early years of a loan.

front money see SEED MONEY.

frozen account account barred by a judicial ruling or legal process from further withdrawals. An account owned by a deceased person is frozen until the lawful heirs of the person's estate can be found. An account that is subject to a legal dispute is frozen until the legal ownership has been determined by a court of law. In the securities industry, the term refers to a customer's account blocked from further trading because of trading violations. See also BLOCKED ACCOUNT.

full coupon bond see CURRENT COUPON.

full faith and credit expression for the commitment by a state, local, or national government to pledge its taxing authority, plus nontax revenues, in payment of principal and interest on outstanding debt securities. For example, a GENERAL OBLIGATION BOND is backed by the issuing municipality's AD VALOREM taxing power. U.S. Treasury obligations and some federal agency securities also are backed by this pledge.

full recourse type of indirect lending in which a dealer sells or assigns installment sales contracts to a bank or finance company with an unconditional guarantee. The dealer assumes full responsibility for repayment and agrees to indemnify the bank if the borrower defaults.

full service bank bank offering the public most, if not all, of the services traditionally expected of banking institutions. The AMERICAN BANKERS ASSOCIATION has used the name in advertising promoting the commercial banking industry. Services typically found in full service banks include consumer credit, mortgage financing, commercial lending, trust services, and corporate agency services, such as funds transfer and securities registration.

full service broker brokerage firm offering investors a full line of brokerage, asset management services and investment advice. Full-service firms generally have a research department that furnishes reports to institutional clients and retail clients, and a buy or recommended list for all clients. DISCOUNT BROKERAGE firms, in contrast, only execute orders to buy or sell securities.

fully amortizing loan loan in which regular payments of principal are sufficient to fully pay off the loan by the maturity date, without additional payments. For example, a 30-year fixed rate or adjustable rate conventional mortgage loan.

functional cost analysis annual survey by the Federal Reserve Board of the costs of banking services, and open to banking institutions on a voluntary basis. The functional cost analysis, comparing various asset, income, and cost ratios, is the only widely available measurement of the cost of providing banking products, such as deposits, withdrawals, and transit items. Functional costing measures the cost of providing each item, and can be readily compared to prior years. Although useful, functional cost analysis has a number of flaws. The number of participants is generally small and costs are based on ledger balances, which ignore balance sheet entries such as cash items (checks) in the process of collection.

functional regulation concept that regulation of financial institutions should be divided along functional lines, rather than consolidated with a single regulatory agency. Thus, a bank's securities activities would come under the regulatory purview of the Securities and Exchange Commission. Banking activities would be regulated by state and/or federal bank regulatory agencies and insurance would be subject to oversight by the appropriate state insurance commissioner.

funds
1. cash or its equivalents, drafts and money orders. The term generally applies to short-term money market instruments and securities that are readily convertible into cash.
2. trader's jargon for Canadian dollar, abbreviated Can$ or $C.

funds availability see AVAILABLE BALANCE.

funds management management of net funds available for investment and external funds purchased from other banks. Funds management attempts to match the cash flow needs of a bank against maturity schedules of its deposits as loan demand increases or decreases. Funds management is more of a Treasury function than ASSET-LIABILITY MANAGEMENT, which deals mainly with control of *interest rate risk* and *liquidity risk*, and the pricing of loans in specific time periods.

Funds management examines the mix of funds raised by a bank, including large dollar deposits, nondeposit borrowings, and credit advances from a Federal Reserve Bank or Federal Home Loan Bank. Its aim is supplying funds sufficient to meet the bank's asset growth objectives at the lowest funding cost, and at acceptable levels of risk (credit risk, liquidity risk, and interest rate risk).

On the asset side of the balance sheet, funds management deals with the control of discretionary portfolios by the corporate treasurer, including the investment securities portfolio and trading account assets. On the liability side, it focuses on wholesale sources of funds, including credit advances from a Federal Reserve Bank or Federal Home Loan Bank, and hedging techniques, such as interest rate futures and interest rate swaps to control these balance sheet exposures. Also called *balance sheet management*. See also LIABILITY MANAGEMENT.

funds transfer

1. moving funds between related accounts or to a third party account.

2. external transfers between an originating financial institution and receiving financial institution. The term funds transfer covers all types of interbank ELECTRONIC FUNDS TRANSFER, including the Federal Reserve's Fed Wire (FEDERAL WIRE); the interbank AUTOMATED CLEARING HOUSE (ACH) system, a nationwide network of electronic clearing houses owned by groups of banks, or individual banks; and the CLEARING HOUSE INTERBANK PAYMENTS SYSTEM (CHIPS) in New York City, through which the majority of international trade payments involving U.S. financial institutions and overseas banks are channeled. The Fed Wire and the CHIPS networks account for more than 90% of transfers of funds on an annual basis. All other forms of payment, including checks, cash, and credit cards, collectively account for less

than 10% of total dollar value, but about 99% of the transactions in the economy.

This is because payment networks like Fed Wire and CHIPS are a convenient way to transfer large amounts of money, quickly and safely. Fed Wire payments are immediate settlement transfers, and are good funds when the receiving bank's reserve account is credited; CHIPS payments have same day funds availability; Automated Clearing House payments usually are considered good funds on a next-day basis; and checks take anywhere from one day to several days to clear.

fungible financial instrument equivalent in value to another, and easily exchanged or substituted. A dollar bill loaned has the same value as a dollar paid back. Bearer securities and stocks issued in the same class have this quality, as well as exchange traded options and mortgages in a pool of loans supporting a mortgage backed security.

furthest month in futures trading, the farthest month from the contract delivery date. It is the most distant of the contract delivery months in financial instruments or commodities approved for trading by a futures exchange. Treasury bills, for instance, are traded in three-month intervals. A contract calling for delivery in 18 months is the furthest month, while a three-month contract is a nearby contract or NEAREST MONTH.

future advance mortgage clause allowing the lender to advance funds after the initial loan closing and disbursement of funds, without executing a new mortgage deed or taking additional collateral. Most common in construction financing, for example, a CONSTRUCTION MORTGAGE secured by the building financed. Construction advances are made at specific stages of completion according to a preset schedule, and ordinarily take precedence over liens recorded after the loan closing date, but before the additional funds are disbursed. See also OPEN-END MORTGAGE.

future dating see VALUE DATING.

future estate see FUTURE INTEREST.

future interest interest in land or personal property giving the holder the right of possession, though not ownership. A vested interest conveys the right to claim, as of a specific date, assets held in trust, for example, an employee's interest in a corporate pension plan, payable upon retirement; a contingent interest transfers ownership only when specific events occur, for example, the death of the grantor or creator of a trust. See also REMAINDERMAN.

futures commission merchant (FCM) firm or person engaged in soliciting or accepting orders for the purchase or sale of futures contracts. A futures commission merchant accepts cash or securities for margin trading, subject to the rules of a futures exchange, and must be licensed by the Commodities Futures Trading Commission.

futures contract negotiable contract to make or take DELIVERY of a standardized amount of a commodity or financial instrument during a specific month, under terms and conditions established by a federally regulated futures exchange market where trading takes place. Futures contracts are often used as a HEDGING device against interest rate risk. Mortgage lenders who believe that mortgage rates are falling might sell 90-day forward contracts in Government National Mortgage Association (Ginnie Mae) pass-through securities; if they think rates are rising, they can buy futures contracts. At contract delivery time, the price of the futures contract and the cash price of the mortgages should cancel each other out. Normally, in futures trading the seller of a contract (known as a *short*) will notify the exchange of his intention to deliver contracts to a buyer (called the *long*) as the contract delivery month draws near. Of course, buyers and sellers of futures contracts have the option of exchanging an expiring contract for a new one, which is what most participants in the futures market actually do, rather than take delivery. See also OPTION.

futures exchanges commodities market where futures contracts in financial instruments or real commodities (wheat, soybeans) are traded. Stock and bond indexes and options also are traded on these exchanges.

Major financial futures exchanges around the world are the following: Chicago Board of Trade; Chicago Mercantile Exchange/International Monetary Market; Commodity Exchange Inc., New York; Mid-America Commodity Exchange Inc., Chicago; New York Futures Exchange; Sydney Futures Exchange, Sydney, Australia; the International Futures Exchange (Bermuda) Ltd.; Financial Futures Market, Montreal Stock Exchange, Montreal, Quebec; Toronto Stock Exchange Futures Market; Winnipeg Commodity Exchange; London International Futures Exchange; London Metal Exchange; Hong Kong Commodity Exchange; and the Gold Exchange of Singapore; and the Tokyo International Financial Futures Exchange.

G

gap amount by which INTEREST SENSITIVE ASSETS differ from IN-
TEREST SENSITIVE LIABILITIES for a designated time period, for
example, the net difference between loans and deposits maturing
in one year or less. An excess of liabilities over assets means
there are more liabilities than interest earning assets, resulting in
a NEGATIVE GAP. The opposite, an excess of interest earning assets compared to deposits, is a POSITIVE GAP. See also GAP MAN-
AGEMENT; GAPPING; REPRICING OPPORTUNITIES.

gap financing see BRIDGE LOAN.

gap management measurement of the difference in the repricing sensitivities of assets and liabilities. The repricing difference (gap) between maturing pools of assets and liabilities is an
indicator of the effect of interest rates on current income. Gap
management, a commonly used tool in ASSET-LIABILITY MANAGE-
MENT, attempts to manage these pools to achieve a satisfactory
level of profitability at an acceptable risk. This is done by matching pools of funds with loans, deposits, or investments. Gap
analysis has two drawbacks: collecting all the necessary data,
and making reasonable estimates about future interest rates, a
notoriously inaccurate exercise. See also MATCHED MATURITIES.

gapping acquiring assets with anticipated maturities, or durations, longer or shorter than the liabilities used to fund those
assets. This is the conventional circumstances of bank lending,
in other words, borrowing short and lending long. Bankers fund
long-term loans, such as home mortgages, with short-term deposits. The resulting interest rate risk is managed through ASSET-
LIABILITY MANAGEMENT.

garnishment process granted by a court order by which a
lender obtains, directly from a third party such as an employer,
part of an employee's salary in satisfaction of an unpaid debt.

Part of the employee's salary will be taken out in each pay period until the debt is fully paid. See also ATTACHMENT; WAGE ASSIGNMENT.

Garn-St Germain Depository Institutions Act

federal law enacted by Congress in 1982 authorizing banks and savings institutions to offer a new account, the MONEY MARKET DEPOSIT ACCOUNT—a transaction account with no interest rate ceiling to compete more effectively with money market mutual funds; gave savings and loan associations the authority to make commercial loans; and gave federal regulatory agencies the authority to approve, for the first time, interstate acquisitions of failed banks and savings institutions.

The following are highlights of the numerous provisions of the act:

(1) savings and loan associations were authorized to make commercial, corporate, business, or agricultural loans up to 10% of assets after Jan. 1, 1984.

(2) the deposit interest rate differential, allowing savings and loans and savings banks to offer rates on interest-bearing deposit accounts 1/4 of 1% higher than commercial banks was lifted, as of January 1984.

(3) the act authorized a new capital assistance program, the Net Worth Certificate Program, under which the Federal Savings and Loan Insurance Corp. and the Federal Deposit Insurance Corp would purchase capital instruments called Net Worth Certificates from savings institutions with net worth to assets ratios under 3%, and would later redeem the certificates as they regained financial health.

(4) the act permitted savings associations to offer checking accounts (demand deposit accounts) to individuals and business checking accounts to customers who had other accounts.

(5) savings and loans were authorized to increase their consumer lending, from 20% to 30% of assets, and to expand their dealer lending and floor-plan loan financing.

(6) the act raised the ceiling on direct investments by savings institutions in nonresidential real estate from 20% to 40% of assets, and also allowed investment of 10% of assets in education loans for any educational purpose, and up to 100% of assets in state and municipal bonds.

(7) the act pre-empted state restrictions on enforcement by lenders of due-on-sale clauses in most mortgages for a three-

year period ending October 15, 1985, and authorized state chartered lenders to offer the same kinds of alternative mortgages
permitted nationally chartered financial institutions.

(8) authorized the Comptroller of the Currency to charter
Bankers' Banks, or depository institutions owned by other
banks.

(9) made state chartered industrial banks eligible for federal
depository insurance.

(10) raised the legal lending limit for national banks from
10% to 15% of capital and surplus.

gateway means by which users of one computer system can
gain access to another without making a separate connection.
Gateway access is commonly used in AUTOMATED TELLER MA-
CHINE (ATM) systems, whether available through a single financial institution or an operator of an ATM network. Financial
institutions that are members of a regional ATM network are
able to link into other regional networks or to national ATM
networks, and other EFT based services such as electronic POINT
OF SALE systems through a single gateway. See also SWITCH.

general account
1. general ledger account for assets or liabilities other than accounts of bank customers, such as loans and deposits.
   2. Federal Reserve term for brokerage accounts subject to
   REGULATION T margin requirements, which regulates broker
   loans for purchase or short sale of securities. The Fed requires that broker loans secured by marginable stock be made
   from this account. See also TREASURY GENERAL ACCOUNT.

general agreements to borrow (GAB) arrange-
ments whereby members of the GROUP OF TEN countries make
loans to the INTERNATIONAL MONETARY FUND (IMF) in their own
currencies to finance drawings by a member of the G-10 group.
Switzerland has also joined in the accord. The G-10 countries,
and Switzerland, have since decided to make the GAB funding
commitment available to all members of the IMF.

general endorsement see BLANK ENDORSEMENT.

general examination detailed examination of a bank by
its regulator. National banks are examined every two years by
the Comptroller of the Currency, state banks by state banking
departments. The Federal Reserve Board examines state banks
that are MEMBER BANKs in the Federal Reserve System.

general ledger central accounting record of an organization, summarizing changes in financial position as transactions
are posted during an accounting period. Accounts owned by a
bank's customers are kept separately in the bank's bookkeeping
department on subsidiary accounts, or control accounts, which
are used to update the general ledger. Control accounts may list
customer accounts by type, maturity, collateral, and so on, although most banks follow the accounting format required by the
Comptroller of the Currency and other regulatory agencies in
listing accounts for the Reports of Condition and Income (call
reports). The general ledger is also the basis for financial disclosures in the CALL REPORT filed with banking regulatory agencies,
stockholders, and other outside organizations.

general lien lien against a borrower's personal assets, as opposed to a claim against real property. The lender may use the
lien to seize property in satisfaction of a debt, including assets
not specifically covered by the obligation.

generally accepted accounting principles
(GAAP) accounting rules and conventions defining acceptable
practices in preparing financial statements. The FINANCIAL AC-
COUNTING STANDARDS BOARD (FASB), an independent self-regulatory organization, is the primary source of accounting rules followed by auditors and certified public accountants. The aim of
GAAP accounting principles is uniformity in financial statements. Compare to REGULATORY ACCOUNTING PRINCIPLES.

general mortgage bond bond secured by a BLANKET
MORTGAGE on all mortgageable property of the issuing corporation. Commonly used by railroads, a general mortgage may not
necessarily have priority of claim over other liens on specific
assets or parcels of land.

general obligation bond state or municipal bond backed by the issuer's full faith credit and taxing authority. Also called a G-O Bond. General obligation bonds are normally issued to finance nonrevenue producing public works projects, such as schools, roads, and public buildings, although some G-O projects do generate revenue, for example, a bond financing a water or sewage treatment plant. A bond having no restrictions as to dollar amount of taxes or tax rate that can be assessed to make debt service payments to bondholders is known as an *unlimited tax bond*. Often, however, local governments are restricted by local or state regulations limiting property taxes that can be raised to make bond principal and interest payments; such a bond is called a LIMITED TAX BOND. See also PRIVATE PURPOSE BOND; PUBLIC PURPOSE BOND; REVENUE BOND.

general partner co-owner of an unincorporated business, who holds a share of the firm's profits or losses, and is fully liable for its debts. Also, the managing partner in a venture capital limited partnership. A general partner has unlimited personal liability for the debts of the partnership. See also LIMITED PARTNERSHIP.

generic securities securities backed by newly issued mortgages or other loans. They are less valuable to investors than SEASONED SECURITIES.

gen-saki short-term money market in Japan, used as a secondary market for repurchase and resale of medium-term and long-term corporate and government bonds. The gen-saki market, which is open to corporations as well as financial institutions, evolved because there is no secondary market in Japan for treasury securities issued by the Bank of Japan.

geodemographic marketing marketing technique that draws from U.S. Census data to divide the population in a given area into identifiable segments, based on income, life-style, or other attributes, for direct mail or telemarketing solicitation. Also called *target marketing*. In marketing of financial services, a bank using geodemographic marketing is able to identify communities with the best prospective new accounts customers, and match that list against its existing customer base or CUSTOMER INFORMATION FILE. The premise behind target marketing or geodemographic marketing is that the neighborhood is an insight into individual net worth, important to financial institutions. Several of the largest banks have applied it successfully in selling credit cards to high net worth individuals.

gift causa mortis gift of personal property by a person anticipating death. The gift, which is legally effective only after the donor's death, can reduce inheritance taxes that would otherwise be payable. Contrast with GIFT INTER VIVOS.

gift inter vivos gift of property between living persons, made during the donor's lifetime, as opposed to a GIFT CAUSA MORTIS. The gift is irrevocable, provided the donor relinquishes ownership and makes the gift without reference to his death. See also INTER VIVOS TRUST.

gift tax graduated federal tax, also imposed by some states, on property transfers by gift during the donor's lifetime. Gifts subject to the tax include irrevocable living trusts. The tax, paid by the donor, is based on fair market value.

GI loan popular name for a Department of Veterans Affairs guaranteed mortgage, authorized under the Serviceman's Readjustment Act of 1944. GI loans, guaranteed up to a certain amount, are all used for residential purposes such as buying a home or a condominium unit, refinancing, or making home improvements. Unlike most conventional mortgage loans, these loans are ASSUMABLE MORTGAGES—transferable to a new mortgagor when a house is sold. The Department of Veterans Affairs, a cabinet-level agency succeeding the Veterans Administration, also makes direct loans to qualified veterans.

gilt-edged British pound sterling bonds (gilts), issued by the Bank of England, and known as gilts in the market, as these securities have little risk of default. Also, AAA-rated U.S. corporate bonds.

Ginnie Mae See GOVERNMENT NATIONAL MORTGAGE ASSOCIATION.

Ginnie Mae pass-through mortgage backed security giving the holder a proportional interest in a pool of residential mortgages, guaranteed by the GOVERNMENT NATIONAL MORTGAGE ASSOCIATION. Ginnie Mae securities are called pass-throughs because the originating banks, mortgage bankers, and savings institutions pass all principal and interest, plus repayments, directly to the investor. There is no reinvestment of principal, as there is in mortgage backed bonds.

Ginnie Mae securities are collateralized by Department of Veterans Affairs guaranteed and Federal Housing Administration insured mortgages. There are two different types of Ginnie Mae securities available to investors. GNMA I certificates remit payments directly from the issuer to the investor on the 15th of each month. The holder gets a separate payment of principal and interest for each certificate issued. GNMA II securities remit payments through Chemical Bank in New York, which acts as a central paying agent. Payments on GNMA IIs are made on the 20th of each month. These securities, unlike GNMA I's, are backed by guaranteed loans from geographically dispersed multiple loan pools, and pay a coupon interest rate that can vary up to 1%. Originating financial institutions deduct a servicing fee of $1/2$ of 1% before remitting mortgage payments to Ginnie Mae. (The servicing fee on GNMA II pass-throughs can vary from $1/2$ of 1% to 1.5%) Ginnie Mae securities are called *modified pass-through* securities because the COUPON RATE (also called the *production rate*) of the securities is reduced by the issuer's servicing fee. Because Ginnie Mae securities are backed by the FULL FAITH AND CREDIT of the U.S. government, these issues have a wide SECONDARY MARKET. Futures contracts in Ginnie Maes have been traded on the Chicago Mercantile Exchange since 1972. See also PARTICIPATION CERTIFICATE; SECONDARY MARKET.

giro electronic payment system widely used in Europe and Japan for consumer bill payments. Unlike the CHECK system in the United States, which is a debit-based system, giros are credit transfers. In giro systems, a payment order automatically transfers funds from the consumer's account to the creditor's account and notifies creditors when the transfer is made. Multiple payments from a single giro are also possible.

Glass-Steagall Act federal law enacted by Congress in 1933 forcing a separation between commercial banking and investment banking. This act, which required commercial banks to dispose of their securities affiliates, bears the same name as the BANKING ACT OF 1933, and is part of the landmark 1933 act. Since then, the name Glass-Steagall has been more commonly used when referring to the four sections of the banking act (Section 16, 20, 21, and 32) pertaining to underwriting and sale of securities.

Highlights of the Glass-Steagall Act are the following:

(1) Section 16, prohibiting Federal Reserve MEMBER BANKS from purchasing equity securities, and also barring these banks from underwriting and dealing in any securities, except U.S. Treasury and federal agency securities, and general obligation securities of states and municipal governments.

(2) Section 20, prohibiting Federal Reserve System member banks from affiliating with firms that are engaged principally in the underwritng and sale of corporate bonds and equity securities.

(3) Section 21, making it a crime for underwriters of corporate securities to also accept deposits.

(4) Section 32, prohibiting interlocking directorates between member banks and securities firms.

In the 1980s banks began chipping away at the Glass-Steagall barrier, gaining Federal Reserve Board approval to underwrite limited amounts of ASSET-BACKED SECURITIES corporate bonds, and commercial paper through bank holding company affiliates; act as INVESTMENT ADVISOR to corporate clients; and sponsor MUTUAL FUND issues and offer DISCOUNT BROKERAGE services. Securities underwriting by holding company affiliates was authorized by a 1987 Federal Reserve Board ruling, allowing banks to underwrite securities through bank holding company affiliates. The Fed's interpretive ruling of bank securities powers under Section 20 of the Glass-Steagall Act has been upheld by the U.S. Supreme Court. See also PERMISSIBLE NONBANK ACTIVITIES; SECURITIES AFFILIATE.

globalization interdependence of buyers and sellers of financial instruments in financial centers around the world. This phenomenon is due mainly to several factors: (1) the maturation of the EUROCURRENCY markets since the 1960s; (2) dramatic changes in trading room technology in recent years, providing market makers with near instantaneous access to current market data on commodities and financial instruments; (3) a desire by financial institutions to expand lending and other activities beyond geographic boundaries; and (4) a desire to control balance sheet risk through INTEREST RATE SWAPS and other financial swap agreements.

For example, the growing use in international financial markets of marketable debt instruments, principally in the EURO-BOND market, as opposed to traditional bank lending, as a financing vehicle for major corporate borrowers, and also sovereign governments. The shift away from bank credit instruments, such as Note Issuance Facilities, toward Floating Rate Notes and Eurocommercial paper began in the early 1980s, and was aided by the strong secondary market in Eurobond financings. Both commercial banks and investment banks participate in this market. Outside the United States, U.S. commercial banks are not confined by Glass-Steagall Act limitations on securities underwriting, and are active participants in the Eurobond market.

Advances in INFORMATION TECHNOLOGY allowed traders in foreign exchange and other money market instruments to manage positions on a 24-hour basis, by moving their trading book to a different financial center at the close of trading. This practice, known as *passing the book*, permits financial institutions that make markets in New York, London, or Tokyo, for instance, to maintain a single trading book listing positions, limits, and exposures for the entire firm, rather than keeping separate books in each trading center.

gnomes popular name for 15-year fixed rate Participation Certificates sold by the Federal Home Loan Mortgage Corporation (Freddie Mac). Gnomes are PASS-THROUGH SECURITIES collateralized by mortgage payments from biweekly mortgages.

go-around process of soliciting competitive quotes from dealers when the Federal Open Market Committee buys (or sells) securities in the open market, in carrying out the Fed's monetary policy. The go-around, a telephone survey by the Open Market Desk at the Federal Reserve Bank of New York, signals the Fed's intention to do business with primary government securities dealers. Buying securities increases bank reserves, or funds available for bank lending; selling securities has the opposite effect.

going long originating mortgage loans without a firm commitment from a SECONDARY MARKET investor. If interest rates are stable, a lender may hold these loans in his own portfolio or try to place them with a buyer at a later date. In the securities industry, buying securities for investment or speculation, with no immediate plans of reselling.

going short hedging strategy whereby a bank obtains either a FORWARD COMMITMENT or a STANDBY COMMITMENT from a SECONDARY MARKET buyer to purchase loans before the loans actually are booked. By getting a commitment first, the lender is able to lock in a mortgage rate if interest rates are expected to rise or fall. In the securities industry, selling a security not actually owned by the investor—a SHORT SALE—anticipating that the open position created by the sale can be closed when the security is later purchased at a lower price.

gold card Visa or MasterCard credit card with a minimum credit line of $5,000, and frequently higher. These cards have a higher annual fee than standard bank credit cards, and are marketed to consumers with above average incomes. Sometimes called a prestige card or premium card.

Also, the American Express Gold Card, which differs from bank issued cards. American Express issues the card, but the credit line is usually arranged separately, by a bank acting as an agent for the card issuer, and varies among banks. American Express Travel Related Services Co. issued the first gold cards in 1966 and has claimed a proprietary right to the name, a claim the courts have not upheld.

gold certificate certificate issued by the U.S. Treasury Department to Federal Reserve Banks, certifying ownership of official U.S. gold reserves. Except for certificates kept for educational displays, no paper certificates actually are issued; these are bookkeeping credits. When the Treasury purchases gold and wants to replenish its dollar balances, it issues gold certificates to the Federal Reserve Board, which are kept in a separate gold certificate account. Federal Reserve Banks use gold certificates to settle payments between reserve banks, carried in the books of the INTERDISTRICT SETTLEMENT account.

gold exchange standard international monetary exchange system, a variation of the GOLD STANDARD in which central bank reserves are held in gold BULLION and in reserve currencies that are convertible into gold. Some economists believe the gold standard acts as a brake on inflation, because commodity prices are linked to gold. From the 1930s until 1971, the U.S. dollar was convertible into gold at $35 an ounce, and foreign exchange rates were fixed, or pegged, to the dollar. In 1971 the United States finally abolished the convertibility of the U.S. dollar into gold, ushering in the floating exchange rates that are the basis of the international monetary system as it exists today. See also INTERVENTION.

gold fixing process by which the daily price is set for gold traded on the spot market. It occurs in London, Paris, and Zurich at 10:30 A.M. and 3:30 P.M. London time of every business day. This price is the average price at which all major bid orders are filled, and is set by gold trading specialists at gold trading financial institutions operating in these cities.

gold-indexed investment any investment whose price and yield are dependent one way or another on the daily spot market fluctuations in the price of gold. Besides gold futures and gold options, these can be gold mutual funds, gold stocks, bank certificates of deposit, and so on.

gold option right to buy or sell any amount of gold bullion in the future if a specific price is reached. To exercise this right the investor or speculator pays an agreed upon sum to the option seller. These options are quoted on the Commodity Exchange Inc. New York; the Mid-America Commodity Exchange; and the Philadelphia Stock Exchange.

gold standard monetary system that pegs or fixes the value of a nation's currency unit to a fixed amount of gold bullion. Paper currency in such systems is convertible freely into gold. The gold standard was introduced in Great Britain in 1821 and was the basis for the U.S. monetary system from the 1870s to 1971, when the U.S. Treasury Department announced it would no longer back the U.S. dollar, for foreign exchange purposes, with its gold reserves. (The Gold Act of 1934 abolished the right of U.S. citizens to exchange paper currency for gold.) The gold standard insures a fixed rate of exchange in international trade, while limiting the amount of paper currency a central government can issue for domestic spending. Its main drawback is that it hinders the ability of a government to control the supply of money and it makes it very difficult for a country to isolate itself from depressions or inflation in the economies of its major trading partners. A country experiencing a large BALANCE OF PAYMENTS deficit may thus find it impossible to properly address the situation without coming off the gold standard. See also GOLD EXCHANGE STANDARD.

gold stock monetary gold reserves maintained by the U.S. Treasury. It consists of (1) monetized gold, or the total of GOLD CERTIFICATE credits issued by the Treasury to Federal Reserve Banks; and (2) nonmonetized gold, or gold bullion against which no certificates have been issued. The value of the Treasury's gold supply is carried on the books at $42.22 a troy ounce, the official U.S. government price set in 1973. The Treasury's gold stock does not include gold reserves held by the EXCHANGE STABILIZATION FUND, U.S. gold subscriptions to the INTERNATIONAL MONETARY FUND, and gold held as EARMARKED RESERVES at the Federal Reserve Bank of New York for foreign and international accounts.

good delivery securities industry term for a certificate bearing the proper endorsement and signature guarantee, and meeting other requirements of National Association of Securities Dealer's Uniform Practice Code, making it transferable by delivery to the buyer, who is obligated to accept it.

good faith
1. unsecured loan made on the basis of the borrower's reputation in the community, called a *character loan*.
2. in BAD DEBT collection, an agreement by the lender to modify efforts to recover the amount owed if the borrower makes certain payments or delivers collateral.
3. legal requirement that a lender extend credit in the belief that the borrower will repay the debt according to the terms of the loan agreement.
4. lender's reasonable estimate of mortgage closing costs, which must be listed in a CLOSING STATEMENT, as required by banking regulation.

5. token sum of money given to indicate interest in fulfillment of a contract, called good faith money. In a real estate transaction, it is known as EARNEST MONEY.

good money
immediately available funds, or FEDERAL FUNDS. The term is applied to interbank funds transfers over the Federal Reserve's Fed Wire, available for withdrawal the same day, as opposed to CLEARING HOUSE FUNDS, which take a minimum of 1-2 days to clear.

goodwill
1. intangible asset representing the difference between the purchase price of an asset and its fair market value. Goodwill is created when a bank pays a premium to acquire the assets of another bank in a take-over transaction. For example, bank ABC pays the shareholders of bank XYZ $100 per share for XYZ's outstanding common stock, which has a book value per share of only $50. Bank ABC reports the difference ($50) as goodwill. Goodwill is also created when a bank pays a premium above estimated market value to acquire loans, credit card accounts, and so on.

   Goodwill is a non-tax-deductible asset. It has no independent market or liquidation value, and accepted accounting principles require that it be written off (amortized) over the time period in use. Goodwill and other intangibles do not qualify as Tier 1 bank CAPITAL after December 31, 1992, under RISK-BASED capital guidelines.
2. informally, an expression for good customer relations, employee morale and a well-respected business name.

gourde
national currency of Haiti.

government bond
long-term debt securities of the United States government, given the highest rating available. The term refers to Treasury bonds, which have original maturities of 10 to 30 years, and Series EE and Series HH Savings Bonds.

government depository
bank eligible to accept government deposits. Banks so designated are Federal Reserve Banks, national banks, and state chartered member banks in the Federal Reserve System. Commercial banks act as agents of the U.S.

Treasury by holding tax receipts in a TREASURY TAX AND LOAN ACCOUNT, which allows the Treasury to leave funds on deposit locally until needed. See also PLEDGING REQUIREMENTS.

Government National Mortgage Association (GNMA) government owned corporation, an agency of the U.S. Department of Housing and Urban Development. The corporation, known informally by its nickname, Ginnie Mae, was organized in 1968 under the Housing and Urban Development Act, which separated the GNMA from the FEDERAL NATIONAL MORTGAGE ASSOCIATION. The GNMA guarantees timely payment of principal and interest on securities backed by pools of mortgages that are guaranteed by the Department of Veterans Affairs or insured by the Federal Housing Administration, making Ginnie Mae securities among the safest mortgage backed securities for investors. The corporation also subsidizes nonprofit public housing by purchasing low-interest rate loans that are resold to investors.

This agency, along with the FEDERAL NATIONAL MORTGAGE ASSOCIATION (Fannie Mae) and the FEDERAL HOME LOAN MORTGAGE CORP. (Freddy Mac), helped foster the development of the secondary market for residential mortgages, thereby increasing the amount of money available for mortgage lending. See also GINNIE MAE PASS-THROUGH; MORTGAGE BACKED SECURITIES; SECONDARY MORTGAGE MARKET.

governments negotiable securities issued by the U.S. Treasury Department, including Treasury bills, notes, and bonds. Also, federal agency securities, many of which are backed by the FULL FAITH AND CREDIT of the U.S. government.

grace period
1. time period allowed for making payments on a loan. Payments made after the due date, but within this 10-15 day period are considered timely payments, and not subject to late charges or other penalties.
2. in credit cards, the time period, ranging anywhere from 10 to 25 days, in which interest is not charged on current purchases. Also called *free period*. Some credit card issuers, though, allow a grace period only on paid-up accounts with no balances carried over from the previous month.

3. in international banking, the length of time during which the borrower is excused from making loan principal payments. For example, multilateral soft loans to developing countries are long-term loans arranged through the World Bank, with lenient credit terms and grace periods that are measured in years.

graduated payment mortgage (GPM)

fixed rate mortgage with low payments in the early years, and higher payments later on, designed to meet the financing needs of young home owners with growing incomes. Also known in the trade as a "Jeep" mortgage. The most popular versions of the GPM are 30-year mortgages with payments that rise by a fixed amount each year for the first five to ten years and then level off. Lenders usually charge a slightly higher rate on a GPM than a CONVENTIONAL MORTGAGE, because part of the interest due is deferred until the later years. Even though borrowers ultimately pay more for a GPM, the lower initial payments make this kind of mortgage more affordable to home buyers whose incomes could not support a conventional mortgage loan. A variation is the adjustable rate graduated payment mortgage, which has an interest rate that is adjusted every three to five years. See also ADJUSTABLE RATE MORTGAGE; ALTERNATIVE MORTGAGE INSTRUMENTS.

grandfathered activities

activities prohibited by law, regulation or agreement, but approved for organizations that were already engaged in those activities as of a specific date. Entry by other firms is, however, disallowed.

In banking, the term is used widely in reference to activities of certain bank holding companies, allowed to continue by the Bank Holding Company of 1956 and its 1970 amendment, or by subsequent legislation. For example, the Competitive Equality Banking Act of 1987 banned the NONBANK BANK, a type of bank that slips through the legal definition of a bank, but allowed companies already owning one of these quasi-banks to keep them operating without having to register with the Federal Reserve Board as bank holding companies.

grantor

1. person who executes a deed conveying property to another, or who creates a trust instrument. Also called *settlor*.
2. writer or seller of an option contract, either a call option or a put option. A call option conveys the right to buy the underlying securities; a put option gives the right to sell.

grantor trust any trust other than one created by a WILL. In the SECONDARY MORTGAGE MARKET and securitized asset sales market, a grantor trust is a legal, passive entity through which pass-through securities are sold to investors. Grantor trusts are not subject to taxation.

green book

1. U.S. Treasury Department publication listing procedures to be followed in handling DIRECT DEPOSIT payments of government benefits and other payments through the AUTOMATED CLEARING HOUSE (ACH) system.
2. economic forecast outlining different economic scenarios, prepared by the Federal Reserve Board staff for members of the FEDERAL OPEN MARKET COMMITTEE at a regular meeting of the FOMC.

gridlock condition in a wire transfer network where the inability of one bank to meet its obligations due other banks may cause similar failures at other banks. This domino-like effect could in theory topple an entire group of banks like a house of cards; a kind of risk known as SYSTEMIC RISK, or payment system risk.

Wire transfer systems such as the CLEARING HOUSE INTER-BANK PAYMENTS SYSTEM guard against this outcome through a system of mutually agreed upon BILATERAL CREDIT LIMITS; limiting the debit total each CHIPS bank is willing to accept from other banks in the system. See also OVERDRAFT CAP.

gross coupon the interest rate earned on mortgages underlying a mortgage backed security, for example, the rate earned by mortgages underlying a PASS-THROUGH SECURITY as opposed to the COUPON RATE on the bonds.

gross estate property in a decedent's estate before payment of debts, estate taxes, and other expenses. After these expenses and funeral costs are deducted, beneficiaries are paid from the amount remaining, which is the net estate.

gross margin
1. **Banking.** Synonymous with SPREAD or yield. The difference between the lender's cost of funds, and the rate paid by the borrower, including upfront fees, usage fees, and cancellation fees.
2. **Finance.** A disclosure on the Profit and Loss (P&L) statement of the borrower, synonymous with gross profit; the difference between sales and gross earnings.

gross spread underwriter's margin in issuing new securities, or the difference between the price at which securities are sold to the public and the price paid by the underwriter to the issuer. The difference, the selling cost, includes the manager's fee and selling concession (the discount offered) to members of the underwriting syndicate.

group banking form of HOLDING COMPANY in which a management group has control of several existing banks. Each bank in the group has its own board of directors, but the holding company coordinates the activities of all banks in the group, and owns a majority of capital stock in member banks. See also BANKERS' BANK; CHAIN BANKING; INTERLOCKING DIRECTORATE.

Group of Seven international group comprised of finance ministers of the seven leading industrial democracies who meet to coordinate economic and monetary policy. The group, also known as the G-7, includes Japan, West Germany, France, Britain, Italy, Canada and the United States. Organized in 1986.

Group of Ten group of major industrial countries, members of the International Monetary Fund (IMF), that coordinate monetary and fiscal policies through GENERAL AGREEMENTS TO BORROW and other activities. The ten are Belgium, Canada, France, Italy, Japan, the Netherlands, Sweden, the United Kingdom, the United States, and West Germany. Switzerland, an associate member of the IMF, has announced its intention to join as a full-fledged member. Also called the *Paris Club*.

Group of 24 see ORGANIZATION FOR ECONOMIC COOPERATION AND DEVELOPMENT.

growing equity mortgage (GEM) mortgage with a fixed interest rate but varying monthly payments. Monthly payments of principal and interest rise monthly, semi-annually, or yearly according to an agreed upon schedule, with extra payments used to reduce the loan principal and shorten the loan term. Also called a rapid payoff mortgage. See also ALTERNATIVE MORTGAGE INSTRUMENT.

guarani national currency of Paraguay.

guaranteed loan loan guaranteed as to repayment of principal and interest by a federal agency, such as the Department of Veterans Affairs or the Small Business Administration. Also, a student loan guaranteed by the Student Loan Marketing Association. In most guaranteed loan programs, the guarantor insures repayment of 90% of the principal, and the lender assumes credit risk for the remainder. The guarantor usually collects a fee from the lender.

guaranteed mortgage certificate (GMC) mortgage backed bond, backed by a pool of mortgages, issued by the Federal Home Loan Mortgage Corporation (Freddie Mac) since 1975. The bonds, representing an undivided interest in a pool of residential mortgages, have a guaranteed average life, and pay principal and interest semiannually. The investor receives full payment of principal if the underlying mortgages prepay at a rate faster than the guaranteed minimum rate.

guaranteed student loan see EDUCATION LOAN; STUDENT LOAN MARKETING ASSOCIATION.

guarantor
1. person or corporation who guarantees payment by another. Also known as a SURETY. A guarantor becomes a co-endorser and assumes liability in event of default.
2. corporation that provides assurances, either through a LETTER OF CREDIT or the strength of its own balance sheet, to step in and pay the outstanding obligation of, for example, a municipal bond issuer. See also FINANCIAL GUARANTEE.

3. Federal Home Loan Mortgage Corp. MORTGAGE SWAP in which mortgage lenders exchange loans for Freddy Mac PARTICIPATION CERTIFICATES.

guaranty three-party agreement, involving a promise by one party (the guarantor) to fulfill the obligation of a person owing a debt if that person fails to perform. The guaranty (also spelled guarantee) is a CONTINGENT LIABILITY of the guarantor. See also FINANCIAL GUARANTEE.

guaranty fund

1. mutual savings bank reserve fund required by some states as cushion against short-term losses. The fund is set aside from current earnings. Also called a *surplus account*.

2. privately sponsored deposit insurance fund, the predecessor of federal deposit insurance. Even after federal deposit insurance was enacted in 1933, private guaranty funds co-existed with federal insurance programs for many years until the mid-1980s when a series of savings and loan failures in Ohio and Maryland forced the private insurers to liquidate. About 10% of credit union shares, however, are still privately insured, and the Deposit Insurance Fund of Massachusetts provides deposit insurance for uninsured (above $100,000) deposits in that state not covered by the Federal Deposit Insurance Corporation.

guardian person who has legal responsibility for care of a minor, or a person incapable of managing his affairs. This right may be conveyed by a court, or it may be a natural guardianship, for example, a parent providing for a child under legal age. Guardianship terminates when the minor, also called a ward, reaches legal maturity—21 years of age—or if the guardian's authority terminates.

guilder national currency of the Netherlands, the Netherlands Antilles, and Suriname.

gulf riyal national currency of Dubai and Qatar.

H

haircut

1. valuation formula used by broker-dealers in computing net capital positions. A dealer's haircut is an estimate of potential losses, taking into account credit risk, market risk, time to maturity, and other factors. Haircuts vary according to class of security: ranging from 0% haircut for U.S. Treasury securities, 30% for equities, to 100% for issues in default, where total loss is probable. Haircuts in government securities trading are based on weekly yield volatility, as tabulated by the Federal Reserve Bank of New York. Dealer capital requirements are governed by the Securities and Exchange Commission's Rule 15c3-1. The lowest haircuts are given to securities considered least likely to default, for example, Treasury bills.

2. in lending, difference between the amount advanced by a lender and the market value of collateral securing the loan. For example, if a lender makes a loan equal to 90% of the dollar value of marketable securities, the difference (10%) is the haircut. Also called *haircut financing*.

3. spread in a repurchase agreement, or the difference between the actual market value and the value actually used in a RE-POSSESSION.

half life

number of years needed for one half of the underlying loan principal in a mortgage backed security to be repaid. Half lives are determined by interest rate volatility, borrower prepayments, and to some extent by geographic region. Some areas of the United States have higher rates of housing turnover than others, so mortgages in these areas have considerably shorter half lives. Through the mid-1970s, when mortgage loan rates did not change often, half lives were fairly predictable. For example, the half life of a pool of mortgages backing a GINNIE MAE PASS-THROUGH security was presumed to be 12 years. The half life of a so-called CURRENT COUPON mortgage is closer to 10 years, but heavy prepayments can shorten half lives to as little as 4 to 5 years. In general, when interest rates fall, borrowers refinance at substantial savings in interest costs, causing half lives to drop. Rising rates have the opposite effect. Borrowers hold on to their loans for a longer period and half lives lengthen. See also AVERAGE LIFE; DURATION.

handle trader's shorthand where the big figure is eliminated from a trade quote. Quotes are in fractions: 1/16 bid, 3/16 offered.

handling charge see INTERCHANGE RATE.

hard currency
1. currency expected to remain stable, if not appreciate in value, in relation to other currencies; also a currency that is readily CONVERTIBLE, or exchanged for the currency of another country. A sizable portion of international trade and bank lending is denominated in hard currencies; central banks keep a portion of their reserves in these currencies. Also called STRONG CURRENCY.
2. gold bullion of gold coins, as opposed to paper money, which is not convertible into an equivalent amount of gold or other precious metal.

hazard insurance property insurance carrying protection against losses from fire, certain natural causes, vandalism, and malicious mischief. Home owners generally maintain hazard insurance coverage through regular mortgage payments, a portion of which goes into an ESCROW account for insurance and property taxes. Mortgage lenders require hazard insurance coverage before a loan is made.

H bond see SAVINGS BOND.

HH bond see SAVINGS BOND.

head teller bank teller whose duties include supervising other tellers, controlling cash in tellers' drawers, preparing a daily cash report for the general ledger, and helping other tellers find a difference if end-of-day debits and credits are out of balance. Actual duties vary by financial institution.

hedge/hedging financial technique to offset the risk of loss from price fluctuations in the market. Hedgers employ a variety of techniques, including futures contracts, options on futures, and interest rate swaps. An investor wanting protection against a fall in price can sell forward contracts (a LONG HEDGE); in the futures market, to protect against a rise in price, the investor buys forward contracts (a SHORT HEDGE). For example, a borrower in the money market can use INTEREST RATE FUTURES as protection against increases in short-term rates with a short or sell hedge, by selling an interest rate contract for future delivery. If rates happen to rise between the contract sale date and the delivery date, the value of the futures contract will drop and the hedger can make a gain by buying back, at a lower price, the contract sold earlier.

Other forms of hedging involve purchase of interest rate and currency options, INTEREST-ONLY (IO) SECURITIES and PRINCIPAL-ONLY (PO) STRIPS, and RESIDUAL tranches of a COLLATERALIZED MORTGAGE OBLIGATION. See also ARBITRAGE; COVERED INTEREST ARBITRAGE; CROSS-HEDGE; DERIVATIVE MORTGAGE BACKED SECURITIES; SHORT SALE.

Herfindahl index mathematical index for determining the potential anticompetitive effects of a bank merger. The index, devised by economist Orris C. Herfindahl, computes market concentration by adding up the squares of the market share owned by banks in a given market. If there are six banks in a market, with market shares of local deposits of 30%, 25%, 20%, 15%, 5%, and 5%, the square of each yields a total figure of 2,200, which is the size of the market in that area. A merger by the two largest banks might be viewed as anticompetitive, but a merger of the bottom two would not be. The weakness of the index, however, is that it is only an approximation. The Herfindahl formula can also be applied to loans or other accounts.

high-grade bond bond rated triple-A or double-A by Standard & Poor's or Moody's rating services. It may be supported by a CREDIT ENHANCEMENT, such as a letter of credit to obtain a high debt rating. See also INVESTMENT GRADE.

high ratio loan mortgage loan in which the amount advanced by the lender is close to the appraised value of the property. Generally, any mortgage with a loan-to-value ratio higher than 80% is considered a high ratio loan. Lenders often require the borrower to obtain MORTGAGE INSURANCE.

hit the bid expression for a seller's willingness to accept the bid price offered by a quoting buyer. The opposite is TAKE THE OFFER.

hold see ACCOUNT HOLD; CHECK HOLD.

holdback portion of a construction loan that is not funded until the project is nearing completion, or the borrower has satisfied certain performance requirements, such as leasing a majority of the units in the building. The amount kept back often is equal to the construction firm's expected profit when the building is completed.

holder in due course party who becomes the good faith holder of a NEGOTIABLE INSTRUMENT (such as a check, note, or draft), for value received, without knowledge of any claims against it, or that the instrument was dishonored when presented for payment, or in any way defective. Under the UNIFORM COMMERCIAL CODE, the body of law governing legal contracts, the person holding a check endorsed by another is the presumed legal owner, and can sue in his or her own name. A person accepting a THIRD PARTY CHECK is a holder in due course, and holds legal title to the instrument, regardless of any prior claims. By contrast, a good faith buyer of an asset does not necessarily acquire title; for example, an innocent buyer of a stolen car never gains title to the car.

A bank acquiring installment loan contracts, as a holder in due course, from a retailer or other lender, can be held liable in some cases for any claims by the original borrower against the seller of the note. This is the Federal Trade Commission's *holder in due course* rule, intended to prevent abusive credit practices. The rule, issued in 1976, says the holder of a note must honor warranties of the original seller. This means a consumer cannot be required to make payments in situations where the seller of the note refused to honor a manufacturer's guarantee on merchandise that turned out to be defective, or the seller refused to perform work, such as home improvements, financed by an installment note.

hold harmless clause clause in a construction mortgage or loan contract relieving the borrower from liability in unforseen events, such as labor strikes or natural disaster, that limit or inhibit the borrower in meeting contractual obligations.

holding company corporation that exercises control over another company, by owning enough voting shares of outstanding common stock, or that controls several related companies. A holding company form of organization allows a bank to engage in business activities outside the normal deposit taking and lending functions of banking, such as discount brokerage, leasing or securities underwriting, without running afoul of state or federal laws prohibiting nonbank commercial activities.

Commercial bank holding companies, first authorized by the BANKING ACT OF 1933, are regulated by the Federal Reserve Board. The BANK HOLDING COMPANY ACT of 1956, gave the Federal Reserve Board the power to regulate multibank holding companies; a 1970 amendment extended Federal Reserve regulation to one-bank holding companies. The Fed has the authority, for example, to approve activities under Federal Reserve REGULATION Y, that are held to be closely related to banking and qualify as service enhancements a bank can offer through a HOLDING COMPANY AFFILIATE. There often are limitations on these nonbanking activities; banking and commerce still do not mix.

A savings and loan holding company, owning two or more savings and loan associations, is supervised by the OFFICE OF THRIFT SUPERVISION. A mutual holding company, approved by several states, is a holding company owning a mutual savings bank. A mutual holding company can be a purely mutual institution owned by its depositors, or a quasi-public institution selling a minority of its stock to the public, depending on state law. See also CHAIN BANKING; GROUP BANKING; PERMISSIBLE NONBANK ACTIVITIES; SECURITIES AFFILIATE.

holding company affiliate bank or nonbank company owned by a BANK HOLDING COMPANY or savings and loan holding company. Certain nonbanking activities, such as operating a mortgage company, a leasing company, or a data processing subsidiary, have been authorized by the Federal Reserve Board under REGULATION Y if in the board's judgment they are "closely related to banking" and a "proper incident thereto." See also HOLDING COMPANY.

holdovers transit checks in collection that, for one reason or another, are delayed until the next processing cycle, which is usually the next business day, for bundling in cash letters and presentment to a clearing house or directly to the paying bank for collection. Most holdovers are found in large clearing banks.

holiday float see FLOAT.

hologram foil strip containing a three-dimensional image that appears on Visa and MasterCard credit cards and debit cards. An anti-counterfeiting device, holograms are now required on all bank cards bearing the Visa or MasterCard logo.

home banking interactive terminal-based service that allows bank customers to check balances, transfer funds between accounts, pay bills, and do other banking services electronically from their homes. Also called video banking. Telephone bill payment was the earliest form of home banking, followed in the early 1980s by systems utilizing personal computers, or keyboard type devices using a television screen as a visual monitor. Home banking services are found mostly in New York and a few other major cities. See also VIDEOTEX.

home equity credit (loan) loan secured by equity value in a borrower's home. Also called an *equity credit line*. A home equity loan allows the home-owner to tap into the accumulated equity in his home—the difference between the current fair market value and the amount secured by a first mortgage—by writing checks that are drawn against a line of credit. The borrower is given a special set of checks. Writing a check or using the credit card creates a lien on the property; the outstanding balance is paid down by making installment payments to the lender. Home equity loans may be fixed rate, or have floating rates that are tied to a cost of funds index. Most home equity loans require an initial sign-up fee and an APPRAISAL of the property to determine the LOAN-TO-VALUE RATIO. Equity credit policies vary regionally, but a common practice is to set the upper limit on equity lines at an amount equal to 60–80% of the current market value of a home, less the outstanding mortgage balance. See also SECOND MORTGAGE.

home improvement loan consumer loan, usually secured by collateral or a mortgage, taken out to finance alterations, remodeling, or structural renovations to an existing dwelling. These loans are generally short-term, though in some cases may be for much longer periods. See also HOME EQUITY LOAN; SECOND MORTGAGE.

Home Mortgage Disclosure Act see REGULATION C.

honor
1. payment of a a check when presented or agreement to pay a time draft at a future date. See also ACCEPTANCE.
2. acceptance, by a merchant, of a bank card or travel & entertainment (T&E) card offered as payment for goods or services.

hot card bank card that cannot be honored for payment, most often because the card has been reported lost or stolen, or has been cancelled by the issuer. Hot cards are listed in the combined Visa and MasterCard WARNING BULLETIN.

hot money
1. interest-sensitive deposits in domestic accounts, such as short-term bank CDs, that are subject to withdrawal at maturity if another bank offers a higher rate. Much of the interest-sensitive money flowing in and out of banks is owned by corporate or institutional investors who seek out the currency and country offering the best return. When rates fall, funds are often withdrawn on short notice.
2. surplus funds that banks purchase or sell to each other in the money market, normally on an overnight or short-term basis, such as FEDERAL FUNDS or overnight repurchase agreements. See also MANAGED LIABILITIES.
3. uninsured deposits, for example certificates of deposit, in amounts above the $100,000 federal deposit insurance limit. Depositors seeking the highest return look for banks and savings institutions paying the highest nationally advertised rate on short-term CDs, and can withdraw funds from a bank in distress, causing a shortage of funds. See also BROKERED DEPOSIT.
4. bank teller's bait money: specially marked bills in a teller's drawer, meant to help identify cash taken in robberies.

Housing and Urban Development, Department of (HUD) cabinet-level federal agency, founded in 1965, that promotes housing development in the United States through direct loans, mortgage insurance and guarantees. The FEDERAL HOUSING ADMINISTRATION, which insures mortgage loans originated by private lenders, and the GOVERNMENT NATIONAL MORTGAGE ASSOCIATION (Ginnie Mae), which guarantees residential mortgages pooled for resale in the secondary mortgage market, are within HUD. Ginnie Mae was separated from the FEDERAL NATIONAL MORTGAGE ASSOCIATION and established as a wholly owned federal agency under HUD by the Housing Act of 1968. Other HUD-assisted programs finance the construction of subsidized public housing, and rehabilitation of single family and multifamily housing. See also MUTUAL MORTGAGE INSURANCE FUND.

housing authority bond short-term note or long-term bond issued by a public housing authority and guaranteed as to repayment of principal and interest by the U.S. Department of Housing and Urban Development. Also called Public Housing Authority bonds or PHA bonds. The bonds finance construction of low- and moderate-income housing, paying competitive rates.

housing starts award of a building permit for construction of new residential multifamily housing. The volume of housing starts, gauging consumer demand for residential mortgages, is one of the 12 leading economic indicators compiled by the U.S. Department of Commerce.

HUMPBACKED YIELD CURVE

humped yield curve unusual situation where medium-term rates are higher than rates on short-term and long-term instruments. Also called a bell-shaped yield curve. For example, the yield curve where yields on three-month Treasury bills are lower than those on six-month bills, but comparable to yields on three- and four-year Treasury bonds, and higher than yields on five- to 30-year Treasury bonds.

hurdle rate

1. in capital budgeting, the minimum rate of return or INTERNAL RATE OF RETURN. If the expected rate of return is below this rate, the project is rejected or re-evaluated.
2. BREAK-EVEN YIELD.

hyperinflation economic condition characterized by rapidly rising prices of freely traded goods, and declining purchasing power, threatening economic stability and ability to repay EXTERNAL DEBT. The term usually is applied when consumer prices are rising at rates in excess of 50% per month, particularly in developing countries. Also called *runaway inflation.*

hypothecation

1. **Banking.** Offer of stocks, bonds, or other assets owned by a party other than the borrower as COLLATERAL for a loan, without transferring title. If the borrower turns over the property to the lender, who holds it in safekeeping, the action is referred to as a *pledge*; if the borrower retains possession, but gives the lender the right to sell the property in event of default, it is a true hypothecation.
2. **Securities.** The pledging of negotiable securities to collateralize a broker's MARGIN loan. If the broker pledges the same securities to a bank as collateral for a broker's loan, the process is referred to as *rehypothecation.*

identification any means of verifying a bank's customer, for example, the drawer (maker) of a negotiable instrument or the person initiating an electronic funds transfer. Also, any industry assigned number identifying a paying bank (the ABA TRANSIT NUMBER or CHECK ROUTING SYMBOL), or the owner of marketable securities.

1. bank customer's signature on a check, either as drawer or endorser. Banks have an obligation to examine paid checks for proper endorsement, but this is now done on an exception basis.
2. in electronic transfers of funds, a sending bank's password, called an issuer KEY, used in place of a bank officer's signature. See also MESSAGE AUTHENTICATION CODE.
3. PERSONAL IDENTIFICATION NUMBER (PIN) assigned to a bank account.
4. biometric identification, a means of identifying bank customers by unique physical characteristics, such as voice, fingerprint, or handwriting. The most promising of these new technologies is signature dynamics, which identifies handwriting.
5. personal information known by the account holder, such as mother's maiden name, recorded on a SIGNATURE CARD when a new account is opened.
6. Social Security Number of an individual or federal TAXPAYER IDENTIFICATION NUMBER of an organization.
7. BANK IDENTIFICATION NUMBER (BIN).
8. MACHINE READABLE characters such as the MAGNETIC INK CHARACTER RECOGNITION (MICR) line printed on the bottom edge of bank checks.
9. CUSIP NUMBER.

illiquid asset not easily sold for cash, for example, a loan with a limited secondary market. Such loans can, however, be sold through private placement with an investor, sometimes at a discount from face value.

Also, assets that are not counted toward a bank's core capital, such as real estate owned through foreclosure and nonmarketable securities.

immediate beneficiary beneficiary of a trust who is entitled to receive immediate benefits, which may be unrestricted or limited to trust income. Contrast with ultimate beneficiary, the person named to receive the final distribution from the trust.

immediate credit check given same-day funds availability when presented to a Federal Reserve Bank for collection. Only banks in a city where the Fed has a Reserve Bank or branch, called a RESERVE CITY BANK, are given immediate availability on checks cleared by the Fed, as as opposed to the normal two-day DEFERRED AVAILABILITY on most checks. Also, banks usually give same-day credit to ON-US checks, or checks drawn against accounts in the same bank where they are deposited.

immediate order see FILL OR KILL.

immunization actions to safeguard a portfolio against risk. Any kind of portfolio can be immunized to produce a desired return, independent of changes in interest rates or bond prices. A bond portfolio is said to be immunized when the DURATION, that is, the expected term of a bond, matches the investor's holding period. Banks can immunize the balance sheet by holding approximately equal amounts of assets and liabilities for a defined period of time. More generally, immunization can refer to investment strategies, such as interest rate and currency swaps to minimize investment risk.

impaired capital condition where a bank's total paid-in capital is less than the stated value, through excessive loan losses or other unsound practices. If the impairment is severe, a bank may be called upon by a regulatory agency's capital call to make up the deficiency by raising new capital or go into liquidation.

impaired credit bank loan where full repayment is considered uncertain. An impaired credit is classified as a DOUBTFUL LOAN, SUBSTANDARD, or LOSS, depending on the severity of the impairment.

implied volatility degree of volatility implied by the market price of an option. Some options traders deal in volatility, buying options when their implied volatility is low and selling options when their implied volatility is high. By using the BLACK SCHOLES MODEL, an investor who knows the option price, the strike price and other factors, can determine the price volatility.

imputed interest interest that legally may be considered part of the principal of a debt, if the interest paid is less than the amount estimated for tax purposes by the Internal Revenue Service.

inactive account account with infrequent deposits or withdrawals. If no activity is recorded for a specified period, other than crediting of interest, it is considered a DORMANT ACCOUNT and removed from the file of active accounts.

inadvertent error clerical or billing error that, although a technical violation of consumer protection laws, does not give cause to a civil liability complaint if a bank can assert the error was unintentional, was made in good faith despite safeguards to prevent such mistakes, and then corrects the error. For example, a lender may assess a LATE CHARGE on a mortgage payment even though the payment was received during the allowed grace period.

INAS network for exchange of bank card authorizations among financial institutions affiliated with MASTERCARD INTERNATIONAL. Full name: Interbank National Authorization System. See also INET.

incentive pricing transaction pricing intended to encourage consumers to use certain kinds of banking services for routine transactions, and not others. For example, a lower fee for getting cash at an automated teller than writing a check for cash.

income capital certificate (ICC) financial instrument devised by the Federal Savings and Loan Insurance Corporation to help troubled thrift institutions. Thrifts needing to raise their equity capital issue ICC notes to the FSLIC in exchange for cash or promissory notes. The notes are retired as the institution rebuilds its net worth and gains financial strength.

income limits maximum amounts that moderate income or low income families may earn to qualify for subsidized rental housing or a low-interest mortgage. Limits are based on family size and geographic location.

income property mortgage see COMMERCIAL MORTGAGE.

income statement financial statement showing a summary of a firm's financial operations for a specific period, including net profit or loss for the period in question. It usually is accompanied by a BALANCE SHEET listing the firm's assets and liabilities for the same period. Income statements are included in quarterly 10Q reports and annual 10K reports filed with the Securities and Exchange Commission.

inconvertible currency or security that cannot be freely exchanged for another, or sold for cash. In foreign exchange, currencies that are not traded easily for other currencies, or exchanged for gold, because of EXCHANGE CONTROLS restricting transfer or ownership of these currencies. An inconvertible currency is less desirable to investors in other countries than a freely CONVERTIBLE currency.

incorporated trustee trust company or bank trust department authorized to act as a FIDUCIARY for a trust account, as opposed to an individual who is appointed trustee.

incremental cost of funds see MARGINAL COST OF FUNDS.

indenture

1. written agreement specifying the terms and conditions for issuing bonds, stating the form of the bond being offered for sale, interest to be paid, the maturity date, call provisions and protective covenants, if any, collateral pledged, the repayment schedule, and other terms. It describes the legal obligations of a bond issuer and the powers of the bond TRUSTEE, who has the responsibility, under the TRUST INDENTURE ACT of 1939, for ensuring that interest payments are made to registered bondholders.

2. mortgage or deed of trust securing a lien against real property, specifying covenants and conditions, as agreed by the seller (the grantor) and the buyer.

independent bank locally owned and operated commercial bank. It derives its sources of funds from, and it lends money to, the community where it operates, and is not affiliated with a multibank holding company. Also called *community bank.*

Independent Bankers Association of America (IBAA) see TRADE ASSOCIATION.

index

1. **In general.** A numerical figure adjusted periodically to reflect changes in the quantity of goods produced, prices paid, loan interest rates, by comparing current activity to a base year, previous month, or previous year. The Consumer Price Index, measuring changes in prices paid for consumer goods, is a widely used example.

2. **Banking.** The interest rate used as the base rate in pricing variable rate loans, often called a COST OF FUNDS INDEX. In an ADJUSTABLE RATE MORTGAGE, the borrower's loan rate is reset periodically at a MARGIN above the index rate. Numerous index rates are used in bank lending, for example, the Federal Home Loan Bank Board's cost of funds index or the National Average Mortgage Contract Rate Index.

3. **Economics.** A statistical measure of the rate of change in the economy, for example, the index of leading economic indicators, which tends to anticipate changes in the business cycle.

4. **Securities.** An indicator of financial market performance, for example, the Standard & Poor's 500 Index of industrial stocks, or the Dow Jones Industrial Average.

indexed investment see GOLD INDEXED INVESTMENT; MARKET INDEX DEPOSIT.

indication

1. **Banking.** A notation next to a money market dealer's price quote signifying that the quotation is for information only, and the dealer is unwilling to do business (make a market) at that price.
2. **Securities.** A willingness to buy securities in registration from an underwriter—an expression of interest.

indirect liability see CONTINGENT LIABILITY.

indirect loan loan sold by a dealer or a retailer of goods, to a third party financial institution that owns the loan contract as a HOLDER IN DUE COURSE and collects principal and interest payments from the borrower. Commercial banks and finance companies buy installment contracts from dealers at a discount from the face value on the notes. See also DEALER FINANCING; FLOOR PLANNING.

individual proprietor see SOLE PROPRIETOR.

individual retirement account (IRA) personal retirement account allowing qualifying individuals to set aside a portion of annual income on a tax deferred basis. Individuals may contribute up to $2,000 a year (up to $2,250, if an individual has a nonworking spouse), deducting IRA contributions from adjusted gross income in federal tax returns. Interest income on the principal amount accumulates tax free, and account assets are not taxed until withdrawals begin. According to IRS rules, an individual can begin taking money out of an IRA account at age 59$^1/_2$, but withdrawals, taxable at ordinary income tax rates, must begin no later than age 70$^1/_2$. Distributions from an IRA before age 59$^1/_2$ are subject to a 10% early withdrawal penalty.

The Tax Reform Act of 1986 imposed new eligibility rules on IRAs, limiting the full tax deduction on IRA contributions to individuals with adjusted gross incomes of $25,000 or less, or persons filing joint returns having incomes of $40,000 or less. IRA contributions of individuals earning up to $35,000, married couples with an adjusted gross income up to $50,000 ($10,000 if filing a separate return) are only partially deductible, as of the 1987 tax year. The tax-deferral benefits of an IRA account are also limited to persons who are not covered by a corporate pension plan, profit sharing plan, or 401(k) employee savings plan. Individuals earning over $35,000 a year, and married couples earning over $40,000, can still make nondeductible contributions (up to $2,000 a year per individual) that earn interest on a tax-free basis. Funds invested in an IRA can be put in bank accounts, stocks, bonds, mutual funds, and other forms of investments. See also 401 (k) PLAN; INDIVIDUAL RETIREMENT ACCOUNT ROLLOVER; KEOGH PLAN; SELF-DIRECTED IRA.

individual retirement account rollover provision in the U.S. tax code allowing the owner of an INDIVIDUAL RETIREMENT ACCOUNT to transfer assets of the account, without penalty, into another IRA account or qualified retirement plan if the funds are reinvested within 60 days. Also called *rollover IRA*. The same rule applies to early distributions of pension fund shares, profit sharing plans, and other tax qualified employee savings plans. This provision allows individuals to shift assets from one form of investment to another, without having to pay the 10% IRS penalty on early withdrawals.

indorsement see ENDORSEMENT.

industrial bank state chartered finance company that makes loans and raises funds by selling investment certificates or investment shares to the public. Also called an *industrial loan company*. Industrial banks were originated by Arthur Morris, an entrepreneur who opened the first Morris Plan Bank, as these consumer finance companies were once called, early in the twentieth century to make small loans to industrial workers. Loans are often secured by CHATTEL MORTGAGE or backed by a cosigner's signature. Industrial loan companies do not have checking accounts, but many offer NOW accounts, and, since 1982, have been eligible for federal deposit insurance.

industrial development bond municipal bond issued by a state or local government, or by a development agency, to finance the private industrial projects generating tax revenues and certain public works projects. These bonds are of two types: development bonds financing the renovation or improvement of public facilities, and industrial revenue bonds, for which a private corporation is responsible for payments to bondholders. Industrial bonds are subject to special IRS rules governing the tax exemption of interest. The tax exemption on many of these bonds, other than bonds financing airports, water treatment plants, and certain other public works related projects, was eliminated by the Tax Reform act of 1986. Bond ratings on revenue bonds are based on the credit rating of the private corporation backing the lease or rental agreement covering the facilities, because the ultimate source of repayment is the corporation, rather than the bond issuer. See also PRIVATE PURPOSE BOND; PUBLIC PURPOSE BOND.

industrial revenue bond see INDUSTRIAL DEVELOPMENT BOND.

INET network for exchange of bank card debit and credit transactions among financial institutions affilated with MASTERCARD INTERNATIONAL. Full name: Interbank Network for Electronic Transfer. MasterCard's card authorization system (INAS) and net settlement system (INET) are now combined in worldwide data communications network known as BankNet.

inflation economic condition characterized by rapid rises in prices and wages. The result is diminished purchasing power, and frequently a lower rate of savings as wage earners put more of their disposable assets in consumption, and less in long-term savings. In modern economics, there are two distinct types of inflation: cost-push inflation and demand-pull inflation. In cost-push inflation, wage increases lead industries to raise prices to cover the cost of new wage contracts, resulting in a cyclical pattern of higher wages and prices—the so-called *wage price spiral*; in demand-pull inflation, high demand for credit (bank loans) is said to cause rising prices, stimulating growth in the Gross National Product that pulls up prices even more. Some economists believe that demand-pull inflation can be controlled by a combination of Federal Reserve MONETARY POLICY and U.S. FISCAL POLICY, for example, a TIGHT MONEY policy by the Federal Reserve and controls on federal spending. Cost-push inflation, on the other hand, is thought to be controllable more by slowing the growth rate in the economy than specific monetary or fiscal policy actions. See also DEFLATION; DISINFLATION; HYPERINFLATION.

information technology computer based information management systems allowing a financial institution to collect information from many different sources and develop a composite picture about its customers, its market position in different financial centers, and its net exposure in those markets. Updating of customer records is a continuous process, as financial transactions are recorded. This allows more informed decision-making, giving rise to the saying that information about money balances is as important to financial managers as money itself.

initial margin see MARGIN.

inside director member of a firm's board of directors who is also a member of its management committee, such as the president or chief executive officer, as opposed to outside directors appointed for their reputation in the community. Directors of banking institutions can be removed by federal banking regulators if they abuse their office, in contrast to directors of nonfinancial companies.

insider information legal term for information not available to the general public, but known by inside directors, principals in a firm planning a takeover of another company, and others. Securities printers as well as brokers or securities analysts with access to nonpublic information that could influence an investor's decision to buy, sell, or hold a security, have been held to be insiders. Trading in takeover stocks with the expectation of making a profit using undisclosed, market sensitive information is termed *misappropriation* of nonpublic information by the Securities and Exchange Commission, and forbidden by SEC Rule 10b-5. Officers, directors, and other corporate insiders owning at least 10% of a company's stock must report trades to the SEC.

insider lending loans to directors and officers of a bank, which must be reported to bank regulators under the Financial Institutions Reform Act of 1978. Banking laws also require that loans to insiders be made at the same rate and credit terms as loans to other borrowers.

insolvency inability to pay debts as they mature, or as obligations become due and payable. A person may still have an excess of assets over liabilities, but be insolvent if unable to convert assets into cash to meet financial obligations.

A financial institution, such as a bank, generally is considered to be insolvent if its ratio of capital to assets is at, or close to, zero, or if its capital assets, including common stock, are of such poor quality that its continued existence is uncertain. See also ACT OF BANKRUPTCY; BANKRUPTCY.

installment contract written agreement to pay for goods purchased, in payments of principal and interest at regularly scheduled intervals. Also called installment sales paper and installment paper. See also CONDITIONAL SALES CONTRACT.

installment credit loan repaid with interest owed, in equal periodic payments of principal and interest. Installment loans are fully amortizing loans, repayable over a fixed amortization schedule in monthly installments. These loans can be secured by personal property—for example, an auto loan—but not real estate. If the loan is to a consumer, disclosure of finance charges is required by federal consumer protection laws. See also CHATTEL MORTGAGE; CONDITIONAL SALES CONTRACT; CONSUMER CREDIT; PERSONAL LOAN.

installment note promissory note underlying an INSTALLMENT CREDIT agreement, calling for periodic payments of principal and interest to pay off the debt.

institutional lender financial institution or institutional investor that invests its own funds, or funds under management, in corporate equities and debt securities, government securities, residential mortgages, commercial real estate, or mortgage backed securities. Frequently, these investors buy mortgage loans, either whole loans or pools of loans packaged as securities, and also new securities offerings sold through private placement. In the SECONDARY MORTGAGE MARKET, savings and loan associations, savings banks, life insurance companies, commercial banks, and pension funds act as institutional lenders.

instructing bank bank that initiates a transfer of funds as instructed by a customer, as opposed to an advising bank, which notifies the sender that payment has been made. Also called the *ordering party*.

instrument legally enforceable agreement between two or more parties, expressing a contractual right or a right to the payment of money. Practically all documents used in credit are instruments, e.g., checks, drafts, notes, bonds. See also NEGOTIABLE INSTRUMENT.

instrumentality government agency issuing marketable securities backed by the FULL FAITH AND CREDIT guarantee of the government. The term is normally used in connection with notes, certificates, and bonds issued by U.S. government agencies, such as the Export-Import Bank, the Government National Mortgage Association, or the Small Business Administration, but can refer more generally to any government agency.

insufficient funds designation for a bounced check, a check written for an amount larger than the collected balance in the maker's checking account. Also called NON SUFFICIENT FUNDS (NSF). If dishonored, the check is returned to the PAYEE's bank.

insurance trust IRREVOCABLE TRUST created to receive the proceeds of a life insurance policy, normally established to avoid paying estate taxes. Trust assets are payable to the beneficiary at the death of the insured. A life insurance trust provides additional liquidity to the insured, but has the disadvantage that the person named as beneficiary cannot borrow against the policy, and must survive a gift to the trust by three years.

insured account account at a bank, savings and loan association, or other savings institution guaranteed against loss by a deposit insurance fund. Accounts in federally insured depository institutions are protected up to $100,000 in principal balance. Commercial bank accounts and mutual savings bank accounts are insured by the BANK INSURANCE FUND; savings and loan and federal savings bank accounts by the SAVINGS ASSOCIATION INSURANCE FUND, and credit union accounts by the National Credit Union Share Insurance Fund.

Federal deposit insurance was enacted in the 1930s when a wave of bank failures threatened to undermine the banking system. Savings and loans (S&Ls) in some states were insured until 1985 by private guaranty funds, but since then many of these S&Ls have opted for federal insurance programs. With the exception of accounts in some state credit unions, nearly all deposit accounts, representing more than 99% of all deposits in financial institutions, are federally insured.

insured financial institution bank or savings institution that is a member of the Federal Deposit Insurance Corporation's deposit insurance plan. National banks and state banks are required to insure deposits with the Bank Insurance Fund. Deposits in savings and loans and federal savings banks are protected by the Savings Association Insurance Fund, and credit unions by the National Credit Union Share Insurance Fund.

insured loan residential mortgage loan protected against credit risk by the FEDERAL HOUSING ADMINISTRATION (FHA). In event of default, the FHA indemnifies the holder of the mortgage for part, or all, of the unpaid principal. FHA-insured loans generally have a high ratio of loan to value, and frequently are pooled for sale to institutional investors as GINNIE MAE (Government National Mortgage Association) PASS-THROUGH CERTIFICATES. The FHA charges a fee for insuring mortgages. Interest rates on FHA insured loans are set slightly below prevailing market rates on conventional mortgage loans. See also CREDIT ENHANCEMENT; FINANCIAL GUARANTEE; GUARANTEED LOAN.

intangible asset balance sheet asset having no physical properties, but thought to represent some future economic benefit to its owner. Intangibles, such as GOODWILL, bank card service marks, patents, franchises, and so on, are noncurrent assets amortized over the period held.

integrated circuit card see SMART CARD.

Interagency Country Exposure Review Committee committee of U.S. banking regulators that sets a uniform rating system to evaluate COUNTRY RISK for U.S. banks that are large foreign lenders. The committee is composed of nine members drawn from the Federal Reserve Board, the Comptroller of the Currency, and the Federal Deposit Insurance Corporation. The committee classifies nonperforming foreign loans as substandard, value impaired, or loss. Banks with loans rated as value impaired would, for example, be required to set aside funds in a special reserve account.

Inter-American Development Bank (IADB) development bank, organized in 1959, to foster economic development in Latin America by arranging project financing with its own funds and loans by private banks. Membership, originally limited to member countries of the Organization of American States, has since been broadened to include the governments of 26 Latin American countries, the United States, Japan, and 14 European countries.

interbank bid rate see LONDON INTERBANK BID RATE.

interbank deposits deposit held by one bank for another bank, usually a correspondent. Each bank holds a DUE TO ACCOUNT in the name of the other bank. Also called *reciprocal deposits*. An account on the books of a foreign correspondent is a NOSTRO ACCOUNT to the bank owning the account, and a VOSTRO ACCOUNT as viewed by the foreign correspondent.

interbank market market in which banks buy and sell money market instruments, such as bankers' acceptances, commercial paper, and certificates of deposit, usually with maturities of less than one year. There are numerous examples: the FEDERAL FUNDS market in the United States, where banks sell EXCESS RESERVES to each other, generally on an overnight basis; the foreign exchange market; and the Eurocurrency deposit market. Trading is done over-the-counter through informal networks of brokers and dealers.

interbank rate see FEDERAL FUNDS RATE; LONDON INTERBANK OFFERED RATE.

interchange exchange of transactions between financial institutions participating in a bank card network, based on a common set of rules. Examples are the Visa and MasterCard national bank card systems and regional automated teller machine networks. Card interchange allows a bank's customer to use a bank credit card at any card honoring merchant, and gain access to multiple automated teller machine systems from a single ATM. See also INTERCHANGE RATE.

interchange rate fee paid by one bank to another to cover handling costs and credit risk in a bank card transaction. Interchange fees generally flow toward the bank funding a transaction and assuming some risk in the process. In a credit card transaction, the interchange fee, also known as the *issuer's reimbursement fee*, is paid by the bank purchasing (or accepting) the merchant's sales drafts (the MERCHANT BANK) to the card issuing bank, who then bills the cardholder. The interchange fee, a percentage of the transaction amount, is derived from an accounting formula that takes into account authorization costs, fraud and credit losses, and the average bank cost of funds, and is periodically revised. In automated teller and electronic debit point-of-sale systems, interchange flows in the opposite direction; when a consumer gets cash at an automated teller machine, the terminal owning bank collects the fee.

interdistrict settlement account clearing account maintained by the Federal Reserve Board in Washington, D.C., for settlement of interbank transfers of funds among the 12 Federal Reserve Banks. As transactions are made, each Reserve Bank's settlement account is increased (debited) by a due from entry, or reduced (credited) by a due to entry. These accounting entries are settled daily on a net basis, reducing the need to transfer funds between Reserve Banks.

interest money paid for the use of money, expressed as a percentage rate for the period of time in use, generally an annual rate. Bank interest is both an amount paid to attract deposit funds, and a finance charge for money loaned to borrowers. Prior to the federal Truth in Lending Act of 1968, lenders used widely differing methods of calculating loan interest. Since then, interest due on consumer loans must be computed in terms of an ANNUAL PERCENTAGE RATE (APR), utilizing interest rate tables from the Federal Reserve Board or from financial publishers, and the total cost of borrowing disclosed when a loan is made. Federal regulation of credit was intended to make it easier for consumer to shop for credit. Loan interest paid over the term of a loan may in fact be less than the total FINANCE CHARGE cost of borrowing if the lender charges a commitment fee or discount points payable in advance.

In the 1980s, as deposit interest rates were deregulated, the cost of funds for bank lenders became more unpredictable. This led many lenders to emphasize variable rate loans, especially in longer-term loans such as home mortgages, in which the rate of interest is indexed to a cost of funds index or money market rate.

See also ADD-ON INTEREST; COMPOUND INTEREST; DAILY INTEREST; DISCOUNT; EXACT INTEREST; PRECOMPUTED INTEREST RATE; PRIME RATE; RULE OF THE 78s; SIMPLE INTEREST; USURY.

interest margin see NET INTEREST MARGIN.

interest only loan

1. commercial loan or line of credit paying interest at regular intervals until maturity, when the entire balance is due. These loans do not require AMORTIZATION, unlike conventional mortgages or installment loans. Apartment buildings in New York City are often financed through interest-only loans. The take-out lender arranging a permanent mortgage assumes responsibility for collecting the entire debt, including the unpaid principal. A REVOLVING CREDIT loan to a business also can be an interesting loan. The borrower makes regular interest payments, and pays down the loan principal during the annual out of debt period, when the borrower is required to be free of debt. See also BALLOON MATURITY; BULLET LOAN.

2. HOME EQUITY CREDIT line deferring payment of loan principal for a specified period, say five years. The borrower can then refinance the loan at current interest rates or begin making regular payments of principal and interest. See also NEGATIVE AMORTIZATION.

interest-only (IO) strip mortgage security consisting of the interest rate portion of a STRIPPED MORTGAGE BACKED SECURITY. The holder receives interest payments based on the current value of the underlying loan collateral. Most often used as a hedging device in periods of high interest rates, as the performance of an IO strip varies inversely to mortgage prepayments. High prepayments on underlying loans can return less to the holder than the dollar amount invested. See also PRINCIPAL-ONLY (PO) STRIP.

interest rate cost of CREDIT, expressed as a percentage rate, computed from the ratio of INTEREST TO PRINCIPAL. Some interest rates are set by supply and demand in the money market, for example, the rate paid by the U.S. Treasury Department when it auctions Treasury bills. Interest rates on bank loans are administered rates, which means they are determined by the lender. The bank PRIME RATE, for example, is determined independently by each bank, even though many banks follow the actions of money center banks in repricing their prime rate. Variable interest rates, such as the rate charged in an Adjustable Rate Mortgage, are determined from an INDEX rate, or COST OF FUNDS INDEX, that by regulation must be outside the control of the lending institution. See also ANNUAL PERCENTAGE RATE; BASE RATE; LEGAL RATE OF INTEREST; USURY.

interest rate cap

1. contractual agreement protecting a borrower against a rise in interest rates. In exchange for an upfront fee paid when the funds are advanced, the lender agrees to hold any rate increases to a preset ceiling. For example, a borrower taking out a loan priced at a spread above the London Interbank Offered Rate (LIBOR) for 90-day Eurodollar deposits pays a cap fee to insure that the loan interest rate does not exceed a preset rate anytime during the life of the loan. The cap seller (the lender) agrees to pay the purchaser (the borrower) the difference between LIBOR and the STRIKE PRICE of the cap when LIBOR rises above that price. Interest rate caps are priced as option contracts, generally using an options pricing formula.

   Most commercial lenders hedge against the interest rate risk created by the cap by buying an offsetting cap from another financial institution, by exchanging a floating rate obligation for a fixed rate obligation in an INTEREST RATE SWAP, or by hedging—selling futures short—in the financial futures market. If interest rates happen to rise, the lender can then sell the futures contract at a higher price. The easiest way to buy protection against interest rate risk is to buy another cap. A bank selling a 15% cap on a $100 million loan could protect itself by taking an identical cap from another lender. Compare to COLLAR.

2. in an ADJUSTABLE RATE MORTGAGE, contractual limits on interest rate adjustments above an INDEX. For example, ANNUAL CAP and LIFE OF LOAN CAP.

interest rate futures contract giving the holder the right to buy or sell a financial instrument at a specific price at a given future date. Interest futures began in 1975 when the Chicago Board of Trade began trading futures contracts on Ginnie Mae mortgage backed pass-through certificates. Later commodities exchanges added futures contracts in Treasury bills, notes and bonds, and commercial paper. Financial institutions utilize futures contracts as a hedging device, to minimize interest rate risk in periods of rising or falling rates.

interest rate mismatch see GAP; MISMATCH.

interest rate options contract giving the right, but not the obligation, to buy or sell a financial instrument paying a fixed rate of interest at a specified price and future date. Option contracts in standard amounts of financial instruments, at a standard STRIKE PRICE and expiration date, are traded on securities and commodities exchanges, or are arranged in the over-the-counter market by a commercial bank or investment bank. Interest rate options, also called *debt options* or *fixed income options* are traded on the American Stock Exchange and the Chicago Board Options Exchange. Financial instruments traded include U.S. Treasury bills and Treasury bonds. Over-the-counter option contracts, often used when hedging a bond portfolio, are written by commercial banks and investment banks for Treasury notes and bonds, mortgage backed securities, and money market instruments.

Another type of interest rate option allows option trading in FINANCIAL FUTURES contracts. For instance, the buyer of a call option in Treasury bond futures takes a long position in Treasury bonds of a specific maturity. Futures options in Treasury bonds are traded on the Chicago Board of Trade, whereas options in Eurodollar futures are traded on the International Monetary Market at the Chicago Mercantile Exchange and the London International Financial Futures Exchange.

interest rate risk risk that an interest-earning asset, such as a bank loan, will decline in value as interest rates change. Longer maturity, fixed rate loans (for example, 30-year conventional mortgages) are more sensitive to price risk from changes

INTEREST RATE SWAP

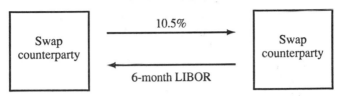

Notional amount: $10 million.
Maturity: 5 years.
Payment frequency: both fixed and floating rate payments
  are made semiannually.

Source: Recent Innovations in International Banking (Bank for International Settlements, 1986).

in rates than variable rate loans. Another type of interest risk is
REINVESTMENT RISK, or the possibility that maturing loans cannot be replaced by new loans earning the same interest rate.

interest rate sensitivity see INTEREST RATE RISK.

interest rate swap contract in which two counter-parties
agree to exchange interest payments of differing character based
on an underlying NOTIONAL PRINCIPAL amount that is never exchanged. There are three types of interest swaps: coupon swaps
or exchange of fixed rate for floating rate instruments in the
same currency; BASIS SWAPs or the exchange of floating rate for
floating rate instruments in the same currency; and cross currency interest rate swaps involving the exchange of fixed rate
instruments in one currency for floating rate in another.
    Typically, a swap contract exchanges long-term fixed rate
obligations for a short-term floating rate instrument in the same
currency. In its simplest form, the two parties to an interest rate
swap exchange their interest payment obligations (no principal
changes hands) on two different kinds of debt instruments, one
being a fixed interest rate, the other being a floating rate.
    For example, the Student Loan Marketing Association (Sal-
lie Mae) may want to swap rates with a mutual savings bank—a
mutually beneficial transaction, as Sallie Mae, a highly rated

institution because of its status as a federal agency, prefers floating rate to match short-term loans in its student loan portfolio. Sallie Mae can sell fixed rate debt at a relatively low cost, whereas the mutual savings bank prefers to match its long-term fixed rate mortgages with fixed rate funds.

interest sensitive assets bank assets, principally loans, that are subject to changes in interest rates, either at maturity or when they are repriced according to an INDEX rate. Repricing of these assets is pegged or indexed to the upward or downward fluctuations of a publicly disclosed rate or cost of funds index, such as the six-month Treasury bill, the bank prime rate, and so on. Examples are variable rate consumer loans, variable rate demand loans, and adjustable rate mortgages. See also ASSET-LIABILITY MANAGEMENT; DURATION; GAP; INTEREST SENSITIVE LIABILITIES; REPRICING OPPORTUNITIES.

interest sensitive liabilities short-term DEPOSIT instruments paying floating, as oppposed to fixed, rates of interest. Since REGULATION Q interest rate ceilings were abolished under the Monetary Control Act of 1980, a significant portion of bank deposits are rate sensitive, including the six-month MONEY MARKET CERTIFICATE, the MONEY MARKET DEPOSIT ACCOUNT, and the SUPER NOW ACCOUNT. Phaseout of deposit interest rate ceilings in 1986 and removal of most penalties for early deposit withdrawals have led to increased volatility in the supply of deposits funding bank loans and new techniques to manage INTERBANK RATE RISK. See also ASSET-LIABILITY COMMITTEE; ASSET-LIABILITY MANAGEMENT; FUNDS MANAGEMENT; INTEREST SENSITIVE ASSETS.

interim loan see CONSTRUCTION MORTGAGE.

interim statement
1. **Banking.** A customer's checking account statement, dispensed by a self-service banking terminal, listing account debits and credits since the last regular account statement was mailed, and current collected balance. Also called *mini statement* or *snapshot statement*.
2. **Finance.** A financial statement reporting activity for an accounting period less than an organization's fiscal year, for example, the quarterly 10Q report filed with the SEC.

interlocking directorate commercial bank or savings institution having individuals on its board of directors who also serve on the board of an unaffiliated competitor in the same marketplace. The Financial Institutions Regulatory Act of 1978 prohibits management interlocks by banks in the same Metropolitan Statistical Area (MSA), but exempts smaller banks, and also permits interlocks of up to 49% of a bank's management officers.

intermediary

1. financial institution, such as a bank or savings and loan, that acts as a conduit between suppliers of funds (depositors) and users of funds (borrowers). See also FINANCIAL INTERMEDIARY.
2. in the SWAP market, a commercial bank or investment bank that makes a market in interest rate and currency swaps to earn fees or trading profits.

intermediate targets monetary targets, either monetary growth or interest rates, that the Federal Reserve sets as objectives of its MONETARY POLICY. In recent years, the Fed has shifted its focus from controlling the rise and fall of the Fed Funds rate to emphasis on monetary targets and growth in the nation's money supply. Money supply is one of these targets, although other economic indicators are also closely watched, including total federal funds trading, net borrowed reserves and total reserves, plus total debt in the economy. See also OPERATING TARGETS.

intermediation process of transferring funds from an ultimate source to the ultimate user. A FINANCIAL INSTITUTION, such as a bank, intermediates credit when it obtains money from a depositor and relends it to a borrowing customer. The opposite is DISINTERMEDIATION, the withdrawal of deposit funds when savers expect to earn a higher yield through direct investment such as stocks or bonds. See also FINANCIAL INTERMEDIARY.

internal capital generation rate rate at which a bank generates equity capital, computed by dividing retained earnings (net income less dividends) by the average balance of stockholders equity for a given accounting period.

internal rate of return (IRR) average annual yield earned by investment during the period held. It can be: (1) the effective rate of interest on a loan; (2) the discount rate in DIS-COUNTED CASH FLOW analysis; or (3) the rate that adjusts the value of future cash receipts earned by an investment so that interest earned (cash inflow) is equal to the original cost (cash outflow). The IRR is arrived at through trial and error calculation, using a mathematical formula, and in financial instruments is equal to the YIELD TO MATURITY.

International Bank for Reconstruction and Development (IBRD) international lending organization, popularly known as the World Bank, founded at the Bretton Woods economic conference in 1944 initially to finance the reconstruction of Europe following World War II, and more recently to provide developing countries with long-term, low-interest credit for industrial development when private financing is unavailable. The World Bank works closely with the INTERNATIONAL MONETARY FUND (IMF) and has 149 member countries. The World Bank finances its operations through member subscriptions, sale of its own securities, and net earnings. Most World Bank loans are made at variable interest rates pegged to its current cost of funds. Member countries must also be IMF members. In recent years, the World Bank has redefined its traditional role. The bank has set aside funds for new loans, in response to the world debt crisis, and has added its guarantee to new bank loans made to less developed countries. See also MULTILATERAL DEVELOPMENT BANKS; WORLD BANK GROUP.

International Banking Act of 1978 federal law, enacted by Congress in 1978, placing U.S. branches and agencies of foreign banks under supervision of U.S. banking regulators. Foreign banks are eligible for federal deposit insurance, are required to maintain noninterest earning reserve account balances and submit to periodic bank examinations, and are subject to the same branching limitations as domestic banks. See also EDGE ACT CORPORATION; FOREIGN BRANCHES.

international banking facility (IBF) separate banking center in a U.S. domestic bank or office of a foreign bank, authorized by the Federal Reserve Board in 1981 to participate in Eurocurrency lending through a separate set of accounts.

Essentially, an IBF is an in-house shell branch (a separate book of assets and liabilities) that makes loans to foreign customers, other IBFs, and U.S offices and foreign offices of an IBF parent bank. IBF deposits, limited to non-U.S. residents, other IBFs, and banks owning an IBF, are free from reserve requirements, federal deposit insurance assessments, and some state income taxes. See also OFFSHORE BANKING UNIT.

international depositary receipt (IDR) negotiable bank-issued certificate representing ownership of stock securities by an investor outside the country of origin. An international depositary receipt, or IDR, is the non-U.S. equivalent of an AMERICAN DEPOSITARY RECEIPT. These instruments have been used since the 1970s to facilitate international trading in securities. The securities backing the receipt remain in the custody of the issuing bank or a correspondent.

International Development Association see WORLD BANK GROUP.

International Monetary Fund (IMF) international organization, formed at the Bretton Woods economic conference in 1944, to maintain monetary stability in the world community. It has 146 members, including the United States. The IMF works closely with the INTERNATIONAL BANK FOR RECONSTRUCTION AND DEVELOPMENT (the World Bank), but directs its attention toward payment of external debts owed by countries with balance of payments deficits, rather than project financing.

The IMF makes loans in the form of drawings (SPECIAL DRAWING RIGHTS (SDRs) by member countries. In recent years, the IMF has linked its lending activities to stringent internal restraints aimed at bringing inflation rates and the world debt crisis under control by reducing imports and increasing exports. In restructuring of debt owed by less developed countries, the IMF also has added its guarantee to private bank loans and made direct loans to encourage banks to renew maturing loans. Loans by the IMF are technically purchases of foreign currencies and SDRs, and repayments are repurchases by IMF members of their own currencies with SDRs or foreign exchange. See also GENERAL AGREEMENTS TO BORROW.

International Organization for Standardization (ISO) organization acting as a central clearinghouse for industry standards drafted by national standard setting organizations. The American National Standards Institute, based in New York City, is the U.S. representative of ISO.

international reserves acceptable international means of payments between CENTRAL BANKS, mainly in gold, certain currencies (such as the dollar), and SPECIAL DRAWING RIGHTS at the International Monetary Fund.

interpretive letter rules of bank regulatory agencies or other administrative agencies that normally take effect as soon as they are issued. Interpretive letter rulings, although not binding as law, are closely watched in the banking industry for indications of new marketing opportunities or authority given by banking regulators for banks to expand their activities in related financial services, such as brokerage and insurance. For example, the Federal Reserve Board's 1989 ruling allowing bank securities affiliates to underwrite corporate bonds.

interstate banking banking expansion across state lines through bank holding company acquisitions. Interstate expansion of commercial banking companies began in the mid-1980s when state legislatures enacted laws permitting holding company acquisitions on a reciprocal basis with other states. Thus, a bank holding company in Connecticut was free to acquire a bank in Massachusetts if Massachusetts law extended the same privilege to Connecticut banking companies. The legal basis of these reciprocal interstate banking laws is the 1966 DOUGLAS AMENDMENT to the Bank Holding Company Act, which gave state legislatures the power to decide when, and under what circumstances, they would explicitly permit interstate acquisitions. The McFADDEN ACT, the 1927 federal act prohibiting interstate branching remains in effect. So, using the above example, the Connecticut banking company cannot legally accept deposits from its own customers at branch offices of the bank it acquired in its neighboring state. Nor can it open new branch offices in Massachusetts under its own name. Even though deposit taking is still restricted, interstate banking allows multistate holding companies to pool capital and other resources, allow subsidiary banks to market a wider array of products and services, and diversify the holding company's loan and deposit base.

Interstate banking legislation has evolved in three distinct phases: REGIONAL INTERSTATE BANKING, allowing mergers by bank holding companies in a geographic region, for example, New England, or the Southeast, and excluding all other states; regional expansion under state laws with a NATIONAL TRIGGER, allowing mergers with banks in any other state after a certain date; and eventually unrestricted nationwide interstate banking. As of 1989, more than two thirds of the states had interstate banking laws with national trigger dates set to expire by 1991 or 1992. See also SUPER-REGIONAL BANK.

intervention action by central bankers to manipulate currency rates in the foreign exchange markets, or maintain an orderly market. Central banks intervene through buying or selling currencies or engaging in currency swaps with other central banks. For example, the Federal Reserve might sell dollars and buy a foreign currency when the exchange value of the dollar is too high, in relation to other currencies; buying dollars and selling another currency in the open market has the opposite effect. In the September 1985 Plaza Agreement, held at the Plaza Hotel in New York, central bankers in the Group of Seven countries agreed to actively intervene in the markets to lower the value of the U.S. dollar, in relation to other major currencies.

Most central banks intervene in the currency markets to one degree or another. The Federal Reserve, acting through the foreign exchange desk of the Federal Reserve Bank of New York, and the U.S. Treasury's EXCHANGE STABILIZATION FUND participate equally in financing exchange market intervention. Exchange market intervention has no effect on bank reserves kept by U.S. banks at Federal Reserve banks. See also CURRENCY BAND; EXCHANGE STABILIZATION FUND; SWAP NETWORK.

inter vivos trust from the Latin, "between the living," a gift of property from one living person to another, as opposed to a TESTAMENTARY TRUST created by a will. Also called *living trust*.

intestate without a will; a person who dies leaving property but without providing for disposition of his or her estate in a will. A court-appointed representative called an ADMINISTRATOR will be appointed to distribute the deceased's property according to state law.

in the money option contract resulting in a net gain if exercisable at a market price above the option STRIKE PRICE of a call option or below the option price of a put option. See also AT THE MONEY; OUT OF THE MONEY.

intrinsic value net benefit to the holder of an option contract from exercising the option immediately. It is the difference between the underlying price and the option's exercise price. An option generally sells for at least its intrinsic value.

inventory financing working capital loan to finance the purchase of inventory for resale. As the inventory is sold, the loan is gradually paid off. Inventory financing includes floor planning and warehouse financing. Loans secured by receivables command a higher BORROWING BASE than inventory, because receivables are one step closer to cash and qualify for a higher credit advance. See also ASSET-BASED LENDING.

inverse floater mortgage backed bond, usually part of a COLLATERALIZED MORTGAGE OBLIGATION (CMO) bearing an interest rate that declines as an index rate, for example, the LIBOR rate, increases. An inverse floater may have a FLOOR and a CAP. Also called a *reverse floater*.

inverted market futures market where the nearer months are selling at premiums to the more distant months.

inverted yield curve unusual money market condition where short-term rates are higher than long-term rates, resulting in a negatively sloping yield curve. The yield curve, under normal market conditions, is positively sloping, meaning that longer maturity instruments carry a higher rate than shorter maturities. The yield curve inverts when the Federal Reserve tightens credit. This holds down the supply of lendable funds in the banking system, when demand for short-term business credit is rising. This pushes up short-term interest rates. Long-term rates, on the other hand, are influenced more by inflationary expectations than the Fed's monetary policy. A negatively slop-

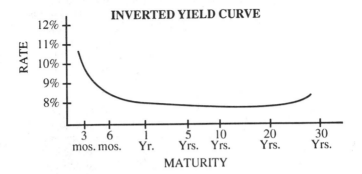

INVERTED YIELD CURVE

ing yield curve is a temporary phenomenon, lasting an average of 15 months or less, and is often viewed as a sign that the economy is weakening or heading into a recession.

investment advisor person or firm supplying buy-sell recommendations and market information to investment clients. Investment advisors are required to register with the Securities and Exchange Commission, and, under the Investment Advisors Act of 1940, disclose any conflicts of interest in recommendations they offer. In general, banks may give limited amounts of investment advice to retail customers, but there are few legal restrictions on investment advice to institutional accounts, such as pension funds, investment management firms and also corporate accounts.

A bank sponsoring a mutual fund can act as the fund's advisor, deciding what investment choices to make, but is prohibited by the GLASS-STEAGALL ACT from acting simultaneously as a fund's advisor and distributor. For this reason, banks issuing mutual fund shares have relied on regulated investment companies to market the securities offered for sale.

investment banking sale and distribution of a new offering of securities, carried out by a financial intermediary (an investment banker), who buys securities from the issuer as principal, and assumes the risk of distributing the securities to investors. The process of purchasing and distributing securities is known as UNDERWRITING. Normally, several investment bankers take part in a securities offering, each agreeing to sell a portion of the securities proposed for sale, and, in return, collecting a portion of the underwriting fee or SPREAD. The GLASS-STEAGALL ACT of 1933 prohibited commercial banks from underwriting securities, and required banks to sell their underwriting affiliates, because of abuses by some commercial bankers in selling securities to their own customers. Also, Congress was concerned that banks taking excessive risks might wipe out their equity capital.

Recent rulings from the Federal Reserve Board, however, have softened this barrier, allowing commercial banks to underwrite issues of asset-backed securities, such as mortgage securities, and sell these directly to the public. Commercial banks have been authorized by the Fed to underwrite limited amounts of corporate bonds, commercial paper, and municipal industrial development bonds through holding company affiliates. A bank SECURITIES AFFILIATE, also known as a Section 20 affiliate, from the section of the Glass-Steagall Act authorizing them, must be capitalized separate from a bank holding company and limit its activities in approved securities to not more than 10% of the dollar value of all securities eligible for bank underwriting. See also ALL OR NONE; BEST EFFORT; FIRM COMMITMENT; STANDBY UNDERWRITING.

investment company company that invests in securities issued by other companies and sells shares to individual investors. Under Securities and Exchange Commission rules, there are four types of regulated investment companies: open-end funds (mutual funds) that regularly sell and redeem their shares; closed-end funds, many of which are listed on stock exchanges, and sell a fixed number of shares; face-amount certificate companies, paying a specific sum to on stated maturity dates to certificate holders; and unit investment trusts, which issue redeemable securities representing an interest in specific securities.

Mutual funds are further divided into load funds, which charge the investor a sales commission, ranging from as little as $1^3/_4$% to a high of around $8^1/_2$% of the face value of shares purchased, and no-load funds that do not impose a charge for purchase or redemption of securities. See also BACK-END LOAD; FRONT-END LOAD; INVESTMENT COMPANY ACT; 12b1 MUTUAL FUND.

Investment Company Act of 1940 federal law, enacted by Congress in 1940, requiring companies that market pooled investment funds to the public to register as investment companies with the Securities and Exchange Commission. The act also sets standards for disclosure of financial information, pricing of shares offered to the public and allocation of portfolio investments, and prohibits a regulated investment company from changing its policies without shareholder approval.

investment credit federal tax credit resulting from ownership of capital equipment. The tax credit is taken in the year the asset is placed in service. Also called *investment tax credit* or ITC. The ITC was repealed by the Tax Reform Act of 1986 for all equipment placed in service after 1985, unless the equipment qualified under special transitional rules. The ITC was originally intended to compensate owners of equipment and equipment lessors for their capital costs.

investment grade description of a high-quality corporate or municipal bond, assigned a rating of AAA to BBB by Standard & Poor's and Fitch's Investors Service. (Moody's Investors Service assigns ratings of Aaa and Baa, respectively.) Investment grade securities are those rated Baa or better or BBB or better. These bonds are considered suitable investments for banks, trust departments, and fiduciaries, such as pension funds. U.S. Treasury securities and federal agency securities are also considered investment quality securities for financial institutions. Bonds rated lower than BBB may often carry a higher yield, but are speculative investments. See also JUNK BOND.

investment letter agreement between the buyer and seller in a PRIVATE PLACEMENT of securities, stating that securities are being purchased for investment and will not be offered for resale to the public any time during a specified period, normally two years. Also called a *letter of intent*. These securities, while exempt from SEC registration requirements, may later be sold to the public under SEC Rule 144, provided the securities are held for at least two years and certain other conditions are met. Securities sold under a letter of intent are known as letter stocks or letter bonds.

investment securities marketable securities held by a bank in its portfolio of balance sheet assets. Investment securities, along with bank loans, are the principal source of bank earnings, and generally serve two key functions: as a source of bank LIQUIDITY, or funding to meet loan demand or customers' needs for cash; and also as an additional source of earnings from the capital gains realized when portfolio securities are sold. Bank investment grade securities also are acceptable collateral in meeting PLEDGING REQUIREMENTS for holding federal government deposits, and also deposits of state and local governments. Bank investment securities are carried at amortized BOOK VALUE, or original purchase cost less amortization or accretion to par value.

Eligible securities that a bank legally can hold as investments include U.S. Treasury securities, federal agency obligations, debt securities of state and local governments, stock in Federal Reserve banks, plus certain other types of investment grade debt (but not corporate securities). The Glass-Steagall Act, for instance, prohibits national banks and state member banks from investing in equity securities of nonfinancial corporations. As a general rule, banks can own stock in bankers' banks, Edge Act corporations, foreign banks and other companies offering bank-like services, and can hold other investment grade debt so long as securities owned do not exceed 10% of a bank's capital and surplus.

Excluded from the investment securities portfolio are TRADING ACCOUNT ASSETS, and other securities a bank is eligible to purchase in securities underwriting for resale to the public or to other financial institutions, and also securities held under repurchase agreements. Assets held in the trading portfolio are marked to market daily. See also BARBELL PORTFOLIO; BOND SWAP; LADDERED PORTFOLIO.

involuntary bankruptcy petition by a sufficient number of creditors, claiming a debtor has commited an ACT OF BANKRUPTCY, or is not paying debts on time, asking a bankruptcy court to distribute assets to pay obligations. Also called a *creditor's petition*. An involuntary bankruptcy petition can be filed by as few as one creditor; but if the debtor has 12 or more creditors, signatures of at least three creditors are needed. Creditors can file petitions under any chapter of the code: a Chapter 7 LIQUIDATION of the debtor's assets, a REORGANIZATION under Chapter 11, or a Chapter 13 repayment plan. Creditors' petitions are allowed against any business or individual except nonprofit organizations and farmers. Once a petition has been accepted by the court, it is handled as if it were a VOLUNTARY BANKRUPTCY filed by the debtor. See also BANKRUPTCY; PRIORITY OF LIEN.

involuntary lien judgment lien, lien for unpaid taxes or special assessment by a municipality that attaches to a real property without consent of the owner, in contrast with a MORTGAGE lien, which is voluntary.

irrevocable letter of credit letter of credit, valid for a stated period of time, that may be cancelled or amended only by agreement of all parties to the credit. The issuing bank waives its right to revoke a letter of credit prior to the expiration date, unless the consent of the beneficiary is obtained.

irrevocable trust trust that cannot be revoked by the person creating it, except with approval of the BENEFICIARY, as opposed to a REVOCABLE TRUST, in which the trust instrument can be modified or terminated at will.

issue
1. securities sold by a corporation or government on a particular date or during an offering period, identifiable by maturity date or class of security.
2. to sell or privately place an offering of securities.
3. to approve a credit instrument, for example, a letter of credit, or approve and mail a bank card to a consumer.
4. a person's direct descendents who stand first in line to inherit an estate.

issuer
1. corporation, government, or other legal entity having the authority to offer its own bond, note, or stock certificate for sale to investors.
2. financial institution that issues credit or debit cards, for example, Visa or MasterCard credit cards, or automated teller machine debit cards. Card issuers authorize transactions on issued and outstanding cards, and mail monthly activity statements to cardholders.
3. bank that approves a letter of credit on behalf of a particular customer, valid for a stated period.

item banking term for negotiable instruments, such as checks or drafts, representing uncollected funds. In electronic transfers of funds, for example, an Automated Clearing House (ACH) credit or debit transaction, an item is an electronic record of funds moving from one bank to another.

itemized statement account activity statement with a line-by-line transaction summary, generally in chronological order, listing account debits, credits, and service charges during an accounting period. If the account is a bank card account, the account statement lists merchant names next to each entry, and terminal locations, for example, automated teller machines, if a debit card is used.

J

jeep see GRADUATED PAYMENT MORTGAGE.

joint account
1. bank account owned by two or more persons, who equally share rights and liabilities of the account. Ownership of joint accounts can be set up in either of two ways: (1) a joint tenancy account (commonly used by husband and wife), in which either, acting separately, can make deposits or withdrawals at any time, and when one owner dies, the full account passes to the surviving owner; (2) tenants in common (commonly used by business partners), in which the approval of both owners is needed to make withdrawals. If one owner dies, the other shares the account equally with the deceased owner's estate. See also JOINT TENANTS WITH RIGHT OF SURVIVORSHIP; TENANCY IN COMMON; TENANCY BY THE ENTIRETY.
2. investment banking account formed by several underwriters acting as a syndicate. See also JOINTLY AND SEVERALLY; SEVERALLY BUT NOT JOINTLY.

joint custody see DUAL CONTROL.

joint endorsement
endorsement by two or more persons, needed to negotiate a check payable to more than one individual. Many banks require signatures by both owners of a dual account before cashing a U.S. government check, for example, an IRS tax refund.

jointly and severally
1. legal term for the liability of two or more individuals, who each agree to repay an obligation. A creditor holding an unpaid note has the option of suing each person individually or all of them as a group.

2. in UNDERWRITING of municipal bonds, expression for a bond offering in which each member of a syndicate is liable for a portion of any unsold securities, in addition to its own participation. Also called an *undivided account* or Eastern Account. See also SEVERALLY BUT NOT JOINTLY.

joint note promissory note signed by two or more makers, payable in installments or at maturity. If unpaid, the lender must bring legal action against the borrowers collectively.

joint tenants with right of survivorship ownership of bank accounts, real property, or personal property by two or more people, each having full right of usage—the most common form of property ownership by married persons. When a married couple opens a JOINT ACCOUNT, say a checking account, each has unlimited access, and can withdraw funds to the full amount in the account. When one owner dies, the property automatically passes to the co-owner, avoiding probate although estate taxes may be payable. Distinguish from TENANCY BY THE ENTIRETY.

joint venture commercial undertaking by two or more organizations that agree to work together for a specific purpose. Joint ventures in the financial services industry encourage innovation by helping to overcome the high initial capitalization costs of new products and services, thereby allowing competing banks to realize economies of scale by working together, rather than separately. For example, a shared AUTOMATED TELLER MACHINE (ATM) network, in which financial institutions in a given market allow unrestricted access to their ATMs by customers of other institutions. Many of these ATM systems are operated as nonprofit ventures, jointly owned by participating banks and savings institutions.

From a legal viewpoint, financial industry joint ventures are considered to be within federal ANTITRUST LAWS as long as they are pro-competitive rather than anti-competitive, that is, they do not discourage participation by nonmember financial institutions.

judgmental credit analysis approval or denial of a credit application, based on the lender's evaluation of the credit application, and credit experience with similar applicants, instead of a CREDIT SCORING model that estimates the probability of debt repayment. As defined by Federal Reserve REGULATION B, a judgmental system is any method of credit approval other than an empirically derived, statistically-based scoring model. Even when scoring systems are used, though, lenders frequently OVERRIDE the model, as when they approve a loan the system rejected.

judgment lien court order placing a lien on a debtor's real property as security for a debt owed to a judgment creditor. The award, which encumbers the property to the extent of the judgment, may be appealed to a higher court. A lien against personal property is an ATTACHMENT.

jumbo certificate of deposit high-yield CERTIFICATE OF DEPOSIT with a principal amount of $100,000 or more, paying a rate adjusted weekly to money market rates. Jumbo CDs may be issued in negotiable form, transferable to a new owner before maturity, although many jumbo CDs are not negotiable. The principal amount of CDs over the $100,000 limit on federal deposit insurance is not insured, a risk compensated for by their higher yield, which makes these CDs appealing investment vehicles to corporations, pension funds and other institutions investors seeking higher money market returns on short-term CDs. See also BROKERED DEPOSITS; SAFEKEEPING CERTIFICATE.

jumbo mortgage mortgage exceeding the maximum amount a secondary market conduit such as Fannie Mae or Freddy Mac will purchase from a mortgage banker or mortgage originator, and usually carrying a higher interest rate. For example, the dollar limit on loans eligible for purchase in 1990 by the Federal Home Loan Mortgage Corp. (Freddie Mac) was $187,450.

junior mortgage MORTGAGE that is subordinate to earlier mortgages, for example, a second mortgage if there is an outstanding first mortgage. If the borrower defaults, holders of junior mortgages will be paid only after prior lien holders have been satisfied.

junior security security with a claim on the assets and earnings of the issuer that is lower in priority, and contingent on payment to the holder of a SENIOR SECURITY. In priority order, claims are generally ranked and paid as follows: mortgage bonds, debentures, preferred stock, and common stock.

junk bond bond issued by companies whose credit ratings are below investment grade, and generally given a bond rating of BB or lower by bond rating agencies. Also called *high-yield bond*. Bond ratings higher than BB are possible, though, through over-collateralization. To attract investors, junk bonds pay a higher interest rate than INVESTMENT GRADE bonds and are regarded as speculative investments, because the bond issuers either are unknown in the market or are well-known companies that are highly leveraged. The bonds pay higher yields because the credit risk is greater than in investment grade issues. Junk bonds are frequently issued by companies to finance a LEVERAGED BUYOUT, a transaction in which investors acquire a company by issuing new debt, using the company's assets as collateral. The takeover debt is retired by selling assets or is paid off from company earnings.

jurisdiction legally recognized authority to hear cases and decide issues submitted for review. The term frequently comes up in discussions concerning legally permissible banking activities, as different banking agencies have overlapping authority. For example, the Federal Reserve Board regulates bank holding companies, but many banking companies have opted for state banking charters, as opposed to NATIONAL BANK charters from the Office of the Comptroller of the Currency, to get banking powers not available to national banks. Jurisdictional disputes arising from these differences frequently are settled by a third party—the federal courts.

In international banking, determination of jurisdiction is crucial to resolving issues arising from cross-border loans to foreign borrowers, who may insist that any legal disputes be settled according to the laws of the borrower's country, not the foreign lender.

K

Keefe Bank Index composite of 24 money center and regional banks compiled by Keefe Bruyette & Woods, a New York investment banking firm specializing in bank stocks. The index is an unweighted index of banks and bank holding companies that tracks earnings, dividends, and market price performance of the group. It is used by securities analysts to monitor the relative performance of individual holdings of bank stocks.

Keogh Plan tax-deferred savings plan allowing self-employed persons and employees of a business to save money for retirement. Owners of a Keogh make regular or annual contributions, up to 15% of net profits or maximum of $30,000, to a profit sharing plan or pension plan under a qualified trustee. A Keogh account must be set up by December 31, although contributions for a calendar year may be made any time until the April 15 filing deadline for federal tax returns. Individuals owning a Keogh may also participate in a corporate pension plan and have an Individual Retirement Account. Withdrawals from a Keogh may be made after age 59¹/₂, and starting no later than 70¹/₂. Early withdrawals are subject to federal income taxes and a tax penalty.

key set of instructions governing the encryption and decryption of electronic messages. Each financial institution participating in a wire transfer system or electronic funds transfer network, such as an ATM network, has a unique identification key, called an issuer's key. See also KEY MANAGEMENT.

key currency currency used in international trade settlement, or as a reference currency in setting exchange rates. Key currencies are the U.S. dollar, or, more broadly, any currency issued by one of the GROUP OF SEVEN countries. Central banks hold a portion of their reserves in a key currency.

key management in data processing and electronic funds transfer, the control of identification codes unique to each financial institution in a network. Banks never transmit a key in the clear, that is in unencrypted form, but use a commonly accepted encryption formula to prevent unauthorized access. Periodically, banks change their codes, called issuer KEYS, for security reasons.

key man insurance insurance policy protecting a small business or partnership against business losses from the death or disability of a principal owner. Lenders sometimes require partnerships or closely held corporations to take out such insurance naming the lender as loss payee before extending credit if they believe the loss of a key employee will hinder a firm's ability to repay a bank loan.

Keynesian economics economic theory originated by the British economist John Maynard Keynes (1883-1946), and his followers. Keynes maintained that governments should use the power of the budget to maintain economic growth and stability, and overcome the recessionary cycles common in most western economies. Toward this purpose, Keynes argued, in his work *The General Theory of Employment, Interest and Money* (1935), that governments become active managers of the economy, by manipulating taxation and spending policies. According to the Keynesian view, deficit spending stimulates private sector development in periods when the economy is under-performing.

Critics of Keynesian economics, especially the monetarists, say that economic stability is best achieved by controlling credit and growth in the MONEY SUPPLY. Monetarists fault Keynesian economics for relying too much on government spending and taxation policies, which they say over-stimulates the economy, causing high inflation rates and contributing to the boom and bust cycles in the economy that have occurred since the mid-1970s. See also FISCAL POLICY; MONETARIST; SUPPLY SIDE ECONOMICS.

key rate interest rate that controls, either directly or indirectly, bank lending rates and the cost of credit paid by borrowers. In the United States, the DISCOUNT RATE and the FEDERAL FUNDS (Fed Funds) rate are key rates regulated by the Federal Reserve System's MONETARY POLICY.

key ratio ratio used by financial analysts in evaluation of a bank's statement of financial condition and income. Ratios examined include: the capital to assets ratio; ratio of loan loss reserves to total loans; liquidity ratios; and performance ratios, such as return on assets (ROA), return on equity (ROE), and the earnings per share ratio. Key ratios give a general indication of bank performance and can be compared to prior year figures.

kicker extra feature in a loan, beyond ordinary payments of interest, demanded by a lender as a condition for extending credit. The effect is to increase the yield over the term of the financing. From a legal viewpoint, kickers have to be disclosed in consumer loans as part of the finance charges, and in some instances may violate state usury laws.

In real estate finance, a kicker is an equity participation in the gross receipts from rental property, or an ownership stake in the property itself. In an EQUITY KICKER, the lender gets a given interest rate, plus a percentage of the rent over a certain dollar amount. Other forms of kickers are stock warrants exercisable at a future date, and rights to purchase securities.

kiting see CHECK KITING.

koruna national currency of Czechoslovakia.

krona national currency of Iceland and Sweden.

krone national currency of Denmark and Norway.

kwacha national currency of Malawi and Zambia.

kwanza national currency of Angola.

kyat national currency of Burma.

L

L measure of monetary liquid assets, published monthly by the Federal Reserve Board, including M3 monetary aggregates, Eurodollars owned by U.S. residents, commercial paper, savings bonds and marketable Treasury securities, and federal agency obligations. This index is compiled for information purposes, and is not actively managed by the Fed, as its components are less influenced by the Fed's OPEN MARKET COMMITTEE actions than deposits held in financial institutions.

laddered portfolio bond investment portfolio holding equal amounts of each security in each maturity range over, say a ten-year period. In rising rates, assets can be shifted to longer maturities. Money market and foreign exchange traders also utilize portfolio laddering in listing maturities, either day-by-day or month-by-month, of outstanding contracts so they can more easily control the maturity gap or mismatch between different portfolio assets. Contrast with BARBELL PORTFOLIO.

lagged reserves RESERVE accounting system whereby depository institutions maintain reserve account balances with a Federal Reserve Bank against checking account and other transaction account deposits outstanding two weeks earlier. The Federal Reserve System followed this method of calculating reserves from the late 1960s until 1984, when it changed the method for calculating reserves to CONTEMPORANEOUS RESERVES, to maintain a more consistent monetary policy and control over monetary aggregates making up the money supply. Time deposit accounts are still reported with a two-week lag. A lagging indicator is an economic indicator that trails or lags behind the business cycle. For example, factory inventories of finished goods, interest rates, consumer prices, and the gross national product all tend to follow advances and declines in the business cycle, rather than move in advance of the economy, as LEADING INDICATORS do.

lagging indicator economic indicator that trails or lags behind the business cycle. For example, factory inventories of finished goods, interest rates, consumer prices, and the gross national product all tend to follow advances and declines in the business cycle, rather than move in advance of the economy, as LEADING INDICATORS do. The U.S. Bureau of Economic Analysis tracks six lagging indicators, including the bank prime rate, outstanding consumer loans, and outstanding commercial and industrial loans.

land flip type of real estate fraud in which undeveloped property is resold from one owner to another, ordinarily at prices well above the fair market value. Typically, the property changes hands many times within a few days, and is sold each time at a higher price. Financial institutions that make real estate loans to land developers, take equity positions through direct investments, risk losses if real estate securing a loan suffers a decline in value.

late charge penalty assessed for delinquent payments on a mortgage or installment loan after a GRACE PERIOD of 10 to 15 days has elapsed. A loan payment due on the first of the month is subject to a penalty if not paid by the 15th day of the month. Late fees are calculated as a percentage of the outstanding balance, and, if unpaid, usually may not be added in the loan interest due.

laundered money see MONEY LAUNDERING.

lead bank
1. bank arranging a loan SYNDICATION, in which several banks buy participations. The lead bank collects a management fee for assembling the syndicate and arranging the financing terms. In the Eurobond market, a bank that acts as agent for members of an underwriting syndicate.
2. investment bank managing an underwriting of securities. Also called a lead manager or managing underwriter.

3. bank holding the primary deposit or lending relationship with an organization, normally a corporation with a multibank servicing agreement for its credit and cash management needs. See also CONCENTRATION BANK.

leading indicator economic indicator believed to anticipate changes in the business cycle, by peaking or bottoming out before general business conditions change direction. Leading indicators precede changes in the economy by 1 to 12 months. The U.S. Commerce Department's Bureau of Economic Analysis tracks the following indicators: the MONEY SUPPLY, changes in business credit employment statistics; new investments; business formations and business failures; corporate profits and stock prices; and business inventories. See also LAGGING INDICATORS.

leads and lags language in a contract or credit agreement allowing a company to either lead (accelerate) or lag (delay) payment of foreign trade obligations to trading partners or overseas subsidiaries. A decision to pay early or pay late is determined largely from an importer's perception of the monetary strength of the currency it is billed in. If currency devaluation is feared, importers try to accelerate their payments.

lease contract giving the right of possession and use of an asset for a specified period in exchange for payments. The party owning the leased property is the lessor, the party using it is the lessee, and the lease payments are rentals. A lease contract may be written for a single piece of equipment, or it may be a master lease governing a continuing arrangement, regardless of the equipment leased. There are several commonly used types of leases.

A tax-oriented lease, sometimes called a TRUE LEASE, gives the lessor the tax benefits of ownership, transferring the use of tax depreciation deductions, and in some cases, investment tax credits, from the lessee to the lessor in exchange for lower rental payments. All others, including FINANCE LEASEs, are nontax leases and are treated as conditional sales contracts for tax purposes. On the lessor's books a lease is treated very much like a loan. Thus, the lessee can deduct only the interest portion of the rentals. See also ALTERNATIVE MINIMUM TAX; CAPITAL LEASE; OPERATING LEASE; RESIDUAL VALUE; SALE AND LEASEBACK.

leaseback see SALE AND LEASEBACK.

leasehold tenant's right to leased property. The tenant enjoys certain rights of occupancy, but does not hold claim to the property's title. For example, a tenancy at will, giving occupancy for the term of a lease.

ledger balance customer's account balance as it appears on a BANK STATEMENT. The ledger balance differs from the AVAILABLE BALANCE representing total funds as available for use. The sole purpose of ledger balances, or total credits less debts during an accounting period, is to facilitate the reconciliation of book balances.

legal entity partnership, corporation, or other organization having the capacity to negotiate contracts, assume financial obligations, and pay off debts. In contrast with natural persons, legal entities are chartered by the states where they are organized. A corporation is a person in the eyes of the law, and it is responsible for its actions. It can be sued if it fails to live up to an agreement.

legal lending limit maximum amount a bank can lend to a single borrower. National banks are limited to 15% of capital and reserves on unsecured loans (25% of capital if fully secured); bank holding companies can lend a bank affiliate up to 10% of the capital and surplus of the affiliate, or up to 20% of the capital of all affiliates owned by the same holding company. Under the Financial Institutions Reform, Recovery and Enforcement Act of 1989, savings and loans are required to follow the same lending limits to a single borrower as national banks.

legal list securities approved by a state banking department as acceptable investments for mutual savings banks, pension funds, insurance companies, and other FIDUCIARY institutions. To protect investors and depositors, only high quality debt and equity securities are generally included. As an alternative, some states apply the PRUDENT MAN RULE.

legal opinion written opinion by an attorney stating that a proposed bond issue bond complies with applicable securities laws. In a municipal bond offering, the opinion also states that the issuer has a legal right to issue the securities proposed for sale, and also whether the bonds are exempt from state and local taxes. The issuer must obtain this statement before a new issue can be floated. Municipal bond issuers usually print the legal opinion on the back of each certificate.

legal owner person who has a legally enforceable claim to an estate or property. This claim may be only a lien, as, for example, a lender's SECURITY INTEREST in collateral pledged by a borrower. Contrast with *equitable owner*, the person recognized by common law as the owner of the property in question.

legal rate of interest highest rate of interest that a lender may legally charge on borrowed funds. Also called the USURY rate. The legal rate is set by law in each state, except in special situations where Congress has preempted the actions of state legislatures. Such pre-emption usually expires within a specified time period. Interest charges in excess of the legal rate are considered usurious and are subject to stiff penalties, even to forfeiture of interest and principal in some states. In many states, the legal rate of interest is also the rate, usually set by state statute, at which debts that don't have any agreed interest rate—judgments, overdue taxes—accrue interest. This rate is rarely the highest rate allowed by law for any debt.

legal reserves portion of demand deposit and time deposit account balances, plus cash in a bank's vault, that can be used to meet RESERVE REQUIREMENTS of the Federal Reserve System. Legal reserves must be kept in a prescribed form, either as vault cash or a deposit in a checking account at a district Federal Reserve Bank.

Legal reserves are a source of bank liquidity, because they cannot be converted to cash to pay depositors. The Federal Reserve Board regulates credit in the banking system by adjusting the reserve requirements that banks are required to keep. Raising the reserve requirement drains credit, because banks have to keep a higher percentage of deposit accounts in a noninterest earning account at the Fed; lowering the reserve requirement expands credit because banks then have more funds to put out in new loans.

Some states also require state chartered banks to set aside funds in reserve accounts, although state regulations are generally more lenient. The MONETARY CONTROL ACT OF 1980, which extended reserve requirements to state banks, phased in over an eight-year period, allows state banks to use their checking account in a Federal Reserve Bank to meet state reserve requirements, if allowed by state law.

legal tender money recognized by law as acceptable payment for debts owed to creditors. Also called *lawful money*. In the United States, legal tender is all forms of circulating paper money, mostly Federal Reserve Notes, and coins. The term literally means that money offered, tendered, as payment has the backing of the government and must be accepted by a creditor, unless a contract calls for another method of payment. See also FIAT MONEY.

lek national currency of Albania.

lempira national currency of Honduras.

lender liability legal doctrine that says a bank can be held legally accountable for a borrower's financial losses relating, directly or indirectly, to actions taken by the lender. According to the doctrine, a bank could be held accountable if it makes a loan in bad faith, declines to renew an existing line of credit after promising to do so, interferes with the debtor's business, or improperly forecloses on a loan without giving adequate notice. All of these actions could, depending on circumstances, be viewed as grounds for a lender liability lawsuit, although the debtor would have to demonstrate that the lender's actions resulted in actual losses.

Lender liability is a complex topic, and is best explained by an illustration: suppose that a bank were to make a five-year loan to a fast food franchise operator, knowing that the borrower is a poor credit risk and may not be able to repay the amount borrowed according to the terms offered by the lender. The borrower pledges, as security for the loan, the franchisee's LICENSE TO OPERATE, which the lender can seize and sell in satisfaction of the debt in the event the borrower defaults. A year later, the borrower does, in fact, default on the loan, and the lender sells the franchise license at a below-market price to a local businessperson. Under lender liability rules, the borrower is free to sue the lender, claiming the lender did not act in good faith, and loaned more than the borrower could reasonably pay back, causing him to suffer a financial loss. Although this may be an extreme case, lender liability suits claiming breach of contract, wrongful sale of assets, and so on, have been filed in the courts.

In view of lender liability claims in recent years, lenders can no longer rely on traditional views of acceptable conduct in extending credit and collecting repayment once a loan has been made.

lender of last resort lender who acts as the ultimate source of credit to the banking system. In the United States this role is carried out by the 12 Federal Reserve Banks, which supply credit through the Federal Reserve DISCOUNT WINDOW. Reserve credit is supplied in a variety of forms, including short-term ADJUSTMENT CREDIT to banks needing funds to maintain their reserve requirements, as well as longer-term SEASONAL CREDIT and EXTENDED CREDIT to banks needing funds for a longer period. On occasion, the Fed has loaned money to troubled banks, and even troubled savings institutions, if it believes that failure to do so would undermine public confidence in the banking system. The Federal Reserve is authorized by the MONETARY CONTROL ACT of 1980 to make discount window loans to savings and loan associations and other nonbank financial institutions. Before borrowing from the Fed, though, a savings institution would have to use up all other forms of credit, including credit advances from the Federal Home Loan Banks. Direct loans by the Fed to nonfinancial companies, although authorized by the Federal Reserve Act, have not taken place since the 1930s.

Bank borrowing from the Fed can be quite large. In 1985, the Bank of New York borrowed $22 billion from the Federal Reserve Bank of New York to cover an temporary overdraft in its Reserve Account caused by a computer malfunction in the bank's government securities clearing business. In European countries, the lender of last resort is generally the Ministry of Finance, rather than the central bank, and in the Eurobond market there is no lender of last resort.

lender participation see KICKER.

leone national currency of Sierra Leone.

less-developed country (LDC) country whose state of economic development is characterized by a low national income, a high rate of population growth and unemployment, and dependence on commodity exports. The majority of nations in Asia, Africa, and Latin America, fit this model, which is why they are known collectively as developing countries or third world countries. LDCs generally pay more for the goods they import from more economically advanced nations than they receive in payments. To make up the shortfall or deficit in balance of payments, these nations must resort to bank loans from private banks and from international credit sources, such as the INTERNATIONAL MONETARY FUND.

letter of advice

1. written instructions from one bank to another, directing that a payment be made at a specified future date. For example, a letter instructing a WIRE TRANSFER payment to a third party.
2. written confirmation of a transfer of funds by BANK DRAFT or ELECTRONIC FUNDS TRANSFER to a third party, given normally to both the person receiving the payment and the person initiating the transaction.

letter of credit (L/C)

credit instrument issued by a bank guaranteeing payments on behalf of its customer to a BENEFICIARY, normally to a third party but sometimes to the bank's customer, for a stated period of time and when certain conditions are met. A letter of credit substitutes the bank's credit for the credit of another party, for example, an importer or exporter, who is authorized to write drafts up to a specified amount, payable by the issuing bank. Letters of credit are widely used in banking, originating with the commercial letter of credit in trade financing. Importers and exporters wanted assurances that merchandise delivered would be paid for by the buyer, a requirement that was met by obtaining a bank letter of credit. The buyer purchases a letter of credit, which is then forwarded to a correspondent bank in the city where payment is to be made. In trade financing, the bank drafts authorized under the issuing bank's letter of credit are frequently accepted by another bank, creating a BANKER'S ACCEPTANCE, and become credit obligations of the accepting bank.

There are several major varieties of letters of credit, each serving a different purpose. An IRREVOCABLE LETTER OF CREDIT cannot be cancelled before a specific date without agreement by all the parties involved, whereas a revocable letter of credit can be amended at any time by the issuing bank. A CONFIRMED LETTER OF CREDIT carries the endorsement of both the issuing bank and its correspondent, guaranteeing payment of all drafts written against it; an unconfirmed letter of credit, carries no such guarantee that a correspondent will honor drafts presented for payment. A STANDBY LETTER OF CREDIT is a contingent (future) obligation of the issuing bank to make payment to the designated beneficiary if the bank's customer fails to perform as called for under the terms of a contract. Standby letters, for this reason, are considered OFF-BALANCE SHEET LIABILITIES in computing bank capital-to-asset ratios. See also BACK-TO-BACK LETTERS OF CREDIT; CREDIT ENHANCEMENT; DOCUMENTARY COMMERCIAL BILL; RED CLAUSE LETTER OF CREDIT; SIGHT DRAFT; TIME DRAFT; TRAVELER'S LETTER OF CREDIT.

letter of intent see INVESTMENT LETTER.

leu national currency of Romania.

lev national currency of Bulgaria.

level payment amortization fixed-term LOAN with periodic payments that remain constant over the term of the loan. A portion of each payment goes to payment of interest, and the balance amortizes, or reduces, the outstanding principal. If the loan has a variable rate, the term may be extended if interest rates rise. Or there may be a BALLOON PAYMENT at maturity. See also AMORTIZATION SCHEDULE.

leverage money borrowed to increase the return on invested capital.
  1. **Banking.** The use of funds purchased in the money market or borrowed from depositors to finance interest-bearing assets, principally loans. What banks do, in effect, is invest their depositors' money in loans at rates high enough to cover the lender's cost of funds and operating expenses, and yield a profit margin or SPREAD. Leverage increases when bank assets grow at a faster rate than equity capital, such as common stock, which acts as a cushion against losses. To keep leverage from getting too high, which might happen if banks grow

too rapidly or made too many risky loans, commercial banks and savings institutions have to keep minimum levels of equity capital in relation to total assets. See also CAPITAL; CAPITAL RATIOS; LIQUIDITY.

2. Finance. The use of debt or senior securities to get a higher return on owner's equity capital. A firm issuing long-term bonds may be able to earn a higher rate of return from the the bond proceeds, which are often invested in capital equipment, than what it pays the bondholders in interest. The result is financial leverage or capital leverage, because any increase in earnings benefits the corporate owners, not the bondholders. Issuing bonds has several advantages, provided the issuer can meet the debt service payments. Bond interest payments are tax deductible, although stock dividends are not, and a bond issue does not dilute the value of shareholders' equity. A bond issuer that is too highly leveraged, though, risks default.

leveraged buyout (LBO) takeover of a company using the acquired firm's assets and cash flow to obtain financing. Typically, these transactions are done by conglomerates selling or spinning off an unwanted subsidiary to the company's managers and outside investors. The buyers of an LBO financing are said to take private the target company. Leveraged buyouts are risky for the buyers if the purchase is highly leveraged. An LBO can be protected from volatile interest rates by an INTEREST RATE SWAP, locking in a fixed interest rate, or an interest rate CAP, which prevents the borrowing cost from rising above a certain level. LBOs also have been financed with high-yield debt, or JUNK BONDS, and have also been done with the interest rate capped at a fixed level and interest costs above the cap added to the principal. For commercial banks, LBOs are attractive because these financings have large up-front fees. They also fill the gap in corporate lending created when large corporations begin using commercial paper and corporate bonds in place of bank loans.

leveraged lease long-term lease in which the lessor borrows most of the funds needed to acquire the asset financed from a third party, usually a bank or insurance company. The lessor makes an equity investment equal to, say, 20% of the equipment's original cost, and borrows the remaining 80% by issuing nonrecourse notes to the lenders, and writes a noncancellable lease for the equipment.

The lessor makes an assignment of the lease and lease rental payments to the lender, who is entitled to repossess the asset if the lessee happens to default. A leveraged lease is a true lease for tax purposes, because the lessor, as owner of the asset, is entitled to all of the tax benefits of ownership, including accelerated depreciation write-offs, deduction of INTEREST payments on the bank loan, and the INVESTMENT CREDIT, if any, for purchase of the asset. Banks write leveraged leases for their own customers through the leasing subsidiary of a bank holding company. See also ASSET-BASED LENDING; CAPITAL LEASE; FINANCE LEASE; OPERATING LEASE; REGULATION Y.

liability

1. **General.** A legally enforceable claim on the assets of a company, excluding owner's equity, or the property of an individual, calling for a transfer of assets at a determined future date. Also, any item appearing on the right hand side of a double-entry accounting system or balance sheet.

2. **Banking.** The funds owed by a bank, including time deposits and demand deposits, borrowings from a Federal Reserve Bank or other banks, and Federal Funds in the interbank market. Deposit liabilities, representing claims by a bank's customers on the assets of the bank, are the major source of funds for bank lending. Other liability categories include MANAGED LIABILITIES, or deposits that banks actively solicit from other banks; BROKERED DEPOSITs, which usually are certificates of deposit secured through a broker-dealer; and OFF-BALANCE SHEET LIABILITIES, which are liabilities that are not direct obligations on the issuing bank, but represent contingent obligations that may become payable in the future.

liability ledger central record of a bank's outstanding loans and discounts to all borrowers, maintained in a bank's loan department. The liability ledger can be a sub-ledger to a bank's computerized GENERAL LEDGER accounting system, or in non-automated systems, individual ledger cards for each borrower. The aggregate total of outstanding loans is the major portion of a bank's EARNING ASSETS.

liability management management of bank liabilities, including deposits, to support lending activities and achieve balanced growth in earnings and bank assets without excessive liquidity risk. Liability management involves accepting money from depositors, and securing additional funds from other financial institutions, for use in lending and investing. Other tools of liability management are interest rate hedging against unexpected market moves, and maintaining a controlled gap between asset and liability maturities for controlled speculation on interest rate shifts.

In banking, active management of the liability side of the balance sheet began in the early 1960s when commercial banks began issuing negotiable certificates of deposit, which could be sold to other holders prior to maturity, to solicit funds from other institutions in the money market. See also ASSET-LIABILITY MANAGEMENT; FUNDS MANAGEMENT; MANAGED LIABILITIES.

LIBOR see LONDON INTERBANK OFFERED RATE.

licensee bank that is granted the right by a licensing authority to distribute financial services in its market area. For example, a bank that issues Visa or MasterCard credit cards. A license may preclude local financial institutions from offering competing services, or be nonexclusive.

license to operate grant of permission to undertake a particular occupation or carry out a business activity, subject to regulation or supervision by the licensing authority. Licenses are granted by state or federal agencies, and also by private concerns, as when a business authorizes another to use its name as a franchise operator. Licenses granted by government authority imply professional competence and ability to meet certain standards set by law or regulation. In real estate law, a license conveys the right of access to property, for example an easement, but does not transfer right of possession to the licensee.

lien creditor's claim against property to secure repayment of a debt. A lien encumbers the borrower's property pledged as security, up to the amount of the debt, and guarantees the lender's right to collect payment through legal means. For example, a MORTGAGE gives a lender the right to initiate FORECLOSURE proceedings against a borrower in DEFAULT on the mortgage loan. A lien holder has a prior claim than creditors whose claims are not secured by the borrower's assets. See also INVOLUNTARY LIEN; JUDGMENT LIEN; MECHANIC'S LIEN; SECURITY INTEREST.

life estate freehold estate giving the person owning it the right to receive income of the estate until death. The beneficiary cannot sell the property and the estate terminates at death.

lifeline banking limited package of retail banking services offered at a relatively low fixed monthly cost. The concept originated in the early 1980s when consumer advocates began pressuring financial institutions to offer low-cost services to senior citizens and low-income depositors. The term preferred by bankers is *basic banking*, and these accounts generally are available to all depositors. A basic banking checking account usually includes check writing up to a certain number of checks per month and limited bank teller visits, but unrestricted access to accounts at automated teller machines. The customer pays a flat monthly fee. More frequent teller visits or check writing triggers an additional charge.

life of loan cap contractual provision in an ADJUSTABLE RATE MORTGAGE limiting the interest rate increase over the amortized life of the loan. For example, a 10% interest rate with a 5% lifetime cap may not increase more than 5% while the loan is outstanding. See also ANNUAL CAP; PAYMENT CAP.

lift a leg in financial futures, money market and commodity market trading and foreign exchange, closing out one side of a long-short hedge before liquidating the other side. Also called legging out. A trader holding a STRADDLE, is said to *leg out* by selling either side of the transaction.

LIMEAN see LONDON INTERBANK MEDIAN AVERAGE RATE.

limit
1. LEGAL LENDING LIMIT on loans to a single borrower. National banks and savings and loan associations cannot make unsecured loans greater than 15% of capital, and secured loans above 25% of capital.

2. bank's own internal credit limit in loans to a single borrower, for example, a guidance line of credit. The guidance line is never disclosed.
3. consumer's CREDIT LIMIT, as in credit cards.
4. in FOREIGN EXCHANGE, a daily trading limit: the maximum amount a dealer is willing to trade or deposit with another bank. Also, a central bank's limit on long or short open positions.
5. COUNTRY LIMIT.
6. in electronic funds transfers, a BILATERAL CREDIT LIMIT negotiated by two banks to prevent overdrawing a Reserve Account at a federal reserve Bank.
7. limit up/limit down: in commodities markets and financial futures, the largest daily price change allowed by a futures exchange.

limited partnership business in which an individual or party who participates in its affairs as a minority investor receives a share of the profits (or losses) that is limited by agreement. A limited partner has no role in managing the concern, and has limited liability, as opposed to the unlimited liability of a GENERAL PARTNER. Limited partnerships were a popular form of tax shelter in the 1970s and early 1980s. The use of limited partnerships in venture capital financing, oil and gas exploration, and other investment oriented partnerships was curtailed by the Tax Reform Act of 1986, which limited the tax deductibility of losses from so-called passive investments. An investor could no longer reduce a tax liability by deducting passive losses from adjusted gross income.

limited purpose trust company state chartered trust company that performs specific trust functions. For example, the DEPOSITORY TRUST COMPANY (DTC) in New York, which holds securities certificates in safekeeping so banks and securities firms can participate in book entry settlement of securities trades, and the Participants Trust Company, a depository for mortgage-backed securities.

limited recourse finance
1. financing arrangement where the lender can require the borrower to repay only in special conditions that are spelled out in the LOAN AGREEMENT itself, and otherwise must look to the

collateral as a source of repayment. Borrowers may have to pay more for limited recourse financing. See also NONRECOURSE LOAN.

2. indirect lending arrangement where a dealer sells installment sales contracts to a bank, which assumes responsibility for collection of the debt as a HOLDER IN DUE COURSE, and the dealer's liability for losses incurred by the bank is limited by contract. The bank's RECOURSE against the dealer expires after a specified period.

limited service bank

1. banking facility in a UNIT BANKING state that is located away from the bank's main office. These offices may accept deposits, but do not make loans or offer trust services.

2. bank that is limited by charter or by regulation to offering only certain services to the public. For example, a NONBANK BANK can either accept consumer deposits or make commercial loans, but cannot do both simultaneously. See also LIMITED PURPOSE TRUST COMPANY.

limited tax bond general obligation MUNICIPAL BOND secured by a pledge of tax receipts from a specific revenue source, usually real estate property taxes, a portion of the real estate taxes, or a group of specific taxes. Contrast with an unlimited tax bond, which is backed by the general taxing authority of the issuer.

line of credit commitment by a bank to lend funds to a borrower up to a specified amount over a specified future period. Lines of credit are reviewed annually, and do not require fees or compensating balances unless the line is guaranteed by the lender. Bank lines are considered good until further notice and may be withdrawn at the bank's option. When the borrower is officially notified of the credit available, the line is referred to as an *advised* line. When the maximum credit is kept internal by the lender, and not disclosed, it is a *guidance* line. In a commercial line of credit, the borrower is usually required to keep 10% to 20% of the available line in a COMPENSATING BALANCE. See also CHECK CREDIT; HOME EQUITY CREDIT; OVERDRAFT; REVOLVING CREDIT.

linked savings account SAVINGS ACCOUNT that has an account number related to a transaction account, usually a checking account or NOW account. Sometimes called a *package account*. The depositor can keep the bulk of funds in the savings account and transfer money between accounts, and may qualify for lower checking account service charges or free checking. Balances on both accounts and interest earned are reported monthly in a COMBINED STATEMENT. See also AUTOMATIC TRANSFER; SWEEP ACCOUNT.

liquid asset cash or its equivalents—any asset that is readily convertible to cash. For example, Treasury bills, short-term marketable securities, demand deposits, and time deposits nearing maturity. Liquid assets can be sold quickly without significant loss. See also NEAR MONEY.

liquidation

1. conversion of assets into cash or inventory into accounts receivable to meet current obligations and service long-term debt of an organization. When an obligation is paid off it is said to be liquidated.
2. termination of a business by selling its assets and distributing the proceeds to meet current liabilities and claims of creditors. Debts are paid in order of priority and remaining assets distributed on a pro rata basis to owner or shareholders. In a VOLUNTARY BANKRUPTCY petition, filed under Chapter 7 of the Bankruptcy Code, the debtor's assets are distributed to meet creditors' claims, in order of priority. A group of creditors can also file an INVOLUNTARY BANKRUPTCY petition, to force the sale and distribution of the debtor's assets.
3. closing out a LONG POSITION or a SHORT POSITION.

liquidator see RECEIVER.

liquidity

1. ability of an organization to meet its current financial obligations. In banking, adequate liquidity means being able to meet the needs of depositors wanting to withdraw funds and borrowers wanting to be assured that their credit or cash needs will be met. Liquidity is also measured in terms of debt capacity or borrowing capacity to meet short-term demands for funds. See also LIQUIDITY RATIOS.

2. quality of an asset that is readily convertible into cash, with minimal loss in value. Short-term securities, such as Treasury bills that are easily sold to other investors at relatively narrow spreads between bid and asked quotes, and in reasonably large trading volumes, are said to be highly liquid.

3. characteristic of a market where a large amount of securities, futures contracts, and so on, can easily be traded with minimal price distortions occurring. Strong markets are characterized by stable prices and relatively narrow bid-asked spreads. Thin markets have wide spreads and extreme trading volatility. See also DEPTH OF THE MARKET.

liquidity diversification see LADDERED PORTFOLIO.

liquidity preference theory in KEYNESIAN ECONOMICS, the desire by investors to hold their money in liquid assets, such as checking accounts, rather than nonliquid assets (stocks, bonds, real estate). This preference is explained by: (1) a transactional motivation, or the desire to keep money available for spending as needed; (2) a precautionary motivation, characterized by the reluctance to keep money tied up in assets not readily convertible to cash; and (3) the speculative motive, a belief that interest rates may be going up in the future. According to the Keynesian theory, INTEREST is the payment to investors to persuade them to give up their liquidity. Longer-term investments, therefore, would command higher rates over shorter-term investments. This premium is known as the liquidity premium. Contrast with EXPECTATIONS THEORY.

liquidity ratios key financial ratios measuring a bank's application of interest-earning deposit liabilities to fund loan growth, expressed as a percentage. There are four primary liquidity ratios: cash and unpledged marketable securities divided by total assets; total deposits divided by borrowed funds; volatile funds divided by liquid assets; and total loans divided by total deposits (most commonly used). A low ratio of loans to deposits indicates excess liquidity, and potentially low profits, compared to other banks. A high loan-to-deposit ratio presents the risk that some loans may have to be sold at a loss to meet depositors' claims.

liquidity risk risk that a bank will have to sell assets at a loss to meet cash demands, for example, depositors' demands for funds. Liquidity risk is generally explained as a ratio comparing available liquidity to the demand for funds.

lira national currency of Italy, Turkey, and Malta.

lis pendens Latin for a pending suit, a legal notice warning all parties that there is a lawsuit that may affect rights in certain property. The notice is published in a newspaper. See also LITI-GATION.

litigation process of filing a law suit in the appropriate jurisdiction to settle a legal dispute or controversy. By filing a suit, one litigates the contested matters. Contrast with ARBITRATION.

living trust see INTER VIVOS TRUST.

load sales charge levied by an investment company to cover the selling broker's commission—up to $8^{1}/2\%$ of invested funds. The sales commission is expressed as the difference between the selling price of shares in an open-end investment fund (a MU-TUAL FUND) and the NET ASSET VALUE of the shares. In a fund with an $8^{1}/2\%$ sales load, only $91^{1}/2\%$ of the principal is invested. Some funds charge a distribution fee, called a 12b1 fee after the SEC ruling allowing mutual funds to charge these fees. Other funds charge a redemption fee, and are known as BACK-END LOAD funds. A fund with a FRONT-END LOAD charges a broker commission when the sale is made. A mutual fund with no sales commission is a NO-LOAD FUND.

load fund mutual fund that charges the investor a sales commission, called a load, as opposed to a NO-LOAD FUND. The sales commission may be due at the time of the sale (a FRONT-END LOAD), or payable at redemption of the securities (a BACK-END LOAD).

loan money advanced to a borrower, to be repaid at a later date, usually with interest. Legally, a loan is a contract between a buyer (the borrower) and a seller (the lender), enforceable under the UNIFORM COMMERCIAL CODE in most states. The terms and conditions for repayment of a loan, including the finance charge or interest rate, are specified in a loan agreement. A loan may be payable on demand (a DEMAND LOAN), in equal monthly installments (an installment loan), or may be good until further notice or due at maturity (a TIME LOAN).

There are various methods lenders use to categorize loans, both for internal control and for reporting lending activity to governmental agencies, for example, classification by maturity, industry, security, and type of borrower. Bank loans are normally classified by: (1) COMMERCIAL & INDUSTRIAL LOANs to business organizations; (2) interbank loans, which are mostly FEDERAL FUNDS transactions, from one bank to another; (3) LOAN PARTICIPATIONS, or loans to a single borrower shared by several banks; (4) real estate loans, which may be subdivided into construction loans and long-term MORTGAGE loans; and (5) loans to consumers, such as auto loans and other forms of consumer installment credit. See also CONSUMER CREDIT; CREDIT; LOAN PARTICIPATION; PARALLEL LOAN; SECURED LOAN; SYNDICATION; TERM LOAN; TIME LOAN; UNSECURED LOAN.

loan application see CREDIT APPLICATION.

loan commitment see COMMITMENT.

loan committee
management committee that evaluates and approves or declines loan applications exceeding the lending authority of an individual loan officer. This committee first examines LOAN DOCUMENTATION and the borrower's financial statements to assure that a pending loan meets the bank's LOAN POLICY standards and regulatory guidelines. Then the lender makes a binding COMMITMENT to fund the loan and disburse the loan proceeds to the borrower. The loan committee also carries out the lender's periodic CREDIT REVIEW of maturing loans, and decides what collection efforts should be taken to restore past-due loans and other NONPERFORMING LOANS to satisfactory payment condition.

loan covenant see COVENANT.

loan documentation
documents evidencing a LOAN or extension of credit, including the PROMISSORY NOTE, disclosure of credit terms, and the lender's FINANCING STATEMENT listing collat-

eral pledged as loan security, for example a mortgage deed, motor vehicle title, stocks, deposit accounts, and so on. Also included are the borrower's CORPORATE RESOLUTION and loan guarantees.

These documents, detailing the history of a loan, are kept for later review by the LOAN COMMITTEE and by field examiners from the lender's primary supervisory agency. Credit-related documents, including the borrower's FINANCIAL STATEMENT, BUSINESS PLAN, and other papers used by lenders in evaluating creditworthiness are kept in the borrower's CREDIT FILE.

loan fee lender's fee for making a loan, either at the COMMITMENT time, or as funds are advanced at specific stages, as in construction financing. There are different types of loan fees: an annual fee to maintain a line of credit; a COMMITMENT FEE to hold available the unused portion of a loan or line of credit; and a UTILIZATION FEE paid for the amount of credit actually drawn down against an approved line. See also COMPENSATING BALANCE.

loan grading loan classification system, or credit scoring system, that assigns ASSET QUALITY ratings to a loan portfolio, based on comparative evaluation of outstanding loans. For example: (1) not reviewed; (2) satisfactory (an acceptable business credit); (3) special mention (missing documentation); (4) substandard (normal repayment in jeopardy); (5) doubtful (full repayment questionable); and (6) loss (complete write-off).

Many lenders use the National Bank Examiner Risk Classification System in assigning risk ratings to commercial loan portfolios, because they are required to use this format in reporting loan quality in the REPORT OF CONDITION filed quarterly with a bank supervisory agency. See also ADVERSELY CLASSIFIED ASSETS; NONACCRUAL ASSET; NONPERFORMING LOAN.

loan ledger see LIABILITY LEDGER.

loan limit
1. LEGAL LENDING LIMIT on loans to a single borrower—not more than 15% of capital and surplus for national banks (secured loans) and generally 10% to 20% for state chartered banks.

2. authority of a bank lending officer to make a loan without obtaining prior approval from the bank's LOAN COMMITTEE.

loan loss provision noncash expense item charged to a bank's earnings when adding to the allowance, or LOAN LOSS RESERVES, for possible bad debt. The loan loss provision is reported on a bank's INCOME STATEMENT.

loan loss reserves valuation reserve against a bank's total loans on the balance sheet, representing the amount thought to be adequate to cover estimated losses in the loan portfolio. When a loan is charged off, it is removed from the loan portfolio as an earning asset, and its book value is deducted from the reserve account for loan losses. Lenders also set aside reserves for a nonaccrual loan, in which interest and principal payments are no longer being collected. Recoveries from the liquidation of collateral repossessed from the borrower are credited to the reserve account. The TAX REFORM ACT OF 1986 limited the tax deduction of loan loss reserves held by banks with assets over $500 million.

loan participation sharing of a loan by a group of banks that join together to make a loan too large for any one bank to handle. Also known as *participation financing*, loan participations are arranged through CORRESPONDENT banking networks in which smaller banks buy a portion of the overall financing package. Large syndications may run into hundreds of millions of dollars, and involve more than one hundred different banks. Syndications are also a convenient way for smaller banks to book loans that would otherwise exceed their *legal lending limits*. By selling most of the financing to an UPSTREAM correspondent, the local bank earns fee income from servicing the loan, and is able to retain other banking relationships, such as checking accounts.

loan policy loan underwriting guidelines, and the written documentation setting forth these standards, as determined by a bank's senior loan committee. A bank's loan policy also establishes minimum credit standards in booking new loans, policies and procedures in treatment of past-due and delinquent loans, and more generally, the type of customer a bank wants as a borrower.

loan production office (LPO) banking office that takes loan applications and arranges financing for corporations and small businesses, but does not accept deposits. Loan applications are subject to approval by the lending institution. Banks have used LPOs to establish a presence in states that did not permit an out-of-state bank to offer full banking services.

loan register journal in which time loans are recorded in chronological order, and consecutively numbered. Also called a *maturity tickler*. Shortly before the maturity date, the borrower is notified by mail, or by a personal visit from a loan officer, that the loan is about to come due. See also NOTE NOTICE.

loan review see CREDIT REVIEW.

loan sales sale of loans or loan participations to an investor without the knowledge of the borrower. Loans, if competitively priced, may sell at par or at a slight premium. If originated at rates below current market rates, loan participations are typically sold at a discount from face value. A bank selling participations in 8% fixed rate loans will have to sell them off at a discount if the competitive market rate on similar loans is 10%. See also ASSET SALES.

loan shark lender, other than a regulated financial institution, who makes a business of lending money at rates above legally permitted interest rates. For example, a $5 loan on Monday to be repaid Friday for $6—an annual percentage rate of 1040%, not including interest compounding. Loan sharking was a pervasive activity through much of the nineteenth century, leading to the formation of cooperative associations, such as mutual savings banks and credit unions, to arrange small loans at reasonable interest rates. State small loan laws generally prohibit loan sharking, although state laws differ on what is, or is not, an excessive rate of interest.

loan strip short-term credit advance made under a long-term lending commitment. For example, a 90-day term loan made under a five-year revolving line of credit. Banking regulators treat a participation in a loan strip as a borrowing if the original investor does not want to renew and another cannot be found. In that event, strips are considered deposits and are subject to reserve requirements under Federal Reserve Regulation D.

loan-to-value ratio relationship, expressed as a percent, between the principal amount of a loan and the appraised value of the asset securing the financing. In a residential mortgage loan, this is the percentage value of the property the lender is willing to finance with a mortgage. For example, a $160,000 mortgage on a $200,000 house has a loan-to-value ratio of 80%. Lenders customarily set upper limits on the loans they are willing to make, and may require borrowers taking mortgages approaching the appraisal value of the property—generally any mortgage loan with a loan-to-value ratio above 80%—to take out PRIVATE MORTGAGE INSURANCE as added security.

local check check deposited in the same Federal Reserve REGIONAL CHECK PROCESSING CENTER as the paying bank, even if payable through a bank located outside the region. For example, credit union SHARE DRAFT payable through a commercial bank. The CHECK ROUTING SYMBOL on the check tells whether the check is paid through a local bank.

lock box post office box used by organizations to accelerate collection of receivables. Checks are routed to a designated P.O. box number, where they are picked up several times during the day, separated from the envelopes, and submitted to the check collection system for conversion into cash receivables. Many large banks offer lock box processing as a cash management service to corporate customers. A lock box can be retail, designed for remittance processing for consumer accounts, or wholesale, in which payments from other corporations are collected and submitted through DEPOSITORY TRANSFER CHECK or electronic debit into a concentration account for investment and disbursement as needed.

lock box network lock box service to corporate customers that is offered by a group of banks working together. For examples, U.S. $ Network (14 cities covered by 7 banks), Imagenet (8 cities covered by 7 banks), and Accelanet (4 cities covered by 2 banks).

locked market said of a market where the bid price equals the asked price. This occurs in very competitive markets, and for only brief periods. The market will unlock, and bid- asked quotes will diverge, after the trades are made.

lock-in period

1. time period, usually 30 to 60 days, a mortgage lender agrees to hold the mortgage rate and points payable by the borrower to the rate quoted when the application was taken. Also called *rate lock*. It is not the same as a loan COMMITMENT, although some commitments may contain a lock-in provision. This protects the borrower against rate increases if interest rates rise before the loan closing takes place. Lenders may charge a flat fee or a percentage of the mortgage loan, or add a fraction of a percentage point to the loan's interest rate.
2. period of time in which a mortgagor cannot refinance a mortgage without paying a penalty to the lender.

Lombard rate interest rate set by banks in West Germany on loans collateralized by securities. The term is used officially in reference to the lending rate set by the Bundesbank, the West German central bank, which sets its Lombard rate .05% above its discount rate. Informally it is used by European banks in referring to loans backed by a pledge of securities.

London interbank bid rate (LIBID) key interest rate at which major banks in the London Interbank Market are willing to borrow funds from each other, as opposed to the lending rate (the LONDON INTERBANK OFFERED RATE) quoted by banks willing to lend surplus Eurodollar deposits. The bid rate is the lower of the two interest rates.

London interbank median average rate (LI-MEAN) median average between the bid rate (LIBID) and the offered rate (LIBOR) in the Eurocurrency market.

London interbank offered rate (LIBOR) KEY RATE in international bank lending. LIBOR is the rate at which major banks in London are willing to lend Eurodollars to each other. It is used to determine the interest rate charged to creditworthy borrowers. LIBOR rates, based on daily quotes at 11 A.M. (London time) from five major London banks, are fixed

rates quoted for specific maturities. The lending rate in the Euro-markets (LIBOR) and the borrowing rate (LIBID), are quoted for the U.S. dollar and other Eurocurrencies, generally for fixed-term borrowings, such as three months, six months, and so on. Actual rates can vary because different reference banks are used. Syndicated Eurocredits facilities, such as Revolving Underwriting Facilities (RUFs), underwritten by several Euro-banks, are quoted as spreads above LIBOR.

long coupon
1. bond interest payment for a period longer than the standard six-month interest payment period, normally the first interest coupon. Contrast with SHORT COUPON.
2. bond with an original maturity of ten years or more, for example, the 30-year U.S. Treasury bond.

long date forward
speculative foreign exchange contract involving forward positions longer than one year. Trading is highly risky as there may not be a willing counterparty to take the opposite position.

long hedge
1. purchase of a FUTURES CONTRACT to lock in the price of a commodity or financial instrument. Also called a *buy hedge*. In buying a futures contract, an investor agrees to buy the underlying commodity or financial instrument in the cash market. For example, an investor holding a $5 million bond portfolio maturing in two months can lock in the reinvestment rate with a long hedge. See also SHORT HEDGE.
2. strategy to lock in current yield, anticipating a drop in notes, with purchase of a futures contract or call option.

long position
1. currency, security, or financial instrument owned outright by a dealer, indicating a net asset position. A dealer holding $5 million in U.S. dollars would say, "I am long in dollars." The opposite is a SHORT POSITION, or a net deficit. In financial futures, the term refers to a trader's market position when purchasing a FUTURES CONTRACT without closing out the position by making an offsetting sale; in options, a call option that has not been exercised or allowed to expire.

2. securities held by a broker-dealer, either for a customer or its own trading account.

long-term
1. loan with an original maturity of more than 10 years, for example, a 30-year conventional mortgage loan.
   2. obligations, such as bonds, that will not become payable for a year or more.
3. holding period (at least one year) for owning securities that qualifies, under Internal Revenue Service rules, for treatment as a long-term capital gain (or loss). Rates on long-term gains are identical to tax rates on short-term gains.

long-term debt generally refers to debt maturing in five years or more. For example, the residential mortgage and fixed term home equity loans.

losing the points in foreign exchange trading, market condition that exists when the buying price in the forward market is lower than the SPOT MARKET selling price. For example, when the spot market currency rates for U.S dollars and West German deutschmarks are $1 (U.S.) = $1.6450 and the one-month forward rates are $1 = $1.6510, the difference is .0050. If a trader buys at the higher spot rate and sells at the one-month forward rate, he is losing the points. Contrast with EARNING THE POINTS.

loss
1. loan written off as uncollectible, and assigned to the workout committee if a commercial loan, or to the collection department if the loan is made to a consumer. Also, the formal classification by bank examiners on loans with no tangible value.
2. sale of an asset at less than its acquisition cost or fair market value.
3. write down of a loan considered partially, or fully, uncollectible.
4. in accounting, an operating loss as when costs exceed net proceeds from a transaction, or expenditures are greater than revenues for an accounting period.

loss reserve see LOAN LOSS RESERVES.

lost card bank card reported missing by the cardholder of record, or a card that was never received and is presumed to have been lost in the mail. To get a replacement card, the cardholder will have to sign an affidavit, a legal document.

lost in transit

1. checks, drafts, or other negotiable instruments lost in the clearing process.

2. sales draft lost between a bank card processing center and either the card issuing bank or the merchant processing bank.

lump-sum distribution single payment to an account beneficiary, for example, the beneficiary of a retirement account, as opposed to scheduled payments at regular time intervals. The holder of an INDIVIDUAL RETIREMENT ACCOUNT, for example, can either reinvest the assets of the account in a rollover account, or the proceeds can be recognized as ordinary income, and taxed at an average rate over a ten-year period.

M

M1 narrowest measure of the MONEY SUPPLY. M1 includes currency held by the public, plus travelers' checks, demand deposits, other checkable deposits (including negotiable order of withdrawal (NOW) accounts, Automatic Transfer of Savings (ATS) accounts, and credit union share draft accounts).

M2 MONEY SUPPLY measure that includes M1 plus savings and small denomination time deposits, Money Market Deposit Accounts, shares in Money Market Mutual Funds held by individual investors, overnight repurchase agreements, and certain overnight Eurodollar deposits.

M3 MONEY SUPPLY measure that includes M2 plus large time deposits, large denomination repurchase agreements, shares in Money Market Mutual Funds held by institutional investors, and certain Eurodollar deposits in foreign branches of U.S. banks.

machine readable capable of being read by a mechanical device without additional processing. Machine readable characters on preprinted checks—the MAGNETIC INK CHARACTER RECOGNITION (MICR) line—permit high-speed check sorting and remittance processing. Other examples are the bank card MAGNETIC STRIPE, magnetic computer tape, the retail industry Universal Price Code (UPC), and Optical Character Recognition (OCR).

macroeconomics branch of economics that deals with the economy as a whole and attempts to explain how key economic variables, such as incomes, prices, unemployment, and productivity, are influenced by FISCAL POLICY and MONETARY POLICY. Contrast with *microeconomics*, or the study of a particular industry or sector of the economy, for example, the housing industry.

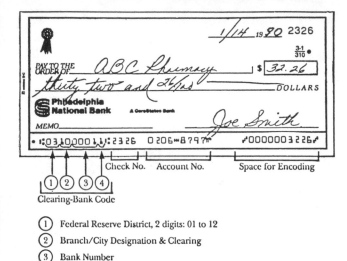

Check No.   Account No.   Space for Encoding

Clearing-Bank Code

① Federal Reserve District, 2 digits: 01 to 12

② Branch/City Designation & Clearing

③ Bank Number

④ Parity Check Digit (for reading error control)

MAGNETIC INK CHARACTER RECOGNITION

Source: Bernell K. Stone, *One to Get Ready*, p.3. © 1988 by Bernell K. Stone.

magnetic ink character recognition (MICR)

machine readable characters used to encode checks so they can be read electronically and processed by check sorting equipment. The MICR line on bank checks refers to the machine readable characters in the bottom edge. The MICR line standard was adopted in 1959 with the cooperation of the Federal Reserve Board and check printers; it enabled banks to standardize the routing and transit numbers identifying the paying banks, and automate the handling of checks. MICR coding includes the paying bank's number, ABA TRANSIT NUMBER; CHECK ROUTING SYMBOL; and the serial number and amount of the check. See also ENCODING.

magnetic stripe

strip of magnetic tape, affixed to bank credit and debit cards, encoded with cardholder identifying information, such as the PRIMARY ACCOUNT NUMBER and card ex-

MAGNETIC STRIPE

Track 1	Airline Ticketing
Track 2	ABA Bank Card Track
Track 3	Off-line Transactions

piration date, permitting automated handling of transactions. The bank card industry standard for magnetic stripes allows three separate tracks of encoded data:

Track 1: developed by the International Air Transportation Association for automation of airline ticketing;

Track 2: developed by the American Bankers Association for the automation of financial transactions; and

Track 3: developed by the thrift industry for financial terminals operating in an OFF-LINE mode (not connected to a host processor) for transaction authorization.

mail float clearing delays that slow the PRESENTMENT of out-of-town checks to the paying bank. Mail float is the time lag attributed to checks and CASH LETTERS arriving from distant points.

mail teller teller of a bank that is responsible for receiving, sorting, and proving deposits arriving by mail. In larger banks, deposits from customers and correspondents are as heavy as volume of deposits taken at the teller line.

maintenance fee periodic charge to maintain an account, such as a credit card annual fee or a monthly checking account service charge, to cover the cost of servicing the account and statement preparation. Checking account fees may be waived if the customer keeps a certain minimum balance.

maintenance margin

1. in futures, money that a customer must keep in a MARGIN account when a position is outstanding. It is usually lower than the initial margin posted. If position losses exceed the maintenance margin, the exchange issues a margin call requiring the customer to post additional margin to bring the level of equity above the maintenance margin level.

2. in securities, the margin requirement a brokerage customer must maintain at all times in a brokerage account with a debit balance. Also called minimum maintenance. Federal Reserve REGULATION T requires an initial $2,000 deposit in a brokerage account and sets the margin requirement (50% since 1974) to cover margin trading on a customer's account.

maintenance requirements dollar amount that a bank or brokerage customer must keep as margin capital in a trading account. The customer can borrow against the total value of securities in the account, but may be required to post additional margin if the value of the margin falls below a prescribed level. Maintenance requirements are a selective credit control used by the Federal Reserve Board, and are implemented through Federal Reserve REGULATION T and REGULATION U. In general, margin levels are set at 50% of market value, but can be raised or lowered as needed.

major industry identifier first digit in the PRIMARY ACCOUNT NUMBER that is printed on the front of a BANK CARD or TRAVEL & ENTERTAINMENT card. Cards issued by banks and other financial institutions generally have account numbers beginning with the number 4 or 5; those issued by nonbank companies, such as travel & entertainment companies, have account numbers beginning with 3.

maker person who writes a CHECK, signs a PROMISSORY NOTE or other negotiable instrument, and assumes primary liability for payment. The maker of a check is also known as the DRAWER.

managed currency any currency whose EXCHANGE RATE is influenced by central bank INTERVENTION in the exchange markets, as opposed to interaction of supply and demand in the free market. Most major currencies are managed to one degree or another when central banks buy and sell their own currency to maintain market stability and carry out MONETARY POLICY. See also CLEAN FLOAT; DIRTY FLOAT; EXCHANGE CONTROLS.

managed liabilities deposits, other than CORE DEPOSITS, that banks actively solicit from other banks, or from brokers, to maintain adequate levels of LIQUIDITY. Managed liabilities are deposits that can be increased or decreased at will, such as negotiable time deposits of $100,000 or more, with maturities under one year; Eurodollar and other Eurocurrency borrowings; repurchase agreements against Treasury securities and federal agency securities; and Federal Funds purchased, to meet a bank's needs for funds to pay off maturing deposits and fund new loans.

Such borrowings can be increased or decreased as needed to meet temporary funding gaps between maturing assets and liabilities. The negotiable CD, which evolved in the period when Regulation Q imposed interest rate caps on all deposits except those above $100,000, is typically sold in $1 million pieces. These certificates of deposit pay interest at maturity, and usually have an original maturity of one to three months. See also BROKERED DEPOSIT; LIABILITY MANAGEMENT.

managing underwriter commercial bank or investment bank representing an UNDERWRITING GROUP in purchase and distribution of a new securities offering. The managing underwriter arranges the selling group; files the necessary registration papers with the Securities and Exchange Commission; acts as AGENT for the selling group, as authorized by the AGREEMENT AMONG UNDERWRITERS; decides the portion of the offering, or ALLOTMENT, to be assigned each member; and acts to stabilize the price of the securities during the offering period. For his or her services, the managing underwriter is paid an extra fee from the syndicate's gross profit. Called LEAD BANK in the Eurobond market. See also BEST EFFORT; NEGOTIATED UNDERWRITING.

mandatory convertible subordinated debt or CAPITAL NOTE that is convertible into common stock at a future date. Conversion is required by the bond agreement and is not at the option of the bondholder. Mandatory convertible notes count toward secondary (Tier 2) capital and minimize the dilution effect of new issues on shareholder value, and interest paid on notes is tax deductible. EQUITY COMMITMENT NOTES, first issued by Manufacturers Hanover Corp. in 1982, are multiyear notes with detachable stock warrants, exchangeable for common stock at maturity. EQUITY CONTRACT NOTES, first issued by Morgan Guaranty & Co., Inc. in 1982, require the issuer to redeem the notes with a new issue of common stock at specific intervals.

mandatory sharing state laws that require financial institutions placing AUTOMATED TELLER MACHINES other customer activated ELECTRONIC FUNDS TRANSFER (EFT) terminals in branch offices or OFF-PREMISE locations to make these terminals available to customers of other financial institutions. Some states mandate sharing of all customer activated EFT terminals, regardless of location. See also SHARED NETWORK.

margin
Banking:
1. difference between a bank's borrowing rate and lending rate when it makes a loan; also known as the lending SPREAD. Contrast with NET INTEREST MARGIN.
2. proportion of the asset pledged as security, for example, inventory or accounts receivable, that a bank will lend against. The difference between the market value and loan value is also called a HAIRCUT. If the collateral declines in value, additional margin will be required.
3. constant value added to the INDEX rate of an ADJUSTABLE RATE MORTGAGE to compute the current interest rate.

Futures: money or securities put up as a good faith deposit assuring that a future contract will be fulfilled. Also known as a security deposit, as in the initial margin and MAINTENANCE MARGIN required when a futures position is open.

Securities: money deposited with a broker that serves as partial payment when purchasing securities. The Federal Reserve Board's REGULATION T sets a MAINTENANCE MARGIN, currently 50%, in purchases or short sales of securities. Margin may be put up in cash or eligible securities. Individual broker-dealers may impose higher margins in trades of OVER-THE-COUNTER securities.

marginal cost of funds incremental cost or differential cost of each additional dollar borrowed. It is the cost of funding one more loan, assuming that the cost of funds remains unchanged. Under conventional cost accounting theory, the marginal cost of acquiring new funds decreases as scale economies are achieved. Put another way, the marginal cost of funds varies inversely to the capital base of financial intermediaries because the larger banks, which as a rule have larger loan portfolios, can tap into the capital markets and money markets with greater ease than smaller ones. See also POOLED COST OF FUNDS.

margin call demand by a securities broker-dealer or a futures clearing house to a clearing member for additional funds or collateral to offset position losses in a MARGIN account. If a bank loan is secured by marginable securities the lender may call the loan if the customer fails to post additional collateral or pay down the loan. If the margin call is on securities, the customer is asked to post more cash or eligible securities by a certain time the following day, or the account is sold to satisfy the outstanding loan.

marital deduction portion of an estate that may pass to the surviving spouse exempt from federal estate taxes. The ECONOMIC RECOVERY TAX ACT OF 1981 permitted an unlimited marital deductions, eliminating the double taxation of assets inherited by a surviving spouse. There are many types of marital deductions, such as the federal income tax deduction for a nonworking spouse.

market
1. aggregate of supply and demand that brings together informed buyers and sellers, and sets the public price for products or services. For example, the CREDIT market, the foreign exchange market, the MONEY MARKET the mortgage market, and the SECONDARY MARKET.
2. public place, such as a stock exchange, or futures exchange, where trading takes place. It implies the presence of market makers who are willing to buy or sell for their own account, or for customers, at quoted prices. Futures exchanges are open outcry markets, where prices are set by direct interaction (hand signals) by traders on the trading floor. Securities exchanges, where listed securities are sold, involve trading by brokers or dealers acting on behalf of buyers or sellers, who maintain contact with the trading floor by telephone.
3. to sell anything of value to a willing buyer at a mutually agreeable price.

market discipline concept that financial institutions should be self-regulated, rather than regulated by government agencies. Market discipline substitutes the free market for the supervisory activities of banking industry regulators, in setting the rates banks pay to attract deposits, and even in the kinds of products that financial institutions sell to the public. In practice, though, intervention by banking regulations can never be ruled out completely. For example, money center banks and large regional banks are generally recognized as being too big to fail, because the failure of a large bank would have a disruptive effect on the economy.

market index deposit SAVINGS ACCOUNT or CERTIFICATE OF DEPOSIT that pays a rate of interest tied to a commodity or a market index. Also known as an indexed deposit account or indexed CD. The yield may be linked to a stock index, such as the Standard & Poor's 500 Index, or other broad gauge measure of the economy. Market index deposits are federally insured deposits, and at maturity pay either a guaranteed minimum return or the fixed portion of any gain in the market index over the life of the deposit, whichever is greater.

marketing business activities relating to delivery of goods and services from sellers to purchasers, and also from businesses to consumers to meet demands of the market. Bank marketing, or selling in the past relied heavily on retail branch networks to distribute financial services, but in recent years banking institutions have employed a variety of marketing approaches, including direct mail and telemarketing. Competition from nonbank financial intermediaries since the mid-1970s has led depository financial institutions to experiment with employee sales incentives and other tactics in an attempt to instill more of a sales culture in bank marketing. See also AFFINITY CARD; CAUSE RELATED MARKETING; MARKET RESEARCH; PERSONAL BANKER; PLATFORM AUTOMATION; RELATIONSHIP BANKING.

market maker person who stands ready to execute buy and sell orders on behalf of customers or his own account, or BOOK. A market maker is someone who assumes trading risk by taking possession of the asset traded, and who executes transactions at publicly quoted prices. A market maker's bid and asked spreads are not so large as to preclude transactions at the prices quoted.

In organized exchanges, such as the stock market or futures market, market makers are licensed by a regulating body or by the exchange itself.

market order order to buy or sell securities at the best available price—at the market—the most common way of executing trades.

market rate of interest rates of interest on deposits and other investments resulting from the demand for and supply of funds in the money market. Market rates are reported in daily newspapers, as collected by various reporting agencies, for example, the Bank Rate Monitor Index and Donoghue's Money Fund Index.

market research systematic collection and analysis of data relating to sale and distribution of financial products and services. Market research is an early step in the marketing process, and includes an analysis of market demand for a new product, or for existing products, as well as appropriate methods of distributing those products. Techniques in market research include telephone polling and focus group interviews to determine customer attitudes, pricing sensitivity, and willingness to use delivery alternatives. Most large banks have their own market research departments that evaluate not only products, but their BRICK AND MORTAR branch banking networks through which most banking products are sold.

market risk risk that an asset will decline in price, resulting in a financial loss to the holder when the asset is sold. Banks try to minimize market risk through a variety of HEDGING techniques, such as futures, options, and swaps.

market segmentation theory theory of interest rates that says short-term and long term markets act independently of each other and that investors have fixed maturity preferences. Also called *segmented markets theory*. Supporters of this theory maintain that short-term and long-term rates are distinct markets, each with its own buyers and sellers, and are not easily substituted for each other. See also EXPECTATIONS THEORY; LIQUIDITY PREFERENCE THEORY.

market to book value ratio of the market value of a security, for example, common stock, to its book value. An indication of performance of common stock equity, after accounting for such factors as dilution of common stock equity after a merger and market reaction to unexpected gains or losses and changes in operating income.

market value highest price that a marketable asset will bring in an open and competitive market, assuming that both buyer and seller are informed and acting independently. Also called FAIR MARKET VALUE. In theory, this is the highest price a seller is willing to accept and the lowest price a buyer is willing to pay. It may differ from the APPRAISAL VALUE. See also MARK TO THE MARKET.

markka national currency of Finland.

mark to the market daily adjustment of an account or investment to reflect actual MARKET VALUE market value, as opposed to historic accounting value or BOOK VALUE. Securities and futures are revalued on a daily basis, but bank loans and investments other than securities are evaluated and marked down only when there is a change in the credit relationship with the borrower, or the loan collateral has deteriorated in value.

Massachusetts rule see PRUDENT MAN RULE.

MasterCard International member-owned nonprofit corporation that licenses financial institutions to issue MasterCard bank cards and market related products and services. Its principal assets are the MasterCard trademarks; global communications network, BankNet, for authorization and settlement of bank card transactions for member banks; and a nationwide AUTOMATED TELLER MACHINE network, Cirrus System Inc.

master mortgage standard mortgage documentation filed by mortgage originators in public land records. The master mortgage simplifies the recording of liens, as mortgages have become increasingly complex in recent years, and also facilitates sales of loans in the secondary mortgage market.

master note see REVOLVING CREDIT.

master trust custody arrangement whereby a bank or trust company manages pension fund assets for a group of related companies under a single trustee account. A master trust agreement facilitates the administration of defined benefit pension plan assets, including purchase and sale of securities; reporting to corporate plan sponsors, as required by the Employee Retirement Income Security Act, and distribution of retirement benefits to individuals covered by the plan. A master trust arrangement facilitates plan accounting when multiple investment managers are used.

matched book portfolio of assets and portfolio of liabilities having equal maturities. The term is used most often in reference to money market instruments and money market liabilities. In contrast, an *unmatched book* is referred to as a short or long book.

matched maturities in bank ASSET-LIABILITY MANAGEMENT, the funding of loans with deposits of approximately equal durations to minimize interest rate risk. Also called matched funding. This is the contractual gap approach to funds management, carried out by matching maturities on opposite sides of the balance sheet in a given reporting period. For example, all 90-day loans are matched against liabilities expected to mature or reprice in 90 days. The difference between maturing assets and maturing liabilities is the contractual gap, which will be different for each calendar period. Matched funding gets more difficult as maturities lengthen. A bank could, for example, try to fund its five-year car loans with five-year Certificates of Deposit, but this is often difficult to achieve. A bank cannot prevent its depositors from withdrawing their money before the CD maturity date. Also, a bank may find it advantageous to deliberately MISMATCH maturities when it believes interest rates are about to change. Maturity matching is more common in the Eurocurrency market where Eurodollar deposits, for instance, have fixed maturities, and can be matched easily against fixed term liabilities.

matched sale repurchase agreement FEDERAL OPEN MARKET COMMITTEE practice in which the Fed sells government securities, usually Treasury bills, to a primary securities dealer, and agrees to repurchase the securities later. Trades are exercised by the Open Market Desk at the Federal Reserve Bank of New York, from the Fed's System Open Market Account. The initial sale reduces EXCESS RESERVES in the banking system and limits the ability of banks to make new loans and investments. Later, when the Fed buys back the securities, the flow of reserves is reversed, according to the requirements of the original sale. Matched sale repurchase agreements are used by the Fed for correction in temporary aberrations in reserves, as opposed to outright purchases and sales, which generally are for long-term effect. Maturities of these buy-sell arrangements are from 1 to 15 days, and ordinarily do not exceed 7 days. Also called a REVERSE REPURCHASE AGREEMENT. See also MONETARY POLICY; OPEN MARKET OPERATIONS; REPURCHASE AGREEMENT.

maturity date date on which the principal balance of a loan, debt instrument or other financial security is due and payable to the holder. Also, the date on which a TIME DRAFT is payable.

maturity gap see GAP; GAPPING.

maturity tickler see LOAN REGISTER.

May Day May 1, 1975, the date when fixed brokerage commissions were abolished in the securities industry in the United States. Passing of fixed commissions led to DISCOUNT BROKERAGE trading by firms that executed orders but gave no investment advice, and accelerated the diversification by securities firms into financial services, in which they began competing directly with banks and thrift institutions.

McFadden Act law enacted by Congress in 1927 giving states the power to regulate bank branching, including branching by national banks. The intent of the act was to put national banks and state chartered banks on a competitively equal footing in their ability to open new branches. In effect, the McFadden Act prohibited interstate expansion by any bank, since state banks were limited to branching within the borders of their home state. National banks are allowed to open branch offices within states, with the approval of the Comptroller of the Currency, but only to the same extent that state laws permitted branching by state banks. State banks that are members of the Federal Reserve System are also subject to McFadden Act limitations, except that state member banks must also obtain approval of the Federal Reserve Board of Governors to establish branch offices. See also INTERSTATE BANKING; REGIONAL INTERSTATE BANKING.

mechanic's lien enforceable claim, permitted by law in most states, securing payment to contractors, subcontractors and suppliers of materials for work performed in constructing or repairing a building. The lien, which attaches to real property, plus buildings and improvements situated on the land, remains in effect until the workmen have been paid in full, or in event of liquidation, gives the contractor PRIORITY OF LIEN ahead of other creditors.

Member, Appraisal Institute (MAI) professional designation by the American Institute of Real Estate Appraisers of the National Association of Realtors, given to real estate appraisers who meet qualifying standards and are certified by the institute.

member bank depository financial institution that is a member of the FEDERAL RESERVE SYSTEM. National banks are required to be members of the Federal Reserve, and state chartered commercial banks and mutual savings banks have the option of becoming members. Member banks are required to: (1) purchase stock in their district Federal Reserve Bank equal to 6% of their PAID-IN CAPITAL and paid-in surplus. (2) keep a portion of their demand deposits and time deposits in LEGAL RESERVES at a Federal Reserve Bank; (3) honor checks drawn on the bank and presented to a Reserve Bank for collection; and (4) comply with federal banking regulations, and if a state chartered bank, accept supervision and examination by the Federal Reserve System. Member banks also elect 6 of the 9 directors in each of the 12 district Federal Reserve Banks, and are permitted to borrow funds at the Federal Reserve DISCOUNT WINDOW.

memo entry debit or credit to a customer's account that is recorded to the bank's transaction journals at a different time than when the transaction actually occurred. Journal entries are entered to the general ledger usually at the end of the day. Many banks that operate electronic banking services, such as automated teller machines, do not record ELECTRONIC FUNDS TRANSFER (EFT) transactions in an on-line fashion, but record them to a memo file, sometimes called a *strip file*, which is used to update customer accounts.

memorandum of understanding voluntary agreement by a bank or savings institution, negotiated with a supervisory agency, to refrain from a particular activity deemed by the regulatory agency to be an unsound banking practice. A memorandum of understanding is not necessarily an admission of wrongdoing, but indicates a willingness to take corrective action in the future.

mercantile agency organization that supplies credit information to businesses and to financial institutions in response to a request for a credit history on an individual or business organization. For example, credit information companies affiliated with the Associated Credit Bureaus of America, such as TRW, Trans Union Credit Information; DUN & BRADSTREET, the oldest of the mercantile credit agencies; and credit interchange associations, such as the National Association of Credit Management. Mercantile agencies furnish information on debt repayment and credit history, collected voluntarily from a wide number of reporting companies.

In consumer credit, federal law prohibits a credit information company from giving out a person's credit records for purposes other than an extension of credit, or when a consumer requests a copy of his or her credit history.

merchant person, firm, or corporation that has a contractual relationship with a card issuing bank to accept bank cards for payment of goods and services.

merchant agreement written agreement between a retail merchant and a card processing bank. The merchant agreement spells out the merchant's rights and warranties with respect to accepting bank cards, the merchant discount rate, and procedures to follow in handling chargebacks and other disputed transactions.

merchant bank

1. credit card processing bank that accepts bank card sales drafts from a retail merchant. The merchant processor converts the merchant's sales drafts to deposits, and collects a processing fee called a *merchant discount*. If the transaction was initiated by a customer at another bank, the merchant bank submits the sales draft information through the bank card INTERCHANGE system, collecting the amount of the draft, less the interchange fee, from the card issuing bank. See also MERCHANT DISCOUNT RATE.

2. European or British investment bank that engages in MERCHANT BANKING.

merchant banking

form of banking where the bank arranges credit financing, but does not hold the loans in its investment portfolio to maturity. A merchant bank invests its own capital in leveraged buyouts, corporate acquisitions, and other structured finance transactions. Merchant banking is a fee based business, where the bank assumes market risk but no long-term credit risk. A common form of banking in Europe, merchant banking is gaining acceptance in the United States, as more banks originate commercial loans and then sell them to investors rather than hold the loans as portfolio investments. A banque d'affaire is a French merchant bank, which has more powers than its British counterpart.

merchant discount rate

fee charged a merchant for processing bank card sales drafts and crediting the funds to the merchant's account. The merchant discount is a percentage of net sales on the card, and is negotiated individually with each merchant. If the merchant discount rate is 2% of net sales, the merchant processing bank remits $98 of a $100 sales transaction to the merchant, and keeps $2 as its fee. More commonly, the bank gives the merchant $100 and charges a $2 fee at the end of the month. See also INTERCHANGE.

merchant fraud

scheme to defraud a bank card plan, often a merchant working in collusion with someone else. A common form is WHITE PLASTIC fraud, a scheme in which the merchant submits phony sales drafts to a processing bank and then splits the sales draft income with the person supplying the account numbers that were charged.

merchant number identification code that identifies card honoring merchants in a bank card plan. Merchants are issued a specially encoded card that is used for end-of-day transaction settlement, in tallying their daily sales volume for reporting to their card processing bank.

merger combination of two or more organizations through pooling of common stock, cash payment to the bank being acquired, or a combination. Managements in both banks generally consent to mergers in the banking industry, or in the case of a bank acquiring a failed institution, the approval of bank regulatory agencies is necessary. A merger is called an ACQUISITION when one of the parties to the transaction, usually but not always the larger one, takes over a smaller company and consolidates the two organizations into a single entity. See also POOLING OF INTERESTS; PURCHASE ACQUISITION.

message authentication code (MAC) unique security code, created by an ALGORITHM and used in ELECTRONIC FUNDS TRANSFER (EFT) to ensure that the information has not been tampered with, and that the sender of a message is in fact the originating bank. See also KEY MANAGEMENT.

messenger bank employee whose job is collection, by direct presentment, of checks, notes, and drafts that are not drawn on clearing house banks and thus are not collectible through a clearing house. Messengers also collect special items from brokerages and corporations, such as drafts with stocks or bonds attached. Collection by messenger is frequently known as *collections by hand*.

metropolitan statistical area (MSA) federally designated geographical unit consisting of an urbanized area with a central city of at least 50,000 residents and a regional population of 100,000. Many MSAs cross state boundaries. For example, the Washington, D.C. MSA contains parts of northern Virginia and southern Maryland. Some advocates of interstate banking believe that banks should be allowed unrestricted branching within these regions. Formerly called standard metropolitan statistical area.

mezzanine bracket popular name for the underwriters in an underwriting syndicate who subscribe to the second largest portion, following the lead manager, and are listed below the lead manager in TOMBSTONE advertising announcing the transaction in newspapers. Other underwriters, including co-managers, participating in the deal are listed in alphabetical order beneath the major underwriters.

mezzanine financing

1. in corporate finance, a LEVERAGED BUYOUT or restructuring financed through subordinated debt, such as preferred stock or convertible debentures. This type of financing is very popular in merger & acquisitions, as the transaction is financed by expanding equity, as opposed to debt. Holders of the securities are also assured of having a greater role in managing the resulting company.
2. second or third level financing of companies financed by venture capital. The mezzanine financing is senior to the venture capital financing, but junior to bank financing, and adds creditworthiness to the firm. It generally is used as an intermediate stage financing, preceding the company's initial public offering (IPO), and is considered less risky than start-up financing.

microfilm photographic process that copies checks and other documents for record keeping and storage. Microfilmed copies of cancelled checks, which banks are required to keep for seven years, are considered valid proof of payment by the Internal Revenue Service. Documents filed with the Securities and Exchange Commission are available on microfilm from private sources. Microfilming of bank records is being replaced gradually by document image processing, in which physical documents are converted into computer readable digital images that are stored on optical laser disks for rapid retrieval.

middle rate median average of BID and OFFER prices quoted by foreign exchange dealers. For example, say the bid price of a given currency versus the U.S. dollar is $1 = 1.6510 and the offer price is $1 = 1.6520. Traders will say, "Can we do business in the middle?"—at $1 equal to 1.6515. ($1 = 1.6515.)

midgets popular name for 15-year Government National Mortgage Association (Ginnie Mae) pass-through securities collateralized by pools of biweekly mortgages. As with 30-year Ginnie Mae pass-through securities, Midget pools have a minimum principal of $1 million.

mini-branch specialized branch office that offers a limited number of banking services, less than what is available at a full-service branch. A mini-branch, generally smaller than a conventional branch, may have only an AUTOMATED TELLER MACHINE for taking deposits and dispensing cash, and may refer loan applications to another branch. Also called *convenience branch*.

minimum balance amount required in an account to earn interest, qualify for special services, or waive service charges. Accounts that fall below the minimum balance may be subject to service charges if the average balance is below that threshhold, or if the account falls below that balance at any time. To get a free checking account, for instance, a customer may have to keep a certain amount in the account at all times or maintain an equivalent amount in other accounts. Cost accounting systems may give customers an earnings credit for funds kept on deposit. Others, instead, work with a flat charge per check or account. See also AVERAGE BALANCE; TARGET BALANCE.

minimum payment smallest payment a credit cardholder can make toward reducing the outstanding balance owed, while meeting the terms and conditions of the cardholder agreement. In most bank credit card plans, the minimum acceptable payment generally is 1/36 of the outstanding balance.

mini-statement see INTERIM STATEMENT.

minor person under legal age, the age when he or she attains full civil rights. The legal age is 18 in most states, but may be 21 in some states.

mint bureau of the U.S. Treasury that manufactures coins, and holds the U.S. Treasury Department's gold bullion reserves in safekeeping. The Treasury's Assay Office is supervised by the Bureau of the Mint.

misencoded payment incorrectly entered encoded in a bank's proof and transit department with an incorrect dollar amount. A misencoded check will become a REJECT and will have to be processed manually as an exception item.

mismatch situation in ASSET-LIABILITY MANAGEMENT when interest-earning assets and interest expense liabilities do not balance. Also known as a *mismatched book*. An example is when an asset is funded by a liability of a different maturity. The conventional circumstances in banking are that banks and savings institutions borrow short and lend long. This means funding 30-year mortgages with short-term deposits, expecting that short-term deposits can be rolled over at maturity dates. Contrast with MATCHED MATURITIES.

mis-sent items checks sent by error to the wrong bank for payment. These are usually returned to the sending bank, delaying payment of these checks.

missing payment loan payment made within the allowed grace period, but, for one reason or another, not posted to the proper account. If not corrected in time, the error may result in the posting of a LATE CHARGE against the account.

mixed deposit deposit at a teller window, night depository, or at an automated teller machine, containing both cash and checks. Contrast with SPLIT DEPOSIT.

mobile home certificate mortgage backed security issued by the GOVERNMENT NATIONAL MORTGAGE ASSOCIATION (Ginnie Mae) representing an undivided interest in pools of mobile home loans insured by the Federal Housing Administration or guaranteed by the Veterans Administration. Mobile home certificates loans have the same full-faith guarantee of timely payment of interest and repayment of principal as Ginnie Mae securities backed by single-family homes. However, yields on mobile home paper are based on much shorter maturities (average life: five to nine years) than Ginnie Mae pass-through certificates backed by residential mortgages.

model mathematical characterization of a process, market condition, or set of variables that is used to determine how each would behave under different scenarios. A pricing model uses hypothetical data to simulate real market conditions, in both present value and at different points in the future. Such models are widely used in ASSET-LIABILITY MANAGEMENT, credit scoring, loan pricing, interest rate futures, and financial swaps. See also BLACK SCHOLES MODEL; ECONOMETRICS; SIMULATION; WHAT-IF CALCULATION.

modified pass-through certificate security that represents an undivided interest in pools of mortgages, backed by federally guaranteed loans of the same maturity and coupon date. When a mortgage banker has collected at least $2 million in mortgages, the loans are deposited in a custodian bank and a certificate is issued against the mortgages. Payments of principal and interest are made monthly to certificate holders, and are guaranteed by the Government National Mortgage Association regardless of whether payments are received or not, as borrowers pay down the loans. There is no holding back of interest payments as with collateralized mortgage obligations and mortgage backed bonds.

modified payoff deposit insurance payoff whereby uninsured depositors, persons holding deposits exceeding $100,000 per account, receive only a portion of their claim against the assets of a failed bank. The modified payoff was introduced by the Federal Deposit Insurance Corporation in the early 1980s to cope with bank failures where a sizeable portion of the deposits were rate sensitive BROKERED DEPOSITs that paid well above rates offered by competing institutions.

modulus 10 digit mathematical formula for computing an account number CHECK DIGIT and used to verify the accuracy of check routing/transit numbers. The check digit is computed by subtracting the check digit calculation from the next higher multiple of 10, hence the name "modulus 10 digit."

monetarist economist who believes that control of the MONEY SUPPLY is the key to managing the boom and bust cycles in the economy. Monetarists, most notably Milton Friedman and his followers, maintain that recessions are caused by declines in the rate of expansion in the money supply. The monetarist school of economic thought says that setting annual targets for growth in the money supply, say 3%-4% annually, is the best means to achieve stable growth in the economy and control inflation. As an economic theory, though, monetarism has its drawbacks. Critics say monetarism ignores other factors, such as government spending and taxation, and bank credit, which are equally important. During the Great Depression in the 1930s it was impossible to make the money supply grow because no one wanted to borrow or use money, even though banks had plenty of money to lend. Attempting to increase bank credit and the money supply was known as "pushing on a string." A monetary policy focusing on controlling the monetary aggregates (M1, M2, and so on) can achieve one objective (a lower inflation rate) at the expense of extreme volatility in interest rates and an economic recession, as the Federal Reserve found during the 1979-1982 period. Finally, there is still no inclusive definition of the money supply itself; consequently, the money supply is observed by the Federal Reserve, but is only one indicator of the effectiveness of monetary policy.

Monetary Accord of 1951 agreement between the U.S. Treasury Department and the Federal Reserve Board of Governors that enabled the Fed to pursue an active MONETARY POLICY, independent of the Treasury and the federal government. Before 1951, the Fed had to assure low cost Treasury financing by purchasing Treasury securities at a set price. Afterward, the Federal Reserve Open Market Committee was able to purchase as much, or as little, of Treasury securities offered for sale by the Treasury Department as it wanted, instead of having to buy whatever the Treasury issued at the prevailing rate. Also known as the Treasury Fed Accord.

monetary aggregates see MONEY SUPPLY.

monetary base sum of reserve accounts of financial institutions at Federal Reserve Banks, currency in circulation (currency held by the public and in the vaults of depository institutions). The major source of the adjusted monetary base is FEDERAL RESERVE CREDIT. The monetary base, as the ultimate source of the nation's MONEY SUPPLY, is controllable, at least to some degree, by Federal Reserve MONETARY POLICY. The adjusted monetary base is compiled weekly by the Federal Reserve Board and the Federal Reserve Bank of St. Louis, and is adjusted seasonally.

Monetary Control Act Title 1 of the DEPOSITORY INSTITUTIONS DEREGULATION AND MONETARY CONTROL ACT OF 1980. The Monetary Control Act phased in reserve requirements for all depository institutions over an eight-year period, and granted universal access to the Fed DISCOUNT WINDOW by federally insured depository institutions. It also allowed the Fed to impose supplemental reserves as needed to carry out monetary policy.

The Monetary Control Act, by phasing in universal RESERVE REQUIREMENTS, significantly broadened the Federal Reserve's authority to manage bank reserves and required the Fed to charge explicit prices for Reserve Bank services such as check collection. It is the first major change in Fed policymaking since the FEDERAL OPEN MARKET COMMITTEE was created in the 1930s to centralize the Fed's OPEN MARKET OPERATIONS with the Federal Reserve Board of Governors. See also PRIVATE SECTOR ADJUSTMENT FACTOR.

monetary policy actions by the FEDERAL RESERVE SYSTEM to influence the cost and availability of credit, with the goals of promoting economic growth, full employment, price stability, and balanced trade with other countries. Through its monetary policy decisions, the Fed tries to regulate both interest rates and the nation's MONEY SUPPLY. Monetary policy is carried out by the FEDERAL RESERVE BOARD and the FEDERAL OPEN MARKET COMMITTEE, the 12-member committee (including all 7 governors of the Federal Reserve Board), which directs the open market purchase and sale of government securities for the 12 Federal Reserve Banks. The Federal Reserve Board chairman appears before Congressional committees twice a year, in February and July, to report on Federal Reserve monetary policy objectives, as required by the 1978 Humphrey-Hawkins Act. These addresses are watched closely for indications of a change in monetary policy.

The Fed has at its disposal three distinct tools of monetary policy: the purchase or sale of securities through OPEN MARKET OPERATIONS, its power to set financial institution RESERVE REQUIREMENTS, and the DISCOUNT RATE paid by banks and savings institutions when they borrow from one of the district Federal

Reserve Banks. Monetary policy can be characterized as being either tight credit or easy credit. When the Fed is worried that the economy is growing too fast or prices are rising too rapidly, it tightens up reserve positions by selling government securities or allowing maturing securities to run off. This process is known as *draining reserves*. If, on the other hand, the Fed becomes concerned that the economy is not growing fast enough, or is headed into a recession, it can inject new reserves into the banking system by buying securities from securities dealers. By buying, instead of selling, securities, the Fed is expanding, rather than contracting the supply of bank reserves, thereby making it easier for banks to meet their reserve requirements and make new loans.

In addition to monetary policy, the Fed also has several selective credit controls regulating the cost of credit. These include the MARGIN requirements on securities purchased through broker-dealers, and the highly effective MORAL SUASION, whereby the Fed tries to persuade bankers to go along with its recommendations through informal pressure. Until 1981, the Fed also had the power to selectively impose surcharges on discount window borrowings, and also impose reserve requirements on assets of nonbank financial intermediaries, such as money market mutual funds. This authority has since expired. Although monetary policy differs from the federal government's FISCAL POLICY, carried out by its tax and spending policies, both share a common objective: balancing aggregate demand in the economy against aggregate supply, as measured by the gross national product, employment, and interest rates, thereby keeping inflation and unemployment under control. See also INTERMEDIATE TARGETS; MONETARIST; MONETARY BASE; OPERATIONAL TARGETS.

monetary targets see OPERATIONAL TARGETS.

money anything commonly accepted as a LEGAL TENDER currency for payment of debts. Money has been defined any number of ways, but it generally serves three distinct purposes, depending on how it is used: (1) as a medium of exchange for payments between consumers, businesses, and government; (2) as a unit of account for measuring purchasing power, or the prices paid for goods and services; and (3) as a store of value for measuring the economic worth of current income deferred for spending in future years.

In the United States, paper currency (FEDERAL RESERVE NOTE), coins, and checking account balances are examples of money. Other forms of money are commodity money (gold and silver bullion and coins, brightly colored shells and so on), and BARTER, the trading of goods and services without monetary exchange. Today, paper currency represents only a fraction of the nation's money stock; about three fourths of the MONEY SUPPLY is held in the form of bookkeeping debits and credits representing demand deposit (checking) account balances in commercial banks. See also CURRENCY IN CIRCULATION; FIAT MONEY; MONETARY BASE; MONEY SUPPLY; NEAR MONEY.

money center bank bank located in a major financial center that participates in both national and international money markets. Money center banks offer regional banks and community banks access to master trust, foreign exchange, and depository services, as well as check clearings, through CORRESPONDENT banking networks. Money center banks are found mainly in New York, Chicago, and San Francisco, and also in London and other world financial centers.

money laundering acceptance of large cash deposits from individuals or businesses when the money is suspected of being used for illicit purposes. Under the BANK SECRECY ACT, financial institutions are required to report cash deposits of $10,000 or more, and multiple deposits from the same depositor that added up to $10,000. Such transactions are reported to the Treasury and the U.S. Secret Service.

The Money Laundering Control Act of 1986 further requires that banks and savings institutions have in place a reporting system to monitor cash transactions under $10,000. Under new federal regulations, some cash transactions under $10,000 are reportable in certain states.

money market market where short-term debt securities are issued and traded. The money market is an informal network of dealers and institutional investors, rather than an organized market like the New York Stock Exchange. A bank selling certificates of deposit, for instance, is engaged in money market activities. Money market securities are generally short-term, typically less than 90 days, and are highly liquid investments issued by firms with good credit ratings. Participants include government securities dealers, banks and other financial institutions, and managers of money market funds. An important part of the global money market is the Euromarket, a largely unregulated market where financial instruments in various currencies are actively traded outside the country of origin. See also MONEY MARKET INSTRUMENTS.

money market certificate (MMC) nonnegotiable certificate of deposit with a minimum denomination of $2,500 and an original maturity of at least seven days. Prior to January 1983, when the MMC was deregulated, the account was a six-month CD requiring an initial deposit of $10,000 to open an account, and paying a rate tied to the yield on six-month U.S. Treasury bills. With deregulation, maturities and rates paid depositors are set by management policy in individual financial institutions, not by government regulation. See also MONEY MARKET DEPOSIT ACCOUNT; NINETY-DAY SAVINGS ACCOUNT; PASSBOOK; STATEMENT SAVINGS ACCOUNT.

money market deposit account (MMDA) high-yield savings account authorized by the GARN-ST GERMAIN DEPOSITORY INSTITUTIONS ACT OF 1982 to allow depository financial institutions to be fully competitive with money market mutual funds in attracting consumer deposits. The MMDA pays a market rate of interest with no regulatory limit so long as the account balance stays above $1,000. (When the balance drops below $1,000, the MMDA pays the same rate of interest as a NEGOTIABLE ORDER OF WITHDRAWAL (NOW) account.)

Bank customers can make an unlimited number of deposits into an MMDA, transfer balances in person or at an automated teller machine as often as they want, but write only three checks a month, limited by regulation. Federal regulations permit three additional preauthorized transfers a month, such as telephone bill payments to merchants.

Banks and savings institutions also have the right to require a seven-day NOTICE OF WITHDRAWAL before approving withdrawals or transfers, but most have waived this requirement. Consequently, MMDA accounts are considered liquid assets, paying rates competitive with money market mutual funds, even though individual bank rates will vary, depending on active financial institutions competing in a given market. See also

MONEY MARKET CERTIFICATE; MONEY MARKET FUND; SUPER NOW ACCOUNT.

money market fund (MMF) mutual fund that invests in short-term debt instruments, such as acceptances, Treasury bills, commercial paper, and negotiable certificates of deposit. Most funds invest in high-quality paper, although some funds have purchased noninvestment grade securities to offer a better yield. Money market funds, managed by investment companies registered with the Securities and Exchange Commission, typically buy paper with maturities of 60 days or less. A fund sells shares to investors, who receive regular interest payments. The amount of interest earned by an investor depends on several factors, including the general level of interest rates, the management fee or commissions charged by the fund's manager, and whether there are redemption fees present. The fee structure in a money market mutual fund and investment characteristics of the portfolio are spelled out in the fund PROSPECTUS. See also DONOGHUE'S MONEY FUND AVERAGE; MONEY MARKET DEPOSIT ACCOUNT.

money market instruments debt instruments issued by private organizations, governments, and government agencies, generally with maturities of one year or less. Such instruments are highly liquid investments, and include Treasury bills, bankers' acceptances, commercial paper and short-term tax-exempt municipal securities, and negotiable bank CDs. Money market instruments are actively traded in the money center financial markets in New York, London and Tokyo. Futures contracts on U.S. Treasury bills and certain other money market instruments are traded in the financial futures markets.

money market preferred stock class of PREFERRED STOCK with a floating dividend rate. The dividend is reset every 49 days—the minimum time interval that holders own the stock, while claiming the 70% dividend tax exclusion—by investors who tender bids for the stock at a specific dividend rate. Money market preferred issues are meant to insure that preferred stock issues trade at, or close to par value, but have been known to fail if an offering fails to attract enough bids at the dividend rate desired by the issuer. Under the financial regulators' risk-based capital rules, Money market preferred stock does not count toward a bank's primary capital or Tier 1 capital. See also ADJUSTABLE RATE PREFERRED STOCK.

money market rates interest paid depositors who invest in money market instruments or federally insured deposits paying market rates of return. Money rates are reported in daily newspapers, and include such key rates as broker call loans, the federal funds rate, rates on bankers' acceptances, Eurodollar time deposits, the 3-month and 6-month Treasury bill rate, and the London Interbank Offered Rate (LIBOR).

money multiplier relationship between the MONETARY BASE and the MONEY SUPPLY. The multiplier explains the money supply has expanded through the banking system by distribution of excess reserves. When a bank makes a loan, it creates money, because part of the loan becomes a new deposit.

The relationship between the monetary base and the money supply is determined by the reserve ratio of required reserves, and by the leakage of deposits from the checking account portion of the money supply into currency, government deposits, foreign deposits, and other forms of deposits that might not be counted in the official money supply aggregate in question. For example, time deposits are spilled over from M1 as savers move excess funds from liquid assets into higher-yielding investment accounts.

In practical terms, banks create money through the multiplier effect. For example, a 12% reserve requirement multiplies a $100,000 deposit several times if the money is left in a bank, because the bank can relend the money to customers seeking loans. However, because banks tend to keep excess reserves on hand, the multiplier effect is never fully achieved. See also FRACTIONAL RESERVES.

money order instrument of exchange issued for a fee, often used by persons who do not have checking accounts to pay bills or send money to someone in a distant city. Money orders are issued by post offices and financial institutions, usually in amounts under $500, and carry both the payee's name and the payer. Those issued by a bank are drawn on the issuing bank or a correspondent.

money supply total amount of money available for transac
tions and investment in the economy. Also known as the *money
stock*. The Federal Reserve Board uses various statistical measures to measure the various forms of money that make up the
money supply. The monetary aggregates in the money supply are
updated weekly by the Federal Reserve Board.

In the early 1980s, the nationwide introduction of interest-
bearing checking accounts, permitted by the Depository Institutions Deregulation and Monetary Control Act of 1980, caused
the Federal Reserve Board considerable problems in estimating
the actual rate of growth in the money supply. Negotiable Order
of Withdrawal (NOW) accounts, approved for all depository financial institutions as of January 1981, and Super NOW accounts, allowed in January 1983, combine the transaction account features of a checking account, and the interest earning
benefits of a savings account.

When the Fed is pursuing an expansive MONETARY POLICY,
banks are able to make more loans, which stimulates growth in
the money supply, because business borrowers keep part of their
loans in the form of bank deposits.

Since 1983, when the monetary aggregates were last revised, the components of the money supply have been the following:

M1: currency held by the public, plus travelers' checks,
demand deposits, Negotiable Order of Withdrawal (NOW) accounts, Super NOW accounts, Automatic Transfer Service
(ATS) accounts, and credit union share drafts.

M2: M1 plus savings and small denomination time deposits,
Money Market Deposit Accounts, money market mutual fund
shares owned by individual investors, overnight repurchase
agreements, and certain overnight Eurodollar deposits.

M3: M2 plus large time deposits, large denomination term
repurchase agreements, shares in money market mutual funds
owned by institutional investors, and certain Eurodollar deposits.

L: long-term liquid assets, including M3, plus nonbank investments in U.S. savings bonds, short-term Treasury securities,
commercial paper, and bankers' acceptances.

money transfer see WIRE TRANSFER.

monthly compounding of interest see COMPOUND INTEREST.

monthly statement ACCOUNT STATEMENT mailed to a customer that lists debits, credits, service charges, and account adjustments during the prior month. A checking account statement includes a list of checks written, deposits, and electronic debits and credits at an ATM, along with cancelled checks. A credit card statement is a descriptive billing statement listing account charges and finance charges that apply to revolving balances if there is an outstanding balance. A consolidated statement summarizes end of month balances in several accounts as of the date the statement was prepared.

Moody's Investors Service investment advisory service, a subsidiary of Dun & Bradstreet Inc., that publishes financial manuals analyzing corporate securities that are sold to the public. Moody's also rates the investment quality of commercial paper, and bonds and short-term tax-exempt notes issued by states and municipalities.

Moody's Investment Grade ratings assigned to municipal notes range from MIG1 (best quality) to MIG4 (adequate quality); all four are considered investment quality securities for banks. Moody's ratings on corporate bonds and preferred stocks, plus certain common stocks, are graded from Aaa (highest quality) to Caa (lowest quality). Securities rated Baa or better are considered investment quality.

moral obligation bond tax-exempt bond issued by a municipality or state financing authority, secured by revenues from the project financed, plus a nonbinding pledge by the state legislature. In the event that project revenues are insufficient to meet debt service payments, the legislature is authorized to step in and appropriate funds in the future to cover principal and interest payments to bondholders. The state's commitment to service the bonds is moral, rather than contractual, as legislatures have no legal obligation to do so if the original OBLIGOR defaults.

moral suasion persuasion by oral or informal pressure, carried out by central bankers and heads of government agencies to convince bankers to do something, or refrain from doing something. Moral suasion is a selective credit control used from time to time by the Federal Reserve Board, for example, when the Fed wants commercial banks to continue making loans to securities broker-dealers to shore up public confidence in the soundness of the financial markets, as happened after the October 1987 stock market crash. Moral suasion, which stops short of legal remedies and formal rule making, can at times be highly effective because of the ANNOUNCEMENT EFFECT Federal Reserve policy has on the markets.

moratorium
1. condition when a borrower declares his inability to repay some or all of an outstanding debt, or when the borrower ceases paying the debt service—interest—on a loan. If a moratorium is declared by a sovereign borrower, it generally leads to rescheduling of the loan with a longer term. See also SOVEREIGN RISK.
2. legal moratorium on a proposed activity, for example the one-year moratorium in the Competitive Equality Banking Act of 1987 on securities underwriting by bank holding company affiliates.

Morris Plan bank see INDUSTRIAL BANK.

mortgage debt instrument giving conditional ownership of an asset, secured by the asset being financed. The borrower gives the lender a mortgage in exchange for the right to use the property while the mortgage is in effect, and agrees to make regular payments of principal and interest. The mortgage lien is the lender's security interest, and is recorded in title documents in public land records. The lien is removed when the debt is paid in full. A mortgage normally involves real estate and is a long-term debt, normally 25 to 30 years, but can be written for much shorter periods.

Originally written exclusively as fixed-rate fully amortizing loans, mortgages have evolved into more flexible contracts. Since the mid 1970s, the financial industry's funding sources have become more volatile and market sensitive, and legislation and regulation have relaxed the prohibitions on alternative types of mortgage financing, such as variable rate and adjustable rate mortgages. Recent innovations in packaging of mortgage loans for resale in the SECONDARY MORTGAGE MARKET to investors have helped to create a national market for mortgage lending and

a wide variety of synthetic financial instruments, such as the
COLLATERALIZED MORTGAGE OBLIGATION, a multiclass security
consisting of several different mortgage backed bonds that have
payment characteristics quite different from the mortgages securing the bonds.

See also ADJUSTABLE RATE MORTGAGE; ALTERNATIVE MORT-
GAGE INSTRUMENT; BALLOON MORTGAGE; BIWEEKLY MORTGAGE;
CHATTEL MORTGAGE; CONVENTIONAL MORTGAGE; DERIVATIVE
MORTGAGE-BACKED SECURITIES; GRADUATED PAYMENT MORT-
GAGE; GROWING EQUITY MORTGAGE; INTEREST-ONLY (IO) SECURI-
TIES; INVERSE FLOATER; MORTGAGE-BACKED BOND; MORTGAGE-
BACKED CERTIFICATE; MORTGAGE-BACKED SECURITIES; NEGATIVE
AMORTIZATION; PORTABLE MORTGAGE; PRICE LEVEL ADJUSTED
MORTGAGE; PRINCIPAL-ONLY (PO) STRIP; REVERSE MORTGAGE;
ROLLOVER MORTGAGE; SHARED APPRECIATION MORTGAGE; ZERO-
COUPON MORTGAGE.

mortgagee lender who arranges mortgage financing, collects
the loan payments, and takes a SECURITY INTEREST in the property financed.

mortgagor borrower in a mortgage contract who mortgages
the property in exchange for a loan and gives the title to the
property to the MORTGAGEE.

mortgage-backed bond bond collateralized by a pledge
of mortgages and payable from the issuer's general funds. Because the market value of the collateral must exceed the outstanding bond principal, additional collateral may be required if
the market value of the underlying mortgages declines. Unlike
mortgage pass-through securities, which convey an ownership
interest in a pool of mortgages, ownership of a mortgage-backed
bond, and usually servicing rights, are retained by the issuer,
although mortgage servicing can be sold, at a price, to a third
party. Also, for tax purposes, mortgage- backed bonds are
treated as issuer debt rather than as a sale of assets. Mortgage-
backed bonds also have a more predictable maturity than pass-
through securities, thus giving the bondholder a kind of call protection against early redemption. See also PAY-THROUGH
SECURITY.

mortgage-backed certificate certificate backed by a MORTGAGE POOL, collateralized by mortgage loans, and guaranteed as to payment of principal and interest. A mortgage certificate, also known as a *pass-through certificate*, conveys a proportional interest in a pool of mortgage loans. Certificates are issued by the Government National Mortgage Association, (Ginnie Mae), the Federal National Mortgage Association (Fannie Mae), the Federal Home Loan Mortgage Corporation (Freddie Mac), and also by financial institutions or private mortgage conduits issuing mortgage certificates in their own name. Mortgage certificates are often pledged as security for COLLATERALIZED MORTGAGE OBLIGATION (CMO) bonds. See also PARTICIPATION CERTIFICATE.

mortgage-backed securities investment grade securities backed by a pool of mortgages or trust deeds. Principal and interest payments on the underlying mortgages are used to pay semiannual interest and principal on the securities. Income from the principal and interest payments on the underlying mortgages are used to pay off the bonds.

Most mortgage-backed securities, such as COLLATERALIZED MORTGAGE OBLIGATIONS and REAL ESTATE MORTGAGE INCOME CONDUITS, consist of multiclass obligations that are divided into different classes of bonds to appeal to different investor needs. Because some mortgage pools will pay off faster than others, mortgaged-backed securities are typically issued as a series of several different bonds, each having a different maturity date. See also ACCRUAL BOND; CONTROLLED AMORTIZATION BOND.

mortgage banker Banker who originates mortgages for resale to investors. Mortgage bankers derive their income much like merchant bankers, from the origination fees and servicing income. Loans are sold in one of two ways: by private placement of whole loans or pools of loans with a single investor, typically an institutional investor, such as an insurance company; or by issuing securities that are backed by mortgage loans. Mortgage bonds are traded in the public markets, and are rated by the debt rating agencies. Also called mortgage company.

Mortgage Bankers Association of America see TRADE ASSOCIATION.

mortgage broker person who brings borrower and lender together, earning a commission. A mortgage broker may also place loans with investors, but he does not collect the mortgage payments.

mortgage cash flow obligation multiclass pay-through bond, similar to a COLLATERALIZED MORTGAGE OBLIGA-TION (CM), and is an unsecured general obligation of the issuer. Payments received on a mortgage pool are applied to paying principal and interest on the obligation. Mortgage cash flow obligations, through, differ from CMOs; in contrast to a CMO, a mortgage cash flow obligation is not secured by a lien on the mortgages in the pool. Investors rely on the issuer's contractual obligation to use the cash flow from the mortgage principal and reinvestment income to meet debt service payments on the bonds.

mortgage conduit see CONDUIT.

mortgage discount amount paid in advance by a mortgagor, computed as a percentage of the loan principal. Also called DISCOUNT POINT , points, or new loan fee. Points, usually paid at the mortgage closing, increase the lender's yield from the mortgage loan.

mortgage insurance
1. federal or private insurance program that protects mortgage lenders against default risk. The mortgage insurance premium is paid by the borrower. Federal insurance coverage is administered by the Federal Housing Administration, and private mortgage insurance programs are administered by private insurance companies. Private mortgage insurance is provided by specialized insurance companies. The largest private insurer is the mortgage Guaranty Insurance Corp. (MGIC) of Milwaukee, Wisconsin, better known as *Magic* in the mortgage industry.
2. declining premium term life insurance, paid by the mortgagor, that pays off the loan in the event the mortgagor dies before the loan is fully repaid. Mortgage insurance is sold through financial institutions as an additional service to their mortgage customers.

mortgage interest deduction see TAX DEDUCTIBLE INTEREST.

mortgage note written promise to repay a mortgage loan plus interest. The MORTGAGE gives the lender a security interest in the mortgaged property. The mortgage note is the PROMISSORY NOTE stating the principal amount due, the rate of interest, and the terms for repayment of the funds advanced. The borrower signing the note, and any cosigners, are personally liable for repayment of the debt.

mortgage pool group of residential mortgage loans classi-fied by original maturity date and type of mortgage (i.e., fixed rate conventional, adjustable rate) for sale to investors in the secondary mortgage market.

mortgage REIT REAL ESTATE INVESTMENT TRUST that sup-plies funds to the residential housing market by lending capital to real estate developers. Mortgage REITS borrow from banks and institutional investors and relend to developers at a higher inter-est rate, and frequently take equity participations in the cash flow income from the projects they finance.

mortgage revenue bond tax-exempt bonds issued by state and local governments and by state housing finance agen-cies to finance the sale or repair of single family homes. Also called mortgage subsidy bonds. These bonds are payable from revenues derived from repayments of interest on mortgage loans financed from the proceeds of the bonds. Since 1980 the issu-ance and structure of these bonds has been controlled by federal law. These offer below market financing to income-qualified borrowers.

mortgage servicing performing the required duties of a mortgage seller, such as collecting payments, curing delinquen-cies, releasing the lien on full payment, foreclosing in event of default, and confirming that taxes are paid and insurance is in force. Servicing may be done by the lender or by a company acting for the lender. The mortgage servicer acts as escrow agent for the holders of mortgage pass-through securities and mort-gage backed securities.

mortgage swap exchange of mortgage loans for participation certificates or pass-through securities backed by the same mortgages. Mortgage lenders, mostly thrift institutions, swap mortgages with the Federal National Mortgage Association (Fannie Mae) or the Federal Home Loan Mortgage Corporation (Freddie Mac), acquiring securities guaranteed by Fannie Mae or Freddie Mac, to improve ASSET QUALITY, obtain acceptable collateral for REPURCHASE AGREEMENTS and REVERSE REPURCHASE AGREEMENTS, get low-rate assets off the balance sheet, or for other reasons.

Mother Hubbard clause see CROSS-COLLATERAL.

multibank holding company bank holding company that owns, or has a controlling interest in, several banks. The Bank Holding Company Act of 1956 brought multibank holding companies under the supervision of the Federal Reserve Board. With few exceptions, multibank holding companies were restricted by branching laws to owning banks in a single state. The arrival of SUPER REGIONAL BANKS in the 1980s changed that restriction, opening the door to eventual unrestricted interstate banking. See also BANK HOLDING COMPANY; McFADDEN ACT; REGIONAL INTERSTATE BANKING.

multicurrency note facility short-term or medium-term Euronote financing denominated in several currencies. The facility allows the borrower to choose the currencies to draw in successive rollover periods, when the loan is refinanced. It is the riskiest credit facility for the borrower, because the lender has the right to set the currency in which the loan will be paid off. The loan will reprice periodically, say every six months, in different currencies, depending on the lender's perception of currency risk in the transaction

multilateral development bank international financial institution organized to provide financial and technical assistance to foster economic development in less developed countries. These institutions are financed by member contributions and borrowings in the world financial markets. In terms of scope they may be global (the World Bank Group), regional (the

Latin American Development Bank or Asian Development
Bank), or specialized institutions (the Caribbean Development
Bank or the East African Development Bank).

multilateral netting

1. international money management technique whereby a company with subsidiaries in several countries is able to net out
   credits and debits between the subsidiaries in various countries, leaving only the balance to be settled. This makes it
   easier to meet a payroll and make intercompany transfers,
   and reduces the need to acquire foreign currency.
2. method of reconciling trading or clearing activity in which
   parties holding mutual obligations settle their obligations to
   each other on a net funds basis, typically at the end of a day.
   For example, a stock exchange or a bank clearing house.

multinational corporation
corporation owning sub-
sidiary companies operating in several countries. A generally
accepted definition is a corporation or enterprise that derives at
least 25% of its annual sales from facilities outside its country of
origin. Developing countries, including the NEWLY INDUSTRIAL-
IZED COUNTRIES, have also encouraged formation of multinational corporations on their soil. Many multinationals are chartered in tax haven countries for trading and investing on a global
basis.

multiple options funding facility (MOFF)
me-
dium-term Euronote financing allowing the borrower to choose
from several funding options, i.e., a medium-term project financing allowing the option of using different guidelines for
pricing, such as prime rate, banker's acceptance rate, and Eurodollar rate. Such options, however, must be listed clearly in the
original loan agreement.

municipal bond
debt instrument that is an obligation of a
state or municipality, and also political subdivisions and agencies
fo these governments. There are several classifications of municipal bonds, including a GENERAL OBLIGATION BOND and a REV-
ENUE BOND. Special assessment bonds are bonds payable from
assessments from benefitted property owners, covering such
things as streets and sidewalks. A special tax bond is a bond
issued for a special purpose, for which proceeds of a special tax

are pledged, but not the taxing authority of the issuer. Water and other utility bonds are payable primarily from utility revenues, but are also supported by taxing authority—so-called double barreled obligations.

Certain classes of municipal bonds issued after August 1986, called PRIVATE PURPOSE BONDS, are fully taxable bonds if, for example, more than 10% of the proceeds from the bond issue are used for private development (as opposed to public improvements, such as highway development), and the debt service is paid by private business organizations. See also INDUSTRIAL DEVELOPMENT BOND; PRIVATE PURPOSE BOND; PUBLIC PURPOSE BOND.

municipal bond insurance financial guarantee protecting a municipal bond issue against default risk. Coverage is purchased from a number of private insurance companies, such as AMBAC Indemnity Corporation, and the Municipal Bond Insurance Association. Bonds insured by these firms, which offer to purchase the bonds at par in event default occurs, enjoy an AAA rating, enabling government agencies to issue bonds at a lower cost. Insured bonds ordinarily have a lower yield than uninsured bonds as the cost of insurance typically is passed on to the holder. When a bond defaults, it is paid off immediately so that even if principal is recovered, interest from the date of default to maturity is not earned. See also FINANCIAL GUARANTEE.

municipal note short-term debt instrument, generally with a maturity of less than one year, issued by state or local government, and repayable from the general fund of the issuer or a defined revenue source. Notes are issued for a variety of purposes: revenue anticipation notes and tax anticipation notes help the issuer overcome a cash flow shortage. See also BOND ANTICIPATION NOTE; TAX ANTICIPATION NOTE.

municipal revenue bond see REVENUE BOND.

Municipal Securities Rulemaking Board (MSRB) self-regulatory organization established by the 1975 amendments to the SECURITIES ACT OF 1934. The board sets rules for trading of municipal bond by broker-dealers and bank dealers, and provides an arbitration service. Its rules are approved by the Securities and Exchange Commission and enforced by the

National Association of Securities Dealers and bank regulatory agencies. Its 15-member board is comprised of securities firms, bank dealers, and the public, each having equal representation.

mutual association nonstock financial institutions, such as a SAVINGS AND LOAN ASSOCIATION, that is owned by savers holding claim to funds on deposit, who are known as *members*. Members have no claim to the earnings of the association, but elect directors to its board of trustees. Other forms of mutual associations are credit unions, mutual savings banks, and cooperative banks.

mutual company nonstock savings bank, insurance company, or savings and loan. The term also has been used in reference to open-end investment companies, which are also known as mutual funds. In a mutual company, profits, after deduction of business expenses, are set aside for the benefit of the depositors of a financial institution, and the policyholders of a mutual insurance company, or are held as surplus reserves to maintain liquidity.

mutual fund investment company that pools money from its shareholders in stocks, bonds, government securities, and short-term money market instruments. Mutual funds can also invest in other marketable assets, such as futures, options, and collectibles. A mutual fund is also known as an open-end investment company, meaning that there is a continuous offering of new shares and redemption of outstanding shares.

When shares are sold, the fund's capitalization increases; it decreases when shares are redeemed by investors. (Unlike a CLOSED-END FUND, shares are not traded on organized exchanges.) The owners of a mutual fund own proportional shares in the entire pool of securities in which the fund invests, and pay taxes on distributions from the fund. Most mutual fund shares are redeemable at current NET ASSET VALUE, although some have a BACK END LOAD or redemption charge when shares are liquidated. In any mutual fund, the value of shares owned depends on current market value of the portfolio, which is generally repriced daily. See also MONEY MARKET FUND.

mutual mortgage insurance fund government sponsored mortgage insurance administered by the FEDERAL

HOUSING ADMINISTRATION, which insures mortgage loans on one- to four-family residential housing. The plan is designed to be self-funding; the FHA collects premiums from mortgagors and pays lender claims on losses from mortgage defaults. See also PRIVATE MORTGAGE INSURANCE.

mutual savings bank (MSB) state chartered nonstock savings institution organized primarily to accept deposits from individuals and make residential mortgage loans. In 1989 mutual savings banks were operating in 16 states. Management is by a board of trustees. These savings institutions offer checking and other transaction account services, and also make consumer loans, commercial loans, and commercial mortgages, and invest in limited amounts of corporate bonds and corporate stock. State banking departments are the primary regulators of mutual savings institutions. See also FEDERAL SAVINGS BANK.

mutual wills separate wills by two people, with similar language, for example, by husband and wife, each naming the other as beneficiary of his or her estate, or naming a common beneficiary.

naked option option written by a buyer or seller who does not own the underlying asset; either a LONG POSITION by the writer of a call option or a SHORT POSITION by the writer of a put option. Naked options can be written for securities, currencies, commodities, and indexes, and have limited profit potential and unlimited risk, although the holder's risk is limited to the life of the option. Writers of naked options assume a higher level of risk, along with greater profit potential.

naked position market position of someone holding an un-hedged position. For example, someone holding an outright LONG POSITION or SHORT POSITION in financial futures that is not hedged by an offsetting position, SPREAD transaction, or part of an ARBITRAGE deal. Also the holder of a NAKED OPTION. The holder is at risk to changes in market prices.

naked reserve carrying no reserves against deposits. Federal Reserve Banks have been free of any reserve requirements against deposits or Federal Reserve Notes issued since 1968. Under prior regulation, Fed banks had to keep reserves in gold certificates equal to 25% of Federal Reserve notes issued.

national association when used in a bank's name, indicates a NATIONAL BANK chartered by the Office of the Comptroller of the Currency. Usually abbreviated N.A.

National Association of Federal Credit Unions (NAFCU) see TRADE ASSOCIATION.

National Association of Securities Dealers (NASD) nonstock membership organization formed under the Securities Act of 1934 to act as primary regulator of securities sold in the OVER-THE-COUNTER market. A self-regulatory organization, NASD issues the rules of fair practice governing practices by broker-dealer firms in the OTC market. Its members include securities broker-dealers and underwriters other than commercial banks. The NASD governs its members in trading policies and procedures, listing of new issues, and customer relations. It also licenses broker- dealers. Bankers who accept customer orders in discount brokerage operations must pass an NASD qualifying examination, and have a NASD Series 7 license.

National Automated Clearing House Association (NACHA) see TRADE ASSOCIATION.

national bank commercial bank chartered by the federal government, as opposed to a state banking department. A national is chartered and supervised by the COMPTROLLER OF THE CURRENCY, a member of the FEDERAL DEPOSIT INSURANCE CORPORATION, and is required by the Federal Reserve Act to purchase stock in its district Federal Reserve Bank as a MEMBER BANK in the Federal Reserve System.

National banks originally came into existence in the 1860s under the National Bank Acts of 1863 and 1864 when the federal government, lacking a uniform national currency, approved the chartering of banks that would issue their own notes (national bank notes) backed by U.S. government bonds, and imposed a 10% tax on bank notes of state chartered banks. (In response to the new federal tax, state chartered banks persuaded their depositors to begin writing checks instead of taking out their money in cash. Of course, this led eventually to paying bills by check, and the check payment system as we know it today.) National bank notes have been retired from circulation since 1935.

About 30% of U.S. commercial banks have national charters, but national banks have economic power beyond what the numbers indicate, holding more than two thirds of the total deposits in federally insured commercial banks. See also DUAL BANKING.

National Bank Surveillance System (NBSS)
computerized monitoring system used by the Office of the Comptroller of the Currency to monitor changes in condition as

reported in call reports of national banks. The NBSS also is useful for bank examiners as an advance warning device for any changes in financial performance by national banks.

National Council of Savings Institutions see
TRADE ASSOCIATION.

National Credit Union Administration (NCUA)
independent federal agency established by federal law in 1970 to charter and supervise federal credit unions. The NCUA is governed by a three-member board, appointed by the president for six-year terms. Its responsibilities include examinations of federal credit unions; management of the National Share Insurance Fund, which provides deposit insurance for federal credit unions and many state credit unions; and the CENTRAL LIQUIDITY FACILITY, a source of short-term funds for credit unions. The chairman of the NCUA is a member of the policy coordinating body of federal financial regulators, the FEDERAL FINANCIAL INSTITUTIONS EXAMINATION COUNCIL.

national currency any approved currency issued by a central bank or monetary authority as the official unit of account for valuation of foreign exchange and payment of debts. Also called monetary unit. In the United States, Federal Reserve Notes issued by the Federal Reserve Banks are the the official national currency. See also LEGAL TENDER.

National Housing Act federal act in 1934 creating the FEDERAL HOUSING ADMINISTRATION providing mortgage insurance and below-market financing for home buyers, and the FEDERAL SAVINGS AND LOAN INSURANCE CORPORATION. FHA mortgage insurance protects against default risk in mortgage loans with loan-to-value ratios up to 80%, and mortgages amortized by periodic payments over a 30-year term. FHA-insured mortgage loans are purchased in the secondary market by the GOVERNMENT NATIONAL MORTGAGE ASSOCIATION.

national trigger statutory date in state laws permitting regional interstate banking whereby bank holding companies will be allowed to acquire banks in other states on a nationwide basis, opening the door to nationwide INTERSTATE BANKING. The majority of states have approved interstate mergers only on a regional basis, but some have pending national trigger dates that are set to occur by the early 1990s.

natural guardian parent, either the father or mother, recognized by law as the lawful guardian, as opposed to an appointed guardian, who is named by a court or a will to care for a child under legal age.

nearest month nearest active trading month of a financial futures market, as opposed to FURTHEST MONTH. Also called nearby month.

near money liquid assets, such as time deposits, Treasury bills, and other short-term government securities, that are easily converted to cash on short notice. Near money is, however, excluded from the narrowest definition of the MONEY SUPPLY, because, unlike checking accounts and cash, it does not function as a medium of exchange in everyday purchases of goods and services.

negative amortization increase in the PRINCIPAL of a loan, when the loan payments are insufficient to pay the interest due. The unpaid interest is added to the outstanding loan balance, so the principal increases, rather than decreases, as payments are made. This situation typically occurs in an ADJUSTABLE RATE MORTGAGE with an ANNUAL CAP limiting any increases in the interest rate, and also in a GRADUATED PAYMENT MORTGAGE (GPM), which has low initial payments so moderate-income borrowers can afford to make the loan payments.

negative authorization approval of a bank card transaction in which the customer's account number is compared against a list of cancelled accounts numbers. This file is called a *negative file*. The opposite is POSITIVE AUTHORIZATION, in which each request for authorization is checked against the account holder's transaction file.

negative carry
1. funding gap that occurs when interest earned on a loan is less than lender's COST OF FUNDS. Also called negative cost of carry. Though rare today, such a situation occurred in the

early 1980s when mortgage lenders were financing fixed rate mortgages at rates below rates paid depositors on six-month certificates of deposit. In many states, lenders were restrained by usury ceilings from charging higher interest rates.

2. situation where the net yield on a dealer's inventory, or a mortgage banker's loan portfolio, is less than the interest rate paid to finance the assets owned. For example, a bond yielding 10% purchased with funds borrowed at 12%. The opposite is POSITIVE CARRY. Also called *negative cost of carry*. See also NEGATIVE AUTHORIZATION.

negative convexity see CONVEXITY.

negative gap repricing or duration mismatch in which interest sensitive liabilities exceed interest sensitive assets. A bank whose interest sensitive liabilities reprice more quickly than interest sensitive assets is said to be liability sensitive.

negative pledge clause in a bond INDENTURE whereby the issuing corporation or government agrees not to pledge assets, unless the holders of bonds or debentures are at least equally secured. Also called covenant of equal coverage.

negative value in credit analysis, any credit related factor that would cause a lender to turn down a credit application, such as adverse information in a credit bureau report, or a bankruptcy filing. The Equal Credit Opportunity Act prohibits credit discrimination on the basis of noncredit factors, such as marital status, race, national origin, or persons receiving public benefits. See also PROHIBITED BASIS.

negative verification auditing system whereby a letter regarding balances, loans, or other information is sent to a bank's customer. A reply is called for only if there is a difference between the information reported by the bank and the customer's own records. The information is assumed to be correct, unless the customer disagrees and responds in ten business days.

negative yield curve yield curve where short-term rates are higher than long-term rates. Also known as an INVERTED YIELD CURVE. A negative yield curve occurs in periods of high

interest rates brought on by high inflationary expectations. When anticipating a rapid rise in short-term rates, investors generally prefer to keep their funds invested for short periods to avoid capital losses and to maximize their current return on investment. See also POSITIVE YIELD CURVE.

negotiable certificate of deposit large-denomination CERTIFICATE OF DEPOSIT ($100,000 or more) issued by a commercial bank. Negotiable CDs are issued as interest-bearing time deposits, paying the holder a fixed amount of interest at maturity. These negotiable instruments are typically held by institutional investors, insurance companies, and financial institutions. There is an active secondary market for negotiable CDs of the 25 largest U.S. banks. Maturities vary from 14 days to 12 months, with the average maturity being about 3 months. CDs sold in the secondary market generally trade in round lots of $1 million or more, and frequently $5 million. Negotiable CDs also have been issued in DISCOUNT form, paying the holder the face value at maturity. See also EURODOLLAR CERTIFICATE OF DEPOSIT.

negotiable instrument written order to pay, such as an acceptance, check, bill of exchange, or promissory note, transferable from one person to another, provided certain conditions are met. When a person cashes a check, he negotiates the check by signing his name on the back and presenting it to a bank, thereby becoming the legal owner of funds represented by the writing on the face of the check. He may take the funds as cash or deposit the money into an account. Checks are negotiable by ENDORSEMENT and delivery (also called PRESENTMENT) to the paying bank, which is then obligated to pay the check. If an instrument is payable to the bearer, for example, a bearer stock or bearer bond, negotiation is done by simply presenting the instrument.

Under Article 3 of the UNIFORM COMMERCIAL CODE, an instrument is negotiable if it is: (1) a written instrument signed by the endorser or maker; (2) an unconditional promise to pay a certain amount of money, either on demand or at a future date; and (3) payable to the holder or bearer. A person who becomes a HOLDER IN DUE COURSE of a negotiable instrument by delivery, or by delivery and endorsement, has an unrestricted claim to the instrument, and can sue other people in his or her own name.

See also CHECK; DEMAND DEPOSIT; DISHONOR; DRAFT; NOTICE OF WITHDRAWAL; PROTEST; THIRD PARTY CHECK; WRONGFUL DISHONOR.

negotiable order of withdrawal (NOW) account
interest-bearing transaction account that combines the payable on demand feature of checks and investment feature of savings accounts. A NOW account is functionally an interest paying checking account. The NOW account began in Massachusetts in 1974 when mutual savings banks offered interest bearing transaction accounts (NOW accounts) to compete with commercial banks. These accounts, which paid a rate of interest equivalent to that of passbook accounts (5$\frac{1}{2}$%), were authorized nationwide for all depository institutions by the 1980 Monetary Control Act. A noninterest bearing NOW account is a NINOW account. See also SUPER NOW ACCOUNT.

negotiated underwriting
sale of securities through exclusive bid by an underwriter, as opposed to COMPETITIVE BID underwriting by several underwriting groups. In negotiated underwriting, the MANAGING UNDERWRITER and the securities issuer agree on the spread, or the difference between the purchase price and the initial public offering price. This form of underwriting is most common in municipal revenue bonds, corporate bonds, and common stock offerings, whereas the alternative, competitive bid underwriting, is preferred—and sometimes required by statute or regulation— in municipal general obligation bonds.

nest egg
savings account holding funds that are not needed for immediate spending, also known as rainy day money. Ordinarily put in time savings account earning a market rate of interest.

net asset value (NAV)
1. in MUTUAL FUNDs, the per share value of assets in a fund, computed by subtracting liabilities from the portfolio value of securities held, plus cash and accrued earnings, and dividing the total by the number of outstanding shares. This is the value all shareholders would receive if all issued shares were redeemed. In a no-load fund, this value is the bid price quoted in the mutual fund listings in daily newspapers. In a load fund, the bid price is figured by adding the sales com-

mission to the NAV. Mutual funds compute net asset value daily, based on closing prices on the previous business day. The asked or offered column in tables in a mutual fund prospectus shows the price after load is added.

2. tangible book net worth of a corporation's securities, usually stated as net value per share. For example, the book value of common stock is the difference between the accounting value of outstanding stock and all liabilities plus intangibles, such as goodwill and depreciation, divided by the number of shares issued. This value, also called tangible book value, also is computed for bonds, preferred stock, and so on, and is unrelated to market value.

net balance see PAYOFF STATEMENT.

net borrowed reserves statistical measure indicating a shortage of reserves in the banking system. A net borrowed reserves position always is expressed as a negative number, meaning there are more funds borrowed nationally at the Federal Reserve DISCOUNT WINDOW than EXCESS RESERVES available for bank lending. This is usually a sign that the Federal Reserve Board is tightening credit and that interest rates may be rising, although interest rate trends also depend on the demand for credit.

net charge-off gross amount of loans charged off as bad debt, less recoveries collected from earlier charge-offs. Net charge-offs are computed as a percentage of gross loans outstanding recorded, less unearned income and LOAN LOSS RESERVES for charged-off loans. Poor credit quality loans that are not worth keeping on the books are purged from the loan portfolio, usually monthly or quarterly. A minus sign before the net charge off amount means recoveries have exceeded charge-offs for an accounting period.

net demand deposits total of demand deposit (checking) accounts in a bank, less checks in the process of collection, legal reserves, and demand deposits due from other banks.

net free reserves statistical measure indicating a surplus of reserves in the banking system, indicating that the Federal Reserve Board is pursuing an easy money policy and that interest rates may ease a bit, or stay about the same. Contrast with NET BORROWED RESERVES.

net interest cost (NIC) total interest cost of an offering to a bond issuer, including both coupon interest and premium or discount, and usually expressed as the total interest to maturity, using a straight line arithmetic computation that does not factor in the time value of money. The formula for calculating net interest cost is: Total Coupon Interest Payment + Discount (or − Premium)/ Bond Maturity in years.

net interest margin (NIM) difference between the average aggregate rate earned on a loan or investment portfolio, less the average rate of aggregate liabilities and capital. The margin between the interest rates earned in bank assets and notes paid on deposits and other liabilities is a key measure of overall bank profitability.

net interest yield see NET INTEREST MARGIN.

net operating income (NOI) earnings reported by a bank or bank holding company, after deducting normal operating expenses, but before taking gains or losses from sale of securities, other losses and charge-offs, and additions to the reserve account for possible loan losses. Normally, NOI refers to earnings before federal income taxes are paid. Also called *net earnings* or *net income*.

net payoff see PAYOFF STATEMENT.

net settlement in electronic payment systems, settlement of interbank transactions on a net, end-of-day, basis between reserve accounts of banks participating in a clearing house. Credit and debit transactions are recorded on the clearing house books throughout the business day; final settlement of the net transactions—credits, less debits—occurs when funds due a bank are credited to its reserve account by a Federal Reserve Bank. This is the common settlement procedure in Automated Clearing Houses and the Clearing House Interbank Payments System (CHIPS).

net settlement risk see RISK.

netting written bilateral contract between two parties or more under which any obligation to each other to deliver securities, currency, or other assets on a given date is automatically amalgamated with all other obligations for the same asset, as of the same value date, in effect legally substituting one single net amount for the previous gross obligations. Netting is usually carried out as netting by novation, in which existing obligations are rolled into a new master agreement for settlement of transactions. In financial swaps, for instance, banks and securities firms use a master swap agreement with each customer, so all outstanding swaps are covered by a single contract. See also NOVATION.

network terminals, computers, and processors connected together by telephone lines or cable for the purpose of approving financial transactions. Among the numerous bank-to-bank networks are, AUTOMATED TELLER MACHINE (ATM) networks, which are electronic banking systems comprising numerous bank-owned ATMs, each connected directly or indirectly to a central computer facility called a SWITCH that routes transactions to the appropriate bank for approval and posting to customer accounts. Other examples of banking networks are AUTOMATED CLEARING HOUSE networks, electronic POINT-OF-SALE systems, the Federal Reserve's FEDERAL WIRE (FED WIRE), and the CLEARING HOUSE INTERBANK PAYMENTS SYSTEM (CHIPS). See also FUNDS TRANSFER; INFORMATION TECHNOLOGY; STAND-IN PROCESSING.

net worth owner's equity in a business, computed as accounting assets, less liabilities. In a depository financial institution, it is generally identical to CAPITAL, and includes capital, surplus and undivided profits in a stockholder-owned institution, and general reserves in a mutual institution. Net worth in a stockholder-owned bank often includes common stock, preferred stock, and certain classes of MANDATORY CONVERTIBLE debentures that are convertible into common stock equity according to a fixed schedule.

net worth certificate capital assistance certificate authorized by the GARN-ST GERMAIN DEPOSITORY INSTITUTIONS ACT OF

1982 to assist savings institutions in meeting mandatory net worth requirements. The assistance takes the form of a paper for paper exchange in which an eligible institution issues capital instruments called Net Worth Certificates to the Federal Home Loan Bank Board or the Federal Deposit Insurance Corporation. These promissory notes would be counted as part of the issuer's net worth, and are backed by the resources of the federal insurance funds. They are payable in cash only if the issuer is liquidated. Otherwise, the notes are to be retired as the issuer's financial position improves. Authority to issue net worth certificates was extended until October 1991 by the Competitive Equality Banking Act of 1987.

net yield

1. profit (or loss) from an investment, after deducting out-of-pocket costs and reserves for losses.
   2. YIELD TO MATURITY of a security, taking into account the purchase price, the coupon rate, and number of years to maturity. Treasury bills and municipal bonds are quoted on a net yield basis.

new balance in credit cards, the balance owed after an unpaid balance is carried over from the previous month and new purchases plus finance charges are added.

new cedi national currency of Ghana.

new Israeli shekel national currency of Israel.

newly industrialized country (NIC) developing country whose economy is supported to a greater or lesser degree on exports from internally generated industrial production, rather than on agricultural products or commodities. For example, Argentina, Brazil, South Korea, Mexico, and Taiwan.

new money

1. deposit of funds into a new account, often representing money transferred from another bank.
   2. in a Treasury refunding, the amount by which the par value of securities offered exceeds that of maturing obligations.

new rupiah national currency of Indonesia.

New York Clearing House Association oldest and largest bank clearing house association in the United States, founded in 1853. The New York Clearing House, owned by 11 money center banks, is operator of the CLEARING HOUSE INTERBANK PAYMENTS SYSTEM (CHIPS), which handles about 90% of international payments involving U.S. financial institutions, and the New York Automated Clearing House, one of the few regional ACH facilities that does not use the data processing services of a Federal Reserve Bank.

New York dollars funds payable in New York from interest and other charges, from deposit accounts at a New York bank, as in a correspondent banking relationship. Any check payable at a bank in New York City.

New York Futures Exchange see FUTURES EXCHANGES.

New York interest interest computed by the exact number of days in a month, rather than a 30-day month or other combinations. Contrasting is Boston interest, which is ordinary interest computed on the basis of a 30-day month.

New York Mercantile Exchange see FUTURES EXCHANGES.

New York Stock Exchange (NYSE) largest and oldest stock exchange in the United States, located at 11 Wall Street in New York City. The New York Stock Exchange, also known as the Big Board, is the most influential stock exchange, listing securities of the largest U.S. corporations, including the 30 firms listed in the Dow Jones Industrial Average. The NYSE is a self-regulatory organization with a 20-member board of governors who regulate the trading activities of its 1300 members. See also AMERICAN STOCK EXCHANGE.

next day funds funds available for withdrawal or transfer the next business day, subject to the settlement rules of the payment system used. Also called CLEARING HOUSE FUNDS. This is the earliest date that checks cleared through a local clearing house association and most AUTOMATED CLEARING HOUSE payments are available for reinvestment. Contrast with SAME DAY FUNDS.

next of kin person in the nearest blood relationship to a decedent, who inherits the decedent's property, as provided by state law, if there is no will. Surviving spouses usually are not considered next of kin, unless state law says otherwise.

niche bank that services only a segment of the market in its geographic region, or that offers a limited number of services to its special advantage. Community banks are niche banks in the sense that they offer credit and deposit services to local customers, but they rely on correspondent banks for more sophisticated products, such as foreign exchange and letters of credit.

night cycle second operating shift used by regional automated clearing house in processing inter-regional ACH transmissions, ordinarily between 10 P.M. and 1:30 A.M. Night cycle processing, commonly used by corporations to move funds into bank CONCENTRATION ACCOUNTS, gives next day funds availability (same day if after midnight), and is subject to a Federal Reserve processing surcharge for items handled.

night depository bank vault accessible by key for merchant deposits after banking hours and on weekends. Many banks have night collection boxes for deposit of daily cash, checks, and credit card sales drafts. Some even have an AUTOMATED TELLER MACHINE next to the street level depository giving the merchant an on-the-spot transaction receipt. Deposits are later proved by bank employees and credited to the merchant's account.

ninety-day savings account passbook savings account with an original maturity of exactly 90 days. The rate paid depositors is sometimes linked to the 90-day Treasury bill. Deposits are subject to a 7-day withdrawal notification, and if left on deposit, are rolled over for another term

no account check returned by the paying bank to the originating bank (the drawee bank) because the check writer has no account to pay checks presented for collection. A no account memo is attached.

no-action letter administrative review letter by the Securities and Exchange Commission (SEC). In a no-action letter the agency declines to rule on the legality of a proposed activity, and will not undertake civil or criminal action if the activity takes place as proposed. SEC no-action letters generally are viewed favorably by those requesting comment because it means the agency will not oppose the activity unless the relevant facts change. These letter rulings are specific to each case, and are applicable only to the facts outlined.

no funds see NOT SUFFICIENT FUNDS.

no-load fund mutual fund that does not carry a sales commission charge or load. Such funds are typically sold directly by the fund's sponsor and distributor, rather than through broker-dealer networks. Some no-load funds, however, have an annual distribution fee covering selling costs, called a 12b-1 fee, that substitutes for a FRONT-END LOAD.

nominal interest rate

1. **Banking.** stated rate of interest earned or paid, ignoring compounding of interest or other factors. The nominal rate of a SAVINGS ACCOUNT or TIME DEPOSIT is less than the EFFECTIVE ANNUAL YIELD. A mortgage may have a contractual rate of 9%, but an ANNUAL PERCENTAGE RATE (APR) of 9.38% because loan application fees and prepaid DISCOUNT POINTS are included in the computation of the APR.

2. **Investments.** stated rate of interest on an investment or security, without adjusting for inflation or inflationary expectations, as opposed to real interest rates. The real rate of interest is equal to the nominal rate less inflation.

nominee registered owner of a stock or bond if different from the beneficial owner, who acts as holder of record for securities and other assets. Typically, this arrangement is done to facilitate the transfer of securities when it is inconvenient to obtain the signature of the real owner, or the actual owner may not wish to be identified. Nominee ownership simplifies the registration and transfer of securities held under a corporate name, and often is done by banks, trust companies, custodians, and fiduciaries for institutional or individual clients.

nonaccrual asset asset, usually a loan, that is not earning the contractual rate of interest in the loan agreement, due to financial difficulties of the borrower. Also called DOUBTFUL LOAN. Nonaccrual assets are loans in which interest accruals have been suspended because full collection of principal is in doubt, or interest payments have not been made for a sustained period of time. A reserve for possible loan losses is set aside for these loans, and any payments received from the borrower are applied first to principal, and then to loan interest due. According to the guidelines of banking regulators, a loan with principal and interest unpaid for at least 90 days is considered a nonaccrual loan, unless the lender has adequate collateral. Consumer loans and residential mortgage loans are generally exempted from these guidelines. For bank bookkeeping purposes, a nonaccrual loan is recorded as a CASH BASIS LOAN, that is, a loan in which interest is credited as earned income only when payments are collected from the borrower. See also NONPERFORMING LOAN; RENEGOTIATED LOAN; WORKOUT AGREEMENT.

nonamortizing loan see INTEREST-ONLY LOAN; NEGATIVE AMORTIZATION.

nonassumption clause clause in a mortgage contract prohibiting ASSUMPTION of the mortgage by a third party, at the same rate and payment terms, without the prior approval of the lender. Also known as a DUE ON SALE CLAUSE.

nonbank bank bank that accepts deposits or makes commercial loans, but does not engage in both activities at the same time. By limiting its operations to either deposit taking or lending, a nonbank bank slips through the legal definition of a bank as defined by the BANK HOLDING COMPANY ACT OF 1956, and thus is not subject to federal laws regulating ownership of banks. The Competitive Equality Banking Act of 1987 closed that loophole by banning new charters of nonbank banks after August 1987, imposed a 7% annual growth cap on existing banks, and amended the Bank Holding Company Act to include, in the legal definition of a bank, financial institutions with federally insured deposits. Existing nonbank banks were grandfathered, and their deposits are insured by the Federal Deposit Insurance Corporation, although they are limited to a 7% asset growth and certain other restrictions limiting cross-marketing of services by a parent company. Nonbank owners of a nonbank bank were exempted from compliance with the Bank Holding Company Act.

During the 1980s bank holding companies exploited the nonbank bank loophole to expand their services to states other than their home state, and nonfinancial companies used it to market consumer financial services such as credit cards and deposit accounts nationwide.

nonborrowed reserves measure of banking system reserves, consisting of TOTAL RESERVES (member bank deposits in Federal Reserve Banks, plus vault cash), less funds borrowed (BORROWED RESERVES) at the Federal Reserve Discount Window. Since October 1979, the Federal Reserve Board has focused its MONETARY POLICY on movement of nonborrowed reserves. The amount of nonborrowed reserves is computed weekly by the Federal Reserve. See also NET FREE RESERVES.

noncallable bond or preferred stock that cannot be redeemed by the issuer prior to maturity or before a date specified in the bond indenture. Most bonds are noncallable for the first five years, and U.S. Treasury bonds generally cannot be called until they are close to maturity. The bond indenture agreement in most corporate bonds protects holders from loss of income from early redemptions by requiring issuers to pay a premium above par value that is at a maximum at the FIRST CALL DATE and diminishes afterward. In fact, yields on most corporate bonds are quoted from the first date a bond becomes callable. Yield is quoted to the first call date when the trading price is above par and an early call involves loss of principal. See also YIELD TO CALL.

noncash item check or other negotiable instrument handled as a COLLECTION ITEM, and not credited to the customer's account until payment has been received from the paying bank. For example, checks with special instructions, maturing bankers' acceptances, and foreign checks (TRANSIT ITEMS).

noncompetitive bid bid in a U.S. Treasury securities auction that does not require the purchaser to compete with other bidders. Also called noncompetitive tender. Instead, noncompetitive bids are filled at the weighted average price of competitive bids. Noncompetitive bidding allows smaller investors to take part in Treasury auctions, without having to bid on the same terms as large government securities dealers who make markets in Treasury securities through competitive bids. In Treasury bill auctions, for instance, noncompetitive bids range from $10,000, the minimum bid, to as high as $1 million. This is intended to make it easier for smaller investors to buy Treasury securities, reducing the advantage of institutional buyers who employ large staffs to keep in touch with minute by minute market price changes in the money market.

nonconforming loan SECONDARY MORTGAGE MARKET term referring to residential mortgage loan exceeding the loan size specifications of the Federal National Mortgage Association and the Federal Home Loan Mortgage Corporation for purchasing loans in the secondary mortgage market. Because Fannie Mae and Freddy Mac are limited by federal law to purchasing loans not exceeding a certain dollar amount ($187,450 in 1990), private sector mortgage conduits have stepped in to purchase loans valued between $250,000 and $500,000.

noncredit services services performed for corporate customers, or for other banks via a correspondent banking relationship, that do not involve the extension of credit and payment of finance charges. Such services include check collection, cash management, trust services, and provision of account summary information by telephone or electronic terminal. Noncredit services are a major source of fee income, supplementing interest income earned on outstanding loans.

nonfeasance failure to carry out an obligation, such as timely repayment of a loan as called for in a loan agreement. Contrast with misfeasance, the improper performance of a lawful act, and malfeasance, the carrying out of an illegal or improper act.

noninterest expense salaries, rental of equipment, leases of buildings and equipment, and taxes and other related expenses, including the LOAN LOSS PROVISION for anticipated bad debt. Noninterest expenses are the fixed operating costs in a bank, which may be offset by fee income from loan originations, late charges on loans, annual fees, and credit facility fees, or through noncredit services.

noninterest income net income derived from fee-based banking services, such as corporate cash management, check collection, and consumer annual fees on credit cards, and also monthly service charges on deposit accounts. Also included are many new activities, such as fees from participations in mutual fund commissions, investment advisor fees in merger & acquisition activities, and securities underwriting fees.

nonlegal investments securities that do not conform to the statutory requirements—the legal list investments—for mutual savings banks and for trust companies. These are generally sub-investment quality securities.

nonmember bank state chartered bank that is not a MEMBER BANK in the Federal Reserve System. Nonmember banks have the option of becoming Federal Reserve member banks, but may not meet the Fed's strict requirements for membership. They may otherwise wish to take advantage of more lenient state regulations, including more liberal guidelines in some states for accounting of LEGAL RESERVES that banks keep as a portion of their deposit accounts. State banks can also charge an exchange fee for paying a check drawn on another bank, though most, in fact, do not. State nonmember banks at the same time have some of the benefits of member banks, including access to the Federal Reserve DISCOUNT WINDOW when they need to borrow to meet short-term demands for funds.

nonmonetary transaction any transaction that does not have a dollar value or result in a transfer of funds, such as a change of name or address, an automated clearing house (ACH) notification of change, or an ACH prenotification—the zero-dollar transaction as required before initiating automated clearing house credits such as direct deposit of payroll or benefits.

nonnotification loan loan by a bank or commercial finance that is securitized by accounts receivable, and where the original debtor is not notified that the account has been pledged. Such loans are on a recourse basis; that is, if the receivables are not paid, the borrower is still liable.

nonpar item check that a paying bank honors at a discount from its par value (face value) when presented by another bank for collection. Nonpar checks are cleared through correspondent banks. In modern banking, this rarely occurs, although nonpar banking, or the practice of discounting drafts and notes drawn on other banks, was commonplace until the Federal Reserve Check Collection System was created in 1916. Banks that are members of the FEDERAL RESERVE SYSTEM are required by regulation to accept checks cleared through the Fed at par value, as do nearly all state chartered banks. The relative handful of nonpar banks that remain mostly are small, independently owned banks in rural areas.

nonperforming loan loan that is not performing according to the original terms of the borrower's loan agreement. The nonperforming loan category includes all loans with a renegotiated interest rate, loans past due 90 days or more, nonaccrual loans, and real estate acquired through foreclosure. The total of nonperforming loans usually is expressed as a percentage of the lender's total loan portfolio.

There are various definitions of this term, depending on the loan involved, and the lender's policy. When the principal and interest payments on a loan are past due by 90 days or more, the loan is said to be nonperforming, and the borrower is in a state of DEFAULT. Before a loan gets to that stage, however, a lender usually takes action to protect his security interest, by asking for more collateral or even demanding payment in full. See also DELINQUENCY; NONACCRUAL ASSET; WORKOUT AGREEMENT.

nonpersonal time deposit time deposits, including money market deposit accounts, held by a depositor other than a natural person. Nonpersonal time deposits include term savings accounts owned by corporations, deposits representing the proceeds of a promissory note or banker's acceptance, deposits owned by Edge Act Corporations and Agreement Corporations, and deposits owned by foreign banks. They are subject to RE-SERVE REQUIREMENTS of Federal Reserve REGULATION D.

nonpossessory lien see LIEN.

nonpurpose loan bank loan, collateralized by pledge of securities, in which the proceeds of the note are to be used for purposes other than purchase of stocks or bonds. Banks are required by Regulation U to have a borrower execute a purpose statement regardless of the use of the loan, whenever a loan is secured directly or indirectly by securities in a margin account.

nonrecourse status of a HOLDER IN DUE COURSE who has no claim against a previous holder to compel payment if the instrument is dishonored, if the prior endorsement contains the words without recourse or if the person holding title to the note was not in fact a holder in due course.

nonrecourse loan

1. loan where the lender's source of repayment is the cash flow generated by a project financed by the loan or the collateral securing the loan. The nonrecourse form of financing commonly is used in FACTORING of accounts receivable. The lender fully assumes the credit risk, and frequently reserves the right to approve a loan before it is accepted for nonrecourse treatment. If the borrower defaults, the lender's only recourse is to foreclose on the collateral backing the loan; the borrower is not liable personally for repayment. In a nonrecourse mortgage loan, for example, the lender must look to the collateral, rather than the borrower, as the ultimate source of repayment.

2. dealer FLOOR PLANNING arrangement in which the liability of the dealer, for example, an auto dealer, is limited to warranties about the genuineness of the paper offered for sale, vehicle title, and so on. The dealer cannot be required to buy back defaulted installment contracts from the lender, as he or she would be required in RECOURSE financing.

3. agricultural loan in which the lender is legally barred from taking action against the borrower if the loan collateral (the farmer's crop), is insufficient to repay the loan. This type of

financing is done through the federal government's direct loan program for farmers.

nonrecurring gain (or loss) any profit or expense that is not likely to occur again, as when a bank is liquidating a business or divesting an investment portfolio and writes off a portion of the uncapitalized expenses, or sells its headquarters building and records the resulting capital gain in the quarter in which the transaction occurred. A nonrecurring gain is a one-time event in accounting terms. If an expense item, it is sometimes called an extraordinary charge.

nonrevolver

1. bank credit card customer who pays a credit card bill in full every month, within the allowed GRACE PERIOD, thereby avoiding finance charges. Also called a *convenience* cardholder, because the credit card is being used as a convenient substitute for cash or checks.
2. LINE OF CREDIT that can be drawn only once, unlike a revolving line of credit that can be drawn against, and repaid, any number of times while in effect.

no protest instructions by one bank to another collecting bank not to object to items in case of nonpayment. The sending bank stamps on the face of the item the letters NP. If it cannot be collected, the collecting bank returns the item without objection.

nostro account *our account* in Latin, meaning an account kept by a bank or company in the currency of the country where the money is held, with the equivalent dollar amount noted in another column. Contrast with VOSTRO ACCOUNT.

notary public public officer authorized to administer oaths and witness documents, such as affidavits, property conveyances, and protest notices as when a bank refuses to honor a negotiable instrument. A notary's seal authenticates a document.

note

1. legal evidence of a debt or obligation. A financial instrument consisting of a promise to pay (PROMISSORY NOTE), rather than an order to pay, a bill of exchange, or a certificate of indebtedness, a BOND.

2. dishonored bill of exchange presented by a notary, and if still not paid or accepted, it is NOTED.

note issuance facility (NIF) revolving credit arrangement in the Euromarket, whereby the borrower issues short-term promissory notes (Euronotes) in its own name, generally with maturities of three to six months. A group of underwriting banks guarantees the availability of funds by agreeing to purchase any unsold notes at each ROLLOVER date, or by writing a standby line of credit. NIFs offer companies the flexibility of short-term financing, and give lenders an opportunity to meet credit needs of borrowers without being required to purchase any unsold notes. The revolving line of credit is often negotiated through a single bank that in turn sells participations to other members of the underwriting syndicate. See also REVOLVING UNDERWRITING FACILITY; STANDBY NOTE ISSUANCE FACILITY; TENDER PANEL.

note notice notice of a maturing loan, stating the amount due, the maturity date, and collateral pledged, that a lender mails as a reminder to the borrower several days before the maturity date. Also called notice of maturity. For example, in a 30-day TIME LOAN, the borrower is notified 10 days before the loan is payable. The loan officer handling the account also is notified.

notice of dishonor declaration signed by a notary public that a check, draft, or bill of exchange has been presented for collection and the drawee bank declines to make payment. See also PROTEST.

notice of withdrawal written notice of a depositor's intention to withdraw funds from an interest bearing account. Banks may require customers to give notice seven days before withdrawals from time deposit accounts, and also Negotiable Order of Withdrawal (NOW) accounts. Most banks, however, waive the notice requirement in NOW accounts.

notice to creditors written notice posted in newspapers asking creditors of an estate, or a debtor, to present their claims in court. A notice to creditors is filed in bankruptcy proceedings and in adjudication of estates. In a bankruptcy case, notice to creditors precedes the first meeting of creditors, where creditors who are owed payment are invited to present their claims.

notional principal principal balance underlying a SWAP transaction, and the amount used to compute swap payments in an INTEREST RATE SWAP or CURRENCY SWAP. Once the obligation to pay interest is separated from the principal on the underlying security, it becomes a notional amount, and is the fictitious principal generating the cash flows in a swap agreement. The two parties to a swap agreement trade the cash flow yield, not the notional amount. For example, a 10% yield on $1 million in notional principal yields $100,000 in interest a year. Interest payments accrue as with any ordinary interest-bearing security, even though the investor in fact receives only interest payments.

not sufficient funds (NSF) check that may not be paid or honored because the balance in the payor's account is less than the written amount on the check. Synonymous with INSUFFI-CIENT FUNDS.

novation
1. substitution of a new contract or obligation for an existing one, and the discharge of the existing obligation. The exchange adjusting or altering existing mutual obligations is by mutual agreement, with either buyer or seller paying the difference in market value to equalize the exchange.
2. substitution of one of the principals to an agreement, either the creditor or debtor. Contrast with ASSIGNMENT.

NOW account see NEGOTIABLE ORDER OR WITHDRAWAL (NOW) ACCOUNT.

numerical transit system See ABA TRANSIT NUMBER.

O

obligation

1. legally enforceable duty to pay a sum of money, or agree to do something (or not do something), according to the terms stated in a CONTRACT. The duty of a borrower to repay a loan, and the legal right of a lender to enforce payment.
2. any form of indebtedness evidenced by a written promise to pay.

obligor party who has an obligation to pay a debt, including interest due, by a specified date, or when repayment is demanded. The obligor (also known as obligator) is the debtor or borrower; the party advancing the funds is the lender, creditor, or obligee. In corporate securities, the obligee is the bondholder and the issuing organization is the debtor.

odd date MATURITY DATE in a foreign exchange contract that is neither a spot nor a fixed date. For example, a normal two-month forward contract from April 15 matures on June 15. An odd date would be a June 10 maturity.

odd days interest interest earned in a mortgage or closed-end installment loan during a time interval that is either longer or shorter than other loan payment periods. This normally occurs when a bank funds a mortgage loan in the middle of a month, or when a dealer sells installment credit contracts to a bank, and the bank assumes responsibility for collecting the debt. For accounting purposes, the extra days' interest is added to the first loan payment. If the loan is a fixed payment, fully amortizing loan, all remaining loan installment are even amount payments.

off-balance sheet liabilities obligations that are contingent liabilities of a bank, and thus do not appear on its balance sheet. In general, off-balance sheet items include the following: direct credit substitutes in which a bank substitutes its own credit for a third party, including standby letters of credit; irrevocable letters of credit that guarantee repayment of commercial paper or tax-exempt securities; risk participations in bankers' accept-ances; sale and repurchase agreements; and asset sales with re-course against the seller; interest rate swaps; interest rate options and currency options, and so on.

Under the RISK-BASED CAPITAL guidelines approved by bank-ing regulators for bank holding companies and state member banks, to be fully phased in by 1992, banks are required to hold a portion of equity capital in reserve to meet contingent obliga-tions in off-balance sheet items. This is based on a risk-weighted scale that requires holding more capital in reserve for certain assets, up to 100% of the prevailing capital requirement for cer-tain assets, and as little as 0% for liquid, easily marketable as-sets. Risk weights are determined by multiplying each off-bal-ance sheet item by a conversion factor to yield a credit equivalent amount. Thus, if the required capital-to-asset ratio is 8%, off-balance sheet items given a 100% risk weight would require an 8% capital backing; a 50% risk weighting requires a 4% capital support. Anything qualifying for placement in more than one category is assigned the lowest applicable risk rating.

The risk weights for off-balance sheet items are as follows:

100% risk weight: standby letters of credit, risk participa-tions, asset sales with recourse, risk participations in bankers' acceptances.

50% risk weight: unused portions of loan or lease commit-ments with original maturities of more than one year; Revolving Underwriting Agreements, Note Issuance Facilities.

20% risk weight: short-term commercial letters of credit, and documentary letters of credit collateralized by the underly-ing shipments.

offer price at which the owner of a security, financial instru-ment, or other asset is willing to sell. Also called the asked price. This differs from the BID price, or the price a buyer is willing to pay. The BID AND ASKED quotes are the prices a dealer is willing to pay, and the price a dealer wants to charge, respec-tively. The bid price is always the lower of the two prices. Buy-ers, who can be individual investors or large institutions, pay the offered price, or the price asked by the seller, frequently after negotiating from the original bid-asked quote.

offering circular see PROSPECTUS.

offering price price per share at which a new distribution of securities is offered to the public, also known as the public offering price. In no-load mutual funds, the offering price is equal to the NET ASSET VALUE of the securities offered for sale.

off-host processing of financial transactions away from a bank's central computer in the back office, usually with a NEGATIVE FILE in another computer that functions as an INTERCEPT PROCESSOR, standing between the user and the host computer. Off-host processing facilitates handling of routine consumer transactions, such as credit card or debit card authorizations, where quick response time is considered essential.

Office of the Comptroller of the Currency (OCC) see COMPTROLLER OF THE CURRENCY.

Office of Thrift Supervision (OTS) federal agency established by the Financial Institutions Reform, Recovery and Enforcement Act of 1989 to examine and supervise savings and loan associations and federal savings banks. The Office of Thrift Supervision, replacing the FEDERAL HOME LOAN BANK BOARD as primary regulator of state chartered and federally chartered savings institutions, is a bureau within the U.S. Treasury Department. The Director of Thrift Supervision, the chief operating officer of the OTS, is appointed by the President with Senate confirmation, and is also one of the five directors of the FEDERAL DEPOSIT INSURANCE CORPORATION. The structure of the OTS within the Treasury Department parallels the Office of the Comptroller of the Currency, the federal agency supervising national banks.

officer senior administrative official of a bank, appointed by the BOARD OF DIRECTORS, to implement and carry out its operating rules, including the bank's loan policy. The chairman of the board is the highest ranking officer in a bank or bank holding company, reporting directly to the board of directors, whereas the chief executive officer (CEO) is ordinarily the executive with the most responsibility in day-to-day operations. In many smaller banks, it is not unusual for the CEO to also hold the title of president or even chairman. Under the bank president are other administrative officers: the chief operating officer (COO); the bank CASHIER, who is senior administrative officer (his or her name appears on all official, or cashier's, checks); executive vice presidents; and lesser officers, including senior vice presidents, vice presidents, assistant vice presidents, branch office managers, and calling officers (sometimes called account executives) who market banking services to corporate customers. In most banks the entry-level officer position is administrative officer, a banking officer who, if a lender, is authorized to approve bank loans, up to a certain amount, without prior approval from a loan committee.

official check see CASHIER'S CHECK.

official staff commentary commentary prepared by the Federal Reserve Board staff explaining in question and answer fashion the important sections of consumer protection regulation. The Fed has prepared staff commentaries to explain compliance requirements with Regulation E, covering electronic funds transfers, and Regulation Z, covering consumer credit. Staff commentaries have replaced letter interpretations, whereby the Fed staff attempted to respond to regulatory compliance questions individually.

off-line
1. situation where communication between a NETWORK and terminals connected to it is temporarily interrupted. The network is said to be *down* when this happens. Most ON-LINE electronic banking networks have backup procedures for handling transactions until normal service is restored.
2. PAYMENT SYSTEM in which there is a time delay between the date a transaction occurs and the date the transfer of funds actually takes place. An AUTOMATED CLEARING HOUSE is an off-line system. See also STAND-IN PROCESSING; STORE AND FORWARD.

off-premise banking retail banking services provided away from a bank's main offices or its branches, ordinarily through automated teller machines (ATMs) in convenience stores, shopping centers, corporate office parks, and hospitals. Off-premise banking, often delivered through self-service automated branches or shared ATM networks, is, for many banks, a service alternative to BRICK AND MORTAR banking in branch offices, though it is not necessarily less costly.

offset either of two accounting entries that cancel each other out.

Banking:
1. lender's right to take possession of any bank account balance that a guarantor or debtor may have, through GARNISHMENT. This is known as the right of offset.
2. number encoded on the MAGNETIC STRIPE of a bank card that, when matched with the cardholder's PERSONAL IDENTIFICATION NUMBER (PIN), verifies the remembered PIN as the correct access code. See also PRIMARY ACCOUNT NUMBER.

Futures and options: closing a position by purchase of an equal number of opposite contracts in the same delivery month, or covering a short sale of futures through the purchase of an equal number of contracts in the same delivery month. Either action cancels the obligation to make or take delivery of the underlying commodity or financial instrument.

offshore banking unit (OBU) shell branch owned by a nonresident bank in an international financial center that, by accepting deposits from foreign banks and other OBUs, makes loans in the Eurocurrency market, unrestricted by local monetary authorities or governments. An offshore banking unit cannot, however, take domestic deposits. Since the 1970s these financial units have sprung up in major European cities, the Mideast, Asia, and the Caribbean. The major offshore banking centers for U.S. banks are the Bahamas, the Cayman Islands, Hong Kong, Panama, and Singapore, which offer favorable political, regulatory, and tax treatment. Since 1981, U.S. banks have been permitted many of these same advantages through International Banking Facilities, located in major U.S. financial centers. See also INTERNATIONAL BANKING FACILITY.

off the shelf see SHELF REGISTRATION.

one bank holding company corporation owning at least 25% of the voting stock of a commercial bank. An amendment to the BANK HOLDING COMPANY ACT, enacted by Congress in 1970, extended Federal Reserve supervision of bank holding companies to corporations owning only one bank. Formation of the one bank holding companies, beginning in the late 1960s, gave rise to the leveraged holding company: commercial banks were no longer dependent largely on depositors' funds to underwrite loans and other investments. Bank holding companies are allowed to issue commercial paper, but banks cannot.

This ability to finance bank operations through holding company debt gave banks greater flexibility in raising capital to support a wide variety of activities by the subsidiary bank, and by affiliate companies.

The 1970 law also required nonbank commercial corporations to divest their banking subsidiaries. See also MULTIBANK HOLDING COMPANY; REGULATION Y.

one-day certificate temporary U.S. Treasury Department financing by which the Treasury borrows from the Federal Reserve System when it needs funds. The Treasury issues an interest-bearing certificate called a Special Certificate to the Federal Reserve Bank of New York. No certificates have been issued since June 1979 when federal legislation limited direct Treasury borrowings from the Fed to not more than $5 billion, and required approval by five of the seven governors of the Federal Reserve Board.

one stop banking see FULL-SERVICE BANK.

one stop shopping see FINANCIAL SUPERMARKET.

on-host bank card authorization system in which transactions are compared against the card issuing bank's customer files, as opposed to looking up only bad or dishonored cards. This allows greater control over credit losses, because credit card accounts exceeding their credit limit also are rejected. Also called full positive authorization or POSITIVE AUTHORIZATION.

on-line computer system where customer transactions are posted to a bank's central records, and directly to a customer's account, as they are made. Also known as *on-line transaction* processing or OLTP. Many banks have on-line teller terminals, connected through a computer in a branch office, directly to the back office computer system where customer files are kept. This allows customers to get faster access to their funds when they deposit a check drawn on the same bank; it also means that money is taken out faster when checks are paid.

Many electronic banking systems, including AUTOMATED

TELLER MACHINE (ATM) networks and electronic POINT-OF-SALE systems, are fully on-line systems, meaning that transactions are approved or rejected and funds are transferred between accounts as soon as they are entered into the system. The opposite is OFF-LINE network. See also FUNDS TRANSFER; INFORMATION TECHNOLOGY; PLATFORM AUTOMATION.

on others item see TRANSIT ITEM.

on-us item
1. check payable from funds on deposit at the same bank where it is presented for collection. If there are sufficient funds in the account on which it is drawn (the drawee's account), the check can be cashed or deposited into another account. Also called a house check.
2. electronic funds transfer where the paying and receiving accounts are at the same bank.

open book Euromarket term for NEGATIVE GAP. Also called an unmatched book or short book. If the average duration (maturity) of a bank's liabilities is less than the average duration of its assets, or vice versa, it is said to be running an open book.

open contract futures market contracts that have not been liquidated by subsequent sale or purchase of the underlying instrument, by taking delivery of the instrument, or by taking an offsetting position in futures. Also called OPEN INTEREST.

open-end credit consumer LINE OF CREDIT that may be added to, up to a preset credit limit, or paid down at any time. Also known as *revolving credit* or *charge account credit*. The customer has the option of paying off the outstanding balance, without penalty, or making several installment payments. Bank CREDIT CARD and check OVERDRAFT credit lines are two of the most widely used forms of open-end credit. Contrast with CLOSED-END CREDIT. See also CASH ADVANCE.

open-end fund type of INVESTMENT COMPANY that sells new shares to the public and stands ready to buy back (redeem) its shares at the market price when investors wish to sell. Open-end investment companies are better known to the public as MUTUAL FUNDS, and are so named because these companies are continually creating new shares when they sell securities. Consequently, the NET ASSET VALUE of mutual funds increases or decreases as investors buy shares or redeem them. Funds typically invest in a variety of financial instruments, including common stocks, corporate bonds, tax exempt bonds, and short-term money market instruments. Contrast with CLOSED-END FUND.

open-end investment company see MUTUAL FUND.

open-end lease lease, usually an automobile or vehicle lease, in which payments do not fully amortize the obligation. The monthly payments ordinarily are lower than closed-end lease financing, but the lease requires a BALLOON PAYMENT at maturity. The size of the balloon is disclosed when the lease is taken out.

open-end mortgage clause in a mortgage allowing mortgaged property to be used for additional advances on the same note, up to a preset amount. Subsequent advances are dated back to the recording of the original mortgage deed.

open interest financial futures market contracts that have not been offset by opposite transactions, or fulfilled by delivery of the underlying financial instrument. Even though each futures transaction has a buyer and a seller, in computing open interest only one side of the market is counted. Open interest also refers to options contracts that have not been closed out, offset by opposite transactions, or allowed to expire.

open market account Federal Reserve System's portfolio of U.S. government securities, agency securities, and bankers' acceptances acquired through OPEN MARKET OPERATIONS. The Open Market Account is maintained by the Federal Reserve Bank of New York, following instructions from the FEDERAL OPEN MARKET COMMITTEE, which meets periodically. Also called System Open Market Account.

open market intervention see INTERVENTION.

open market operations purchase or sale of government securities by the Open Market desk at the Federal Reserve Bank of New York, as directed by the FEDERAL OPEN MARKET COMMITTEE.

By buying and selling securities, mostly short-term Treasury obligations, i.e., Treasury bills, the Federal Reserve is able to: (1) meet the public demand for cash by adjusting bank reserves upward or downward, as needed, and (2) influence bank interest rates, including rates such as the Federal Funds (Fed Funds) rate that banks charge for short-term sale of EXCESS RESERVES. Because reserve accounts at Federal Reserve Banks don't earn interest, banks try to hold reserves to a minimum or to the level of required reserves.

When the manager of the Fed's Open Market Desk at the Federal Reserve Bank of New York makes the decision to buy securities, the Fed writes a check on itself to the bank, or other institutional investor holding the securities, and deposits a check in a commercial bank. If the Fed buys $1 billion in Treasury bills, bank reserves are increased by that amount. Selling $1 billion in T-bills has the opposite effect, shrinking the reserves in the banking system, which tends to drive up the cost of credit, and interest rates. Because commercial bank reserve accounts don't earn any interest, banks try to hold their reserves at a minimum. When the Fed is worried that the inflation rate is rising, it pursues a tight money policy by selling securities. Banking reserves are then reduced, and banks have to borrow from the Fed at the DISCOUNT WINDOW to meet the demand for credit. What results is higher interest rates, because the banks pass the added cost along to the borrowers. There is, however, no direct correlation between discount window loans and interest rates. Interest rates do not always move automatically one way or the other when the Fed adjusts credit policies.

The Fed also adds reserves to the banking system to meet the public's seasonal demand for cash, that is, when it anticipates banks will have more checks in the process of collection. This demand for cash varies seasonally; it is highest in December, and lowest in late summer.

For these reasons, open market operations are the most flexible monetary tool the Fed has available in implementing its monetary policy objectives. Because commercial banks have about three fourths of the nation's checking account deposits, the Fed, by managing the level of reserves in the banking system, is able to influence the nation's supply of money (the money supply or money stock), and the cost of credit. Both the Fed Funds rate, which is the market rate banks pay one another for nonborrowed reserves, and the bank prime rate are influenced to a large degree by the Fed's actions in open market operations.

Other tools of monetary policy are the DISCOUNT RATE and RESERVE REQUIREMENTS. See also FISCAL POLICY; MATCHED SALE REPURCHASE AGREEMENT; REVERSE REPURCHASE AGREEMENT; SWAP NETWORK.

open market rates interest rates on various MONEY MARKET INSTRUMENTS that have an active secondary market. Open market rates are influenced by a number of factors, including supply and demand, current interest rates, and also trading arbitrage by market participants.

For example, in the FEDERAL FUNDS market, banks with excess reserves sell funds, usually on an overnight basis, to other banks needing cash to meet their RESERVE REQUIREMENTS. The Fed Funds rate is repriced with each transaction, and is highest during periods of TIGHT MONEY when the supply of NONBORROWED RESERVES in the banking system is reduced by Federal Reserve monetary policy.

Other examples of open market rates are the rates banks pay when they buy Eurodollar deposits from a non-U.S. bank or purchase negotiable certificates of deposits and bankers' acceptances from banks willing to sell funds in the money market.

operating lease LEASE written for a shorter period than the economic life of the leased asset. These leases ordinarily are written by equipment manufacturers, who are expected to take back the equipment and re-lease it to other users. Commercial banks do not make operating leases, as the Federal Reserve's REGULATION Y requires that bank lessors recover at least 75% of the original equipment cost through lease payments of principal and interest. Operating leases are cancellable leases, meaning the equipment can be returned at any time if it becomes obsolete or no longer is needed. See also CAPITAL LEASE; FINANCE LEASE; LEVERAGED LEASE; RESIDUAL VALUE.

operational targets Federal Reserve MONETARY POLICY objectives, expressed in terms of projected changes in monetary aggregates (the MONEY SUPPLY) and credit (NONBORROWED RESERVES). The Federal Reserve Board chairman reports the Fed's intentions, that is, what the Fed expects to achieve through its monetary policy, in twice-annual reports to Congress, as called for by the Full-Employment and Balanced Growth Act of 1978. The growth projections are stated as upper and lower ranges, covering the fourth quarter of one year to the fourth quarter of the following year.

The Fed's ultimate objective in monetary policy is balanced growth in the economy, as measured by changes in the GROSS NATIONAL PRODUCT, the inflation rate, unemployment, and so on. Since 1979, the Fed's near-term focus in monetary policy has been management of credit in the banking system, which it attempts to control through OPEN MARKET OPERATIONS.

opportunity cost present value of the income that could be earned (or saved) by investing in the most attractive alternative to the one being considered. The cost of pursuing one course of action in terms of the foregone return offered by the most attractive alternative. For example, investing in government bonds instead of originating mortgages. Also called *alternative cost*.

option contract granting the right, and not the obligation, to purchase or sell property, or assets during a specified period at an agreed-upon price, called the EXERCISE PRICE or STRIKE PRICE. Options are most common in the stock market, but also are used frequently as a hedging device in managing currency positions in foreign exchange, financial futures, commodities, and stock index futures. Option prices are determined by the interaction of the maturity, volatility, and price of the underlying instrument.

There are two basic types of options:

(1) call option—contract sold for a price that gives the holder the right to buy from the option seller a specified amount of securities at a specified price; and

(2) put option—contract sold for a price that gives the holder the right to sell a specified amount of securities at a predetermined price.

The initial cash paid, or PREMIUM, is determined at the beginning of the option contract. Most put and call options are rarely used. They are allowed to expire unexercised, or are sold before the exercise date in trading activity, based on the rise and fall of option premiums. See also AT THE MONEY; DELTA; IN THE MONEY; OUT OF THE MONEY; STRADDLE.

Options Clearing Corp. (OCC) corporation, owned by the stock exchanges, providing trade comparison and settlement services for all option trades on U.S. securities exchanges. The corporation's prospectus, given to option traders, describes its rules for ethical conduct and outlines trading risks in exchange-traded options. OCC's Intermarket Clearing Corporation also provides a link to the New York Futures Exchange.

order

1. instrument authorizing payment to someone else, such as a CHECK or a DRAFT. Checks are three-party instruments, involving a check writer or MAKER, the financial institution delivering the funds (the payor bank) and the person receiving the payment. A check is different from a NOTE, such as a PROMISSORY NOTE, in that a note is a two-party instrument and merely is a promise to pay, not an order to pay; it is not always negotiable, or transferable to a third party. A check, by definition, is a NEGOTIABLE INSTRUMENT; ownership of a check is transferred by ENDORSEMENT. See also DRAWEE; DRAWER; NEGOTIABLE ORDER OF WITHDRAWAL (NOW) ACCOUNT; PAYOR; PAYMENT ORDER.

2. trading instructions to a broker or dealer. There are several kinds of orders in futures trading, such as market order, which instructs a floor broker to buy or sell contracts in a specific month. A limit order tells the broker to execute an order only if the market reaches or betters that price. An open order is an order that is good until cancelled or executed. A stop order tells the broker to buy or sell at the market when a specific price is reached, either above or below the market price when the order was given. A stop order also is known as a stop out order or stop. Other types of orders commonly used on securities trading are time orders, such as a good until cancelled order, a good for one day order.

ordinary interest interest computed on a 360-day year, using 12 months of 30 days, instead of a 365-day year. For instance, Treasury bill yields are quoted on a 360-day year. Corporate bonds, mortgages, and consumer installment loans with precomputed interest earn ordinary interest. With larger amounts invested, the difference between ordinary interest and EXACT INTEREST (a 365 day year) can be substantial. See also BASIS.

Organization for Economic Cooperation and Development (OECD) official group of 24 nations, including most of the major industrialized countries, that was formed in 1961 to coordinate economic and social policies among its members and promote economic assistance to developing countries. Its members include 18 European countries, Canada, the United States, and Japan. It is based in Paris.

original issue discount (OID) amount that the original issue price of a bond, COLLATERALIZED MORTGAGE OBLIGATION, or other debt instrument is below PAR VALUE or face value. These bonds require special tax treatment from the Internal Revenue Service. The Internal Revenue Service treats the increase in price from the original issue price to par at maturity as interest subject to income tax. Even though no interest is received, taxes are due on the accretion of bond interest. At the extreme, a zero-coupon bond pays no interest at all until maturity.

original maturity term to maturity from the issue date of a bond. It differs from the current maturity, which is the difference in years between the present date and the maturity date. For example, a 30-year bond issued in 1982 has a current maturity of 22 years in 1990.

origination fee fee charged by a lender to cover the cost of handling an application and credit investigation relating to a loan application. The Real Estate Settlement Procedures Act requires that lenders disclose origination and closing costs associated with real estate loans, so consumers can compare fees of different institutions.

Statement 91 of the FINANCIAL ACCOUNTING STANDARDS BOARD (FASB 91) requires financial institutions to treat origination fees, for accounting purposes, as a deferred asset, and amortize loan and lease origination fees over the life of the loan (or lease), rather than in the year the fees are collected. These front-end fees cover direct expenses for credit investigation, documentation, and legal expenses. Previously, financial institutions were allowed to match these front-end costs against fees collected from the borrower or lessor.

originator

1. bank that initiates a wire transfer or automated clearing house payment.

2. bank, mortgage banker or savings institution that makes mortgage loans and then assembles the loans into a pool for resale to an institutional investor.

See also ASSET-BACKED SECURITIES; SECONDARY MORTGAGE MARKET.

out of the money

term used in options trading when the market value of an underlying security or financial instrument is lower than the EXERCISE PRICE of a CALL OPTION (an option to buy) or higher than the strike price of a PUT OPTION (an option to sell). An out-of-the-money option has no benefit or INTRINSIC VALUE, although buyers of these options hope they will move IN THE MONEY by the expiration date. See also AT THE MONEY.

out-of-town check

see FOREIGN ITEMS; TRANSIT LETTER.

outright forward

forward market purchase or sale of foreign exchange without a corresponding SPOT MARKET purchase. For example, buying a one-month, two-month, or three-month contract in a given currency.

outstanding

Banking:

1. checks or drafts that have not been presented to the paying bank for payment, or are still in the process of collection.

2. aggregate amount owed by a bank's credit card holders; this usually is less than total card volume due to early payments by cardholders.

Finance: uncollected funds, or accounts receivable; also unpaid obligations.

Securities: a corporation's capital stock; stock issued and sold to investors, less stock repurchased by the issuer (treasury stock).

over and short

general ledger account where differences in transaction journals are recorded, such as a teller's cash difference. Also known as a difference account. Transaction journals that refuse to balance are one of the daily hazards of banking; the causes usually are bookkeeping or clerical errors, for example, a transposed digit in a teller's transaction log.

overcollateralization type of CREDIT ENHANCEMENT by which an issuer of securities pledged collateral in excess of what is needed to adequately cover the repayment of the securities plus a reserve. By pledging collateral with a higher face value than the securities being offered for sale, for example 125% of principal value, an issuer of mortgage backed bonds can get a more favorable rating from a rating agency and also guard against the possibility that the bonds may be called before maturity because of mortgage prepayments.

overdraft

1. amount by which a check exceeds the AVAILABLE BALANCE in a checking account. Also, the negative account balance that results when a depositor writes checks exceeding the account balance. Legally, an overdraft is a loan, reportable as an extension of credit. Banks are not obligated by law to pay inadvertent overdrafts, though they often make exceptions for customers in good standing. Bank customers who have an overdraft line of credit, called OVERDRAFT PROTECTION, can write checks for more than the account balance whenever they want, without fear that their checks will be returned or they will have to pay overdraft check fees for bounced checks.

2. DAYLIGHT OVERDRAFT to a bank's RESERVE ACCOUNT at a Federal Reserve Bank created when balances transmitted to other banks or third parties exceed the balance in its reserve account. The resulting funds shortage in the reserve account is a temporary situation ordinarily covered by incoming wire transfers from other banks. See also BILATERAL CREDIT LIMIT; OVERDRAFT CAP; UNWINDING.

3. banking system in Great Britain and other European countries where depositors can write checks greater than their average balance, and can even maintain a negative balance, paying interest only on the negative balance. Also called *overdraft banking*.

overdraft cap maximum dollar amount a bank agrees to transmit to other financial institutions over private payment networks and the Federal Reserves FEDERAL WIRE network in a single day. In order to control DAYLIGHT OVERDRAFT exposure, each bank's cap is a multiple of its RISK-BASED CAPITAL. See also BILATERAL CREDIT LIMIT

overdraft protection bank customer's personal credit line that advances funds to cover an OVERDRAFT. The line is activated by writing a check for more than the available balance in the account. Also called CASH RESERVE checking. Overdraft protection allows the check to be honored by the drawee bank. The check writer avoids having to pay NOT SUFFICIENT FUNDS (NSF) charges when temporarily short of funds, but pays daily interest on the loan.

over-extension
1. **Banking.** A loan balance or total credit obligation beyond the borrower's ABILITY TO PAY. In situations where the borrower has taken on more credit than he can handle, a debt consolidation loan (combining several obligations in a single loan repayable over a longer term) may be the only alternative to bankruptcy. As a rule of thumb, borrowers who pay more than one third of their net income to repayment of consumer debt, excluding mortgage debt, may be over-extended in their ability to repay recurring household debt.
2. **Securities.** A trader's purchase of securities above his capital and borrowing power. This situation could lead to losses in a declining market if the trader is unable to meet margin calls.

overlapping debt debt created by a municipality when it issues municipal bonds to fund other development projects by a governmental unit serving the same area. For example, a city may use income from general obligation bonds to service county or school district bonds.

overlying mortgage see JUNIOR MORTGAGE.

overnight money money that is sold in the interbank market by banks with idle funds to those needing temporary funds. The Fed Funds market, where financial institutions sell EXCESS RESERVES from reserve accounts kept at Federal Reserve Banks to one another, is the largest source of overnight funds. Fed funds are due back at the selling bank at the start of business the following day. See also MATCHED SALE REPURCHASE AGREEMENT; REPURCHASE AGREEMENT.

overnight repurchase agreement

1. MONEY MARKET arrangement whereby securities dealers and banks finance their portfolios of Treasury bills, Ginnie Mae mortgage backed securities, and other government securities. The dealer sells securities to an investor, agreeing to buy them back the next day at a higher price. In a repo deal, the dealer either delivers the collateral to the purchaser or has it immobilized by a third-party depository, who issues a trust certificate to the purchaser. The opposite transaction, a REVERSE REPURCHASE AGREEMENT, occurs when the holder of securities sells them to a dealer, with an agreement to buy them back the next day at a higher price. Bank repo deals are exempt from Regulation D RESERVE REQUIREMENTS.

2. arrangement used by the Federal Reserve Bank of New York to create banking industry RESERVEs by engaging in short-term purchases of securities from primary government securities dealers, with an agreement to resell the securities at the end of the stated period. If the securities are returned at the beginning of the next business day, the transaction is an overnight repurchase agreement. See also MATCHED SALE REPURCHASE AGREEMENT; REPURCHASE AGREEMENT.

over-ride

1. decision by a credit analyst or bank lender to approve or decline a credit application, despite the presence of other factors, such as DEROGATORY INFORMATION as released by a credit reporting agency. Over-rides most often occur when a lender grants a loan request, or rejects the application, even though a credit scoring system has determined otherwise. See also CREDIT SCORING.

2. set aside of federal legislation by a state legislature during a specified period of time after enactment of federal legislation. See also PREEMPTIVE RIGHT.

Overseas Private Investment Corporation

independent federal agency created by the Foreign Assistance Act of 1969 to insure, guarantee, and finance private investments in developing countries. Since 1979 OPIC has operated as a unit of the International Development Cooperation Agency.

over-the-counter (OTC)

market for trading securities that are not listed on an organized stock exchange, such as the

New York Stock Exchange or a regional stock exchange. U.S. government securities, corporate bonds, mortgage backed securities, asset-backed securities, and municipal securities also are traded over-the-counter. Trading activity is carried out by broker-dealers who communicate with each other by telephone, and by computer-controlled networks of quotation terminals. In the OTC market, prices are determined by negotiation between buying and selling brokers, rather than auction bidding on the floor of an exchange. Most bank stocks are traded over the counter, although many are listed on major exchanges, as well as regional stock exchanges.

The NATIONAL ASSOCIATION OF SECURITIES DEALERS established market rules for trading in unlisted stocks that are traded over-the-counter. Trading in municipal securities is regulated by the MUNICIPAL SECURITIES RULEMAKING BOARD. Both are self-regulatory organizations, and are exempt from Securities Exchange Commission supervision, with the exception of SEC rules covering fraudulent transactions. The Federal Reserve Board, which regulates margin buying of stocks, publishes a list of OTC stocks that are subject to the margin regulations of Federal Reserve REGULATION T.

owner's paper all forms of mortgages, debt, or second mortgages that are held by the seller rather than a financial institution, for example, a PURCHASE MONEY MORTGAGE. Also called a seller's mortgage.

P

P* statistical measure of the impact of Federal Reserve MONE-
TARY POLICY on the rate of inflation in the economy. The P*
(pronounced P *star*) number tracks the growth of M2, a MONEY
SUPPLY measure, as modified by the VELOCITY OF MONEY. If P*
exceeds P (expected future prices), the Fed can be expected to
tighten bank credit and interest rates, causing the economy to
grow at a slower rate. When P* is less than P, the Fed can ease
its credit policies, allowing bank credit and the money supply to
grow at a faster rate.

The P* formula is:

$$P^* = M2 \times V^* / Q^*$$

where M2 is an official measure of the money supply (checks
plus checkable deposits, savings, and time deposit accounts), V*
is the velocity of M2, or the number of times that money turns
over, and Q* is the estimated value of Gross National Product at
a nominal growth rate of 2.5% a year.

pa 'anga national currency of the Tonga islands.

package mortgage mortgage or deed of trust that covers
personal property, such as furniture, appliances, and other
household items. See also CHATTEL MORTGAGE; WRAPAROUND
MORTGAGE.

paid-in capital
1. **Banking.** The capital stock of a bank, Federal Reserve Bank,
or international development bank subscribed to, and paid by,
its stockholders. Paid-in capital is the amount contributed by
stockholders to obtain a bank charter and commence business. Federal Reserve MEMBER BANKs are required to purchase shares in their district Federal Reserve Bank equal to
6% of their capital and surplus; only 50% of this amount
actually is paid. The remainder, or callable capital, can be
called at any time.

2. Finance. The difference between par value of a corporation's outstanding shares of stock and current market value. This value is adjusted downward when a corporation repurchases its own stock. Contributions in excess of par value or donations not counted toward capital stock are called *capital surplus.*

pair-off hedging technique involving trade of a mortgage backed security to offset a previous trade. In mortgage banking, it allows a lender to buy back mortgages or mortgage backed securities committed to a buyer in the SECONDARY MORTGAGE MARKET.

panic sudden loss of public confidence in the financial markets, characterized by falling prices and business failures. Financial panics occurred at regular intervals in the nineteenth and early twentieth centuries, before the United States had a central bank to regulate the banking system. The most severe panic, occurring in 1907, led to a Congressional investigation and legislation in 1913 that created the FEDERAL RESERVE SYSTEM.

paper generic term for short-term debt instruments, such as bankers' acceptances, commercial paper, and documentary drafts. Short-term obligations are a source of credit to businesses needing temporary financing, for example, an importer who needs bank financing to cover the cost of merchandise until his inventory is sold. Short-term paper with maturities under 90 days is eligible for REDISCOUNT at a Federal Reserve Bank; that is, it can be used as collateral for a Federal Reserve credit advance. See also DISCOUNT WINDOW; ELIGIBLE PAPER.

paper gain (or loss) popular name for unrealized capital gain or loss in an investment portfolio or an open position in options or futures. Also called PAPER PROFITS. Paper gains are determined by comparing the current market price to the original cost of the investment. They are not realized until securities are sold, a futures position is liquidated, or an option to sell is exercised.

paperless entry

1. transfer of funds, initiated by telephone or instruction from a computer terminal rather than a check or draft.

2. electronic deposit of pay or benefit payments from a government agency or private organization into a depositor's account.

See also BOOK ENTRY SECURITY; DIRECT DEPOSIT; ELECTRONIC FUNDS TRANSFER.

paper money

bank notes designated by the U.S. Treasury as LEGAL TENDER for payment of debts, principally FEDERAL RESERVE NOTES. Paper money is also known as FIAT MONEY, because it is not backed by the issuing government's pledge to exchange paper for an equivalent amount of gold or hard currency.

paper profits

see PAPER GAIN (OR LOSS).

parallel loan

four-party loan involving parent companies and their subsidiaries in different countries. A parallel loan is an arrangement to borrow in the currency of one country with a promise to pay interest and principal at a later date. The loan is collateralized by a concurrent loan from a multinational parent company to its affiliate in a foreign country. A parallel loan is similar to a BACK-TO-BACK LOAN, or two-party loan, in that it transfers surplus liquidity from one currency to another. Its main disadvantage is that the lender's right of offset in event of default is unclear, and it is less flexible than a back-to-back loan. The two-party loan is safer from the lender's view because, if the subsidiary defaults, the multinational parent normally is obligated to make good on the loan.

Paris club

see GROUP OF TEN.

parity

1. in foreign exchange trading, absence of a counterproposal to a bid or offer of another party. The term implies that both traders are dealing at exactly the same prices. Thus, they are at par or at parity.

2. PURCHASING POWER PARITY.

3. in financial swaps, the absence of any price difference between two maturity dates of a swap agreement.

participation see LOAN PARTICIPATION; RISK PARTICIPATION.

participation certificate (PC) certificate representing an undivided interest in a POOL of conventional mortgage
loans. Principal and interest payments pass through to the certificate holders each month. For example, a participation certificate
is in the form of a PASS-THROUGH SECURITY that is issued and
guaranteed by the Federal Home Loan Mortgage Corporation.
See also MODIFIED PASS-THROUGH CERTIFICATE; MORTGAGE-
BACKED CERTIFICATE.

partnership agreement see ARTICLES OF PARTNERSHIP.

par value
1. **Securities.** The face value of a security or financial instrument. The par value of a common stock is the nominal value
   assigned by a corporate charter, and has no specific financial
   relevance after the issue date. The par value of a debt security, for example a bond, is very relevant, as that is the price
   that will be paid the bondholder at maturity. The bond coupon
   interest payable semi-annually is a percentage of a bond's par
   value. Preferred stock dividends normally are stated as a percentage of the assigned par value, but also may be determined by auction bidding at periodic intervals. Par value is
   unrelated to market value, which is influenced more by market pricing, YIELD on the securities offered for sale, NET AS-
   SET VALUE, and prices of comparable issues in the secondary
   market. See also ABOVE PAR; ACCRETION OF DISCOUNT.
2. **Banking.** A check collection system where depository institutions exchange checks at face value, without charging a fee
   (called an exchange charge) for accepting checks drawn on
   other banks. Non-par banking was prevalent during the nineteenth and early twentieth centuries. Banks that are member
   banks in the Federal Reserve System are required by the Fed
   to honor checks at face value, and in fact, most banks, even
   nonmember state banks, honor checks at par exchange. The
   Federal Reserve maintains a list, called the par list, of banks
   that pay checks at par.

passbook account at a bank or thrift institution whose ownership is evidenced by entries in a nonnegotiable book that must be
presented with each deposit or withdrawal, and for posting of

interest. In general, a SAVINGS ACCOUNT, although a TIME DE-POSIT account may be in passbook form. Also called bank book. Contrast with STATEMENT SAVINGS account.

passbook loan see SAVINGS ACCOUNT LOAN.

passing the book see GLOBALIZATION.

passive investor investor who lends money or collects a portion of gross income. For example, a LIMITED PARTNERSHIP in a real estate development project. Passive investors may deduct investment losses only if gains from such investments exceed their losses. Income earned by passive investors may become subject to the ALTERNATIVE MINIMUM TAX.

pass-through account method of maintaining required reserves, whereby nonbank financial institutions are able to meet RESERVE REQUIREMENTs by holding deposits in a MEMBER bank that maintains an equivalent deposit at a Federal Reserve Bank. The bank maintaining the pass-through account does not have to be in the same Federal Reserve District as the bank owning the account.

pass-through security security that passes payments from borrowers to investors as loan payments are collected. Its cash flow is from a pool or pools of underlying loans. The issuer remits, or passes through, to the investor monthly payments of principal and interest. Servicing of the underlying loans is usually done by the seller, who is paid a servicing fee. Actual lives of pass-through securities can be shorter than the stated maturity, because in periods of falling interest rates, borrowers pay off their loans early. See also PARTICIPATION CERTIFICATE.

past due loan payment not made as of the scheduled payment date, and subject to late charges after an allowable GRACE PER-IOD. Continued lateness is noted in the borrower's credit history, and may be reported to a credit bureau or credit reporting agency. Past due loans are reported on a bank's CALL REPORT.

pataca national currency of Macao.

payable through draft DRAFT payable through a designated bank, drawing funds from the issuer's own account. The bank, whose name is printed on the face of the draft, verifies neither the signature nor the endorsement, which is the responsibility of the issuer. Payable through drafts are used by corporations to pay freight bills, or by insurance companies to settle claims. A credit union SHARE DRAFT, a check-like negotiable instrument, also is a payable-through draft, often cleared through a correspondent bank.

pay-by-phone SEE TELEPHONE BILL PAYMENT.

paydown
1. partial reduction of a debt, as when a consumer pays off a part of the outstanding balance on a credit card, mortgage, or installment loan.
2. net reduction of a debt when the amount of new securities issued is less than that of a maturing issue.

payee party named as the beneficiary of a CHECK or NEGOTIABLE INSTRUMENT; the person to whom the written amount on the face of the instrument is paid.

payer party responsible for making payment of the amount written on a check, draft, or other negotiable instrument. Also called the maker or writer.

payer bank the bank paying a check, unless the check is payable at another bank and is sent to that bank for payment or collection. Also, a payable through bank, for example, when the writing on a draft (a PAYABLE THROUGH DRAFT) states it's payable through XYZ bank.

paying agent agent, usually a commercial bank, authorized by a securities issuer to make principal payments and periodic interest payments to bondholders. The bank, or banks, acting as paying agent charges a fee for this service. Occasionally, the treasurer of the issuing organization will be designated as paying agent. See also REGISTRAR; TRANSFER AGENT

payment cap clause in an ADJUSTABLE RATE MORTGAGE (ARM) limiting monthly payment adjustments, usually restricting the increase to a percentage of the previous payment. An ARM with a 7¹/₂% payment cap and monthly payments of $100 can increase to no more than $107.50 in the first adjustment period, and $115.56 in the second. See also ANNUAL CAP; LIFE OF LOAN CAP.

payment date

1. date specified in a bond indenture as the interest payment date or interest and principal payment date for a series of bonds.
2. designated VALUE DATE where funds are transferred by prior arrangement, for example, a payroll or Social Security DIRECT DEPOSIT.

payment delay time delay between the date on which borrowers make their mortgage payments and the date investors holding pass-through mortgage backed securities are paid. Because interest is calculated monthly, payment delays result in interest-free delay periods of up to 19 days on Ginnie Mae pass-through securities, 24 days on Fanny Mae participation certificates, and 44 days on Freddy Mac participation certificates, reflecting the actual number of days between payment on the underlying mortgages and payment to the pool investors.

payment order check-like instrument directing a bank to pay a specified sum to a third party, for example, a Negotiable Order of Withdrawal or Payment Order of Withdrawal. ORDERS differ from CHECKS, which are payable on demand; an order legally is a DRAFT that the drawee bank has the option to pay. The bank may require advance notice before honoring a draft, though in practice the withdrawal notice usually is waived.

payment shock said to occur when the monthly payment rises sharply at the first adjustment period in an ADJUSTABLE RATE MORTGAGE (ARM). An ARM with an initial rate of 8% has a monthly payment of $476.95. If the rate increases to 10% in the second year, the payment is $568.82 a month, and if it goes to 12%, the monthly payment rises nearly $200 to $665.43. Consumers can guard against payment shock by taking adjustable rate loans with PAYMENT CAPS limiting the maximum monthly payment, or with interest rate caps that put a ceiling or upper limit on the amount of interest charged.

payment system financial system creating the means for transferring money between suppliers and users of funds, usually by exchanging debits or credits among financial institutions. Also known as a payment mechanism. Checks and drafts commonly are referred to as the paper based payment system; electronic fund transfers, such as AUTOMATED CLEARING HOUSE debits and credits, and Fed Wire transfers, are referred to as the electronic payment system or paperless system.

payoff statement document prepared by a lender when a borrower is considering paying off a mortgage or other loan, showing the number of remaining payments, principal balance due, the daily rate of interest, and amount of interest to be rebated if the borrower prepays. Also called *letter of demand*.

pay-through security mortgage-backed bond collateralized by a POOL of mortgages. Also called a *cash flow bond*. These securities are fully amortizing bonds resembling modified pass-through securities, paying interest at scheduled intervals, monthly or quarterly. An example is a COLLATERALIZED MORTGAGE OBLIGATION. Although paying a somewhat lower yield than a PASS-THROUGH security, pay-through securities generally are safer investments because they are general obligations of the issuer, and are guaranteed by a federal agency or mortgage insurance company.

pay to bearer check, draft, or other NEGOTIABLE INSTRUMENT transferable to the holder by delivery, without endorsement. A BEARER BOND, such as a bond with detachable coupons, is not registered in the name of a particular owner and is payable to whomever receives it in good faith.

pay to order NEGOTIABLE INSTRUMENT that is payable by endorsement and delivery. Pay to order instruments are usually written "Pay to the order of XYZ" or "Pay to XYZ or order." Ownership of a check, under the UNIFORM COMMERCIAL CODE, can be transferred only after the person accepting the check endorses it over to someone else.

peer group classification of commercial banks by asset size and other characteristics. The UNIFORM BANK PERFORMANCE REPORTing system classifies banks by 20 different groups. Within each group, banks are compared to other banks of comparable size with respect to profitability (return on assets), and so on. Peer group analysis is used by banks to assess their financial performance vis-a-vis competing banks in their market. Peer groups are determined from bank size, location, and mix of business, and can have as few as five or six banks, in the case of money center banks, or hundreds of community banks.

peg (pegging)

1. in FOREIGN EXCHANGE, the process by which a government ties the value of its own currency to the currency of another country, usually the currency of its strongest trading partner, or a basket of currencies. For example, the exchange rate of the Mexican peso was pegged for many years to the U.S. dollar. An adjustable peg allows periodic adjustments in exchange rates, to adjust for currency fluctuations; a crawling peg adjusts the pegged currency rate on a more frequent basis, even daily. See also FLOATING EXCHANGE RATE; MANAGED CURRENCY.

2. manipulation to maintain the value of a security or commodity, whereby the price is not permitted to fluctuate above or below a certain preset value, known as the PAR VALUE. Pegging or otherwise fixing the prices of securities traded on national exchanges is unlawful under Section 9 of the Securities Exchange Act of 1934. In commodities trading, however, exchanges may legally restrict daily price fluctuations by setting daily trading limits, pegged to the previous day's settlement price or CLOSE.

penalty clause clause in contracts, loan agreements, and other obligations allowing a financial institution to assess penalties for early withdrawal from a savings account, late payments on an installment loan, or breach of contract. Since interest rate ceilings were lifted in March 1986, the Federal Reserve Board has eliminated the requirement under REGULATION Q that banks impose mandatory penalties on early withdrawals from savings accounts; however, a bank still has the option of charging a penalty if a depositor fails to give advance NOTICE OF WITHDRAWAL, usually seven days in advance, before withdrawing funds from an interest earning deposit account. See also EARLY WITHDRAWAL PENALTY; PREPAYMENT PENALTY.

pension fund fund set up to collect regular contributions from a corporation, government agency, or organization to provide post-retirement income for eligible employees. Employer contributions are set aside in tax-free investments, under authority granted by the Internal Revenue Code. These institutional investors are among the largest investors in the stock market, and also invest in mortgage backed securities, and to a lesser extent, real estate and venture capital limited partnerships. Pension funds are exempt from capital gains taxes and thus any holding period provisions in securities regulations. Pension fund managers are required to follow investment rules, as fiduciaries for pension fund assets held in interest.

perfected lien security interest in collateral securing a debt protected from claims by third parties. To properly file a lien and take a security interest in property owned by the borrower, a lender must file the lien with the appropriate legal authority. Perfection of a lien on real estate is accomplished by recording the mortgage deed of trust in public land records of a municipality, such as a town clerk's office.

Perfecting a lien on stocks, bonds, or other assets owned by the borrower (known as PERSONAL PROPERTY, as opposed to REAL PROPERTY, or real estate) occurs when the lender files a FINANCING STATEMENT (UCC-1) listing the type of collateral securing the loan, and its location, in a designated filing place, generally the office of the Secretary of the State or a county recorder's office.

The lender's financing statement gives the lender priority status ahead of creditors filing subsequent liens, and is valid for a five-year period. The filing date is recorded, and the lender's documents are assigned a file number. These documents contain a detailed record of the collateral pledged or taken by the lender, establishing the lender's claim against assets by the borrower in event that the borrower defaults or goes bankrupt. See also CONTINUATION STATEMENT; PREFERENCE; PRIORITY OF LIEN.

perfect title real estate TITLE free of LIENS, encumbrances, or other defects. Removing prior claims is a legal process known as perfecting a title, allowing sale or assignment to a second party. See also CLOUD ON TITLE; QUIET TITLE ACTION; WARRANTY DEED.

performance analysis comparative examination of return on assets, return on equity, and other KEY RATIOS of bank performance. Performance analysis generally ranks financial institutions by PEER GROUP, or groups of institutions of similar asset size, by deposit base, type of industry primarily served, or by other criteria. A rule of thumb ranking often used ranks banks by community bank, regional bank, large regional bank (SUPER REGIONAL BANK) and MONEY CENTER BANK.

Earnings and other characteristics of performance, such as noninterest expense, net interest income, loan charge off-ratio, and peer group data collected by the Uniform Bank Performance Report, the National Bank Surveillance System, or other means are examined. Bank performance ratings are available from several sources, including Thomson Bank Watch Inc., Sheshunoff & Company, Cates Consulting Analysts, Olson Research Associates, and Veribanc Inc.

Sources of these reports are bank annual reports, CALL REPORT data, and the FORM 10K and FORM 10Q reports filed with the Securities and Exchange Commission. See also FUNCTIONAL COST ANALYSIS; RATIO ANALYSIS; UNIFORM BANK PERFORMANCE REPORT

performance bond
1. bond that calls for specific monetary payment to a beneficiary if the purchaser or maker fails to do something or acts in violation of a contract. It may be a SURETY BOND purchased from an insurance company, or cash held in an ESCROW account by a bank or a third party.
2. STANDBY LETTER OF CREDIT issued by a bank that guarantees the issuing bank will pay a third party BENEFICIARY in the event the bank's customer fails to meet a contractual obligation.

periodic rate finance charge on consumer credit loan balances, expressed as a percentage. The rate is applied daily, monthly, or at other regular intervals. For example, a credit card account may have a rate of 1.5% on unpaid balances in each BILLING CYCLE. Compare to an ANNUAL PERCENTAGE RATE of

18% for a credit card account with a periodic rate of 1.5% and 12 billing periods. The periodic rate must be disclosed in consumer credit applications or borrowing agreements.

periodic statement billing summary listing account activity, mailed at regular intervals, usually monthly. A credit card account statement shows new purchases and cash advances during the previous BILLING CYCLE, the MINIMUM PAYMENT and PERIODIC RATE on unpaid balances. See also COUNTRY CLUB BILLING; DESCRIPTIVE BILLING.

permanent financing long-term mortgage loan, usually covering development costs, construction costs, legal expenses, and other related costs, as opposed to short-term financing, for example, a construction loan. Also known as a TAKE-OUT LOAN. This loan differs from the CONSTRUCTION MORTGAGE that permanent financing is negotiated after development has been completed and a project is ready for occupancy. It is a long-term obligation, generally for periods of ten years or more.

permissible nonbank activities financial services other than deposit taking and lending, approved by the Federal Reserve Board as an acceptable activity for bank holding companies. The Fed has the authority, under the BANK HOLDING COMPANY ACT, and the act's 1970 amendments, to approve nonbanking services that (1) meet a public need, and (2) are "closely related to banking" and "a proper incident thereto." Bank holding companies can offer these services either directly, through a subsidiary bank, or indirectly, through an affiliated company.

Nonbanking activities are approved by the Fed on a case-by-case basis, following the guidelines for bank holding companies spelled out in Federal Reserve REGULATION Y, plus the Fed's assessment of the expected public benefits, and the likely impact on regulated financial institutions. Examples of approved nonbank activities are operating a consumer finance company, mortgage banking, equipment leasing, and securities underwriting.

personal banker bank employee who manages a customer's accounts much as a BROKER manages a client's securities portfolio. Each personal banker services specific customers, opens new accounts, takes loan applications, answers questions about other banking services, and in general acts as a personal financial advisor.

The personal banker system was pioneered by Wachovia Bank & Trust, Winston-Salem, N.C., in the early 1980s. It is based on RELATIONSHIP BANKING, or the concept that banks and thrift institutions can improve their competitive position vis-a-vis nonbank financial institutions by channeling retail sales through highly trained representatives who are knowledgeable about all of their institution's products and services. See also CROSS- SELL; CUSTOMER SERVICE REPRESENTATIVE; PRIVATE BANKING.

personal identification number (PIN) numeric IDENTIFICATION code used by bank customers when making transactions at a self-service electronic banking terminal, such as an automated teller machine. Also known as an *access code* or *security number.* A customer's PIN, a numeric code generally four to six digits in length, is his or her signature when making deposits or withdrawing cash at an ATM, or when transferring funds between accounts in a home banking or telephone bill payment service. PINs are cost effective means of customer identification, although banks continue to experiment with other means, such as signature verification. From a bank security standpoint, PINs pose several problems. Customers who are prone to forgetting their PINs often write their access code on their bank card. Also, the person who successfully uses a PIN to withdraw money from an account may not be the authorized cardholder. See also MAGNETIC STRIPE; PRIMARY ACCOUNT NUMBER.

personal line of credit see LINE OF CREDIT.

personal loan loan granted for personal, family, or household use, as distinguished from a loan financing a business. Also known as a CONSUMER LOAN. Such loans, often made for amounts under $5,000, are usually unsecured, though in some situations the lender may require a co-signer or guarantor. If unsecured, the loan is made on the basis of the borrower's integrity and ABILITY TO PAY. Generally, these loans are used for debt consolidation, or to pay for vacations, education expenses, or medical bills, and are amortized over a fixed term with regular payments of principal and interest. See also INSTALLMENT CREDIT; SAVINGS ACCOUNT LOAN.

personal property tangible and intangible goods, such as furniture, manufacturing equipment, and other assets that are not legally considered as REAL PROPERTY. Personal property is owned by the borrower, and is not fixed or immovable. Also called *personalty*. Personal property can be pledged as loan collateral under a FINANCING STATEMENT filed with a public records office.

personal trust trust created for individuals and their families, typically high net worth individuals, as opposed to CHARITABLE TRUSTs formed by institutions. Other examples are guardianships and reversionary trusts, such as CLIFFORD TRUSTS established during the life of the grantor to reduce tax liabilities or set up an education fund for a minor.

peseta national currency of Spain, Andorra, the Balearic islands, and the Canary islands.

peso national currency of Chile, Colombia, Cuba, the Dominican Republic, Mexico, the Philippines, and Uruguay.

phantom income income represented by ownership in a MORTGAGE POOL, and considered taxable to the holder, even though no cash is received. This may occur when the issuer of a mortgage-backed security keeps part of cash flow from the security to cover the labor and other out-of-pocket costs, or when investors purchase RESIDUAL cash flows from overcollateralization or excess cash flow from mortgage principal and interest payments. REAL ESTATE MORTGAGE INVESTMENT CONDUITS (REMICs), which issue securities from a trust, were designed to overcome this problem.

piggybacking
1. **Banking.** The services a bank makes available to other financial institutions, for a fee. For example, a financial institution that does not have automated teller machines may issue ATM

PHANTOM INCOME

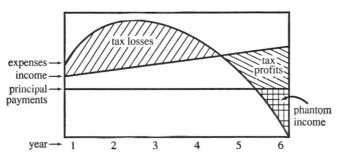

Source: Michael Thomsett, *Webster's New World Investment & Securities Dictionary*, p. 206. © 1986 by Michael Thomsett.

debit cards and arrange to have its cardholders use the ATMs owned by a nearby bank. Also, a bank, acting as agent, may make depository services available to other banks.

2. Securities. The secondary distribution of securities, allowing investors who purchase existing shares in addition to a new offering.

PIN pad numeric key pad a consumer uses to enter a PERSONAL IDENTIFICATION NUMBER (PIN) when paying by DEBIT CARD at a retail merchant or using an AUTOMATED TELLER MACHINE. In a retail purchase the PIN serves as the customer's signature; in fact, it eliminates the need for a signature in electronic POINT-OF-SALE transactions. A correctly entered PIN approves the sale and the transfer of funds from the customer's account to the retailer's account. An incorrect PIN invalidates the transaction.

pip dealer's term for the minimum price change in floating foreign exchange rates. For example, a change in a quoted price from 1.7814 to 1.7815 is equal to one pip.

pipeline expression for loan applications approved by a lender but not actually closed and delivered to a secondary market buyer, or held in the originator's loan portfolio. A mortgage banker refers to loans for which he or she has a FORWARD COMMITMENT to deliver in 30 days, 60 days, and so on, as loans in the pipeline. In the securities industry, a new issue of securities being readied for a public offering. See also CALENDAR; VISIBLE SUPPLY.

piti
short for Principal, Interest, Taxes, and Insurance—the four itemized components of a mortgage payment as listed in a borrower's mortgage statement.

placements see PRIVATE PLACEMENT.

plain vanilla swap U.S.-dollar interest rate swap in which one party receives floating rate payments based on six-month LIBOR and receives fixed rate funds expressed as a spread over the rate on U.S. Treasury securities. The maturity is usually five to seven years and deal size typically is $50 million to $100 million.

platform automation form of banking automation that connects the customer service desk in a bank office with the bank's customer records in the back office. Direct linkage to a CUSTOMER INFORMATION FILE enables branch account officers to book new loan applications directly with the bank's loan processing system, and also permits faster look-up of customer account information to answer questions on rates, new services, and so on. (The term platform originated in the period when banking officers sat at desks on a platform slightly elevated above the main banking floor, but today is used to describe the customer service area in a bank's lobby.) Platform automation in bank branches also can speed the processing time in handling credit applications, because paperwork is reduced. See also BACK OFFICE; PERSONAL BANKER; RELATIONSHIP BANKING.

planned amortization bond see CONTROLLED AMORTIZATION BOND.

pledge transfer or assignment of assets to secure payment of an obligation. Also called a SECURITY INTEREST. The borrower assigns an interest in the property to the lender, which becomes a LIEN on the collateral. If the borrower offers stocks, bonds, or other securities as collateral, the lender generally takes possession or is assigned ownership of the collateral until the loan is paid. See also HYPOTHECATION; MARGIN; PERFECTED LIEN; REGULATION T.

pledged account mortgage (PAM) type of GRADUATED PAYMENT MORTGAGE where principal and interest payments are supplemented by payments from a special savings account. Funds are drawn from the pledged account, acting as additional collateral, during the early years of the loan.

pledging requirements administrative, statutory, or contractual requirement that securities be hypothecated as collateral public fund deposits or serve as a bond or security for specified deposits. Securities backing public deposits are marketable securities, such as U.S. Treasury bills or bonds. Pledged securities generally are kept by the pledging bank in a separate account. They can be placed with an independent trustee, for example, a Federal Reserve Bank, and serve as collateral for deposits by the U.S. government, states, or municipal governments. A minimum amount of hypothecated securities—the pledging ratio of securities to public deposits—must be kept at all times. U.S. Treasury securities generally are counted at face value, commercial paper and bankers' acceptances at 90% of face value, and municipal securities at 80% of value.

plus
1. plus sign (+) following a Treasury note or bond price quote, indicating the quote is expressed in sixty-fourths of a percentage point. A quote of 93.16 means 93 and 33/64 of par. It appears in published quotations as 93.16 +.

2. indicator showing the closing price of a stock or mutual fund published in a daily newspaper is higher than the previous day's close.

point

1. Securities. The trading unit equal to $1 in stock prices or 1% of bond value.

2. Banking. (1) amount equal to one percent of the principal amount of an loan, called a DISCOUNT POINT. This fee, payable at the loan closing, increases the lender's yield on mortgages and other installment loans in relation to other types of investments; for the borrower, it is considered part of the finance charge and is tax deductible in the year the loan is made; and (2) BASIS POINT, or one hundredth of one percentage point.

3. Futures. The minimum price fluctuation, or smallest increment of price movement. In interest rate futures this is expressed as 1/32nd of a percentage point. Also called a TICK. A market move of 3 ticks is equal to a change of 3/32.

4. Foreign Exchange. In price quotes, the fourth place after the decimal point. For example, if $1 = 1.7855 deutschmarks, an exchange rate of $1 = 1.7854 is one point lower. See also PIP.

point-of-sale (POS) retail PAYMENT SYSTEM that substitutes an electronic transfer of funds for cash, checks, or drafts in the purchase of retail goods and services. In a POS system, sales and payment information are collected electronically, including the dollar amount of the sale, the date and place of the transaction, and the consumer's account number. If the transaction is done on a bank credit or debit card, the payment information is passed on to the financial institution or payment processor, and the sales data is forwarded to the retailer's management information system for updating of sales records. Much of the actual processing volume is for credit card sales. See also ELECTRONIC BANKING; POINT-OF-SALE TERMINAL; REGULATION E.

point-of-sale terminal electronic transaction terminal used in an electronic POINT-OF-SALE (POS) system. The terminal interacts with a computer file to approve transactions and transmits sales information for posting against customer accounts. There are two basic types of POS terminals: electronic cash registers that are used by high volume merchants, such as department stores, and dial-up terminals that automatically dial a special telephone number, often a toll-free number, to obtain authorization. NET SETTLEMENT, when the transfer of funds actually takes place, may occur at the same time as the transaction, or soon afterward, or it may occur later in the day in POS systems that operate OFF-LINE in a STORE AND FORWARD mode. This type of system operates off-line, that is the merchant terminal is not connected directly to a central computer for authorization or processing of sales receipts.

point scoring see CREDIT SCORING.

political risk see SOVEREIGN RISK.

pool group of mortgages, consumer loans, commercial loans, or other credit receivables acting as collateral for an issue of bonds, mortgage backed securities, or ASSET-BACKED SECURITIES. Any group of loans with similar qualities, i.e., term to maturity, interest rate, and so on, can be treated as a unit for purposes of securing pass-through securities, pay-through bonds, or multiclass bonds offered for sale to investors. Rules specifying the types of loans eligible for pooling are established by the issuer, and stated in the bond INDENTURE agreement or the issuer's offering circular. See also MORTGAGE POOL.

pooled cost of funds cost of funds formula based on division of the balance sheet into different categories, matching specific interest earning assets with interest sensitive liabilities. For example, the pooling of all interest sensitive assets with maturities of one year or less, and matching these loans against all one-year interest sensitive deposits. An accounting credit is given to the liabilities for the earnings on the asset pool, and the assets are charged a cost reflecting the average cost of the deposit liabilities. This costing formula usually is adjusted for LEGAL RESERVES that banks keep as a portion of their total deposits, regulatory capital-to-asset requirements, fee income collected from checking account customers, and float—uncollected checks. See MARGINAL COST OF FUNDS.

pooling of interests accounting method in a MERGER transaction involving an exchange of voting stock. This is a non-cash, tax-free, transaction in which the parties involved merely exchange equivalent amounts of common stock; it is the method preferred by many bank holding companies. The assets, liabilities and capital of the banks in the transaction are added together without any adjustment for fair market value. The other form of merger, a purchase transaction, involves a cash payment to the owners of the firm or bank being acquired. Pooling transactions have their drawbacks, however, namely the risk that a merger will inflate the amount of common stock issued, which temporarily dilutes common stock equity values and earnings per share. Contrast with PURCHASE ACQUISITION.

portable mortgage mortgage that allows the borrower to transfer the outstanding balance of an existing mortgage loan at the same rate when selling one house and buying another. The borrower pays a premium over fixed rate mortgages of comparable maturity, in addition to title insurance and appraisal fees at the time the mortgage deed is transferred. An advantage to the borrower, however, is the absence of closing costs and DISCOUNT POINTS when buying a new home. See also ASSUMABLE MORTGAGE.

portfolio group of loans or assets, classified by type of borrower or asset under management, For example, the loan portfolio, the investment securities portfolio, or assets managed by a bank trust department. The largest asset portfolio in a commercial bank normally is the loan portfolio, in which loans are classified by borrower—commercial loan, mortgage loan, and consumer installment loan.

portfolio lender lender, frequently a mortgage originator, who holds loans in portfolio until maturity (or until the loans are paid off by the borrower), and does not sell loans to investors in the secondary market. A portfolio lender derives its net income from the loan spread, or difference between its interest earning assets and deposit liabilities, as opposed to a mortgage banker, whose income primarily is from fees.

position

1. **Banking.** (1) bank's net balance of a foreign currency taking into account all assets and liabilities denominated in that currency; (2) mortgage banker's inventory of mortgages held in portfolio, as compared to take-out commitments from investors; and (3) lender's status, either secured by collateral or fully unsecured, in relation to other creditors of a single borrower. See also CASH POSITION; PRIORITY OF LIEN.

2. **Investments.** An investor's stake in a market, in the form of open (unliquidated) contracts. Investors take a view on the market by GOING LONG (buying) or GOING SHORT (selling) securities. A LONG POSITION also is a dealer's inventory of unsold securities. See also SHORT POSITION; SHORT SALE.

3. **Foreign Exchange.** A dealer's inventory in a particular currency. When interest rates in a particular country go down, dealers sell that country's currency; when rates rise, they add to their net position.

positive authorization retail authorization system where all noncash transactions are compared against a bank's customer files for approval. This is a more stringent form of credit approval than a NEGATIVE AUTHORIZATION system, because a positive file may turn down persons who have exceeded the authorized credit limit on a credit card account, but are not delinquent cardholders. See also ZERO-FLOOR LIMIT.

positive carry condition where cost of borrowing is less than the yield on the instrument being financed; also referred to as a positive spread. The opposite is NEGATIVE CARRY.

positive gap maturity or repricing MISMATCH in a bank's assets and liabilities where there are more assets maturing or repricing in a given period than liabilities. A bank with a positive gap is asset sensitive. The opposite is NEGATIVE GAP.

positive yield curve YIELD CURVE in which long-term rates are higher than short-term rates, so-called because yield curve has an upward slope, meaning longer maturities earn a higher rate of interest. Also known as a *normal yield curve*. If the nominal interest rate on Treasury bonds maturing in, say, ten years, is higher than it is for three-month Treasury bills, the yield curve is said to be positive. Under the LIQUIDITY PREFER-

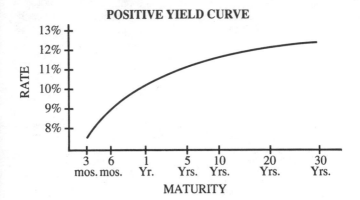

POSITIVE YIELD CURVE

ENCE THEORY of interest rates, savers who commit their funds for a longer period of time expect to earn more interest than if they put their money out short-term. They give up liquidity, or ease of access to their money, in exchange for a liquidity premium (the higher interest rate), which explains why, under normal economic conditions, longer-term rates are higher than shorter-term rates. The opposite is a NEGATIVE YIELD CURVE.

postal float SEE MAIL FLOAT.

post-dated CHECK or negotiable instrument payable on a future date. Checks written with a future date cannot be paid (honored in banking terminology) until that date has passed. Bankers' acceptances and time drafts are always post-dated instruments. Compare to STALE-DATED.

posting transferring accounting entries from journals, or records of original entry, to a general ledger. The date transactions actually are credited to an account, such as cleared checks or bank card transactions, is known as the posting date. Also known as the payment date or execution date. Some bank credit card issuers charge interest on purchases from the date transactions are posted to the cardholder's account. See also MEMO ENTRY.

pound national currency of Bermuda, Cyprus, Egypt, Lebanon, Sudan, and Syria.

pound sterling national currency of the United Kingdom, including Great Britain.

power of appointment right granted to a person acting as TRUSTEE to appoint others to dispose of or distribute an ESTATE according to the terms of a will or a deed of trust. A general power of appointment authorizes the person receiving the property (called the donee) to sell or dispose of it without restriction; a limited power of appointment limits the distribution of the estate to named individuals.

power of attorney legal document authorizing another person to act as agent. The authority granted may be a full power, or it may be limited to certain acts, and it must be witnessed by a notary public. A person selling property may assign power of attorney if unable to attend the real estate closing.

power of sale
1. mortgage clause giving the lender the right to sell the property securing the mortgage if the borrower defaults.
   2. trust power, either express or implied, giving a TRUSTEE the right to sell assets from a trust.

preapproved credit credit card or line of credit that is approved in advance and available for use at any time. Federal banking regulation prohibits mailing unsolicited credit cards, but financial institutions are permitted to mail out applications inviting a consumer to apply for credit. Once the preapproved application is signed and returned, the credit card is mailed. Use of the account is presumed to indicate acceptance of applicable credit terms, including interest rates and annual fees. See also PRESCREENING.

preauthorized payment automatic transfer of funds from a borrower's deposit account to a lender to pay down a loan or obligations owed to third party creditors. A payment schedule is set by written agreement, establishing the amount to be debited, and the date the funds are to be transferred. Payments to third party creditors are sometimes made by preauthorized check, a check-like instrument debiting the borrower's account, but more often are made by electronic transfers. See also AUTO-MATED CLEARING HOUSE; VALUE DATE.

precomputed interest finance charge on consumer installment loans that is computed in advance, and added to the outstanding balance owed by the borrower. The basis of interest calculation is usually the ADD-ON INTEREST method. Contrast with SIMPLE INTEREST.

preemptive right

1. **Banking.** The authority of the Federal Reserve Board to pre-empt the authority of state legislatures to regulate banking when intervention is deemed necessary to maintain stability in the credit markets. An example is the Monetary Control Act of 1980, which authorized the Fed to set aside state usury ceilings at a time when mortgage rates in some states were at, or close to, the legally permitted limits. In most situations, states are authorized to nullify national pre-emption if they pass legislation within three years.

2. **Finance.** The right of stockholders to subscribe to new issues of common stock before a public offering is made, protecting against dilution of ownership. Depositors in a savings institution converting from mutual to stock ownership have the same privilege.

preference transfer of property occurring within 90 days of a borrower's filing of a bankruptcy petition. A preference may be through a lien or security interest, or transfer of property to a creditor. An unsecured loan paid off within 90 days of bankruptcy also may be declared a preference. Bankruptcy trustees have the power to void preferences that impair the POSITION of general creditors, or that undermine the stability of a business through transfer of an obligation. See also SET-OFF CLAUSE; VOIDABLE PREFERENCE.

preferred stock stock that pays a fixed dividend and has claim to assets of a corporation ahead of common stockholders in event of liquidation. Preferred stock is sometimes called *preference stock*. Bank depositors have priority of claim over even preferred stockholders. Banks and bank holding companies have issued several classes of preferred stock, including perpetual preferred stock, which has no stated maturity date and is not redeemable by the holder; and limited life preferred stock, or preferred stock with a stated maturity of at least 25 years.

Under the RISK-BASED CAPITAL guidelines adopted by U.S. banking regulatory agencies for bank holding companies and state chartered banks that are members of the Federal Reserve System, nonvoting preferred stock can be counted as part of a bank's core capital or Tier 1 capital. (Tier 1 capital must equal 4% of a bank's total assets, by January 1, 1993.) Preferred stock elibible for inclusion as Tier 1 capital can be noncumulative preferred stock, equal to 25% of common stock but not auction rate preferred stock, such as MONEY MARKET PREFERRED STOCK. See also ADJUSTABLE RATE PREFERRED STOCK.

premium
1. **Banking.** A noncash incentive offered customers opening a savings account or taking out a loan.
2. **Finance** difference between the face value of a bond and the ABOVE PAR price. The opposite is DISCOUNT. Bonds purchased at a premium are amortized over their expected life; if purchased at a discount, its book value is said to accrete or grow towards par from the date purchased. See also ACCRETION OF DISCOUNT.
3. **Foreign exchange** exchange situation, called AGIO, in which gold or silver coins have a higher exchange value than paper currency of equivalent face value.
4. **Insurance.** An annual, semiannual, or other payment for insurance coverage.
5. **Options.** The price paid by the buyer of an option contract.

prenotification zero dollar entry in the AUTOMATED CLEARING HOUSE system that precedes live transactions. Such messages, known as prenotes, are required by National Automated Clearing House Association rules at least ten days prior to the first live ACH transaction to verify account numbers and related information.

prepayment partial or complete payment of a loan's principal balance by a borrower prior to the maturity date. These early repayments are influenced by economic factors, such as a sharp decline in interest rates, causing borrowers to refinance at lower rates; and also changes in the borrower's family size, relocation, sale of the mortgagor's house, or death of the mortgagor. Commercial loans and installment loans also are paid off early when borrowers refinance. See also PREPAYMENT PENALTY.

prepayment model financial model predicting prepayment on MORTGAGE loans. Some models commonly used are the 12-year life assumption used for Government National Mortgage Association (Ginnie Mae) pass-through securities, the conditional prepayment rate, constant percent prepayment, and the Public Securities Association's standard prepayment model. The Federal Housing Authority model specifies standard prepayment percentages in each year of a mortgage's life. The PSA sets a standard prepayment assumption for each month, expressed as a percentage, and annualizes that number. That number increases if expected prepayment increases steadily from .2% in the first month to 6% in mortgages aged 30 months or more that are expected to prepay. See also AVERAGE LIFE; HALF LIFE.

prepayment penalty fee paid to a lender for the privilege of paying off a loan prior to maturity. A prepayment penalty, which may decline in the years after a mortgage was originally booked, is intended to compensate the lender for loss of income in future years. These are becoming less common as more mortgages are made at adjustable rates that rise or fall according to a COST OF FUNDS INDEX or a bank lending rate, such as the six-month Treasury bill rate, LIBOR, or the bank prime rate. See also ASSUMABLE MORTGAGE.

prescreening activity in credit approval in which a lender compiles a list of prospective new accounts from credit bureau records. Prescreening normally is done by a direct mail firm that is responsible for handling the institution's new account solicitation. The firm matches the bank's credit criteria against credit bureau data on the prospective new accounts. Prescreening reduces the cost of a new accounts mailing, in that only the accounts considered good credit are solicited. These prospects may receive a PREAPPROVED CREDIT offer, inviting them to fill in certain personal information, such as income and credit experience, or they may simply receive an invitation to apply for credit.

presentment demand for payment made to a maker, drawee, acceptor or other payor of a NEGOTIABLE INSTRUMENT. In the case of a demand instrument, such as a CHECK, the UNIFORM COMMERCIAL CODE stipulates that presentment must take place within a reasonable time. In the case of time instruments, presentment takes place at the MATURITY date. Presentment may be done by mail, in person, or through banking channels, such as a local CLEARING HOUSE or the Federal Reserve check collection system.

present value today's value of a payment or a stream of payment amount due and payable at some specified future date, discounted by a compound interest rate or DISCOUNT RATE. Also called the *time value of money*. Today's value of a stream of cash flows is worth less than the sum of the cash flows to be received or saved over time. Present value accounting is widely used in DISCOUNTED CASH FLOW analysis.

previous balance account balance in open-end credit arrangements at the start of a BILLING CYCLE. Finance charges computed on the opening balance increase the lender's overall yield and the borrower's interest payments, because the borrower pays interest on the full amount owed, regardless of whether the initial balance is paid down. Compare to AVERAGE DAILY BALANCE.

price/earnings ratio relationship between the current price of a stock to the earnings over any earnings period. Also known as the *P/E ratio*. The period in question can be the most recent quarter, annualized earnings, next year's projected earnings, and so on. The P/E is calculated by dividing the current stock price by the earnings per share.

The P/E ratio, also known as the *P/E multiple*, measures corporate earnings power and is used by investors to gauge market demand for stocks. The ratio is calculated by dividing the market value by earnings per share for the most recent 12-month period. Companies with a high P/E have greater earnings potential than low P/E stocks, but also are more volatile and somewhat riskier investments.

price level adjusted mortgage (PLAM) form of GRADUATED PAYMENT MORTGAGE in which the rate of interest paid remains fixed, but the outstanding balance is adjusted for inflation according to an appropriate price index. Periodically, according to a time schedule approved by both borrower and lender, the outstanding balance owed is revised for appreciation in property values and monthly payments are revised accordingly. See also ALTERNATIVE MORTGAGE INSTRUMENT.

primary account number (PAN)

14-digit or 16-digit numeric code embossed on the face side of a bank card, and also encoded in the MAGNETIC STRIPE. The primary account number is a composite number containing: the MAJOR INDUSTRY IDENTIFIER of the card isuer; an individual account identifier, which includes part of the account number; and a CHECK DIGIT or code that verifies the authenticity of the embossed account number.

primary capital

equity capital supporting the lending and deposit activities of a bank. This is now called Tier 1 capital, and includes common stock, retained earnings, and perpetual preferred stock and GOODWILL acquired before March, 1988. This is the first part of the two-tier risk-based capital standard adopted by banking regulatory agencies in 1989: 4% primary capital and 4% supplemental capital, for capital-to-asset ratio of 8%.

Under the RISK-BASED CAPITAL guidelines regulations, the total capital requirement for bank holding companies and state chartered member banks in the Federal Reserve system is raised from 5.5% to 8% of assets, although only half of the total need be in primary capital. Capital qualifying as Tier 2 capital, or supplemental capital includes limited life preferred stock, subordinated debt, and loan loss reserves. The risk-adjusted capital guidelines require banks to reserve higher amounts of capital for certain assets on the balance sheet, and also off-balance sheet items, based on a credit risk rating assigned by federal banking supervisors.

primary dealer

government securities dealer reporting its daily trading volume and portfolio positions to the Federal Reserve Bank of New York. Also called a *reporting dealer*. The New York Fed, which manages the Open Market Account desk for the Federal Reserve System, does business only with primary dealers when it sells, or purchases securities in OPEN MARKET OPERATIONS. To be accepted by the Fed as one of the three dozen or so primary dealers, a dealer must be willing to act as a MARKET MAKER in all Treasury auctions of U.S. Treasury bills, notes, and bonds and to maintain adequate capital reserves, as determined by the Fed. Nonbank primary dealers finance their inventories by engaging in REPURCHASE AGREEMENTs and by pledging securities to obtain COLLATERAL LOANS from large banks.

primary deposits see CORE DEPOSITS.

primary market

1. market in which a loan is actually made to the borrower, distinguished from the SECONDARY MARKET, where securities backed by loan receivables are sold to investors. A bank or thrift institution that holds its loans on its own records, and does not engage in secondary market sales, is known as a portfolio lender.
2. market where original issue government securities are sold in public auction by PRIMARY DEALERS. Primary dealers then remarket government securities to investors in the secondary market.
3. market in which newly issued securities are offered for sale, futures contracts are offered for sale, and options are purchased.

primary regulator state or federal agency that is a financial institution's principal supervisory agency. It is usually the same agency that issued a bank or thrift institution's operating CHARTER. Banks and other depository financial institutions must file quarterly statements of income and condition, known as call reports, with their primary regulator, and submit books and records to periodic BANK EXAMINATION.

The Comptroller of the Currency regulates national banks; the Federal Reserve Board regulates bank holding companies and state chartered banks that are members of the Federal Reserve System; and the Federal Deposit Insurance Corporation regulates state chartered banks that are not members of the Federal Reserve System. Savings and loan associations and federal savings banks are supervised by the Office of Thrift Supervision, and STATE BANKS and SAVINGS BANKS by state banking departments. See also DUAL BANKING; FUNCTIONAL REGULATION; REPORT OF CONDITION.

primary reserves cash needed to operate a bank, plus the LEGAL RESERVES required to be held in a Federal Reserve Bank or correspondent bank, plus uncollected checks. Primary reserves cannot be used to cover sudden deposit outflows that might occur in a depositor RUN, or a temporary liquidity crisis. Primary reserves are distinguished from SECONDARY RESERVES, which may be invested in marketable securities, such as Treasury bills and municipal bonds.

prime rate BASE RATE that banks use in pricing short maturity commercial loans to their best, or most creditworthy, customers. Commercial and industrial (C&I) loans are often priced at prime or prime plus a spread. The prime rate is less important today in pricing bank loans to corporate borrowers that have access to the capital markets. Starting in the 1970s, banks began pricing commercial loans at rates below the bank prime to their most creditworthy corporate customers. Many banks, however, still price business loans under $1 million and loans to smaller borrowers at spreads above the prime rate. Alternatives to the bank prime rate are the lender's own cost of funds, and an index rate, such as the London Interbank Offered Rate (LIBOR). Although the prime rate is the definitive best rate for top-quality borrowers, many banks maintain a two-tier pricing system where major corporations and even middle market firms are able to borrow at an even lower rate.

prime underwriting facility (PUF) form of REVOLVING UNDERWRITING FACILITY in which the lender's yield is pegged to the bank prime rate. Typically, a prime underwriting facility is a short-term note having a maturity of one to three years. If the lead bank cannot fully place the loan, it will call on the facility's underwriters to fund the credit.

principal
1. face amount of a loan evidencing the amount repayable, exclusive of interest, according to the terms of the NOTE securing the obligation. See also HOLDER IN DUE COURSE.
2. original amount of a TIME DEPOSIT or savings account on which interest is paid daily, monthly, or at other intervals. See also COMPOUND INTEREST.

3. primary borrower in a loan, as distinguished from the GUAR-ANTOR or co-maker. If the borrower defaults, the guarantor is secondarily liable.
4. person who has controlling interest in a joint venture, corporation, or partnership.
5. person who appoints another to act on his behalf as agent or ATTORNEY IN FACT.
6. property of an estate or investment trust, exclusive of income.

principal exchange rate linked security (PERL)
bond paying semiannual interest, with a yield tied to foreign exchange rates. A reverse PERL is denominated in one currency, and pays interest in another. For example, a yen-denominated bond, paying interest in dollars. Investor's EFFECTIVE YIELD increases if the dollar appreciates against the yen, decreases if the dollar falls in value.

principal-only (PO) strip
mortgage security consisting of the principal portion of STRIPPED MORTGAGE-BACKED SECURITIES. PO strips are created by separating the principal payments from the interest payments collected from a pool of mortgage pass-through securities. The principal payments are combined, regardless of whether principal is paid early or at final maturity.

PO strips are priced and traded at a discount from par value, like zero-coupon issues, rising to par at maturity. PO strips can have high yields if prepayments are stretched out, but can have returns much lower than expected if mortgage prepayments are high. At worst, the return to the investor may never reach the purchase price, resulting in a loss. POs are used mostly to hedge interest rate movements, for example, as a protection against prepayment risk, or the risk of portfolio losses from a sudden increase in mortgage prepayments by mortgagors. See also IN-TEREST-ONLY (IO) STRIP.

priority of lien
order in which creditors are paid when the assets of a borrower are liquidated. Creditor priority is established under the first to file rule in the UNIFORM COMMERCIAL CODE, and is summarized as follows: creditors holding a SECU-RITY INTEREST in collateral are paid before unsecured creditors. As a general rule, holders of secured claims are paid in the order their claims were filed, starting with the earliest recorded lien.

For example, in a VOLUNTARY BANKRUPTCY filed under Chapter 7 of the Bankruptcy Code, the debtor's assets are liquidated to meet unpaid obligations. In general, the bankruptcy estate is distributed as follows: (1) administrative costs, including court costs, trustee's fees, attorney's fees incurred by the debtor; (2) wage claims; (3) costs and expenses incurred by creditors; (4) federal, state and local tax claims; (5) debts having priority under federal law, i.e., claims of secured creditors, followed by claims of general creditors (unsecured creditors.) Creditors holding a perfected security interest are paid before other creditors. See also PREFERENCE; SET-OFF CLAUSE.

prior lien LIEN recorded before other secured claims, and payable ahead of other liens if LIQUIDATION of pledged collateral occurs. A first mortgage has priority over second and third mortgages, known as junior liens. A secured creditor holding a perfected SECURITY INTEREST has priority over liens filed afterward. See also PRIORITY OF LIEN.

privacy see FINANCIAL PRIVACY.

private banking
1. banking services, including lending and investment management, for wealthy individuals. Private banking primarily is a credit service, and is less dependent on accepting deposits than retail banking. See also PERSONAL BANKER; RELATIONSHIP BANKING.
2. nonstock state chartered and state supervised bank that offers banking services to the public. Originally organized as a partnership. Private banking was a common form of banking in the United States in the nineteenth century. Among the private banking firms still in existence is the prestigious Brown Brothers Harriman & Co. in New York.

private conduit legal entity that pools conventional mortgages and other loans for resale in the secondary market, without any financial assistance by a federal agency. For example, Maggie Mae, a conduit owned by Mortgage Guaranty Insurance Corporation, a mortgage insurance company, issues PARTICIPATION CERTIFICATES on conventional mortgages that it insures. Private conduits match lenders and investors, and give lenders originating mortgages that are not federally insured or guaranteed access to national markets for placement of mortgage backed securities. Loan servicing is retained by the seller.

Private Export Funding Corporation (PEFCO) trade finance corporation owned by a consortium of U.S. commercial banks and industrial companies that arranges fixed rate medium-term and long-term loans to foreign buyers. Organized in 1970, the corporation works closely with the Export-Import Bank (Eximbank), which guarantees repayment of PEFCO loans. The corporation finances its activities through the sale of debt securities in the capital markets and by credit lines from member banks and the Eximbank.

private label credit retail REVOLVING CREDIT plans managed for a retailer, independent dealer, or manufacturer by a bank or commercial finance company. Major department and specialty stores also manage their own private label credit programs. If managed by a firm other than the retailer, the servicing company issues the cards, funds the credit receivables, and collects the payments from cardholders. Credit criteria are set by agreement between the retailer and the third party servicing firm. By having a private label credit program, a retailer is able to offer his customers extended payment terms, thereby increasing his sales and accounts receivable turnover. Private label credit plans also build customer loyalty, because retailers are able to send marketing promotions to preferred customers. See also CO-BRANDED CREDIT CARD.

private mortgage insurance (PMI) private insurance protecting mortgage lenders against borrower default. Lenders often require borrowers to obtain mortgage insurance coverage in high-ratio loans (generally, any loan with a loan-to-value ratio above 80%). In the PRIMARY MARKET, PMI insurors provide coverage for the top 20% to 25% of a mortgage loan; in the SECONDARY MARKET, insurors underwrite pool coverage, usually 5% of the pool of the underlying loans in a mortgage backed security.

private placement sale of an entire issue of securities to a small group of investors. Also known as *direct placement*. Private placements to 35 or fewer investors are exempt from Securities and Exchange Commission registration requirements, under the Securities Act of 1933. Investments with tax shelter provisions do, however, have to be registered, as required by the Deficit Reduction Act of 1984. In a private placement transaction, the buyer or buyers sign an INVESTMENT LETTER stating the securities will not be resold for a specified period of time, normally two years. Buyers of private placements include banks, savings and loans, and large institutional investors, such as insurance companies, mutual funds, and pension funds. A proposed SEC rule, Rule 144A, establishes a safe harbor for resale of privately sold securities to institutional investors, without the need to comply with the registration requirements of the Securities Act of 1934.

private purpose bond bond issued by a state or government agency in which more than 10% of the proceeds are to be used by nongovernmental units, and are repaid from revenues from private trade or business. Also called a *private activity bond* or *nonessential bond*. The Tax Reform Act of 1986 exempted private activity bonds issued in rural areas from federal taxes, but most private activity bonds are fully taxable securities. Other exemptions were granted for state housing and education bonds, bonds financing airports, public transportation facilities, and waste treatment or recycling plants. Interest earned on tax-exempt private purpose bonds is also subject to the federal alternative minimum tax. See also INDUSTRIAL DEVELOPMENT BOND; PUBLIC PURPOSE BOND.

private sector adjustment factor (PSAF) pricing markup that adjusts service fees charged by Federal Reserve Bank for check clearing and other services. This markup reflects operational costs, taxes paid, and profit margins of private sector firms. Under the MONETARY CONTROL ACT OF 1980 Federal Reserve Banks are required to charge service fees on check collection and other payment services that prior to 1981 were furnished without charge. The PSAF is based on data collected from major bank holding companies, and is revised annually.

probate validation of a will by a probate court, followed by the appointment of an executor or administrator. A probate court also is known as a court of probate, surrogate's court, ordinary court, or prefect's court. Validation of a will as authentic is the first step in the settlement of an estate. Most states require that a will be signed by at least two witnesses before it can be accepted as a valid document.

problem bank bank with a high ratio of nonperforming loans in proportion to its total capital. Also, a bank with a CAMEL RATING of 4 or 5 on the 1-5 rating scale of bank performance assigned by a supervisory agency after a bank examination. These ratings are not disclosed publicly. Problem banks are examined on a more frequent basis than banks that are in healthy condition.

problem loan see NONACCRUAL ASSET.

proceeds
1. amount given to a borrower after prepaid interest, loan fees, and other costs are deducted.
    2. funds received from the sale of assets, or from the issue of securities, after deduction of selling or marketing expenses incurred.
3. sum collected on a CHECK or other negotiable instrument after deduction of exchange or collection charges.

production credit associations see FARM CREDIT SYSTEM.

profitability see RETURN ON ASSETS; RETURN ON EQUITY.

profit and loss statement see INCOME STATEMENT.

profit center unit of business that contributes both revenues and expenses, which ultimately are recorded on the income statement and balance sheet of its parent organization. For bookkeeping accounting purposes, it is treated as an independent entity, responsible for generating income for the organization and controlling expenses. Because most commercial banks are required to report earnings on a consolidated basis, income from individual business units generally are not disclosed, unless otherwise noted in the annual report. The opposite is a COST CENTER.

pro forma statement hypothetical financial statement showing assets and liabilities, or income and expenses that may be recognized in the future. Pro forma statements also can illustrate projected earnings if a company were to merge with another, or sell off part of its operations. Business firms often are asked to submit pro forma statements when making a loan application. For example, a loan request for bank financing to purchase and carry inventory ordinarily would include a pro forma statement showing the impact of the amount borrowed on current assets and liabilities in the most recent balance sheet. Banks also use pro forma statements to indicate expected revenues from a bank ACQUISITION or MERGER with another bank, from a JOINT VENTURE that involves equity participation with other firms, or anticipated income and cash flow from a new business activity. See also BUSINESS PLAN; FINANCING STATEMENT; PROFIT CENTER.

prohibited basis credit practices that are contrary to the nondiscrimination guidelines contained in the EQUAL CREDIT OPPORTUNITY ACT. The act makes it illegal to approve consumer credit applications in a manner that denies creditworthy applicants access to credit on the basis of race, sex, national origin, age, marital status, or dependence on public assistance. Consumers who assert their rights under the Consumer Credit Protection Act also are protected by the statute. See also EFFECTS TEST; REGULATION B.

promissory note written promise to pay, frequently used in installment loans and commercial loans. A promissory note is the legal evidence of a debt, a promissory note may be transferred to a third party as a NEGOTIABLE INSTRUMENT. The holder of a promissory note who wants payment before the maturity date can negotiate it by endorsing the note and presenting it to the payer for payment. See also ACCOMMODATION PAPER; NOTE; ORDER.

proof and transit collection and reconcilement of checks, drafts, and notes. The oldest form of proof is teller proof, that is the balancing of a teller's cash position at the close of a business day. In check processing, proof and transit have been combined into a single operation involving high-speed check sorting equipment, a READER/SORTER machine that separates checks into different groups, such as checks payable by other banks (on-others checks) and checks payable by the same bank (on-us checks). Checks destined for other banks, known as TRANSIT ITEMS, are encoded with the dollar amount in the MICR line and shipped off to a clearing house to be presented to the paying bank. Proof and transit is a highly automated business, and has made the check a very competitive, low-priced payment mechanism. See also PROOF OF DEPOSIT.

proof of deposit (POD) verification of the dollar amount on a check or draft being deposited. This is done by comparing the handwritten amount on the check to the amount written on the accompanying deposit slip. Proof of deposit is the second step in processing of checks presented for payment, after checks have been separated by a check sorting machine known as a READER-SORTER into on-us and on-others categories, and is the only step in check processing that has not been automated fully. Proof of deposit or proving a check is done manually after checks have been sorted into different categories and the MICR line containing the customer's account number and the bank routing and transit number has been captured by the reader/sorter. See also ENCODING.

proprietary debit card DEBIT CARD issued by a retail merchant for use in electronic transfer of funds. Proprietary cards issued by gasoline retailers give the user the same benefits as cash paying customers, for example, a cash DISCOUNT off the listed price paid by customers paying with credit cards.

proprietary network AUTOMATED TELLER MACHINE network that is limited to customers of a single bank or group of banks. The opposite is a SHARED NETWORK. The two kinds of proprietary networks are those owned by a single financial institution for use by its own customers; and shared proprietary networks, which provide ATM access to a group of institutions, but prohibit access by customers of competing networks. See also MANDATORY SHARING.

prospectus informational document showing the formation of and intent to issue securities, required by the Securities and Exchange Commission. Also called *offering circular*. A prospectus is the legal document stating the purpose of the security issue, describing in detail the primary business of the issuer and the issuer's financial condition, and listing the principal officers. It also describes how shares are offered for sale and dividends paid. A MUTUAL FUND prospectus describes REDEMPTION rights of investors who liquidate their holdings, and also lists management fees, redemption fees, and other charges payable by the investor if the fund being offered is a LOAD FUND. A prospectus is preceded by a preliminary disclosure containing preliminary information printed in red, and hence known as a RED HERRING. The prospectus itself is an offer to sell shares to the public. A prospectus supplement is an additional statement filed with the SEC containing information about the issuer not mentioned previously; supplements are normally issued in conjunction with SHELF REGISTRATION securities and contain further information on the particular issue being sold.

The Securities Act of 1933 requires only that issuers give full disclosure of information pertaining to a proposed offering. The SEC does not approve or disapprove the offering, but it allows the prospectus and the REGISTRATION STATEMENT to clear on the 20th day after the filing date. If the SEC objects to the offering or asks for more information, the 20-day waiting period begins again unless an exception is granted.

protest formal notice that a bank has refused to pay a check or other NEGOTIABLE INSTRUMENT properly and legally presented for payment. Also called a *protest jacket*. Protest is a means of legally proving that presentment was made, but rarely is used. Modern banking systems provide a sufficient AUDIT TRAIL to verify the conditions under which presentment was made. When a check is dishonored by the drawee bank, it can be presented a second time by a notary public or other public official. If the drawee bank still refuses to pay, an official statement is attached to the instrument, legally certifying that presentment was made and that the instrument was dishonored.

provisional credit temporary redeposit of funds in a disputed ELECTRONIC FUNDS TRANSFER while the transaction is investigated. Under the ERROR RESOLUTION procedures in Regulation E, a consumer who claims his bank account was debited erroneously without his or her authorization may challenge the transaction. The consumer's bank has ten business days from he time the complaint is lodged to investigate and if necessary correct the error. If it cannot, the bank must return the funds debited, and it then has up to 45 days in most transactions to investigate the alleged error.

prudent man rule investment standard for trusts and fiduciary investments. The rule, originating in an 1830 court case, states that trustees are free to make investment decisions, applying the same standards—reasonable income and preservation of capital—that a prudent man would use. The rule has been accepted in some states as a guide for trustees. Other states have more formal rules, limiting fiduciaries and bank trust departments to a so-called LEGAL LIST of approved investments.

public offering offering and sale of securities by an issuer, after meeting registration requirements of the Securities and Exchange Commission. Offerings usually are carried out by an underwriting syndicate, according to the terms and conditions in an UNDERWRITING AGREEMENT. Also, the secondary distribution of previously issued shares of securities.

public purpose bond bond issued by or on behalf of a state or local governmental unit that is exempt from state or local taxes under the Tax Reform Act of 1986. The Tax Reform Act defines qualified government as having taxing authority, power of eminent domain, or policing power within its jurisdiction. Such bonds may include GENERAL OBLIGATION BONDS backed by taxing authority, revenue anticipation notes and TAX ANTICIPATION NOTES issued to cover cash flow shortfalls. They are exempt from federal taxes, including the alternative minimum tax but are subject to volume limitations on new issues of tax-exempt securities. Contrast with PRIVATE PURPOSE BOND.

Public Securities Association trade association of dealers in U.S. government securities, mortgage backed securities, and municipal securities. Its members include the primary dealers that buy or sell securities with the Federal Reserve, dealer banks, and nonbank dealers that are market makers in the government securities market, and also the market for mortgage backed securities. Trading and settlement rules are set by the association's uniform code of practices.

punt national currency of the Republic of Ireland.

purchase acquisition accounting method that adds the revalued assets and liabilities of an acquired firm to those of the acquirer. The assets and liabilities of the acquired organization are recorded on the books of the acquirer at FAIR MARKET VALUE. The difference between the purchase price and the net fair market value of assets and liabilities acquired or assumed is carried by the acquirer as GOODWILL. The financial figures of the two entities remain combined going forward, but historical costs are restated. This method ordinarily is used when more than 10% of the purchase price is paid with cash, preferred stock, or debt securities.

purchase and assumption method used by the FED-ERAL DEPOSIT INSURANCE CORPORATION in closing a failed bank and transferring ownership and control to a healthy institution. The acquiring bank purchases the deposits of the failed bank, and assumes responsibility for most of the failed institution's liabilities. The FDIC restores the assets of the acquired bank, either through a cash payment or sale of notes with repayment guaranteed by the insurance agency. Purchase and assumption is the most common method of transferring the assets and branches of a failed bank; it is used only when it is a less expensive option to a LIQUIDATION, in which the FDIC pays depositor claims and disposes of the failed bank's assets to partially recover its liquidation costs. See also MODIFIED PAYOFF.

purchased funds see FEDERAL FUNDS; MANAGED LIABILI-TIES; OVERNIGHT MONEY.

purchase money mortgage mortgage taken by the seller in lieu of full payment in cash, securing the buyer's obligation. A purchase money mortgage, usually given when the buyer is unable to get commercial financing or financial institutions are unwilling to make a loan, is used most often in financing the sale of undeveloped land. Most seller arranged mortgages are short-term loans, repayable within five years.

purchasing power parity economic theory linking currency exchange rates to prices paid for goods and services in any two countries. The theory compares what two currencies can buy in their respective countries at a given rate of exchange. For example, if a basket of goods can be bought with $1,000 in the

United States or 150,000 yen in Japan, the parity of the U.S. dollar to the yen is 1-to-150. If either currency has greater purchasing power, the theory goes, it might be better for buyers to convert yen into dollars, for instance, and buy in the United States. Eventually, prices are adjusted, and parity reset at a different exchange ratio. In reality, though, purchasing power has less influence on exchange rates than interest rates and other economic factors.

purpose statement signed affidavit of a borrower stating the intended use for a loan collateralized by margin securities. Federal Reserve REGULATION U requires banks to obtain a purpose statement (Federal Reserve form U-1) when loans are secured by marketable securities. The borrower agrees not to violate any Federal Reserve regulations on sale or purchase of securities.

put bond MUNICIPAL BOND or other bond that has a sell-back provision, or REDEMPTION privilege, allowing holders to sell their holdings back to the issuer at specific intervals up to five years after the original issue date at specific prices determined at the time of issuance. Also known as an option bond, put bonds were first offered in 1980 to encourage reluctant investors to buy long-term bonds. Put bonds frequently are supported by CREDIT ENHANCEMENTS.

put option contract giving the holder the right, but not the obligation, to sell a security or financial instrument for a specified period of time at a specific price, called the EXERCISE PRICE or STRIKE PRICE. Puts are bought by investors who believe the price of the underlying securities will go down, and they will be able to sell the securities at a higher striking price. The opposite is a CALL OPTION.

pyramiding
1. **Finance.** The use of paper profits to make additional investments, adding to the holder's unliquidated (open) position.
2. **Banking.** Using credit with one financial institution to roll-over outstanding obligations at other creditors without paying down the principal. Eventually, interest payments become so large the debtor is unable to rollover his debts any

longer, and he is often forced to seek protection under the bankruptcy code, or combine obligations in a debt consolidation loan.

3. **Real Estate.** The acquisition of additional properties by refinancing already owned property, and reinvesting the proceeds.

Q

quadratic pricing model financial pricing model, indicating the optimal market for a new product or service, and the optimal price-yield of a new product. The highest profit potential is for a customized product made for a specialized group of clients, such as full-service brokerage, or PRIVATE BANKING, in the upper left quadrant. The lowest price, but highest demand, is the lower right quadrant, where services are more often commodity products, such as discount brokerage, or credit cards.

qualified endorsement endorser's writing on a check limiting his liability in event of nonpayment or nonacceptance of an instrument. It usually is written with the words WITHOUT RECOURSE, or similar words to indicate the endorser is not secondarily liable for payment.

qualified opinion opinion by a certified auditor, stating that the auditor is unable to verify completely the accuracy of the financial records of a bank, because of certain omissions in the records or the limited scope of the audit. A qualified opinion does not necessarily mean, however, that there are serious errors or omissions.

qualifying ratio total monthly housing expenses, including repayment of principal, taxes, and insurance, as a percentage of gross monthly income. Or the borrower's total regular monthly debt as a percentage of gross monthly income. The qualifying ratio is the lender's rule of thumb for determining a borrower's ABILITY TO PAY.

quantity theory of money theory that attempts to correlate the quantity of money and prices in the economy. It attempts to explain how inflation can be controlled by MONETARY POLICY, that is, by control of the money supply. The theory has come under attack because of the existence of quasi-money or near money, and also the ability of nonbank financial institutions

QUADRATIC PRICING MODEL

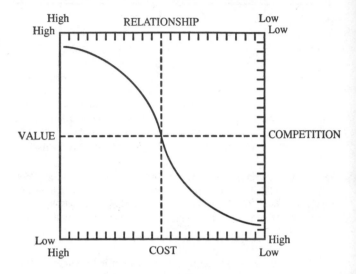

Source: G. Michael Moebs, *Pricing Financial Services* (Dow Jones Irwin, 1986).

to develop and introduce new forms of credit. The quantity theory has gained respect in recent years largely through the work of Milton Friedman of the University of Chicago.

quarterlies interim financial reports on the condition of a publicly held company, released each quarter of its fiscal year.

quasi-public corporation privately operated corporation that fulfills a public mandate, such as purchasing loans in the SECONDARY MARKET, thereby helping to maintain adequate funding sources for lenders. Quasi-public corporations often have government backing behind their debt obligations, and some issue stock that is publicly traded. The FEDERAL NATIONAL MORTGAGE ASSOCIATION (Fannie Mae) was founded to encourage mortgage lending by purchasing mortgages guaranteed by the Federal Housing Administration or insured by the Department of Veterans Affairs, and also conventional home mortgages. The STUDENT LOAN MARKETING ASSOCIATION (Sallie Mae) was started in 1972 to develop a secondary market for student loans. Fannie Mae, a stock corporation, raises capital in the public markets; Sallie Mae meets its financing obligations through sale of debt securities, largely through the FEDERAL FINANCING BANK.

quetzal national currency of Guatemala.

quick assets current assets of a business, excluding inventories, that could be converted into cash if necessary within a short period, usually one year or less. Also known as *liquid assets*.

quiet title action legal action brought to eliminate any interest or claim in a property by others. It is the procedure used to remove title defects from a real estate title when a QUITCLAIM DEED cannot be obtained.

quitclaim deed document in which title, claim, or ownership of property or an estate is relinquished to another, without representing that such title is valid. Usually it contains no convenant or warranty against outstanding claims of previous lien holders.

quotation broker's stated price giving the highest bid to buy or lowest offer to sell. A full quotation displays the price that will be paid (the bid price), and price offered (the offered price). The normal order of listing is bid first, and asked second. The amount of activity is indicated by the spread between bid and asked quotes. Often shortened to "quote."

R

raised check check with the written dollar amount fraudulently changed to a higher figure. To protect consumers and financial institutions the dollar amount is written twice: in numeric form after the words "pay to the order of," and in the maker's handwriting on the line below. When the two amounts differ, the paying bank usually accepts the written out amount—for example, "one thousand one hundred dollars"—as the check writer's intention.

rand national currency of South Africa.

range forward FORWARD EXCHANGE CONTRACT combining the purchase of a specific amount of currency with a futures and option contract. Range forward contracts limit downside losses from currency DEPRECIATION to an agreed amount, while giving the holder the option of participating in upside profits. The two ends of the contract represent the strike price on options contracts.

rap accounting see REGULATORY ACCOUNTING PRINCIPLES.

rate ceiling see USURY CEILING.

rate lock see LOCK-IN PERIOD.

rate of exchange see EXCHANGE RATE.

rate of return
1. yield obtained on invested capital, also known as the RETURN ON EQUITY (ROE), or RETURN ON ASSETS, (ROA), a measure of operating performance.
2. gross annualized yield on a time deposit or certificate of deposit, the EFFECTIVE ANNUAL YIELD, including compounded interest paid or accrued. This differs from the advertised annual rate or NOMINAL INTEREST RATE.

3. EARNINGS PER SHARE—net income plus after-tax interest charges, divided by the number of outstanding shares. Perhaps the single most useful ratio for assessing a firm's overall operating performance.

4. investor's rate of return, measured by changes in current stock prices and dividends.

rate sensitivity see INTEREST RATE RISK.

rating

1. credit standing of an individual or firm, determined by previous credit experience, income needed to pay other creditors, and other factors, such as a favorable CREDIT REPORT. There are four major national credit reporting agencies collecting information on consumer obligations. DUN & BRADSTREET prepares detailed reports on commercial firms, listing capitalization, ownership, total assets, and external debt, among other things.

2. quality assessment of a debt instrument, as determined by a rating agency, based on probability of full repayment. Ratings are given to corporate bonds, municipal bonds, certificates of deposit, commercial paper, and other instruments. See also BANK QUALITY; INVESTMENT GRADE.

ratio analysis

1. analytical tool used in bank PERFORMANCE ANALYSIS by bank performance rating agencies, such as Cates Consulting Analysts, Olson Research Associates, Lace Financial Corp., Sheshunoff & Co., Thomson Bankwatch Inc., Veribanc Inc., and is also extensively used by financial industry regulators. Ratio analysis also is used by leading MERCANTILE AGENCIES, including Moody's, Standard & Poor's, Fitch Investors Service, and McCarthy Crisanti and Maffei, in assigning ratings for corporate debt securities. In lending, ratio analysis is widely used in analyzing pro forma income and balance sheet statements to determine the borrower's ability to take on debt and make regular payments.

Ratio analysis examines performance and overall profitability of banks and bank holding companies. The four general categories of ratios in assessing performance of banks and bank holding companies include: profitability—RETURN

ON ASSETS, RETURN ON EQUITY; capital—CAPITAL RATIO; liquidity—LIQUIDITY RATIO; and asset risk ratio—risk adjusted capital ratio. See also CAMEL RATING.

2. financial ratios used by commercial lenders in analyzing the financial condition of prospective and current borrowers. Trade ratios comparing performance by different firms in specific industries are available from the Robert Morris Associates, the national association of bank credit officers, the U.S. Department of Commerce, and other sources. See also BALANCE SHEET RATIOS.

rational expectations see EXPECTATIONS THEORY.

reader/sorter machine that separates checks received from bank tellers or from other banks, sorting them into different categories. Checks that are payable by other banks (*on others* checks) are pulled out first, and are bundled together in a CASH LETTER for presentment to other banks. The on-others checks are processed first, in order to meet a local clearing house deadline. The on-us checks are sorted out later. A reader/sorter is a key piece of equipment in preparing CASH LETTERS sent to other banks. It sorts, encodes checks, and distributes checks. See also MAGNETIC INK CHARACTER RECOGNITION; PROOF AND TRANSIT; TRANSIT ITEM.

reaffirmation voluntary agreement by a debtor in bankruptcy to pay all or part of a debt, even though the debtor is not legally obligated to do so, and cannot be compelled by his creditors to repay a debt. Under the bankruptcy code, the debtor's attorney files a statement with the court stating that reaffirmation will not harm the debtor financially. Debt reaffirmations are not allowed in Chapter 13 WAGE EARNER PLANS.

real estate investment trust (REIT) investor-owned corporation, trust or association that earns profits for shareholders by managing income producing real estate or lending money to developers. A REIT is exempt from federal corporation taxes, provided that it distributes 90% of its income to investors, although shareholder dividends are fully taxable. Assets of a REIT are managed by one or more trustees who control its acquisitions and investments. An equity REIT owns and operates income property, such as shopping centers and apartment buildings; a MORTGAGE REIT lends money to developers, holding a construction mortgage or long-term mortgage as security.

real estate mortgage investment conduit

(REMIC) mortgage securities vehicle authorized by the Tax Reform Act of 1986 that holds commercial and residential mortgages in trust, and issues securities representing an UNDIVIDED INTEREST in these mortgages. A REMIC, which can be a corporation, trust, association, or partnership, assembles mortgages into pools and issues pass-through certificates, multiclass bonds similar to a COLLATERALIZED MORTGAGE OBLIGATION (CMO), or other securities to investors in the secondary mortgage market. Mortgage backed securities issued through a REMIC can be debt financings of the issuer or a sale of assets. The Tax Reform Act eliminated the double taxation of income earned at the corporate level by an issuer and dividends paid to securities holders, thereby allowing a REMIC to structure a mortgage backed securities offering as a sale of assets, effectively removing the loans from the originating lender's balance sheet, rather than a debt financing in which the loans remain as balance sheet assets. A REMIC itself is exempt from federal taxes, although income earned by investors is fully taxable. As a tax-exempt entity, a REMIC may invest only in qualified mortgages and permitted investments, including single family or multifamily mortgages, commercial mortgages, second mortgages, mortgage participations, and federal agency pass-through securities. Nonmortgage assets, such as credit card receivables, leases, and auto loans are ineligible investments. The Tax Reform Act made it easier for savings institutions and real estate investment trusts to hold mortgage securities as qualified portfolio investments. A savings institution, for instance, can include REMIC-issued mortgage backed securities as qualifying assets in meeting federal requirements for treatment as a savings and loan for tax purposes.

A REMIC can issue mortgage securities in a wide variety of forms: securities collateralized by Government National Mortgage Association (Ginnie Mae) pass-through certificates, whole loans, single-class participation certificates and multiclass mortgage backed securities; multiple class pass-through securities with fast-pay or slow-pay features; securities with a SUBORDINATED DEBT tranche that assumes most of the default risk, allowing the issuer to get a better credit rating; and Collateralized

Mortgage Obligations with monthly pass-though of bond inter est, eliminating reinvestment risk by giving investors CALL PRO-TECTION against early prepayment.

Among the major issuers of REMICS are the Federal Home Loan Mortgage Corp. (Freddie Mac) and the Federal National Mortgage Association (Fannie Mae), the two leading secondary market buyers of conventional mortgage loans, and also privately operated mortgage conduits owned by mortgage bankers, mortgage insurance companies, and savings institutions. See also CONDUIT; GRANTOR TRUST.

real estate owned real estate acquired by a lender through FORECLOSURE in satisfaction of a debt and held in inventory until sold. Also called *other real estate owned (OREO)*. A loan secured by foreclosed real estate is counted as a NONPERFORMING LOAN in reporting loan quality in call reports to bank supervisory agencies. Foreclosed real estate normally is auctioned off through a bidding process. Normally, the lender bids what is owed, and no more. If there are no higher bids, the lender takes the property and it becomes real estate owned.

Real Estate Settlement Procedures Act (RESPA)
federal law requiring lenders to give home mortgage borrowers an estimate of total charges prior to the loan closing. This disclosure is given in a CLOSING STATEMENT. Disclosure under RESPA is mandatory in federal guaranteed or insured residential mortgages, and certain types of commercial real estate loans. It requires lenders to make a good faith estimate of closing costs, prohibits borrower kickbacks and sets guidelines for handling mortgage escrow accounts. RESPA is administered by the Department of Housing and Urban Development, and is enforced by the lender's primary banking regulator.

real interest rate interest rate calculated by subtracting the inflation rate from the stated rate, or NOMINAL INTEREST RATE. The real interest rate, an important tool in comparing effective yields on different investments, can be figured for the current time period, or for future periods by estimating the future inflation rate. Thus, a bond or bank CD earning 11% when the inflation rate is 5% has a (pretax) real interest rate of 6%. As the rate of inflation rises above 5%, the investment begins to lose value because the interest earned falls behind the general increase in prices.

realized profit (or loss) profit or loss when a security actually is sold or otherwise disposed at a price exceeding its purchase price, as distinguished from paper profits.

real money money, usually coinage, as distinguished from paper money accepted as LEGAL TENDER. Also called HARD CURRENCY. Checks, drafts, and other negotiable instruments would not be considered real money.

real property land, buildings, and other kinds of fixed or immovable property. This is classified as real, as distinguished from personal property. In some states, it is synonymous with real estate.

real rate of return rate of return earned by an investment, less the rate of inflation in the country where funds are invested. Also called real interest rate. An investor earning a rate of 8% while the inflation rate is 3%, has a real rate of return of 5%. Rate of return analysis is used in many different economic scenarios, including international capital movements between countries.

rebate
1. UNEARNED INTEREST returned to the borrower when a loan is paid off early. See also RULE OF THE 78'S.
   2. pro-rated share of deposit insurance premium returned to a federally insured bank or savings association when the sum of insurance premiums paid exceeds payouts to depositors from an insurance fund.
3. portion of net sales returned to cardholders by a bank card plan, based on card usage. A plan with a 2% rebate nets the cardholder $2 for every $100 in sales.
4. reduction in a credit card merchant's MERCHANT DISCOUNT RATE for credit card transactions above a certain amount.

recapitalization any major changes in a corporation's paid in capital, resulting from issuance of new shares of stock, REORGANIZATION in bankruptcy, or exchange of common stock shares for bonds and notes, as in a LEVERAGED BUY-OUT. In banking, it is any restructuring of a troubled bank assisted by a deposit insurance fund, as in a BAILOUT of a failing bank, where the insurance fund pays the acquiring bank the difference between the book value of a troubled bank's assets and the estimated market value. The insurance fund may also take an equity position in the restructured bank.

receipt written record of a transaction or payment of a debt. A deposit receipt is a bank customer's copy of the deposit ticket submitted with a check being deposited. A transaction receipt is a customer's copy of a bank card sales draft, or, in an electronic funds transfer, the terminal receipt that is required by REGULATION E. A receipt acknowledging payment of debt is not a promise to pay, and therefore is not a negotiable instrument, but if it is an order to pay, may be transferrable through assignment. See also AMERICAN DEPOSITARY RECEIPT; INTERNATIONAL DEPOSITARY RECEIPT.

receivables financing form of ASSET-BASED LENDING providing seasonal capital to businesses, collateralized by accounts receivables. Receivables loans, like inventory loans, are sources of short-term funds that are used for a variety of purposes, such as financing a business expansion. Receivables are a better form of collateral than inventory from the lender's viewpoint; they demonstrate that the firm has buyers. Receivables are more liquid than inventory; they are one step closer to cash. A lender's primary risk in receivables financing is that the borrower will divert collections away from repayment of the loan. See also BORROWING BASE.

receiver person named by a bankruptcy court to act as agent for a debtor in bankruptcy. The receiver is entrusted with authority to help reorganize the company, or to liquidate it to satisfy obligations to creditors. The receiver is required to maintain the property for the benefit of creditors or others having an equity interest in it, until bankruptcy has been discharged. In a BANK FAILURE the FDIC acts as receiver of the failed bank's assets. See also DEBTOR IN POSSESSION.

receiving bank in the nationwide AUTOMATED CLEARING HOUSE (ACH) system, a bank or other depository institution eligible to receive electronic credit and debit entries from another bank, the ORIGINATOR of an ACH transaction, for posting to a customer's account. Also called *receiving depository financial institution* (RDFI).

recession downturn in a country's economy, measured by a decline in aggregate economic activity. Most economic measures of a recession are at least partly subjective, although a widely held definition says a recession occurs when real GROSS NATIONAL PRODUCT declines in two consecutive quarters. Another indicator of a recession is a sudden rise—at least two percentage points—in the unemployment rate. The National Bureau of Economic Research decides when recessions begin and end, based on an analysis of economic indicators. This often means that a recession can be well underway before policymakers in government and business become aware of it and begin taking corrective actions. See also FISCAL POLICY; MONETARY POLICY.

reciprocal statutes mutually beneficial legislation adopted by two or more states to encourage commerce between them, or for other reasons. For example, state laws approving REGIONAL INTERSTATE BANKING, and also state laws providing comparable treatment of corporation or inheritance taxes. See also UNIFORM COMMERCIAL CODE.

reclamation
1. adjustment for errors in processing of a check or other negotiable instrument incorrectly recorded by a clearing house association. The net difference is either due, or payable by, a clearing member.
2. securities term for the right of a party to collect money or securities from the party on the other side of the transaction if irregularities in settlement are discovered, for example, if certificates are stolen.

record date
1. calendar date used by a bond issuer in determining eligibility to collect future payments of principal and interest. For example, the record date for a holder of a Collaterized Mortgage Obligation is generally one month prior to the payment date.

2. date on which owners of a corporation's stock are declared by the board of directors as eligible to receive dividends payable at a specified future date or vote on corporate issues, as in a RIGHTS OFFERING.

recording (of lien) public acknowledgment of a lien against specific property identified in a mortgage, and recorded in a public land record office. The details of a properly executed legal document, such as a mortgage, deed of trust, or extension of a mortgage are noted, and become part of the public record.

recourse ability of a person owning a negotiable instrument to compel payment. Under negotiable instruments law, recourse conveys the right to collect from a writer or endorser of a negotiable instrument, such as a check or draft. When an installment sales contract is sold to a bank on a recourse basis, the retailer takes full responsibility for the paper if default occurs. In commercial finance, where a lender purchases a merchant's accounts receivables, the finance company reserves the right to charge back any disputed invoices to the customer and debit the customer's account. In contrast, FACTORING is done on a NON-RECOURSE basis; in other words, the factor buying the merchant's credit receivables makes the credit evaluation in advance and assumes all credit risk of nonpayment. See also LIMITED RECOURSE FINANCE; NON-RECOURSE LOAN; WITH FULL RECOURSE.

recovery
1. collection of payment on an obligation previously written off as a loss. Because the loan already was charged against the reserve account for bad debts, recoveries may be credited against the loan loss reserve or allocated to undivided profits. Recoveries may result from payment by the borrower or liquidation of collateral. See also WORKOUT AGREEMENT.
2. improvement in the business cycle, as after a RECESSION.
3. gain in securities prices after a market decline.
4. gain in the value of a currency against other world currencies.

recurring payment regularly scheduled payment of a consumer debt, such as an installment loan, which is payable monthly, a MORTGAGE, which is payable monthly or biweekly, or an insurance premium. Benefits payments to individuals, such as

Social Security payments or pension benefits, also are recurring payments. Recurring payments, which change little in dollar amount, are processible through the AUTOMATED CLEARING HOUSE system. More than 40% of Social Security payments are deposited in this fashion. See also DIRECT DEPOSIT; PREAUTHORIZED PAYMENT.

red clause letter of credit LETTER OF CREDIT allowing the beneficiary of a documentary credit to receive funds for the purchase of merchandise described in the credit. These funds, known as advances, are deducted from the face amount of the draft when the beneficiary presents the letter for payment. Most red clause letters are opened in transactions where the beneficiary is acting as agent for the buyer in the exporting country, and purchases merchandise destined for export.

redemption

1. repayment of a debt security or preferred stock issue by payment of the principal at maturity, or at an earlier date if the issuer calls the security and pays a premium to debt security holders. Also, the liquidation of mutual fund shares by selling shares back to the fund's investment manager at the NET ASSET VALUE price.
2. mortgagor's right, called the EQUITY OF REDEMPTION, to recover foreclosed property by paying principal and interest due, plus the lender's out-of-pocket costs.
3. in bankruptcy, the right of a debtor to reclaim personal property by paying creditors the estimated fair market value of assets secured by a lien.

red herring customary statement, printed in red, on the first page of a prospectus. It is not an offer to sell, but contains the required public disclosures. Also called *preliminary prospectus*. The notice is printed in red on the first page of the preliminary prospectus, and on the face of the preliminary offering circular.

rediscount process by which a Federal Reserve Bank discounts a NEGOTIABLE INSTRUMENT or commercial finance paper, such as a bill of exchange or acceptance that already has been discounted by a bank. Federal Reserve Banks are empowered to accept loans and other bank obligations as collateral for advances at the DISCOUNT WINDOW. As a practical matter, however, rediscounting of commercial obligations accepted by a bank, called ELIGIBLE PAPER, that comply with the Federal Reserve's criteria for discounting, has occurred infrequently in the last 30 years.

redlining discriminatory practice of discouraging mortgages, improvement loans, and other forms of borrowing by home owners and businesses on the basis of race or ethnic background. Originally, such neighborhoods were outlined in red on a map, hence the name redlining. The practice is forbidden by the Community Reinvestment Act and other federal regulations. Lenders also are discouraged from using postal ZIP codes as a credit criterion, because they may inadvertently exclude borrowers whose credit status is protected from discrimination by the Equal Credit Opportunity Act. See also REGULATION B.

reference rate see BASE RATE; FEDERAL FUNDS RATE; LONDON INTERBANK OFFERED RATE; PRIME RATE.

refinance bill see THIRD COUNTRY ACCEPTANCE.

refinance risk risk that a bank will be unable to refinance maturing deposit liabilities when they come due at maturity, at acceptable prices and terms. When banks go to the market to refinance liabilities, the risk is that they may be unwilling or, in extreme rate volatility, unable to acquire deposits necessary for making new investments. Refinance risk applies to money market deposits and corporate debt, such as term debentures. The risk for the institution is that it may not be able to roll over those liabilities at an affordable rate.

refinancing
1. **Banking.** A loan that adds to the principal balance owed, usually for property or home improvements, and alters the payment amount and terms.
2. **Finance.** Issuing new securities at a lower interest rate, or extended maturity. Also called REFUNDING.
3. **Real estate.** To extend existing financing to new properties.

refundable interest interest refunded to a borrower who pays off a loan before the maturity date; refunding of the UNEARNED INTEREST under the RULE OF THE 78's.

refunding

1. process of paying off maturing or outstanding debt with proceeds of a new issue, often at a lower interest cost to the issuer. The U.S. Treasury Department uses the refunding process to replace maturing Treasury bills and notes with new issues.

2. redemption of a corporate or municipal bond issue prior to the maturity date. This can be advantageous to the issuer if interest rates fall, but disadvantageous to the bondholders. Bond issues are refundable if there is a provision in the IN-DENTURE allowing early call or redemption. Some refunding provisions permit early calls with excess funds, but prohibit refunding with the proceeds of a lower interest rate issue.

   A call provision allows the bond issuer to pay part or all of the issue early by paying a specified redemption price to the bondholders. Some long-term industrial revenue bonds, however, are callable except for refunding purposes.

regional bank

bank whose primary business is making loans to customers in a regional or metropolitan area and taking deposits within the state where it is chartered. A regional bank has a broader market focus than a COMMUNITY BANK, but smaller than a MONEY CENTER BANK. See also SUPER-REGIONAL BANK.

regional check processing center (RCPC)

check processing center owned by a Federal Reserve Bank, that services depository institutions located in one of the 12 Federal Reserve districts. Fed check collection centers accelerate the nationwide collection of corporate and personal checks, by sorting and delivering checks to paying banks the same day as received. Checks are delivered to an RCPC by private courier hired by check processing banks. Regional check processing centers also handle collection of checks drawn on the Treasury, postal money orders, and redeemed food stamp coupons, but not cash and securities.

regional interstate banking

banking expansion across state lines through bank holding company acquisitions, permitted by reciprocal legislation in states in a defined geographic region. For example, six New England states adopted legislation in the mid-1980s allowing interstate acquisitions by banks in the New England region, but excluded New York banks. Banks in other regions, in the southeastern United States and the Midwest, soon followed with regional banking arrangements when state legislatures passed enabling legislation.

The legality of these reciprocal statutes was upheld by a U.S. Supreme Court decision in June 1985, when the court turned down an appeal by opponents of regional interstate laws (Northeast Bancorp. v. Board of Governors) challenging a Connecticut law limiting interstate acquisitions to New England. The ruling paved the way to interstate compacts in other regions around the country.

See also INTERSTATE BANKING; NATIONAL TRIGGER; SUPER REGIONAL BANK.

registered bond bond whose owner's name is recorded as a book entry on the books of the issuer or its transfer agent. Bonds registered as to principal and interest are fully registered bonds, paying interest by check from the issuer's agent. Bonds registered as to principal are transferable only by endorsement of the holder. Most new corporate bonds and municipal bonds are issued only in fully registered form. The opposite is a BEARER BOND. Both registered bonds and bearer bonds are negotiable instruments.

registered check check, similar to a MONEY ORDER, purchased at a bank for a fee. Registered checks are used by persons who don't have checking accounts to transfer funds to another, or pay bills. The purchaser writes the payee's name, signs his or her name, and presents the check to a bank teller. The check is payable from funds on deposit, but not certified by the bank. Contrast with CERTIFIED CHECK.

registrar bank or bank trust department authorized by an issuer of securities to maintain records of the number of stock shares or securities cancelled and reissued. The registrar, by ensuring that only the authorized number of stock shares or securities is outstanding at any time, is protecting the holders' interests while performing a service for the corporation. The registrar normally is a commercial bank other than the stock TRANSFER AGENT. See also REGULATION 9.

registration statement document required by the Securities and Exchange Commission for public offerings of securities. The registration statement, required by the Securities Act of 1933, discloses information on the management and financial condition of the issuer, and describes how the proceeds of the offering will be used. The statement also is filed with the appropriate securities exchanges and state securities regulators. Proposed offerings under $500,000 generally are exempt from SEC registration requirements under the 1933 Act. See also SHELF REGISTRATION.

regression analysis statistical techniques that quantify the relationship between two or more variables. The objective is quantitative prediction or forecasting to find out whether or not the variables being examined can be expected to be closely related to a larger population group. Regression analysis is a frequently used statistical tool in ASSET-LIABILITY MANAGEMENT, CREDIT SCORING, and ECONOMETRICS. Much econometric theory relates to theoretical problems arising from the application of various regression models, based on certain assumptions about economic activity.

Regression analysis allows a bank to set credit criteria for the general public, and build a statistical formula predicting how new accounts will perform in the future, that is, their ability to repay debt, by studying a sample of existing accounts. The banker wants to know the credit characteristics of consumers who are good payers, and those who are poor payers. Consumer credit ideally is suitable for statistical tools such as regression analysis because consumer behavior in handling credit is fairly predictable, based on a study of previous credit experience; even the credit losses are predictable.

A credit scoring formula must, however, comply with the equal credit guidelines REGULATION B; and scoring formulas need to be revised periodically, because the underlying assumptions may no longer be valid after five to seven years.

reintermediation flow of funds into banks and other depository financial institutions from competing nonbank investments. This occurs when consumers move funds from money market funds and direct investments into bank money market and time deposit accounts, sometimes to take advantage of federal deposit insurance on accounts in depository institutions. The opposite is DISINTERMEDIATION.

reinstatement restoring a borrower's credit standing to an acceptable condition. Reinstatement occurs when a borrower has cured a delinquency by making past-due payments plus any applicable penalty fees or late charges. If the account is a bank credit card, the customer's account number is removed from a list of accounts—the WARNING BULLETIN—that limits the consumer's ability to use the card. Reinstatement generally is reported to local or national credit bureaus, so that credit reports can be updated accordingly.

Regulation 9 regulation issued by the Comptroller of the Currency allowing national banks to operate trust departments and act as fiduciaries. Under Regulation 9, a national bank is permitted to act as trustee, administrator, and registrar of stocks and bonds, and engage in related activities, such as management of a collective investment fund, as long as these activities do not violate state legislation. See also FIDUCIARY.

Regulation A Federal Reserve Board regulation governing advances by Federal Reserve Banks to depository institutions at the Federal Reserve DISCOUNT WINDOW. Credit advances are available to any bank or savings institution maintaining transaction accounts or nonpersonal time deposits. The Fed has two different programs for handling discount window borrowings: ADJUSTMENT CREDIT to meet temporary needs for funds when other sources, including the Federal Home Loan Banks, are not available; and EXTENDED CREDIT, designed to assist financial institutions with longer-term needs for funds. This category includes SEASONAL CREDIT privileges extended to smaller financial institutions that don't have ready access to money market funds. Fed banks may also extend EMERGENCY CREDIT to financial institutions other than depository institutions where failure to obtain credit would affect the economy adversely.

Regulation B Federal Reserve regulation prohibiting discrimination against consumer credit applicants, and establishing guidelines for collecting and evaluating credit information. Regulation B prohibits creditors from discriminating on the basis of age, sex, race, color, religion, national origin, marital status, or receipt of public assistance. The regulation also requires creditors to give written notification of rejection, a statement of the applicant's rights under the EQUAL CREDIT OPPORTUNITY ACT, and a statement listing reasons for rejection, or the applicant has the right to request the reasons. If an applicant was denied credit because of adverse information in a credit bureau report, the applicant is entitled to receive, at no cost, a copy of the bureau report. Creditors who furnish credit information when reporting information on married borrowers must report information in the name of each spouse. See also CREDIT REPORTING AGENCY; CREDIT SCORING; EFFECTS TEST.

Regulation C Federal Reserve regulation implementing the Home Mortgage Disclosure Act of 1975, requiring depository institutions to make an annual disclosure of the location of certain residential loans, to determine whether depository institutions are meeting the credit needs of their local communities. Specifically exempted are institutions with assets of $10 million or less. Regulation C requires lenders of mortgages that are insured or guaranteed by a federal agency to disclose the number and total dollar amount of mortgage loans originated or purchased in the recent calendar year, itemized by census tract where the property is located.

Regulation D Federal Reserve regulation that sets uniform RESERVE REQUIREMENTS for depository financial institutions holding transaction accounts or nonpersonal time deposits. The reserve requirement on transaction accounts (checking, NOW accounts, share draft accounts, and savings accounts with automatic transfer) of 3% of the first $29.8 million and 12% on anything above that amount. Reserves on time deposits with original maturities of less than $1\frac{1}{2}$ years, owned by corporations (NONPERSONAL TIME DEPOSITS) are subject to a 3% reserve requirement, and time deposits with original maturities of $1\frac{1}{2}$ years are subject to a zero percent reserve requirement. Reserves are maintained in the form of vault cash or a noninterest bearing balance at a Federal Reserve Bank or at a correspondent bank. Reserves on NONMEMBER BANKS were to be phased in over an eight-year period ending in 1988. See also RESERVE REQUIREMENTS; TOTAL RESERVES.

Regulation E Federal Reserve regulation that sets rules, liabilities, and procedures for electronic funds transfers (EFT), and establishes consumer protections using EFT systems. This regulation prescribes rules for solicitation and issuance of EFT debit cards, governs consumer liability for unauthorized transfers, and requires financial institutions to disclose annually the terms and conditions of EFT services. For example, the regulation sets up an error resolution procedure for errors on EFT related accounts. See also ERROR RESOLUTION; PROVISIONAL CREDIT.

Regulation F Federal Reserve regulation requiring state chartered banks with 500 or more stockholders and at least $1 million in assets to file financial statements with the Federal Reserve Board of Governors. In general, these state chartered MEMBER BANKs must file registration statements, periodic financial statements, proxy statements, and various other disclosures of interest to investors. These regulations are substantially similar to those issued by the Securities and Exchange Commission. Information filed under Regulation F is available at the Board of Governors in Washington, D.C., or at the Federal Reserve Bank in the district where a bank is located.

Regulation G Federal Reserve regulation governing credit secured by margin securities extended or arranged by parties other than banks or broker/dealers. It requires lenders to register credit extensions of $200,000, secured by margin stock, or $500,000 in total credit, within 30 days after the end of a quarter. It is one of four regulations covering credit extensions to finance securities transactions. See also REGULATION T; REGULATION U; REGULATION X.

Regulation H Federal Reserve regulation defining membership requirements for state chartered banks that become members of the Federal Reserve System. The regulation sets forth the procedures for state chartered banks to become members of the Federal Reserve System, as well as privileges and requirements for membership. The regulation also requires state chartered banks acting as securities transfer agents to register with the board.

Regulation I Federal Reserve regulation requiring each MEMBER BANK joining the Federal Reserve System to purchase stock in its Federal Reserve Bank equal to 6% of its capital and surplus. Reserve bank stock, which pays interest semiannually, is nontransferable and cannot be used as collateral. When a bank increases or decreases its capital base, it must adjust its ownership of Federal Reserve stock accordingly.

Regulation J Federal Reserve regulation providing the legal framework for collection of checks and other cash items, and net settlement of balances through the Federal Reserve System. It specifies terms and conditions under which reserve banks will receive checks for COLLECTION from depository institutions, and PRESENTMENT to paying banks, and return of unpaid items. The regulation is supplemented by operating circulars issued by Federal Reserve banks.

Regulation K Federal Reserve regulation governing international banking operations by bank holding companies and foreign banks in the United States. The regulation permits Edge Act corporations to engage in a range of international banking and financial activities. It also permits U.S. banks to own up to 100% of nonfinancial companies located outside the United States. The regulation also imposes reserve requirements on Edge Act corporations, as specified in Regulation D, and limits interstate activities of foreign banks in the United States.

Regulation L Federal Reserve regulation prohibiting interlocking director arrangements in MEMBER BANKs or bank holding companies. A management official of a state member bank or bank holding company may not act simultaneously as a management official of another depository institution if both are not affiliated, are very large banks, or are located in the same local area. The regulation provides a ten-year grandfather period for certain interlocks, and allows some on an exception basis, such as organizations owned by women or minority groups, and newly chartered organizations, and in situations where implementing the regulation would endanger safety and soundness.

Regulation M Federal Reserve regulation implementing the consumer leasing provisions of the Truth in Lending Act, and covers leases on personal property for more than four months for family, personal, or household use. It requires leasing companies to disclose in writing the cost of a lease, including security deposit and monthly payments, taxes and other payments, and in the case of an open-end lease, whether a BALLOON PAY-

MENT may be applied. It also requires written disclosure of the terms of a lease, including insurance, guarantees, responsibility for servicing the property, and whether the lessor has an option to buy the property at lease termination.

Regulation N Federal Reserve regulation governing transactions among Federal Reserve Banks, and transactions involving the Federal Reserve Banks and foreign banks and governments.

This regulation gives the board responsibility for approving in advance negotiations or agreements by Reserve Banks and foreign banks, bankers, and governments. A Reserve Bank may, under the direction of the Federal Open Market Committee, undertake negotiations, agreements, or facilitate open market transactions. Reserve banks must report quarterly to the Board of Governors on accounts they maintain with foreign banks.

Regulation O Federal Reserve regulation limiting the amount of credit member banks may extend to their own executive officers. Regulation O also implements the reporting requirements of the Financial Institutions Regulatory and Interest Rate Control Act of 1978 and the Garn-St. Germain Depository Institutions Act of 1982. Each federally insured bank is required to include in its quarterly statement of income and condition the total amount of credit extensions to executive officers and principal shareholders, and the number of such individuals who have received loans equaling 5% of the bank's equity capital or $500,000, whichever is less.

Regulation P Federal Reserve regulation that sets minimum standards for security devices, such as bank vaults, and currency handling equipment, including automated teller machines. A member bank must appoint a security officer to develop and administer a program to deter robberies, thefts, and larcenies, and file an annual compliance statement with its reserve bank.

Regulation Q Federal Reserve regulation prohibiting payment of interest on checking (demand deposit) accounts, and requires depository institutions to clearly state the terms for depositing and renewing time deposits and certificates of deposit, and also any penalties for early withdrawal of savings accounts. Deposit interest rate ceilings under Regulation Q were abolished as of March 31, 1986. Regulation Q does not prevent the paying of interest on NEGOTIABLE ORDER OF WITHDRAWAL (NOW) ACCOUNTS, which are orders to pay, rather than demand instruments, i.e., checks. A bank has discretion on whether to honor NOW drafts.

Regulation R Federal Reserve regulation prohibiting individuals who are engaged in securities underwriting, sale, and distribution from serving as a director, officer, or employee of a member bank. The regulation specifically exempts those involved in government securities trading, including Treasury securities, the International Bank for Reconstruction and Redevelopment, the Tennessee Valley Authority, and general obligations of states and municipalities.

Regulation S Federal Reserve regulation implementing the section of the Right to Financial Privacy Act of 1978 requiring government authorities to pay reasonable fees to financial institutions for financial records of individuals and small partnerships available to federal agencies, in connection with government loan programs or Internal Revenue Service summons.

Regulation T Federal Reserve regulation governing credit extensions by securities brokers and dealers, including all members of national securities exchanges. Broker-dealers may not extend credit to their customers unless such loans are secured by margin securities—securities listed and traded on a national securities exchange, mutual funds, over-the-counter stock designated by the SEC as eligible for trading in the national market system. Generally, a broker-dealer may not extend credit on margin securities in excess of the percentage of current market value permitted by the board.

Regulation U Federal Reserve regulation governing extensions of credit by banks for purchasing and carrying margin securities. Whenever a lender makes a loan secured by margin securities, the bank must have the customer execute a PURPOSE STATEMENT regardless of the use of the loan.

Regulation V Federal Reserve regulation dealing with financing of contractors, subcontractors and others involved in national defense work. The regulation spells out the authority granted to reserve banks under the Defense Production Act of 1950, to assist federal departments and agencies in making and administering loan guarantees to defense-related contractors, and sets maximum interest rates, guaranty fees, and commitment fees.

Regulation W Federal Reserve regulation setting minimum down payments, maximum maturities, and other terms applicable to consumer credit, authorized by executive order during World War II and Congressional legislation in 1947-48. With the repeal of authorizing legislation in 1952, Regulation W was revoked.

Regulation X Federal Reserve regulation extending the provisions of other securities related regulations—Regulation G, T, and U—to foreign persons or organizations who obtain credit outside the United States for the purchase of U.S. Treasury securities.

Regulation Y Federal Reserve regulation governing banking and nonbanking activities of bank holding companies and to the divestiture of impermissible nonbank activities. The regulation spells out the procedures for forming a bank holding company and procedures to be followed by bank holding companies acquiring voting shares in bank or nonbank companies. The regulation also lists those nonbank activities that are deemed closely related to banking and therefore permissible for bank holding companies.

Regulation Z Federal Reserve regulation implementing the consumer credit protections in the Truth in Lending Act of 1968. The major areas of the regulation require lenders to:

—give borrowers written disclosure on essential credit terms including the cost of credit expressed as a finance charge and an annual percentage rate.

—respond to consumer complaints of billing errors on certain credit accounts within a specified period.

—identify credit transactions on periodic statements of open-end credit accounts.

—provide certain rights regarding credit cards.

—inform customers of the RIGHT OF RESCISSION in certain mortgage-related loans within a specified period.

—comply with special requirements when advertising credit.

Regulation AA Federal Reserve regulation establishing procedures for handling consumer complaints about alleged unfair or deceptive practices by a state member bank. Complaints should be submitted in writing to the Director of the Division and Community Affairs at the Board of Governors in Washington, D.C.

Regulation BB Federal Reserve regulation implementing the COMMUNITY REINVESTMENT ACT. Banks are required to make available to the public a statement indicating communities served, the type of credit the lender is prepared to extend, and public comments to its CRA statement.

Regulation CC Federal Reserve Regulation implementing the EXPEDITED FUNDS AVAILABILITY ACT of 1987, setting endorsement standards on checks collected by depository financial institutions. The endorsement standard is designed to facilitate the identification of the endorsing bank and prompt return of unpaid checks. The regulation specifies funds availability schedules that banks must comply with, starting September 1988, and procedures for returning dishonored checks (also known as BAD CHECKS).

regulatory accounting principles (RAP) accounting rules and procedures authorized in the 1980s by the Federal Home Loan Bank Board to assist savings and loan associations with low NET WORTH in meeting regulatory capital requirements. RAP accounting differs from GENERALLY ACCEPTED ACCOUNTING PRINCIPLES (GAAP) in several key areas. Under RAP accounting, a savings institution can: (1) write off GOODWILL over a longer period; (2) amortize gains (or losses) from sale of assets over the remaining time to maturity; (3) include the unrealized gains from appreciation in real estate holdings as part of its net worth; (4) increase its regulatory net worth by selling special capital certificates to the Bank Board under the board's NET WORTH CERTIFICATE program, authorized by the Garn-St Germain Depository Institutions Act; and (5) include mutual capital certificates and subordinated debt as part of its net worth.

RAP accounting allows savings institutions to accelerate the recognition of income from sale of discounted mortgages as they revert towards par, and to defer loss write-offs over a longer period, for example, 30 years. For example, an S&L selling 30-

year fixed rate mortgage loans earning 8% in a market where rates on new loans are 12%, is permitted under RAP to write off the difference, representing an interest loss of 4% a year, over the remaining life of the mortgages. This differs from GAAP, which says that gains or losses from ASSET SALES must be recorded at the time of the transaction. The FINANCIAL INSTITUTIONS REFORM, RECOVERY AND ENFORCEMENT ACT OF 1989 excludes goodwill from an S&L's capital base after 1995. Supervisory goodwill, the premium paid by the acquirer of a troubled S&L, may count as core capital until 1992.

reinvestment risk uncertainty about investment opportunity rates that may prevail at some future date. In lending, it is the risk that a bank will be unable to reinvest interest-earning assets at current market rates. An asset with an interest coupon carried at an above market rate may not easily be reinvested at a comparable rate at maturity, or when the borrower repays it early. When interest rates decline, borrowers tend to repay loans early or refinance at lower rates.

rejection see CREDIT DENIAL.

reject items checks, drafts, or electronic payments that cannot be processed when presented for payment. There are various causes of reject items: an unreadable MICR line on a damaged check; misencoding of the dollar amount or account number; an incorrect routing/transit number; a stale-dated or post-dated check; insufficient funds (NOT SUFFICIENT FUNDS) in an account being debited; or the absence of an account at the receiving institution. Right items require special handling. See also PRENOTIFICATION; PROOF AND TRANSIT.

relationship banking concept in financial services marketing whereby an account officer or CUSTOMER SERVICE REPRESENTATIVE tries to meet all of a consumer's needs, or to the extent permitted by regulation. Relationship banking is an attempt to advance the sales culture in bank marketing beyond order taking to a more pro-active form of direct selling. Instead of selling financial services one at a time, an account officer attempts to gain an understanding of the consumer's needs and offer services that fulfill those needs. Commercial banks and other financial institutions have attempted to apply the concept of relationship banking through PERSONAL BANKER and PRIVATE BANKING programs. See also PLATFORM AUTOMATION.

release written notification discharging a claim by a creditor. A release of lien discharges secured property from a lien, indicating that the borrower has paid off the loan or substituted other collateral. A release clause in a mortgage or deed of trust stipulates that the property may be released from a mortgage lien if the buyer pays off the mortgage, or certain other conditions are met. A release of mortgage is recorded in public land records. See also SATISFACTION OF MORTGAGE.

remainderman person who has a FUTURE INTEREST in the estate created by a trust, either as a contingent interest when a life tenant surrenders a claim to the estate, or a vested interest that becomes effective at a specified future date.

REMIC see REAL ESTATE MORTGAGE INVESTMENT CONDUIT.

remittance
1. payment toward satisfaction of a debt, whether in cash or cash equivalents, such as checks, drafts, and other negotiable instruments.
2. payment on an installment loan or open-end credit account, forwarded through the mail to a LOCK BOX, along with a remittance document, a machine readable billing document encoded with the customer's account number, and the amount due, plus any late charges, if the loan payment is delinquent.
3. PROCEEDS from a check submitted to another bank for COLLECTION.

remittance letter see TRANSIT LETTER.

remote disbursement see DELAYED DISBURSEMENT.

remote service unit (RSU) freestanding AUTOMATED TELLER MACHINE in a supermarket or other location, where consumers can deposit or withdraw funds. The term originated in the 1970s when the Federal Home Loan Bank Board began approving applications from savings and loan associations to operate self-service ATMs away from branch offices.

renegotiated loan loan in which the original payment terms have been altered due to a deterioration in the borrower's financial condition. This usually involves extending the loan maturity or lowering the interest rate to avoid FORECLOSURE on collateral assigned by the borrower, or charging-off the loan as uncollectible. See also NONACCRUAL ASSET; TROUBLED DEBT RESTRUCTURING.

renegotiated rate mortgage see ROLLOVER MORTGAGE.

renewal substitution of a new PROMISSORY NOTE for a maturing one. If the old note is surrendered, it legally is considered a NOVATION. Renewal of a loan is accompanied by cancellation of a maturing note and making of a new one, which is then recorded on the bank's records. Renewal may also mean an extension of the maturity of an existing loan.

reorganization

1. restructuring of a corporation's financial assets under Chapter 11 of the Bankruptcy Code to return the company to profitability. The debtor corporation, known as the DEBTOR IN POSSESSION if no bankruptcy trustee is named, remains in operation and attempts to work out a plan for repayment of debts under supervision of the Bankruptcy Court. Creditors are prevented from seizing assets of the debtor to satisfy their claims, and must agree to a reorganization plan submitted by the debtor. If no acceptable plan can be worked out, the corporation's assets can then be liquidated, or sold off, to meet its unpaid obligations. Any corporation other than a bank or an insurance company, or a municipal government, may file a bankruptcy petition under Chapter 11. See also CRAMDOWN; CREDITORS' COMMITTEE; INVOLUNTARY BANKRUPTCY.

2. combination of two or more related business organizations, resulting in a new corporate structure, but leaving the business units intact. For example, two subsidiary banks of a bank holding company can merge into a single bank. The transaction is similar to a POOLING OF INTERESTS.

repatriation return of financial assets deposited in a foreign bank or foreign branch of a domestic bank to a home country. Repatriation of assets denominated in a foreign currency may be impeded by EXCHANGE CONTROLS limiting the ability of residents of another country to transfer assets.

reporting days days on which DEPOSITORY institutions report their deposit liabilities to a Federal Reserve Bank for the purpose of maintaining RESERVE REQUIREMENTS. Most banks and thrifts are required to adjust their RESERVE ACCOUNT balances the same week they report changes in net transaction accounts (checking, NOW accounts, and so on). This accounting procedure is known as CONTEMPORANEOUS RESERVES reporting, and has been in use since 1984. Time deposit accounts still are reported with a two-week lag (LAGGED RESERVES). Depository institutions with deposits under $15 million report quarterly, and those with reservable deposits of $2 million or less are exempt from any reserve requirements.

report of condition bank balance sheet, plus additional schedules detailing major balance sheet and off-balance sheet items, as of a specific date. Banks are required by regulation to file sworn statements of financial condition on the last day of each calendar quarter at the request (call) of a state or federal regulatory agency, hence the name CALL REPORT. The call report also includes the bank report of income and stockholder dividends. A copy of the call report filed by all federally insured banks also is forwarded to the FEDERAL DEPOSIT INSURANCE CORPORATION, which makes these reports available in magnetic tape format six months after each quarterly filing. Tapes can be ordered from the National Technical Information Service, Springfield, Virginia.

Bank call reports are one of the two primary forms of bank supervision by regulatory agencies, the other being on-site visits by bank examiners. Quarterly filing of the Report of Condition allows a regulator to monitor the financial condition of banks with a higher than normal percentage of nonperforming assets, and schedule more frequent examinations if necessary. All three federal banking agencies, the Federal Reserve Board, the Comptroller of the Currency, and the FDIC, have uniform reporting guidelines, complied by the FEDERAL FINANCIAL INSTITUTIONS EXAMINATION COUNCIL, for filling out call reports. Smaller banks and bank holding companies under $150 million in assets are required to file less detailed reports than regional banks and money center banks. Full name: Reports of Condition and Income.

repossession seizure of collateral securing a loan in default. Repossession occurs most often when other attempts to persuade the borrower to make payments that are past due fail to cure the loan delinquency. In most jurisdictions, repossession of collateral in which a lender has a security interest is done by obtaining a deficiency judgment or court order authorizing the lien holder to reclaim the property.

repricing opportunities
1. days when bank loans or deposits are subject to a change in interest rate. Interest rates in variable rate consumer loans and adjustable rate mortgages may reprice at scheduled intervals, for example, semiannually or annually, based on changes in an INDEX rate. Other loan and deposit rates can change more frequently, sometimes even daily. A bank with more one-year deposit liabilities changing rates than one-year assets is said to be liability sensitive; if more one-year assets reprice than liabilities, it is asset-sensitive.
2. maturity date of a certificate of deposit or other time deposit that can be renewed (rolled over) at a different rate.

repudiation intentional refusal to pay an obligation, usually the act of a government or a government agency. Repudiation differs from DEFAULT or MORATORIUM.

repurchase agreement contract to sell and subsequently repurchase securities at a specified date and price. Also known as a *repo*, *RP*, or *buyback agreement*. The Federal Reserve's Open Market Desk engages in repurchase agreements when it buys government securities from dealers, who agree to repurchase them by a specified date and at a specified price. Buying Treasury securities on a temporary basis adds reserves to the banking system, raising the level of NONBORROWED RESERVES. Repurchase agreements involving the Fed have maturities of 15 days or less, most often 7 days or less, and are frequently overnight transactions. The dealers usually have the option to terminate the agreements before maturity. The Fed also accepts repurchase agreements from foreign banks wishing to invest dollars overnight. Financial institutions also engage in repurchase agreements to maximize earnings on Treasury securities on a short-term basis. See also MATCHED SALE REPURCHASE AGREEMENT; OVERNIGHT REPURCHASE AGREEMENT; RETAIL REPURCHASE AGREEMENT.

required balance see COMPENSATING BALANCE.

rescheduling process of negotiating new loans to replace existing obligations, either by lengthening maturities, deferring of loan principal payments, or reducing interest rates, where the alternative is DEFAULT by the borrower and seizure of collateral by the lender. In commercial lending, rescheduling can take the form of a TROUBLED DEBT RESTRUCTURING, in which the lender offers the borrower a concession, such as a lower rate of interest, that it would not consider ordinarily.

   In loans to less developed (LDC) countries, debt rescheduling is often carried out jointly with financial aid agreements, such as multi-year STRUCTURAL ADJUSTMENTS supervised by the International Monetary Fund, which are intended to encourage internal economic reforms and increased private sector participation in the economy of the debtor nation. See also BUYBACK; DEBT FOR BOND SWAP; DEBT FOR EQUITY SWAP.

rescind see RIGHT OF RESCISSION.

reservable deposits transaction accounts, savings accounts, and nonpersonal time deposits subject to RESERVE REQUIREMENTS under Federal Reserve Board REGULATION D.

reserve funds set aside in anticipation of future payments or obligations.
   1. **Accounting.** A valuation reserve from retained earnings to cover anticipated future payments. Also called an ALLOWANCE.
   2. **Banking.** There are two basic types of reserves, PRIMARY RESERVES, including cash needed to operate a bank, and cash and deposits at a Federal Reserve Bank to meet the required RESERVE RATIO, and secondary reserves. Required reserves are listed in the balance sheet under the asset category "cash and due from other banks." Secondary reserves are funds that

can be kept in liquid investments, Treasury or municipal bonds, and can be sold readily if necessary. There is, however, no category labeled secondary reserves on the balance sheet of a bank. See also LOAN LOSS RESERVES.

3. **Mortgage Banking.** A fund established by a bond issuer that may be used by the trustee of a series of mortgage backed bonds to make principal and interest payments, or to pay administrative expenses. Also known as a debt service fund.

reserve account noninterest earning balance that DEPOSITORY financial institutions maintain with a Federal Reserve Bank or with a CORRESPONDENT bank to satisfy the Fed's RESERVE REQUIREMENTS on transaction accounts. Aside from their value to the Fed when it implements its MONETARY POLICY objectives, reserve account balances play a central role in the exchange of funds between depository institutions. Large dollar-value payments between financial institutions are processed through the Federal Reserve Communication System, also known as FEDERAL WIRE or Fed Wire, which routinely handles a daily volume exceeding $500 billion. These interbank transfers are made from reserve accounts. Banks with excess balances in a reserve account—balances greater than the required ratio of reserves to transaction account deposits—routinely sell these excess balances, known as FEDERAL FUNDS or Fed Funds, in the short-term MONEY MARKET to get a higher yield on temporarily idle balances. Fed Funds usually are sold on an overnight basis and are due back at the start of business the next day. Banks that have Fed Funds to sell generally are community banks with relatively low loan growth; buyers of Fed Funds typically are large regional or money center banks whose demand for short-term capital often exceeds their deposit liabilities. See also BORROWED RESERVES; CONTEMPORANEOUS RESERVES; EXCESS RESERVES; RESERVE RATIO; TOTAL RESERVES.

reserve account computation see REPORTING DAYS.

reserve city bank bank located in a city with a Federal Reserve Bank or branch office. Also, any commercial bank with demand deposits of $400 million or more. These banks generally maintain higher reserve account balances than banks located outside reserve bank cities, which are called country banks. The

Association of Reserve City Bankers represents the interests of Reserve City Banks regarding Federal Reserve regulation of the banking system.

reserve for loan loss see LOAN LOSS RESERVES.

reserve ratio ratio of RESERVE ACCOUNT balances to total deposits subject to RESERVE REQUIREMENTS. With the exception of very small institutions (those with reservable deposits of $2.4 million or less) all banks, thrifts, and credit unions are required to maintain reserve balances equal to 3% of nonpersonal time deposits and Eurocurrency deposits—and 12% on any balances above that. Time deposits with original maturities of 1½ years or more are exempt from reserves. Nonmember depository institutions (state banks and savings institutions) can maintain a pass-through account at a MEMBER BANK acting as a CORRESPONDENT for the reporting bank.

reserve requirements balances that DEPOSITORY financial institutions must maintain at a Federal Reserve Bank, in cash, or at a CORRESPONDENT bank. Reserves do not earn interest and may be in vault cash or checking account at a Federal Reserve bank. A commercial bank that is a MEMBER of the Federal Reserve System must place its reserves directly with the nearest Fed bank. Nonmember banks have the option of holding reserves with the nearest Fed bank or in a PASS-THROUGH ACCOUNT with a correspondent. The Federal Reserve Board's REGULATION D sets the required RESERVE RATIO reserves to transaction account deposits (checking accounts and other checkable deposits, such as Negotiable Order of Withdrawal or NOW accounts, credit union share draft accounts, and savings accounts allowing automatic transfers). In addition, the Fed has the right to impose special supplemental reserves of up to 4%, after first consulting with other regulatory agencies, in situations where the Fed believes it necessary to increase reserves to carry out monetary policy. The Board of Governors may also, after consulting with Congress, impose a reserve of any ratio on any bank liability in periods of extraordinary circumstances for up to 180 days. See also BORROWED RESERVES; EXCESS RESERVES; FRACTIONAL RESERVES; NONBORROWED RESERVES; TOTAL RESERVES.

residential mortgage mortgage collateralized by a one-
to four-family dwelling, and ordinarily owner-occupied. The
typical mortgage loan is a CONVENTIONAL MORTGAGE loan by a
bank or thrift institution.

residual cash flows resulting from the difference between the
income stream generated by a POOL of mortgages and the cash
flow necessary to fund a series of COLLATERALIZED MORTGAGE
OBLIGATION bonds. Also known as equity. These excess amounts
accrue to the CMO issuer, or to a CMO trustee if it has been
sold.

residual value anticipated value or fair market value of an
asset at the expiration of a lease. Fair market value is determined
by agreement, or by APPRAISAL. In an OPEN-END LEASE, a consumer lease often used in auto financing, the lessee has the option of buying the car at its assumed residual value. Under Federal Reserve REGULATION Y, bank holding companies are
permitted to assume residual values not greater than 25% of an
asset's acquisition cost.

Resolution Funding Corporation government-
sponsored corporation established by the Financial Institutions
Reform, Recovery and Enforcement Act of 1989 to raise funds
for use in liquidating insolvent savings and loan associations.
The Resolution Funding Corp., also called Refcorp., is authorized to borrow $30 billion by issuing long-term 30-year zero-
coupon securities. Principal value of securities offered for sale is
to be paid by $1.2 billion from the S&L industry. Interest on
RFC bonds will be paid by the RTC, the savings industry, and
from U.S. Treasury funds. The FIRREA also authorized an additional $20 billion in direct Treasury borrowings, to be used in
liquidating insolvent S&Ls.

Resolution Trust Corporation (RTC) government-
sponsored corporation established by the Financial Institutions
Reform, Recovery and Enforcement Act of 1989 to transfer assets of insolvent savings and loan associations to financially
sound institutions, and to liquidate troubled real estate and other
assets. The RTC, to be managed by the Federal Deposit Insurance Corporation, has responsibility for managing the assets and
liabilities of savings institutions that become insolvent between

1989 and August 1992. The RTC will derive its funding from the Federal Home Loan Banks and the Resolution Funding Corporation; it also has a $5 billion line of credit with the U.S. Treasury Department. The agency's authorization as a receiver of insolvent savings associations is to expire in 1996. Afterward, its assets are to be transferred to the SAVINGS ASSOCIATION INSURANCE FUND.

respondent bank that regularly buys check processing and other services from a CORRESPONDENT bank. Also known as a downstream bank. Purchased services can include securities clearing and trading, check processing, and foreign exchange trading. A respondent bank, which usually is a community bank, may also maintain its RESERVE ACCOUNT in a PASS-THROUGH ACCOUNT at a correspondent, or sell a participations in loans exceeding its legal lending limit, or buy participations in loans originated by other banks.

response time elapsed time in seconds in response to a terminal inquiry to approve or disapprove an authorization request. Promptness in responses is critical in ON-LINE consumer-oriented banking services, such as electronic point-of-sale, and electronic banking systems.

restricted asset account or other balance with limited right of access or withdrawal. For example, a BLOCKED ACCOUNT.

restricted card list See WARNING BULLETIN.

restricted market exchange rate heavily controlled by government action, but influenced to some extent by free market interaction. A currency that is pegged to another currency's rate of exchange; for example, the Luxembourg franc is pegged to the Belgian franc. A restricted market is less controlled than a BLOCKED CURRENCY market, and much less than a free market (CLEAN FLOAT) exchange rate.

restrictive covenant see COVENANT.

restructured loan see RENEGOTIATED LOAN.

retail banking banking services offered to the general public. Retail banking services are a group of financial services that includes installment loans, residential mortgages, equity credit loans, deposit services, and individual retirement accounts. In contrast with WHOLESALE BANKING or corporate banking, retail banking is a high volume business with many service providers competing for market share. Some retail banking services, for example, credit cards, are among the most profitable services offered by financial institutions. Many nonfinancial corporations have established retail banking subsidiaries through acquisition of a NONBANK BANK or through marketing bank-like services such as ASSET MANAGEMENT ACCOUNTS to their own clients. See also CONSUMER CREDIT; FINANCIAL SUPERMARKET INSTALLMENT CREDIT.

retail repurchase agreement type of REPURCHASE AGREEMENT marketed by financial institutions to their retail customers. Retail repurchase agreements were popular in the period prior to the abolition of REGULATION Q. A financial institution would purchase funds from retail depositors, and buy back the funds after a specified period. The transactions were collateralized by the institution's portfolio of government securities. The borrower's only risk was that retail repos are investments, not deposits, and are not covered by federal deposit insurance.

retained earnings undistributed earnings that have not been paid to stockholders or transferred to a surplus account. Retained earnings are part of a bank's net worth, or capital and surplus. In a bank, there is little, if any, distinction between capital and surplus, because all amounts contributed by common stockholders over the nominal value of their equity goes into the surplus account. See also PAID-IN CAPITAL.

return items checks, drafts, or notes returned unpaid to the originating bank because they may result in a loss if honored. They are returned by the drawee bank so that the originator can correct any errors or irregularities and then present the items a second time for collection.

return on assets (ROA) net income divided by total assets. Return on assets is a KEY RATIO of profitability, indicating how efficiently a financial institution's assets are employed.

return on equity (ROE) net income divided by total equity; it is a profitability ratio measuring how well equity capital is invested.

revaluation adjustment in the value of a country's currency relative to currencies of other nations. SPECIAL DRAWING RIGHTS, resulting in a higher exchange rate in relation to others' currencies. In a revaluation, a country's central bank raises the official exchange rate of its national currency in relation to other currencies. This ordinarily is done by a country with a substantial BALANCE OF PAYMENTS surplus. The opposite is DEVALUATION.

revenue anticipation note (RAN) short-term debt security issued by a municipality to finance operations, repayable from anticipated future revenues, such as sales tax. These notes are usually a general obligation of the issuing government, and interest income is tax-exempt to the holder. See also TAX ANTICIPATION NOTE.

revenue bond MUNICIPAL BOND or state bond issue paying principal and interest from the revenues of an income generating project, such as a toll bridge, highway, hospital, or other public facility that is built with the proceeds of the financing. Income generated by the facility goes first toward meeting debt service on the bonds, i.e., paying interest to bondholders and retiring the bonds at maturity. Unlike general obligation bonds, revenue bonds are not backed by the FULL FAITH AND CREDIT, or taxing authority, of the bond issuer. As a rule, revenue bonds are considered tax exempt to bondholders in the issuing state. Commercial banks, under the Banking Act of 1933 (the Glass-Steagall Act) are authorized to underwrite, and trade in limited amounts of revenue bonds through separate securities affiliates, as authorized by the Federal Reserve Board. See also SECURITIES AFFILIATES.

reverse floater see INVERSE FLOATER.

reverse mortgage MORTGAGE in which the borrower receives periodic payments from the lender, based on the accumulated equity in the underlying property. A reverse mortgage provides retirement income to older borrowers whose mortgages are paid in full, or who have substantial equity. There are several types of reverse mortgages, although these are not widely available due to special problems in underwriting these loans and uncertainty about how the loans will be repaid. The ultimate source of repayment is the borrower's estate. Reverse mortgages may be structured as rising debt loans with periodic advances to the borrower, or disbursed in a lump sum payment. If the mortgage loan is structured as a life annuity, it commonly is referred to as a *reverse annuity mortgage* or RAM. In a RAM, the borrower purchases a single premium annuity and receives a monthly distribution; the mortgage lender takes title to the mortgaged property at the death of the mortgagor.

A second type of reverse mortgage is the life estate transaction in which the home owner sells a house but is granted a life estate and receives immediate cash. A third variation is the SALE AND LEASEBACK transaction. These loans pose some problems for lenders as there is no standard method for underwriting the loans or distributing the loan proceeds. Also, loan collection may pose problems because it still is unclear how a lender will be able to collect full payment at maturity. Foreclosure actions may create unwanted and negative publicity for lenders. See also ALTERNATIVE MORTGAGE INSTRUMENT; HOME EQUITY CREDIT.

reverse repurchase agreement securities transaction involving a purchase of securities by a dealer, with an agreement to resell the securities back at an agreed price at a later date. The borrowing is collateralized by a pledge of securities. Reverse repurchase agreements are often used by the Federal Open Market Committee, in carrying out Federal Reserve monetary policy, and are known as MATCHED SALE REPURCHASE AGREEMENTs. When the Fed wants to drain credit from the banking system (an action normally undertaken to control inflation in the economy), it sells Treasury securities out of its portfolio to dealers and to banks, with the stated agreement to buy back the securities sold at a higher price on a specified date. The difference between the selling price and the repurchase price is the dealer's yield or profit in the transaction.

Reverse repurchase agreements also are used by securities dealers to finance their inventory by buying securities, for example, Ginnie Mae mortgage backed pass-through securities, from a bank or savings institution, and agreeing to re-sell the securities at an agreed-upon price at a later date. In effect, the financial institution is borrowing from the dealer, and can make money on the transaction if cash from the sale can be re-invested in instruments earning a higher rate of interest for the term of the repurchase agreement. Contrast with DOLLAR ROLL.

reverse swap transaction on the secondary swap market. A reverse swap offsets the interest rate or currency exposure on an existing swap. It can be written with the original counterparty or with a new counterparty. Either way, it typically is executed to realize capital gains.

revocable letter of credit see LETTER OF CREDIT.

revocable trust agreement providing transfer of property to heirs that may be altered or revoked any time during the life of the grantor. Estate taxes are paid at the death of the grantor, but the estate does not have to go through probate. Beneficiaries may have the unrestricted use of the property while the trust agreement is in effect. Contrast with IRREVOCABLE TRUST.

revolver cardholder in a bank credit card plan that pays down principal on outstanding balances, and interest, over several months. The opposite is a NONREVOLVER.

revolving credit

1. LINE OF CREDIT extended to a business; a credit facility that is good for a stated period of time, but does not have a fixed repayment schedule. The borrower may draw down the line at any time, or repay it in full without penalty. The borrower usually pays a COMMITMENT FEE that secures the line of credit when the application is taken by the lender. Contrast with EVERGREEN LOAN.

2. CREDIT CARD, checking account CASH RESERVE, or other consumer credit arrangement that gives consumers the option of borrowing against a pre-approved line of credit. There is no charge when the account is not used. When used, the borrower pays a finance charge on outstanding balances, as stated in the credit agreement or credit contract. A finance charge of 1.5% per month, for example, is equal to an ANNUAL PERCENTAGE RATE of 18%. A monthly rate of 1.65% equals 19.8% APR. In credit card plans, there are several methods of computing finance charges. The most common is the average daily balance method, in which the interest rate is

calculated on the daily average of the previous month. Another is the previous balance method. Revolving check credit plans are written like checks, but draw funds from a bank card account. Check credit and checking account cash reserve advances begin accruing interest payable from the date of the transaction (unlike credit cards, where billing on new charges ordinarily is deferred during a GRACE PERIOD of 15 to 25 days) and are payable in the next billing cycle. See also REGULATION Z.

revolving underwriting facility (RUF) medium-term Euronote facility, usually between three and seven years maturity, that guarantees the overseas sale of short-term promissory notes (the Euronotes) issued by the borrower at or below a predetermined interest rate. The revolving credit portion of an RUF is usually done through a single bank, known as the arranger. Typically, the arranger commits itself to a very small share of the total financing (less than 10%) and acts as placement agent for marketing the Euronotes. The Euronotes generally have maturities of one to six months, and are sold through a TENDER PANEL of commercial banks and investment banks. The revolving credit banks agree to purchase any unsold notes at a given Eurodollar spread over LIBOR. The borrower pays interest only on amounts actually drawn. See also EUROCOMMERCIAL PAPER; STANDBY NOTE ISSUANCE FACILITY.

rial national currency of Iran, Oman, and Yemen.

riel national currency of Cambodia.

right of foreclosure lender's right to take over mortgaged property, and cancel the mortgagor's interest if the mortgagor fails to meet terms of the mortgage note, such as timely payments of principal and interest.

right of redemption right of a mortgagor to recover mortgaged property from a judicial sale or foreclosure by paying the lender the outstanding principal and interest due, plus the lender's costs in foreclosure. Also, the right of a debtor in bankruptcy to redeem personal property by paying creditors the fair market value of assets securing their lien.

right of rescission option given a borrower in a loan secured by real estate to cancel the loan contract after a three-day cooling-off period. Rescission delays the actual funding commitment for a home equity loan or other real estate secured loan for that three-day period. In open-end equity secured loans, the right of rescission is applied once, at the outset of the loan, under the current interpretation of the TRUTH IN LENDING ACT. See also REGULATION Z.

right of survivorship right of a surviving married spouse to claim co-owned property, when assets are owned in a joint tenants relationship.

rights offering offer by a corporation to sell a new offering of securities, normally common stock to its shareholders, proportionate to their holdings. Usually an offer to sell newly issued shares or additional shares, at a lower price than the publicly offered price. The offer expires after a certain date if not exercised. The issuer is often required by statute to limit the dilution of stockholder value when new shares are offered for sale.

risk uncertainty that an asset will earn an expected rate of return, or that a loss may occur. Because banks invest much of their funds in interest sensitive assets, primarily loans, there are several categories of risk, including:

capital risk—risk that a deterioration in asset quality from loan losses will impair a bank's capital, requiring sale of new stock to meet regulatory capital requirements;

credit risk—the possibility that the borrower will be unable to make regular payments of principal and interest, and may default;

delivery risk—the possibility that the buyer or seller of an instrument or foreign exchange may be unable to meet obligations at maturity;

exchange risk—the possibility of a loss on an uncovered position resulting from an appreciation or depreciation of a foreign currency;

INTEREST RATE RISK—risk that an interest earning asset (for example, a bank loan) will decline in value as market interest rates change;

LIQUIDITY RISK—risk that a bank will have insufficient cash or short-term marketable assets to meet needs of depositors and borrowers;

operations risk—the possibility that a data processing failure from fire, other natural disaster, or from other causes (for example, a computer hacker gaining access to bank records) will impede or prevent a bank from maintaining normal service;

political risk—the possibility that political instability in a debtor nation will make it difficult for that country to make regular payments on a loan. Also known as SOVEREIGN RISK; and

payments system risk—the possibility that the failure of a major bank, or its inability to honor payment commitments in a wire transfer network will have a domino effect on other banks, causing similar failures elsewhere. Also known as SYSTEMIC RISK.

See also BASIS RISK; COUNTRY RISK; REFINANCE RISK; REINVESTMENT RISK.

risk assets

1. **Banking.** Bank assets subject to change in value, due to changes in market conditions or changes in credit quality at various REPRICING OPPORTUNITIES. Examples are maturing bank CDs and bank lines of credit with a FLOATING INTEREST RATE.
2. **Finance.** Equity capital, especially capital in troubled companies that may become subordinated to claims of bondholders.

risk-based capital
capital regulations adopted by the Federal Reserve Board, the Comptroller of the Currency, and the Federal Deposit Insurance Corporation for bank holding companies and state chartered banks that are member banks in the Federal Reserve System. The OFFICE OF THRIFT SUPERVISION sets risk-weighted capital rules for savings and loan associations. The aim of risk-based capital, to be fully phased in by January 1, 1993, is to: (1) encourage banks to keep a sufficient cushion of equity capital, including common stock, to support balance sheet assets; (2) include off-balance sheet items in the computation of capital adequacy; (3) eliminate disincentives to holding low-risk, liquid assets; and (4) set uniform international guidelines for bank capital adequacy in the GROUP OF TEN countries.

In the United States, the risk-based capital formula raises the mandatory capital from 5.5% of assets to 8%, 4% of which must be in Tier 1 capital (common stock plus noncumulative preferred stock); and 4% in other types of qualifying capital, including loan loss reserves, perpetual preferred stock, hybrid capital instruments, such as MANDATORY CONVERTIBLE debentures, and subordinated debt.

The risk-based guidelines, approved by the Basle Committee on Banking Regulations and Supervisory Practices (the Basle Supervisors' Committee), are a fundamental change in calculation of bank capital from previous measures of calculating capital adequacy. It shifts capital determination from the liability side of the balance sheet to the asset side, using a formula that assigns specific risk weights to different groups of assets. A bank's risk-based capital ratio is computed by dividing its qualifying capital by its weighted risk assets. Assets given a 100% risk rating, such as commercial loans and consumer installment loans, require an institution to maintain total equity capital (Tier 1 and Tier 2 capital) equal to 8% of the asset's book value. So-called riskless assets, having a risk rating of zero (cash, U.S. government securities), require no capital held in reserve.

The risk weights for balance sheet assets are summarized as follows:

—0% risk weight: cash, gold bullion, loans guaranteed by the U.S. government, balances due from Federal Reserve Banks.

—20% risk weight: demand deposits, checks in the process of collection, risk participations in bankers' acceptances and letters of credit, and other short-term claims maturing in one year or less.

—50% risk weight: 1-4 family residential mortgages, whether owner occupied or rented; privately issued mortgage backed securities and municipal revenue bonds.

—100% risk weight: cross-border loans to non-U.S. borrowers, commercial loans, comsumer loans, derivative mortgage backed securities, industrial development bonds, stripped mortgage backed securities, joint ventures, intangibles (including grandfathered goodwill* plus interest rate contracts (forward rate agreements), and exchange rate contracts (currency swaps, cross currency swaps, and so on).

Bank holding companies with total assets under $150 million are exempted from compliance with the risk-based capital regulations. See also OFF-BALANCE SHEET LIABILITIES.

* GOODWILL acquired before March 12, 1988 is excluded from the computation of bank capital after December 31, 1992. Goodwill owned by S&Ls is excluded after January 1, 1995.

risk-based deposit insurance concept that relates deposit insurance premiums paid by DEPOSITORY institutions to the riskiness of their asset portfolios. Banks that engage in high-risk or speculative activities would, in theory, have to pay a higher insurance premium than institutions that follow prudent banking practices. Variable insurance premiums, in place of the flat rate insurance premiums, would also reduce the inequity in the current deposit insurance system that in effect subsidizes poorly performing banks. Implementation of risk based insurance poses problems, however, because it is difficult to require a capital impaired bank to pay higher insurance premiums than healthy banks. See also MARKET DISCIPLINE.

risk management
1. procedures to manage a bank's exposure to various types of risks associated with banking. This is done through a combination of internal policies, contractual arrangements with insurance companies for BANKER'S BLANKET BOND coverage, DIRECTORS & OFFICERS INSURANCE, and SELF-INSURANCE to reduce the costs from accidental loss.
2. corporate service sold by commercial banks. Risk management is a set of services, rather than a specific product, aimed at controlling financing risk, including credit risk, and interest rate risk, through hedging devices, financial futures, and interest rate caps. The aim is to control corporate funding costs, budget interest rate expense, and limit exposure to interest rate fluctuations.

risk participation sale by a bank of its participation in a contingent obligation of assets, for example, a bank's participation in a BANKER'S ACCEPTANCE or a STANDBY LETTER OF CREDIT. The originating bank remains liable to the beneficiary for the full amount of the transaction if the obligor fails to pay when payment is demanded. These are treated as off-balance sheet transactions in computing risk-weighted capital, and are not included in a bank's equity capital under the risk-based capital guidelines.

riyal national currency of Saudi Arabia.

Robert Morris Associates see TRADE ASSOCIATION.

rollover

1. time savings account or certificate of deposit that is renewed for another term at the prevailing interest rate.

   2. profit-sharing plan, 401(k) plan, individual retirement account, or other type of deferred income plan that is reinvested within the permitted 60-day period, according to Internal Revenue Service Rules, in which assets may be transferred without tax penalty from one form of investment to another.

3. EURODOLLAR term loan, which is periodically repriced at an agreed spread over a market index rate, usually LIBOR.

4. **Foreign Exchange.** The sale and purchase of currency for one business day. These transactions take various forms, depending on the trade dates and delivery dates involved. If the trade is made today for delivery tomorrow, the transaction is an overnight rollover, usually involving money market instruments, for example, a repurchase agreement. Other rollover transactions include a SPOT NEXT, a TOMORROW NEXT (TOM NEXT), and SWAP. See also SHORT DATE FORWARD.

5. **Banking.** To extend the maturity of, or to renew, a loan or obligation.

rollover mortgage

mortgage in which the finance charge periodically is adjusted. A renewable rate mortgage is a short-term loan that must be renewed periodically, say every three to five years, and the interest rate adjusted to reflect market rates at renewal. The best known example is the Canadian Rollover mortgage, where the loan is renegotiated at a new rate every five years. This is the predominant type of residential mortgage in Canada. Also known as a renegotiable rate mortgage. See also ALTERNATIVE MORTGAGE INSTRUMENTS.

roly poly certificate of deposit

multi-year CERTIFICATE OF DEPOSIT, consisting of a series of six-month CDs that are rolled over at successive maturity dates, hence the name roly poly. The purchaser of a roly poly CD, normally sold in minimum denominations of $5 million, is obligated to hold the instrument until maturity.

rounding

1. **Banking.** In consumer credit, the allowed tolerance in computing the ANNUAL PERCENTAGE RATE (APR) finance charge disclosed in loan agreements. Federal Reserve Regulation Z allows rate variations as much as 1/8 of 1% above, or below, the exact interest rate. For example, an annual percentage rate of 10.3333 may be stated as 10.33%, 10.3%, or 10.25%.

2. **Finance.** The practice of shortening publicly disclosed information by adjusting a figure upward or downward to the nearest whole number. The practice simplifies disclosures in annual reports, for example, when zeroes are omitted, and conveys the same information as the fully expressed data to the casual observer.

routing/transit number See ABA TRANSIT NUMBER; CHECK ROUTING SYMBOL.

rubber check slang term for BAD CHECK; a check drawn on an account with insufficient funds. Also known as a bounced check. A bank may pay the resulting OVERDRAFT if the customer has a satisfactory credit relationship with the bank or an overdraft line of credit. The customer may still be liable for overdraft charges to cover the bank's costs in processing the check.

ruble national currency of the Soviet Union.

Rule of 72 method commonly used to approximate the time required for a sum of money to double at a given rate of interest. The rule of 72 is computed by dividing the interest rate by 72. For example, a savings account earning 10% will double in less than $7\frac{1}{2}$ years ($72 \div 10 = 7.2$ years).

Rule of the 78's mathematical formula used in computing the interest rebated when a borrower pays off a loan before maturity. The Rule of 78's, also known as the Sum of the Digits, is applied mostly to consumer loans in which the finance charges were computed using the ADD-ON INTEREST or DISCOUNTED INTEREST method of interest calculation.

The formula for calculating rebates works as follows: add up the number of months for which payments are scheduled; in a 12-month installment loan, the total is 78. This number, divided by the number of payments to be made, equals the finance charge for that month. In the first month, the borrower has use of the whole amount borrowed, and the finance charge is 12/78 of the total interest; in the second month, it is 11/78, and so on. A $3,000 loan, paid in 15 equal installments of $225, has an interest payment of $28.13 in the first month, $26.25 in the second, and only $1.87 in the final month. Thus, under the add-on method, the finance charges in the early months are higher than later on, which means that paying off an installment loan early doesn't necessarily reduce the amount of interest the borrower would have paid. The TRUTH IN LENDING ACT, however, requires that lenders disclose how the finance charge will be computed if the debt is paid in full before maturity, so borrowers can weigh different financing alternatives before signing a loan agreement. See also SIMPLE INTEREST.

run

1. unexpectedly large series of withdrawals at a bank, resulting from depositor fears of the soundness of the institution. A so-called silent run is triggered not by a single event, for example, rumors of a bank failure, but by depositors withdrawing their money to earn a better rate elsewhere.
2. list of securities offered for sale to investors, or bank certificates of deposit sold to other institutions or investors in the SECONDARY MARKET for bank deposit liabilities. Also, a dealer's list of bid and asked quotes.

runoff

1. reduction of a loan portfolio as loans are paid off at scheduled maturity dates, or when borrowers prepay their loans. Loan portfolio runoffs accelerate when interest rates are declining, and borrowers refinance at lower rates.
2. early withdrawal of SAVINGS ACCOUNT or TIME DEPOSIT balances. When depositors take their funds out of depository institutions to put their money in direct investments, such as stocks, bonds, or mutual funds, the outflow of funds from banking institutions is known as DISINTERMEDIATION.

rupee national currency of India, the Maldives, Mauritius, Nepal, Pakistan, the Seychelles, and Sri Lanka.

rupiah national currency of Indonesia.

S

safe deposit box storage facility maintained in the vault area of a bank that is rented to customers for SAFEKEEPING of personal valuables. Access to a safe deposit box is controlled through dual keys, one kept by the customer and one by the bank, and signature cards. Date of entry is recorded on a signature card. If the safe deposit box is rented by a corporation, a separate corporate resolution must be obtained before access is granted. Safe deposit box contracts usually contain a disclaimer limiting the bank's liability to the bank's failure to provide adequate protection facilities. A bank ordinarily is not responsible for loss of personal valuables, and has no knowledge of the contents of a safe deposit box. See also DUAL CONTROL; SIGNATURE CARD.

safe harbor
1. Securities and Exchange Commission Rule 10b-18, known as the *safe harbor rule*, allowing companies to repurchase their own securities without fear of being charged with securities manipulation.
2. type of tax-oriented lease, called safe harbor leasing, permitted by the Economic Recovery Tax Act of 1981, giving the investor a tax position safe from challenge by the Internal Revenue Service. Companies were permitted to sell their tax benefits accruing from new asset purchases through sale-leaseback agreements with profitable companies seeking tax benefits from ACCELERATED DEPRECIATION and the INVESTMENT CREDIT. These tax benefits have since been eliminated by the Tax Equity and Fiscal Responsibility Act of 1982 and the Deficit Reduction Act of 1984.

safekeeping
1. agency account managed by a trustee for holding securities, such as stock certificates. A bank holds in its vaults stock certificates and other securities and returns them at the request of a holder. Safekeeping requires a bank to maintain an itemized record of property in its possession and to issue a

receipt for securities held. Distinguish from custody, in which a bank buys, sells, and receives securities when instructed. See also CUSTODY ACCOUNT.

2. SAFE DEPOSIT BOX where personal valuables are kept.

3. CHECK SAFEKEEPING. See also TRUNCATION.

safekeeping certificate document evidencing ownership of a security or certificate of deposit transferred to a new NOMINEE. The certificate is proof of ownership and also represents the holder's claim against the person holding the instrument. For example, an AMERICAN DEPOSITARY RECEIPT, representing ownership in registered or unregistered securities that are issued outside the United States and traded on a non-U.S. stock exchange; a certificate issued by a brokerage firm when a BROKERED DEPOSIT, normally a CD paying a market rate of interest, is placed by a broker with a bank or savings institution. See also INTERNATIONAL DEPOSITARY RECEIPT.

safety and soundness objective of financial industry regulation. Federal and state supervision of banking is designed to provide a financially stable industry that meets the public's credit and other financial needs, as well as to prevent RUNS or PANICS by providing depositors with assurances that their funds will be protected from loss. Federal deposit insurance, for example, protects depositors' accounts from loss in event of financial institution failure. Supervision is done through periodic site visits and examination of a bank's records, and also through filing of CALL REPORT data with an institution's PRIMARY REGULATOR.

salary reduction plan voluntary savings plan that automatically deducts a predetermined amount from a person's wages for investment in a savings plan on a tax deferred basis. Salary reduction plans are known by various names, such as 401(k) savings plans—the names come from a section of the tax code, defined benefit contribution plans. Funds set aside in a salary reduction plan may be invested in bank savings or money market account, mutual fund, guaranteed investment contract plans, tax free bonds, or other securities.

sale and leaseback sale of an asset, usually real estate, and agreement to lease it back from the purchaser on a long-term basis. In commercial finance, this type of financing arrangement strengthens the seller's balance sheet, because a capital asset is sold and converted into cash or a receivable.

It may, however, result in a forfeiting of depreciation and tax benefits. Typical sale-leaseback transactions may involve refinancing of a bank's headquarters building or other facilities. The sale is recorded as a onetime nonrecurring gain.

sale repurchase agreement see MATCHED SALE RE-PURCHASE AGREEMENT.

sales literature brochures, pamphlets, and other printed booklets containing information on rates, savings accounts, and other banking services, found near the teller counter in a bank or branch office. If the products described are listed securities, sales literature is provided for general disclosure only, and is not an offer to sell. A PROSPECTUS for mutual fund shares, on the other hand, discloses terms and conditions under which securities may be sold to the public, and redeemed, and is available on request in banks offering mutual funds.

Sallie Mae see STUDENT LOAN MARKETING ASSOCIATION.

same day funds funds that are available for transfer or withdrawal the same day as presented and collected, subject to net settlement of accounts between presenting and remitting banks, or sending and receiving banks. FEDERAL FUNDS transferred from one bank to another over the Federal Reserve Wire Network (Fed Wire) are same day funds, as are transfers through the CLEARING HOUSE INTERBANK PAYMENTS SYSTEM in New York. On the other hand, AUTOMATED CLEARING HOUSE transfers are available for withdrawal the following day and are known as next-day funds.

samurai bond yen-denominated bond issued in Japan by a foreign borrower. These bonds are unsecured obligations of the issuer and generally have minimum maturities of five years or longer. They are used primarily by corporate borrowers to raise capital in the yen market at reasonable cost. Samurai bonds were first issued in 1970 by the Asian Development Bank. Twenty-five percent of primary issue securities can be purchased by foreign investors; there are no secondary market restrictions. See also EUROBOND; YANKEE BOND.

satisfaction of mortgage document releasing a MORT-GAGE lien, indicating the borrower has paid the debt in full. Also known as a discharge of mortgage or mortgage release. The release of lien is also noted in public land records.

satisfactory loan in which payments are being made on time, loan covenants are met, the collateral is priced right (at fair market value), and the loan is performing "as agreed" in the original loan agreement.

savings account interest bearing DEPOSIT account without a stated maturity, as opposed to a TIME DEPOSIT. Funds can be deposited or withdrawn at will, and most savings accounts pay interest from day of deposit to day of withdrawal. The account holding financial institution may require up to seven days' notice before approving withdrawals; most, however, have waived this right.

There are two broad types of savings accounts: a MONEY MARKET DEPOSIT ACCOUNT (MMDA), allowing the depositor up to six transfers a month (including three by check, draft, or debit card); and an ordinary savings account, such as a STATEMENT SAVINGS ACCOUNT or PASSBOOK account. In both an MMDA and passbook or statement savings, the depositor can make unlimited number of transfers for loan payments and transfers to another account owned by the same depositor, or make account withdrawals by mail, at a teller window, or at an automated teller machine. A deposit account having more than three transfers to third parties, by check, draft, and so on, is a TRANSACTION AC-COUNT in the eyes of bank regulators, and is reportable as part of a bank's deposits subject to reserve requirements. MMDA accounts and other savings accounts are exempt from this requirement.

savings account loan COLLATERAL LOAN secured by savings account up to the amount advanced to the borrower. Also called a passbook loan, these are relatively secure and risk-free consumer loans. The lender takes possession of the passbook, or places a hold on the account equal to, or greater than, the amount of the loan, and has right of offset (set-off) against the funds in the account.

savings and loan association state or federally chartered financial institution that is required by law to making a certain percentage of its loans (currently 70%) as home mortgages. Also known as a THRIFT INSTITUTION and, in the United Kingdom, a building society. Savings and loan associations may be mutually owned, or stock corporations. Originally, savings and loans were organized in the nineteenth century as voluntary associations that pooled the savings of members to finance land acquisition. The current regulatory structure of savings and loans was created in 1933 under the Home Owners Loan Act, which established the FEDERAL HOME LOAN BANK BOARD. In the years since Congress enacted the MONETARY CONTROL ACT in 1980 and the GARN-ST GERMAIN DEPOSITORY INSTITUTES ACT in 1982, savings and loans have expanded their traditional role as residential mortgage lenders. This legislation gave savings and loans the power to make consumer loans, issue credit cards, and offer a variety of commercial loans to the extent permitted by law. Mutual savings and loans associations are, in theory, owned by the depositors. Many savings and loans are owned by stockholders, through direct ownership or through savings and loan holding companies.

Savings Association Insurance Fund (SAIF)

deposit insurance fund operated by the FEDERAL DEPOSIT INSURANCE CORPORATION, insuring deposits in federal savings and loan associations, federal savings banks, and state savings and loans up to $100,000 per account. The SAIF assumed the assets, liabilities, and obligations of the FEDERAL SAVINGS AND LOAN INSURANCE CORPORATION for financially sound savings and loan associations and federal savings banks, under the FINANCIAL INSTITUTIONS REFORM, RECOVERY AND ENFORCEMENT ACT OF 1989. The act also authorized increases in deposit insurance premiums paid by SAIF-insured institutions to replenish reserve assets in the fund. Insurance premiums paid by SAIF-insured financial institutions are set bv the Federal Deposit Insurance Corporation. Savings institutions insured by the SAIF have a new insurance logo stating that deposits are "backed by the full faith and credit of the United States Government."

savings bank depository financial institution that accepts consumer deposits and invests its assets primarily in residential mortgages and high-grade securities. Savings banks are found in

16 states mostly in the Northeast, can be owned by depositors as MUTUAL SAVINGS BANKS or stock savings banks issuing common stock to the public. Financial deregulation in the 1980s gave savings banks the right to offer checking accounts and credit cards, make commercial loans and consumer loans, discount brokerage, and invest in real estate. Savings banks today offer banking services competitive with many commercial banks. The GARN-ST GERMAIN DEPOSITORY INSTITUTIONS ACT OF 1982 gave state chartered savings banks the option of converting to federal charter and switching deposit insurance from the Federal Deposit Insurance Corporation to the Federal Savings and Loan Insurance Corporation, and authorized FEDERAL SAVINGS BANKS. See also SAVINGS AND LOAN ASSOCIATION.

savings bank life insurance (SBLI) life insurance sold by savings banks in New York, Massachusetts, and Connecticut. Several types of insurance coverage are available: term life, whole life, limited payment life, and annuities. Insurance is sold over the counter, without sales commissions. The cost of coverage generally is less than comparable insurance from commission paid agents, although there are state imposed limits on the amount of insurance that can be purchased.

savings bond U.S. government bond earning variable, market-based interest that is sold to the public through depository financial institutions and Federal Reserve Banks. Savings bonds are issued in denominations from $50 to $10,000 and are available in two forms. Series EE bonds, replacing the Series E bond in 1980, are sold at discount, and pay a rate of interest calculated at 85% of the market average on Treasury securities maturing in five years, or the rate in effect when the bond was purchased, whichever is higher. Since November 1986 the minimum rate has been 6%. Series EE Bonds purchased after 1989 are exempt from federal and state taxes if used for education expenses.

Series HH Bonds, sold in denominations of $500 to $10,000, are available only from a Federal Reserve Bank or the Commissioner of Public Debt. These bonds can be purchased in exchange for maturing Series E and Series EE Bonds, and U.S. Savings Notes (called Freedom Shares). Series HH Bonds are current income bonds, paying interest semiannually and have a term to maturity of ten years. Interest on Series EE Bonds is reportable annually, but reporting may be deferred until the bonds are cashed or at the maturity date. Series HH Bonds pay semiannual interest and also permit bondholders to defer federal income tax until the HH Bonds are sold or mature. Savings bond interest is subject to federal tax in the year a bond is redeemed, but is exempt from state and local taxes.

savings certificate CERTIFICATE evidencing ownership of a TIME DEPOSIT account paying a fixed rate of interest. A savings certificate is a retail CERTIFICATE OF DEPOSIT that normally is issued in denominations of $500 or more, and has a stated maturity. It is nonnegotiable, or transferable by assignment to another owner. A receipt is issued to the certificate holder, and the instrument is recorded in the issuing bank's ledger accounts. See also ALL SAVERS CERTIFICATE; MONEY MARKET CERTIFICATE; SMALL SAVER CERTIFICATE.

savings club see CLUB ACCOUNT.

scenario analysis in mortgage backed securities, evaluation that projects expected total RETURN on a security under different interest rates. The calculation of expected return is based on collection of principal and interest, reinvestment income on interim cash flows, and price appreciation or depreciation of the remaining principal balance until maturity. Seenario analysis attempts to limit INTEREST RATE RISK.

schedule
1. list of rates paid on deposit accounts.
2. funds AVAILABILITY SCHEDULE stating when deposited checks become good funds.
3. list disclosing minimum balances and fees charged to an account, for example, the average monthly balance needed to get a free checking account.
4. list of mortgage certificates transferred to a trustee for use as collateral in COLLATERALIZED MORTGAGE OBLIGATION bonds.
5. in factoring, a list detailing accounts being financed, signed by the borrower, that periodically is updated.
6. SCHEDULED ITEMS.

scheduled items nonperforming loans and leases, real estate owned through foreclosure, and other problem assets. These are noted on a separate schedule on a bank's CALL REPORT under the heading ADVERSELY CLASSIFIED ASSETS (doubtful loans, special mention substandard or loss), and give an indication of the soundness of a lender's loan portfolio. Classification as a scheduled item does not necessarily mean that a loss is expected; for example, some loans with a high loan-to-value ratio are listed, also loans with missing documentation or improperly filed security agreements that may become problem loans if the borrower becomes delinquent.

schilling national currency of Austria.

scrip
1. certificates, coupons, and other documents that have no monetary value, but are assigned a nominal value.
2. paper receipts dispensed by a consumer activated electronic terminal that substitutes for cash in retail establishments. The terminal prints a coupon and debits the consumer's account for the amount of the sale. The coupon is redeemable for goods or services, and also is the customer's sales receipt.
3. temporary stock certificate or dividend payable in short-term promissory notes to conserve cash.

seasonal adjustment adjustment for periodic swings in statistical data or changes in supply and demand. Data collected are adjusted or converted to an annual rate, a process that smooths out the differences from one period, or time series, to the next. For example, the volume of bank debits (checks and check-like drafts, including Negotiable Order of Withdrawal accounts, written by businesses and consumers) is higher in December than the following month's total, due mostly to year-end holiday shopping. Seasonal adjustment would reduce the December number, while raising the January figure. If there is no change in trends, both numbers would be identical. Seasonal adjustments also reveal a secular trend showing the cyclical movements of business data. An adjustment factor in annually reported data is unnecessary, as seasonal influence is no longer relevant.

Several statistical methods are used in adjusting reported data for seasonal trends; one of the most widely used is the ratio to moving average method, which divides the original data for a full year by 12. The most recent month (January in this example) is then added, the January data from the prior year deleted, and the total is again divided by 12, yielding the arithmetic mean. Specific ratios are then computed by dividing the original data in each period by the full trend cycle to arrive at an index of seasonally adjusted data.

seasonal credit

1. credit arrangement, usually a LINE OF CREDIT, allowing corporate borrowers to finance inventory and receivables, purchase supplies, and pay wages during a manufacturing and sales cycle. The borrower has the option of using the line of credit anytime during a specified period, usually two years, and then becomes conventional REVOLVING CREDIT. A line of credit may, however, be less enforceable than a revolving line of credit.

   The commitment fees and compensating balances the borrower pays to obtain a standby line are a less expensive way to borrow than a fixed term loan because the borrower draws only what is needed, and can pay down the outstanding balance at any time.

2. extended credit, supplied by the DISCOUNT WINDOW at a Federal Reserve Bank for periods up to 90 days. Federal Reserve banks make these advances under certain conditions to smaller financial institutions that have a demonstrated seasonal need for funds or have difficulty raising funds from the national money market.

seasoned loan loan that has been on the books for at least a year and has a satisfactory payment record. Mortgage loans that have been on the books for a period longer than a year command a permium over unseasoned loans when sold in the SECONDARY MORTGAGE MARKET.

seasoned securities securities that have a track record, that have been on the books at least one year, and that are traded in the secondary market. Seasoned securities are worth more to investors than securities that are less well known to investors.

seasoning aging of a mortgage or loan, expressed as elapsed time since origination. Mortgage loans that have a satisfactory payment record of at least one year, known as SEASONED LOANS, are more easily sold in the SECONDARY MARKET to investors than loans with payment characteristics that have not been established.

secondary liabilities see CONTINGENT LIABILITY.

secondary market the market where existing loans, marketable securities, and other assets are sold to investors, either directly or through an intermediary.
1. **Mortgages.** The nationwide SECONDARY MORTGAGE MARKET for purchase and sale of existing mortgages; the market in which mortgages are originated is the primary market. See also SECURITIZATION.
2. **Money Market.** The market where marketable debt instruments are offered by dealers for resale to new investors. For example, the dealer market in negotiable CERTIFICATES OF DEPOSIT (CDs) is concentrated in 25 dealers based in New York. Trades in negotiable CDs between dealers and their customers are in lots of $1 million or more.

secondary mortgage market national market where residential mortgages are assembled into pools and sold to investors. The secondary market, which originated with the FEDERAL NATIONAL MORTGAGE ASSOCIATION and the FEDERAL HOME LOAN MORTGAGE CORPORATION, and the GOVERNMENT NATIONAL MORTGAGE ASSOCIATION, supplies additional liquidity to mortgage lenders. Mortgages are sold through established CONDUITS that assemble pools of loans for resale or through private placement of loans directly with an investor. The secondary mortgage market, although dominated by the federal agencies, also includes private mortgage companies that buy conventional mortgages from mortgage originators, for resale as part of a COLLATERALIZED MORTGAGE OBLIGATION, or through a REAL ESTATE MORTGAGE INVESTMENT CONDUIT. By the late 1980s, more than half of mortgages originated in the United States were sold to other investors in the secondary market.

The single most important contribution of the secondary mortgage market is the creation of a national market for resale of residential mortgages. This assures that mortgage originators, regardless of where they are located, have access to pools of capital managed by pension funds, insurance companies, and other institutional buyers of mortgage backed bonds. Home buyers are assured an adequate supply of mortgage financing, as the secondary market sales lessen the possibility that a lending institution will become loaned up and cease making new loans. The maturing of the secondary market, beginning in the late 1960s with the organization of the GOVERNMENT NATIONAL MORTGAGE ASSOCIATION, has fostered other developments: standardized mortgage loan documentation; greater diversification in mortgages available from lenders, because most secondary market agencies have purchase programs for fixed rate, adjustable rate, and biweekly mortgages; and the beginnings of a national mortgage market, in which loan originators, some operating multistate or even nationwide networks of mortgage origination offices, are able to make new loans at competitive rates, and quickly sell loans under forward delivery commitments for sale to investors. Nongovernment conduits, or organizations that buy loans from correspondents, became active in the 1980s, for example, Maggie Mae, created by Mortgage Guaranty Insurance Corp., a mortgage insurance company, or HOMAC (Home Mortgage Access Corp.), organized by the National Home Building Association.

See also COMPUTERIZED LOAN ORIGINATION; MORTGAGE BACKED BOND; MORTGAGE BACKED SECURITIES; MORTGAGE BANKER; PASS-THROUGH SECURITY; PAY-THROUGH SECURITY; PRIVATE CONDUIT; PRIVATE MORTGAGE INSURANCE.

secondary reserves assets invested in short-term marketable securities, usually Treasury bills and short-term government securities. LEGAL RESERVES kept in a Federal Reserve Bank don't earn interest, but secondary reserves are a source of supplemental liquidity. These earn interest and can be used to adjust a bank's reserve position. If loan demand is slow, deposit funds often are invested in short-term securities that are easily converted to cash. Secondary reserves are not listed as a separate balance sheet item. See also MANAGED LIABILITIES; RESERVE REQUIREMENTS.

second mortgage mortgage that is subordinate to the lien created by a FIRST MORTGAGE, but senior to subsequent liens. Sometimes called a *second trust*, a second mortgage normally has a repayment term much shorter than a first mortgage, a fixed amortization schedule, and may have a balloon payment. The holder of a second mortgage has rights secondary to the holder of a first mortgage lien in event of foreclosure. In a second mortgage, interest due is computed on the entire principal balance owed, which is advanced to the borrower after the required three-day rescission period. A second mortgage is, in effect, an installment loan secured by the borrower's real estate, and technically, a CLOSED-END CREDIT arrangement with a predetermined repayment table or AMORTIZATION SCHEDULE. Contrast with HOME EQUITY CREDIT.

Second mortgages are used for a variety of borrowing needs, including home improvement, investment in a business, and raising cash. Second mortgages also are commonly used to make a larger down payment in a first mortgage if taken out when a home is purchased. See also RIGHT OF RESCISSION.

secured credit see SECURED LOAN.

secured credit card bank credit card that is backed by a savings account. The issuer places a hold on the savings account credit card equal to the cardholder's credit line, and reserves the right to use the deposit account to pay off credit card bills if the cardholder is unable to pay. Secured credit cards normally are issued only to persons whose ability to pay, based on credit history, is uncertain.

secured creditor party that holds some form of collateral or claim to assets. A mortgage lender holds a security interest in a borrower's residence. A bank taking a SECURITY INTEREST in a borrower's assets is a secured creditor.

secured loan LOAN that is collateralized by assignment of rights to property and a SECURITY INTEREST in personal property or real property taken by the lender. A mortgage borrower (the mortgagor) gives the lender a MORTGAGE in the property financed. A business loan can be secured by cash, inventory, receivables, marketable securities, or other acceptable COLLATERAL. In event the borrower fails to repay according to the original credit terms, the lender can take legal action to reclaim, and sell, the collateral. Contrast with UNSECURED LOAN, which is backed only by the borrower's promise to pay—a promissory note. See also ASSET-BASED LENDING; FINANCIAL STATEMENTS; SECURITY AGREEMENT; SIDE COLLATERAL.

Securities Act of 1933 act passed by Congress requiring registration of securities intended for sale to the public in interstate commerce or through the mail. The issuer must disclose relevant financial and other information, such as the offering price and the number of shares offered in a REGISTRATION STATEMENT filed with the Securities and Exchange Commission. (The public disclosure of an offering is called a PROSPECTUS.) State chartered banks and national banks were exempted from the registration and disclosure requirements of the 1933 act, under the theory that banks already were under sufficient scrutiny by banking regulators. What this means, of course, is that securities issued by a bank holding company must be registered with the SEC, but securities issued by a holding company's subsidiary bank are exempted. State and local bonds also are exempted from SEC registration requirements.

All issuers of securities for sale to the investing public are, however, still subject to compliance with anti-fraud provisions in the 1933 act making it a crime to make misleading statements to obtain money through fraud or other means. The SEC uses these anti-fraud provisions to impose its powers on otherwise exempt organizations such as municipalities and financial institutions.

securities affiliate bank holding company AFFILIATE authorized to underwrite limited amounts of commercial paper, municipal revenue bonds, plus securities backed by credit receivables and mortgages. Also called a Section 20 affiliate, from the section of the GLASS-STEAGALL ACT allowing a bank to affiliate with firms that are not engaged principally in the purchase and sale of corporate debt. A Federal Reserve Board ruling in April 1987, allowing bank securities affiliates to underwrite commercial paper, revenue bonds, and other securities, was challenged in federal court by securities broker-dealers (Securities Industry Association v. Board of Governors), but upheld in 1988 by the U.S. Supreme Court. Bank securities affiliates were permitted to underwrite and deal in corporate debt securities as long as revenue from underwriting these securities did not exeed a certain percentage of total revenue generated by a securities affiliate. In 1989, underwriting of corporate debt securities was capped, by Federal Reserve regulation, at 10% of total underwriting volume in a securities affiliate. The Federal Reserve Board has since expanded its ruling, allowing bank securities affiliates to underwrite corporate bonds.

The Federal Reserve ruling notwithstanding, most U.S.

banks cannot underwrite corporate securities through securities affiliates. This underwriting cap effectively limits bank underwriting of corporate debt to money center banks and large regional banks that are primary dealers in the U.S. government securities market, an approved banking activity under the Glass-Steagall Act. Many of these banks have consolidated all of their securities activities in separate holding company affiliates to take fuller advantage of the Fed's ruling. Before approving bank applications to underwrite securities, the Federal Reserve conducts an on-site audit to ensure that securities affiliates are not financed by depositors' money or holding company debt, and that firewalls restricting transactions between a bank and its securities affiliate have been established. See also ASSET-BACKED SECURITIES; SECURITIZATION.

Securities and Exchange Act of 1934 act passed by Congress establishing the Securities and Exchange Commission, an independent agency, to enforce federal securities laws. The act extended the registration and disclosure requirements of the Securities Act of 1933 to all companies with securities listed for sale on a national exchange, as well as other companies with assets over $1 million and more than 500 shareholders. These companies must file a registration application with the exchange and the SECURITIES AND EXCHANGE COMMISSION. The act also required disclosure of proxy solicitations, in which an organization attempts to vote the shares of other shareholders.

The act also established provisions regulating margin trading, authorizing the Federal Reserve Board of Governors to set limitations on credit extensions for purchase of securities. It also required registration of broker-dealers and exchanges in the OVER-THE-COUNTER market. Finally, the act gave the SEC authority to subpoena books and records, authorized criminal prosecutions by the Department of Justice, and allowed the SEC to issue orders, after notice and hearings, barring members of securities firms from trading listed securities, and also barring individuals from employment from registered firms.

Securities and Exchange Commission independent regulatory agency established in 1934 to oversee the administration of federal securities laws. With limited exceptions, the Commission has authority to regulate issuance and trading of publicly offered securities, and require issuers to give investors sufficient information to make informed decisions. The commission is headed by a bipartisan group of five commissioners, appointed by the President to serve five-year terms.

Securities Investor Protection Corporation (SIPC)
nonprofit, government sponsored membership corporation chartered in 1970 to protect the customer of insured broker-dealers, up to $500,000 per account. The SIPC has no supervisory powers and does not assist failing firms. The corporation, which is funded by member assessments and portfolio income, also has a line of credit with the U.S. Treasury. Five of its seven governors are appointed by the President; the remaining two are named by the Board of Governors of the Federal Reserve System and the secretary of the treasury. In addition to SIPC insurance, many broker-dealers also guard against losses through private insurance.

securities loan
1. bank loan collaterized by marketable securities. Such loans are regulated by Federal Reserve Regulation T if made by broker-dealers, by Regulation U if made by banks, and Regulation G if made by other organizations. These regulations set margin limits on credit that may be extended against various kinds of securities.
2. bank's loan to a broker, known as a broker loan or BROKER CALL LOAN.

securitization
conversion of bank loans and other assets into marketable securities for sale to investors. Securities offered for sale can be purchased by other depository institutions or nonbank investors. More broadly, corporate financing through Floating Rate Notes and Eurocommercial paper, replacing bank loans as a means of borrowing, is a form of securitization.

By securitizing bank loans and credit receivables, U.S. financial institutions are able to remove bank assets from the balance sheet if certain conditions are met—boosting its capital ratios, and make new loans from the proceeds of the securities sold to investors. The process effectively merges the credit markets (for example, the mortgage market in which lenders make new mortgages) and the capital markets, because bank receivables are repackaged as bonds collateralized by pools of mortgages, auto loans, credit card receivables, leases, and other types of credit obligations. As banks look to investors as the ultimate holders of the obligations created by bank lending, banks as an industry are inclined to act more as sellers of assets, rather than portfolio lenders that keep all the loans they originate in their own portfolio. Securitization also redefines the bank definition of ASSET QUALITY, and loan underwriting standards, because lenders will be looking at loan quality more in terms of their marketability in the capital markets than probability of repayment by the borrowers.

For regulatory reporting purposes, a loan that is converted into a security and sold as an asset-backed security qualifies as a sale of assets. The seller retains no risk of loss from the assets transferred and has no obligation to the buyer for borrower defaults or changes in market value of securities sold. Asset transfers where the buyer has RECOURSE against the selling institution are treated as *financings* or a borrowing secured by assets. Securitization of bank assets is further complicated by Securities and Exchange Commission regulations, and accounting guidelines. Tax counsel is advised in structuring new issues for market. See also ASSET SALES; ASSET-BACKED SECURITIES; CONSUMER RELATED RECEIVABLES SECURITIES.

security
Banking:
1. Personal assets or property that can be pledged as COLLATERAL; also, a good faith GUARANTY by a co-maker to pay an obligation if the borrower defaults. See also SECURITY AGREEMENT.
2. Physical safeguards, internal audits, and written procedures to insure safety of customer assets and account records. Such procedures must comply with minimum standards set by the Federal Deposit Insurance Corporation and the Comptroller of the Currency.

Finance: Certificate evidencing ownership of equity (stock), ownership of a debt obligation payable (bond), and the rights to ownership implied by options and warrants. Securities, when pledged as collateral, may be used to obtain bank financing.

security agreement
document giving a lender a SECURITY INTEREST in assets or property pledged as COLLATERAL. This agreement, signed by the borrower, describes the collateral

and its location in sufficient detail so the lender can identify it, and assigns to the lender the right to sell or dispose of the assigned collateral if the borrower is unable to pay the obligation. The security agreement may contain loan COVENANTS governing the advancement of funds, and a schedule for repayment of principal and interest, or require the borrower to obtain insurance coverage for the assets pledged.

The security agreement may cover nonpossessory liens in intangible property such as accounts receivable, or a possessory lien, in which the lender holds the collateral, for example, stock certificates, until the loan is fully paid. In some loans, the security agreement is also the FINANCING STATEMENT filed with a public records office, if it has the signatures of both borrower and lender.

security interest lender's claim to assets pledged by a borrower securing payment of an obligation. A lender's interest, also known as A LIEN, is said to attach to the borrower's property, and consists of two limited rights: FORECLOSURE and PRIORITY. A lender who files a FINANCING STATEMENT, which is often the same document as the SECURITY AGREEMENT, with the appropriate state or county official gives legal notice to other creditors that a lien has been filed. This process, known as *perfecting a lien*, commonly is done in commercial lending of a lien that is valid against claims of other creditors and most third parties. See also PERFECTED LIEN.

seed money
   Real Estate: The initial capital contributed by a project developer. Also called front end money.
   Venture Capital: The initial capital investment in a new company by venture capital. Venture capitalists generally retain rights or warrants to common stock, when the sponsored company issues stock in an initial public offering. This level of financing precedes intermediate MEZZANINE FINANCING, or second-stage financing. See also START-UP FINANCING.

segmentation
   1. division of a pool of mortgages into groups with similar rate and prepayment characteristics, such as a COLLATERALIZED MORTGAGE OBLIGATION, in securitizing bank loans, or converting bank assets into marketable securities for sale on the

SECONDARY MARKET. This enhances the value of the securities to investors, as securities offered for sale offer the investor more options than conventional mortgage backed passthrough certificates. These options include fast-pay or slow-pay mortgage backed bonds and residual interests in the excess cash flow from mortgage bonds.

2. in market research, process of dividing the population into groups of households for preparation of mailing lists and direct mail advertising. Market segmentation, known as GEODEMOGRAPHIC MARKETING in the direct mail industry, allows a financial institution to identify the best prospects for new products and services, based on income, life-style, and other characteristics.

segregation

1. SECURITIES AND EXCHANGE COMMISSION rule that broker-dealers maintain separate customer accounts for purposes of obtaining MARGIN credit from a bank, and may not combine customers' accounts except with the customers' approval. See also COMMINGLED FUNDS.

2. requirement by the Comptroller of the Currency, the Federal Reserve Board, and the Federal Deposit Insurance Corporation that banks maintain their investment portfolios separate from securities held as TRADING ACCOUNT ASSETS on behalf of customers and other banks, or for the bank's own account. Transfers between the two must be properly recorded.

3. separation of accounts under management by a bank trust department acting in a FIDUCIARY capacity for trust accounts.

seigniorage difference between the cost of materials in coins (the ASSAY value), and the face value. Since 1965, when the U.S. Treasury Department switched from silver coins to sandwich coins with a copper core, its seigniorage, or profit margin, in minting new coins has been very high.

self-dealing

1. **Banking.** The situation where a lender fails to exercise normal DUE DILIGENCE in approving loans to bank officers or directors, makes loans to insiders at abnormally favorable terms, or illegally accepts kickbacks in exchange for making a loan. See also INSIDER LENDING.

2. Trusts. The situation where a TRUSTEE sworn to protect the assets of another person or the ESTATE of a decedent consummates a transaction out of self-interest as opposed to his duty as a FIDUCIARY.

self-directed IRA
INDIVIDUAL RETIREMENT ACCOUNT that gives the investor the option of switching from one form of investment to another, such as stocks, fixed income securities, and short-term or long-term savings accounts in a bank or savings institution. The account holder also has the option of managing the portfolio, as well as directing funds into various forms of investments.

self-insurance
protecting against loss by setting aside funds from earnings, as opposed to buying an insurance policy. This form of insurance is often used when self-funding for possible losses is less costly than conventional insurance coverage, or when coverage by an insurance company is unavailable, or available only at great cost. A self-insurance plan, for example, can be set up to cover general liability, workers' compensation, or liability of bank directors and officers, and sometimes is a pooling arrangement sponsored by a trade association. Some companies have funded self-insurance through wholly-owned subsidiaries in offshore financial centers, for example, the Bahamas or the Cayman Islands. Self-funding of DIRECTORS & OFFICERS' (D&O) INSURANCE is permitted in some states. These plans can be funded by reserving assets (earnings) to meet future claims, or pay-as-you-go unfunded plans where claims are charged to current earnings when paid.

self-liquidating loan
short-term WORKING CAPITAL loan that is repaid from the liquidation of inventories. It is used to finance seasonal borrowing needs of a business needing capital to acquire inventory, by a farmer or other business needing bank financing to buy seed, fertilizer, and other supplies. The borrower repays the loan as inventory is converted into cash or a farm crop is sold. Early in the twentieth century, commercial banks made only short-term loans, and self-liquidating loans were a common variety. See also EVERGREEN LOAN.

self-regulatory organization
business organization that sets its own rules for fair conduct, licenses or approves

firms engaging in market making activities, and supervises the activities of market participants. Examples are the NATIONAL ASSOCIATION OF SECURITIES DEALERS, the MUNICIPAL SECURITIES RULEMAKING BOARD (MSRB), the NEW YORK STOCK EXCHANGE, and the AMERICAN STOCK EXCHANGE. MSRB rules are subject to the approval by the Securities and Exchange Commission, and are enforced by the National Association of Securities Dealers (for nonbank dealers), and by banking regulatory agencies for financial institutions.

self-service banking system in retail banking whereby consumers perform many routine banking transactions themselves, without going to a bank teller. The supporting theory is that many banking services, such as account withdrawals and deposits, can be automated, generating a stable, and growing, source of CORE DEPOSITS at low acquisition cost. At sufficient transaction volumes, self-service banking lowers the cost of serving the customer and provides greater customer convenience, because consumers are no longer restricted to doing their banking during business hours and have access to their accounts through automated teller machine networks. See also AUTOMATED TELLER MACHINE; CUSTOMER ACTIVATED TERMINAL; HOME BANKING; POINT-OF-SALE; TELEPHONE BILL PAYMENT; 24-HOUR BANKING.

sell down portion of a syndicated financing offered to interested buyers outside the underwriting group. Sell down financing can be a LOAN PARTICIPATION in a multilender commercial & industrial loan, or in securities underwriting whereby a portion of the offering is distributed through a SELLING GROUP acting as agents for the underwriter. In general, the higher the sell down, the greater the yield for the lead manager or lead underwriter.

seller financing see PURCHASE MONEY MORTGAGE.

seller-servicer secondary mortgage market term for a mortgage lender approved by the FEDERAL NATIONAL MORTGAGE ASSOCIATION or the Federal Home Loan Mortgage Corporation to sell mortgages in the SECONDARY MORTGAGE MARKET, and collect monthly principal and interest payments from mortgagors. The selling institution forwards mortgage loans, maintains mortgage records, and collects a servicing fee, generally 3/8 of 1%, for work performed.

selling group securities dealers who affiliate with an underwriting group on an agency basis to assist in distribution of a new offering of securities. Members collect a commission or concession fee for securities placed. The group ordinarily includes members of the original underwriting group. It may be required in some instances to purchase any unsold portion of the offering.

sell short SEE SHORT SALE.

semiannual interest interest payable twice a year. Bond interest is payable semi-annually.

sender net debit cap limit imposing a maximum ceiling on the aggregate debit position a financial institution will incur during a business day in wire transfers to other financial institutions. Also called OVERDRAFT CAP. This cap can be applied to the sender's payments made on a particular network or a single cap covering all transfer activities across Fed Wire and private wire networks. See also DAYLIGHT OVERDRAFT.

senior debt debt that has priority of claim ahead of other obligations. A first mortgage holder is payable before a creditor holding a second mortgage, in a foreclosure action. A lender holding a perfected SECURITY INTEREST has a claim against the borrower's assets that has priority over subsequent lien holders. Senior debt securities have claim to assets of a corporation before SUBORDINATED DEBT in event of liquidation. See also PRIORITY OF LIEN; SENIOR SECURITY.

senior security security that has a claim against earnings or assets, and must be paid before other holders of other securities. Bonds have priority over preferred stock, and preferred stock has precedence over common stock.

Separate Trading of Registered Interest and Principal (STRIPS) book-entry zero-coupon U.S. Treasury security, sold through broker-dealers since 1985. A STRIPS issue accumulates interest over the life of the bond, and pays interest in a lump sum at maturity. A dealer or investor holding full- coupon Treasury securities may return them to the Treasury for stripping. The Treasury returns a zero-coupon security. The process also works in reverse. That is, a dealer can turn in the required number of zero-coupon bonds and receive a full-coupon security. See also COUPON STRIPPING.

sequestered account deposit account impounded by court order under due process of law, and from which funds cannot be disbursed without prior approval. These accounts usually are kept under a separate file.

serial bond bond issued as one of a set of bonds, each having a specific maturity. Serial bonds, commonly issued by state and municipal governments, are bonds that allow the issuer to amortize bond principal over several years, by issuing bonds at periodic intervals, at, say, every six months. Each bond has its own maturity date, set by a schedule in the initial offering. Contrast with TERM BOND.

series
1. group of bonds issued as part of a group of bonds under a single INDENTURE. Bonds offered for sale may be issued in the same year or have a different maturity, accrual schedule, and interest rate, as stated in the prospectus or prospectus supplement. Electric utility bonds and revenue bonds typically are issued in a series over an extended period of time. A COLLATERALIZED MORTGAGE OBLIGATION (CMO) normally is subdivided into of several sets of mortgage-backed bonds, called TRANCHES (from the French, meaning slice), each having its own yield to maturity. The tranches in a CMO series usually are denoted by a different letter or number.
2. options term for call options and put options on the same underlying security, at the same expiration date and exercise price (STRIKE PRICE).

service bureau CORRESPONDENT bank or third party service firm that performs data processing, credit card billing, securities safekeeping, or other functions that are too expensive for a smaller bank to perform by itself. More than half the commercial banks in the United States, and a majority of the THRIFT INSTITUTIONS, rely on third party service organizations to record daily transactions to customer records and general ledger accounts. See also FACILITIES MANAGEMENT.

service charge bank charge to a customer's account, as when an account balance falls below a certain MINIMUM BALANCE, a check is returned for insufficient funds, or for servicing an account. Bank fees are meant to cover the cost of maintaining a depositor's account, or performing a specific service requested by a customer. Banks also impose service fees for late payments on loans and credit card purchases above the cardholder's credit line. Other service charges include the annual charge for renting a safe deposit box and transaction fees for using an automated teller machine. See also TARGET BALANCE.

service corporation subsidiary of one or more banks or thrift institutions that performs services other than deposit taking for its owners and outside customers. These may be services the owners cannot perform directly, or services a bank is forbidden by regulation from performing directly. These latter include PERMISSIBLE NONBANK ACTIVITIES that bank holding companies may engage in through separate subsidiary companies. The Garn-St Germain Depository Institutions Act allowed bank service corporations to engage in these bank related activities and savings and loan service corporations to directly invest in real estate development.

service subsidiary see SERVICE CORPORATION.

servicing
1. collection of principal and interest payments and management of collateral on loans sold in the SECONDARY MARKET. In a mortgage PASS-THROUGH SECURITY, the loan originator collects monthly payments, makes certain claims or warranties as to the condition of the loans, and agrees to buy back mortgages not conforming with these specifications. The loan originator or a master servicer (if serving rights are sold) acts as a servicing agent for the mortgage trustee, and collects a fee ranging from 1/4 of 1% to 1/3 of 1%. Many

financial institutions sell servicing rights to specific pass-through securities to a third-party service corporation. See also SELLER-SERVICER.

2. collateral control in ASSET-BASED LENDING, by which a lender (or a factor in FACTORING) monitors its collateral position. Collateral control, also known as policing, can be done by the lender or by a third party. It (1) assures an account is in good standing; (2) confirms shipments of goods; (3) protects against diversion of funds; and (4) provides a monthly AGING SCHEDULE of receivables.

servicing agreement contract between a financial institution, as agent, and an institutional buyer, as PRINCIPAL, when a loan is sold in the SECONDARY MARKET. The agreement, in general, covers the duties, fees, and audit requirements expected of the seller, covering (1) the seller's fiduciary role as a trustee to collect and remit borrower payments; (2) the seller's agreement to post a fidelity bond and carry ERRORS AND OMISSIONS INSURANCE; and (3) the buyer's right to conduct periodic audits of the selling institution's books and records.

set-off clause

1. common law right of a lender to seize deposits owned by a debtor for nonpayment of an obligation. A bank lending $5,000 to a borrower who has $2,500 on deposit at the same bank will set-off $2,500, and file an unsecured claim for the remaining $2,500. An exception is consumer credit transactions, where the right of set-off is prohibited by the TRUTH IN LENDING ACT. A consumer who refuses to pay a credit card bill, claiming the merchandise ordered was defective, is thus protected from collection efforts by the card issuing bank by seizing deposits equal to the debt owed.

2. settlement of mutual debt between a debtor in bankruptcy and a creditor, through offsetting claims. Instead of receiving cash payment, debtors credit the amount owed against the other party's obligations to them. This allows creditors to collect more than they otherwise would have collected under a debt repayment plan approved by a bankruptcy court.

settlement

1. **Banking.** The accounting process recording the respective debit and credit positions of the two parties involved in a transfer of funds. Funds are available for use and may be drawn at any time afterward. Funds transferred through Fed Wire are available for use at the time the transfer occurs, and are settled by adjusting the RESERVE ACCOUNT balances of the sending and receiving banks. Checks, automated clearing house transfers, and other payments between banks are settled on a provisional basis, because the possibility exists that the person initiating the transfer of funds may not have sufficient funds to cover the payment, or the payment cannot be processed for various reasons. See also NETTING; NET SETTLEMENT.

2. **Real Estate.** The CONVEYANCE or transfer of property to a purchaser, and recording of the mortgage lien on the property deed by the bank financing the transaction. Also known as a mortgage *closing*.

3. **Securities.** The delivery of securities by a selling broker, and payment by the buying broker, normally five business days (regular way delivery) after the transaction date. Settlement can sometimes take longer than five days, especially in new issues of tax-exempt bonds.

settlement date

1. **Banking.** The date that funds transferred through the Federal Reserve Fed Wire, or private network are deposited in a customer's account and available for use. Fed Wire and CLEARING HOUSE INTERBANK PAYMENTS SYSTEM (CHIPS) transfers are settled the same day. Automated clearing house transfers are settled the next day. See also FINALITY OF PAYMENT.

2. **Securities.** The date that securities sold actually changes hands. Under regular way settlement, transfer of ownership occurs five days after the transaction. Under seller's option settlement, delivery of securities in completion of a trade can be delayed up to 60 days from the trade execution date.

settlement option

1. **Foreign Exchange.** A contract in which the seller has the option to settle a FORWARD CONTRACT at any time within a specified period.

2. **Securities.** A seller's option to deliver securities at any time from five days after the transaction date (known as regular way corporate settlement) to as late as 60 days after the transaction date.

settlement price in futures, the figure determined by the closing range of prices and used to calculate trading gains or losses. Settlement prices are used to determine gains, losses, margin calls, and invoice prices for deliveries. Also, the price of a financial instrument underlying an option contract when then the contract is exercised.

severally but not jointly arrangement commonly used in corporate UNDERWRITING in which each member of a selling group assumes responsibility for selling a share of the total offering, but is not responsible for actions of the other parties. Each member of the selling group is responsible for a portion of the original contract, but not for any unsold shares. Also called a *divided account* or *Western Account*. See also JOINTLY AND SEVERALLY.

share account account offered by a CREDIT UNION, paying earnings to its members as dividends rather than INTEREST. The major forms of share accounts are regular share accounts, an interest bearing account similar to personal savings accounts at banks and savings institutions; SHARE DRAFT ACCOUNTs, an interest bearing account permitting withdrawals or transfers by writing drafts against the account; money market accounts, often called money market share accounts and share certificate accounts, which are similar to term savings accounts. Credit union shares are subject to RESERVE REQUIREMENTS if they allow more than three telephone transfers or preauthorized transactions a month.

shared appreciation mortgage (SAM) residential mortgage combining a fixed rate of interest at below market rates, and lender participation in any equity appreciation in the mortgaged property. A shared appreciation mortgage has a low monthly payment, as compared to a fixed rate CONVENTIONAL MORTGAGE, and typically is a short-term (under five years) loan. This type of mortgage is appealing to mortgagors who borrow in periods of high interest rates, expecting to refinance later on at a lower rate. See also ADJUSTABLE RATE MORTGAGE; ALTERNATIVE MORTGAGE INSTRUMENT.

shared network electronic banking system, such as an AUTOMATED TELLER MACHINE network, that is open to customers of any financial institution in a geographic region. Distinguish from PROPRIETARY NETWORK. Sharing rules, to comply with the Justice Department's guidelines on EFT joint ventures, must allow participation by any financial institution wishing to join.

share draft account transaction account similar to a NEGOTIABLE ORDER OF WITHDRAWAL ACCOUNT, or NOW account, that is offered by credit unions. Members of a credit union can gain access to their share balances by writing drafts on the accounts. These check-like drafts are authorized for federally insured credit unions under the Consumer Checking Account Equity Act of 1980.

shelf registration popular name for the Securities and Exchange Commission rule allowing securities issuers to file registration statements and sell the securities in a PUBLIC OFFERING at a later date. The SEC's Rule 415, adopted initially in 1982, allows issuers to register securities they expect to sell within two years of the initial effective date, without having to file additional registration statements with each offering.

This allows issuers to act quickly when the market seems ready without the delays of registration, possibly getting a better price for its securities offered for sale. Under SEC Rule 415, issuers are expected to file amendments disclosing any changes in financial condition. Delayed offerings originally were used by corporations, but the SEC also has approved their use by limited partnership tax shelters, employee benefit plans, and issuers of mortgage pass-through certificates.

shell branch foreign branch of a U.S. chartered bank that acts as a booking office for financial transactions carried out beyond U.S. borders. Ledgers of the shell branch usually are maintained at the main office of a U.S. bank. Often located in offshore banking centers, in particular the Bahamas and the Cayman Islands, shell branches provide access at low cost to the Eurocurrency markets. An INTERNATIONAL BANKING FACILITY is a domestic shell branch of a U.S. bank, allowing its owner to participate in the syndicated Eurocredit market without regulatory hindrance. See also OFFSHORE BANKING UNIT.

sheriff's sale public AUCTION of a borrower's assets seized in a FORECLOSURE order obtained from a court, and carried out by a sheriff or other court officer. Assets pledged as loan collateral and secured by attachments, liens, or mortgages may be sold at auction.

Sherman Antitrust Act see ANTITRUST LAWS.

shipping preparing and submitting mortgage documents to an investor in fulfillment of a standby commitment or forward commitment to sell mortgages in the SECONDARY MORTGAGE MARKET.

short book see UNMATCHED BOOK

short coupon
1. bond interest payment for a period less than the standard six months. Normally, only the first interest payment of a new issue has a short coupon, as computed from the ACCRUED INTEREST payable from the issue date until the first coupon payment date.
2. bond with a relatively short remaining term to maturity, usually under two years. See also LONG COUPON.

short date forward FORWARD EXCHANGE CONTRACT in the foreign exchange markets involving a sale and delivery contract ranging from one week to one month after the trade date. Contrast with SPOT NEXT; TOMORROW NEXT. See also ROLLOVER.

short hedge investment strategy to fully or partially eliminate the risk of a decline in value. The opposite is a LONG HEDGE.
1. purchase of call options or sale of put options. A put option limits position losses to the cost of the option. A call option protects against rising interest rates, or falling prices, in a future time period.

2. sale of futures contracts to limit the downside risk of ownership of a commodity or financial instrument. The futures contract is approximately equal in value to the underlying financial instrument.

short position dealer's net deficit of commodities, securities, financial instruments, and so on. A short position occurs when a dealer over-sells, anticipating falling prices with the expectation of buying back the assets sold at a lower price.

short sale

1. sale of a security not owned in anticipation of making a profit by purchasing the security later at a lower price, and delivering the security in completion of the short sale. The trade is completed by delivery of a borrowed certificate that is delivered to the buyer, completing the transaction at the time of the original sale. A regular way short sale occurs when the seller has no other position in the security; a short sale against the box occurs when the seller has an offsetting long position and wants to postpone tax losses until the following year. The box is securities industry jargon for securities owned by the seller, but held in safekeeping by a broker-dealer.

2. in futures, taking a market position by selling a futures contract in a financial instrument not owned by the seller, in anticipation of a price decline.

short-term financing

1. loan or credit facility with a maturity of one year or less.

2. credit arrangement extended to a MORTGAGE BANKER, to finance an inventory of loans that are resold to investors. These include short-term lines of credit from a commercial bank, called a warehouse line; commercial paper issued by mortgage bankers, known as COLLATERAL TRUST NOTES.

short-term gain in computing capital gain (or loss), an investment held for a period of less than 12 months if acquired after 1987, as opposed to a LONG-TERM INVESTMENT owned for a longer holding period. Previously, the holding period for short-term investments was six months.

short-term investment funds generic name for pooled investment funds that invest in short-term money market instruments or government bonds. Also called short-term funds. Examples are money market mutual funds, collective investment funds managed by bank TRUST DEPARTMENTS, and tax-exempt funds that invest in securities issued by state and local governments. Many of these funds have minimal investment requirements, can be bought or sold at any time, and are highly liquid investments. Collective investment funds, for example, are composed largely of assets that mature in 91 days or less, and are payable on demand.

short-term paper
1. notes, drafts, bills of exchange, or promissory notes that have original maturities up to nine months to a year, excluding days of grace or renewal. COMMERCIAL PAPER, for example, is a promissory note with an original maturity of less than 270 days, although in practice most issues of commercial paper is for shorter periods.
2. promissory notes or installment notes payable within a year.

side collateral pledge of assets or deposits that does not fully collateralize a loan. A lender making a $5,000 commercial loan may place a hold on $1,000 in marketable securities. Personal guarantees, such as a promise not to mortgage or sell property owned by the borrower, also are a form of side collateral, and are worth only as much as the character of the borrower. Side collateral rarely is taken in consumer credit arrangements.

sight draft bill of exchange or draft that is payable when presented. Used when the seller of goods wants to retain control of the goods being shipped to an importer or exporter, either for credit reasons or to retain title. Money is payable at sight, or when the completed documents are presented, or within a specified period called days of grace. See also TIME DRAFT.

signature card card that a customer signs when opening an account at a financial institution. It identifies the depositor. Copies of signature cards are kept in the branch offices. It is also a dual control device, controlling access to safe deposit boxes. Two signatures are required to open a safe deposit box: the customer's and a bank employee's.

signature loan unsecured loan backed only by the borrower's signature on a PROMISSORY NOTE. No collateral is taken by the lender. These generally are loans to individuals with good credit standing who are known by the lending officer. Also known as a *good faith loan* or *character loan.*

signature on file bank card billing system in which cardholders actually do not sign the sales draft authorizing a charge to their account. Instead, the merchant or merchant processing bank approves the transaction by matching the cardholder's address supplied by the merchant to a home mailing address, according to bank records. Signatures are not actually compared. This form of cardholder IDENTIFICATION is used most often by mail order merchants, and by hotel chains when billing additional charges after a hotel guest has checked out. If the customer disputes a charge, he or she signs an affidavit.

signature verification examination of a signature on a negotiable instrument to determine whether the handwriting is genuine, and whether the person signing the check is authorized to use the account. Banks have a legal responsibility to examine checks and drafts presented for payment, but as a practical matter, signatures of check makers and endorsers are examined only on an exception basis. See also IDENTIFICATION.

silver certificate U.S. paper currency, issued by the U.S. Treasury Department rather than the Federal Reserve Banks, as circulating money until 1967, when they were replaced by the FEDERAL RESERVE NOTE as the United States official LEGAL TENDER. Until then, silver certificates were redeemable for an equivalent amount of silver.

simple interest interest computed only on the principal balance, without compounding. Simple interest for a year on $100, borrowed at 8% interest, is $8. If interest is compounded daily, the finance charge is $8.33. Simple interest computation is the basis of variable rate consumer lending, and also is used widely in mortgage lending. When interest payments on loans are calculated on a simple interest basis, the borrower pays finance charges on the principal balance actually used. Interest

calculated under the ADD-ON INTEREST method speeds up the rate
of interest payment in the early years of a loan. See also BANK
DISCOUNT RATE; COMPOUND INTEREST.

Simplified Employee Pension Plan (SEP) type
of pension plan that allows small businesses or sole proprietors
to set aside up to 15% of gross annual salary on a tax deferred
basis for retirement savings. Funds can be contributed to an individual retirement account or to an annuity. Employees contributing to a SEP are also entitled to claim a tax deduction for their
annual contribution.

simulation in ASSET-LIABILITY MANAGEMENT, a technique of
using operating account balances to test various pricing models
and RUNOFF scenarios and to determine in advance how the asset
portfolio (loans) and liability portfolio (deposits) are likely to
perform under different interest rate and pricing situations. The
purpose is to test earnings performance under different interest
rate hypotheses. See also FORECASTING; SCENARIO ANALYSIS;
WHAT-IF CALCULATION.

single interest insurance insurance policy that pro-
tects a lender's SECURITY INTEREST in a vehicle or automobile
financed by an installment loan. Also known as vendor single
interest insurance, the policy names the lender as loss payee.
Such insurance coverage is sometimes required of marginally
creditworthy borrowers, and is payable in one installment, or
over the life of the loan.

sinking fund
1. **In general.** Money accumulated in a custodial account to retire debt instruments according to a predetermined schedule,
   regardless of pricing changes in the secondary market. Some
   sinking fund requirements must be satisfied by redemption of
   a specific amount of the issue during a specified year. In
   other cases, the sinking fund requirement can be met through
   purchases of the issue in the open market.
2. **Mortgage Backed Securities.** A provision in an INDENTURE
   calling for scheduled amortization of mortgage backed
   bonds, subject to prepayment activity. For example, a CON-
   TROLLED AMORTIZATION BOND tranche in a Collateralized
   Mortgage Obligation (CMO).

skip account delinquent borrower who moves without leaving a forwarding address. Lenders hire professional collectors, known as skip tracers, to locate a skip and try to collect the amount owed or extract a promise to pay.

skip payment privilege

1. clause in a consumer loan agreement giving the borrower the option of omitting one or more payments, provided the lender is notified in advance.
2. option in some credit card plans allowing the cardholder to defer payments due in December until the following month, after the end-of-year holiday shopping season has ended.

slow loan

1. classification of loans that are considered doubtful, with questionable repayment. A bank may set aside cash assets against such loans in its LOAN LOSS RESERVES.
2. working capital loan to a firm with an extended accounts receivable cycle; i.e., a firm that takes a long time to convert assets into cash. For example, an agricultural loan.

Small Business Administration (SBA) independent federal agency chartered in 1953 to provide financial assistance to small businesses. The SBA makes direct loans to borrowers who are unable to obtain conventional financing, participates in loans originated by financial institutions, and also guarantees loans made by banks and other financial institutions. Typically, the SBA guarantees 85% of a small business loan. The agency also provides disaster assistance to small businesses and financial counseling to minority-owned businesses. The SBA also licenses, regulates, and provides venture capital assistance to a SMALL BUSINESS INVESTMENT COMPANY. The SBA can make direct loans up to $750,000 and guarantee loans up to $1 million.

small business investment company company licensed by the Small Business Administration to provide equity capital and long-term loans, subsidized by the SBA, to small businesses. An SBIC may lend money to, or buy stock or convertible debentures in, firms with less than $5 million in assets, net worth of not more than $2½ million, and after-tax net income not exceeding $250,000. Originally SBICs had special IRS

tax treatment, allowing stockholders to write off credit losses against ordinary income. The Small Business Administration matches the capital contribution of investors in an SBIC, which is permitted to make loans equal to four times its initial capital.

small saver certificate (SSC) fixed-rate TIME DEPOSIT with no minimum balance and a maturity of 18 months. The Small Saver Certificate was originally authorized in 1980 so banks and savings institutions could compete with money market funds for consumer deposits under $10,000 (the minimum deposit for a six-month Money Market Certificate), and are paid a rate based on the average yield of U.S. Treasury securities with comparable maturities. In October 1983, interest rate ceilings on time deposits with maturities longer than 31 days were removed, eliminating the need for the SSC.

smart card bank card containing a computer chip for identification, special purpose processing, and data storage. The computer chip has the ability to perform various computations, such as validating the cardholder's PERSONAL IDENTIFICATION NUMBER (PIN), authorizing retail purchases, verifying account balances, and storing personal records. A smart card's internal memory may also store pertinent information on a consumer's relationship with a bank, broker, insurance company, or medical history— a personal data base that is updated every time the card is used. Also called *chip card* or *memory card*. See also MAGNETIC STRIPE.

Smithsonian Agreement agreement by members of the GROUP OF TEN countries in December 1971 to adopt FLOATING EXCHANGE RATES. The conference, held at the Smithsonian Institution in Washington, D.C., was prompted by the collapse of the fixed exchange rates that had existed since 1944 under the Bretton Woods agreement, and indirectly by the decision of the United States to abandon the gold exchange standard. The Smithsonian conference led to an agreement in 1972 by the members of the European Economic Community to limit currency movements within a narrow band called the SNAKE, which attempted to manage currency fluctuations in the European community by pegging exchange rates to the strongest currency in the EEC.

smurf slang term for a person who carries out cash transactions in a MONEY LAUNDERING scheme. A smurf, also known as a runner, attempts to deposit cash in small amounts (under $10,000) to disguise the owners of the cash or to conceal the ultimate purpose for which the money will be used.

snake exchange rate system in the Western European countries, adopted in 1972 as a more flexible form of FIXED EXCHANGE RATES. The exchange rate of each country participating in the European Economic Community was allowed to fluctuate up or down within certain upper or lower limits, called a CURRENCY BAND. When one nation's currency repriced vis-a-vis an external currency, the exchange rates of all currencies in the snake moved accordingly. Within, the snake generally follows the West German Deutschmark, the strongest currency in the group.

snapshot statement see INTERIM STATEMENT.

Society for Worldwide Interbank Financial Telecommunications (SWIFT) nonprofit, cooperative organization that facilitates the exchange of payment messages between financial institutions around the world. SWIFT was organized in 1973 by a group of European bankers who wanted a more efficient method than telegraph wire (telex) or mail to send payment instructions to correspondent banks. Among its 1,000 plus members are U.S. money center and regional banks, and major banks in Europe, Latin America, Africa, Asia, and Australia. SWIFT began operations in 1977, providing the framework for an international communication system between financial institutions, using common terminals and standard communication protocols. In 1988, access to the SWIFT network was expanded to broker-dealers and securities firms, and securities transfers and redemptions were added to SWIFT's network services.

By itself, SWIFT is not a payment system; a SWIFT message is merely an advice, an instruction to transfer funds to a specified account at another bank. The exchange of funds between banks takes place on domestic funds clearing systems. In the United States, interbank transfers of funds are handled by the Federal Reserve System's FEDERAL WIRE network or by the CLEARING HOUSE INTERBANK PAYMENTS SYSTEM (CHIPS).

soft currency see WEAK CURRENCY.

soft dollar

1. payment for banking services with balances, for example, a COMPENSATING BALANCE, as opposed to paying in fees or explicit bank SERVICE CHARGES.
2. payment of brokerage fees through commission revenue rather than direct payment to a broker. A broker collecting a full fee often will use part of the revenue to pay for other services delivered to the client, such as a subscription to a financial service, or third party investment advice.
3. in a real estate project, prepaid interest and fees paid by an investor in a real estate project that is tax deductible against the current year's income.

soft loan extended term project financing made at below-market rates, especially in loans to developing countries. Soft loans are made by the special lending facility of a multilateral development bank (for example, the Asian Development Fund and the African Development Fund) or the International Development Association, an affiliate of the World Bank. Typically, soft loans have extended grace periods in which only interest or service charges are due, longer (up to 50 years) amortization schedules, and lower interest rates than conventional bank loans. Access to the soft-loan window is limited to developing countries with low per capita incomes, and developing countries experiencing balance of payment problems.

sol national currency of Peru.

sole proprietor unincorporated business owned and controlled by one person, ordinarily under a business name (doing business as) other than the owner's. Sole owners are treated as individual accounts, and may open interest-bearing checking accounts, unlike corporations.

solvency

1. **Finance.** The ability of a borrower to pay personal obligations or debt service payments as scheduled, or on demand if not subject to a fixed schedule. See also ABILITY TO PAY.
2. **Banking.** The excess of a bank's assets over liabilities, also known as NET WORTH. See also CAPITAL ADEQUACY.

sovereign risk risk of default by a foreign central government or agency backed by the FULL FAITH AND CREDIT of the government. A famous banker once said, "Sovereign nations don't go broke." But they can refuse to pay their obligations to creditor banks, making it extremely difficult for a bank to collect full repayment of its loans. A sovereign borrower cannot be sued without its permission.

Since the mid-1980s, when Mexico defaulted in 1982 on its loans to foreign banks, banks in the GROUP OF TEN countries have worked jointly with the International Bank for Reconstruction and Development (the World Bank) and the INTERNATIONAL MONETARY FUND to find ways to restructure loan payment terms and reduce the external debt burden of less developed countries. Among the options proposed were debt for equity swaps, government guarantees of principal and/or interest repayments, and partial write-off of nonperforming loans by creditor banks. In 1989, Mexico's banks agreed to a debt restructuring plan, assisted by $5.5 billion in financial aid from the World Bank and the International Monetary Fund, that would guarantee payment of principal and interest on Mexico's external debt. See also STRUCTURAL ADJUSTMENT.

special drawing rights (SDR) type of international money created by the INTERNATIONAL MONETARY FUND and allocated to its member nations. Although SDRs are only accounting entries, and are not backed by paper money or precious metal, they are an international reserve asset. The SDR is made up from a basket of major currencies; the dollar value of SDRs is computed daily by multiplying these currencies by their dollar exchange rate in London, and adding (U.S.) $.54. A nation that has a balance of payments deficit can use SDRs, subject to certain International Monetary Fund (IMF) conditions, to settle debts to another nation or to the IMF.

special mention potentially weak loans or assets presenting an unwarranted credit risk, but less risky than SUBSTANDARD ASSETS. Bank loans are classified as special mention assets when the lender fails to supervise a loan properly or maintain sufficient documentation, or otherwise has deviated from acceptable and prudent lending practices. Assets listed for special mention generally reflect weaknesses in administration, servicing, or collection, as opposed to credit weaknesses, which are noted in examination reports as ADVERSELY CLASSIFIED ASSETS.

special provision addition to loss reserves for loans considered doubtful. When loans finally are written down, the loan loss reserve account and gross loans are reduced accordingly. These loans have doubtful repayment prospects, and are expected to be charged off as a loss. For example, loans to a less developed country with interest in arrears or loans secured by nonperforming real estate.

specie money in the form of coins, usually gold or silver, as opposed to PAPER MONEY. Also called HARD CURRENCY. Since the gold standard was abolished in the 1930s, gold coins, aside from their higher instrinsic value and demand as collectibles, no longer have any special worth as a standard of value in world trade.

speculation risk taking by buying securities in the hope of realizing a large capital gain or profit. Speculators realize they are putting capital at risk, and may experience a higher loss than ordinary investors, who seek a reasonable return on investment and preservation of capital. In general, the shorter the time period a security is owned, the more speculative the investment. Nearly all market makers in the foreign exchange markets and the financial futures markets, who buy and sell for their own account, are speculators who expect to make a profit from price swings. Speculators also trade in Treasury Bonds to take advantage of short-term price action. See also PAIR-OFF; SHORT SALE.

speculative securities
1. securities rated as sub-investment paper by an investment advisory service, and thus an unsuitable investment for a bank investment portfolio or trust department. Speculative securities are rated by Standard & Poor's as grade BB or lower, and by Moody's Investors Service as Ba or lower.
2. investment security subject to loss of interest or principal, or both. Banking regulators have discouraged investing in certain types of derivative mortgage backed securities, unless these are used as a hedging device to limit interest rate risk.

These include STRIPPED MORTGAGE BACKED SECURITIES—such as INTEREST ONLY (IO) STRIPS and PRINCIPAL-ONLY (PO) STRIPS—and also trading in WHEN-ISSUED securities, that is, buying a security in the interim between the announcement date and the offering date, in the hope of making a quick profit.

speed shorthand reference for prepayment of mortgages underlying mortgage backed securities. There are various mathematical formulas for calculating loan prepayment which directly influence the YIELD TO MATURITY on mortgage backed securities: the Federal Housing Authority's prepayment model; the Public Securities Association's Standard Prepayment Model; and Single Monthly Mortality, developed by First Boston Corporation. A prepayment assumption forecasts projected cash flows when a COLLERALIZED MORTGAGE OBLIGATION initially is priced and offered to investors. As the CMO portfolio ages, these cash flows in turn determine the expected maturity (DURATION) and AVERAGE LIFE of the issue.

split deposit deposit where the customer presenting an endorsed check receives part of the amount being deposited in cash. Split deposits are a major source of teller errors and potential fraud in customer statements. Contrast with MIXED DEPOSIT.

split level balance
1. in bank credit cards or consumer lines of credit, an outstanding balance above which a lower interest rate can be charged. For example, a credit card may have a finance charge of 15% APR on balances up to $2,000, and a 13% rate on any outstanding balance above $2,000. The split rate is meant to encourage consumers to use credit cards for major purchases, because only a portion of the amount due is payable every month.
2. deposit total in a savings account or other interest-bearing account that determines the interest rate paid. A split balance can be the minimum balance needed to earn interest, or avoid service charges, for example, a $2,500 average balance requirement in a NEGOTIABLE ORDER OF WITHDRAWAL (NOW) ACCOUNT. Accounts with balances under $2,500 would be treated as ordinary checking accounts, earning no interest. See also TARGET BALANCE; TIERED RATE ACCOUNT.

spot in FOREIGN EXCHANGE trading, on the spot delivery to meet immediate orders for purchase or sale of a currency at current market prices, normally in two business days. The rate quoted is the spot rate. For example, a dealer may agree on Tuesday to sell U.S. dollars and buy Japanese yen for current delivery. The contract is completed on Thursday, when funds are exchanged and delivery takes place. The majority of foreign exchange current delivery contracts are settled with two-day delivery. An exception is the Canadian dollar and Mexican peso contracts traded in North American markets, where the delivery date is one business day forward; Tuesday orders are filled on Wednesday. See also SPOT MARKET; SPOT NEXT.

spot market market for immediate delivery and payment in cash, as opposed to future delivery, of commodities, foreign exchange, or financial instruments. Also called the CASH MARKET. Delivery normally occurs two days after the trade date. In financial futures, the term can also refer to futures contracts deliverable in the current month.

spot next FOREIGN EXCHANGE term for purchase of currency for delivery on the day after the SPOT date. For example, U.S. dollars purchased on Monday for delivery on Thursday, three days after the trade date. The delivery price is adjusted for the extra day. A spot one week contract calls for delivery one week after the trade date; a spot fortnight contract calls for two-week delivery. See also TOMORROW NEXT.

spread
1. **Banking.** The net difference between the interest earned on bank loans and other assets, and a bank's cost of funds, or interest rate paid depositors for their funds and other interest-bearing liabilities. Contrast with MARGIN.
2. **Securities.** (1) in underwriting, the difference between the purchase price paid by a dealer acting as principal to an issuer of securities and the price paid by investors when a new offering of securities is sold. Also known as GROSS SPREAD; and (2) the difference between bid and asked prices on stocks or bonds traded OVER-THE-COUNTER.
3. **Futures.** The simultaneous purchase and sale of futures contracts in the same financial instrument for delivery in different months, or in different but related markets.

   4. **Finance.** A put and call option on the same security.
   5. **Foreign Exchange.** The difference in price between a bid and offer. In the spot market it is known as *spot spread*.

spreadsheet

1. accounting worksheet organized by rows and columns, providing a two-way system for analyzing related accounts. An organization's income statement and balance sheet are based on data collected in this format. For example, an entry in a row might represent a debit, an entry in a column represents a credit. Adding up the rows and columns gives a summary total for the accounting period in question. If used to post original account entries, it is a transaction journal or account ledger. Summary totals from these subsidiary ledgers are later posted to the GENERAL LEDGER. For example, a bank's LIABILITY LEDGER listing commercial loans on the books might list all interest payments received and posted to the ledger, past due interest, noninterest expense, and noninterest income.
2. electronic spreadsheet, often used as a forecasting tool to project the impact of interest rate changes on a deposit or loan portfolio during future time periods, and test various what-if hypotheses or interest rate scenarios in each of those periods. Because of its flexibility, computer simulation based on spreadsheet modeling has become an important part of budgeting, financial planning, and ASSET-LIABILITY MANAGEMENT.

square position foreign exchange term indicating a dealer's purchase commitments in a given currency are offset by sell commitments. The dealer's inventory is balanced, neither a LONG POSITION nor a SHORT POSITION.

squeeze see TIGHT MONEY.

stabilization

1. **Monetary Policy.** The actions of a CENTRAL BANK to limit currency fluctuations in the FOREIGN EXCHANGE markets, by purchasing or selling currency reserves to other central banks. When a central bank intervenes in the open markets and sells reserves of its nation's currency, the value of that currency against other currencies tends to decline or remain

about the same. Stabilization funds, for example, the EX-CHANGE STABILIZATION FUND maintained by the Federal Reserve Bank of New York, are national government units involved in foreign exchange operations. See also PEG (PEGGING); SWAP NETWORK.

2. Underwriting. The actions by a DEALER or issuer of a security to prevent a security from falling below the initially offered price in the period between the registration date and the date these securities have been sold in the public market. Some dealers make an active market in these so-called WHEN ISSUED securities.

stale-dated check presented to the paying bank six months or more after the original issue date. Banks are not required by the Uniform Commercial Code to honor stale-dated checks and can return them to the issuing bank unpaid. The maker of a check can discourage late presentment by writing the words "not good after X days" on the back of the check. See also POST-DATED.

Standard & Poor's investment advisory service, a subsidiary of McGraw Hill, that supplies debt ratings on ASSET-BACKED SECURITIES, corporate and MUNICIPAL BONDS, COMMERCIAL PAPER, common stock, and preferred stock. The company also compiles various market indexes—the best known being the Standard & Poor's 500 Index of major industrial firms—and publishes investment guides, including the Standard & Poor Bond Guide, the BLUE LIST of offered municipal bonds (published through a subsidiary). The company rates Tennessee Valley Authority bonds, but does not review other government backed obligations. Rated securities are more easily sold to investors, and issuers voluntarily submit their offerings for review. Ratings, once published, are reviewed once a year. Standard & Poor's also maintains the CUSIP NUMBER system used to identify securities issued in certificate form, under a contract with the American Bankers Association.

Standard & Poor's assigns 12 different ratings for corporate bonds and asset-backed securities. It also assigns ratings to CERTIFICATES OF DEPOSIT. Corporate debt securities and municipal bonds are rated from AAA (the highest quality) to D, bonds that are in default of principal, interest, or both.

A bond rating of AAA means the issuer has sufficient income to pay principal and interest over the 5- to 40-year lifetime of the bonds. Commercial paper is rated A1, A2, A3, B, although only the top three grades are relevant because issuers usually will not attempt to market lower grade paper. A grading of NCR (no contract rating) means the issuer has not asked for a rating. A rating of P (for provisional) assigned revenue bonds indicates that repayment is contingent on project completion.

Certificates of Deposit issued by banks and savings institutions are assigned ratings under S&P's Qualified CD Rating Service. These are given ratings ranging from AAA to CCC for long-term CDs (over a year) and A1+ to D for CDs with maturities under a year. (The letter Q following a rating indicates a rating is based on public sources.) See also DUN & BRADSTREET; MERCANTILE AGENCY; MOODY'S INVESTORS SERVICE; RATING.

standard of value one of the properties of MONEY, a test of moneyness. A stable national economy depends on an accepted, uniform medium of exchange allowing suppliers and users of funds to set a fair value (price) on money loaned from one party to another, or on goods sold in open, competitive markets. Gold is the ultimate standard, although today most Western currencies no longer are backed by gold, i.e., exchangeable for gold coins or bullion equal to the face value of paper currency. The United States abandoned the gold standard domestically with the Gold Reserve Act of 1934, and internationally in 1971 when it signed the SMITHSONIAN AGREEMENT, which initiated FLOATING EXCHANGE RATES between the major Western countries. See also AGIO; BARTER; BULLION; LEGAL TENDER; MONEY.

standard prepayment commonly used prepayment model in mortgage backed securities, based on an assumed rate of prepayment each month of the unpaid principal balance of a pool of new mortgage loans. For example, this model might assume an annual prepayment rate of 0.2% in the first month in the life of the mortgage loans, and 2% in subsequent months until the 30th month. Afterward, a prepayment rate of 6% annually is assumed. Also known as *constant prepayment rate*.

standard risk
1. an acceptable loan using normal credit standards. Also called a satisfactory credit. This credit classification indicates the asset in question has satisfactory asset quality and borrower

liquidity. The borrower has the capacity to repay scheduled debts as called for by a promissory note.
2. risk rating given bank assets requiring 100% of risk-based capital for computing capital adequacy. For example, commercial loans, consumer installment loans, and most off-balance sheet assets.

standby commitment
1. nonbinding commitment by the FEDERAL NATIONAL MORT- GAGE ASSOCIATION to purchase a specified number of mortgages in the secondary mortgage market. Loans offered for sale during the standby period may be converted to mandatory commitment at any time during the term of a standby. A commitment fee of $1\frac{1}{2}$% is paid by the mortgage originator, depending on the length of the commitment.
2. bank lending commitment, convertible to line of credit.

standby letter of credit
letter of credit that represents an obligation by the issuing bank on a designated third party (the BENEFICIARY), that is contingent on the failure of the bank's customer to perform under the terms of a contract with the beneficiary. Also called a PERFORMANCE BOND. A standby letter of credit is most often used as a CREDIT ENHANCEMENT, with the understanding that, in most cases, it will never be drawn against or funded. As a contingent liability of the issuing bank, standby letters are OFF-BALANCE SHEET LIABILITIES, and the issuing bank must reserve a portion of its capital equal to 100% of the standby letter, under RISK-BASED CAPITAL regulations.

standby note issuance facility (SNIF)
credit facility that arranges project financing through secondary obligations, rather than primary ones. A standby facility guarantees payment if the original note issuer defaults. It is often used by weak credit borrowers, who pay a commission to the guarantor, who is secondarily liable if the primary issuer defaults. This as an off-balance sheet item in financial reporting. See also REVOLV- ING UNDERWRITING FACILITY.

standby underwriting
form of UNDERWRITING whereby the selling group agrees to purchase any outstanding shares of securities that have not been purchased after shareholders have

exercised their preemptive rights to purchase new securities or exchange new securities for old ones, as in a REORGANIZATION OR RECAPITALIZATION. When the underwriter remarkets securities purchased through underwriting, he is acting as a DEALER. See also ALL OR NONE; BEST EFFORT.

standing mortgage interest-only loan with no amortization of principal during the life of the loan. The principal is payable at maturity in a balloon note. Contrast with LEVEL-PAYMENT AMORTIZATION.

stand-in processing in ON-LINE financial networks, such as automated teller machine (ATM) networks, a processing alternative that is used when the normal on-line processor in an EFTS system is not available. A negative or positive file is used to identify valid accounts and to approve or deny transactions.

standstill agreement agreement whereby a lender makes no further collection efforts on an unpaid loan, acting in the belief that FORECLOSURE would jeopardize the ability of a borrower in financial difficulty to repay any portion of the debt. Such agreements are found most frequently in agriculture loans and loans secured by real estate, where both parties agree that a renegotiated loan is better than a defaulted borrower. The lender and borrower negotiate new credit terms that may include a lower interest rate and rescheduling of payment terms. See also TROUBLED DEBT RESTRUCTURING; WORKOUT AGREEMENT.

start-up financing money used to start a business or purchase assets. Banks tend to view entrepreneurial ventures cautiously and rarely make loans to newly organized businesses without taking COLLATERAL, and if the business venture is a corporation, personal guaranties of the starters. If the entrepreneurs obtain VENTURE CAPITAL financing, a bank loan typically serves as a second level of funding; the bank loan becomes a source of WORKING CAPITAL loan to finance conversion of inventory or receivables into cash receipts, whereas the venture capital funding is a source of longer-term EQUITY capital that ultimately becomes the source of profit to the owners if the firm becomes successful. See also BUSINESS PLAN; CO-MAKER; CORPORATE RESOLUTION; FINANCING STATEMENT; GUARANTOR; KEY MAN INSURANCE; SECURITY AGREEMENT; SECURITY INTEREST.

state and local bonds long-term bonds issued by municipal govenments, local taxing districts, and state government
agencies. These bonds, sometimes referred to collectively as
MUNICIPAL BONDS, generally are tax-exempt from federal income
taxes on interest earned, although certain classes of bonds issued
after August 1986 are subject to federal taxes on interest income.
The Tax Reform Act of 1986 placed annual limits on the amount
of fully tax-exempt bonds issued by a state or local agency.

Classifications of these bonds include GENERAL OBLIGATION
BONDS, REVENUE BONDS, INDUSTRIAL REVENUE BONDS, MORT-
GAGE REVENUE BONDS. See also PRIVATE PURPOSE BOND; PUBLIC
PURPOSE BOND; TAXABLE MUNICIPAL BOND.

state bank corporation chartered by a state to engage in commercial banking, and subject to supervision under banking laws
in the chartering state. State banks differ from NATIONAL BANKS,
which are chartered and supervised by the Comptroller of the
Currency. State banks have access to Federal Reserve services,
such as check collection, currency and coin delivery, and the
Federal Reserve Fed Wire, and can become member institutions
in the Federal Reserve System. Only about 1,000 state banks
have become Federal Reserve MEMBER BANKS.

Regulations in some states give state chartered banks
more authority than national banks to engage in selected nonbank activities, such as insurance underwriting and brokerage,
securities underwriting, and real estate investments, which accounts for the diversity of banking under the DUAL BANKING system. Supervision of state chartered banks is shared by STATE
BANKING DEPARTMENTS and the FEDERAL DEPOSIT INSURANCE
CORPORATION, which insures deposits of most regulated financial institutions. The FDIC also requires state banks to follow
Federal Reserve Board regulations, even if they are not Federal
Reserve Member Banks. This effectively extends the Fed's jurisdiction, for instances in regulating consumer credit, to all federally insured commercial banks.

state banking department agency that charters and
supervises state banks. The chief officer in this department is the
designated superintendent of banks or has a similar title. The
Conference of State Bank Supervisors is the national association
of state bank superintendents.

stated maturity latest date on which holders of COLLATER-ALIZED MORTGAGE OBLIGATION (CMO) bonds will be paid in full, assuming there are no prepayments on mortgages backing the bonds. The date printed on a bond is its stated maturity. A typical CMO issue has several maturity classes (called TRANCHES) that cover a range of maturity assumptions: a fast pay bond with maturities up to five years; an intermediate pay bond maturing in 5 to 10 years; a slow pay bond maturing in 20 to 25 years; and a Z-Bond (or accrual bond) that pays out at the maturity of a 30-year mortgage. See also AVERAGE LIFE.

statement detailed record of a customer's account, listing debits, credits, transfers between related accounts, and service charges during the preceding month. A checking account statement lists checks by the date paid, bank teller deposits, and electronic deposits (for example, a payroll direct deposit); AUTO-MATED TELLER MACHINE withdrawals and deposits; preauthorized debits (for example, a loan payment automatically deducted each month); and the beginning and end-of-month account balance. A DESCRIPTIVE STATEMENT lists the payee's name next to each account entry, for example, the merchant name in a bank credit card statement. A COMBINED STATEMENT lists account balances in related accounts, for example, checking and savings accounts that are maintained under a single account number. See also BANK STATEMENT; PERIODIC STATEMENT; STATE-MENT SAVINGS ACCOUNT.

statement analysis detailed examination of a borrower's balance sheet and cash flow to determine ability to repay bank debt. A key part of the process is close examination of financial ratios, such as receivables turnover. Unaudited financial statements may require additional verification. See also BALANCE SHEET RATIOS; TURNOVER RATIOS.

statement balance
1. account balance as of the date summary statements are prepared and mailed to customers. Checking account statements list all checks paid before the date the statement is prepared. The ending balance may differ from the actual balance in the account, because checks that have not yet cleared are not

included. By comparing the bank statement with checks listed in a checkbook, the customer can verify the accuracy of the account statement.

2. outstanding balance owed on a CREDIT CARD account.

3. closing balance in a deposit account, including interest earned, less service charges.

statement of account see ACCOUNT STATEMENTS; STATEMENT.

statement of condition see REPORT OF CONDITION.

statement savings account savings account where deposits, withdrawals, and interest credited are recorded as computer entries. The customer receives a periodic statement of account, showing deposits, withdrawals, and interest earned up to the posting date, but does not receive a passbook evidencing ownership of the account.

statement stuffer marketing brochure in a customer's ACCOUNT STATEMENT, containing a brief sales message and a short-form application or toll-free telephone number. Statement stuffers are an inexpensive way to market additional products to bank customers or promote special rates on savings accounts.

static gap the simplest measure of short-term net interest exposure, or difference between assets and liabilities of comparable repricing periods. It generally is calculated for periods under one year, in multiple periods, or time frames of 0 to 30 days, 31 to 90 days, or 91 to 180 days. By itself, interest rate gap is an imprecise measurement, because it fails to consider interim cash flows, loan prepayment, average maturity, and other factors. Contrast with DYNAMIC GAP.

statute of frauds legislation adopted in most states stipulating that certain contracts must be in writing to legally be enforceable. The purpose is to prevent fraudulent transactions. For example, Article II of the UNIFORM COMMERCIAL CODE stipulates that contracts for sale of goods for $500 or more must indicate terms of the agreement in writing and be signed by the party owing the agreed amount.

statute of limitations state laws specifying the time period within which parties taking judicial action to enforce rights must file the claims. The period varies depending on the type of claim: if based on statute, the claim must be filed within a certain number of years of the action in question; if based on written contract, a longer period is allowed—up to six years in most states for contract claims, and five years for civil liability (TORT) claims. The statutory period for filing claims, however, varies according to state jurisdiction. Claims filed after the statutory period ends are barred.

stock ownership interest in a corporation, evidenced by physical certificates authorized and sold to the public by the issuer. Common stock entitles the owners to receive regular dividends if declared by the board of directors, to vote at annual shareholder meetings, or to authorize other persons to vote on their behalf. Preferred stock usually has no voting rights, pays limited dividends, but has priority claim over common stock to earnings (dividends) and assets (liquidation value) of the corporation. See also ABOVE PAR; COUPON; PAR VALUE; STOCK PURCHASE OPTION.

stock purchase option employee benefit authorizing purchase of shares of common stock issued by their employer, usually at a price discounted from the book market value. The option may be exercised anytime during a ten-year period. Sometimes called a stock-bonus trust. See also EMPLOYEE STOCK OWNERSHIP PLAN.

stock split increase in the number of shares to be offered for sale, done by amending a corporate charter. The amendment approves an increase (a split up) in the number of common shares or a decrease, called a split down or reverse stock split. The transaction does not increase equity capital, as the stated par value of shares owned is reduced proportionately. In a reverse split, the issuer reduces the number of shares outstanding. Compare to RIGHTS OFFERING.

stop order order to buy or sell at the market when a definite price is reached, either above or below the price in effect when the order was given. Also called *stop out order*. It is not always possible to execute a stop order at the current market price. In a falling market, for example, a stop order calling for sale at 40 becomes a market order at that price, but the next sale may be at 39 or lower. The security is offered for sale at the market price.

stop out price lowest price the U. S. Treasury Department accepts in an auction of a new issue of Treasury securities. Securities sold at this price pay the highest yield. When the Treasury auctions securities, it accepts tenders starting at the highest bid price and continues to fill bids at gradually lower prices until the entire amount of securities has been sold. Usually, the Treasury also reports the percentage of stop out bids accepted in an auction of new securities.

stop payment order by the maker of a check that payment should not be honored. Stop payment orders directing the drawee to dishonor a specific check may be given by telephone or in writing. Under the Uniform Commercial Code, stop payment orders that have been confirmed in writing by the check writer or maker are valid for six months.

stopped account see ACCOUNT HOLD.

store and forward computer facility in an ELECTRONIC FUNDS TRANSFER system that temporarily holds transactions in a batch file, before forwarding them to the host computer for interbank settlement and posting to customers' accounts.

story paper investment that because of its newness in the market, does not have a strong track record, and may not carry a rating by a rating agency. More often than not, story paper is sold on the basis of the seller's persuasive abilities than on the safety and yield of the bond or investment itself. This creates paper risk, because the investor may end up holding something different from what was originally sold, and file a lawsuit against the seller. For example, unscrupulous sales tactics by some municipal bond salesmen in the early 1970s led to a Congressional investigation, and the formation of the MUNICIPAL SECURITIES RULEMAKING BOARD in 1975 to supervise the municipal bond market. Contrast with SEASONED SECURITIES.

straddle simultaneous purchase of a call option and a put option with the same exercise date and exercise price. This is an option position designed to profit from an expected increase in the price volatility of the underlying instrument.

straight bond noncallable bond, such as a Treasury bond, Eurobond, or savings bond.

straight credit
1. LETTER OF CREDIT requiring presentation on or before the expiration date at the office of the paying bank. Drafts are honored in favor of the beneficiary only.
2. loan that is backed or secured only by the borrower's promise to pay. Also known as a GOOD FAITH LOAN.

street name securities term for a registered security held in the name of a bank, brokerage firm, or another third party as NOMINEE, as opposed to a registration in the owner's name. Street name registration eliminates the need to deliver certificates to a selling broker when transferring securities.

strike price dollar price at which the holder of a call option can buy the underlying securities, or the holder of a put option can sell, anytime during the life of the option contract. Also called *striking price* or EXERCISE PRICE.

strip security created by separating the corpus, or bond principal, from the interest coupons, or interest payments. The stripping is done by a trust fiduciary. Principal payments are grouped together to make large denomination securities, and interest payments grouped with other interest payments of the same date to make other large securities, which are then sold to investors in smaller denominations. Separating the interest coupons effectively creates a ZERO-COUPON SECURITY, a bond that pays no interest until maturity. An investor buying a ten-year $1,000 Treasury Bond, yielding 9%, pays $415 and at maturity receives the full face value of the bond.

In U.S. Treasury securities, there are two general classes of strip securities: so-called generic STRIPS, short for SEPARATE TRADING OF REGISTERED INTEREST AND PRINCIPAL, which are direct obligations of the U.S. Teasury Department, and synthetic strips, which are sold through brokerage houses. U.S. Treasury securities actually are not stripped of coupon interest payments, but are sold at true discount. Zero-coupons issued by brokerage houses have such colorful acronyms as CATS (Certificate of Accrual on Treasury Securities, issued by Salomon Brothers), and TIGR (Treasury Income Growth Receipts, issued by Merrill Lynch.) See also STRIPPED MORTGAGE-BACKED SECURITIES.

stripped mortgage-backed securities mortgage-backed instrument consisting of two distinct classes: INTEREST-ONLY (IO) SECURITIES and PRINCIPAL-ONLY (PO) SECURITIES. In its purest form, the mortgage-backed security is converted into an INTEREST-ONLY strip, where the investor receives 100% of the interest cash flow, and a principal only strip, in which the investor receives 100% of the principal cash flows. Both are highly interest rate sensitive. An interest-only strip will increase in value when interest rates rise, and a principal-only strip will increase in market when rates decline. POs are more subject to prepayment risk for this reason. Alternative forms of IOs and POs are made up of differing amounts of principal and interest to suit individual investor or market requirements.

See also ASSET-BACKED SECURITIES; COLLATERALIZED MORTGAGE OBLIGATION; RESIDUAL; SPECULATIVE SECURITIES.

strong currency currency that lenders are willing to accept as payment, other than their own national currency. Also, a convertible currency trading in the exchange markets at a premium vis-a-vis other convertible currencies. Lenders have no legal obligation to accept payment in a strong currency. Central banks maintain a portion of their reserves in strong currency deposits. In foreign exchange trading, a strong currency trades at a premium in relation to a WEAK CURRENCY. Also known as a *reserve currency*.

structural adjustment medium-term credit facility originated by the World Bank in 1979 to assist developing countries in gaining economic self-sufficiency. This form of lending is aimed at reducing a debtor nation's CURRENT ACCOUNT DEFICIT, rather than financing new projects. Under these multiyear agreements, debtor nations postpone repayment of principal to later years when the debt service can be more easily absorbed by a stronger, growing economy. The basis of structural adjustment credit is the borrower's agreement to encourage private development, stimulate exports, and promote economic diversification with the ultimate aim of resuming positive economic growth.

structuring MONEY LAUNDERING scheme whereby cash in excess of $10,000 is deposited without being reported in several transactions under that amount. Cash transactions that ordinarily are reportable under the Money Laundering Control Act of 1986 are restructured in several ways. SMURFs, or the runners in a money laundering scheme, attempt to restructure cash transactions by making several small deposits instead of one large one; by asking for cash back so the final transaction amount is under $10,000; and by purchasing cashier's checks, all under $10,000, at several banks, which are later deposited in a single account. If structuring is suspected, however, bank tellers still are required to fill out a CURRENCY TRANSACTION REPORT. Such transactions are reportable not only to banking authorities, but also to the U.S. Secret Service and the IRS.

student loan see EDUCATION LOAN.

Student Loan Marketing Association publicly traded corporation established in 1972 to increase the availability of student loans by purchasing loans in the SECONDARY MARKET. The corporation, also known as Sallie Mae, guarantees college education loans under the federal Guaranteed Student Loan Program, and under the Health Education Assistance Program. Sallie Mae purchases a 90% interest in loans guaranteed by the corporation, and finances its secondary market activities by issuing medium-term notes and floating rate notes. Sallie Mae obligations are exempt from state and local taxes.

subchapter M section of the Internal Revenue Code authorizing favorable tax treatment of regulated investment companies. Companies that choose this form of organization are not required to pay income taxes on realized gains and investment income distributed to shareholders if they: (1) distribute not less than 90% of their net investment income (interest and dividends, less expenses) in any taxable year; (2) derive at least 90% of gross income from dividends, interest, and gains from sale of securities; and (3) comply with other percentage limitations on short-term gains from securities held less than three months. Nonregulated investment companies are taxed on net income and realized gains.

subchapter S business concern chartered as a corporation that is taxed as a partnership. An S corporation can use the CASH BASIS of accounting, has 35 or fewer shareholders, and corporate gains (or losses) from operations are taxed to the shareholders as individuals. Also known as a small business corporation.

subject offer offer that is not a firm commitment to sell, but is intended for information purposes only, or to solicit a counteroffer from a willing buyer.

subject to collection check drawn on an out-of-town bank and deposited, with IMMEDIATE AVAILABILITY of funds, to a customer in good standing, or one who has sufficient balances to cover the deposit. The deposit is made with the understanding that if the check bounces for any reason, the amount deposited will be charged back to the customer's account. See also AVAILABILITY.

subject to mortgage assignment or transfer of real estate where the purchaser agrees to take over monthly payments of principal and interest, but does not assume personal liability for the obligation. If the purchaser defaults, the lender must attempt to collect the debt from the original borrower, through FORECLOSURE on the property, or other means. The original mortgage remains intact, and property title is not passed on to the purchaser. Contrast with ASSUMPTION.

subject to verification deposit accepted for IMMEDIATE AVAILABILITY credit, as for example, a check drawn on and deposited in the same bank, that may be adjusted later if an error is discovered. For example, if the check amount differs from what the customer wrote on the deposit ticket, or when a bank's customer makes a cash deposit at an AUTOMATED TELLER MACHINE

(ATM). Envelope deposits at an ATM must be verified by bank employees to see that the deposit matches the amount claimed by the customer.

subordinated debt debt having a claim against the issuer's assets that is lower ranking, or junior to, other obligations, and is paid after claims to holders of senior securities are satisfied. Credit has differing levels of claim, depending on how a financing is structured; thus, an obligation can be senior to one claim, but subordinate to another. For example, a subordinated debenture is junior to a mortgage backed bond, but has precedence over dividend payments to stockholders.

A REAL ESTATE MORTGAGE INVESTMENT CONDUIT (REMIC), which invests in a pool of mortgages, typically sells interests in these mortgages through multiclass senior/subordinated securities to improve the marketability of REMIC securities. The subordinated debt class absorbs all the credit risk and default risk of one or more senior debt classes. Subordinated obligations also are used commonly in MEZZANINE LEVEL financings arranged in corporate leveraged buyouts and restructurings.

subordination agreement

1. agreement signed by a co-maker placing an interest in property owned jointly with a borrower behind the lender's security interest in pledged collateral. Lenders in states recognizing the TENANTS IN COMMON form of property ownership ordinarily require co-makers to sign a promissory note or a subordination agreement if the borrower defaults.
2. instrument acknowledging that a creditor's claim is secondary to claims of other creditors. Thus, under s subordination agreement, a loan by an officer of a corporation to the firm has a secondary claim to assets after a bank loan. The agreement assures that a bank loan will be paid off first.

subrogation substitution of one creditor for another in settlement of a claim or obligation, or transfer of ownership, as when a mortgage is sold in the secondary market.

subscription offer to purchase securities, that may be exercised any time during a specified waiting period, usually one to two months after they are initially offered.

subsidiary

1. corporation controlled through partial or complete ownership of its voting stock by another company, known as the parent company. Bank owned subsidiary companies are reportable in a bank's REPORT OF CONDITION filed with its primary regulatory agency. A company with 50% or more of its outstanding stock owned, directly or indirectly, by a bank is a majority owned subsidiary. A significant subsidiary of a reporting bank is a company in which the parent bank has a 5% equity capital interest, or a company that contributes at least 5% of the parent bank's gross operating income or 5% of its pretax income (or loss). Banks and other depository financial institutions report income on a consolidated basis, including earnings of subsidiary companies.

2. corporation, owned by a bank holding company, offering nonbanking services, such as equipment leasing or securities underwriting, as approved by the Federal Reserve Board under Section 4(c)(8) of the Bank Holding Company Act. A company owned by a bank holding company, rather than a bank itself, generally is referred to as a bank AFFILIATE, to avoid being confused with bank-owned subsidiaries. Holding company ownership of these nonbanking affiliate companies also serves to protect a bank's insured deposits from operating losses in uninsured activities, such as bond underwriting.

   The Bank Holding Company Act requires bank holding companies to maintain an 80% interest in subsidiary corporations, and to get approval of the Federal Reserve Board before acquiring more than a 5% interest in a company engaged in a business other than accepting deposits and making loans. See also SECURITIES AFFILIATE; SERVICE CORPORATION.

substandard

1. bank loan or other interest-earning asset that is protected inadequately by current net worth and paying capacity of the borrower, or the collateral pledged. Loans classified as substandard are characterized by the distinct possibility that the lender will sustain some loss if the deficiencies are not corrected. Some loss of interest is anticipated, or may have already occurred, but loss of principal is considered unlikely. See also ADVERSELY CLASSIFIED ASSETS; DOUBTFUL LOAN; LOSS.

2. country risk classification for cross-border loans to a debtor nation, in which the country involved has not met external

debt payments, accepted an economic adjustment program recommended by the International Monetary Fund, or negotiated a rescheduling of debts with its creditors.

substitution

1. replacement of one creditor by another, also known as SUBROGATION.
   2. replacement of collateral securing a broker's call loan with other collateral of equal value.
2. acquisition of a borrower's tangible property through FORECLOSURE. The lender takes collateral in exchange for the defaulted loan.
3. in the SECONDARY MORTGAGE MARKET, an investor's right to have the selling financial institution replace a nonperforming loan with another.
4. the exchange of a new contract for an existing one, as in a NOVATION.

sucre national currency of Peru.

sunset clause language in a state law stating the law expires at a specified date, unless renewed by act of the state legislature. Legislation in several states raising or abolishing interest rate ceilings on credit card finance charges contains such clauses.

Super NOW account transaction account combining features of the NEGOTIABLE ORDER OF WITHDRAWAL (NOW account) and the MONEY MARKET DEPOSIT ACCOUNT. Authorized for depository institutions in January 1983, Super NOWs have no interest rate ceilings, but a seven-day withdrawal notice may apply. In addition, they have unlimited deposit and withdrawal capability, but are available only to depositors eligible for NOW accounts, excluding for-profit businesses.

super regional bank bank holding company operating subsidiary banks in two or more states. The American Banker, a daily newspaper, defines a super-regional bank as a non-MONEY CENTER BANK ranking in the top 100 banking companies in the United States that has merged across state lines to establish a full commercial banking presence in another state. Super regional banks originated in New England and the southeastern United

States in the mid-1980s under state legislation permitting RE-
GIONAL INTERSTATE BANKING. Currently they are found in all major geographic regions of the country.

super sinker bond tranche in a Collateralized Mortgage Obligation (CMO) or other mortgage-backed security with a
shorter average life than other bonds in the same offering. These
bonds are retired at a faster than normal rate by early borrower
prepayments, reducing the cash flow uncertainty. Super sinker
bonds are also a common feature in MORTGAGE REVENUE BONDS.
These housing related bonds are attractive to investors who believe that mortgage rates will fall while new housing construction increases. See also CONTROLLED AMORTIZATION BOND.

supervisory merger consolidation of two or more financial institutions, supervised by a bank regulatory agency, in
which a weak institution is acquired by a stronger one. The supervisory agency may arrange assistance to the acquiring bank
by purchasing some or all of the bad loans in the troubled institution, or giving the acquirer of a failing bank or savings institution guarantees against losses for a limited period. See also BAIL-
OUT.

supply side economics economic theory popularized in
the 1970s that maintained policy objectives for growth in the
economy can be met through tax incentives encouraging businesses to make productive investments. Supply side economists
emphasize the importance of tax cuts and tax credits, which they
argue stimulates AGGREGATE SUPPLY encouraging suppliers to
produce more, and individuals to earn more as opposed to stimulating AGGREGATE DEMAND for goods and services by consumers
and businesses. In other words, people will work more because
they can produce more. Supply siders argue that the economic
stimulus of tax cuts and tax credits will offset revenue losses
from cuts in marginal tax rates. In the early 1980s, supply side
economics was a politically attractive solution to the stagflation
(double-digit inflation accompanied by stagnant growth) characteristic of the late 1970s. It is counter to the KEYNESIAN ECO-
NOMICS school; supply siders reject the Keynesian multiplier ar-
gument that relates tax cuts to increases in aggregate demand.

surcharge

1. extra charge imposed on those who purchase with a credit card instead of cash. Credit card surcharges are forbidden by the Truth in Lending Act amendments of 1975, which did allow discounts for cash payments.

2. charge assessed by a Federal Reserve bank for access to the nighttime processing cycle of an AUTOMATED CLEARING HOUSE, commonly used by banks to move excess funds from ZERO-BALANCE ACCOUNTs into concentration accounts for corporate customers.

3. DISCOUNT WINDOW surcharge imposed by a FEDERAL RESERVE BANK, on short-term adjustment credit. Used in the early 1980s as a selective credit control to control inflation, the Fed's authority to use surcharges expired in November 1981.

surety guaranty of debt repayment or fulfillment of contractual obligation. Borrowers unable to obtain credit under their own name often have a third party sign the application. Under a surety agreement, the lender can look first to the surety or guarantor for payment if the borrower defaults. A surety who pays a borrower's debt takes an assignment of the creditor's rights through SUBROGATION and can attempt to recover that payment from the borrower.

surety bond agreement by an insurance company to take the place of a defaulted contractor in a development project, and take corrective action, if necessary, to finish the project. The insurance company also may be compelled to pay for damages resulting from default. Surety bonds commonly are required on municipal development projects financed by general obligation bonds or revenue bonds. A surety bond also is required to put a STOP PAYMENT order on an official bank check, such as a CASHIER'S CHECK. Also called an *indemnity bond*.

surplus

1. EQUITY of a corporation, including stock issued at a premium over its par value or stated value, representing the excess of assets over liabilities, including capital stock. The preferred term is capital surplus. In banking, there is little difference between equity capital and surplus, because amounts contrib-

uted by stockholders over the par value of their stock are counted as part of the capital account in computing CAPITAL ADEQUACY and the bank's NET WORTH.

The Comptroller of the Currency requires national banks to have surplus of 20% over the PAID IN CAPITAL stock before obtaining a charter. Also, national banks must allocate at least 10% of the previous six month's earnings to the surplus account before paying shareholder dividends.

2. net profits of a corporation after payment of dividends. Also called earned surplus, undistributed profits, or RETAINED EARNINGS.

surplus reserves

1. Accounting. The portion of cash surplus that has not been allocated to a particular account.

2. Banking. Reserve account balances above the legal RESERVE REQUIREMENTS. Also known as EXCESS RESERVES. Also, unallocated reserves of banks belonging to a clearing house association.

surveillance

1. monitoring system that alerts banking regulators to sudden changes in a bank's condition. The Comptroller of the Currency has an electronic early warning system, the NATIONAL BANK SURVEILLANCE SYSTEM (NBSS), that watches changes in a national bank's financial condition compared to banks of similar size. The NBSS system helps the Comptroller's office keep track of banks in need of special attention.

2. video cameras and other security systems used to monitor teller line and automated teller machine transactions. Film from monitoring systems can be used to document robberies, unauthorized withdrawals, and other disputed transactions.

suspension

1. revocation of a bank's charter by a supervisory agency.

2. bank closing ordered by banking or governmental authorities to control a RUN on a bank, or when a bank is declared insolvent.

3. temporary halt in trading of a security, or trading activity on a stock exchange in advance of a news announcement or to correct an imbalance of buy and sell orders.

    4. debt repayment MORATORIUM declared by a debtor nation, for example, a temporary halt in interest payments.

sustainable growth
    1. noninflationary, stable growth in the economy with full employment: an objective of Federal Reserve MONETARY POLICY.
    2. income from a firm's operations in future accounting periods that can support debt repayment. It implies a rate of growth expected from retained earnings without external financing, and without altering financial leverage. Lenders usually ask for copies of financial statements before extending or renewing a LINE OF CREDIT.

swap
    1. Foreign Exchange. The simultaneous buying and selling of a currency in approximately equal amounts for different maturity dates. The swap price is the difference in price between the two maturity dates of the swap.
    2. agreement to exchange interest payments in a fixed rate obligation for interest payments in a floating rate obligation (an INTEREST RATE SWAP), or one currency for another (a CURRENCY SWAP), and reverse the exchange at a later date. A cross-currency swap is the exchange of a fixed rate obligation in one currency for a floating rate obligation in another. A swap agreement is based on a NOTIONAL PRINCIPAL amount, or an equivalent amount of principal, that sets the value of the swap at maturity, but is never exchanged. The notional principal sets the value of the interest payments in a swap. Rules governing financial swaps are set by the International Swap Dealers Association, a self-regulatory organization.

      Interest rate and currency swaps are used by bankers and investment managers to minimize borrowing costs, to fund bank loans with liabilities of approximately equal durations, to gain liquidity (in a currency swap) in one currency versus another; to hedge portfolio risk or raise capital in foreign markets, and also to generate trading profits. Swaps most often are used for funding purposes or for creating assets, and have some advantages when compared to bank loans or deposits in ASSET-LIABILITY MANAGEMENT. Unlike loans or deposits, swaps are not disclosed on the balance sheet of the issuing bank, although banks must still reserve a portion of their equity capital to cover their outstanding swap agreements under RISK-BASED CAPITAL guidelines. See also ASSET SWAP; BASIS SWAP; SWAP NETWORK.

3. BOND SWAP.

4. MORTGAGE SWAP.

swap network reciprocal short-term credit agreement between central banks to stabilize currency prices through INTERVENTION in the foreign exchange market. A central bank obtains foreign exchange by swapping its national currency with a trading partner and, at a future specified date, reversing the transaction, i.e., the central bank obtains domestic currency in return for foreign exchange.

swaption option contract on an INTEREST RATE SWAP. The contract gives the buyer the option to execute an interest rate swap on a future date, thereby locking in financing costs at a specified fixed rate of interest. The seller of the swaption, usually a commercial bank or investment bank, assumes the risk of interest rate changes, in exchange for payment of a swap premium.

Swap Transferring Risk with Participating Element (STRIPE) hedging technique combining an INTEREST RATE SWAP and an INTEREST RATE CAP. Also called *a participating swap*. A percentage of the amount financed, say 50%, is borrowed at a fixed rate; the rest is financed at a floating rate with an agreed-upon cap. If rates fall, the borrower participates in half of the benefits from dips in interest rates on the 50% portion covered by the cap. The borrower also is protected from upward swings in interest rates by the cap on the FLOATING RATE NOTE portion of the debt. The borrower also does not pay a fee on the swap agreement; instead, the lender prices the fixed rate portion of the loan above the rate the borrower would get in a straight interest rate swap. See also CAP; COLLAR; FLOOR.

sweep account transaction account that offers convertibility of balances above some minimum into a higher-yielding savings or investment instrument. A typical sweep account could be a Negotiable Order of Withdrawal (NOW account) on which 5.25% interest is paid on the first $2,000 on deposit. Balances above the specified amount periodically are transferred into a money market mutual fund or repurchase agreement. If the

NOW account falls below the minimum balance, some funds in the higher yielding account are liquidated and transferred back to the NOW account. Sweep accounts were popular in the early 1980s when deposit interest ceilings were still in effect, but are being replaced by Super NOW accounts. A variation is the repurchase agreement, or sweep repo, in which funds are moved from a depositor's account and invested in government securities. The transaction is reversed on the next banking day, and the customer's funds, plus interest, are recredited to the deposit account.

sweetener
1. **Banking.** The additional consideration paid by a borrower in periods of high interest rates and TIGHT MONEY, or by a marginally creditworthy borrower. For example, payment of an additional point (one percentage point of the principal amount borrowed) during periods of high loan demand. Also, the pledge of additional securities by a broker to finance securities trading for customers.
2. **Finance.** The addition of a conversion privilege on securities, making them convertible into common stock, and thus more valuable to investors.

SWIFT see SOCIETY FOR WORLDWIDE INTERBANK FINANCIAL TELECOMMUNICATIONS.

swingline short-term BACKUP LINE of credit that can be called at very short notice, and normally is arranged by a bank for an issuer of COMMERCIAL PAPER. The line provides contingency financing to cover potential shortfalls that may result if the proceeds of a sale are insufficient to retire the debt incurred in issuing the paper, or if the issuer is unable to ROLL OVER an issue of maturing paper.

swing loan see BRIDGE LOAN.

switch
1. **Foreign Exchange.** The intended effect of intervention in currency markets by central monetary authorities. Switching policy is intended to reverse the rate at which a nation's currency flows out of, or is absorbed by, domestic markets, and has further impact on a nation's balance of trade.

2. **Futures.** Liquidating an existing position and simultaneously reinstating a position in another futures contract of the same type. Known as *switching*.

3. computer facility in shared ELECTRONIC FUNDS TRANSFER networks that routes transactions between a terminal and a card issuing bank's host computer. A switch in front clears all transactions processed through a network; a switch behind clears only transactions initiated by customers of other financial institutions—on others transactions. See also STAND-IN PROCESSING.

4. **Foreign Trade.** The practice of exporting or importing goods through a third country. This commonly is done when the destination country is short of U.S. dollars and the intermediary country has available dollars and is willing to exchange the destination country's currency. Switch transactions must conform with various laws covering export licenses. See also THIRD COUNTRY ACCEPTANCE.

5. **Mutual Funds.** Moving assets from one fund to another, within a family of funds.

syndicated loan see SYNDICATION.

syndication

1. **Banking.** Project financing common in the Eurobond and Euronote markets, whereby a group of commercial bankers and investment bankers each agrees to advance a portion of the funding. Typically, the financing is arranged by a single bank at narrow interest rate spreads above the lender's cost of funds. The syndicator acts as investment manager, collecting a loan origination fee or commitment fee from the borrower, and arranging for the sale of Euronotes to other banks in the group. Typically, the syndicator keeps only a small portion of the total financing, generally less than 10% of the total value of the loan.

   The syndicated loan differs from a LOAN PARTICIPATION because the syndicate members are known at the outset to the borrower. Syndication also separates the lead banker from the group of financial institutions that ultimately fund the obligation. See also NOTE ISSUANCE FACILITY; REVOLVING UNDERWRITING FACILITY; TENDER PANEL.

2. **Securities.** A group of investment bankers who purchase a new offering of securities from an issuer for resale to the

investing public at a fixed price. Also called the *purchase group* or *underwriting group*. Operating rules of the investment syndicate, led by a MANAGING UNDERWRITER, are spelled out in the AGREEMENT AMONG UNDERWRITERS. The purchase group, which may include commercial bankers, differs from the SELLING GROUP.

3. **Investments.** The purchase of shares in investments promising tax avoidance, or reinvestment of earnings without paying income taxes, usually through LIMITED PARTNERSHIP participations in real estate, oil and gas exploration, and so on, sold through an investment syndicate or a broker-dealer. The Tax Reform Act of 1986 sharply curtailed so-called passive losses in tax shelter investments.

synthetic security any combination of financial instruments producing a market instrument with different characteristics than could otherwise be achieved, for example, higher yield, better liquidity, or interest rate protection. These securities mimic conventional financial instruments that may or may not be available to investors. Most such deals are PRIVATE PLACEMENTS involving two investors, and usually are created through INTEREST RATE SWAPS, for example, creating a synthetic FLOATING RATE NOTE by matching a fixed rate bond and an interest rate swap. See also ASSET SWAP.

systemic risk possibility that failure of one bank to settle net transactions with other banks will trigger a chain reaction, depriving other banks of funds and preventing them from closing their positions in turn. Carried out to its logical extreme, the possibility exists that institutions that have had no business dealings with the failed bank ultimately will be affected in a general shutdown of normal clearing and settlement activity, a condition known as payment system GRIDLOCK. High dollar payment networks have special rules designed to prevent system-wide settlement failures from occurring. See also FEDERAL WIRE; NET SETTLEMENT; OVERDRAFT CAP.

T

tail
1. in U.S. Treasury auctions, the price spread between the average competitive bid on bills, notes, and bonds sold in Treasury auctions and the STOPOUT PRICE.
2. money market term for a financial instrument partially financed by a REPURCHASE AGREEMENT. For example, a dealer buys a 90-day Treasury bill and sells a 30-day repurchase agreement. The maturity difference between the two is the tail.
3. **Finance.** The figures appearing after the decimal point in a bond quotation. For example, in a bid of $95.3712, the tail is .3712. Bond prices also are quoted in dollars plus 32/100 of a dollar.
4. **Estates.** The property inherited by direct descendents, for example, children or grandchildren of a decedent. Called an *estate in tail*.

taka
national currency of Bangladesh.

take a position
popular expression for the activities of someone who speculates in the market, with the expectation of making a profit. A position may be long or short at the end of a trading day. A dealer buys securities, foreign exchange, or money market instruments as inventory, with the expectation of selling them later at a profit. If held for account of other institutions or for customers, the securities are listed as part of the bank's TRADING ACCOUNT ASSETS. Also called *taking a view*.

take down
1. **Banking.** An advance of money to a borrower under a CREDIT agreement or COMMITMENT to lend. A borrower who draws $20,000 against a $70,000 revolving line of credit takes down the line by the amount used.
2. **Municipal Bonds.** The price, discounted from par value, at which members of an underwriting syndicate offer to sell. The difference is the underwriter's profit.

3. **Underwriting.** The portion of an offering of securities each member of an underwriting syndicate agrees to purchase for resale to investors. Also, the price paid by underwriters in a new offering of securities.

take-out

1. trading profit from the sale of a block of securities and purchase of another at a lower price. The difference can be reinvested or taken as profit.
2. bid made to the seller of a security intended to buy out his or her position. See also LOCKED MARKET.
3. in lending, to pay off a borrower's other creditor, by replacing a short-term loan with a longer maturity loan, taking out the other lender. See also TAKE-OUT COMMITMENT.

take-out commitment agreement between a mortgage banker and a long-term investor under which the latter agrees to purchase a mortgage at a specific future date. The investor, called a TAKE-OUT LENDER, is typically an insurance company or other financial institution. See also TAKE-OUT LENDER; TAKE-OUT LOAN.

take-out lender financial institution that extends a long-term MORTGAGE on real property that replaces the interim financing, or construction loan arranged by a savings and loan, bank, or mortgage banker. The institution extending the long-term loan, or permanent financing, is often an insurance company or institutional investor willing to make a long-term investment in income producing property of realizing a capital gain from the eventual sale of the property, in addition to cash flow from rental payments by property tenants.

take-out loan permanent financing, usually structured as an amortizing, fixed payment mortgage, on an office development, housing project or mixed use income producing property. A recent innovation is the ZERO-COUPON MORTGAGE, in which interest is due and payable in one lump installment or BALLOON PAYMENT at maturity.

take the offer expression for buyer's willingness to accept the offered price of a quoting seller. The opposite is HIT THE BID.

taking delivery

1. liquidating a futures position and taking (paying for) securities or commodities underlying a futures contract, when a futures contract is open at maturity. This rarely happens in futures trading; the underlying commodities or financial instruments actually are delivered only in about 3% of all futures contracts. Futures traders are more interested in short-term market gains than in the instrument or commodity being traded. See also DELIVERY NOTICE.

2. in securities settlement, when a buyer pays for securities purchased, which normally occurs on the *regular way* settlement date, five days after the trade date.

tala national currency of Samoa.

tandem loan SECONDARY MORTGAGE MARKET program by which the GOVERNMENT NATIONAL MORTGAGE ASSOCIATION (Ginnie Mae) purchases mortgages originated at below-market rates and resells the loans at market prices to the FEDERAL HOME LOAN MORTGAGE CORPORATION (Freddie Mac) or the FEDERAL NATIONAL MORTGAGE ASSOCIATION (Fannie Mae). The Ginnie Mae Tandem Program provides financial assistance to developers of nonprofit public housing projects. Ginnie Mae pays the difference between the price paid by Fannie Mae or Freddie Mac and the original purchase price, enabling public housing authorities to obtain mortgage financing at affordable cost.

tangible asset real property or personal property, such as buildings, machinery, and real property. Tangible assets are distinguished from intangible assets such as trademarks, copyrights, and goodwill, and natural resources (timberlands, oil reserves, and coal deposits). Also includes accounts receivable of a concern. Tangible and intangible assets are recorded separately on the balance sheet. Physical assets are depreciated over their useful life; intangibles are amortized. The book value of wasting assets, such as coal, gas, or oil is reduced through depletion. Accounting rules are vague on this distinction between tangibles and intangibles. Generally, any asset not expressly defined as an intangible is considered a tangible asset.

tangible net worth equity capital (common stock) of a bank, less goodwill and other intangibles. Also called total net worth. It is an indication of the borrowing capacity or strength of a bank or a savings institution. The Financial Institutions Reform, Recovery and Enforcement Act of 1989 required savings and loan associations to maintain tangible capital (common stock plus retained earnings) equal to 1.5% of total assets. See also CAPITAL RATIOS.

tangible property see TANGIBLE ASSET.

target balance desired balance in a deposit account that meets minimum standards for profitability, or the BREAK-EVEN YIELD. There are various formulas for pricing deposit accounts to cover servicing costs. If a checking account is priced separately from other deposit accounts, a bank may insist that the customer keep a minimum balance in the account at all times, say $1,500, to qualify for service charge-free checking. A bank may waive service charges for those customers who have a high-balance savings account, for example, a $10,000 money market certificate, or combination of accounts that are kept on deposit, or a COMPENSATING BALANCE kept by a corporation.

target rate
1. rate set by a bank's ASSET-LIABILITY COMMITTEE as a desirable objective in repricing maturing deposits or loans. See also REPRICING OPPORTUNITIES; RUNOFF.
2. INTERNAL RATE OF RETURN, also known as the hurdle rate in capital budgeting.

tax abatement reduction in AD VALOREM real estate taxes granted by a municipality or local taxing authority resulting from an easement, exercise of eminent domain by the taxing authority, natural disaster, or other reasons.

taxable equivalent yield total income, including income earned on tax-exempt securities (municipal bonds). This restates nontaxable income earned in the investment portfolio on a basis that is comparable to taxable income before any taxes actually are paid, excluding PRIVATE PURPOSE BONDS acquired after December 31, 1982, which no longer are tax-exempt.

taxable estate portion of an inheritable estate subject to estate taxes, after deducting allowable expenses incurred in settling the estate, including funeral expenses, taxes owed, and marital and charitable deductions.

taxable municipal bond private activity municipal bond or industrial revenue bond that is subject to federal and state income taxes at the ordinary tax rate. Also called a nonessential function bond, or PRIVATE PURPOSE BOND. The Tax Reform Act of 1986 repealed the tax exemption for bonds financing convention centers, sports facilities, and other quasi-municipal facilities. Interest income on bonds issued after August 7, 1986 that exceed state caps on issuance of tax-free municipals is fully taxable. Certain investors also are subject to the ALTERNATIVE MINIMUM TAX on interest income from private activity bonds. Taxable municipals generally pay higher interest rates than other munis, but are protected from early redemption by call protection features. Such bonds may also be exempt from state and local taxes in the state where they are issued. States that exhaust their allowed limit of tax-exempt bonds frequently issue taxable bonds, generally to finance private development. See also PUBLIC PURPOSE BOND.

tax and loan account see TREASURY TAX AND LOAN ACCOUNT.

tax anticipation bill (TAB) U.S. Treasury bill sold on an irregular basis, and scheduled to mature in periods of heavy tax receipts. No tax anticipation bills have been issued since 1974. Instead, the Treasury has raised money on an irregular basis through the sale of CASH MANAGEMENT BILLS, which usually are reopenings or sales of additional amounts of bills. Cash management bills, like tax anticipation bills, are intended to finance the Treasury's funding requirements until tax payments are received.

tax anticipation note (TAN) short-term note issued by states and municipalities to finance current operations, with repayment from anticipated tax receipts. Also called a tax anticipation warrant. These notes are issued at a discount, have maturities of a year or less, and mature either at a specific future date or when property and other taxes are collected. Tax anticipation notes hold first claim on tax receipts when collected. See also REVENUE ANTICIPATION NOTE.

tax-deductible interest

1. interest payments on first mortgages, home equity lines of credit, and second mortgages, subject to a cap—the original purchase price of the borrower's house, plus improvements. Equity loans taken out for medical expenses or education are not subject to these restrictions. Advances on equity loans taken down before August 15, 1986 are not restricted, provided the funds were actually advanced to the borrower.
2. consumer interest payments, subject to a phaseout: 65% of interest charges in 1987, 40% in 1988, 20% in 1989, 10% in 1990, and 0% in years thereafter.

tax-deferred annuity investment vehicle generally used to create income for retirement, usually sold through an insurance company. The annuity pays a guaranteed rate of return, and federal income taxes on the pretax dollars invested are deferred until retirement. Such annuities can be single payment or multiple payment plans, or may be structured so they are payable to the surviving beneficiary named by the policyholder.

tax-deferred savings savings or investment plan that allows an individual to set aside a portion of current income in a designated savings plan, and defer payment of income taxes on principal amount and earned interest. An INDIVIDUAL RETIREMENT ACCOUNT (IRA) permits individuals with gross annual incomes of $25,000 or less, to set aside up to $2,000 a year in a savings or investment account and begin withdrawing the funds at age 59½. Others with income over $25,000 ($40,000 if filing joint return) can defer taxability of interest, but not the principal balance of an IRA contribution. Account withdrawals are taxed at the ordinary tax rate. See also ALL SAVERS CERTIFICATE; 401(K) PLAN; KEOGH PLAN.

tax-exempt bond municipal bond that is not taxed by the federal government and is free from state and local taxes in most states if purchased by an in-state resident. Most general obligation municipal bonds are exempt from state and local taxes in the states where they are originated, and certain bonds are triple tax exempt, regardless of where they originate. Five states (Texas, Nevada, Alaska, South Dakota, and Wyoming) do not tax municipal bonds issued by other states. If the yield differential is high enough, a taxable bond issued out of state actually may pay a better return to the investor. See also TAXABLE MUNICIPAL BOND.

tax-free rollover reinvestment of a tax-advantaged savings account, such as an INDIVIDUAL RETIREMENT ACCOUNT, within the statutory 60-day period allowed by the IRS for reinvestment without penalty. Amounts that are not reinvested are subject to a 10% penalty payment.

tax lien INVOLUNTARY LIEN on real estate for nonpayment of income taxes or property taxes. Tax liens have priority over bank liens securing the same property, placing the lender at a less than advantageous position in attempting to collect a debt from a delinquent borrower who also owes back taxes.

tax loss carry back (carry forward) tax benefit allowing an individual or organization to reduce a tax liability by applying net operating losses incurred in the current fiscal year against income reported in earlier years. IRS tax rules permit carrying back losses (the excess of allowable deductions over gross income) over the three prior years, resulting in a tax refund. A tax loss carry forward, on the other hand, is an operating loss charged against income in future years.

In general, banks are subject to the same rules as other corporations in computing a tax loss carry back or carry forward, under the TAX REFORM ACT OF 1986, except for losses attributable to bad debt. Starting in 1987, a bank can apply a net operating loss to taxable income in the previous three years, or forward 15 years. The Tax Reform Act repealed the old ten-and-five rule (ten years back and five years forward). However, the ten-year carry back for net operating losses caused by bad debts is retained through 1993.

Individuals can apply capital gains losses in any year above the standard income tax deduction to future years' income until the carry forward loss is offset by income or capital gains, but unlike corporations, cannot carry back losses to reduce a previous year's tax liability. See also CARRY FORWARD/CARRY BACK.

tax opinion legal opinion issued by a bond issuer's tax attorney stating, for computation of federal income tax, how a collateralized mortgage obligation will be treated by its holders. In municipal bonds, the tax opinion also states that the bond conforms to statutes making the bond interest exempt from federal income taxes.

tax-oriented lease see TRUE LEASE.

taxpayer identification number (TIN) IRS identification number needed before most bank accounts can be opened. For individuals and sole proprietors, the tax number is the individual's Social Security number. A business tax identification number is the employer's identification number, required of corporations, nonprofit organizations, associations, and partnerships. A bank's liability for noncompliance with the IRS rule after January 1, 1984 is $50 per account. A bank must also withhold 20% of the interest earned on the account in a special escrow account. See also BACKUP WITHHOLDING.

tax planning minimization of tax liability through personal FINANCIAL PLANNING, investing in tax deferred investments, tax-exempt securities, or tax shelters offsetting capital gains from passive investments, such as real estate investment trust. Contrast with tax evasion, the willful nonpayment of taxes legally owed. See also FINANCIAL PLANNING.

tax preference items tax deduction giving the holder special tax benefits, which must be computed in calculating the ALTERNATIVE MINIMUM TAX (AMT) liability under federal tax laws. The AMT is due if the amount owed using the AMT calculation is greater. Preference items include, for individuals, capital gains from exercise of stock options, and for corporations, deductions for accelerated depreciation, investment tax credits, and increases in loan loss reserves by banks and savings institutions.

Tax Reform Act of 1986 act passed by Congress that simplified the tax code and eliminated some deductions. The Tax Act of 1986 was the most significant change in the tax structure of the United States in over 50 years.

Important provisions include:

—lowered the top corporate tax rate from 46% to 34%, the individual tax rate from 50% to 28%.

—set a new corporate ALTERNATIVE MINIMUM TAX on depreciable expenses such as accelerated depreciation on capital equipment.

—imposed a 5% surcharge, effective in 1988, for some taxpayers.

—limited the special deduction for loan loss reserves in banks above $500 million in assets. Larger banks may claim losses only when loans are written off.

—limited the deduction of interest payments on residential mortgages to principal homes and second homes, granted after August 15, 1986.

—reduced the annual limit on individual contributions to 401(k) employee savings plans from $30,000 a year to $7,000 a year.

—eliminated the 15% investment tax credit previously allowed equipment lessors.

—restricted the use of passive tax shelters to income gains or losses from investment portfolios, instead of a taxpayer's gross income.

—limited foreign tax credits on non-U.S. investments, including financial services income, passive investments, and dividends from foreign corporations in which a U.S. corporation has a minority interest. A transition period for the new tax rules extends through 1994.

—allowed net operating losses to be carried back three years and forward 15 years, except for losses attributable to bad debts. Bad debt losses retain the ten-year carry back through 1993.

— authorized sale of mortgage backed securities through Real Estate Mortgage Investment Conduits (REMICs).

—eliminated the 100% deduction of the interest attributed to tax-exempt obligations (municipal bonds) acquired after August 7, 1986.

—imposed a 20% corporate alternative minimum tax on nonessential municipal bonds issued after August 7, 1986.

—prohibited use of cash basis accounting by banks after 1986, phased in over a four-year period.

—retained the accelerated cost recovery system for depreciating assets. However, machinery and equipment must be depreciated over a longer period.

—increased the recovery period for residential real estate, for depreciation purposes, from 19 years to 27½ years, and from 19 years to 31½ years for commercial real estate. Both will be depreciated under the straight line basis under the new law.

—limited fully deductible INDIVIDUAL RETIREMENT ACCOUNTS to taxpayers not covered by a qualified pension plan, or individuals whose gross income is less than $40,000 on joint returns (less than $25,000 for taxpayers filing as singles).

—taxed Clifford Trusts to the trust grantor, and required that trusts and estates follow the calendar year for tax purposes.

—limited tax deductions from passive real estate tax shelters.

—eliminated the use of the installment method for sales made under revolving credit plans.

—phased out the deductibility of consumer interest charges over a five-year period. The new law permits taxpayers to deduct 65% of interest charges in 1987, 40% in 1988, 20% in 1989, 10% in 1990, and zero in 1991.

—limited deduction of only 80% of business related expenses.

tax swap see BOND SWAP.

teaser rate
1. low initial mortgage rate that lenders charge for an ADJUSTABLE RATE MORTGAGE. The rate is less than the rate charged for standard fixed rate mortgages, and lower than the fully-indexed rate on adjustable rate mortgages. The lower payment in turn makes mortgage financing more available to more potential home owners. The rate typically is reset to the market rate after a period of several months to a year.
2. high initial rate offered depositors who invest in savings accounts paying money market rates. When MONEY MARKET DEPOSIT ACCOUNT (MMDA)s were first introduced in December 1982 (but not yet approved for purposes of accepting deposits), certain banks offered rates as high as 21% through repurchase agreements that were rolled into MMDAs when these high rate accounts became legal.

technical analysis forecasting price movements by analysis of trading volume, supply and demand, short-term and long-term market trends, and other market related factors. An important premise in technical analysis is that certain price-volume factors repeat themselves, and can be illustrated graphically by chart patterns, a process known as charting. For example, a point and figure chart, showing the upward and downward movement of a security in a given time period; an ascending top, showing continually rising prices and the beginning of a price rally; a head and shoulders pattern, depicting the reversal of a trend; and a double top, signaling the end of a rally. First used by commodities traders, charting is a frequently used analytical tool in the stock market, foreign exchange, and financial futures. Technical analysis differs from fundamental analysis, which examines financial information, such as company earnings and capital formation, and is concerned foremost with the financial strength and profitability of an issuer of securities.

Technical analysts believe that, by diagramming the movement of a market, they can determine market swings in advance. According to the theory, the best time to sell (take a short position) is the start of a major downtrend; the best time to buy is when prices, and trends, are heading upward. The drawback with this methodology is that chart patterns often are recognized after the fact, that is, after events have run their course. Second, the trend charts can themselves be misleading, giving the appearance of order and stability to otherwise volatile markets.

telegraphic transfer see WIRE TRANSFER.

telephone bill payment banking service allowing customers to pay merchant bills, verify account balances, and transfer funds between accounts by giving verbal instructions to a customer service representative or using a touch-tone telephone. Also called *bank-by-phone* or *pay-by-phone*. As a financial service, telephone bill payment attracted a small and loyal customer base, but failed to attract a sizable number of users largely because it is limited to bill payments and account transfers. Also, most consumers did not view paying bills by check as an inconvenience.

Telephone bill payment was popularized in the mid-1970s by savings and loan associations that wanted to offer their customers transaction accounts even though, at the time, they legally couldn't offer checking accounts, so the payments were instead taken out of savings accounts. Telephone bill payment services are offered by many commercial banks and savings institutions in the expectation that checks might eventually be replaced by electronic transfers, although check displacement so far has been minimal. See also ELECTRONIC FUNDS TRANSFER; HOME BANKING; TELEPHONE TRANSFER.

telephone order

1. verbal instruction (TELEPHONE TRANSFER) to move funds from one bank account to another, or from one bank to another, by check or electronic transfer, such as a payment over the Federal Reserve's Fed Wire network.
2. mail-order purchase charged to a bank card or travel and entertainment card. No signature is required, and the customer has the same consumer rights and obligations as when making a purchase in person. See also SIGNATURE ON FILE.

telephone transfer transfer of account balances from one account to another, or from payor to recipient made by TELEPHONE ORDER, rather than traditional written authorization or instrument. The accounts being debited can be checking, savings, or, if three or fewer telephone transfers per month, money market deposit accounts. See also TELEPHONE BILL PAYMENT.

teletext one-way video information service allowing subscribers to read news, market data, weather and other information from a central data base via an alphanumeric keyboard or terminal. It differs from two-way communication, which is called VIDEOTEX. See also HOME BANKING.

teller bank employee who accepts deposits, cashes checks, and performs other banking services for the public. In most financial institutions, tellers work from behind a counter or enclosure. Large banks assign teller functions by job description: a MAIL TELLER processes incoming bank deposits arriving through the mail; a loan teller keeps a record of payments to customer accounts; and a note teller handles the collection of funds on notes and drafts payable by other banks. See also CUSTOMER SERVICE REPRESENTATIVE; HEAD TELLER.

teller's check see CASHIER'S CHECK.

temporary loan short-term WORKING CAPITAL loan to finance a firm's inventory or receivables. These loans have maturities generally under one year, and are evidenced by a PROMIS-

SORY NOTE taken or a WARRANT issued by the borrower. A temporary loan can be unsecured or secured by a lien on the firm's assets. Working assets acquired through temporary financing eventually will be converted into cash through the firm's trade cycle, when it sells inventory for cash or collects its receivables. See also COLLATERAL LOAN; TERM LOAN.

tenancy by the entirety joint ownership of property by husband and wife, recognized in some states. Each has equal rights of possession and enjoyment, and right of survivorship when the other spouse dies. Although similar to joint tenancy, the most common form of property ownership by married couples, tenancy by the entirety treats the estate as a unit, which means that neither spouse can sell assets without the other's consent. Also, creditors cannot force the sale of property to satisfy debts of either spouse. The surviving spouse inherits the entire estate. See also COMMUNITY PROPERTY; JOINT TENANTS WITH RIGHT OF SURVIVORSHIP; TENANCY IN COMMON.

tenancy in common joint ownership of property by two or more persons, without right of survivorship. This form of property ownership most often is used by partners in a business partnership, and by unrelated persons holding title to real property. Each party has an indivisible share of the property; when they die, their share is inheritable by their heirs, not by the other tenants. Also called *tenants in common*. See also COMMUNITY PROPERTY, JOINT TENANTS WITH RIGHT OF SURVIVORSHIP; TENANCY BY THE ENTIRETY.

tender
1. BID or request for project financing.
2. notice by the seller of a futures contract of his intention to deliver a commodity or financial instrument.
3. offer of payment owed to a creditor; an offer to settle up an obligation. For example, to tender a check.
4. LEGAL TENDER or cash offered in payment of an obligation.
5. offer to purchase securities at a specified price, called a TENDER OFFER.

tender offer publicly announced offer to purchase securities at a stated price and for a specified period. It is an invitation to shareholders of a company to sell their shares at the offered price, regardless of whether the issuer approves or disapproves of the offer being tendered. The offering price is often at a premium over the market price, as in a corporate takeover attempt.

tender panel financing method used in sale of promissory notes (Euronotes) through a REVOLVING UNDERWRITING FACILITY (RUF). A syndicate, consisting of up to 15 to 20 commercial banks and investment banks, is authorized by a borrower (or the borrower's agent) to solicit bids on a BEST EFFORT basis for project financing. The panel acts as a selling agent for the banks arranging a credit facility.

    The tender panel sale allows placement of Euronotes with a large number of investors seeking medium-term (five to seven years) paper. It also separates the originating bank from the banks actually purchasing the notes, thereby spreading the credit risk among a large number of participants. The originating bank's participation in the offering is small, often as little as 10% of the total financing. See also MULTICURRENCY NOTE FACILITY; MULTIPLE OPTIONS FUNDING FACILITY; NOTE ISSUANCE FACILITY; PRIME UNDERWRITING FACILITY; STANDBY NOTE ISSUANCE FACILITY; TRANSFERABLE UNDERWRITING FACILITY.

tenor
1. shorthand reference for maturity on a note or financial instrument.
    2. designates the time when a draft is payable: on sight (when presented), a given number of days after presentment, or a given number of days after the date of the draft.
3. terms set for payment of a draft, i.e., when delivered (a SIGHT DRAFT) or at a future date (a TIME DRAFT).

term
1. maturity of a LOAN or DEPOSIT, expressed in months. Short-term obligations or investments generally are less than a year; long-term instruments may have maturities from 1 year to 30 or 40 years.
2. any condition specifying how a loan is to be repaid, for example, the ANNUAL PERCENTAGE RATE finance charge, monthly payment, number of payments, BALLOON PAYMENT, and so on.

term bond bond with a single maturity date, as opposed to a SERIAL BOND. Generally, the issuer makes mandatory payments into a SINKING FUND in the years prior to maturity. Bond issuers meet sinking fund requirements by purchasing the issued security in the open market, redeeming the bonds at market prices, which may be lower than the sinking fund call price. This sinking fund provision spreads the issuer's liability of a GENERAL OBLIGATION BOND over the life of the bond; issuers of REVENUE BONDS are able to match debt service payments with bond revenues.

term federal funds RESERVE ACCOUNT balances purchased for periods longer than a single day, but generally less than 90 days. Banks purchase Fed funds for an extended period when they see their borrowing needs lasting several days, or they believe short-term rates may rise and they want to lock in the current rate. Fed funds purchased for an extended term, like overnight Fed funds, are not subject to RESERVE REQUIREMENTS and sometimes are preferred to other purchased liabilities of comparable maturity. See also BROKERED DEPOSIT; MANAGED LIABILITIES; REPURCHASE AGREEMENT.

terminal
1. point of entry in a data communications network. Electronic funds transfer terminal devices are AUTOMATED TELLER MACHINES, teller terminals, retail POINT-OF-SALE TERMINALs, personal computers in home banking, and touch-tone telephones in automatic telephone bill payment. Sometimes referred to as an *electronic window* in corporate CASH MANAGEMENT. See also PLATFORM AUTOMATION; TREASURY WORKSTATION.
2. authorization device that approves transactions charged to bank credit cards, deposit accounts, retail private label accounts, or travel and entertainment cards. Most of these are inexpensive devices that automatically dial a central computer to obtain authorization, hence the name *dial-up terminal*. See also AUTHORIZATION CODE.

termination statement statement releasing a lender's claim or SECURITY INTEREST in a borrower's assets when a debt is fully paid, and terminating a previously filed FINANCING STATEMENT. The Uniform Commercial Code requires secured lenders to sign a termination statement, generally known as Form UCC-3 to clear the borrower's name of leins listed in public records.

term loan fixed-term business loan with a maturity of more than one year, providing an organization with working capital to acquire assets or inventory, or to finance plant and equipment generating cash flow. The term loan is the most common form of intermediate-term financing arranged by commercial banks, and there is wide diversity in how it is structured. Maturities range from one year to 15 years, although most term loans are made for one- to five-year periods. Term loans are paid back from profits of the business, according to a fixed amortization schedule. Term loans may be secured or unsecured, and carry a rate based on the lender's cost of funds, the federal funds rate, LIBOR, or the bank PRIME RATE. Loan interest normally is payable monthly, quarterly, semiannually, or annually.

Most business loans contain both affirmative and restrictive COVENANTs that impose certain conditions on the borrower that permit acceleration of the maturity if the loan conditions are violated. The lender may, for example, restrict cash dividends paid and loans taken out by corporate officers, and usually will require the borrower to maintain the business in good order, keep adequate insurance, and file quarterly financial statements with the bank. Larger borrowings often are financed by several banks through a SYNDICATION arrangement. See also DEMAND LOAN; SECURED LOAN; SECURITY AGREEMENT; SECURITY INTEREST.

term mortgage nonamortizing MORTGAGE, usually with a maturity under five years, that provides for interest-only payments for a specified period, after which the outstanding principal balance is due and payable in a lump-sum BALLOON PAYMENT. See also STANDING MORTGAGE.

term repurchase agreement repurchase agreement with a maturity of more than one day. Also known as a *term repo*. Banks and savings institutions that have excess cash to invest often buy government securities instead of certificates of deposit, which have a minimum maturity of seven days. In a repurchase agreement, the bank buys securities from a dealer, or from a nondealer bank, with an agreement to sell back the securities later at a predetermined price. The difference between the purchase price and the resale price represents the payment of interest. Term repos may pay higher yields than overnight repos, because the seller assumes interest rate risk for a longer period than an overnight repo.

testamentary trust TRUST established by the terms of a WILL. After the death of the TESTATOR, it becomes an IRREVOCABLE TRUST. This kind of trust is useful if the testator wishes to set aside funds for the education of children who are minors or have just reached the age of majority. The trust is placed in the hands of a trustee, who may be an individual or a bank trust department.

testator person who has died leaving a valid will, providing for distribution of assets to heirs. Sometimes called *settlor*. Compare with TRUSTOR.

test number numeric prefix in an electronic wire transfer payment or payment instruction identifying the originating bank. Also called an issuer KEY or *test key*. The number changes with each transmission between banks, according to a predetermined ALGORITHM or mathematical formula, making it difficult for unauthorized persons to gain access to sensitive bank account information. See also ENCRYPTION; MESSAGE AUTHENTICATION CODE.

thin market market characterized by few bids and offers, wide bid-asked spreads, and fluctuating prices. A thin market is said to have a shallow depth and weak demand for trading, and wider price fluctuations than a strong market, where bid-asked spreads are narrow, and prices move upward or downward within a more or less predictable range. Also called *weak market*.

third country acceptance in international trade, a BANKERS ACCEPTANCE drawn on a bank in a country other than the country of the importer or exporter, and paid in the national currency of the accepting bank. Third country acceptances, also called *refinance bills*, often are used by exporters to obtain bank financing at competitive rates. Since the mid-1970s, Japanese and South Koreans have financed a large portion of their ex ports, including exports to European countries, through bankers' acceptances denominated in U.S dollars, which accounts for much of the growth of these acceptances in the last decade.

third market see OVER-THE-COUNTER.

third party check

1. check transferred by ENDORSEMENT and the words "pay to the order of—." The new holder has the same legal rights as the original endorser, and is free to negotiate the check himself, either by endorsing the back of the instrument and depositing it, or by exchanging it for cash at a bank teller. The Uniform Commercial Code allows transfer of a check to a new owner any number of times. In practice, however, multiple endorsed checks are uncommon, and banks may be reluctant to accept them without verifying signatures of endorsers.
2. CHECK or DRAFT payable to someone other than the check writer (the MAKER of the instrument) or the person who initially negotiates the check by endorsing the back of the instrument.
3. PAYABLE THROUGH DRAFT. Credit Union SHARE DRAFTS often are paid by a commercial bank, which then debits the credit union's account after paying drafts presented for payment, as are drafts that are written against a money market mutual fund.

third party credit credit facilitating the sale of merchandise and services that is arranged by someone other than the seller. Retail merchants accept bank credit cards and travel and entertainment cards as payment for merchandise, which often is less costly than extending credit directly, because the merchant is relieved of the expense of funding the credit receivables and collecting the payments. In return for payment of a MERCHANT DISCOUNT, computed as a percentage of net sales, the merchant can get immediate credit for bank card sales slips deposited with a bank. If the merchant discount rate is 2%, the merchant gets $98 for every $100 in credit sales. As long as the merchant follows the terms of the credit agreement, the merchant also is not liable for credit or fraud losses. See also PRIVATE LABEL CREDIT; REVOLVING CREDIT.

third party payment see THIRD PARTY TRANSFER.

third party transfer payment made out to and deposited in the account of someone other than the person who initiates the payment, or who initially receives it. Such payments may be THIRD PARTY CHECKS transferred by endorsement, written or oral instructions directing a bank to pay a consumer's bills, or electronic payments. See also TELEPHONE BILL PAYMENT.

thrift institution savings and loan association or savings bank whose primary function is encouragement of personal savings (thrift) and home buying through mortgage lending. Also known as a *savings institution*. Credit unions, which are member owned cooperative associations operating under a common affiliation also generally are considered thrift institutions. The traditional commitment of savings institutions to financing long-term loans with short-term deposits, from their origins early in the nineteenth century, has made them more sensitive to fluctuating interest rates than COMMERCIAL BANKs, which have more diversified loan portfolios.

During the early 1980s, banking industry deregulation allowed savings and loans to invest a greater percentage of their assets in consumer loans, commercial loans, and direct real estate investments. A significant portion of mortgage loans originated by savings and loans is in the form of ADJUSTABLE RATE MORTGAGES, as opposed to 30-year fixed-rate CONVENTIONAL MORTGAGES. The Depository Institutions Deregulation and Monetary Control Act of 1980 allowed savings institutions to offer Negotiable Order of Withdrawal (NOW) accounts and the Garn-St Germain Depository Institutions Act of 1982 expanded this transaction account power to checking accounts for individuals and businesses. The 1982 act also allowed savings institutions to offer the MONEY MARKET DEPOSIT ACCOUNT, an interest-bearing transaction account competitive with MONEY MARKET FUNDS. Asset Diversification, although intended to encourage savings and loans to invest their deposits in shorter maturity assets, encouraged many S&Ls to take greater risks. Many savings and loans suffered losses in the 1980s from excessive investments in real estate, which depleted their net worth and drained reserves from the Federal Savings and Loan Insurance Corporation, the savings and loan deposit insurance fund.

The FINANCIAL INSTITUTIONS REFORM, RECOVERY AND ENFORCEMENT ACT of 1989 committed $50 billion in federal assistance, including $20 billion in direct U.S. Treasury obligations, to liquidate hundreds of insolvent savings and loans and restore the savings and loan insurance fund to sound financial condition. The act also restructured the federal agencies regulating the savings and loan industry, replacing the Federal Home Loan Bank Board with a new supervisory agency, the OFFICE OF THRIFT SUPERVISION, and creating a new deposit insurance fund, the SAVINGS ASSOCIATION INSURANCE FUND, in place of the insolvent Federal Savings and Loan Insurance Corporation. The Office of Thrift Supervision, headed by the Director of Thrift Supervision, is a bureau of the U.S. Treasury Department. The act also raised from 60% to 70% the percentage of assets—the so-called qualified thrift lender test—that savings institutions must hold to qualify for a savings and loan charter. Qualifying assets include residential mortgage construction loans, home improvement and repair loans, mobile home loans, and mortgage-backed securities. See also FEDERAL HOUSING FINANCE BOARD; FEDERAL HOME LOAN BANK SYSTEM; RESOLUTION FUNDING CORPORATION; RESOLUTION TRUST CORPORATION.

Thrift Institutions Advisory Council advisory body established by the Monetary Control Act of 1980 to advise the Federal Reserve Board of Governors on the needs of savings institutions. This panel is composed of representatives of savings banks, savings and loan associations, and credit unions.

throwback rule in trusts, an IRS rule requiring that trust assets distributed in any taxable year in excess of the amount allowed that year are, for tax purposes, treated as if the income was earned and distributed in a prior year. In other words, they are thrown back to the previous year, or years.

tick minimum price fluctuation in bond or interest rate futures trading; 1/32 of a percentage point. Treasury bill and bond quotes are given in increments of 32nds. The decimal equivalent of 1/32 of a $1,000 bond is $31.25, 2/32 is $62.50, and so on. More generally, the term also applies to price movements of precious metals, stocks, and commodities.

tiered rate account savings account that pays a rate of interest scaled according to the amount invested in the account. Typically, the higher the balance in the account, the higher the rate. Savings accounts with longer terms generally pay higher rates than accounts with shorter terms.

tight money market condition that exists when the Federal Reserve, acting through the FEDERAL OPEN MARKET COMMITTEE, reduces the amount of credit available to the public through the banking system. During periods of tight credit, borrowers face stricter lending standards at rising interest rates, although interest rates may in fact be quite reasonable considering market demands for credit.

When the System Open Market Desk at the Federal Reserve Bank of New York sells Treasury securities, the supply of bank reserves diminishes and the FEDERAL FUNDS rate that banks charge each other for overnight borrowings tends to rise. This is sometimes known as *draining reserves.* Rising interest rates are the result of tight Federal Reserve MONETARY POLICY, and also excessive growth in the economy, creating an inflationary situation of too much demand and not enough goods and services to meet market demands. See also EASY MONEY; INTERMEDIATE TARGETS; NONBORROWED RESERVES.

time deposit

1. deposit account paying interest for a fixed term, with the understanding that funds cannot be withdrawn before maturity without giving advance notice. Also known as an *investment account* or *time certificate of deposit.* Time deposit accounts, evidenced by either a paper certificate or a statement mailed to the depositor when interest is paid, normally pay a fixed rate of interest, and have maturities of seven days to seven years or longer. The notification of withdrawal requirement ordinarily is waived for consumer deposits, though not for large dollar corporate time deposit accounts. Consumer withdrawals still are subject to an EARLY WITHDRAWAL PENALTY, and partial loss of interest. Federal Reserve REGULATION Q requires that account withdrawals within six days after being deposited be subject to a loss of six days' interest. Time deposit accounts owned by a corporation (NONPERSONAL TIME DEPOSITS) are subject to RESERVE REQUIREMENTS, but at a lower rate than transaction accounts, such as checking accounts. See also CERTIFICATE OF DEPOSIT; NINETY-DAY SAVINGS ACCOUNT; PASSBOOK.

2. time deposit open account, an interest bearing deposit account allowing multiple deposits, but limited right of withdrawal before maturity. For example, club accounts, such as Christmas Clubs and vacation clubs. The deposit is evi-

denced by a ledger entry on the books of the depositing financial institution.

time draft DRAFT (bill of exchange) payable to a third party on a specified or determinable future date, as opposed to a SIGHT DRAFT. A BANKER'S ACCEPTANCE is an example of a time draft.

time loan short-term business LOAN that is payable in full at a specified maturity date, e.g., 30, 60, 90, or 120 days. Interest on this type of loan ordinarily is deducted (discounted) in advance when the loan is made. It differs from a DEMAND LOAN in that the lender cannot call or demand repayment of a time loan before the maturity. Time loans are repaid from turnover of assets, for example, the sale of inventory or collection of accounts receivable. See also DISCOUNT; TERM LOAN.

time-out condition in an ON-LINE banking network where a customer activated terminal fails to respond to a transaction request within a specified time limit, known as the RESPONSE TIME. The terminal then disconnects from a host processor, and the customer will have to retry the transaction.

time-sale financing form of indirect lending (DEALER FINANCING) in which a bank or other third party purchases installment sales contracts at a discount from face value from a dealer, and the borrower makes payments to the lender. This usually is done in conjunction with dealer FLOOR PLANNING.

time value of money see PRESENT VALUE.

title legally valid claim to ownership of real property, evidenced by deed, certificate of title, or bill of sale. A lender will extend MORTGAGE financing to a buyer only if the seller holds uncontested ownership of the property in question. Most states treat a mortgage as a lien against the title held by the lender, or MORTGAGEE, but some states recognize a mortgage as a binding obligation of the borrower, or the MORTGAGOR named in the title. See also TITLE COMPANY; TITLE DEFECT; TITLE INSURANCE; TITLE SEARCH.

title company firm that verifies ownership of real property, often done in connection with a conveyance of real property from buyer to seller. The valid owner is determined through a thorough examination of property records in a TITLE SEARCH. The company issues a title certificate, based on its examination.

title defect legal claim, circumstance, or other condition that makes it difficult to identify the true owner of real property or transfer title to another. Also called a CLOUD ON TITLE or clouded title, as when ownership has not been recorded properly, or when secondary liens have not been removed after the obligations have been paid. See also TITLE INSURANCE; TITLE SEARCH.

title insurance insurance against losses resulting from a TITLE DEFECT discovered after property has been conveyed from buyer to seller and a new mortgage taken out by the buyer. This protects the borrower against claims not identified in the title search, or claims not specifically listed as exemptions to the title insurance policy.

title search process of verifying the actual owner of real property by a careful review of public land records, usually conducted by a professional title abstractor. This investigation also determines whether there are any outstanding liens or encumbrances binding on the property, and results in issuance of an abstract of title by the title company. See also TITLE; TITLE DEFECT; TITLE INSURANCE.

tombstone slang term for financial advertising listing acquisitions, new securities offered for sale, listing the underwriting parties in order of their participation—with managing partners listed at the top and participating members below. The name derives from the minimal artwork in financial ads. It lists only the relevant data of the parties to the transaction. Such ads are not an offer to sell, as securities regulations prohibit explicit advertising, other than through a PROSPECTUS.

tom next see TOMORROW NEXT.

tomorrow next (tom next) foreign exchange and money market term for trades executed tomorrow for delivery on the next business day. For example, a currency purchased on

Tuesday is deliverable on Thursday, or the SPOT delivery day plus one day. Also known as ROLLOVER or T/N. The spot market price for two-day delivery is adjusted by a premium to account for the extra day. See also SPOT NEXT.

topping up clause language in a BACK-TO-BACK loan, or a two-currency loan, protecting the lender from currency devaluations. The borrower is required to make additional payments of, say 5% in the depreciating currency if the value of that currency declines by that amount. Such provisions can cause problems if the party on the other side of a back-to-back loan has no use for the additional currency, or is required to report topping up payments as additional income. Dependence on these special payments has been reduced by passing the credit risk to a bank, in exchange for payment of a fee.

Torrens certificate certificate of property ownership issued by government agencies in some states. Originated by Sir Robert Torrens, an Australian land reformer, the Torrens system permits property transfers without the need for title searches. It also simplifies title searches; under the Torrens system, a title discovered after the certificate is issued is no longer valid.

tort wrongful act, other than a breach of CONTRACT, causing one party to suffer a property loss or bodily injury. Such cases are argued in civil courts, although criminal prosecution also is possible in some cases. A person committing a tort is liable for damages.

total capital PRIMARY CAPITAL (Tier 1) capital plus secondary capital, in calculation of risk adjusted capital base.

total lease obligation total of all direct costs of a consumer lease, including monthly rentals, interest, and any contingent payments (BALLOON PAYMENTs) due at the end of the lease, and fair market value (residual value) of the property at lease termination. Federal Reserve REGULATION M requires disclosure of closing costs in consumer leases. The lessor must also tell the lessee whether the lease contains a purchase option available at the end. An OPEN-END LEASE may require a balloon payment, depending on the value of the property, although the Consumer Leasing Act limits such payments to no more than three times the average monthly payment.

total reserves sum of the deposits that depository institutions may count toward their legal RESERVE REQUIREMENTS. Included in the calculation are reserve account balances on deposit with a reserve bank during the most recent week, currency and coin in a bank's vault, including cash in transit to or from reserve banks. The Monetary Control Act requires most depository institutions to keep reserve balances either directly or indirectly with the central bank.

total return annual adjusted yield on a fixed income investment, taking into account capital gains, dividends, or interest paid, and the investor's tax bracket. Total return is usually expressed as a percentage. For corporate bonds, total return is the equivalent of the YIELD TO MATURITY calculation; for stocks, future capital appreciation is projected using the current PRICE EARNINGS RATIO. Mutual funds use a formula worked out by the Securities and Exchange Commission in advertising fund performance.

In mortgage-backed securities and asset-backed securities, total return differs from the yield to maturity calculation because the total return calculation takes into account reinvestment income and borrower prepayments. When interest rates are falling, borrowers tend to prepay their mortgages and refinance their loans at current interest rates, causing investor yields on conventional mortgage-backed securities to drop. See also CASH FLOW YIELD.

Totten trust informal trust in which assets deposited into an account are controlled by the person creating the trust, the GRANTOR, and held in trust for another, who is named as BENEFICIARY. When the account owner dies, the account is transferred to the beneficiary, but taxed as part of the grantor's estate. If the account is jointly owned, the regulations covering joint accounts apply. When all the owners of the account die, the beneficiary becomes the lawful owner.

trade acceptance see BANKER'S ACCEPTANCE.

trade association nonprofit mutual benefit organization formed to provide services for its members, promote education and professional standards, and influence governmental agencies through lobbying. There are numerous trade groups representing commercial banks and savings institutions in the United States, operating at the state level and nationwide. Nationally, the largest banking trade group is the AMERICAN BANKERS ASSOCIATION, which has over 12,000 member banks.

At the state level, affiliates of the American Bankers Associations, the U.S. League of Savings Institutions, and other national trade groups play an active role in lobbying before state legislatures and regulatory agencies.

Major trade groups in banking are the following:

—American Association of State Savings and Loan Supervisors, Washington, D.C., representing regulators of state chartered savings and loan associations.

—Association of Bank Holding Companies, Washington, DC, representing holding companies registered with the Federal Reserve Board under the Bank Holding Company Act.

—Association of Thrift Holding Companies, representing companies owning or controlling S&Ls, based in Washington, D.C.

—Association of Reserve City Bankers, Washington, D.C., representing executive officers of commercial banks holding correspondent deposits for other banks, and generally located in cities with a Federal Reserve Bank.

—Bank Capital Markets Association, Arlington, Virginia, representing bankers involved in trading marketable financial instruments and foreign exchange. Formerly, the Dealer Bank Association.

—Bankers Association for Foreign Trade, Washington, D.C., representing commercial banks active in international banking and trade finance.

—Bank Marketing Association, Chicago, Illinois, an organization serving financial marketing officers of commercial banks, affiliated with the American Bankers Association.

—Conference of State Bank Supervisors, Washington, D.C., serving supervisors of state chartered commercial banks and savings banks, and dedicated to maintaining the DUAL BANKING financial system.

—Consumer Bankers Association, Arlington, Virginia, representing commercial banks and savings institutions active in the retail financial services industry.

—Credit Union National Association, Madison, Wisconsin, representing the majority of U.S. credit unions, through state credit union leagues.

—Electronic Funds Transfer Association, Alexandria, Virginia, a multi-industry association representing financial institutions, service organizations, and manufacturers dedicated to promotion of electronic payment services.

—Independent Bankers Association of America, Washington, D.C., representing independently owned commercial banks. About half of the 13,000 commercial banks in the United States are IBAA members.

—National Association of Bank Women Inc., Chicago, Illinois, a group representing women holding executive positions in banking institutions.

—National Association of Federal Credit Unions, Arlington, Virginia, representing federal credit unions chartered by the National Credit Union Administration.

—National Bankers Association, Washington, D.C., a trade group representing minority-owned banks.

—National Automated Clearing House Association, Herndon, Virginia, a trade group promoting uniform rules and standards for AUTOMATED CLEARING HOUSE associations.

—National Council of Savings Institutions, Washington, D.C., representing about 500 savings banks and savings and loan associations.

—Robert Morris Associates, Philadelphia, Pennsylvania, representing commercial loan and credit officers at banks and savings institutions.

—United States League of Savings Institutions, Washington, D.C., representing savings and loan associations, which account for the major portion of the thrift industry in the United States. See also AMERICAN INSTITUTE OF BANKING; BANK ADMINISTRATION INSTITUTE.

trade confirmation see CONFIRMATION.

trade date date an order is executed to buy or sell securities, financial instruments, or commodities. It precedes the date funds are transferred to settle the transaction (the SETTLEMENT DATE) by one day in options trading, two days in most foreign exchange trading, and five days in stock market trading. See also DELIVERY DATE; RECORD DATE.

trade paper see ACCEPTANCE; SHORT-TERM PAPER.

trader party who buys or sells securities, financial instruments, or commodities on behalf of customers, or for his or her own account. A trader may be a broker, dealer, or speculator, and may or may not take overnight positions.

trade reference credit reference furnished by a credit reporting agency listing credit experience of a firm's trade suppliers, including trade terms, highest credit balance or amount due in the previous year, amounts past due, the terms of sale, and payment history. The report serves as a general credit reference of an organization, and its ability to meet current obligations. See also DUN & BRADSTREET; MERCANTILE AGENCY.

trade report see CREDIT REPORT.

trading account assets separate account managed by banks that buy (underwrite) U.S. government securities and other securities for resale at a profit to other banks and to the public, rather than for investment in the bank's own investment portfolio. Trading assets are segregated from the investment portfolio. They are recorded separately when acquired until they are disposed of or sold, and are recorded at the price in effect when these securities are purchased or sold. Trading assets held for other banks are marked to market (adjusted to current market value) while held by a bank. See also SECURITIES AFFILIATE.

trading flat see FLAT.

trading limit maximum number of futures contracts that may trade in a day's trading session, as determined by a trading exchange and the Commodities Futures Trading Commission. Limits generally are based on price, and vary according to markets, and may be adjusted depending on market conditions. See also MARGIN.

trading range range between high and low prices, or bids and offers, recorded during a stated time period, for example, a daily trading session on a stock exchange, an over-the-counter market, or a foreign exchange market. A trading range also can be from January 1 to the latest date, the last 12 months, and so on.

trading the basis see BASIS.

tranche

1. one of the classes of debt securities issued as part of a single bond or instrument, from the French word tranche, meaning slice. Securities often are issued in tranches to meet different investor objectives for portfolio diversification. For example, a COLLATERALIZED MORTGAGE OBLIGATION is a mortgaged-backed security issued with several different bond tranches issued under a single bond indenture, ranging from a fast-pay bond to a long-term slow-pay bond (called the ACCRUAL BOND, or the Z-bond.) Each is paid off consecutively; as one bond matures, the next is paid down in a stepping stone progression. Each tranche has a different coupon and maturity, and is identifiable by a different CUSIP NUMBER.
2. separate borrowings or funding commitments under a TERM LOAN or other credit facility. A multicurrency loan will be structured with a U.S. dollar tranche, a deutschmark tranche, and so on. World Bank advances to a sovereign borrower are structured in tranches.
3. single maturity CERTIFICATE OF DEPOSIT sold by a lead bank, which is then divided into smaller denominations for placement with investors.
4. gold tranche: first 25% of a member country's contribution to the International Monetary Fund, normally in gold bullion.
5. reserve tranche: deposit balances subject to RESERVE REQUIREMENTS.

transaction

1. any event that causes a change in an organization's financial position or net worth, resulting from normal business activity. It is recorded on the general ledger by debit or credit tickets.
2. advance of funds, as in a credit card cash advance, purchase of goods at a retailer, or when a borrower activates a revolving line of credit. See also STANDBY COMMITMENT.
3. activities affecting a deposit account, such as a deposit of funds or a withdrawal, carried out at the request of the account owner

transaction account

1. deposit account from which the account holder is permitted to make withdrawals or transfers by negotiable or transferable instrument, payment order of withdrawal, TELEPHONE TRANSFERS, or similar means to make transfers to third parties.
2. demand deposit, NOW account, SUPER NOW ACCOUNT, and other accounts accessible by negotiable instrument, and subject to RESERVE REQUIREMENTS, as defined by the Monetary Control Act of 1980, with a Federal Reserve Bank or CORRESPONDENT.

transfer

1. moving funds from one account to another, as from checking to savings.
2. electronic payment from one bank to another through the AUTOMATED CLEARING HOUSE system.
3. large dollar payment from one bank to another through the Federal Reserve Fed Wire or the Clearing House Interbank Payments System in New York.
4. real estate CONVEYANCE from buyer to seller that takes place at a mortgage closing.
5. clause in a LETTER OF CREDIT allowing the BENEFICIARY to make the proceeds of the credit available to a third party (secondary beneficiary). The secondary beneficiary is obligated to present the draft to the advising or paying bank to receive payment.
6. moving stocks, bonds, or other securities from one owner to another, and recording the change of ownership on registration papers.
7. ASSUMPTION of a mortgage by a new borrower.

transferable letter of credit LETTER OF CREDIT giving the BENEFICIARY the option of making part or all of the credit available to third parties (secondary beneficiaries). The credit may be transferred only with approval of the issuing bank, and must be stated clearly in the letter of credit documentation, provided it is designated expressly as a transferable credit.

Transferable Underwriting Facility (TRUF)

Euronote facility allowing the original underwriter, the project manager, to reserve the right to transfer the commitment to another agent willing to assume financial responsibility. This transfer of authority has to be done with the consent of all the original parties to the facility, and is both a transfer of responsibility and management.

transfer agent company that issues, registers, and redeems securities on behalf of the issuer. The agent, usually a commercial bank, also maintains records of changes in ownership, cancels old securities, updates these records when securities are sold, and ensures that new offerings of securities are not overissued. If the securities offered for sale are bonds, the agent is known as a REGISTRAR. See also AMERICAN DEPOSITARY RECEIPT; BOOK ENTRY SECURITY; CUSTODIAN; DEPOSITORY TRUST COMPANY.

transfer of mortgage ASSIGNMENT of mortgage by either the borrower (the MORTGAGOR) or the lender (the MORTGAGEE). The person receiving the property may take it SUBJECT TO MORTGAGE, i.e., on the condition that the original borrower maintains the existing mortgage, replaces it with another, or may assume the mortgage at the same rate and terms. In that event, the new owner becomes liable for repayment of the debt. See also ASSUMABLE MORTGAGE.

transfer pricing value placed on transfers within an organization, used as a means of allocating costs to various profit centers. Transfer pricing is used widely in multioffice banks and bank holding companies, serving these important functions: (1) price setting for services performed by business units; (2) a means of evaluating financial performance by business units; and (3) determining the contribution to net income by profit centers in the organization.

An example is determining a bank's internal cost of funds, or the cost assigned bank deposits supplied by retail branch offices to its commercial lending division. The retail branches traditionally are suppliers of funds, and commercial lenders traditionally are users of funds. Transfer pricing schemes also are widely used in pricing bank holding company services supplied to affiliate banks, for example, check processing, data processing, and funds supplied by a holding company to a subsidiary bank or a nonbank affiliate company. In lending, transfer pricing can be used as a form of internal credit rationing, by arbitrarily assigning the lowest cost of funds to the least risky loans, encouraging lenders to make loans that are profitable to the bank as well as low-risk. Transfer pricing schemes generally follow one of three cost accounting approaches: (1) market price; (2) cost-based price, generally the marginal cost of funds; or (3) negotiated price, a price determined through negotiation by buyer and seller. Historic cost, on the other hand, normally is used for reference only, and generally is not used in internal pricing.

transfer tax

1. **Securities.** The tax levied by several states and the federal government on sales or transfers of securities, payable by the seller, determined by the location of the TRANSFER AGENT, not the place where the transaction occurs.
2. **Real Estate.** The taxes paid to a state or local government to cover the costs of recording a property deed in public land records, payable by the seller when the property is sold.
3. **Estates.** The federal or state taxes assessed in settlement of an estate, usually nine months after the date of death. ESTATE taxes are federal taxes on the decedent's property, whereas inheritance taxes are state taxes payable by the heirs named in the decedent's will.

transit department department in a bank where checks or drafts issued by out-of-area banks are sorted, bundled together, and sent out (presented) to the DRAWEE bank for payment. Checks from distant banks routinely are honored, and a temporary hold is placed on the deposit until funds are received (SUBJECT TO COLLECTION) from the issuer. Banks send these checks, called TRANSIT ITEMS, to a FEDERAL RESERVE BANK or Federal Reserve REGIONAL CHECK PROCESSING CENTER or to the check issuing bank for collection. See also ABA TRANSIT NUMBER; CASH LETTER; CHECK ROUTING SYMBOL; DEFERRED AVAILABILITY; DIRECT SEND; PROOF OF DEPOSIT; REGULATION CC.

transit item CHECKS or DRAFTS issued by a financial institution other than the bank where it is deposited. Also called *on-others items*. These are separated from checks written by a bank's own customers (ON-US ITEMS) and are submitted to the DRAWEE bank by direct PRESENTMENT (direct send), through a local clearing house, or a FEDERAL RESERVE BANK or REGIONAL

CHECK PROCESSING CENTER. Checks drawn on other banks normally are sorted and submitted for collection before checks drawn by a bank's own customers are posted to accounts.

transit letter documentation accompanying checks or drafts submitted for collection, listing the number of checks (items) being sent and the total dollar amount of the checks. A CASH LETTER accompanies checks presented to other banks for payment; a REMITTANCE letter is used when the sending bank does not have an account at the receiving bank.

transit number see ABA TRANSIT NUMBER.

transmittal letter document sent with securities tendered for sale, checks and other negotiable instruments presented for COLLECTION, letters of credit, and so on, explaining the purpose of the transaction and detailing any instructions for special handling.

transposition error error caused by reversing two or more digits of an amount while posting a transaction. If two adjacent numbers are switched, the resulting error is always divisible by nine. If a teller's closing balance is off by $63, the error probably was caused by switching the numbers 70 and 7, 81 and 18, or 92 and 29.

travel & entertainment (T&E) card charge card used to pay for hotel, airline, and other business related expenses. The first travel card was issued in 1950 by Diners Club, followed by American Express in 1958. Travel cards differ from bank credit cards in several ways: they typically are 30-day charge accounts, with payment due in full before the next billing cycle; the account holder receives copies of the original sales drafts (called COUNTRY CLUB BILLING) with the monthly billing statement; and some T&E card plans, usually corporate cards, give the cardholder a quarterly summary of charges to the card. See also GOLD CARD.

traveler's check SIGHT DRAFT issued through banks acting as sales agents, or sold directly to the public. The purchaser pays for the checks in advance, and signs the drafts twice—once when ordering the drafts and once when cashing them. The drafts are payable by the issuing company, sold in denominations of $10 to $100 and in numerous foreign currencies, and insured against loss or theft. They readily are accepted in lieu of cash by merchants, and may be cashed at bank offices in the United States and most foreign countries. Travelers' checks were first issued by American Express Co., which uses the spelling traveler's cheque.

traveler's letter of credit LETTER OF CREDIT addressed to the issuing bank's correspondents, authorizing them to honor drafts drawn by the bearer up to the authorized credit line. Also called a circular letter of credit. Payments are endorsed by the issuer's correspondents on the reverse side of the letter of credit when they negotiate the drafts. This type of credit often is used to cover travel expenses and usually is prepaid by the customer. See also TRAVELER'S CHECK.

treasurer's drafts see PAYABLE THROUGH DRAFT.

Treasury bill short-term U.S. Treasury security issued in minimum denominations of $10,000 and usually having maturities of 13, 26, or 52 weeks. Investors purchase bills at prices lower than face value (at discount). The return to the investor who holds it to maturity is the difference between the price paid and the face value at maturity. Treasury bills are the securities most frequently purchased or sold by the Federal Reserve when it carries out OPEN MARKET OPERATIONS.

The formula for computing the discount price on U.S. Treasury bills, which are issued at a price less than par value or face value, is as follows:

Discount in dollars = Days to Maturity / 360 X Discount Basis

Thus, a six-month Treasury bill selling at a 7% discount has a discount price of $35 per $1,000 of maturity value.

The BOND EQUIVALENT YIELD of a 180-day Treasury bill, which allows comparison with interest-bearing securities, is as follows:

Discount/ Purchase Price X 365/180 = 7.35%

The Treasury Department also auctions from time to time short-term CASH MANAGEMENT BILLS with maturities up to 50 days that are sold to institutional buyers in lots of $1 million or more. These have replaced Treasury certificates of indebtedness and Tax Anticipation Bills as short-term debt instruments.

Treasury bond long-term U.S. Treasury securities usually having initial maturities of ten years or more and issued in denominations of $1,000 or more. Bonds pay interest semiannually, with principal amount paid at maturity. The 30-year Treasury bond, also known as the Treasury long bond, is considered a bellwether for fixed income securities and long-term interest rates in general.

Treasury certificate coupon bearing special certificates of indebtedness with maturities of less than one year. The Treasury Department borrows from the Federal Reserve System from time to time, by issuing these short-term certificates to the Federal Reserve Bank of New York. The certificates cover overdrafts on the Treasury's account maintained at FEDERAL RESERVE BANKs. Legislation in June 1979 authorized Treasury borrowings from the Fed only in unusual circumstances, and when the borrowings are approved by the Federal Reserve Board of Governors.

Treasury general account (TGA) general checking account for the U.S. Treasury Department maintained at the Federal Reserve Bank of New York. All official U.S. government disbursements are made from this account. The account also holds dollars credited to the Treasury in the form of monetized gold. See also TREASURY TAX AND LOAN ACCOUNT.

Treasury investment growth receipt see STRIP; ZERO COUPON SECURITY.

Treasury note intermediate-term, coupon bearing U.S. Treasury securities having initial maturities of less than ten years and issued in denominations of $1,000 or more, depending on the maturity of the issue. Notes pay interest semiannually, and the principal amount is payable at maturity.

Treasury securities generic term for interest bearing obligations of the U.S. government issued by the Treasury as a means of borrowing money to meet government expenditures not covered by tax revenues. Marketable Treasury securities fall into four categories: TREASURY BILLS, with maturities of 91 to 365 days; TREASURY BONDS, with maturities of ten years or longer; and TREASURY NOTES, with maturities between one and ten years.

These currently are issued in book entry form only. Ownership of book entry securities is maintained on the computers of the Federal Reserve Bank of New York. The purchaser receives a statement (a receipt), rather than an engraved certificate.

treasury stock previously issued shares of stock repurchased and held by the issuer. In banking, treasury stock, whether carried at cost or par value, is deductible from a bank's equity capital, and is reportable under undivided profits in the REPORT OF CONDITION.

Treasury tax and loan (TT&L) account checking account balances maintained by the U.S. Treasury Department at 14,000 depository institutions, primarily commercial banks. Federal withholding taxes are payable through TT&L accounts. A large portion of tax receipts are deposited into these accounts. Some Treasury balances may be kept in interest bearing deposits in local banks. See also TREASURY GENERAL ACCOUNT.

treasury workstation microcomputer based information management system allowing a corporate treasurer to automate the daily BALANCE REPORTING of collected balances, investment of idle funds in the short-term money market, and disbursement of funds to trade creditors. The overall aim is improvement in productivity, and eventual integration of funds management and corporate accounting systems, such as order entry and invoicing. See also CASH MANAGEMENT; CONTROLLED DISBURSEMENT; DELAYED DISBURSEMENT; ELECTRONIC DATA INTERCHANGE.

trend analysis in credit analysis, detailed examination of a company's financial ratios and cash flow for several accounting periods to determine changes in a borrower's financial position. Trend analysis is a key part of credit underwriting, and is a useful and necessary tool in determining whether the borrower's financial strength is improving or deteriorating. Key ratios examined include debt coverage ratio, turnover ratio (conversion of inventory and receivables to cash), and the QUICK ASSETS ratio or quick ratio (current assets divided by current liabilities). See also BALANCE SHEET RATIOS; TURNOVER RATIOS.

triggering term consumer credit term that, when used in credit promotion literature or advertising, must disclose certain pertinent information, as required by the TRUTH IN LENDING ACT. Consumer finance charges, for example, must be disclosed as an ANNUAL PERCENTAGE RATE (APR) to give consumers uniform credit information and compare rates charged by different lenders. Also covered by the rule are annual fees, closing costs, and contingent credit costs, such as balloon payments.

troubled bank bank that has an above normal percentage of NONPERFORMING LOANS when compared to banks of comparable size, and may have a negative net worth (or an excess of liabilities over assets). Troubled banks are listed on the bank regulator's PROBLEM BANK list.

troubled debt restructuring condition where a lender grants a concession to a borrower in financial difficulty. The Statement of Financial Accounting Standards No. 15 (FASB 15) divides debt restructuring of nonperforming loans, where the loan payments are past due 90 days or more, into two categories: (1) loans where the borrower transfers assets to the lender; and (2) those where credit terms are modified. The latter includes foreclosures, reductions in the interest rate, extension of the maturity date, and forgiveness of principal and/or interest payments. Typically, the lender negotiates a WORKOUT AGREEMENT with the borrower to modify the original credit terms rather than initiate foreclosure proceedings against the delinquent borrower. See also ADVERSELY CLASSIFIED ASSETS; CASH BASIS LOAN; LOSS; NONACCRUAL ASSET; SPECIAL MENTION; STAND-STILL AGREEMENT; WRITE OFF.

troubled loan NONPERFORMING LOAN, also known as a *sour loan*. There are several warning signals: thin margins, liquidity questions, adverse business and employment conditions, insufficient (under margin) collateral, insufficient income. Payments of interest and/or principal may have been renegotiated or restructured. See also ADVERSELY CLASSIFIED ASSETS; SPECIAL MENTION; TROUBLED DEBT RESTRUCTURING.

true interest cost (TIC)

1. ANNUAL PERCENTAGE RATE cost of credit, including finance charges, credit life insurance, discount points, and prepaid interest. The federal TRUTH IN LENDING ACT requires lenders to disclose in consumer credit loan agreements the true cost of credit, using a standard method of computing the borrower's finance charge, plus loan application fees and other costs of borrowing. The true interest cost of a $4,000 installment note at 10% interest payable over 36 months is $645.80. Thus, the total cost of the loan, including interest, is $4,645.80.

2. actual cost of issuing a bond, taking into account the present value (time value) of money. The TIC, commonly used in municipal bond offerings, is the rate of interest, compounded semiannually, required to discount the payments of principal and interest to bondholders to the original purchase price. Compare to NET INTEREST COST.

true lease LEASE that meets the Internal Revenue Code and accounting tests allowing the lessor to claim the tax benefits of ownership. Also known as a *tax-oriented lease*. The lessor is permitted to depreciate the asset over its lifetime and claim any unused tax credits; the lessee can deduct the lease payments as a capital expense from ordinary income taxes. A lease qualifying for tax treatment ordinarily is a multiyear, LEVERAGED LEASE, for example, a lease of capital equipment to an airline or manufacturer. See also CAPITAL LEASE; FINANCE LEASE; OPERATING LEASE.

truncation

1. banking service in which cancelled checks or drafts are held by the customer's bank, or by another bank in the check collection system, and are not returned to the check writer with the ACCOUNT STATEMENT. Checks can be truncated, or stopped, at the bank where a check is first deposited, or by a Federal Reserve Bank. If done by a bank for its own customer, it is known as CHECK SAFEKEEPING. Interbank check truncation, or truncation involving large numbers of banks, eliminates the physical handling of checks, but requires banks to follow new rules governing the rights and liabilities of banks presenting checks for payment and banks paying the

items on behalf of customers. Eventually, significant reductions in check processing costs are possible if large numbers of banks participate in check truncation programs.

2. dropping one or more digits in calculating interest accrued on savings accounts. For example, 1.677754 truncated after the fourth decimal becomes 1.6777. The opposite is ROUNDING.

trust

1. fiduciary relationship involving two parties, whereby the second party has responsibility for handling property for the benefit of someone else. The trust business has three broad categories: personal trusts, institutional management trusts created under an INDENTURE, and MASTER TRUST arrangements in which a fiduciary, usually a bank, manages the record keeping for a corporate pension fund. There are four types of personal trusts: a TESTAMENTARY TRUST created by a will; an IRREVOCABLE TRUST in which the person creating the trust (the GRANTOR) transfers property to a trustee but does not have the right to cancel the agreement; a short-term trust, such as a CLIFFORD TRUST created to set aside funds for education of the grantor's children; and a revocable living trust that may be terminated by the grantor at any time. See also ACTIVE TRUST; BLIND TRUST; CHARITABLE TRUST; DEED OF TRUST; INTER VIVOS TRUST; PASSIVE TRUST; TRUST ACCOUNT; TRUST COMPANY; TRUST DEPARTMENT; TRUSTEE; TRUST INDENTURE ACT OF 1939.

2. business combination that attempts to restrain competition in a given market through monopoly control of manufacturing, processing, or distribution of goods and services. See also ANTITRUST LAWS.

trust account shorthand name for all types of accounts handled by a bank's TRUST DEPARTMENT or by a TRUST COMPANY. See also ESTATE; GUARDIAN; TOTTEN TRUST; TRUST; UNIFORM GIFT TO MINORS ACT.

trust company corporation organized for the purpose of accepting and executing trusts, and acting as trustee under wills, as executor or guardian. State chartered trust companies also may offer banking services, such as taking deposits and making loans, depending on their charter. Trust companies also act as fiscal agents for corporations, paying stock dividends and bond interest payments, and as fiscal agents or paying agents for state and local governments that have borrowed funds in the municipal bond market. Many trust companies also accept deposits, make loans, and perform other banking services. Federal law permits NATIONAL BANKS to engage in trust activities. State chartered trust companies may become members of the Federal Reserve System and be insured by the Federal Deposit Insurance Corporation. Trust companies are regulated by state law.

trust department department in a bank or savings institution engaged in management of TRUST ACCOUNT assets for personal trust, employee benefit trusts, and corporate accounts and AGENCY services for trust clients. Smaller trusts are managed commonly as COMMINGLED FUNDS or common account trusts, as it is uneconomical to manage them separately. Bank trust departments also settle estates for individuals and act as TRANSFER AGENTS for corporations. Trust account funds are managed separately and accounted for separately from other assets managed by a bank. See also EMPLOYEE RETIREMENT INCOME SECURITY ACT; MASTER TRUST; REGULATION 9; TRUST COMPANY; TRUSTEE.

trust deed see DEED OF TRUST.

trustee
1. person named to administer a trust for a BENEFICIARY according to the terms established by the donor.
   2. financial institution, usually a TRUST COMPANY or the TRUST DEPARTMENT in a commercial bank that holds collateral for the benefit of bondholders. The trustee collects principal and interest payments, invests the cash between payment dates, and disburses funds to pay principal and interest on issued and outstanding bonds.
3. BANKRUPTCY TRUSTEE, named by a bankruptcy judge to handle the assets of a debtor in bankruptcy.

Trust Indenture Act of 1939 federal law, an amendment to the Securities Act of 1933 that requires issuers of corporate bonds, mortgage backed bonds, and other debt instruments to disclose terms and conditions under which securities are issued. These disclosures are contained in an INDENTURE agreement, a document specifying the legal obligations of the issuer and any restrictions, such as call provisions applying to the securities. The act requires issuers to name a corporation to administer terms of the indenture. The trustee, who must be free of conflict of interest, also makes semiannual disclosures of pertinent information to the securities holders. The act also prohibits impairment of the holders' right to sue individually, and requires the trustee to make available a list of the holders so they can communicate with one another. The act also exempts securities (mostly municipal bonds) that are not subject to securities registration requirements.

trustor person who establishes a TRUST for the benefit of another, and turns property over to a TRUSTEE for distribution to the BENEFICIARY. Also known as a donor or settlor.

trust receipt

1. written agreement used extensively in letter of credit financing, often extended to a buyer or other importer of goods. The buyer promises to hold the property received in the name of the bank arranging the financing, although the bank retains title to the goods. Trust receipts allow an importer to take possession of the goods for resale before paying the issuing bank.

2. type of SECURITY AGREEMENT now part of Article 9 of the UNIFORM COMMERCIAL CODE that controls credit extensions to sellers of durable goods. The seller, say an automobile dealer, has possession of the cars in the dealer's showroom and pays the lender from a trust account as the cars are sold. The lender may also take a FINANCING STATEMENT from the dealer before making the loan. See also FLOOR PLANNING; INDIRECT LOAN.

Truth in Lending Act act passed by Congress in 1969 requiring lenders to disclose key terms in extensions of credit. The act, part of the Consumer Credit Protection Act, requires lendors to disclose the method of computing finance charges, the conditions under which a finance charge may be imposed, and the finance charge expressed as an ANNUAL PERCENTAGE RATE. These credit terms must be disclosed clearly and conspicuously in consumer credit applications. The act also requires that borrowers who sign credit agreements giving the lender a security interest in the borrower's home have the right to rescind the contract within three business days. This is known as the borrower's RIGHT OF RESCISSION. The Truth in Lending Act, the earliest of the federal consumer protection statutes, has been amended several times, and has been copied in several states by state laws containing similar consumer protections. See also ADVERSE ACTION; EFFECTS TEST; EQUAL CREDIT OPPORTUNITY ACT; FAIR CREDIT REPORTING ACT; REGULATION B; REGULATION M; REGULATION Z.

truth in savings concept that financial institutions be required by regulation to disclose information on deposit account rates and adopt a uniform method of calculating rates paid depositors, to allow the consumer to more easily compare deposit interest rates. This has been proposed as legislation in several states and also in Congress. These proposals would require all depository institutions to disclose specific information on annual percentage rate, effective annual yield, and so on when requested, and before a deposit account is opened.

tugrik national currency of Mongolia.

turnaround purchase and sale of securities, commodities, and financial instruments in a single day, as by a speculator taking profits from short-term market shifts. The trader does not hold the securities in his portfolio overnight. See also DAY ORDER.

turnkey project real estate development project in which the builder assumes all risk until a certain point has been reached, usually at completion of the project or where the building is ready for occupancy. Permanent financing by a TAKE-OUT LENDER can be arranged at that point, provided certain conditions are met.

turnover ratios financial ratios related to sales or volume, for example, accounts receivable turnover; also known as efficiency ratios, for example, assets turnover, conversion of receivables into cash. These measure efficiency of converting assets into cash. See also LIQUIDITY RATIOS.

12b1 mutual fund mutual fund that uses part of its assets to cover sales and marketing expenses, named after the 1980 SECURITIES AND EXCHANGE COMMISSION ruling allowing the practice. Instead of charging the customer an up-front commission, or a sales LOAD as high as 8½%, the mutual fund manager assesses an annual charge, usually less than 1% of a mutual fund's net asset value. Originally, fund managers thought they could reduce average expenses by using fund assets to cover management fees and other expenses, thereby lowering costs paid by shareholders as a fund grew in size. The SEC requires disclosure of 12b1 fees in a mutual fund prospectus, a requirement that caused some fund sponsors to switch from 12b1 fees to BACK-END LOAD funds with redemption charges when fund shares are sold by an investor. So-called 12b1 funds have been popular with banks because some mutual fund sponsors have been willing to share these sales fees to help offset a bank's marketing costs.

24-hour banking self-service banking extending beyond normal banking hours by obtaining cash, making deposits, and transferring money between accounts at AUTOMATED TELLER MACHINES. The development of shared ATM networks, both nationally and internationally in the 1980s, has made it possible for a consumer to perform at least some routine banking functions anywhere in the country and, to some extent, on an international scale.

twenty-percent rule commercial bank practice of requiring corporate borrowers to maintain average deposit balances equal to 20% of their borrowings under a revolving line of credit or term loan. Also known as a COMPENSATING BALANCE. Today, fixed balance requirements in bank lending are a thing of the past; in actual practice, compensating balances vary from 10% of borrowings to 25%, or may be waived altogether in lieu of bank service charges. The exact ratio of deposits to borrowings depends on interest rates and local market conditions. Banks require balances, which serve as a liquidity cushion for both borrower and lender, compensate the lender for servicing the loan, and tend to weed out uncreditworthy borrowers.

two-name paper popular name for trade paper—trade acceptances and BANKERS' ACCEPTANCEs—carrying two signatures, either as drawer or endorser. Also known as *double name paper*. In the event the issuer cannot pay a banker's acceptance, the bank accepting the obligation is liable for payment.

two-party loan see BACK-TO-BACK LOAN; PARALLEL LOAN.

two-sided market market where a dealer is willing to quote both a bid and an asked price, or stands ready to make a market on both sides of a transaction, either as buyer or seller. This kind of market usually is found in the government securities market and the over-the-counter stock market, rather than the municipal bond market, which normally is a one-way market. Municipal securities tend to be less marketable than U.S. Treasury obligations, which actively are traded and have a strong secondary market. Some muni bond dealers, however, quote bid and asked prices on longer maturity term bond issues.

U

UCC-1 statement see FINANCING STATEMENT.

ultra vires acts actions beyond the powers of a corporation, as stated in its charter, or the laws of the state where it is incorporated. These acts are not defensible in a court of law, leaving a corporation open to shareholder and third party lawsuits. Broadly defined, an ultra vires act is any act prohibited by a corporation's charter, or an excessive use of powers granted. See also ARTICLES OF INCORPORATION.

unauthorized investment investment that is not approved specifically by a trust instrument establishing a trust, as opposed to NONLEGAL INVESTMENTS by a trust company or a bank's TRUST DEPARTMENT. An investment, if not authorized, may meet state laws regulating investments by fiduciaries, but still violates the intent of the person creating the trust. See also LEGAL LIST.

unauthorized transfer cash withdrawal or transfer of funds, using a bank DEBIT CARD, from a consumer's deposit account by someone other than the cardholder. REGULATION E limits the consumer's liability to not more than $50, provided the consumer notifies the bank within 60 days of discovering the loss. Otherwise, the consumer's total liability may be as much as $500. In situations where the cardholder made it easy for someone else to withdraw money from a bank account without his approval, say by writing his personal access code or PIN number on the card itself, the consumer may have difficulty persuading his bank to correct the error. Liability in wrongful use of PIN numbers is, however, a legally ambiguous area, and is still open to dispute. See also ERROR RESOLUTION; PROVISIONAL CREDIT; UNAUTHORIZED USE.

unauthorized use use of a CREDIT CARD by someone other than the authorized cardholder, for example, after a bank credit card has been lost or stolen and purchases not approved by the

cardholder are charged to the account. Federal Reserve REGULA-
TION Z limits the cardholder's liability in such situations to not
more than $50, although many banks waive even the $50 fee
because attempting to collect such a token amount is usually not
worth the effort. The TRUTH IN LENDING ACT does limit credit
card issuance to consumers who have filled out an application,
or have responded to a direct mail invitation to apply for a credit
card. See also UNAUTHORIZED TRANSFER.

unbundling bank service pricing in which account activity is
separated into different categories and account SERVICE CHARGES
imposed for each activity. Thus, checking account customers are
charged a fee for each check paid and each cash withdrawal from
an automated teller machine, as opposed to a monthly account
maintenance fee. In unbundling service pricing, a bank may also
calculate an EARNINGS CREDIT rate on balances in deposit accounts, which can then be used to reduce the charges for un-
bundled services. The purpose in unbundling is to price bank
services so each earns a profit, or has a measurable loss, and
also to impose service charges fairly on all bank customers. Un-
bundled pricing also is a potential source of fee income, or noninterest income, which can be used to meet noninterest expenses, such as employee salaries. Contrast with account
BUNDLING.

unclaimed balances balances left idle in a bank account,
and considered abandoned property. Ownership may revert to
the state after a specified period, usually five years, under state
ESCHEAT laws. Also called a DORMANT ACCOUNT.

uncollected funds
1. checks or drafts that have not been paid by the drawee bank.
   Also called *uncollected items*. FEDERAL RESERVE FLOAT (FED
   FLOAT) is the time interval created when Federal Reserve
   Banks pay these checks before they are in turn paid by the
   payer bank. Federal Reserve Banks report these clearing
   checks as cash items in the process of collection in their
   weekly Statement of Condition.
   Federal Reserve REGULATION CC requires banks to follow
   a uniform schedule of funds availability, even if funds have
   not been collected from the paying bank: a local check drawn
   on a bank in the same Federal Reserve check processing dis-

trict is to be available for withdrawal funds three business days after a check is deposited; nonlocal checks are to be usable funds in seven business days; and the first $100 of any check deposited, the next business day. See also CHECK HOLD; DEFERRED AVAILABILITY; IMMEDIATE AVAILABILITY.

2. check that cannot be paid by the drawee bank because the maker's account does not have enough funds to cover the check. Also called NOT SUFFICIENT FUNDS.

uncovered option see NAKED OPTION.

underlying financial instruments that must be delivered in completion of an option or futures contract. For example, the underlying may be fixed rate securities, foreign exchange or equities of futures contracts (if the security is an option on a futures contract).

underlying lien claim having priority over claims of other creditors, and is repayable before subsequent obligations are fully paid. A first MORTGAGE has priority over second and third mortgages, which are known as junior liens. A lender may ask a borrower to sign a SUBORDINATION AGREEMENT making a bank loan repayable ahead of other obligations, for example, a loan by the individual borrower to a closely-held corporation or partnership in which the borrower is a principal owner.

underlying mortgage see UNDERLYING LIEN.

underwater loan loan that has a market value less than its book value. If sold in the secondary market, the lender would suffer a loss. Loans sink because the borrower is delinquent in payments; the coupon interest rate is below the rate on loans of similar quality and comparable maturities; or the loan collateral is worth less than the loan principal, or is not the principal source of repayment. For example, a lender holding a long-maturity auto loan, say a five-year loan, may find the market value of the car is below the remaining unpaid principal.

underwriting
Banking:
1. detailed credit analysis preceding the granting of a loan, based on credit information furnished by the borrower, such

as employment history, salary, and financial statements; publicly available information, such as the borrower's credit history, which is detailed in a CREDIT REPORT; and the lender's evaluation of the borrower's credit needs and ABILITY TO PAY. See also CREDIT SCORING; CORPORATE RESOLUTION; LOAN COMMITTEE; LOAN POLICY.

2. purchase of corporate bonds, commercial paper, U.S. Treasury securities, municipal general obligation bonds by a commercial bank or dealer bank for its own account, or for resale to investors. Bank underwriting of corporate securities is carried out through separate holding company affiliates, called SECURITIES AFFILIATEs or Section 20 affiliates (taken from the section in the GLASS-STEAGALL ACT allowing banking companies to purchase limited amounts of corporate bonds, mortgage backed securities and asset- backed securities for resale to investors).

Securities: process of purchasing securities for resale to investors. Securities are brought to the market by negotiated underwriting with the issuer, or by making competitive bids as in the auctions for U.S. government securities. Most corporate bonds and stocks, debt securities of U.S. government agencies and municipal bonds sold through negotiated underwriting. U.S. Treasury securities (Treasury BILLS, NOTEs and BONDs) are sold through auction market bidding by primary government securities dealers approved by the Federal Reserve Bank of New York. When a dealer bank purchases Treasury securities in a quarterly Treasury bond auction, it acts as underwriter and distributor. Treasury Securities purchased by a primary dealer are held in a dealer bank's TRADING ACCOUNT ASSETS portfolio, and often resold to other banks, and to private investors. Other forms of underwriting are ALL OR NONE, BEST EFFORT underwriting, and STANDBY UNDERWRITING. See also DUTCH AUCTION; GLASS-STEAGALL ACT; PRIVATE PLACEMENT; PUBLIC OFFERING.

Insurance: agreement by an insurer to accept risk of loss from property damage, accidental death, and so on, in exchange for payment of a premium.

underwriting agreement agreement between the managing underwriter, acting as agent for the UNDERWRITING GROUP, and the securities issuer. The agreement sets forth the responsibilities of all parties to the proposed sale and the initial price of securities offered to the public, and specifies whether the underwriter will buy any or all of the unsold securities. The issuer pays the cost of filing registration papers with the SECURITIES AND EXCHANGE COMMISSION, and the securities PROSPECTUS detailing terms of the public offering. Contrast with AGREEMENT AMONG UNDERWRITERS.

underwriting group association of commercial banks and investment banks that purchases a new offering of securities, generally for immediate resale to investors through a public offering. Also called an underwriting *syndicate*. Members of the underwriting group, acting through an AGREEMENT AMONG UNDERWRITERS, purchase the offering at an agreed price for resale at the public offering price. The group signs a purchase offer, or an UNDERWRITING AGREEMENT with the issuer that defines the terms of the proposed offering, and the amount to be purchased by each member of the group. See also NOTE ISSUANCE FACILITY; STANDBY UNDERWRITING; TENDER PANEL.

underwriting spread dollar difference between the amount paid by the UNDERWRITING GROUP in a new issue of securities and the price at which securities are offered for sale to the public. It is the underwriter's profit margin, usually expressed in points per unit of sale (bond or stock). Spreads may vary widely, and are influenced, among other factors, by the underwriter's expectation of market demand for the securities offered for sale, interest rates, and so on. See also GROSS MARGIN; YIELD SPREAD.

undivided interest

1. unrestricted claim of ownership to the assets of a corporation or partnership, as in a joint tenant account or TENANCY IN COMMON account. Each owner has a claim to the whole asset base. See also JOINT TENANTS WITH RIGHT OF SURVIVORSHIP.
2. SECONDARY MARKET term for an investor's claim of ownership in WHOLE LOANS purchased WITHOUT RECOURSE from a mortgage originator, mortgage pass-through certificates, or mortgage-backed bonds, such as COLLATERALIZED MORTGAGE OBLIGATIONS. The investor's claim to the underlying mortgages comes before all other claims.

undivided profits cumulative earnings that have not yet been distributed to shareholders as DIVIDEND payments, or carried over to the SURPLUS account; the term excludes reserves for contingencies and loan losses. It is the equivalent of retained earnings in corporate accounting.

unearned discount finance charges received when a loan is made and recognized as income at a later date. Finance charges in DISCOUNT notes are deducted from the loan proceeds, or the amount actually loaned to the borrower. In accounting terms, an unearned discount is a liability on the books of the lender until the loan matures. Under ACCRUAL BASIS accounting, deferred interest is unrealized income, and is deducted from gross loans carried on a bank's books so it does not overstate earnings.

unearned interest interest income received by a bank, though not actually recognized as accrued, or earned income. Consumer INSTALLMENT LOANS where the finance charges are computed using the ADD-ON INTEREST method, and DISCOUNT loans, with prepaid finance charges, are loaded in the early months with interest payments that the lender cannot count as income. If the borrower repays the loan early, part of the interest paid must be given back in a REBATE. The early interest payments gradually are amortized over the life of the loan, and credited as interest income.

Also, fees paid by either of the parties to a SWAP agreement, are unearned interest, for example, an interest rate swap. See also RULE OF THE 78'S; UNEARNED DISCOUNT.

unencumbered free of creditor's liens; property with a clean title, which may be sold or conveyed to another party, and is so noted on the TITLE certificate.

uniform bank performance report analytical survey prepared by the FEDERAL FINANCIAL INSTITUTIONS EXAMINATION COUNCIL, based on call reports filed quarterly. The report primarily is for bank management use as a tool in self-analysis. It emphasizes trends in profitability, asset quality, liquidity, and asset-liability management (sources and uses of funds). The report uses financial ratios to show the impact of management decisions and changing economic conditions on a bank's balance sheet and earnings, and also a bank's ability to cover losses with future earnings, ASSET QUALITY, or condition of the loan portfolio, and the adequacy of transfers to LOAN LOSS RESERVES to cover anticipated bad debt. The data in this report are collected by a survey of commercial banks, and shared with participating banks, though it is not publicly disclosed, unlike call report data. See also DECISION TREE; OFF-BALANCE SHEET LIABILITIES; PEER GROUP; RATIO ANALYSIS.

Uniform Commercial Code (UCC) set of standardized state laws governing financial contracts. The code was drafted by the National Conference of State Law Commissioners, and was adopted in the 1950s by most states and the District of Columbia. (Louisiana, the only state which has not fully ratified the code, has adopted Article 3 of the UCC, dealing with CHECKS, DRAFTS, and NEGOTIABLE INSTRUMENTS.) The code has nine separate sections, called articles. The most important of these are Article 3, dealing with negotiable instruments; Article 4, dealing with bank DEPOSITS and COLLECTIONS; Article 5, dealing with LETTERS OF CREDIT; Article 7, dealing with WAREHOUSE RECEIPTS and other documents of TITLE; Article 8 and Article 9, dealing with SECURED LOANS.

The most recent addition to the UCC, Article 4A, dealing with corporate-to-corporate electronic payments, such as wire transfers and automated clearing house credit transfers, was presented to state legislatures in 1989. Article 4A does not address consumer transactions, deferring to the ELECTRONIC FUNDS TRANSFER ACT and Federal Reserve REGULATION E for regulation of consumer payments.

Adoption of the code by state legislatures made it easier for lenders to extend credit secured by PERSONAL PROPERTY, such as a firm's equipment or receivables, as opposed to MORTGAGE loans secured by real estate. The code also cleared up some ambiguities and differences in state laws, and required contracts for sale or purchase of goods worth $500 be in writing to be enforceable. See also FINANCING STATEMENT; PERFECTED LIEN; SECURITY AGREEMENT; SECURITY INTEREST.

Uniform Consumer Credit Code law adopted in some states setting standards for consumer credit agreements. The code, applying to consumer credit agreements and installment sales contracts for amounts under $25,000, specifies creditor's remedies when a borrower defaults, and contains borrower protections against unfair or unlawful practices by a creditor.

Several states have in addition adopted their own versions of the federal TRUTH IN LENDING ACT to protect borrower's rights and equal access to credit.

Uniform Fiduciaries Act see FIDUCIARY.

Uniform Gift to Minors Act law adopted in most states allowing transfers of property to a minor, supervised by an adult, usually a parent, acting as a CUSTODIAN. Gifts to minors must be irrevocable, and are taxed to the minor, not the DONOR. The custodianship ends when the child reaches legal age.

Interest and dividend income earned by a child exceeding $1,000 is taxable, under the Tax Reform Act of 1986, at the highest tax rate of the parent. This is the so-called kiddie tax, intended to discourage transfers of assets to avoid paying taxes.

Uniform Partnership Act law adopted in many states covering the distribution of assets in partnerships. Unless the partners state otherwise, they will share equally in the profits and surplus remaining after liabilities are paid. A tenancy in partnership similar to a joint tenant agreement is created, giving each partner the right to use jointly owned property. These rights are not assignable, and partners are not liable for personal obligations of another partner. See also ARTICLES OF PARTNERSHIP.

uniform settlement statement see CLOSING STATEMENT.

uninsured depositor depositor who has checking or savings account deposits in a federally insured bank or savings institution exceeding the $100,000 deposit insurance ceiling per depositor. Depositors holding accounts with principal amounts exceeding the $100,000 limit, for example, a JUMBO CERTIFICATE OF DEPOSIT, risk losing part of their principal and interest earned if the institution holding their account becomes insolvent and its assets are liquidated. The Federal Deposit Insurance Corporation has, when conditions warranted, paid uninsured depositors of a failed bank the full amount of their deposit; in other bank liquidations depositors received only a pro rata share of their uninsured deposit above the $100,000 ceiling.

Despite the limitation of $100,000 in deposit protection, it is still possible for an individual to have more than $100,000 in fully insured deposits—by owning a joint account with someone else, or by holding an account in trust for another and naming that person as beneficiary. Contributions to an INDIVIDUAL RETIREMENT ACCOUNT or KEOGH account are exempt from the deposit insurance limits, and each can be insured separately for $100,000, i.e., a married couple can each have a $100,000 account, plus a joint account and an IRA account, and have $300,000 in fully insured deposits.

unit banking banking system in several states that prohibits branching, or operation of more than one full-service banking office by state chartered or national banks. Banks operating in these states, located principally in the Midwest, are sometimes referred to as unit banks. Thrift institutions, including savings and loans and credit unions, are unaffected by branching laws covering commercial banks. Limited branching laws, most prevalent in the Midwest and the Southwest, encouraged chartering of large numbers of small, independently owned state banks, and large MUILTIBANK HOLDING COMPANIES owning numerous unit banks. Branching laws in most of these states have been eased in the last several years, permitting geographic expansion, for example, county-wide or statewide branching. See also BRANCH BANKING; CHAIN BANKING; McFADDEN ACT.

unit investment trust see INVESTMENT COMPANY.

universal banking banking system in several European countries where commercial banks make loans, underwrite corporate debt, and also take equity positions in corporate securities. For example, in West Germany commercial banks accept time deposits, lend money, underwrite corporate stocks, and act as investment advisors to large corporations. In Germany, there has never been any separation between commercial banks and investment banks, as there is in the United States.

The advantages of this type of banking system have been debated. Universal banking permits better use of customer information and allows banks to sell more services under one roof as a FINANCIAL SUPERMARKET. The main disadvantage is that universal banking permits concentration of economic power in a handful of large banking institutions that hold equity positions in companies that are also borrowers of funds.

universal numerical system see ABA TRANSIT NUMBER; CHECK ROUTING SYMBOL.

unlawful loans loans made for amounts in excess of the legal lending limit to a single borrower; loans made at a rate exceeding state USURY laws; insider loans to directors or officers that are made in excess of levels permitted by federal regulation; and loans that are illegal according to banking statutes. See also ULTRA VIRES ACTS.

unlimited liability liability of general partners and sole proprietor owners of a company extending to their entire assets, including personal property. This contrasts with the limited liability of stockholders in a corporation, or the liability of limited partners in a joint venture, whose potential losses are limited to the extent of their investment.

unlimited mortgage see OPEN-END MORTGAGE.

unlisted security see OVER-THE-COUNTER.

unmatched book
1. asset-liability imbalance that occurs when the maturity of a bank's assets differs from its balance sheet liabilities. Also called a *mismatched maturity*. Refers to the situation where a bank's deposit liabilities have a shorter term than the assets (bank loans) funded by those liabilities. An asset-liability gap can be positive or negative, depending on whether the asset maturity is shorter or longer than the liability maturity.
    In the Euromarket, the term is synonymous with open book or short book, and also applies to unmatched currency exposure, for example, owning more pound sterling liabilities than pound sterling assets. See also MISMATCH.
2. foreign exchange FORWARD MARKET or SPOT MARKET purchase that has not been executed, or vice versa.
3. in FOREIGN EXCHANGE trading, a currency mismatch, for example, holding more liabilities than assets in British pound sterling.

unpaid balance outstanding LOAN balance or CASH ADVANCE that is still due and payable. It may be the current balance on a loan, credit card account, or a past due balance, including late charges, if payments are missed. A balance unpaid more than 30 days may be reported as PAST DUE to a CREDIT REPORTING AGENCY.

unperfected security interest security interest in which the holder of lien has not taken all of the necessary steps to assure validity of claim, as required under the Uniform Commercial Code. This can happen when a lender fails to properly record a FINANCING STATEMENT attaching a lien to the borrower's property, fails to discover a previously filed lien in public records, or does not file a CONTINUATION STATEMENT extending an existing financing statement.

The lender risks not being able to collect the full value of its claim if its position as a secured creditor is challenged by another party. Courts generally will recognize the validity of an unperfected claim in litigation involving the lender and its borrower, but an unperfected lien may not stand up to challenge by a third party.

unrealized profit (or loss) paper profits (or losses) from securities owned, which actually have not been made or collected. Also called paper gain or loss. Accounting rules state that unrealized losses of marketable securities caused by a market decline must be recognized in the holder's income statement, even though the securities or futures contract have not been sold. In banking, this applies only to TRADING ACCOUNT ASSETS held by a bank for its own trading account or a third party. Paper profits in an investment portfolio or trust account are realized when the securities are sold.

unsecured creditor general creditor of a debtor filing a VOLUNTARY BANKRUPTCY petition, who does not hold a SECURITY INTEREST in the debtor's assets or backing by a MORTGAGE. In a Chapter 7 LIQUIDATION, general creditors are paid a pro rata share of the bankruptcy ESTATE after claims of secured creditors are satisfied, which means that most general creditors can receive substantially less than the value of their claim.

unsecured debt debt offering backed only by the creditworthiness and reputation of the issuer, and not supported by COLLATERAL. See also COMMERCIAL PAPER; DEBENTURE; NOTE; SUBORDINATED DEBT.

unsecured loan loan granted on the strength of the borrower's credit history or reputation in the community, earnings potential, and other assets owned, even if unpledged, rather than a pledge of assets as COLLATERAL. Assignment of collateral, as in a MORTGAGE, is not required. The borrower signs a PROMISSORY NOTE stating the terms and conditions under which the loan will be repaid. The lender may ask a CO-MAKER or GUARANTOR to sign the note, pledging to repay the loan if the borrower defaults. Also called a *character loan* or *good faith loan*. See also FIVE C's OF CREDIT; SIDE COLLATERAL.

unwinding

1. to close out a market position by executing an offsetting order canceling that position.

   2. disengaging from a speculative foreign exchange FORWARD MARKET or LEADS AND LAGS position.

3. in futures, simultaneous liquidation of both short and long positions when the pricing spread between the cash and futures market closes, or returns to normal. If the spread tightens up, the long and short positions would be reversed again. Also known as *spread trading*.

4. removing a bank's WIRE TRANSFER payments to other banks in the event the bank is unable to cover its end-of-day NET SETTLEMENT obligations to other banks.

upfront fee see ORIGINATION FEE.

upstream

1. CORRESPONDENT bank that buys LOAN PARTICIPATIONS exceeding the legal lending limit of a community bank, also called the DOWNSTREAM bank or respondent bank. Typically, correspondent banks offer other banking services for community banks, such as check collection, foreign exchange, and arrange LETTER OF CREDIT financing.

2. loan or transfer of funds, for example, earnings or capital, from a subsidiary to its parent company, a term widely used in banking to denote the internal movements of funds within a bank holding company. Corporate dividends in a multibank holding company are paid out of funds transferred to the holding company by its operating banks.

usable funds see AVAILABLE BALANCE.

usance period of time between the date a bill of exchange is presented and the date it is paid. In a strict sense, the term means the time allowed by custom for the period of bills of exchange in trade between two particular countries, which can be anywhere from two weeks to two months or longer. Today, it means the time period for which any bill is drawn, or its TENOR.

use
  1. Banking. The ability to draw from a bank line of credit or loan.
  2. Trusts. An informal agreement giving beneficial ownership of property legally owned by another person; the forerunner of the modern TRUST. Differs from nominal ownership of property put in the care of a TRUSTEE for enjoyment by the BENEFICIARY named in a trust.

U.S. depository FEDERAL RESERVE BANK or commercial bank holding balances in safekeeping for the U.S. Treasury Department or federal agencies. The Treasury Department maintains TREASURY TAX AND LOAN ACCOUNTS in 14,000 commercial banks for collection of federal taxes and licensing fees. Federal Reserve Banks also buy and hold Treasury securities that are not purchased by government securities dealers at regular Treasury auctions; the reserve banks also buy Treasuries from dealers in carrying out Federal Reserve monetary policy. See also TREASURY GENERAL ACCOUNT.

U.S. League of Savings Institutions see TRADE ASSOCIATION.

U.S. savings bond see SAVINGS BOND.

U.S. treasury securities see TREASURY SECURITIES.

usury charging loan interest higher than the rates allowed by law. Interest rates in consumer credit contracts are controlled by state law, and the highest permitted rate is called the usury rate or the usury ceiling. Since the early 1980s, many state legislatures have recognized that statutory controls of consumer credit, rather than protecting consumers from unscrupulous lenders, often make it more difficult for consumers to obtain credit. Lawmakers, consequently, have revised state statutes to allow interest rates to be set by market competition, rather than specified by laws. Several states have abolished usury ceilings; most states have raised the interest ceilings to encourage more rate competition among financial institutions, and most of these laws have a SUNSET CLAUSE calling for periodic review every three to five years. Some states, including New York, Delaware, and South Dakota have no limits on consumer credit. New York does, however, have a criminal usury ceiling of 25%, a maximum rate of interest that lenders may charge on consumer credit. Many states abolished these limits in the early 1980s, when the high interest rates made it unprofitable for lenders to make consumer loans, and also to keep banks from moving their credit card operations to states with more liberal statutes.

State usury laws generally are enforceable only through civil suits filed by debtors claiming excessive interest charges. Most state laws have stiff penalties for illegal interest, ranging from forfeiture of interest owed on the entire loan balance, or forfeiture of both principal and interest. Commercial credit in most states is exempt from usury statutes; agricultural credit is unregulated, though not exempt from state interest rate controls.

usury rate see USURY.

utilization fee annual fee charged by a lender against the portion of a revolving line of credit or TERM LOAN actually used by the borrower. Contrast with COMMITMENT FEE.

utilization rate portion of a revolving line of credit actually advanced to the borrower and on which interest is paid. It is the basis for assessing the annual UTILIZATION FEE the borrower pays to maintain the line of credit.

V

valuation reserve special account set up to offset changes in one or more accounts, for example, accumulated depreciation from depreciable fixed assets or dividends payable. When a bank believes a loan is uncollectible, it sets aside a portion of earnings equal in value to the estimated difference between the loan and the market value of the bad loan in the special account for LOAN LOSS RESERVES. If the loan is charged off as a worthless asset, the bank writes down the loan portfolio and the reserve account by an equal amount. See also EARMARKED RESERVES.

value see APPRAISAL; FAIR MARKET VALUE; STANDARD OF VALUE.

value compensated purchase or sale of foreign currencies between two banks in which both parties agree to fix the values of the currencies exchanged at the spot rate price on the settlement date. This minimizes exchange risk, as the buyer agrees to reimburse the seller for any difference in currency values, provided that each bank agrees not to make payment to a third party on the actual settlement date. Trades ordinarily are confirmed by cable advice.

value date
Banking:
1. date that a customer can use funds deposited in an account.
2. calendar date on which a transfer of funds through FEDERAL WIRE, AUTOMATED CLEARING HOUSE, or electronic settlement network becomes available for use as good funds by the receiving bank or its customer. Fed Wire transfers are effective immediately, and are available as good funds the same day as transmitted by the sending bank. Automated Clearing House transactions generally are available the next day. These dates may be same day, next day, or some specified date in the future. See also NET SETTLEMENT.
Foreign Exchange: date on which foreign exchange bought and sold must be delivered, and the delivery price paid in local

currency. This is usually two days. In the Eurobond market, it is the seventh calendar date after the transaction date. See also DELIVERY DATE; SPOT NEXT; TOMORROW NEXT.

value dating process of initiating electronic payments prior to the date that funds actually are credited to the customer's account. It is used most often in DIRECT DEPOSIT programs, for example, electronic deposit of Social Security benefits into a beneficiary's account, or payroll direct deposit.

value impaired loan to a foreign borrower that is rated as a NONPERFORMING LOAN because the borrower is delinquent in interest payments six months or more. It is not in compliance with an INTERNATIONAL MONETARY FUND debt restructuring program and there is little immediate prospect for compliance; it has not met debt rescheduling terms for more than a year, or there is little prospect for orderly restoration of debt service in the near future.

VA mortgage see VETERANS LOAN.

variable rate certificate CERTIFICATE OF DEPOSIT carrying a yield set at a spread over a bare rate—for example, the current 90-day CD rate— and adjusted quarterly. These were introduced in the United States in 1975. Yields are pegged to an interest rate INDEX, commodity prices, and so on. See also MARKET INDEX DEPOSIT.

variable rate loan consumer installment loan or commercial loan carrying an interest rate that fluctuates according to changes in an INDEX rate. Also called a *floating rate loan*. The rate paid by the borrower may rise or fall, depending on changes in MONEY MARKET rates such as the six-month Treasury bill, or the bank PRIME RATE. Most adjustable rate consumer loans are level payment loans, and rates are revised quarterly or semiannually. If the loan rate falls, the installment NOTE is paid early; if rates rise, there is an additional BALLOON PAYMENT. Variable rate consumer loans generally are medium-term loans used in automobile financing, home improvement, home equity lines of credit, or unsecured personal loans.

Variable rate commercial loans are adjusted against changes in a BASE RATE, for example, the banker's acceptance rate or the

London Interbank Offered Rate (LIBOR). The base lending rate is typically a money market rate, determined by the buyers and sellers of excess funds in the short-term credit markets. See also ADJUSTABLE RATE MORTGAGE.

variable rate mortgage see ADJUSTABLE RATE MORT-GAGE; ALTERNATIVE MORTGAGE INSTRUMENT.

vault armored storage facility meeting minimum security standards set by the Federal Reserve Board (REGULATION P). It is used for storage or safekeeping of customer valuables in SAFE DEPOSIT BOXES, a bank's portfolio of investment grade securities, such as TREASURY BONDS, and cash balances (VAULT CASH) sufficient to meet daily cash needs.

vault cash cash in a bank's vault that is used for day-to-day business needs, such as cashing checks for customers. On premises cash can be counted as a portion of bank LEGAL RESERVES to meet RESERVE REQUIREMENTS of the Federal Reserve System.

velocity of money number of times that money balances turn over in the economy. It is an attempt to measure national income against spending habits by showing the relationship between money and spending on goods and services. This usually is expressed as the ratio of gross national product to the amount of money available for spending (called the money stock). An increase in velocity means that money is being held, on average, for shorter periods of time, indicating a growing demand for money and general economic expansion. A decrease means that money is being spent less rapidly, and that consumers are more inclined to hold onto their dollars than spend them. A larger velocity of money can also mean a higher number of consumer transactions. See also MONETARY POLICY.

vendor express marketing name adopted by the U.S. Treasury Department's Financial Management Service (FMS) for electronic payments to vendors doing business with the federal government. The FMS is the fiscal agent for most federal agencies handling the majority of payments to government contractors. Vendor Express payments are processed through the AUTO-MATED CLEARING HOUSE system using the CASH CONCENTRATION & DISBURSEMENT payment format, plus a single addendum record for invoice and payment related information. Under Vendor Express, FMS intends to pay a majority of the federal government's suppliers with electronic payments, rather than checks.

vendor single interest insurance see SINGLE INTEREST INSURANCE.

vendor's lien seller's right to reclaim property sold to a buyer if the purchaser falls behind in payments, for example, a seller's lien on real estate sold through a PURCHASE MONEY MORTGAGE. Seller's liens are a carryover from common law, and are relatively uncommon in the United States. See also MECHANIC'S LIEN.

venture capital initial money invested in high-risk companies or small companies specializing in new technologies, often in return for an equity position in the firm. Also called *risk capital*. Start-up companies generally go through three stages of financing: initial START-UP FINANCING or seed money to a newly organized company; second-tier financing or MEZZANINE LEVEL financing to firms showing potential for positive growth; and finally, an initial PUBLIC OFFERING by successful companies issuing common stock to the public. Venture capitalists recoup most of their investment in start-up companies by taking common stock WARRANTs, and by taking capital appreciation gains from stock sold at a public offering. Frequently, venture financing is arranged in tandem with a WORKING CAPITAL line of credit from a commercial bank to meet short-term borrowing needs.

verification
Banking:
1. employer's confirmation of a borrower's annual income, requested by a lender when screening a CREDIT APPLICATION.
2. auditing procedure whereby the accuracy of bank records is checked by direct contact with customers. Verification, also called CONFIRMATION, can be positive or negative. In negative verification, a bank customer is asked only to notify the bank of bookkeeping errors; in positive verification, the customer is asked to verify an account balance as of a specific date.

3. validation of a PERSONAL IDENTIFICATION NUMBER when a bank card is used at an automated teller machine or point-of-sale terminal.

Accounting: auditor's review of financial statements by comparing journal entries to actual documents, such as cancelled checks, copies of loan documentation, and so on.

vested interest right of beneficial interest in real or personal property, which may be deferred for enjoyment in future years. For example, an interest in the assets of a pension fund, trust fund, and so on. Participants in a company's DEFINED BENEFIT PENSION PLAN gain the right to the employer's contributions to the plan after a vesting period normally after ten years of employment. Pension funds must comply with certain Internal Revenue Service rules before they qualify as employee benefit plans eligible for special tax treatment as tax-exempt investment funds.

veterans loan education loan or MORTGAGE partially guaranteed as to repayment of principal and interest by the Department of Veterans Affairs, providing below-market financing with no down payment to veterans of the U.S. armed services. As an incentive to lenders, the Department of Veterans Affairs (formerly the Veterans Administration) guarantees 80% of 30-year residential mortgage loans against default by the borrower. Lenders may charge interest rates up to a ceiling set by the department. Veterans loans may be paid off at any time without penalty, and are assumable by another borrower at the same rate if the borrower sells a home. See also FEDERAL HOUSING ADMINISTRATION.

video banking generic name for information delivery systems allowing two-way communication from a consumer-owned computer, television set, or specially designed VIDEOTEX hardware to a financial institution to pay bills, compare rates on investment accounts, and so on. See also HOME BANKING.

videotex two-way communication connecting a computer and a home TV screen, personal computer, or videotex terminal via telephone lines. Also spelled videotext. Users can make banking transactions, order airline tickets, or buy merchandise from participating retailers, entering commands from an alphanumeric keypad. Examples of commercial videotex systems are the Minitel system in France and Prodigy in the United States. See also HOME BANKING.

Visa member-owned association, based in San Mateo, California, that licenses Visa service marks to financial institutions issuing Visa CREDIT and DEBIT cards, and provides net settlement services for its members through its BASE I authorization and BASE II transaction settlement networks. Formerly National BankAmericard Inc. (until 1977), Visa manages a global electronic communications network, called VisaNet, connecting financial institutions, merchant authorization terminals, and automated teller machines around the world. In recent years, Visa has expanded its operations from bank cards to electronic banking, acting as a payment processor for point-of-sale debit card and automated clearing house (ACH) transactions for financial institutions in several states. Full name: Visa International Services Association. See also MASTERCARD INTERNATIONAL.

visible supply calendar of new issues of MUNICIPAL BONDS coming to market in the next 30 days, used as a measure of available investments in gauging market acceptance of new issues. Also called *thirty-day visible supply*. Originally, a commodities market term, the term has been adapted to municipal bonds and other types of debt securities offered to investors. Municipal bond issues offered for sale in the dealer market are advertised in the BLUE LIST.

voidable preference transfer of assets by a debtor filing a VOLUNTARY BANKRUPTCY petition in favor of one creditor at the expense of other secured creditors. If the transfer was made in the 90-days prior to filing the petition, or was made in anticipation of a bankruptcy filing, the bankruptcy trustee may set aside the preference.

volume
Futures. The number of transactions in a futures contract (one side only) during a specified period of time. A market with a high number of contracts is good for trading.

Banking.

1. aggregate purchases and cash advances on a credit card program during an accounting period. Outstanding credit receivables usually are less because some cardholders will pay off their credit card bill every month.
2. dollar amount of loans booked by a lender during a calendar or reporting period.

Securities. The aggregate number of shares traded on an exchange during a given day.

voluntary bankruptcy legal proceeding whereby a debtor voluntarily files a petition for relief from creditors in a federal bankrupcy court. The debtor's property is placed in the hands of a court appointed trustee, who distributes assets to pay debts owed to creditors. A business intending to remain in operation can act as its own trustee (called a DEBTOR IN POSSESSION) if no bankruptcy trustee is named. When a petition is filed, an automatic stay prohibits creditors from making further collection efforts until a debt has been discharged, a repayment plan is accepted by creditors, or a petition is dismissed by the bankruptcy court. Individuals and businesses other than railroads, municipalities, banks, and savings institutions can file petitions under any of the three main chapters in the bankruptcy code: a Chapter 7 LIQUIDATION, in which the debtor's assets are sold to pay creditors; a Chapter 11 REORGANIZATION, normally filed by a business; or a Chapter 13 WAGE EARNER PLAN filed by persons with regular income who agree to make partial payments toward their obligations. Contrast with INVOLUNTARY BANKRUPTCY. See also BANKRUPTCY; CREDITORS' COMMITTEE; REAFFIRMATION; REDEMPTION.

voluntary conveyance see FORECLOSURE.

voluntary termination cancellation of a swap contract by mutual agreement of the counterparties, usually involving a lump-sum payment from one party to the other.

voluntary trust type of living trust (an INTER VIVOS TRUST) in which the person setting up the trust (the settlor) retains legal title of the gift transferred to the beneficiary, even though the beneficiary has actual title and possession. Contrast with GIFT INTER VIVOS.

vostro account account used by a bank to describe a demand deposit account maintained with it by a bank in a foreign country. It is the NOSTRO ACCOUNT of the other bank, and is used primarily to arrange FOREIGN EXCHANGE transfers between the respective banks.

voting trust certificate receipt issued to shareholders of a company in REORGANIZATION placing voting rights in the hands of a few individuals, who are known as voting trustees. Shareholders owning common stock exchange their shares for voting trust certificates giving them the same rights of ownership and equity as before, but give up the right to vote their shares during the period of time the voting trust remains in effect. A voting trust is a limited life trust, normally expiring after five years, but can be extended by mutual agreement of shareholders and the trustees.

voucher
1. document authorizing disbursement of cash to cover a liability.
2. legally acceptable evidence of debt repayment, for example, cancelled checks, remittance documents, and so on. See also ACQUITTANCE.

voucher check CHECK with a detachable form indicating the reason for payment. The party who endorses deposits the check and retains the attached stub as a record of payment. In trade credit, the amount appearing on the payment stub is the posting medium for crediting the seller's accounts receivable ledger, and the buyer's accounts payable ledger.

W

wage assignment clause in a loan agreement allowing the lender to attach the borrower's wages if the borrower defaults, without notifying the borrower.

wage earner plan popular name for a debt repayment plan under Chapter 13 of the Bankruptcy Code. Also called a *rehabilitation*. The debtor voluntarily agrees to repay over a three- to five-year period a portion of obligations due creditors in exchange for a promise by creditors to refrain from further collection efforts. Court supervised repayment plans help debtors earning a regular income restore their credit ratings without liquidating their personal or financial assets. See also LIQUIDATION.

wage garnishment see GARNISHMENT.

waiting period popular name for the SECURITIES AND EXCHANGE COMMISSION rule mandating a 20-day cooling-off period dating from the filing of the REGISTRATION statement and a preliminary PROSPECTUS. The regulatory intent is to encourage disclosure to potential investors, but not actual selling. The SEC allows the offering to clear the registration process by not objecting to anything disclosed in the registration papers. Any objection by the SEC automatically would restart the 20-day period, unless the agency has accelerated the process.

waiver a voluntary relinquishment of a right to property owned, claim against another's property, or to any legally enforceable right. In banking, the term has numerous meanings, such as an agreement not to charge a credit card annual fee during the first year after a new card is issued, or an agreement to forgo overdraft charges on bad checks.

waiver of demand see WAIVER OF NOTICE.

waiver of exemption clause in a loan agreement whereby the borrower waives a right to exempt personal or real property from attachment or seizure in the event of default. This credit practice was prohibited by banking regulatory agencies in 1985.

waiver of notice

1. agreement by the endorser of a CHECK, DRAFT, or NOTE to accept legal responsibility, without being notified formally, in the event the original maker defaults. Also called *waiver of demand.*

2. waiver of a bank's customary right to be notified formally when it presents ELIGIBLE PAPER (drafts, acceptances) for REDISCOUNT at the Federal Reserve DISCOUNT WINDOW. Endorsement by the bank is legally considered a waiver of demand, notice, and protest by the Federal Reserve, should the original signer default on the notes.

Wall Street popular name for the financial district in New York City where the New York Stock Exchange, the American Stock Exchange, leading securities firms, and several major banks and insurance firms are located. In a more generic sense the term is broader in scope, referring to the investment banking and securities brokerage industry regardless of where the firms involved actually are located.

ward an incompetent person or a child whose affairs are put in the hands of a GUARDIAN appointed by a court, who acts as a FIDUCIARY. The child's guardian administers the child's estate on behalf of the child until the child reaches the age of adulthood.

warehouse

1. bonded storage facility where commodities, finished goods, or works in process are under a WAREHOUSE RECEIPT. Also called a *field warehouse.*

2. swap maker's book listing inventory of swaps to be held or traded, either for other financial institutions or to profit from position taking. A bank that manages a swap book is known as a MARKET MAKER.

warehouse financing see ASSET-BASED LENDING; INVENTORY FINANCING.

warehouse receipt document giving proof of ownership of goods held in inventory, for example, unfinished goods temporarily stored in a field warehouse by a manufacturer. The receipt is a TITLE document for its holder, and may be either negotiable or nonnegotiable. A negotiable warehouse receipt is deliverable to the bearer or to another party named; a nonnegotiable receipt specifies to whom the stored goods are deliverable. Most warehouse receipts are issued in negotiable form, making them eligible as collateral for WORKING CAPITAL loans from a bank. See also ASSET-BASED LENDING; INVENTORY FINANCING; UNIFORM COMMERCIAL CODE.

warehousing

1. holding of mortgages by a MORTGAGE BANKER on a short-term basis until the loans are sold to an investor. The mortgage originator finances the inventory of unsold loans with a short-term line of credit, using the mortgages as loan collateral. This form of financing commonly is used by mortgage bankers to raise working capital funds until mortgages held in inventory are sold to a permanent investor, the TAKE-OUT LENDER.

2. temporary storage of transactions by an AUTOMATED CLEARING HOUSE (ACH) or a financial institution, as for corporate customers. ACH associations may hold transactions for financial institutions up to 31 days prior to the VALUE DATE when funds actually are moved.

3. pledging a MORTGAGE as collateral for short- term loans, usually called a hypothecated mortgage.

4. interest carryover in an ADJUSTABLE RATE MORTGAGE subject to a periodic rate cap. When a rise in borrowing costs exceeds the interest rate cap, lenders may defer interest payable to future time periods if allowed by the mortgage contract.

warm card bank card with restricted usage. Withdrawals or deposits may be permitted, but not both. An example can be a deposit-only card, allowing merchants to deposit their daily cash receipts at a night depository and get a transaction receipt from an AUTOMATED TELLER MACHINE.

warning bulletin paper listing of over-limit or past-due credit card accounts and stolen cards, compiled weekly by Visa and MasterCard and mailed in a joint bulletin to credit card accepting merchants. Merchants are instructed to obtain authorization before accepting the cards listed. Also called *cancellation bulletin*, *hot card list*, or *restricted card list*. See also ZERO-FLOOR LIMIT.

warrant

1. short-term interest bearing note issued by a state or local government to pay debts, repayable from a defined income source. For example, notes issued in anticipation of future tax revenues (a TAX ANTICIPATION NOTE) or future cash receipts (a REVENUE ANTICIPATION NOTE).

2. certificate giving the bearer the right to buy securities, gold, or other commodities at a stated price for a stated period or at any time in the future. Also called a *subscription warrant*. The offered price usually is above the market price, in contrast to a rights offer of newly issued securities at below market prices. These instruments are offered to the public in negotiable form, and are traded freely on the stock exchanges. They differ from STOCK PURCHASE OPTIONS, which normally are offered only to the issuer's employees.

3. CURRENCY WARRANT. The yield and price of the instruments covered are fixed at the time of the original sale.

warranty statement, either written or implied, that assertions made in completion of a contract are true. For example, a seller's claim in a WARRANTY DEED that the property being sold has a marketable title. In mortgage banking, a lender's claim that loans offered for sale to a secondary market CONDUIT meet the buyer's specifications for pooling with other loans and are not in arrears. Under a warranty agreement, the buyer has recourse against the seller. A SELLER-SERVICER of loans sold in the secondary mortgage market agrees to buy back an agreed-upon portion of losses from borrower defaults.

warranty deed deed conveying the seller's interest in real property to the buyer. The seller, also known as the grantor, certifies that the title on property being conveyed is free and clear of defects, liens, and encumbrances. If a third party claim is not exempted specifically, the buyer (the grantee) may sue the seller for the damages caused by the defective title.

wash sale

1. sale and repurchase of securities within a short period of time to give the appearance of trading activity, sometimes done by stock manipulators to give the impression of trading activity and to raise stock prices. Sales between two people to boost prices, and induce investors to buy, are now prohibited by stock exchange rules.

2. disallowed tax loss resulting from sale of a security at a loss in a 30-day period, followed by a repurchase of the same or a substantially identical security, or purchase of a call option, in the next 30 days. Internal Revenue Service rules disallow tax losses involving sale and purchase of the same or substantially identical securities within a 61-day period. To be dissimilar, securities must have different interest rates, voting power or earnings power, or, in the case of bonds, different maturities. Only traders are exempted from the IRS rule that losses from wash trading have to be recognized when the trades took place.

wasting trust TRUST account that allows the TRUSTEE to use part of the trust PRINCIPAL to make payments to a BENEFICIARY if the interest income is insufficient. The term also applies to trusts that invest largely in WASTING ASSETS such as oil and gas reserves.

watch list

1. list of banks regarded by bank examiners as having earnings problems or IMPAIRED CAPITAL. These generally are banks given a rating higher than 3 on the CAMEL RATING scale used by federal banking regulators to identify banks needing closer supervision. (A CAMEL rating is a composite score, based on five criteria: Credit, Assets, Management, Earnings and Liquidity). A CAMEL rating of 4 or 5 indicates financial weaknesses in the balance sheet, such as a higher ratio of nonperforming loans to total assets than banks of similar size. If uncorrected, these problems could impair a bank's future viability. A bank placed on the watch list is considered a TROUBLED BANK, and is examined more frequently by bank supervisory agencies than other banks. (In contrast, a bank given a CAMEL rating of 1 is a bank with strong earnings and few nonperforming assets.) In any event, a CAMEL rating is never disclosed publicly.

2. list of banks issuing CERTIFICATES OF DEPOSIT to the secondary market that have potentially weak balance sheets, compiled by credit rating agencies, such as Standard & Poor's.

3. list of countries whose ability to meet debt service payments on external debt is followed closely by federal banking agencies for changes in financial condition. The list, a rating of COUNTRY RISK associated with loans to developing countries, is compiled by the INTERAGENCY COUNTRY EXPOSURE REVIEW COMMITTEE, whose members are drawn from the Federal Reserve Board, the Comptroller of the Currency, and the Federal Deposit Insurance Corporation.

4. any list of loans or credit exposures compiled by a bank for internal monitoring. For example, a maturity tickler of time loans maturing in the next 30 days and commercial loans with a perfected SECURITY INTEREST due to expire in the next six months, unless renewed.

watermark stripe bank card MAGNETIC STRIPE using a proprietary design to thwart card counterfeiting. The Watermark stripe developed by Thorn EMI Malco, Garrison, MD, has a proprietary design that imprints each magnetic stripe with a unique signature, making counterfeiting extremely difficult. Despite its security properties, though, the Malco stripe has not been accepted widely in the banking industry.

weak currency currency said to be a less desirable form of payment than other currrencies. Weak currency countries have frequent currency devaluations against currencies of major trading partners, balance of payment deficits, or political instability. These currencies generally trade at a discount in relation to currencies of economically developed countries. Foreign exchange dealers generally do not make markets in weak currencies, except for currency speculation. A dealer who expects a weak currency to decline in value may sell that currency short, making a profit from the difference in exchange rates.

Acceptability of one currency versus another is dependent, of course, on local market conditions. The Portuguese escudo, for example, may be a weaker currency than the U.S. dollar, but its relative weakness may not be significant enough to discourage exporters from accepting it as payment. Contrast with STRONG CURRENCY.

weak market see THIN MARKET.

Wednesday scramble last-minute buying or selling of FEDERAL FUNDS on the day that banks report their deposit account balances subject to RESERVE REQUIREMENTS. Banks temporarily short of reserves make up the shortfall by buying overnight funds—Fed Funds—from a bank with EXCESS RESERVES. Federal Funds purchased ordinarily are returned to the selling bank at the opening of business the following day.

weekly reporting banks

1. large commercial banks that report their balance sheet assets and liabilities to FEDERAL RESERVE BANKS on a weekly basis. The consolidated asset and liability positions of these banks and their domestic subsidiaries, known as the Weekly Consolidated Condition Report, is released every Wednesday by the FEDERAL RESERVE BOARD. The report lists balance sheet conditions as of the Wednesday two weeks earlier. As of 1989 there were nearly 300 federally insured banks filing weekly reports of condition.
2. money center banks in New York City reporting their financial condition every Wednesday to the Federal Reserve Bank of New York. The New York Fed publishes the consolidated assets and liabilities of nine money center banks, including domestic subsidiaries.

weighted average coupon (WAC) weighted average of the underlying COUPON interest rates of mortgage loans or other loans backing ASSET-BACKED SECURITIES or MORTGAGE BACKED SECURITIES, as of the issue date, using the balance of each mortgage as the weighting factor. This calculation is used only when the underlying loans have variable interest rates. WAC is computed by multiplying the coupon rate of each mortgage or mortgage backed security by its remaining balance, adding the products, and dividing the result by the remaining balance.

weighted average life see AVERAGE LIFE.

weighted average maturity (WAM) weighted AVERAGE LIFE of the remaining terms to maturity of the underlying loans of a mortgage certificate at the issue date, using the balance of each loan as the weighting factor. Weighted average maturity is computed by multiplying the maturity of each mortgage in a given pool by its remaining balance, adding the products and dividing the result by the remaining balance. The Federal National Mortgage Association and the Federal Home Loan Mortgage Corporation use WEIGHTED AVERAGE REMAINING TERM instead of WAM, when referring to mortgage backed securities.

weighted average remaining term (WART) remaining term of MORTGAGE-BACKED SECURITIES or ASSET-BACKED SECURITIES at any given point in their life. It is affected by prepayments and must be adjusted monthly. It is sometimes used interchangeably with WEIGHTED AVERAGE MATURITY. Weighted Average Remaining Term is used by the Federal Home Loan Mortgage Corporation (Freddie Mac), instead of Weighted Average Maturity, in computing the remaining term in mortgage participation certificates and strip participation certificates.

what-if calculation forecasting computation that allows testing of different hypotheses for repricing assets and acquiring funds. These hypothetical calculations usually are executed with a spreadsheet program using a microcomputer. In asset-liability management, a what-if calculation can estimate the difference between maturing assets and liabilities for different time periods in the future. These models also can forecast changes in pro forma financial statements under different interest rate scenarios, and are an analytical tool used in credit analysis.

when issued securities term for when and if issued, referring most often to conditional trading in bonds or other securities in the interval between the announcement date and the actual date of issue. Securities dealers trade offerings of new securities, stock splits, and government securities, among others, in the period before the effective listing date. Although the U.S. Treasury Department tries to discourage trading in Treasury securities on a when issued basis, government securities dealers frequently can arrange preauction bond swaps (yield swaps) for the issue to be offered for sale.

white plastic type of credit card fraud in which a merchant knowingly accepts fraudulent transactions. The person initiating the scheme buys merchandise with blank plastic cards stamped with valid account numbers, hence the name white plastic. Afterward the merchandise is sold for cash and the merchant is paid a portion of the cash sale proceeds.

whole loans mortgage loan sold in its entirety, without any participation kept by the seller. The investor assumes all contractual rights and responsibilities, and may pay the seller a SERVICING fee for collecting principal and interest payments. The purchase price usually is discounted when the mortgage COUPON is below current market rates.

whole pools mortgage PARTICIPATION CERTIFICATE representing an UNDIVIDED INTEREST in an entire pool of MORTGAGE loans, rather than a pro rata share, or fractional interest, in the loans packaged for sale to an investor.

wholesale banking banking services offered to corporations with sound financial statements, and institutional customers, such as pension funds and government agencies. Services include lending, cash management, commercial mortgages, working capital loans, leasing, trust services, and so on. Most banks divide wholesale banking into several different businesses: the Fortune 500 and Fortune 1000 market, comprising the 1,000 largest U.S. corporations; the Middle Market, or companies with annual sales of $50 to $250 million; and the small business market, or corporations with sales under $10 million.

Commercial banks, responding to increased market competition from alternative financing sources, such as commercial paper and junk bonds, have begun to place more emphasis on fee-based corporate services, including foreign exchange and securities trading, advisory services in corporate merger and acquisitions, merchant banking, and corporate cash management, and securities underwriting. See also COMMERCIAL AND INDUSTRIAL (C&I) LOAN; COMMERCIAL MORTGAGE; INVESTMENT ADVISOR; LEVERAGED BUYOUT; NONCREDIT SERVICES; SECURITIES AFFILIATE; SECURITIZATION.

widow's allowance allowance of personal property made by a court or by statute to give a widow sufficient funds from an ESTATE for household expenses during the period immediately following her husband's death.

widow's exemption allowed deduction from state inheritance taxes, claimed by a widow for her share of her deceased husband's estate.

wildcat banking period in the first half of the nineteenth century when state-chartered banks issued their own banknotes (paper money). Many of these banks were organized more for the purpose of issuing banknotes than for taking deposits or making loans, and many failed. These abuses led to the National Bank Act of 1864, which authorized national banks to issue currency (national banknotes), and imposed a 10% federal tax in 1866 on banknotes issued by state banks, which effectvely put the wildcat banks out of business. State chartered banks "discovered" deposit banking after this tax was imposed, persuading their customers to leave their funds in the bank and make withdrawals by check.

will formal document distributing the assets of an estate after the death of the person signing it—the TESTATOR. A will is usually written, signed by the testator in the presence of two or more witnesses. Most states also allow oral wills if signed in the presence of the testator by two or more witnesses, and handwritten or holographic wills. Preparing a will has several advantages over leaving an estate INTESTATE: the testator can designate how the estate will be distributed and can establish a TESTAMENTARY TRUST for the benefit of children. A will also allows property or real estate owned by the testator to be sold more easily. See also INTER VIVOS TRUST; TRUST.

window

1. market opportunity for new loans or other combination of events that must be acted upon, or lost forever.
   2. Federal Reserve DISCOUNT WINDOW, so named because bankers used to apply in person at a Federal Reserve Bank teller window for short-term credit advances.
3. period during the day when AUTOMATED CLEARING HOUSE or WIRE TRANSFER payments may be submitted to a Federal Reserve Bank, clearing house, or other processing organization for settlement between banks. See also CUT-OFF TIME.

window dressing special adjustments in financial position to give the appearance of adequate liquidity, often to comply with reporting requirements. It gives the appearance of a healthy balance sheet, whereas actual conditions may state otherwise. For example, an organization might buy U.S. Treasury securities and other cash equivalent securities to build up its cash position.

Window dressing, or sprucing up the balance sheet, takes place just before the statement date, for example, at the end of a fiscal year or quarter, and is intended to add size to the financial institution. Mutual funds sell off securities not preferred by the public, and purchase securities preferred by the public. Fund managers sell junk bonds held for yield, in favor of AAA-rated securities for appearance.

wire fate item checks, notes, or drafts sent to an out-of-town bank with instructions to notify by wire, usually FEDERAL WIRE, as to whether they were paid or not. Notification tells the sending bank when the check actually was paid, which especially is useful if the check is written for a large amount or if the check is being handled as a NONCASH ITEM.

wire transfer order to pay funds electronically by wire or telephone instruction, usually involving a large dollar payment. For example, the Federal Reserve Wire Network (FEDERAL WIRE), and the CLEARING HOUSE INTERBANK PAYMENTS SYSTEM (CHIPS) are wire transfer payment systems. The Federal Reserve Wire Network links Federal Reserve offices, depository institutions, the U.S. Treasury, and other government agencies. It transfers funds, U.S. government securities, and Federal Reserve administrative, supervisory, and monetary policy messages. The Culpeper Switch, a computerized Federal Reserve facility located in Culpeper, Virginia, serves as a central switching system. See also AUTOMATED CLEARING HOUSE; AVAILABILITY; BANK WIRE; ELECTRONIC FUNDS TRANSFER; NET SETTLEMENT; SAME DAY FUNDS; SOCIETY FOR WORLDWIDE INTERBANK FINANCIAL TELECOMMUNICATIONS (SWIFT).

withdrawal
1. taking funds out of a deposit account by writing a CHECK, DRAFT, or withdrawal slip in the case of a time deposit or savings deposit. Certain time deposits and certificates of deposit require a NOTICE OF WITHDRAWAL before funds are with-

drawn in cash or transferred to another account. These may also be subject to an EARLY WITHDRAWAL PENALTY or forfeiture of interest. See also REGULATION Q.

2. substituting new collateral securing a COLLATERAL LOAN, allowing the borrower to take back the original collateral pledged.

withdrawal notice see NOTICE OF WITHDRAWAL.

withdrawal penalty see EARLY WITHDRAWAL PENALTY.

with exchange writing on a CHECK or DRAFT specifying that any collection costs above the face value are payable by the drawee of the check, or the payer of the draft being presented for payment. Sometimes written "payable with exchange".

with full recourse clause in an ASSET SALES agreement whereby a bank selling WHOLE LOANS or LOAN PARTICIPATIONs to an investor agrees to fully reimburse the investor for losses resulting from the purchased loans, for example, by taking back any loans that become delinquent in principal and interest payments.

withholding see BACKUP WITHHOLDING.

with interest bonds or securities paying accrued interest to the bearer. When sold, the buyer pays any interest accrued since the last payment date, in addition to the market price.

without expression for a market characterized by the absence of either bids or offers, indicating a one-way market. If XYZ at $50 was the bid, and there was no offer, the quote would be $50 without. This could be a sign of a bearish market, where traders expect falling prices.

without recourse
In general: phrase meaning that credit risk, or risk of nonpayment, is assumed by the buyer, rather than the seller, of a promissory note or the holder of a negotiable instrument. In negotiable instruments law, the endorser of a check or draft cannot be held accountable for payment to subsequent holders

in the event the MAKER or DRAWER fails to pay, if the endorsement contains the words "without recourse." Such an endorsement is a qualified endorsement under Article 3 of the Uniform Commercial Code. See also HOLDER IN DUE COURSE.

Banking:

1. financing arrangement or dealer FLOOR PLANNING in which the dealer's liability is limited to warranties about the quality of the installment contracts, which the lender purchases at a discount. Defective installment contracts are not charged back automatically to the dealer. A nonrecourse plan may, however, require the dealer to assist in repossessions and collections of delinquent accounts. See also NONRECOURSE LOAN.

2. language in a SECONDARY MARKET sale of loans, certificates of deposit, and so on, in which the seller is under no obligation to reimburse the investor for any losses suffered. Transactions where the buyer can ask for compensation are regarded by bank regulators as financings and do not qualify as sales of assets; the loans or deposits involved must remain on the seller's balance sheet.

Finance: financing agreement in ASSET-BASED LENDING, common in FACTORING, whereby the lending institution cannot charge back unpaid invoices caused by the account debtor's financial instability.

with right of survivorship joint tenant account in which assets of either owner pass to the other tenant when either tenant dies, rather than to the owner's heirs.

won national currency of South Korea.

working capital

1. current assets of an organization, especially cash, accounts receivable, and inventory. Also called liquid capital. Definitions of the term vary. An alternative definition is net working capital, or the excess of current assets over current liabilities. A firm's working capital ratio (current assets divided by current liabilities) is a measure of its liquidity.

2. earning assets of an organization, including marketable securities, receivables, and inventory, which can be converted to cash if needed.

working reserves see FREE RESERVES.

workout agreement mutual agreement by borrower and lender to reschedule loan payments, modify payment terms by extending the original maturity, and so on. This normally is done in lieu of FORECLOSURE action, in which the lender attempts to sell at auction any loan collateral pledged by the borrower. Loans in this stage of negotiations already are covered fully by loan loss reserves and have been written off as BAD DEBT. By negotiating new terms with the borrower, the lender expects to collect more from recoveries than from legal remedies, such as foreclosure, liquidation, and bankruptcy. See also CREDITORS' COMMITTEE; DEBT FOR EQUITY SWAP; STAND-STILL AGREEMENT; TROUBLED DEBT RESTRUCTURING.

World Bank see INTERNATIONAL BANK FOR RECONSTRUCTION AND DEVELOPMENT.

World Bank Group collective name for the INTERNATIONAL BANK FOR RECONSTRUCTION AND DEVELOPMENT (the World Bank) and its affiliates: the International Finance Corporation, organized in 1950 to provide long-term project financing to developing countries; and the International Development Association, formed in 1960 to make long-term (up to 50 years) loans at low interest rates. The International Development Association is supported by periodic contributions from World Bank member countries. The World Bank itself raises capital for lending by selling bonds in the capital markets of member countries and from direct contributions of member governments. See also SOFT LOAN.

worn currency circulating money retired from use as it wears out. The average life of a $1 bill, the most widely circulated FEDERAL RESERVE NOTE, is about 15 to 18 months. Currency no longer fit for use as LEGAL TENDER is removed from circulation and burned by Federal Reserve Banks. Mutilated or partially destroyed currency is redeemable at full face value if more than half the original note is intact.

wraparound mortgage financing arrangement in which an existing mortgage is refinanced, and additional money loaned at an interest rate between the rate charged on the old loan and current market rates. The lender, who agrees to pass through part of the loan payments to the original mortgage lender, combines or wraps the remainder of the old loan with the new loan, and the borrower makes one monthly payment. Wraparound loans generally earn a higher yield for the lender than new mortgage loans because the wraparound lender advances only the difference between the unpaid first mortgage and the combined principal of the two loans, but the wraparound rate is computed on the borrower's total debt. A wraparound mortgage is an alternative to refinancing the entire loan when a borrower needs additional funds.

write down revaluation of securities, loans, or other assets when the market value is lower than the book value at which the asset is carried. Marketable securities carried as TRADING ACCOUNT ASSETS for a bank's trading account or held for other institutions must be adjusted to market value (MARK TO THE MARKET) daily, by either writing down or writing up. Loans and leases are carried to maturity at the original book value, unless a bank is required to write down their value by a banking regulatory agency.

write off
1. accounting process whereby a loan determined to be a worthless asset is removed from the books as an earning asset and charged to the LOAN LOSS RESERVES account. Its book value is written down to zero.
2. process of removing a BAD DEBT or uncollectible loan from the balance sheet.

writer
1. DRAWER of a check, also called the maker.
2. person who sells an OPTION contract, an agreement to buy (a CALL OPTION), or to sell (a PUT OPTION), a specified amount of securities, currency, or commodities at a specified price at a designated future date.

writ of attachment legal document placing a borrower's assets under the control of a court order, for example, when a bank initiates foreclosure action for nonpayment of debt. Basically, a property execution that attaches to assets of a corporation, as distinct from a wage GARNISHMENT, which applies to individuals.

written notice

1. consumer protection clause in the TRUTH IN LENDING ACT stating that consumers have to be notified in writing of any changes in credit terms. This notice may be included in the periodic billing statement, as for example, a change in the method of computing the interest rate in a credit card account. A change in rate applies to the entire balance owed and new purchases, once notification is given and the customer continues to use the account, unless state law says otherwise. See also REGULATION B; REGULATION Z.
2. notice that banks may legally require from customers before paying DRAFTs from a NEGOTIABLE ORDER OF WITHDRAWAL (NOW) account. See also NOTICE OF WITHDRAWAL.

wrongful dishonor failure to pay a CHECK or DRAFT properly endorsed and presented for payment. Under the UNIFORM COMMERCIAL CODE, the payor bank has until midnight of the day after it receives a check to pay or DISHONOR it. A bank may return a check with a missing signature, altered date, and so on, without penalty. If, however, the DRAWEE (the person presenting the check) suffers financially because of the bank's refusal to HONOR an otherwise payable check, the bank may be liable to its customer for damages. The customer must still be able to prove financial harm. See also PROTEST.

X

x-mark signature signature made by a person unable to sign his or her own name. To be legally valid, the signature must be witnessed by another person.

X.9 financial standards committee of the AMERICAN NATIONAL STANDARDS INSTITUTE, a voluntary association, that sets financial industry payment industry standards for banks and other depository financial institutions. Its members include banks, retailers, equipment suppliers, and federal agencies. The AMERICAN BANKERS ASSOCIATION acts as secretariat for the X.9 committee.

X.12 uniform standard for interindustry electronic interchange of business transactions. The purpose of the X.12 committee of the American National Standards Institute is to develop and foster standards for electronic interchange of trade-related transactions, such as order placement and processing, invoicing, payments, and cash application data. The Electronic Data Interchange Association, in Alexandria, Virginia, is secretariat for the X.12 standards committee. See also ELECTRONIC DATA INTERCHANGE.

Y

yankee bond dollar denominated bond issued in the United States by foreign banks and corporations. These bonds, the U.S. equivalent of the EUROBOND, pay semiannual interest, unlike Eurobonds, which pay annual interest, and are registered with the Securities and Exchange Commission. They ordinarily are issued when the domestic market is more favorable to investors than the Euromarket, and offer the foreign investor some degree of protection against fluctuating exchange rates. See also INTERNATIONAL BANKING FACILITY; YANKEE CERTIFICATE OF DEPOSIT.

yankee certificate of deposit negotiable TIME DEPOSIT issued in the United States by a foreign borrower, usually in denominations of $1 to $5 million. These certificates pay a fixed or variable rate of interest for a specified maturity, usually under 12 months, and are sold directly or through dealers. They are unsecured obligations of the issuing institution. See also YANKEE BOND.

yen national currency of Japan.

yen bond any bond denominated in yen, usually issued in the Japanese money market. There are several types of yen bonds. If issued in the Euromarket it is called a Euroyen bond. Yen-denominated bonds issued in Japan to non-Japanese investors are priced by the four major Japanese securities firms, and are known as SAMURAI BONDS. (Contrast with foreign currency Shogun bonds issued in Japan to both Japanese and foreign investors.) Only in the last several years have the Japanese financial markets opened up to non-Japanese investors desiring to tap Japan's balance of trade surplus by borrowing in the Tokyo bond market. A 1984 accord between the U.S. Treasury Department and the Japanese Ministry of Finance was instrumental in opening up the yen market to non-Japanese issuers. See also EUROBOND.

yield return on a loan or investment, stated as a percentage of price. Yield can be computed by dividing return by purchase price, by current market value, or by any other measure of value. In interest-earning investments, such as bank loans or deposits, yield is interest revenue earned divided by the average balance. In fixed income securities, such as bonds, yields fluctuate as bond prices rise or fall, which means that current yields will differ from redemption yields on the same investments.

1. **Banking.** The return earned by a loan portfolio expressed as a percentage. Yield is computed by multiplying the outstanding balances by the ANNUAL PERCENTAGE RATE paid by the borrowers. PREPAYMENTS and CHARGE-OFFS of bad loans will, however, reduce the portfolio return.

2. **Investments.** The income from a BOND, interest-bearing NOTE, or TIME DEPOSIT, expressed as an annualized percentage rate. The nominal yield is calculated from the amount invested multiplied by the interest rate paid and the maturity (Interest = Principal × Rate × Time). The EFFECTIVE ANNUAL YIELD on a time deposit takes into consideration the effect of interest rate COMPOUNDING on the invested principal balance. CURRENT YIELD on a bond is the current COUPON rate of interest in semiannual interest payments, without taking into account whether the bond price is at a premium or a discount in relation to par value. Net YIELD TO MATURITY is based on the amount payable at maturity, taking into consideration the average annual accumulation of interest payments on bonds held to their stated maturity. See also AVERAGE BOND YIELD; BOND EQUIVALENT YIELD; DISCOUNT; TOTAL RETURN; YIELD CURVE.

3. **Securities.** The dividends paid to holders of common or preferred stock as of the dividend paying date, measured as a percentage of current market value. The dividend yield, a ratio comparing the dividend rate to the market price per share of common stock, is computed by the following formula:

dividend yield = annual dividend per share / market price

Thus, a stock selling at $30, paying a $2 annual dividend, has a dividend yield of 6.6%.

yield basis method of quoting the yield on securities that states income earned as a percent, rather than as a dollar amount. MUNICIPAL BONDs issued in different SERIES (as part of a SERIAL BOND) and maturing on different dates, and thus having different prices, are sometimes quoted this way for purposes of comparison, as are railroad equipment trust certificates, and Government National Mortgage Association futures contracts. See also DOLLAR BOND.

yield curve comparison of the market return, or yield, of a security and its maturity. This usually is plotted on a graph showing the comparative yields of similar investments, such as bonds. By depicting the market yield on the vertical axis and the maturity on the horizontal axis, yield comparisons between short-term instruments and long-term instruments are made more easily. The yield curve for U.S. Treasury securities, comparing securities from 3 months to 30 years in maturity, is the benchmark for comparing yields of other fixed income investments. Corporate bonds, mortgage backed bonds, and asset-backed bonds are described as having a yield spread, measured in basis points, over Treasury securities.

Under ordinary conditions the yield curve slopes upward to the right, called a normal yield curve or a POSITIVE YIELD CURVE because long-term investments pay higher yields than short-term instruments and borrowers are (supposedly) willing to pay a premium for long-term funds. When the yield curve is positive, no radical changes in rates are expected.

When short-term rates rise above long-term rates, an IN-VERTED YIELD CURVE or negative yield curve results. Inverted yield curves are characterized by unstable financial conditions, and occur during periods of TIGHT MONEY, when the Federal Reserve drains reserves from the banking system to cool inflationary pressures in the economy. Under such conditions, lenders resist making long-term loans. A flat yield curve is a sign that investors are undecided about which direction rates are moving. See also EXPECTATIONS THEORY; HUMPED YIELD CURVE; LIQUIDITY PREFERENCE THEORY; MARKET SEGMENTATION THEORY; YIELD TO AVERAGE LIFE; YIELD TO CALL; YIELD TO MATURITY.

yield equivalence

1. restatement of rates paid by tax-exempt state and local bonds to arrive at a YIELD that nearly is identical to the after-tax returns on taxable bonds. This is done for clarity in fiscal year reporting, for example, a bank's annual report, and takes into account the holder's current tax rate to arrive at a

yield quote matching the after-tax return on fully taxable securities.

2. in GOVERNMENT NATIONAL MORTGAGE ASSOCIATION (Ginnie Mae) contracts, a price adjustment made when making delivery of SPOT or FORWARD MARKET contracts. Adjusting the contract purchase price allows the seller to satisfy the seller's yield requirements. For example, a mortgage originator may agree to sell Ginnie Mae 10's (10% yield) priced at 110% of par value in lieu of Ginnie Mae 11's if the originator can meet the contract price by delivering securities of approximately the same value. Ginnie Mae trading is done through yield maintenance contracts allowing substitution of underlying collateral as long as the yield called for in the contract is met.

yield to average life annualized percentage return on a bond substituting the AVERAGE LIFE maturity for stated final maturity. This often is used in pricing mortgage backed securities, for example, COLLATERALIZED MORTGAGE OBLIGATIONs, where PREPAYMENT of the underlying mortgages can influence the investor's return, and bonds with SINKING FUND provisions allowing the issuer to buy back, or redeem, its own bonds. See also WEIGHTED AVERAGE MATURITY; WEIGHTED AVERAGE REMAINING TERM.

yield to call annualized percentage return on a bond or note redeemed by the issuer at the earliest possible CALL date. Also known as *yield to first call*. When a security can be called by the issuer at the first call date allowed by the bond INDENTURE, the annualized yield to that date is often substituted for the YIELD TO MATURITY in yield quotations. Although some longer-term U.S. Treasury bonds are callable five years prior to final maturity, as indicated by the hyphenated quote in bond tables, in practice few, if any, Treasury securities have been called prior to maturity. The term yield to first call is used when a bond issue is trading at a premium over the call price and the investor would lose capital. The yield to first call, taking this loss into account, usually is lower than the yield to final call.

Yield to par is used to describe the yield on securities that are issued at a discount or premium in relation their nominal value, or PAR VALUE and are callable at par. See also ADVANCE REFUNDING.

yield to maturity annualized percentage return of a bond held until its stated maturity. Also called the *effective rate of return*. This is a commonly accepted method of comparing yields on bonds with different coupon interest rates, because it assumes that interest income will be reinvested at the current yield and it takes into account any adjustments for bond premium or discount. For this reason it differs from CURRENT YIELD, which may be higher or lower.

Another measure of effective yield of fixed income securities is DURATION, which measures the average time to collection of all payments, including principal and interest of an interest sensitive security, for example, a mortgage backed bond, during the period owned by an investor. Yield to maturity quotes may also differ from an investor's actual return at maturity because they assume constant reinvestment of interest at the currently quoted yield. This may or may not be accurate if the bonds are sold at prices above, or below, their face value, or PAR VALUE. For easy reference, the yield to maturity of a given bond can be found in the bond tables prepared by financial publishers. Certain types of programmable calculators can also be used to compute yield to maturity. See also BOND EQUIVALENT YIELD; YIELD TO AVERAGE LIFE; YIELD TO CALL.

yuan national currency of the Republic of China.

Z

zaibatsu Japanese industrial conglomerate, one of whose members is a major bank providing financing to other members of the group. The bank acts like a treasurer, arranging short-term working capital and taking an equity position in the companies it finances. Its sources of funds are bank deposits, borrowings from the Japanese central bank and borrowings from other banks in the money market. These conglomerates were broken up after World War II and have been replaced by more informal organizations.

zaire national currency of Zaire.

z-bond see ACCRUAL BOND; TRANCHE.

zengin funds transfer system in Japan, operated by the Federation of Bankers Associations of Japan. This electronic payment system links AUTOMATED TELLER MACHINES and branch offices of more than 700 Japanese financial institutions. It facilitates both small value and high value automated credit transfers by banks, corporations, and consumers.

zero-balance account checking account used by corporations to accelerate collection of funds from subsidiaries, or control funds disbursed to pay trade creditors. In a zero-balance collection account, collected balances are transferred by DEPOSITORY TRANSFER CHECK or automated clearing house debit from subsidiary accounts into a central CONCENTRATION ACCOUNT, bringing the collecting account to a zero balance at the end of each business day. Zero-balance concentration accounts are generally used by companies wanting centralized control of cash receipts. In a zero-balance disbursing account, corporate funds are transferred out of a central account to subsidiary accounts for payment to trading partners. Funds to cover the payment are transferred from a control account whenever a payment is made from the zero-balance account. Zero-balance disbursement accounts are typically used by companies that want centralized cash control but decentralized funds disbursement.

zero-coupon convertible bond

1. single payment bond, sold at an original issue discount, that may be exchanged for COMMON STOCK of the issuer when the securities reach a specific price. Liquid Yield Option Notes (LYONs), one variety of these securities, have both a conversion feature and a put option allowing the holder to sell the bonds back to the issuer.
2. single payment MUNICIPAL BOND carrying a conversion feature allowing the holder to switch to a regular interest coupon paying bond after a specific number of years.

zero-coupon mortgage long-term commercial MORTGAGE that defers all payments of principal and interest until maturity. The loan is structured as an accrual note; interest due is rolled into the outstanding principal. At maturity, the borrower must either pay off the note or refinance at current interest rates. The lender arranging financing gets a discounted internal rate of return; the borrower can finance a commercial project with a smaller cash flow, on the expectation that appreciation of the property value over the life of the loan is sufficient to pay off the loan.

zero-coupon security security, usually a bond, paying no interest during its stated lifetime. The holder receives interest paid in one lump sum at maturity. These bonds have no interest coupons attached, but the bond interest accrues and is taxable on a prorated basis each year. This interest deferral is attractive to investors who are not taxed on current income, for example, those investing in tax-deferred savings plans, such as an INDIVIDUAL RETIREMENT ACCOUNT, KEOGH accounts, and so on, or who expect that bond interest when paid will be offset by future expenses, for example, college tuition expenses.

Annual interest earned is treated by the IRS as taxable income, even though there is no cash payment of interest. Thus, the appeal of zero-coupon securities lies in the fact that these securities eliminate REINVESTMENT RISK, or risk of market rates rising or falling, because the interest earned is determined in advance by the interest accruals. Zero-coupon bonds, however, are more volatile in yield than bonds paying coupon interest semiannually.

A number of zero-coupon securities have been issued in recent years. Examples are stripped securities, such as U.S. Treasury STRIPs (Separate Trading of Registered Interest and Principal of Securities), which actually are created by dealers who turn back large blocks of Treasury securities for stripping. The Treasury Department separates the bond CORPUS from interest COUPONs, exchanging the whole-coupon securities for U.S. Treasury STRIPS. Synthetic zero-coupon securities are issued by dealers who separate the principal of Treasury bonds from semiannual interest payments and sell the two pieces separately. A trust receipt is issued to the holder of these discounted securities. Among synthetic strips issued are Certificates of Accrual on Treasury Securities (CATS), Treasury Income Growth Receipts, and ZEBRAs (Zero-coupon Eurosterling Bearer with Registered Accruing Securities) issued in the U.K. Treasury STRIPs are also transferable in BOOK ENTRY SECURITY form, making them slightly more liquid than synthetic strips.

Other variations of the discount, single payment investment are the zero-coupon certificate of deposit, zero-coupon municipal bond and the ZERO-COUPON MORTGAGE. See also ZERO-COUPON CONVERTIBLE BOND.

zero-floor limit RETAIL POINT-OF-SALE authorization system in which all bank card transactions are approved by checking the transactions against either the account balance or the WARNING BULLETIN listing over limit or past due accounts. See also FLOOR LIMIT; NEGATIVE AUTHORIZATION; POSITIVE AUTHORIZATION.

zero gap condition where a bank's INTEREST SENSITIVE ASSETS and INTEREST SENSITIVE LIABILITIES are balanced perfectly for a given time period. This state of equilibrium occurs when maturities of assets and liabilities subject to repricing are matched evenly. In reality, this rarely happens because the dynamics of a competitive market make it difficult to match maturities of deposits and loans (a process called matched funding), and because banks, as credit intermediaries, have to take some maturity risk when they make loans. Banks can, however, control the INTEREST RATE RISK created by maturity imbalances by engaging in

HEDGING tactics, such as FINANCIAL FUTUREs and interest rate SWAPs.

zero-interest loan see ZERO-COUPON MORTGAGE.

zero proof manual bookkeeping procedure in which posting entries are subtracted, one by one, from an ending balance. The posting entries *prove* or balance out when a balance of zero is reached, indicating the account entries have been entered correctly. This method of proof is sometimes used by bank tellers to reconcile posting errors, also known as a teller's difference.

zloty national currency of Poland.

ABBREVIATIONS AND ACRONYMS

ABA	American Bankers Association
ACH	Automated Clearing House
ACRS	Accelerated Cost Recovery Schedule
ACU	Asian Currency Unit
ADR	American Depositary Receipt
AIB	American Institute of Banking
AID	Agency for International Development
AMEX	American Stock Exchange
AMI	Alternative Mortgage Instrument
ANSI	American National Standards Institute
AON	All or None
APR	Annual Percentage Rate
ARM	Adjustable Rate Mortgage
ATM	Automated Teller Machine
ATRR	Allocated Transfer Risk Reserve
ATS	Automatic Transfer Service
BAFT	Bankers Association for Foreign Trade
BAN	Bond Anticipation Note
BIC	Bank Instrument Contract
BIN	Bank Identification Number
BIS	Bank for International Settlements

CAB	Controlled Amortization Bond
C&I	Commercial and Industrial
CAMEL	Credit, Assets, Management, Earnings, Liquidity
CARD	Certificate for Amortizing Revolving Debt
CARS	Collateralized Auto Receivable Securities
CAT	Customer Activated Terminal
CCD	Cash Concentration & Disbursement
CD	Certificate of Deposit
CFTC	Commodities Futures Trading Commission
CHAPS	Clearing House Automated Payments System
CHIPS	Clearing House Interbank Payments System
CIE	Customer Initiated Entry
CIF	Customer Information File
CLF	Central Liquidity Facility
CLO	Computerized Loan Origination
CMO	Collateralized Mortgage Obligation
COFI	Cost of Funds Index
CPR	Conditional Prepayment Rate
CSBS	Conference of State Bank Supervisors
CSR	Customer Service Representative
CTP	Corporate Trade Payment
CTR	Currency Transaction Report
CTX	Corporate Trade Exchange
D&B	Dun & Bradstreet
DES	Data Encryption Standard
DIDC	Depository Institutions Deregulation Committee
DTC	Depository Transfer Check
DTC	Depository Trust Company
ECU	European Currency Unit
EDI	Electronic Data Exchange
EEC	European Economic Community
EET	Electronic Funds Transfer
ERISA	Employee Retirement Income Security Act
ESOP	Employee Stock Ownership Plan
ETC	Export Trading Company
FASB	Financial Accounting Standards Board
FCIA	Foreign Credit Insurance Association
FCM	Futures Commission Merchant
FCS	Farm Credit System
FDIC	Federal Deposit Insurance Corporation
FFB	Federal Financing Bank
FHA	Federal Housing Administration
FHFB	Federal Housing Finance Board
FHLMC	Federal Home Loan Mortgage Corporation
FIRREA	Federal Institutions Reform, Recovery and Enforcement Act

FmHA	Farmers Home Administration
FNMA	Federal National Mortgage Association
FOK	Fill or Kill
FOMC	Federal Open Market Committee
FRB	Federal Reserve Board
FRN	Floating Rate Note
FSLIC	Federal Savings and Loan Insurance Corporation
GAAP	Generally Accepted Accounting Principles
GAB	General Agreements to Borrow
GEM	Growing Equity Mortgage
GMC	Guaranteed Mortgage Certificate
GNMA	Government National Mortgage Association
GPM	Graduated Payment Mortgage
HUD	Housing and Urban Development, Department of
IADB	Inter-American Development Bank
IBAA	Independent Bankers Association of America
IBF	International Banking Facility
IBRD	International Bank for Reconstruction and Development
ICC	Income Capital Certificate
IDR	International Depositary Receipt
IMF	International Monetary Fund
INAS	Interbank National Authorization System
INET	Interbank Network for Electronic Transfer
IO	Interest Only
IRA	Individual Retirement Account
IRR	Internal Rate of Return
IRS	Internal Revenue Service
ISO	International Organization for Standardization
LBO	Leveraged Buyout
LDC	Less Developed Country
LIBID	London Interbank Bid Rate
LIBOR	London Interbank Offered Rate
LIMEAN	London Interbank Median Average Rate
LPO	Loan Production Office
MAC	Message Authentication Code
MAI	Member, Appraisal Institute
M&A	Merger and Acquisition
MICR	Magnetic Ink Character Recognition
MMC	Money Market Certificate
MMDA	Money Market Deposit Account
MMF	Money Market Fund
MOFF	Multiple Options Funding Facility

MSA	Metropolitan Statistical Area
MSRB	Municipal Securities Rulemaking Board
NACHA	National Automated Clearing House Association
NAFCU	National Association of Federal Credit Unions
NASD	National Association of Securities Dealers
NAV	Net Asset Value
NBSS	National Bank Surveillance System
NCUA	National Credit Union Administration
N.G.	Not Good
NIC	Newly Industrialized Country
NIF	Note Issuance Facility
NOI	Net Operating Income
NOW	Negotiable Order of Withdrawal
NSF	Not Sufficient Funds
NYSE	New York Stock Exchange
OBU	Offshore Banking Unit
OCC	Office of the Comptroller of the Currency
OCC	Options Clearing Corporation
OECD	Organization for Economic Cooperation and Development
OPIC	Overseas Private Investment Corporation
OTC	Over-the-Counter
OTS	Office of Thrift Supervision
PAM	Pledged Account Mortgage
PAN	Primary Account Number
PEFCO	Private Export Funding Corporation
PERL	Principal Exchange Rate Linked Security
PIN	Personal Identification Number
PITI	Principal, Interest, Taxes, and Insurance
PLAM	Price Level Adjusted Mortgage
PMI	Private Mortgage Insurance
PO	Principals Only
POD	Proof of Deposit
POS	Point of Sale
PSAF	Private Sector Adjustment Factor
PUF	Prime Underwriting Facility
RAN	Revenue Anticipation Note
RAP	Regulatory Accounting Principles
RCPC	Regional Check Processing Center
REIT	Real Estate Investment Trust
REMIC	Real Estate Mortgage Investment Trust
RESPA	Real Estate Settlement Procedures Act
RFC	Resolution Funding Corporation
ROA	Return on Assets
ROE	Return on Equity

RSU	Remote Service Unit
RTC	Resolution Trust Corporation
RUF	Revolving Underwriting Facility
SAIF	Savings Association Insurance Fund
SAM	Shared Appreciation Mortgage
SBA	Small Business Administration
SBLI	Savings Bank Life Insurance
SDR	Special Drawing Rights
SEP	Simplified Employee Pension Plan
SIPC	Securities Investor Protection Corporation
SNIF	Standby Note Issuance Facility
SSC	Small Saver Certificate
STRIPE	Swap Transferring Risk with Participating Element
STRIPS	Separate Trading of Registered Interest and Principal
SWIFT	Society for Worldwide Interbank Financial Telecommunications
T&E	Travel and Entertainment
TIC	True Interest Cost
TIN	Taxpayer Identification Number
TRUF	Transferable Underwriting Facility
TT&L	Treasury Tax and Loan
UCC	Uniform Commercial Code
WAC	Weighted Average Coupon
WAM	Weighted Average Maturity
WART	Weight Average Remaining Term